THE PRESIDENTIAL ELECTION OF 2016

Hillary Clinton (Democrat) margin of victory

Total electoral votes: 232

less than 5% · 5–10% · more than 10%

Donald Trump (Republican) margin of victory

Total electoral votes: 306

less than 5% · 5–10% · more than 10%

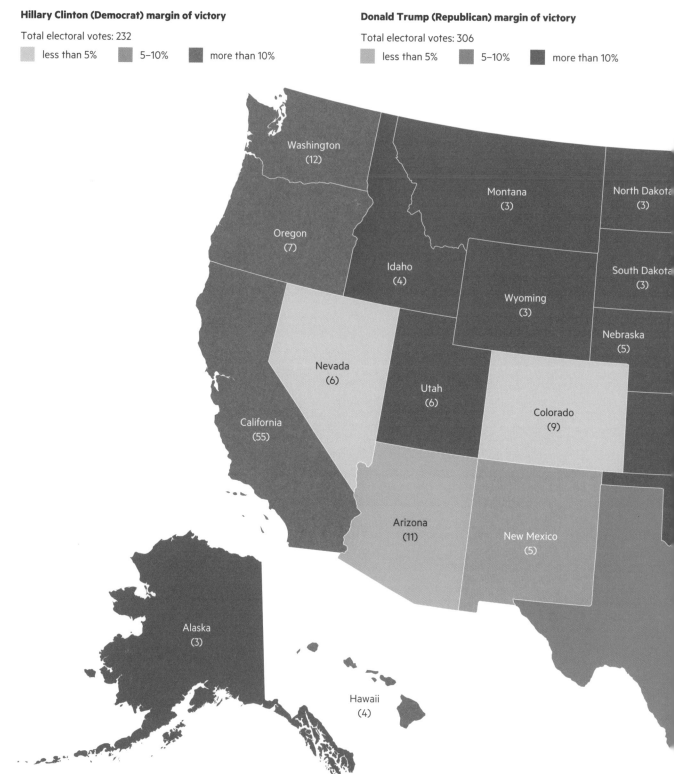

Washington
(12)

Montana
(3)

North Dakota
(3)

Oregon
(7)

Idaho
(4)

South Dakota
(3)

Wyoming
(3)

Nebraska
(5)

Nevada
(6)

Utah
(6)

Colorado
(9)

California
(55)

Arizona
(11)

New Mexico
(5)

Alaska
(3)

Hawaii
(4)

Note: Donald Trump won the electoral college with 304 votes to Hillary Clinton's 227.
Seven electors voted for someone other than their party's candidate.

Maine (3 votes to Clinton, 1 vote to Trump)

Vermont (3)

New Hampshire (4)

Massachusetts (11)

Rhode Island (4)

Connecticut (7)

New Jersey (14)

Delaware (3)

Maryland (10)

District of Columbia (3)

Minnesota (10)

Wisconsin (10)

Michigan (16)

New York (29)

Pennsylvania (20)

Iowa (6)

Ohio (18)

Illinois (20)

Indiana (11)

West Virginia (5)

Virginia (13)

Kansas (6)

Missouri (10)

Kentucky (8)

North Carolina (15)

Oklahoma (7)

Arkansas (6)

Tennessee (11)

South Carolina (9)

Texas (38)

Mississippi (6)

Alabama (9)

Georgia (16)

Louisiana (8)

Florida (29)

American Politics Today

Fifth Core Edition

Fifth Core Edition

American Politics Today

William T. Bianco
Indiana University, Bloomington

David T. Canon
University of Wisconsin, Madison

W. W. NORTON & COMPANY • NEW YORK • LONDON

W. W. Norton & Company has been independent since its founding in 1923, when William Warder Norton and Mary D. Herter Norton first published lectures delivered at the People's Institute, the adult education division of New York City's Cooper Union. The firm soon expanded its program beyond the Institute, publishing books by celebrated academics from America and abroad. By midcentury, the two major pillars of Norton's publishing program—trade books and college texts—were firmly established. In the 1950s, the Norton family transferred control of the company to its employees, and today—with a staff of four hundred and a comparable number of trade, college, and professional titles published each year—W. W. Norton & Company stands as the largest and oldest publishing house owned wholly by its employees.

Editor: Peter Lesser
Project Editor: Linda Feldman
Assistant Editor: Samantha Held
Managing Editor, College: Marian Johnson
Managing Editor, College Digital Media: Kim Yi
Production Manager: Ashley Horna
Media Editor: Spencer Richardson-Jones
Associate Media Editor: Michael Jaoui
Media Project Editor: Marcus Van Harpen
Media Editorial Assistant: Ariel Eaton
Digital Production: Mateus Teixeira
Marketing Manager, Political Science: Erin Brown
Design Director: Jillian Burr
Text Designer: Open, N.Y.
Photo Editor: Catherine Abelman
Photo Researcher: Donna Ranieri
Permissions Manager: Megan Schindel
Permissions Clearer: Elizabeth Trammell
Composition: Cenveo ® Publisher Services
Manufacturing: LSC Communications-Kendallville

Permission to use copyrighted material is included on p. A49.

The Library of Congress has catalogued the full edition as follows:

Names: Bianco, William T., 1960- author. | Canon, David T., author.
Title: American politics today / William T. Bianco, Indiana University,
    Bloomington, David T. Canon, University of Wisconsin, Madison.
Description: New York : W.W. Norton & Company, [2017] | Includes
    bibliographical references and index.
Identifiers: LCCN 2016049890 | ISBN 9780393283594 (hardcover)
Subjects: LCSH: United States—Politics and government.
Classification: LCC JK275 .B53 2017 | DDC 320.473—dc23 LC record available at
https://lccn.loc.gov/2016049890

This edition:
ISBN 978-0-393-28360-0

W. W. Norton & Company, Inc., 500 Fifth Avenue, New York, NY 10110
wwnorton.com
W. W. Norton & Company Ltd., 15 Carlisle Street, London W1D 3BS

2 3 4 5 6 7 8 9 0

For our families,
Regina, Anna, and Catherine,
Sarah, Neal, Katherine, and Sophia,
who encouraged, empathized, and
helped, with patience,
grace, and love.

About the Authors

William T. Bianco

is professor of political science at Indiana University, Bloomington. His research focuses on congressional institutions, representation, and international cooperation in crewed spaceflight. He received his undergraduate degree from SUNY Stony Brook and his MA and Ph.D. from the University of Rochester. He is the author of *Trust: Representatives and Constituents*; American Politics: Strategy and Choice; and numerous articles on American politics. His research and graduate students have received funding from the National Science Foundation and the national Council for Eurasian and Eastern European Research. He has also served as a consultant to congressional candidates and party campaign committees, as well as to the U.S. Department of Energy, the U.S. Department of Health and Human Services, and other state and local government agencies. He was also a Fulbright Senior Scholar in Moscow, Russia, during 2011-12.

David T. Canon

is professor of political science at the University of Wisconsin, Madison. His teaching and research interests focus on American political institutions, especially Congress, and racial representation. He is the author of *Actors, Athletes, and Astronauts: Political Amateurs in the U.S. Congress*; *Race, Redistricting, and Representation: The Unintended Consequences of Black Majority Districts* (winner of the Richard F. Fenno Prize); *The Dysfunctional Congress?* (with Kenneth Mayer); and various articles and book chapters. He served as the Congress editor of *Legislative Studies Quarterly*. He is an AP consultant and has taught in the University of Wisconsin Summer AP Institute for U.S. Government & Politics since 1997. Professor Canon is the recipient of a University of Wisconsin Chancellor's Distinguished Teaching Award.

Contents in Brief

Contents

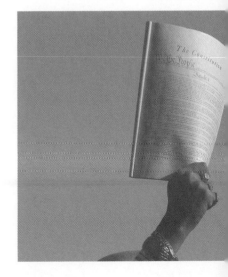

3. Federalism   64

Part II: Politics

6. Public Opinion   190

7. The Media   224

8. Political Parties   252

9. Elections   286

10. Interest Groups   330

Part III: Institutions

13. The Bureaucracy 440

14. The Courts 474

Appendix

Preface

This book is based on three simple premises: politics is conflictual, political process matters, and politics is everywhere. It reflects our belief that politics is explainable, that political outcomes can be understood in terms of decisions made by individuals—and that the average college undergraduate can make sense of the political world in these terms. It focuses on contemporary American politics, the events and outcomes that our students have lived through and know something about. The result, we believe, is a book that provides an accessible but rigorous account of the American political system.

American Politics Today is also the product of our dissatisfaction with existing texts. Thirty years ago we were assistant professors together at the same university, assigned to teach the introductory class in alternate semesters. Though our graduate training was quite different, we found that we shared a deep disappointment with available texts. Their wholesale focus on grand normative concepts such as civic responsibility or their use of advanced analytic themes left students with little idea of how American politics really works, how events in Washington, D.C., affect their everyday lives, and how to piece together all the facts about American politics into a coherent explanation of why things happen as they do. These texts did not engender excitement, fascination, or even passing interest. What they did was put students to sleep.

As with previous editions, the overarching goal of the Fifth Edition is to move beyond simply describing what happens in American politics to explaining behavior and outcomes. In part we wish to counter the widespread belief among students that politics is too complicated, too chaotic, or too secretive to make sense of. More than that, we want to empower our students, to demonstrate that everyday American politics is relevant to their lives. This emphasis is also a response to the typical complaint about American government textbooks—that they are full of facts but devoid of useful information, and that after students finish reading, they are no better able to answer "why" questions than they were before they cracked the book.

In this edition, we maintain our focus on conflict and compromise in American politics—identifying what Americans agree and disagree about and assessing how conflict shapes American politics, from campaign platforms to policy outcomes. Though this emphasis seems especially timely given the 2016 elections and the prospect of continued deadlock in Washington, our aim is to go beyond these events to identify a fundamental constant in American politics: the reality that much of politics is driven by disagreements over the scope and form of government policy, and that compromise is an essential component of virtually all significant changes in government policy. Indeed, it is impossible to imagine politics without conflict. Conflict was embedded in the American political system by the Founders, who set up a system of checks and balances to make sure that no single group could dominate. The Constitution's division of power guarantees that enacting and implementing laws will involve conflict and compromise. Furthermore, the Constitution itself was constructed as one long series of compromises. Accordingly, despite the general dislike people have for conflict, our students must recognize that conflict and compromise lie at the heart of politics.

Throughout the text, we emphasize common sense, showing students that politics inside the Beltway is often strikingly similar to the students' own everyday interactions. For example, what sustains policy compromises made by members of Congress?

The fact that the members typically have long careers, that they interact frequently with each other, and that they only deal with colleagues who have kept their word in the past. These strategies are not unique to the political world. Rather, they embody rules of thumb that most people follow (or are at least aware of) in their everyday interactions. In short, we try to help students understand American politics by emphasizing how it is not all that different from the world they know.

This focus on common sense is coupled with many references to the political science literature. We believe that contemporary research has something to say about prediction and explanation of events that students care about—and that these insights can be taught without turning students into game theorists or statisticians. Our text presents the essential insights of contemporary research, motivated by real-world political phenomena and explained using text or simple diagrams. This approach gives students a set of tools for understanding politics, provides an introduction to the political science literature, and matches up well with students' common-sense intuitions about everyday life. Moreover, by showing that academic scholarship is not a blind alley or irrelevant, this approach helps to bridge the gap between an instructor's teaching and his or her research.

The Fifth Edition builds on these strengths. We've continued to streamline and improve the presentation of text and graphics, and added a new section, "What Do the Numbers Say," that guides students through interpreting quantitative information. Our focus on explanation is hammered home throughout the chapters with new "Why Should I Care" call-outs. New or revised chapter openers use contemporary stories and examples (from student loans to the threats posed by ISIS) to highlight the conflict and compromise theme. We refer to these openers throughout the chapters to illustrate and extend our discussion. The "Take a Stand" sections now explicitly argue both sides of policy questions. Finally, we have added new pull quotes and other sidebar material to enhance the liveliness of the text.

The text continues to be ruthlessly contemporary, but also places recent events in context. Although we do not ignore American history, our stress is on contemporary politics—on the debates, actions, and outcomes that most college students are aware of. Focusing on recent events emphasizes the utility of the concepts and insights that we develop in the text. It also goes a long way toward establishing the relevance of the intro class. The new edition discusses the acceptance of same-sex marriage, the debate over immigration reform, and debates over income inequality—all issues that Americans care about. We have also devoted considerable space to describing the 2016 presidential race, working to show how the contest between Hillary Clinton and Donald Trump fits into a broader theory of how candidates campaign and how voters decide.

Finally, our book offers an individual-level perspective on America's government. The essential message is that politics—elections, legislative proceedings, regulatory choices, and everything else we see—is a product of the decisions made by real flesh-and-blood people. This approach grounds our discussion of politics in the real world. Many texts focus on abstractions such as "the eternal debate," "the great questions," or "the pulse of democracy." We believe that these constructs don't explain where the debate, the questions, or even democracy come from. Nor do they help students understand what's going on in Washington, D.C., and elsewhere, as it's not obvious that the participants themselves care much about these sorts of abstractions—quite the opposite, in fact.

We replace these constructs with a focus on real people and actual choices. The primary goal is to make sense of American politics by understanding why politicians, bureaucrats, judges, and citizens act as they do. That is, we are grounding our description of American politics at the most fundamental level—an individual facing a decision. How, for example, does a voter choose among candidates? Stated that way, it is reasonably easy to talk about where the choice came from, how the individual might evaluate different options, and why one choice might look better than the others. Voters' decisions may be understood by examining the different feasible strategies they employ (issue voting, retrospective evaluations, stereotyping, etc.) and by asking why some voters use one strategy while others use a different one.

By focusing on individuals and choices, we can place students in the shoes of the decision makers, and in so doing, give them insight into why people act as they do. We can discuss, for example, why a House member might favor enacting wasteful pork-barrel spending, even though a proposal full of such projects will make his constituents economically worse off—and why constituents might reward such behavior, even if they suspect the truth. By taking this approach, we are not trying to let legislators off the hook. Rather, we believe that any real understanding of the political process must begin with a sense of the decisions the participants make and why they make them. Focusing on individuals also segues naturally into a discussion of consequences, allowing us to move from examining decisions to describing and evaluating outcomes. In this way, we can show students how large-scale outcomes in politics, such as inefficient programs, don't happen by accident or because of malfeasance. Rather, they are the predictable results of choices made by individuals (here, politicians and voters).

The policy chapters in the Full and Essentials Editions also represent a distinctive feature of this book. The discussion of policy at the end of an intro class often fits awkwardly with the material covered earlier. It is supposed to be a culmination of the semester-long discussion of institutions, politicians, and political behavior, but instead it often becomes an afterthought that gets discarded when time runs out in the last few weeks of class. Our policy chapters explicitly draw on previous chapters' discussions of the actors that shape policy: the president, Congress, the courts, interest groups, and parties. By doing so, these chapters show how all the pieces of the puzzle fit together.

Finally, this book reflects our experience as practicing scholars and teachers, as well as interactions with more than fifteen thousand students in introductory classes at several universities. Rather than thinking of the intro class as a service obligation, we believe it offers a unique opportunity for faculty to develop a broader sense of American politics and American political science, while at the same time giving students the tools they need to behave as knowledgeable citizens or enthusiastic political science majors. We hope that it works for you as well as it does for us.

Features of the
Text and Media Package

The book's "three key ideas"
are fully integrated throughout the text.

- **Politics Is Conflictual** and conflict and compromise are a normal, healthy part of politics. The questions debated in elections and the policy options considered by people in government are generally marked by disagreement at all levels. Making policy typically involves important issues on which people disagree, sometimes strongly; so compromise, bargaining, and tough choices about trade-offs are often necessary.

- **Political Process Matters** because it is the mechanism we have established to resolve conflicts and achieve compromise. Governmental actions result from conscious choices made by voters, elected officials, and bureaucrats. The media often cover political issues in the same way they do sporting events, and though this makes for entertaining news, it also leads citizens to overlook the institutions, rules, and procedures that have a decisive influence on American life. Politics really is not just a game.

- **Politics Is Everywhere** in that the results of the political process affect all aspects of Americans' everyday lives. Politics governs what people can and cannot do, their quality of life, and how they think about events, other people, and situations.

New and revised "How It Works" chapter openers
feature hot-button political issues and pose the kinds of questions students might ask. For example, "When is discrimination legal and when is it not?" (Civil Liberties) and "How do interest groups work? Do lobbying victories always go to the side with the most money?" (Interest Groups).

Organization around chapter goals
stresses learning objectives and mastery of core material.

- **Chapter Goals** appear at the beginning of the chapter and then recur at the start of the relevant sections throughout the chapter to create a more active reading experience that emphasizes important learning objectives.

- **Extensive end-of-chapter review sections organized around the Chapter Goals** include section summaries, practice quiz questions, key terms, and suggested reading lists. Students have everything they need to master the material in each section of the chapter.

Special features for critical thinking
reinforce the three key ideas while introducing other important ways to think about American politics.

- **"How It Works" graphics,** newly redesigned for greater clarity, highlight key political processes and structures and build graphical literacy. The "How It Works in Practice" section of these graphics show how the processes presented play out in a real-world political event.

- **NEW "What Do the Numbers Say?" features** develop quantitative reasoning skills by teaching students to read and interpret data on important political issues and current events.

- **NEW "Why Should I Care?" sections** draw explicit connections between the chapter material and students' lives.
- **NEW "Did you know?" features and pull quotes** give students tidbits of information that may induce questions, anger, and may even inspire students to get involved.
- **Revised "Take a Stand" features** address contemporary issues in a pro/con format and invite students to consider how they would argue their own position on the topic. Each feature concludes with two critical-thinking questions.
- **"Nuts & Bolts" features provide students with concise explanations of key concepts,** like the difference between civil liberties and civil rights, different kinds of gerrymanders, and brief summaries of campaign finance rules. These features provide an easy way for quick study and review.

Tools for a dynamic classroom

- **InQuizitive, Norton's formative, adaptive assessment tool,** accompanies the Fifth Edition of *American Politics Today* and reinforces reading comprehension with a focus on the foundations of government and major political science concepts. Guiding feedback helps students understand why their answers were right or wrong and steers them back to the text. Student knowledge is strengthened through questions that compel analysis of the systems of government, animated and static infographics, and images, charts, and graphs from this text. With InQuizitive, students have the opportunity to achieve the maximum score in a low-risk environment.

  To learn more about InQuizitive, visit http://books.wwnorton.com/books/inquizitive/overview/.

- **Norton Coursepacks are free and open with no access codes,** allowing you to easily bring Norton's high-quality digital content into your existing learning management system. The content is fully editable and is yours to keep forever. The Norton Coursepack for *American Politics Today,* Fifth Edition, contains the following activities and quizzes:
  - **How to Read Charts and Graphs tutorial** that provides students with extra practice and guidance interpreting common representations of data that they will encounter in this textbook and in the world,
  - **Pre- and post-test chapter quizzes** that assess student knowledge of core concepts,
  - **Video exercises** that engage students and help them retain and apply information through significant events,
  - **"How It Works" and "How It Works In Practice" animated graphics** that guide students through understanding political processes and institutions,
  - **Updated simulations** that show students how concepts work in the real world,
  - **"By the Numbers" activities** that give students more practice with quantitative skills and more familiarity with how political scientists know what they know, and
  - **"Take a Stand" exercises** that present students with multiple sides of contemporary debates and ask them to consider and refine their own views based on what they've learned.
- **Test bank** contains more than 1,800 questions tagged to chapter-learning objectives and keyed to Bloom's taxonomy.
- **Instructor's manual** includes chapter outlines, class activities, and discussion questions.
- **Instructor PowerPoints** contains fully customizable lecture slides with clicker questions and "How It Works" and "How It Works in Practice" animated PowerPoint slides for optimal classroom presentation.

Acknowledgments

This edition of *American Politics Today* is again dedicated to our families. Our wives, Regina and Sarah, have continued to accommodate our deadlines and schedules and have again served as our most accurate critics and sources of insight and inspiration. Our children have again been forced to contend with politics and textbook writing as a perennial topic of conversation in their visits home, and have responded with critiques and ideas of their own, which appear throughout the text.

Our colleagues at Indiana University and the University of Wisconsin (and before that, Duke University for both of us) provided many opportunities to talk about American politics and teaching this course.

Bill thanks his colleagues at Indiana University and elsewhere, including Christine Barbour, John Brehm, Ted Carmines, Chris DeSante, Mike Ensley, Bernard Fraga, Russ Hansen, Matthew Hayes, Yanna Krupnikov, Lin Ostrom, Regina Smyth, Will Winecoff, and Jerry Wright, for sharp insights and encouragement at crucial moments. He is also grateful to many teaching assistants who have helped him organize and teach the intro class at three universities. Finally, he thanks the students at the Higher School of Economics in Moscow, Russia, where he taught the introductory class as a Fulbright Scholar in 2012.

David gives special thanks to Ken Mayer, whose daily "reality checks" and consistently thoughtful professional and personal advice are greatly appreciated. Barry Burden, Ben Marquez, Don Moynihan, Ryan Owens, Ellie Powell, Howard Schweber, Byron Shafer, Alex Tahk, Dave Weimer, Kathy Cramer, Susan Yackee, and all the great people at Wisconsin have provided a wonderful community within which to teach and research American politics. John Coleman, who has moved on to become a dean at the University of Minnesota, also deserves special thanks as a former member of the intro American team and good friend and colleague. David would also like to thank the students at the University of Debrecen in Hungary, where he taught American politics as a Fulbright Scholar in 2003–2004, and the Eberhard Karls University of Tübingen, Germany, where he taught as a Fulbright Scholar in 2011–2012. The Hungarian students' unique perspective on democracy, civil liberties, and the role of government required David to think about American politics in a different way. The German students' views on the role of political parties, campaigns, and the social welfare state also provided a strong contrast to the views of his American students.

Both of us are grateful to the political science faculty at Duke University, who, in addition to giving us our first academic jobs, worked to construct a hospitable and invigorating place to research and to teach. In particular, Rom Coles, Ruth Grant, John Aldrich, Tom Spragens, Taylor Cole, and David Barber were model teachers, colleagues, and scholars. We both learned to teach by watching them, and we are better instructors and scholars for it.

We are indebted to the outstanding people at W. W. Norton who have been our full partners through all five editions. Peter Lesser's relentless combination of wit, insight, and expertise is evident throughout the book. Sam Held kept us all on the same page, and was a graceful editor and deadline-enforcer. Steve Dunn was responsible for getting the process started and providing good counsel from beginning to end. Roby Harrington has been a source of constant encouragement and feedback. Linda Feldman has been a superb project editor, bringing to the project her talent for clarity of words and visuals. Cat Abelman put together an excellent photo program. Megan Jackson cleared reprint permissions for the figures and tables. Ashley Horna handled production with efficiency and good humor. Jillian Burr and Open design studio created a beautiful design for the book's interior and cover. Spencer Richardson-Jones and Michael Jaoui's clear vision for the ever-more-complex and rich digital media package has been a major help. We also would like to thank Aaron Javsicas and Ann Shin for their outstanding work on earlier editions. The entire crew at Norton has been incredibly professional and supportive in ways we never knew when we started writing this book. Signing with them fifteen years ago was an eyes-shut home run.

We are also indebted to the many reviewers who have commented on the text.

First Edition Reviewers

Dave Adler, *Idaho State University*

Rick Almeida, *Francis Marion University*

Jim Bailey, *Arkansas State University, Mountain Home*

Todd Belt, *University of Hawaii, Hilo*

Scott Buchanan, *Columbus State University*

Randy Burnside, *Southern Illinois University, Carbondale*

Carolyn Cocca, *SUNY College at Old Westbury*

Tom Dolan, *Columbus State University*

Dave Dulio, *Oakland University*

Matt Eshbaugh-Soha, *University of North Texas*

Kevin Esterling, *University of California, Riverside*

Peter Francia, *East Carolina University*

Scott Frisch, *California State University, Channel Islands*

Sarah Fulton, *Texas A&M University*

Keith Gaddie, *University of Oklahoma*

Joe Giammo, *University of Arkansas, Little Rock*

Kate Greene, *University of Southern Mississippi*

Steven Greene, *North Carolina State University*

Phil Habel, *Southern Illinois University, Carbondale*

Charles Hartwig, *Arkansas State University, Jonesboro*

Ted Jelen, *University of Nevada, Las Vegas*

Jennifer Jensen, *Binghamton University, SUNY*

Terri Johnson, *University of Wisconsin, Green Bay*

Luke Keele, *Ohio State University*

Linda Keith, *University of Texas, Dallas*

Chris Kelley, *Miami University*

Jason Kirksey, *Oklahoma State University*

Jeffrey Kraus, *Wagner College*

Chris Kukk, *Western Connecticut State University*

Mel Kulbicki, *York College*

Joel Lieske, *Cleveland State University*

Steve Light, *University of North Dakota*

Baodong (Paul) Liu, *University of Utah*

Ken Long, *Saint Joseph College, Connecticut*

Michael Lynch, *University of Kansas*

Cherie Maestas, *Florida State University*

Tom Marshall, *University of Texas, Arlington*

Scott McClurg, *Southern Illinois University, Carbondale*

Jonathan Morris, *East Carolina University*

Jason Mycoff, *University of Delaware*

Sean Nicholson-Crotty, *University of Missouri, Columbia*

Timothy Nokken, *Texas Tech University*

Sandra O'Brien, *Florida Gulf Coast University*

John Orman, *Fairfield University*

L. Marvin Overby, *University of Missouri, Columbia*

Catherine Paden, *Simmons College*

Dan Ponder, *Drury University*

Paul Posner, *George Mason University*

David Redlawsk, *University of Iowa*

Russell Renka, *Southeast Missouri State University*

Travis Ridout, *Washington State University*

Andy Rudalevige, *Dickinson College*

Denise Scheberle, *University of Wisconsin, Green Bay*

Tom Schmeling, *Rhode Island College*

Pat Sellers, *Davidson College*

Dan Smith, *Northwest Missouri State University*

Dale Story, *University of Texas, Arlington*

John Vile, *Middle Tennessee State University*

Mike Wagner, *University of Nebraska*

Dave Wigg, *St. Louis Community College*

Maggie Zetts, *Purdue University*

Second Edition Reviewers

Danny Adkison, *Oklahoma State University*
Hunter Bacot, *Elon College*
Tim Barnett, *Jacksonville State University*
Robert Bruhl, *University of Illinois, Chicago*
Daniel Butler, *Yale University*
Jennifer Byrne, *James Madison University*
Jason Casellas, *University of Texas, Austin*
Jeffrey Christiansen, *Seminole State College*
Richard Conley, *University of Florida*
Michael Crespin, *University of Georgia*
Brian DiSarro, *California State University, Sacramento*
Ryan Emenaker, *College of the Redwoods*
John Evans, *California State University, Northridge*
John Fliter, *Kansas State University*
Jimmy Gleason, *Purdue University*
Dana Glencross, *Oklahoma City Community College*
Jeannie Grussendorf, *Georgia State University*
Phil Habel, *Southern Illinois University, Carbondale*
Lori Han, *Chapman University*
Katy Harriger, *Wake Forest University*
Richard Himelfarb, *Hofstra University*
Doug Imig, *University of Memphis*
Daniel Klinghard, *College of the Holy Cross*
Eddie Meaders, *University of North Texas*

Kristy Michaud, *California State University, Northridge*
Kris Miler, *University of Illinois, Urbana-Champaign*
Melinda Mueller, *Eastern Illinois University*
Michael Mundt, *Oakton Community College*
Emily Neff-Sharum, *University of North Carolina, Pembroke*
David Nice, *Washington State University*
Tim Nokken, *Texas Tech University*
Stephen Nuño, *Northern Arizona University*
Richard Powell, *University of Maine, Orono*
Travis Ridout, *Washington State University*
Sara Rinfret, *University of Wisconsin, Green Bay*
Martin Saiz, *California State University, Northridge*
Gabriel Ramon Sanchez, *University of New Mexico*
Charles Shipan, *University of Michigan*
Dan Smith, *Northwest Missouri State University*
Rachel Sondheimer, *United States Military Academy*
Chris Soper, *Pepperdine University*
Walt Stone, *University of California, Davis*
Greg Streich, *University of Central Missouri*
Charles Walcott, *Virginia Tech*
Rick Waterman, *University of Kentucky*
Edward Weber, *Washington State University*
Jack Wright, *Ohio State University*

Third Edition Reviewers

Steve Anthony, *Georgia State University*
Marcos Arandia, *North Lake College*
Richard Barberio, *SUNY College at Oneonta*
Jody Baumgartner, *East Carolina University*
Brian Berry, *University of Texas, Dallas*
David Birch, *Lone Star College, Tomball*
Eileen Burgin, *University of Vermont*
Randolph Burnside, *Southern Illinois University, Carbondale*
Kim Casey, *Northwest Missouri State University*
Christopher Chapp, *University of Wisconsin, Whitewater*
Daniel Coffey, *University of Akron*
William Corbett, *University of Texas at El Paso*
Jonathan Day, *Western Illinois University*
Rebecca Deen, *University of Texas, Arlington*
Brian DiSarro, *California State University, Sacramento*
Nelson Dometrius, *Texas Tech University*

Stan Dupree, *College of the Desert*
David Edwards, *University of Texas, Austin*
Ryan Emenaker, *College of the Redwoods*
John Evans, *University of Wisconsin, Eau Claire*
Brandon Franke, *Blinn College, Bryan*
Rodd Freitag, *University of Wisconsin, Eau Claire*
Donna Godwin, *Trinity Valley Community College*
Craig Goodman, *Texas Tech University*
Amy Gossett, *Lincoln University*
Tobin Grant, *Southern Illinois University*
Stephanie Hallock, *Harford Community College*
Alexander Hogan, *Lone Star College, CyFair*
Marvin King, *University of Mississippi*
Timothy LaPira, *James Madison University*
Mary Linder, *Grayson University*
Christine Lipsmeyer, *Texas A&M University*
Michael Lyons, *Utah State University*
Jill Marshall, *University of Texas, Arlington*

Thomas Masterson, *Butte College*
Daniel Matisoff, *Georgia Institute of Technology*
Jason McDaniel, *San Francisco State University*
Mark McKenzie, *Texas Tech University*
Leonard McNeil, *Contra Costa College*
Melissa Merry, *University of Louisville*
Ann Mezzell, *Lincoln University*
Eric Miller, *Blinn College, Bryan*
Jonathan Morris, *East Carolina University*
Leah Murray, *Weber State University*
Farzeen Nasri, *Ventura College*
Brian Newman, *Pepperdine University*
David Nice, *Washington State University*
Stephen Nichols, *California State University, San Marcos*

Tim Nokken, *Texas Tech University*
Barbara Norrander, *University of Arizona*
Andrew Reeves, *Boston University*
Michelle Rodriguez, *San Diego Mesa College*
Dan Smith, *Northwest Missouri State University*
Christopher Soper, *Pepperdine University*
Jim Startin, *University of Texas, San Antonio*
Jeffrey Stonecash, *Syracuse University*
Linda Trautman, *Ohio University*
Kevin Unter, *University of Louisiana, Monroe*
Michelle Wade, *Northwest Missouri State University*
Michael Wagner, *University of Nebraska, Lincoln*
Adam Warber, *Clemson University*
Wayne Wolf, *South Suburban College*

Fourth Edition Reviewers

Rickert Althaus, *Southeast Missouri State University*
Eric K. Austin, *Montana State University*
Evelyn Ballard, *Houston Community College Southeast*
Jim Battista, *University at Buffalo, SUNY*
Kenneth C. Blanchard Jr., *Northern State University*
Heidi Brockmann, *United States Military Academy*
Adriana Buliga-Stoian, *Mount Mercy University*
Abbe Allen DeBolt, *Sandhills Community College*
John C. Evans, *University of Wisconsin, Eau Claire*
Babette Faehmel, *Schenectady County Community College*
Daniel Fuerstman, *State College of Florida*
Stephanie Hallock, *Harford Community College*
John Hitt, *North Lake College*
Debra Jenke, *Angelina College*
Ronald A. Kuykendall, *Trident Technical College*
Paul Lewis, *Arizona State University*
Mary Linder, *Grayson College*
Michael Lyons, *Utah State University*

Wendy Martinek, *Binghamton University, SUNY*
Melissa Merry, *University of Louisville*
Javan "J. D." Mesnard, *Mesa Community College*
Monique Mironesco, *University of Hawai'i, West O'ahu*
Tim Nokken, *Texas Tech University*
David Parker, *Montana State University*
Sylvia Peregrino, *El Paso Community College*
Blayne Primozich, *El Paso Community College*
Bryan Rasmussen, *Collin College*
Suzanne M. Robbins, *George Mason University*
Susan Roomberg, *University of Texas at San Antonio*
Michael Shamgochian, *Worcester State University*
Geoffrey Shine, *Wharton County Junior College*
Rachel Milstein Sondheimer, *United States Military Academy*
Gregory Streich, *University of Central Missouri*
Jeremy Teigen, *Ramapo College*
Dave Wells, *Arizona State University*

Fifth Edition Reviewers

Leslie Baker, *Mississippi State University*
Evelyn Ballard, *Houston Community College*
Jim Battista, *University at Buffalo, SUNY*
Nathaniel A. Birkhead, *Kansas State University*
William Blake, *Indiana University, IUPUI*

Kenneth C. Blanchard Jr., *Northern State University*
Michael P. Bobic, *Glenville State College*
Ben Christ, *Harrisburg Area Community College*
Rosalyn Crain, *Houston Community College, Northwest College*

Brian Cravens, *Blinn College-Schulenburg*

Stephanie R. Davis, *University of South Carolina*

Christi Dayley, *Weatherford College*

Justin B. Dyer, *University of Missouri*

Jonathan P. Euchner, *Missouri Western State University*

John W. Eyster, *University of Wisconsin, Whitewater*

Eddie Feng, *Weatherford College*

John P. Flanagan, *Weatherford College*

Peter L. Francia, *East Carolina University*

Daniel Fuerstman, *State College of Florida*

Willie Hamilton, *Mt. San Jacinto College*

David Huseman, *Butler County Community College*

Debra Jenke, *Angelina College*

Catherine Johnson, *Weatherford College*

Joshua Kaplan, *University of Notre Dame*

Tim LaPira, *James Madison University*

Alan Lehmann, *Blinn College*

Morris Levy, *University of Southern California*

Michael S. Lynch, *University of Georgia*

Rob Mellen Jr., *Mississippi State University*

Timothy Nokken, *Texas Tech University*

Anthony O'Regan, *Los Angeles Valley College*

Hyung Lae Park, *El Paso Community College*

Donna Rhea, *Houston Community College*

Joseph Romance, *Fort Hays State University*

Sam Scinta, *Viterbo University*

Michael Shamgochian, *Worcester State University*

Lenore VanderZee, *SUNY Canton*

Abram J. Trosky, *United States Coast Guard Academy*

Ronald W. Vardy, *Wharton County Community College; University of Houston*

Gordan Vurusic, *Grand Rapids Community College*

Jeremy Walling, *Southeast Missouri State University*

It is a humbling experience to have so many smart people involved in the process of writing and revising this book. Their reviews were often critical, but always insightful, and you the reader are the beneficiaries of their efforts. In many cases, the improvements in this edition are the direct result of their suggestions. They have our profound thanks.

William T. Bianco
David T. Canon
November 2016

American Politics Today

Fifth Core Edition

"

In a democracy, oftentimes other people win.

— C. J. Cregg, *The West Wing*

Understanding American Politics

How does politics work and why does politics matter?

You have just lived through one of the most interesting presidential elections in American history. For the first time, a major party nominated a woman as their candidate. Even so, the election was won by a newcomer to politics, Republican Donald Trump, who won his party's nomination despite having a deeply problematic past, no political experience, and a campaign style that emphasized insult, innuendo, and attack. The campaign was one of the nastiest ever, exemplified by Trump's repeated threats to jail Clinton if he became president, and his claim that a conspiracy of elites, media companies, and banks were working to rig the election and ensure his defeat. Yet Trump was able to win by rallying voters who wanted change and opposed immigration reform, and by raising questions about Clinton's use of a private e-mail server while secretary of state and vowing to change the "culture of corruption."

For most of you, this is the first presidential election you have paid much attention to, and it would be no surprise if you asked whether American politics always worked this way. Are presidential contests always drawn-out, controversial, and conflictual? Do they typically feature candidates as widely disliked as Clinton and Trump? Do candidates often attack their opponents in intensely personal terms, such as Trump's referring to Clinton as "Crooked Hillary," alleging that she lacked the stamina and the judgment to be president, criticizing her appearance, or claiming she used drugs to enhance her debate performance? How often do significant numbers of party leaders abandon their nominees?

The easy answer is no: the 2016 presidential election is not typical. Trump's focus on general themes such as "make America great again" rather than specific policy proposals, his rejection of well-accepted campaign tactics, his charges of a rigged electoral process, claims of sexual assault against him, the dissention within Republican ranks—all of these things are highly unusual. Even so, political science does a good job of explaining what happened in 2016. Trump's nomination

★

CHAPTER GOALS

Describe the basic functions of government.
pages 4–8

Define *politics* and identify three key ideas that help explain politics.
pages 8–14

Identify major sources of conflict in American politics.
pages 15–20

Explain how the American values of democracy, liberty, and equality work to resolve political conflict.
pages 20–23

📷

The 2016 presidential campaign and the surprising election of Republican Donald Trump highlighted the conflicts deeply embedded in American political life. Issues surrounding race, ethnicity, gender, geography, education, income level, and sexual orientation all seemed to further divide an already polarized country. Now the questions emerge: How will Trump govern? Will the divisions in American politics only become deeper, or will President Trump fulfill his election-night pledge to represent all Americans and work to unite the country?

reflected the relatively extreme policy preferences held by the average Republican primary voter and an anti-Washington mood. The closeness of the general election reflects the role of party identification and economic conditions in vote decisions. And the omnipresent conflict seen in 2016 was not only due to candidates or their campaign strategies—rather, it reflects sharp, sincere underlying differences between the parties (and their supporters) over what the federal government should and shouldn't be doing.

In fact, the outcome of the 2016 elections illustrates how digging below the surface of political events can help to explain why things happen in American politics—the conflicts and the political process that deals with them. But is conflict natural in American politics? Is this how politics really works? And why does politics matter in our lives?

Making sense of American government and politics

The premise of this book is simple: *American politics makes sense.* What happens in elections, in Washington, D.C., and everywhere else—even the 2016 election—has a logical and often simple explanation; we just have to know how to look for it. By the end of this book, we hope you get really good at analyzing the politics you see everywhere—in the news and in your own life.

This claim may seem unrealistic or even naive. On the surface, American politics often makes no sense. Polls show strong support for extreme, unconstitutional, or downright silly proposals. Candidates put more time into insulting their opponents than making credible campaign promises. Members of Congress seem more interested in beating their political opponents than getting something done. Election outcomes look random or even chaotic. And many policy questions, from reforming immigration policy to deciding what to do about climate change, seem hopelessly intractable.

Many people, we believe, have given up on American politics because they don't understand the political process, feel helpless to influence election outcomes or policy

Conflicts within the government—say, over immigration policy—often reflect real divisions among American citizens about what government should do about certain issues. Groups on all sides of controversial issues pressure the government to enact their preferred policies.

making, and believe that politics is irrelevant to their lives. Many people disliked both of the candidates running in 2016, and saw this as more evidence that American politics do not work well. Since you are taking a class on American politics, we hope you have not given up on politics entirely. It is *not* our goal to turn you into a political junkie or a policy expert. You don't need to be completely immersed in politics to make sense of it, but we hope that after finishing this book you will have a basic understanding of the political process and why it matters.

One goal of this book is to help you take an active role in the political process. A functioning democracy allows citizens to defer complicated policy decisions to their elected leaders, but it also requires citizens to monitor what politicians do and to hold them accountable at the voting booth. This book will help you accomplish this important duty by providing the analytical skills you need to make sense of politics, even when it initially appears to make no sense at all.

We are not going to spend much time talking about how American politics should be. Rather, our focus will be on explaining American politics as it is. Here are some other questions we will examine:

- Why don't people vote? Why *do* people vote? How do they decide who to vote for?
- Why do so many people mistrust politicians and the political system?
- Why can't Congress get things done? Why can they get anything done?
- Why is the Supreme Court so political?
- Can presidents do whatever they want? Why can't they do more?
- Is the media biased?

We will answer these questions and many others by applying three key ideas about the nature of politics: politics is conflictual, political process matters, and politics is everywhere. But first, we begin with an even more basic question: Why do we have a government?

Why do we have a government?

As we prepare to address this question, let's agree on a definition: **government** is the system for implementing decisions made through the political process. All countries have some form of government, which in general serves two broad purposes: to provide order and to promote the general welfare.

To Provide Order At a basic level, the answer to the question "Why do we have a government?" seems obvious: without government there would be chaos. As the seventeenth-century British philosopher Thomas Hobbes said, life in the "state of nature" (that is, without government) would be "solitary, poor, nasty, brutish, and short."[1] Without government there would be no laws—people could do whatever they wanted. Even if people tried to develop informal rules, there would be no way to guarantee enforcement of those rules. Accordingly, one of the most important roles of government is policing—making sure that people obey the law and protecting citizens from threats coming from outside the nation.

The Founders of the United States noted this crucial role in the Constitution's preamble: two of the central goals of government are to "provide for the common defense" and to "insure domestic Tranquility." The former refers to military protection against foreign invasion and the defense of our nation's common security interests. The latter refers to law enforcement within the nation, which today includes the National Guard, Federal Bureau of Investigation (FBI), Department of Homeland Security, state and local police, and the courts. So at a minimal level, government is necessary to provide security.

government
The system for implementing decisions made through the political process.

However, there's more to it than that. The Founders cited the desire to "establish Justice . . . and secure the Blessings of Liberty to ourselves and our Posterity." But do we need government to do these things? It may be obvious that the police power of the nation is required to prevent anarchy, but can't people have justice and liberty without government? In a perfect world, maybe, but the Founders had a more realistic view of human nature. As James Madison, one of the founding fathers (and the fourth president of the United States), said, "But what is government itself, but the greatest of all reflections on human nature? If men were angels, no government would be necessary. If angels were to govern men, neither external nor internal controls on government would be necessary."[2] Furthermore, Madison continued, people have a variety of interests that have "divided mankind into parties, inflamed them with mutual animosity, and rendered them much more disposed to vex and oppress each other than to co-operate for their common good."[3] That is, without government, we would quickly be headed toward Hobbes's nasty and brutish state of nature because of differences in opinion about what society should look like. Having a government means that people cannot act unilaterally against each other, but it also creates a new problem: people will try to use the government and its powers to impose their views on the rest of society.

Madison's view of human nature might sound pessimistic, but it was also realistic. He assumed that people were self-interested: we want what is best for ourselves and for our families, and to satisfy those interests we tend to form groups with like-minded people. Madison saw these groups, which he called **factions**, as being opposed to the public good, and his greatest fear was of tyranny by a faction imposing its will on the rest of the nation. For example, if one group took power and established an official state religion, that faction would be tyrannizing people who practiced a different religion. This type of oppression is precisely why many of the early American colonists fled Europe in the first place.

So government is necessary to avoid the anarchy of the state of nature, and the right kind of government is needed to avoid oppression by whoever controls the policy-making process. As we will discuss in Chapters 2 and 3, America's government seeks to control the effects of factions by dividing government power in three main ways. First, the **separation of powers** divides the government into three branches—judicial, executive, and legislative—and assigns distinct duties to each branch. Second, the system of **checks and balances** gives each branch some power over the other two. (For example, the president can veto legislation passed by Congress; Congress can impeach the president; and the Supreme Court has the power to interpret laws written by Congress to determine whether they are constitutional.) Third, **federalism** divides power yet again by allotting different responsibilities to local, state, and national government. With power divided in this fashion, Madison reasoned, no single faction could dominate the government.

To Promote the General Welfare The preamble to the Constitution also states that the federal government exists to "promote the general Welfare." This means tackling the hard problems that Americans cannot solve on their own, such as taking care of the poor, the sick, and the aged and dealing with global issues like climate change, terrorist threats, and poverty in other countries. However, government intervention is not inevitable—people can decide that these problems aren't worth solving. But if people *do* want to address these large problems, government action is necessary because **public goods** such as these are not efficiently provided by the free market, either because of **collective action problems** or for other reasons.

It is easy for two people or even a small group to tackle a common problem without the help of government, but 1,000 people (to say nothing of the more than 320 million in the United States today) would have a very difficult time. They would suffer from the **free rider problem**—that is, because it is in everyone's own interest to let someone else

factions
Groups of like-minded people who try to influence the government. American government is set up to avoid domination by any one of these groups.

separation of powers
The division of government power across the judicial, executive, and legislative branches.

checks and balances
A system in which each branch of government has some power over the others.

federalism
The division of power across the local, state, and national levels of government.

public goods
Services or actions (such as protecting the environment) that, once provided to one person, become available to everyone. Government is typically needed to provide public goods because they will be under-provided by the free market.

collective action problems
Situations in which the members of a group would benefit by working together to produce some outcome, but each individual is better off refusing to cooperate and reaping benefits from those who do the work.

free rider problem
The incentive to benefit from others' work without making a contribution, which leads individuals in a collective action situation to refuse to work together.

do the work, the danger is that no one will contribute, even though everyone wants the outcome that collective contributions would create. A government representing more than 320 million people can provide public goods, such as protecting the environment or defending the nation, that all those people acting on their own would be unable to provide, so people elect leaders and pay taxes to provide those public goods.

Collective action problems are common in modern society. Education is a great example. You benefit personally from your college education in terms of the knowledge and experience you gain, and perhaps from the higher salary you will earn because of your college degree. However, society also benefits from your education. Your employer will benefit from your knowledge and skills, as will people you interact with. If education were provided solely by the free market, those who could afford schooling would be educated, but the rest would not, leaving a large segment of society with little or no education and therefore unemployable. So, public education, like many important services, benefits all levels of society and must be provided by the government for the general welfare.

Now that we understand *why* we have a government, the next question is: *What* does the government do to "insure domestic Tranquility" and "promote the general Welfare"? Many visible components of the government promote these goals, from the police and armed services to the Internal Revenue Service, Federal Reserve, Postal Service, Social Security Administration, National Aeronautics and Space Administration, Department of Education, and Food and Drug Administration. In fact, it is hard to find an aspect of everyday life that does not involve the government in some way, either as a provider of public goods, such as national defense, interstate highways, and national parks, as a protector of civil liberties, as an enforcer of laws and property rights, or as a regulator of individual or corporate behavior.

Two important government functions described in the Constitution are to "provide for the common defense" and "insure domestic Tranquility." The military and local police are two of the most commonly used forces the government maintains to fulfill those roles.

Forms of government

While all governments must provide order and promote the general welfare, there are different types of governments. Greek political philosopher Aristotle, writing in the fourth century bc, developed a classification scheme for governments that is still surprisingly useful. Aristotle distinguished three pure types of government based on the number of rulers versus the number of people ruled: monarchy (rule by one), aristocracy (rule by the few), and polity (rule by the many—such as the general population).

Additional distinctions can be made within Aristotle's third type—constitutional republican governments—based on how they allocate power among the executive, legislative, and judicial branches. Presidential systems such as we have in the

DID YOU KNOW?

64%

of the world's population lives in countries considered to be free or partly free. All countries considered not free are in Asia or Africa.
Source: Freedom House

United States tend to follow a separation of power among the three branches, while parliamentary systems such as the one in the United Kingdom elect the chief executive from the legislature so there is much closer coordination between those two branches.

We can further refine Aristotle's third type by considering the relationships among different levels of the government. In a federal system such as the United States, power is shared among the local, state, and national levels of government. In a unitary system (such as the United Kingdom), all power is held at the national level. A confederation (like Switzerland) is a less common form of government in which states retain their sovereignty and autonomy but form a loose association at the national level.

★

DEFINE *POLITICS* AND IDENTIFY THREE KEY IDEAS THAT HELP EXPLAIN POLITICS

politics
The process that determines what government does.

What is politics?

We define **politics** as the process that determines what government does. You may consider politics the same thing as government, but we view politics as being much broader; it includes ways of behaving and making decisions that are common in everyday life. Many aspects of our discussion of politics will probably sound familiar because your life involves politics on a regular basis. This may sound a little abstract, but it should become clear in light of the three key ideas of this book (see the How It Works graphic in this chapter).

First, *politics is conflictual*. The questions debated in election campaigns and in Washington and the options considered by policy makers generally involve disagreement at all levels. The federal government does not spend much time resolving issues that everyone agrees should be decided in a particular way. Rather, making government policy involves issues on which people disagree, sometimes strongly, which makes compromise difficult—and this is a normal, healthy part of politics. Although compromise may be difficult, it is often necessary to produce an outcome that can be enacted and implemented.

Second, *political process matters*. Governmental actions don't happen by accident— they result from conscious choices made by elected officials and bureaucrats. Politics, as the process that determines what governments do, puts certain individuals into positions of power and makes the rules that structure their choices. The media often cover political campaigns the way they would report on a boxing match or the Super Bowl, focusing on the competition, rivalries, and entertaining stories, which can lead people to overlook the institutions, rules, and procedures that have a decisive influence on politics. Indeed, the political process is the mechanism for resolving conflict. The most obvious example of the political process at work is elections, which democracies use to resolve a fundamental conflict in society: deciding who should lead the country.

Third, *politics is everywhere*. Decisions about what government should do or who should be in charge are integral to society, and they influence the everyday lives of all Americans. Politics helps to determine what people can and cannot do, their quality of life, and how they think about events, people, and situations. Moreover, people's political thought and behavior are driven by the same types of calculations and decision-making rules that shape beliefs and actions in other parts of life. For example, deciding which presidential candidate to vote for is similar to deciding which college to attend. For candidates, you might consider issue positions, character, and leadership ability, while for college you would weigh which school fits your academic goals, how much tuition you can afford, and where different schools are located. In both cases you are making a decision that will satisfy the criteria most important to you.

Three Key Ideas for Understanding Politics

Politics Is Conflictual

Conflict and compromise are natural parts of politics. Political conflict over issues like the national debt, abortion, and health care **reflects disagreements among the American people** and often requires compromises within government.

Political Process Matters

How political conflicts are resolved is important. Elections determine who represents citizens in government. **Rules and procedures determine who has power** in Congress and other branches of government.

Vote aquí

Politics Is Everywhere

What happens in government affects our lives in countless ways. Policies related to jobs and the economy, food safety and nutrition, student loans, and many other areas shape **our everyday lives**. We see political information in the news and encounter political situations in many areas of our lives.

? Critical Thinking

1. **One implication of the idea that politics is conflictual is that politicians** may not want to negotiate compromises on important policy questions. Why do you think politicians sometimes refuse to compromise rather than work together to get things done?

2. **Think back to the discussion** of the 2016 election at the beginning of this chapter. Even though this election was not typical, in what ways does it illustrate the three key ideas described here?

Politics is conflictual

Political scientists have long recognized the central role of conflict in politics. In fact, one prominent theory in the mid-twentieth century saw conflict between interest groups as explaining most outcomes in American politics. The political scientist E. E. Schattschneider argued that the scope of political conflict—that is, how many people are involved in the fight—determines who wins in politics. Others have argued that some conflict is helpful for small groups: if nobody challenges a widely shared but flawed view, people may convince themselves that the obvious flaws are not a problem. Bureaucratic politics, congressional politics, elections, and even Supreme Court decision making have all been studied through the lens of political conflict.[4]

Despite the consensus that conflict in politics is inevitable, most people do not like conflict, either in their personal lives or in politics. You probably have heard people say that the three topics one should not discuss in polite company are money, religion, and politics. Indeed, since the 1950s, political scientists have found strong evidence that people avoid discussing politics in order to maintain social harmony.[5]

Many people apply their disdain for conflict to politicians as well. "Why is there so much partisan bickering?" our students frequently ask. "Why can't they just get along?" Many such comments were voiced during recent negotiations over budgets, surveillance, and foreign policy, and during many other legislative fights in recent years.

This dislike of conflict, and of politics more generally, produces a desire for what political scientists John R. Hibbing and Elizabeth Theiss-Morse call "stealth democracy"—that is, nondemocratic practices such as running government like a business or taking action without political debate. In essence, this idea reflects the hope that everything would be better if we could just take the politics out of politics. Hibbing and

Conflict is inherent in American politics. Here, supporters and opponents of same-sex marriage argue in front of the Supreme Court building in Washington on the day the Court heard arguments in *Obergefell v. Hodges,* the 2015 case that legalized same-sex marriage throughout the nation. #Obergefell #SCOTUS

Theiss-Morse argue that, to combat this belief, we need to do a better job of educating people about conflict and policy differences and that the failure to do so "is encouraging students to conclude that real democracy is unnecessary and stealth democracy will do just fine."[6] Conflict cannot be avoided in politics; ignoring fundamental disagreements will not make conflict go away.

The argument over abortion is a good example. Abortion rights have been a perennial topic of debate since a 1973 Supreme Court decision held that state laws banning abortion were unconstitutional. Surveys about abortion rights show that public opinion spans a wide range of policy options, with little agreement about which policy is best. (In Chapter 6, we will examine the political implications of this kind of broad disagreement.) Such conflicts reflect intense differences of opinion that are rooted in self-interest, ideology, and personal beliefs. Moreover, in such situations, no matter what Congress does, many people will be unhappy with the result. You might expect that politicians will ultimately find a compromise that satisfies everyone, but this is not always true. In many cases, no single policy choice satisfies even a slight majority of elected officials or citizens.

The idea that conflict is nearly always a part of politics should be no surprise. Situations in which everyone (or almost everyone) agrees about what government should be doing are easy to resolve: either a popular new policy is enacted or an unpopular issue is avoided, and the debate moves off the political agenda. Although issues where there is consensus resolve quickly and disappear, conflictual issues remain on the agenda as the winners try to extend their gains and the losers work to roll back policies. Thus, one reason that abortion rights is a perennial issue in campaigns and congressional debates is that there is no national consensus on when to allow abortions, no indication that the issue is becoming less important to citizens or elected officials, and no sign of a compromise policy that would attract widespread support.

An important consequence of the inevitable conflicts in American politics is that compromise and bargaining are essential to getting things done. Politicians who bargain with opponents are not necessarily abandoning their principles; striking a deal may be the only way to make some of the policy changes they want. Moreover, agreement sometimes exists even in the midst of controversy. For example, surveys that measure attitudes about abortion find widespread support for measures such as prohibiting government funding for abortions, requiring parental notification when a minor has an abortion, or requiring doctors who perform the procedure to present their patients with information on alternatives such as adoption.

Another consequence of conflict is that it is almost impossible to get exactly what you want from the political process. Even when a significant percentage of the population is united behind common goals—such as supporters of Barack Obama after the 2012 election, who favored immigration reform and additional control on handguns, or Republicans, who wanted to shrink government and repeal Obamacare—these individuals almost always find that they need to accept something short of their ideal to attract enough support to implement policy change. Republicans, for example, had to accept that Obamacare was here to stay, at least for the moment. The need for compromise does not mean that change is impossible, only that what is achievable often falls short of individuals' demands.

When everyone (or almost everyone) agrees about a policy or problem, the issue is generally dealt with quickly and without much conflict. In a rare example of compromise and cooperation, Republican and Democratic members of Congress along with students, teachers, and administrators applaud as President Obama signs the Every Student Succeeds Act in December 2015, which reduced the federal government's authority over state education standards. #EveryStudentSucceeds

As long as the reason of man continues fallible, and he is at liberty to exercise it, different opinions will be formed.

—James Madison

Political process matters

The political process is often described like a sporting event, with a focus on strategies and ultimately on "winning." In fact, the *National Journal* magazine regularly published a segment titled "The Play of the Day" on its online site. This focus overlooks an important point: politics is the process that determines what government does, none of which is inevitable. Public policy—everything from defending the nation to spending on Medicare—is up for grabs. And the political process determines these government actions. It is not just a game.

Elections are an excellent example of the importance of the political process. Elections allow voters to give fellow citizens the power to enact laws, write budgets, and appoint senior bureaucrats and federal judges. It matters who gets elected. After the 2008 election, when Democrats strengthened their control of Congress and captured the presidency, they enacted a massive economic stimulus package and new policies for alternative energy, global warming, education, health care, regulation of the mortgage and financial sectors, and the plan for fighting the wars in Iraq and Afghanistan. Clearly, political process matters: if the 2008 election had gone the other way, policies in all these important areas would have been significantly different. The same is true for the 2016 election, given the candidates' sharp disagreements on trade, gun rights, immigration, and other issues. Again, elections matter.

Yet politics is more than elections. As you will see, many unelected members of the federal bureaucracy have influence over what government does by virtue of their roles in developing and implementing government policies. The same is true for federal judges, who review government actions to see if they are consistent with the Constitution and other federal laws. These individuals' decisions are part of the political process, even though they are not elected to their positions.

Ordinary citizens are also part of politics. They can vote; donate time or money to interest groups, party organizations, or individual candidates; or demand action from these groups or individuals. Such actions can influence government policy, either by determining who holds the power to change policy directly or by signaling to policy makers which options have public support.

Another important element of politics is the web of rules and procedures that determines who has the power to make choices about government policy. These rules range from the requirement that the president must be born a U.S. citizen, to the rules that structure debates and voting in the House and the Senate, to the procedures for

The political process mattered in the 2016 presidential election, from determining who the candidates were, to affecting which states received the most attention from the campaigns. Here, Hillary Clinton is shown debating Donald Trump.

approving new federal regulations. Seemingly innocuous rules can have an enormous impact on what can or does happen, which means that choices about these rules are actually choices about outcomes. The ability to determine political rules empowers the people who make those choices.

Politics is everywhere

Even though most Americans have little interest in politics, most of us encounter it every day. When you read the newspaper, watch television, go online, or listen to the radio you'll almost surely encounter a political story. When you are walking down the street, you may see billboards, bumper stickers, or T-shirts advertising a candidate, a political party, an interest group, or an issue position. Someone may ask you to sign a petition. You may walk past a homeless person and wonder whether a winning candidate followed through on her promise to help. You may glance at a headline about violence in the Middle East and wonder if America should be "putting boots on the ground" (sending in troops).

Many people have an interest in putting politics in front of us on a daily basis. Interest groups, political parties, and candidates work to raise public awareness of the political process and to shape what people know and want. Moreover, the news media offer extensive coverage of elections and governing and how government policies affect ordinary Americans. Through efforts like these, politics really is everywhere.

Politics is also a fundamental part of how Americans think about themselves. Virtually all of us can name our party identification (Democrat, Republican, or Independent)[7] and can place our views on a continuum between liberal and conservative.[8]

Politics is everywhere in another important way, too: actions by the federal government touch virtually every aspect of your life. Figure 1.1 shows a time line for a typical college student on a typical day. As you can see, from the moment this student wakes up until the end of the day his or her actions are influenced by federal programs, spending, and regulations. As you will see in later chapters, it's not surprising that the federal government touches your everyday life in many ways. The federal government is extraordinarily large regardless of whether you measure spending (nearly $4 trillion a year), number of employees (over two million if you include contract workers and postal service employees), or new regulations (over 80,000 pages per year).[9]

Moreover, the idea that politics is everywhere has a deeper meaning: people's political behavior is similar to their behavior in the rest of their lives. For example, collective action problems occur when you live with roommates and need to keep common areas neat and clean. Everyone has an interest in a clean area, but each person is inclined to

I'll let you write the substance, you let me write the procedure, and I'll screw you every time.
—John Dingell

The idea that "politics is everywhere" means that government actions touch virtually all aspects of our lives, from requiring drone owners to register with the Federal Aviation Administration to mandating equal funding for men's and women's sports in high schools and colleges. Moreover, everyday life often helps us to make sense of politics and politicians, such as Republican presidential candidate Ted Cruz's claim that *Star Trek*'s Captain Picard was a Democrat while Captain Kirk was a Republican. #FAADrones #TitleIX #StarTrek

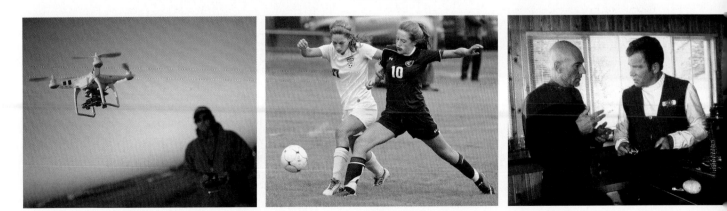

Government in a Student's Daily Life

On a typical day, the government plays a critical role in a student's daily life through federal programs, regulation, and spending. In addition to what is listed here, in what other aspects of your life does government play a part?

7:30	Wake up in dorm funded by federal program.
8:00	Eat cereal regulated by Food and Drug Administration.
8:15	Get dressed in clothing subject to import tariffs and regulations.
8:30	Read weather reports that use data from the National Weather Service.
9:00	Check e-mail using Internet developed with federal funding.
10:00	Drive to school in car whose design is shaped by federal regulations.
10:30	Drive past post office, military recruitment office, and environmental cleanup site.
11:00	Attend lecture by professor whose research receives federal funding.
4:00	Ride home from school on federally subsidized mass transit.
7:30	Pay bursar bill using federally funded student loan.
8:00	Call friend on cellular network regulated by the Federal Communications Commission.
10:00	Watch TV program on station that has federal license.

> **Just because you do not take an interest in politics does not mean that politics will not take an interest in you.**
>
> —Pericles

let someone else do the work. The same principles help us to understand campus protests of tuition hikes, alcohol bans, or changes in graduation requirements in terms of which kinds of issues and circumstances foster cooperation. In each case, individual free riders acting in their own self-interest may undermine the outcome that most people prefer.

Similarly, convincing like-minded individuals to contribute to a political group's lobbying efforts is no easy task. Each would-be contributor of time or money also has the opportunity to be a free rider who refuses to participate yet reaps the benefits of others' participation. Because of these difficulties, some groups of people with common goals remain unorganized. College students are a good example: many want more student aid and lower interest rates on government-subsidized student loans, but they fail to organize politically toward those ends.

This similarity between behavior in political situations and in the rest of life is no surprise; everything that happens in politics is the result of individuals' choices. And the connections between politics and everyday life mean you already know more about politics than you realize.

"Why Should I Care?"

The three key ideas should be the first thing you think of when you are trying to make sense of a political situation. Focusing on conflict helps you to understand what is at stake. Focusing on rules helps to explain the strategies that participants use to achieve their goals. And the idea that politics is everywhere is there to remind you that conflicts over government policy are not something that happen to other people—for better or worse, the outcome of political conflicts can touch virtually all aspects of our lives.

Sources of conflict in American politics

Where does political conflict come from? As mentioned earlier, most people avoid conflict, so you might think politicians would try to minimize it. The reality is that conflict must be addressed in order to find compromise and enact policy. Sometimes, however, disagreements resist resolution because of inherent differences among people and their opinions about government and politics.

Economic interests

People's economic interests today vary widely, and they constitute a source of conflict in politics. In contrast, relative economic equality was a defining characteristic of our nation's early history—at least among white men, since small landowners, businessmen, craftsmen, and their families constituted a large majority of the nation's population. Compared with our European counterparts, the United States has been relatively free from class-based politics. Over time, our nation has become more stratified by class, to the point that the United States has one of the highest levels of income inequality among developed nations. Nonetheless, a commitment to the **free market** (an economic system based on competition among businesses without government interference) and to *economic individualism* (the autonomy of individuals to manage their own financial decisions without government interference) remains central to our national identity.

free market
An economic system based on competition among businesses without government interference.

Despite this basic consensus on economic principles and a history relatively free of class-based politics, there are important differences among American citizens, interest groups, and political parties in terms of their economic interests and favored economic policies. Democratic politicians and activists tend to favor more **redistributive tax policies** (that is, tax policies, such as taxing the rich at higher percentages than the middle class or the poor, that attempt to create greater social equality) and social spending on programs for the poor. Democrats are also more inclined to regulate industry to protect the environment and ensure worker and product safety, but they tend to favor fewer restrictions on the personal behavior of individuals. Republicans favor lower taxes and less spending on social policies. They are also more supportive than Democrats of the free market and less inclined to interfere with business interests, although many Republicans favor regulation of individual behaviors, such as abortion and same-sex marriage.

redistributive tax policies
Politics, generally favored by Democratic politicians, that use taxation to attempt to create social equality (for example, higher taxation of the rich to provide programs for the poor).

Cultural values

Another source of conflict in American politics is differing cultural values. For example, political analysts often focus attention on the **culture wars** in the United States between "red-state" Americans, who tend to have strong religious beliefs, and "blue-state" Americans, who tend to be more secular. (The color coding of the states comes from the election-night maps on television that show the states carried by Republican candidates in red and those won by Democrats in blue—but see "Purple America," the What Do the Numbers Say? feature, for a more nuanced take on this.)

culture wars
Political conflict in the United States between "red-state" Americans, who tend to have strong religious beliefs, and "blue-state" Americans, who tend to be more secular.

Purple America: The 2016 Presidential Election

The media create maps of the country on election night with red states where Republicans win and blue states where Democrats win (see the very first pages of this book). But what do we see if we look beyond the state level to the county level? And what if we look not just at who won and who lost, but which party was stronger relative to the other? This is what this map, created by Robert Vanderbei at Princeton University, shows. The simple view of two Americas—Republican versus Democrat, red versus blue—starts to look a lot more purple.

Democrat

Other

Republican

(c) Robert J. Vanderbei

Think about it

- Which sections of the country were the strongest for Clinton and which were strongest for Trump?
- Which areas are the most mixed (light purple)?
- How do you think the color of the map will shift over the next 20 years as the nation becomes more racially and ethnically diverse?

Source: Provided by Robert J. Vanderbei, Princeton University, "2016 Presidential Election, Purple America," www.princeton.edu/~rvdb/JAVA/election 2016 (accessed 11/14/16).

The debate over income inequality in America and what should be done about it (raising the minimum wage, for example) was one of the important issues that divided Republicans and Democrats in the 2016 elections. #WageAction #FightFor15

Although the precise makeup and impact of "values voters" is still debated, there is no doubt that many Americans disagree on cultural and moral issues. These include the broad category of "family values" (such as whether and how to regulate pornography, gambling, and media obscenity and violence); whether to supplement the teaching of evolution in public schools with intelligent design and creationism; same-sex marriage; abortion; school prayer; the War on Drugs; gun control; school vouchers; immigration policy, including allowing political refugees to enter the country; the federal Common Core curriculum for K–12 schools; and religious displays in public places. These are all hot-button issues that interest groups and activists on all sides attempt to keep at the top of the policy agenda.

Racial, gender, and ethnic differences

Many political differences are correlated with racial, gender, and ethnic differences. For example, over the last generation about 90 percent of African Americans have been strong supporters of Democratic candidates. Other racial groups have been less cohesive in their voting, with their support for a particular party ranging from 55 to 70 percent. Whites tend to vote Republican; Latinos tend to vote Democratic, with the exception of Cuban Americans, who tend to vote Republican; Asian Americans tend to support Democrats with about 70 percent of the vote. A gender gap in national politics is also evident, with women being somewhat more likely to vote for Democrats and men for Republicans.[10] Because these tendencies are not fixed, however, the political implications of racial, gender, and ethnic differences can change over time.

One of the enduring debates in American politics concerns whether ethnic and racial differences *should* be tied to political interests. One perspective reflects the melting pot image of America, which holds that as different racial and ethnic groups come to this country they should mostly leave their native languages and customs behind. This perspective focuses on assimilation into American culture, with the belief that while immigrant groups will maintain some traditions from their native country, our common bonds as Americans are more important. Supporters of this view usually advocate making English the country's official language, oppose bilingual public education, and, if they favor immigration at all, prefer that it be restricted to well-off people from English-speaking countries.

Civil and voting rights contributed to the realignment of the South in the second half of the twentieth century, as more whites began supporting the Republican Party and the Democratic Party came to be seen as the champion of minority rights. Here, blacks and whites in Alabama wait in line together to vote at a city hall after enactment of the 1965 Voting Rights Act.

However, there are varied alternatives to the melting pot view. These range from racial separatists such as the Nation of Islam, whose members see white-dominated society as oppressive and discriminatory, to multiculturalists, who argue that there is strength in diversity and embrace a "tossed salad" version of assimilation (that is, each ingredient remains distinct but contributes to the overall quality of the salad).[11] In general, people holding this viewpoint favor less restrictive immigration laws and oppose policies that encourage immigrants to assimilate.

This debate over culture is one reason why recent discussions about immigration law have been so conflictual—the two sides start from very different premises about the value of diversity. But regardless of how this debate is resolved, our multiracial makeup is clear, as Table 1.1 shows. In fact, trends in population growth suggest that by 2042 whites will no longer constitute a majority of the U.S. population. The extent to which this diversity continues to be a source of political conflict depends on the broader role of race in our society. As long as there are racial differences in employment, education, health, housing, and crime and as long as racial discrimination is present in our society, race will continue to be a source of political conflict.

Many of the same observations apply to gender and politics. The women's movement is usually viewed as beginning in 1848 at the first Women's Rights Convention at Seneca Falls, New York. The fight for women's suffrage and legal rights dominated the movement through the late nineteenth and early twentieth centuries. Beginning in the 1960s and 1970s, feminism and the women's liberation movement highlighted a broad range of issues: workplace issues such as maternity leave, equal pay, and sexual harassment; reproductive rights and abortion; domestic violence; and sexual violence. While progress has occurred on many fronts, gender remains an important source of political disagreement and identity politics. Progress has been made on many fronts, including at the most basic level of electing women to political office. While Clinton failed to win the 2016 presidential election, the new Congress has more than 80 female House members and more than 20 female senators. Even so, these percentages are far lower than in the general population, confirming that gender equality remains an important source of political conflict.

TABLE 1.1

The Racial Composition of the United States

Only about 62 percent of Americans describe themselves as white. Moreover, the proportion of Hispanics and Latinos in the population is about 18 percent and rising, although this category contains many distinct subgroups. What changes would you expect in American politics and federal policy if the actual population in 2060 matches the projections?

	% of population	
	2015	2060
White	61.7	43.6
Hispanic or Latino	17.7	28.6
Black or African American	12.4	13.0
Asian	5.3	9.1
American Indian and Alaska Native	0.7	0.6
Native Hawaiian and Other Pacific Islander	0.2	0.2
Two or More Races	2.1	4.9

Source: Census data aggregated by author. Raw data available at www.census.gov/projections (accessed 6/21/16).

Ideology

Another source of differences in interests is **ideology**: a cohesive set of ideas and beliefs that allows an individual to organize and evaluate the political world. Ideology may seem most obviously related to political interests through political parties, since Republicans tend to be **conservative** and Democrats tend to be **liberal**. While this is true in a relative sense (most Republicans are more conservative than most Democrats), few Americans consider their own views ideologically extreme.[12]

Ideology shapes specific beliefs. Conservatives promote traditional social practices and favor lower taxes, a free market, and more-limited government, whereas liberals support social tolerance, stronger government programs, and more market regulation. However, the picture gets cloudy if we look more closely. **Libertarians**, for example, prefer very limited government—that is, they believe that the government should provide for the national defense and should only have a few other narrowly defined responsibilities. Because they are at the extreme end of the ideological continuum on this issue, libertarians are generally conservative in areas such as social welfare policy, environmental policy, and government funding for education and generally liberal on issues involving personal liberty such as free speech, abortion, and the legalization of drugs. For libertarians, the consistent ideological theme is limiting the role of government in our lives.

Personal ideologies are not always consistent. Someone can be both a fiscal conservative (favoring balanced budgets) and a social liberal (favoring the pro-choice position on abortion and marital rights for gay men and lesbians), or a liberal on foreign policy issues (supporting humanitarian aid and opposing military intervention overseas) and a conservative on moral issues (being pro-life on abortion and opposing stem-cell research). Ideology is a significant source of conflict in politics, and it does not always operate in a straightforward manner. In Chapter 6, we explore whether America is becoming more ideological and polarized, deepening our conflicts and making compromise more difficult.

Even so, there are clear areas of agreement in American politics, even on issues that once divided us. For example, while there is still considerable disagreement over same-sex marriage, public opinion has clearly shifted toward making such unions legal. Along the same lines, two generations ago Americans were divided on the legality of mixed-race marriage, while today very few people would object. Thus, even though conflict is a constant in American politics, it is wrong to say that we are divided into two groups, red and blue, that oppose each other on all issues of significance.

Ideology
A cohesive set of ideas and beliefs used to organize and evaluate the political world.

conservative
One side of the ideological spectrum defined by support for lower taxes, a free market, and a more-limited government; generally associated with Republicans.

liberal
One side of the ideological spectrum defined by support for stronger government programs and more market regulation; generally associated with Democrats.

libertarians
Those who prefer very limited government and therefore tend to be conservative on issues such as welfare policy, environmental policy, and public support for education but liberal on issues of personal liberty such as free speech, abortion, and the legalization of drugs.

DID YOU KNOW?

38%

of millennials call themselves conservative on economic issues, while 33 percent call themselves liberal.
Source: *USA Today*/Rock the Vote Poll

The first step in understanding politics is to determine who wants what. Who is involved in this conflict? What do they, or their side, want? In modern American politics, citizens' demands are often connected to their economic interests, values, race, gender, ethnicity, and ideology. As a result, an individual's group affiliations often tell us a lot about what they want from candidates and the government, and why they want it.

"Why Should I Care?"

Libertarians, including those in the Tea Party, believe in very limited government. These Tea Party activists at the Utah state capitol in Salt Lake City hold a flag with the libertarian motto "Don't Tread on Me" while protesting against high taxes and government programs. #TeaParty #Libertarian #LibertyForAll

EXPLAIN HOW THE AMERICAN VALUES OF DEMOCRACY, LIBERTY, AND EQUALITY WORK TO RESOLVE POLITICAL CONFLICT

democracy
Government by the people. In most contexts, this means representative democracy in which the people elect leaders to enact policies. Democracies must have fair elections with at least two options.

Resolving conflict: democracy and American political values

When we say that rules shape how conflicts are worked out in American politics, most of the time we are referring to formal (written-down) constraints that describe how the actions taken by each participant shape the ultimate outcome. For example, most American House and Senate elections are decided using simple majority rule (whichever candidate gets the most votes wins), while a few states require winners to receive an absolute majority (50% + 1) of votes cast. However, some of the most important rules are not written down—these constitute America's political culture, or a collective idea of how a government and society should operate, including democracy, equality, and liberty.[13]

Democracy

The idea of democracy means that policy disagreements are ultimately resolved through politics—through decisions made by citizens, such as their votes in elections. In the simplest terms, "democracy" means government by the people. As put into practice, this typically means representative democracy rather than direct democracy—that is, the people elect representatives who decide policies and pass laws rather than determining those things directly. There are some examples of direct democracy in the United States, such as the New England town meeting[14] and the referendum process, in which people in a state directly determine policy. But for the most part, Americans elect politicians to represent us, from school board and city council members at the local level, to state legislators and governors at the state level, to U.S. House members, senators, and the president at the national level.

Democracy is not the only way to resolve conflict, nor do all societies have as strong a belief in democracy as in America. One mechanism used by authoritarian governments is to suppress conflict though violence and limitations on freedom. Some governments, such as those of China and Russia, control political outcomes while allowing relatively free markets. The Iranian government is a theocracy, where religious figures have a veto over the government's policy choices. Part of the reason why these governments have remained in place over time is that their citizens have less of a preference for democracy—they favor, for example, a strong leader who can implement policy change without needing elected officials or the people to consent.

Liberty

Democracy means resolving conflict through voting and elections rather than through violence or coercion. When the second president of the United States, John Adams, turned over power to his bitter rival, Thomas Jefferson, after losing a hotly contested election in 1800, it demonstrated that democratic government by the people had real meaning. Democracy depends on the consent of the governed: if the views of the people change, then the government must eventually be responsive to those views or the people will choose new leaders. It also means that citizens must accept election results as authoritative—you have to obey the laws passed by a new Congress, even if you voted for the other party's candidates.

The American ethos is to embrace conflict as a natural consequence of the differences between people and to create a system that gives people the political freedom to express views based on those differences. To the Founders, liberty was the central principle for their new government: they believed that people must have the freedom to express their political views. The Bill of Rights of the Constitution, discussed in Chapter 4, outlines the nature of those liberties: the freedom of speech, press, assembly, and religion, as well as many legal and due process rights protecting individuals from government control. James Madison recognized this essential trade-off between liberty and conflict. He argued that suppressing conflict by limiting freedom was "worse than the disease" (worse than conflict). Therefore, any political system with political freedom will have conflict.

Democracy also means that resolving conflict requires compromise. In a dictatorship, totalitarian state, or monarchy, no compromise is required. The government simply chooses its preferred policies and implements them. Any dissent is either ignored or quashed. Representative democracies must be more open to dissent, or they lose legitimacy. Given the broad range of interests outlined in the previous section, no single group can get its way all of the time. Having a functioning democracy means compromising on issues that we may care deeply about.

liberty
Political freedom, such as the freedom of speech, press, assembly, and religion. These and other legal and due process rights protecting individuals from government control are outlined in the Bill of Rights of the U.S. Constitution.

Equality

Another principle of democracy is equality. Even though the Declaration of Independence boldly declared "all men are created equal," this did not mean that all people were entitled to the same income or even the same social status. Instead, the most widely embraced notion of equality is the equality of opportunity—that is, everyone should have the same chance to realize his or her potential. Political equality also means that people are treated the same in the political system. Everyone has one vote in an election, and everyone is equal in the eyes of the law—that is, we are all subject to the same rules that limit how we can lobby, contribute, work for a candidate, or express our opinions. In practice, political equality has not always existed in America. In our early history, only white men could vote and in many states those men needed to be property owners in order to vote. Slowly, political equality expanded as property requirements were dropped; black men (in 1870, but restrictions persisted into the 1960s), women

equality
In the context of American politics, "equality" means equality before the law, political equality (one person, one vote), and equality of opportunity (the equal chance for everyone to realize their potential), but not material equality (equal income or wealth).

(in 1919), and 18- to 20-year-olds (in 1971) got the right to vote (for more on the expansion of the right to vote, see Chapter 5). Today, although wealthy people clearly can have their voices heard more easily than poor people (through campaign contributions or independent expenditures on political ads), the notion of political equality is central to our democracy.

Like democracy, political equality also contributes to resolving conflict. First, if people know that they will be treated equally by the political system, they are more likely to respect the system. Indeed, one of the triggers for revolutions around the world is reaction against rigged elections or policies that benefit only the supporters of winning candidates. Political equality also gives us cues about how to get involved in politics. Most fundamentally, it suggests that the way to change policy is to elect candidates who share your views, rather than appealing to a friend or relative who works in the government or offering a bribe to a bureaucrat.

While America's political culture has many other aspects, the concepts of democracy, liberty, and equality are central to understanding how American politics works. Agreement on these principles helps to lessen conflicts and limits their scope. For example, when Republican legislators lost the battle to prevent Obamacare from being enacted, they didn't have to worry that Democrats would throw them in jail for opposing the program or force them to pay for health care for everyone else. (Indeed, this equality norm is one reason why Trump's threat to jail Clinton was so controversial.) Rather, the benefits of Obamacare are given to everyone regardless of who they voted for. Moreover, Republicans have a clear path to ending Obamacare: attract enough supporters to win the presidency and enough seats in Congress to repeal the program. Americans have been more willing to grant one another political equality and to take political defeats in stride because there is more agreement on the basic boundaries of political debate. Again, this consensus does not imply there is no conflict—quite the contrary. However, conflict is easier to resolve if it is over a narrower range of options.

In democracies like the United States, voting is one of the most visible ways citizens use the political process to express their opinions and resolve conflict.

Not surprisingly, many aspects of America's political culture will come up throughout this book. You also might want to look out for them when you are watching the news or reading about national politics. When Hillary Clinton talked about the need to provide subsidized college tuition for all Americans, she was emphasizing equality—and when President Trump argues that minimizing government involvement and allowing people more choice would lead to a better system, he is emphasizing liberty. Moreover, as this example suggests, part of the conflict in American politics is over which aspect of political culture should carry the day. The fact that issues such as education were central in recent elections is a reminder of the importance of elections in a democracy, and our belief that elections are one venue where conflicts are debated and resolved.

"Why Should I Care?"

To truly understand American politics, you must understand America's core values: democracy, liberty, and equality. These values set broad limits on how political conflicts will be resolved. Democracy implies that the people are the ultimate authority over political outcomes. Equality means that everyone has an equal share of decision-making power. And liberty implies that people are able to express whatever demands they want and to choose among a wide range of strategies in trying to shape the outcomes of political decisions. Despite conflicts over their interpretations, most Americans believe in these core values, and reminding ourselves of this can help us work toward resolving political conflicts.

Conclusion

By understanding that politics is conflictual, that it is rooted in process, and that it is everywhere, you will see that modern American political life makes more sense than you might have thought. As you read this book, we hope you will learn important "nuts and bolts" of the American political process as well as some political history. In general, however, your reading in this book will focus on contemporary questions, debates, and examples to illustrate broader points about our nation's political system. After all, American politics in its current form is the politics that will have the greatest impact on your life. To return to the case of the 2016 election, regardless of how you feel about the campaign or the outcome, you need to know how things work in order to understand why your preferred candidate won or lost—and to determine what actions you might take to help your cause.

Although you will no doubt disagree with some aspects of American politics and other parts may even make you angry, our goal in this book is to provide you with the tools to understand *why* government operates as it does. We are not arguing that the federal government is perfect or that imperfect responses to policy problems are inevitable. Rather, we believe that any attempt to explain these outcomes, or to devise ways to prevent similar problems, requires an understanding of why they happened in the first place. After reading this book, you will have a better sense of how American politics really works, and why it matters.

STUDY GUIDE

Making sense of American government and politics

Describe the basic functions of government. (Pages 4–8)

Summary

Forms of government can be characterized by the number of people who hold power (many versus few) and the number of levels over which power is distributed (national versus state versus local). Government exists primarily to provide order, although it must do so while avoiding oppression by the rulers. Government also needs to provide public goods because they will be underprovided by the free market.

Key terms

government (p. 5)

factions (p. 6)

separation of powers (p. 6)

checks and balances (p. 6)

federalism (p. 6)

public goods (p. 6)

collective action problems (p. 6)

free rider problem (p. 6)

Practice Quiz Questions

1. **What did Aristotle call "a government ruled by the many"?**
   a. monarchy
   b. aristocracy
   c. polity
   d. unitary system
   e. democracy

2. **Which term describes giving each branch of government power over the other two?**
   a. separation of powers
   b. checks and balances
   c. federalism
   d. plutocracy
   e. unitary system

3. **Which term describes the inability to get individuals to cooperate to achieve a common goal?**
   a. positive externality
   b. the Samaritan's dilemma
   c. collective action problem
   d. principal-agent problem
   e. public goods

What is politics?

Define *politics* and identify three key ideas that help explain politics. (Pages 8–14)

Summary

Conflict in politics cannot be avoided: the American people disagree on nearly every issue on which politicians make policy decisions. Compromise and bargaining are essential to enacting policy, but this means that it is almost impossible to get exactly what you want from the political process. Policy outcomes are also influenced by the policy process itself—different procedures of making policy can lead to different outcomes. Whether it is on the news or influencing most aspects of your life, politics is all around us.

Key term

politics (p. 8)

Practice Quiz Questions

4. **What is the main reason why politicians have a hard time resolving the issue of abortion?**
   a. Politicians don't listen to the people.
   b. The parties are divided on what abortion policy should look like.
   c. Politicians don't know what their constituents' views are.
   d. The country is closely divided on what abortion policy should look like.
   e. Abortion is a relatively new issue.

5. **Which concept describes the idea that actions by the government touch most aspects of your life?**
   a. Politics is understandable.
   b. Politics is conflictual.
   c. Political process matters.
   d. Politics is everywhere.
   e. People have different interests.

6. **Rules, such as those regulating debate in the Senate or limiting who can vote in elections, serve as evidence that _____ .**
   a. politics is understandable
   b. politics is conflictual
   c. political process matters
   d. politics is everywhere
   e. people have different interests

Sources of conflict in American politics

Identify major sources of conflict in American politics. (Pages 15–20)

Summary

Although Americans generally agree on a free market system, there is considerable conflict over how much the government should support tax policies that redistribute wealth. Conflict also arises on cultural grounds, pitting religious "red-state" Americans against the more secular "blue-state" Americans. There is also disagreement on the extent to which racial, gender, and ethnic diversity should be celebrated or minimized.

Key terms

free market (p. 15)
redistributive tax policies (p. 15)
culture wars (p. 15)
ideology (p. 19)
conservative (p. 19)
liberal (p. 19)
libertarians (p. 19)

Practice Quiz Questions

7. Democrats tend to favor _____ tax policies and are _____ inclined to regulate industry.

   a. redistributive; more
   b. conservative; more
   c. redistributive; less
   d. conservative; less
   e. regressive; less

8. Which issue is commonly associated with the culture wars?

   a. the national debt
   b. environmental regulation
   c. affirmative action
   d. the tax code
   e. same-sex marriage

9. An individual who opposes government social welfare policy and supports the legalization of drugs is most likely a _____.

   a. libertarian
   b. socialist
   c. Democrat
   d. Republican
   e. centrist

Resolving conflict: democracy and American political values

Explain how the American values of democracy, liberty, and equality work to resolve political conflict. (Pages 20–23)

Summary

Democracy, liberty, and equality are American political values that are essential for understanding how conflict is resolved. Representative democracies resolve conflict through elections rather than through violence. Although liberty ensures that people will have the freedom to express differing views, democracy is the best system for resolving those conflicts. Political equality ensures that everyone is treated the same before the law and that all votes are equal, and the equality of opportunity means that every person has an equal chance to realize his or her potential.

Key terms

democracy (p. 20)
liberty (p. 21)
equality (p. 21)

Practice Quiz Questions

10. Which type of equality is *not* typically agreed upon in American politics?

   a. equality of opportunity
   b. equality before the law
   c. political equality
   d. one person, one vote
   e. material equality (such as equal income)

11. What did James Madison argue was "worse than the disease"?

   a. giving too much power to state legislatures
   b. allowing people to have too much freedom, which would lead to chaos
   c. giving up liberty to get rid of conflict
   d. allowing politicians to exercise their judgment rather than listen to the people
   e. taking cod liver oil to treat various ailments

Suggested Reading

Dahl, Robert. *A Preface to Democratic Theory*, expanded ed. Chicago: University of Chicago Press, 2013.

Fiorina, Morris P., with Samuel J. Abrams and Jeremy C. Pope. *Culture War? The Myth of a Polarized America*, 3rd ed. New York: Pearson, Longman, 2010.

Gelman, Andrew, David Park, Boris Shor, Joseph Bafumi, and Jeronimo Cortina. *Red State, Blue State, Rich State, Poor State: Why Americans Vote the Way They Do*. Princeton, NJ: Princeton University Press, 2008.

Putnam, Robert D. *Bowling Alone: The Collapse and Revival of American Community*. New York: Simon and Schuster, 2000.

Schattschneider, E. E. *The Semisovereign People: A Realist's View of Democracy in America*. New York: Holt, Rinehart, and Winston, 1960.

2

The Constitution and the Founding

What are the rules of the political game?

Recently, the Constitution itself has become the focus of political debate and conflict. Starting in the 2010 midterm elections and continuing through the last three elections, a popular movement within the Republican Party known as the Tea Party has supported candidates who endorse a return to the Constitution's founding principles. Although the range of views within the Tea Party movement is vast, its supporters generally see the expansion of federal power—which began with Teddy Roosevelt, exploded during the New Deal of the 1930s and Great Society of the 1960s, and continues today with President Obama's health care reform—as constitutional overreach. Many Tea Party supporters see Social Security, Medicare, and the Federal Reserve System as unconstitutional because such policies are not expressly permitted by the Constitution. Jim DeMint, head of the conservative Heritage Foundation and a leading Tea Partier, wrote in 2010: "If President Obama's motto is 'Yes, we can,' the Constitution's is 'No, you can't.' ... Although the Constitution does give some defined powers to the federal government, it is overwhelmingly a document of limits, and those limits must be respected."[1]

To draw more attention to the Constitution, members of Congress took turns reading the document from the floor at the start of the new session of the House of Representatives in 2011. It was the first time in U.S. history that the entire Constitution had been read aloud in Congress. But even this simple gesture proved to be controversial: former representative Jesse Jackson Jr. (D-IL) objected to the "whitewashing" of the document, as the reading excluded all portions of the Constitution that alluded to slavery.[2]

The Tea Party's efforts to establish constitutional limits on government activity have also met resistance from those who challenge the Tea Party's take on the Constitution and the Founding. Rather than considering the Constitution a document that created a limited national government and protected state

Supporters of the Tea Party movement think the federal government has overstepped the powers granted to it by the Constitution. Here, a Tea Party activist holds up a copy of the Constitution to emphasize that point. Throughout American history, debates over the meaning of the Constitution have persisted. #TeaParty

power, these critics argue that it was intended to create a strong national government while limiting state power.[3] Differences of opinion about the Constitution have been part of American politics since the debates over its ratification. Unfortunately, the Constitution itself provides few definitive answers because its language was intentionally written to be general so it would stand the test of time. Consequently, in every major political debate in our history both sides have claimed to ground their views in the Constitution. Proslavery and antislavery factions during the pre–Civil War period, New Deal supporters and opponents during the Great Depression, and civil rights activists and segregationists all claimed to have the Constitution on their side, whether the dispute was over a broad or narrow interpretation of the commerce clause, the Fourteenth Amendment, or the Tenth Amendment. Today's vigorous debate about the proper scope of the national government's powers on issues such as health care, immigration, and economic policy is only the most recent chapter in this perpetual conflict. This debate is likely to shift sharply in the direction of less national power now that Republicans have unified control of government.

The Constitution provides the basis for resolving conflict through elections and representative government rather than by taking up arms. Losers of one round of elections know that they have an opportunity to compete in the next election and that their voices can be heard in another part of the government. The peaceful transition of power and the stability in our political system may be attributed to the hallmark characteristic of U.S. constitutional government: the separation of power across the levels of government (national, state, and local) and within government (legislative, executive, and judicial), and the checks and balances of power across the institutions of government.

This stability does not mean that the Constitution *resolves* our political conflicts. The Founders recognized that self-interest and conflict are inherent parts of human nature and cannot be eliminated, so they attempted to control conflict by dispersing power across different parts of government. This means that parts of the political system are always competing with one another in pursuit of various interests: for example, Republicans in Congress may want to cut spending to balance the budget whereas a Democratic president may want to achieve that goal by using a mix of spending cuts and tax increases. This creates a conflictual process that is often criticized as being

The Founders wanted to create a constitution that was general enough to stand the test of time. Their approach succeeded, and the U.S. Constitution is the oldest written constitution still in use today. However, by leaving some passages open to interpretation they also set the stage for conflict over the meaning of the Constitution. This painting depicts the signing of the document at the Constitutional Convention of 1787.

mired in "gridlock" and "partisan bickering." But that is the system our Founders created. Think about it this way: dictatorships do not have political conflict because dissenters are sent to jail or shot. We experience political conflict because there is free and open competition between different interests and ideas. Why is conflict inherent in our political system? And what does the Constitution say about how we deal with that conflict?

The historical context of the Constitution

★

DESCRIBE THE HISTORICAL CIRCUMSTANCES THAT LED TO THE CONSTITUTIONAL CONVENTION OF 1787

The Constitution was created through conflict and compromise, and understanding the historical context can help clarify *why* the framers made the specific choices they did. The first event that led many American colonists to question the fairness of British rule and shape their ideas about self-governance was the Stamp Act of 1765, which imposed a tax on many publications and legal documents in the colonies. The British Parliament enacted the tax to help pay for the French and Indian War (1754–1763), which those lawmakers thought was only reasonable because the American colonies were benefiting from the protection of British troops. However, many colonists saw this as unfair "taxation without representation" because they had no representation in the British Parliament and thus had no say in the passage of the act. A series of escalating events moved the colonies closer to the inevitable break with Great Britain. These included the British-imposed Tea Act (1773) and the Boston Tea Party later that year, in which colonists dumped tea from the British East India Company into the harbor rather than pay the new tax on tea. The British Parliament responded to the tea party with the Coercive Acts (or Intolerable Acts) of 1774 in a series of moves aimed at making sure the colonists paid for the tea they had destroyed, and designed to break the pattern of the colonists' resistance to British rule. Attempts at a political solution failed, so the Continental Congress declared independence from Britain on July 4, 1776.[4]

The Articles of Confederation: the first attempt at government

Throughout the Revolutionary and early post-Revolutionary era, the future of the American colonies was very much in doubt. While many Americans were eager to sever ties with the oppressive British government and establish a new nation that rejected the trappings of royalty, there was still a large contingent of Tories (supporters of the British monarchy) and probably an even larger group of Americans who wished the conflict would just go away. Although public opinion on the matter is impossible to know, John Adams, the second president of the United States, estimated that the Second Continental Congress was about equally divided between Tories, "true blue" revolutionaries, and "those too cautious or timid to take a position one way or the other."[5] This context of uncertainty and conflict made the Founders' task of creating a lasting republic extremely difficult.

The first attempt to structure an American government, the Articles of Confederation, swung too far in the direction of decentralized and limited government. The

Articles of Confederation
Sent to the states for ratification in 1777, these were the first attempt at a new American government. It was later decided that the Articles restricted national government too much, and they were replaced by the Constitution.

limited government
A political system in which the powers of the government are restricted to prevent tyranny by protecting property and individual rights.

FIGURE
2.1

Constitutional Time Line

The sequence of important events leading to independence and the writing and ratification of the Constitution.

September
First Continental Congress

May
Second Continental Congress

January
First publication of Thomas Paine's *Common Sense*

July
Congress adopts the Declaration of Independence

November 15
Articles of Confederation adopted by Congress, sent to the states for ratification

February 6
Treaty of Alliance with France

October 19
Cornwallis surrenders the British army at Yorktown

March 1
Articles of Confederation are ratified by the requisite number of states

1774   1775   1776   1777   1778   1779   1780   1781

1775–1783 Revolutionary War

Articles were written in the summer of 1776 during the Second Continental Congress, which also authorized and approved the Declaration of Independence. The Articles were submitted to all 13 states in 1777 for approval, but they did not take effect until the last state ratified them in 1781. However, in the absence of any alternative, the Articles of Confederation served as the basis for organizing the government during the Revolutionary War (see Figure 2.1).

In their zeal to reject monarchy, the authors of the Articles did not even include a president or any other executive leader. Instead, they assigned all national power to a Congress in which each state had a single vote. Members of Congress were elected by state legislatures rather than directly by the people. There was no judicial branch; all legal matters were left to the states, with the exception of disputes among the states, which would be resolved by special panels of judges appointed on an as-needed basis by Congress. To limit the power of government, the authors of the Articles gave each state veto power over any changes to the Articles and required approval from 9 of the 13 states on any legislation. Even more important, the states maintained autonomy and did not sacrifice any significant power to the national government; thus, government power was decentralized in the states, rather than centralized in the national government. For example, both the national government and the states could make treaties and coin money.

Congress also lacked any real authority over the states. For example, Congress could suggest the amount of money each state owed to support the Revolutionary army but could not enforce payment. General George Washington's troops were in dire straits, lacking basic food and clothing—to say nothing about the arms and munitions they needed to defeat the British. At first, Congress tried to compel the states to support their own troops, but this appeal failed. Desperate for funds, in 1781 Congress tried to give itself the power to raise taxes, but the measure was vetoed by Rhode Island, which represented less than 2 percent of the nation's population! If France had not come to

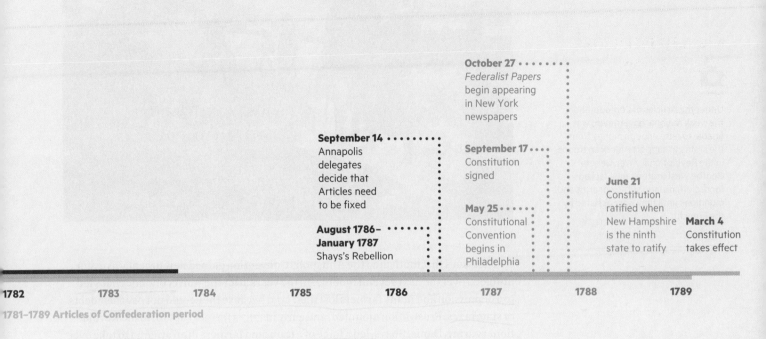

October 27 · · · · · · · ·
Federalist Papers
begin appearing
in New York
newspapers

September 14 · · · · · · · · ·
Annapolis
delegates
decide that
Articles need
to be fixed

August 1786– · · · · · · ·
January 1787
Shays's Rebellion

September 17 · · · ·
Constitution
signed

May 25 · · · · · ·
Constitutional
Convention
begins in
Philadelphia

June 21
Constitution
ratified when
New Hampshire
is the ninth
state to ratify

March 4
Constitution
takes effect

| 1782 | 1783 | 1784 | 1785 | 1786 | 1787 | 1788 | 1789 |

1781–1789 Articles of Confederation period

the aid of the American army with much-needed funds and troops, the weakness of the national government could have led to defeat.[6]

After the Revolutionary War ended with the British surrender at Yorktown in October 1781, the inability to raise revenue through taxes continued to plague Congress. The new government owed millions of dollars in war debts to foreign governments and domestic creditors, so Congress devised a plan to repay the debts over 25 years; but again, it had no way to make the states pay their share. Instead, Congress proposed an amendment to the Articles that would allow it to collect import duties, but New York, the busiest seaport in the nation, did not want to share its revenue and vetoed the amendment. Foreign trade also suffered because of the weak national government. If a foreign government negotiated a trade arrangement with Congress, it could be vetoed or amended by a state government, so that a foreign country wanting to conduct business with the United States might have to negotiate separate agreements with Congress and each state legislature. Even trade among the states was complicated and inefficient: each state could make its own currency, exchange rates varied, and many states charged tolls and fees to export goods across state lines. (Just imagine how difficult interstate commerce would be today if you had to exchange currency at every state line and if the value of your currency varied depending on which state you were in.)

A small group of leaders decided that something had to be done. A group from Virginia urged state legislatures to send delegates to a convention on interstate commerce in Annapolis, Maryland, in September 1786. Only five sent delegates. However, Alexander Hamilton and James Madison salvaged success from the convention by getting those delegates to agree to convene again in Philadelphia the following May. Delegates to the Annapolis Convention also agreed that the next convention would examine the defects of the current government and "devise such further provisions as shall appear to them necessary to render the Constitution of the Federal Government adequate to the exigencies of the Union."[7]

Under the Articles of Confederation, the weak national government was unable to raise enough money from the states to support American troops in the Revolutionary War. General George Washington's men lacked food, clothing, and sufficient arms and munitions until they were assisted by the French.

The issues that motivated the Annapolis Convention gained new urgency as events unfolded over the next several months. In the years after the war, economic chaos led to a depression and many farmers lost their land because they could not pay their debts or state taxes. Frustration mounted, and early in 1787 a former captain in the Revolutionary army, Daniel Shays, led a force of a thousand farmers in an attempt to take over the Massachusetts state government arsenal in Springfield. Their goal was to force the state courts to stop prosecuting debtors and taking their land, but the rebels were repelled by a state militia. Similar protests on a smaller scale took place in Pennsylvania and Virginia. Some state legislatures gave in to the debtors' demands, causing national leaders to fear that Shays's Rebellion had exposed fundamental discontent with the new government. The very future of the fledgling nation was at risk.

Shays's Rebellion
An uprising of about 4,000 men in Massachusetts in 1786 and 1787 to protest oppressive laws and gain payment of war debts. The unrest prompted calls for a new Constitution.

Political theories of the framers

Although the leaders who gathered in Philadelphia in the summer of 1787 to write the Constitution were chastened by the failure of the Articles of Confederation, these men still shared many of the principles that had motivated the Revolution. There continued to be broad consensus on three key principles: (1) popular control of government through a republican democracy, (2) a rejection of monarchy, and (3) limitations on government power that would protect individual rights and personal property (that is, protect against tyranny).

monarchy
A form of government in which power is held by a single person, or monarch, who comes to power through inheritance rather than election.

Republicanism First among these principles was rejection of monarchy in favor of a form of government based on self-rule. Republicanism as understood by the framers is a government in which elected leaders would represent the views of the people. Thomas Paine, an influential political writer of the Revolutionary era, wrote a pamphlet titled *Common Sense* in 1776 that was a widely read[8] indictment of monarchy and an endorsement of the principles that fueled the Revolution and underpinned the framers' thinking. Paine wrote that monarchy was the "most bare-faced falsity ever imposed on mankind" and that the common interests of the community should be served by elected representatives.

republicanism
As understood by James Madison and the framers, the belief that a form of government in which the interests of the people are represented through elected leaders is the best form of government. Our form of government is known as a republican democracy.

The Founders' views of republicanism, together with liberal principles of liberty and individual rights, shaped their vision of the proper form of government. The best expression of these principles is found in the Declaration of Independence:

We hold these truths to be self-evident, that all men are created equal, that they are endowed by their Creator with certain unalienable Rights, that among these are Life, Liberty, and the pursuit of Happiness. That to secure these rights, Governments are instituted among Men, deriving their just powers from the consent of the governed. That whenever any Form of Government becomes destructive of these ends, it is the Right of the People to alter or to abolish it, and to institute new Government.

Three crucial ideas are packed into this passage: equality, self-rule, and natural rights. Equality was not given much attention in the Constitution (in later chapters we discuss how the problem of slavery was handled), but the notion that a government gains its legitimacy from the "consent of the governed" and that its central purpose is to uphold the "unalienable" or natural rights of the people was central to the framers. The "right of the people to alter or abolish" a government that did not protect these rights served both to justify the revolt against the British and to remind the framers of their continuing obligation to make sure that those needs were met. The leaders who met in Philadelphia thought the Articles of Confederation had become "destructive to those ends" and therefore needed to be altered.

Paine, Jefferson, Madison, and other political thinkers of the American Founding broke new ground in laying out the principles of republican democracy, but they also built on the ideas of political philosophers of their era. As mentioned in Chapter 1, Thomas Hobbes argued that government was necessary to prevent people from living in an anarchic "state of nature" in which life would be "nasty, brutish, and short." However, Hobbes's central conclusion was undemocratic: he believed that a single king must rule because any other form of government would produce warring factions. Another influential seventeenth-century philosopher, John Locke, took the notion of the consent of the governed in determining a government's legitimacy in a more democratic direction. He discussed many of the ideas that later appeared in the Declaration of Independence and the Constitution, including natural rights, property rights, the need for a vigorous executive branch that would be checked by a legislative branch, and self-rule through elections.[9] Baron de Montesquieu, an eighteenth-century political thinker, also influenced the framers. Although he did not use the term "separation of powers," Montesquieu argued in *The Spirit of the Laws* (1748) that no two, let alone three, functions of government (judicial, legislative, and executive) should be controlled by one branch. He also argued that in order to preserve liberty, one branch of government should be able to check the excesses of the other branches.

Human Nature and Its Implications for Democracy The most comprehensive statement of the framers' political philosophy and democratic theory was a series of essays written by James Madison, Alexander Hamilton, and John Jay titled the *Federalist Papers*. These essays explained and justified the framework of government created by the Constitution; they also revealed the framers' view of human nature and its implications for democracy. The framers' view of human nature as basically being driven by self-interest led to Madison's assessment that "[i]n framing a government which is to be administered by men over men, the great difficulty lies in this: you must first enable the government to control the governed; and in the next place oblige it to control itself." This analysis, which comes from *Federalist 51*, is often considered the clearest articulation of the need for republican government and a system of separated powers. In *Federalist 10*, Madison described the central problem for government as the need to control factions.

Madison argued that governments cannot control the causes of factions, because differences of opinion—based on the fallibility of reason; differences in wealth, property, and native abilities; and attachments to different leaders—are part of human

"consent of the governed"
The idea that government gains its legitimacy through regular elections in which the people living under that government participate to elect their leaders.

natural rights
Also known as "unalienable rights," the Declaration of Independence defines them as "Life, Liberty, and the pursuit of Happiness." The Founders believed that upholding these rights should be the government's central purpose.

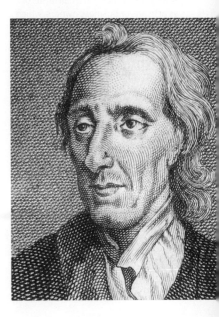

Seventeenth-century political philosopher John Locke greatly influenced the Founders. Many ideas discussed in Locke's writing appear in the Declaration of Independence and the Constitution.

nature. The only way to eliminate factions would be to either remove liberty or try to make everyone the same. The first remedy Madison called "worse than the disease," and the second he found "as impracticable as the first would be unwise." Because people are driven by self-interest, which sometimes conflicts with the common good, government must, however, try to control the effects of factions. This was the task facing the framers at the Constitutional Convention.

Economic interests

Political ideas were central to the framers' thinking at the Constitutional Convention, but economic interests were equally important. First, while there were certainly class differences among Americans in the late eighteenth century, they were insignificant compared with the inequalities found in Europe. America did not have the history of feudalism that had created tremendous inequality in Europe between landowners and propertyless serfs who worked the land. In contrast, most Americans owned small farms or worked as middle-class artisans and craftsmen. Thus, while political equality did not figure prominently in the Constitution, citizens' relative economic equality did influence the context of debates at the Constitutional Convention.

Second, despite Americans' general economic equality, there were significant regional economic differences. The South was largely agricultural, with cotton and tobacco plantations that depended on slave labor. The South favored free trade because of its export-based economy (bolstered by westward expansion) and the slave trade. The middle Atlantic and northern states, however, had smaller farms and a broad economic base of manufacturing, fishing, and trade. These states favored government-managed trade and commercial development.

Despite these differences, the diverse population favored a stronger national government and reform of the Articles of Confederation (see Nuts & Bolts 2.1). Creditors

The economic context of the American Founding had an important impact on the framing of the Constitution. Most Americans worked on small farms or as artisans or business owners, which meant that economic power was broadly distributed. This woodcut shows New York City around the time the Constitution was written, viewed from upper Manhattan.

Comparing the Articles of Confederation and the Constitution

Issue	Articles of Confederation	Constitution
Legislature	Unicameral Congress	Bicameral Congress divided into the House of Representatives and the Senate
Members of Congress	Between two and seven per state (the number was determined by each state)	Two senators per state; representatives apportioned according to population of each state
Voting in Congress	One vote per state	One vote per representative or senator
Selection of members	Appointed by state legislatures	Representatives elected by popular vote; senators appointed by state legislatures
Chief executive	None (there was an Executive Council within Congress, but it had limited executive power)	President
National judiciary	No general federal courts	Supreme Court; Congress authorized to establish national judiciary
Amendments to the document	When approved by all states	When approved by two-thirds of each house of Congress and three-fourths of the states
Power to coin money	Federal government and the states	Federal government only
Taxes	Apportioned by Congress, collected by the states	Apportioned and collected by Congress
Ratification	Unanimous consent required	Consent of nine states required

wanted a government that could pay off its debts to them, southern farmers wanted free trade that could only be efficiently promoted by a central government, and manufacturers and traders wanted a single national currency and uniform interstate commerce regulations. However, there was a deep division between those who supported empowering the national government and those who still favored strong state governments and a weak national government. These two groups became known as the Federalists and the Antifederalists. Now the stage was set for a productive but contentious convention.

Federalists
Those at the Constitutional Convention who favored a strong national government and a system of separated powers.

Antifederalists
Those at the Constitutional Convention who favored strong state governments and feared that a strong national government would be a threat to individual rights.

The politics of compromise at the Constitutional Convention

★

ANALYZE THE MAJOR ISSUES DEBATED BY THE FRAMERS OF THE CONSTITUTION

The central players at the Constitutional Convention were James Madison, Gouverneur Morris, Edmund Randolph, James Wilson, Benjamin Franklin, and George Washington, who was the unanimous choice to preside over the convention (despite his initial decision not to attend). Several of the important leaders of the Revolution were not present. Patrick "Give me Liberty, or give me Death!" Henry was selected to attend

James Madison argued that it is beneficial to put the interests of one group in competition with the interests of other groups, so that no one group can dominate government. He hoped to achieve this through the separation of powers across different branches of the national government and across the national, state, and local levels.

but declined to do so, as he opposed any changes in the Articles, saying he "smelled a rat." Indeed, those who were opposed to a stronger national government largely avoided the convention. Other prominent leaders who did not attend included Thomas Jefferson and John Adams, who were working overseas as U.S. diplomats, and Thomas Paine, who was back in England. Moreover, John Hancock and Samuel Adams were not selected to attend. The delegates met in secret to encourage open, uncensored debate.

Although there was broad consensus among the delegates that the Articles of Confederation needed to be changed, there were many tensions over the issues that required political compromise (see Nuts & Bolts 2.2). Among them were the following:

- majority rule versus minority rights
- large states versus small states
- legislative power versus executive power (and how to elect the executive)
- national power versus state and local power
- slave states versus nonslave states

These complex competing interests meant that the delegates had to focus on pragmatic, achievable solutions rather than on proposals that represented particular groups' ideals but that could not gain majority support. Robert A. Dahl, a leading democratic theorist of the twentieth century, argues that it was impossible for the Constitution to "reflect a coherent, unified theory of government" because so much compromising and vote trading was required to find common ground.[10] Instead, the delegates tackled the problems one at a time, holding lengthy debates and multiple votes on most issues. The most important initial decision they made was to give up on the original plan to revise the Articles of Confederation; instead, they decided to start from scratch with a new blueprint for government.

Majority rule versus minority rights

A central problem for any representative democracy is protecting minority rights within a system ruled by the majority. The framers did not think of this issue in terms of racial and ethnic minorities (as we might today), but in terms of regional and economic minorities. How could the framers be sure that small landowners and poorer people would not impose onerous taxes on the wealthier minority? How could they guarantee that dominant agricultural interests would not impose punitive tariffs on manufacturing while allowing free export of farmed commodities? The answers to these questions can be found in Madison's writings on the problem of factions.

Madison defined a faction as a group motivated by selfish interests against the common good. If these interests prevailed, it could produce the very kind of tyranny that the Americans had fought to escape during the Revolutionary War. Madison was especially concerned about tyranny by majority factions because, in a democracy, minority tyranny would be controlled by the republican principle: the majority could simply vote out the minority faction. If, however, the majority always rules, majority tyranny could be a real problem. Given the understanding of selfish human nature that Madison so clearly outlined, a populist, majoritarian democracy would not necessarily produce the common good. However, if too many protections were provided to minority and regional interests, the collective interest would not be served because constructive changes could be vetoed too easily, as under the Articles of Confederation.

Madison's solution to this problem provided the justification for our form of government. He argued that to control majority tyranny, factions must

Major Compromises at the Constitutional Convention

Conflict	Position of the Large States	Position of the Small States	Compromise
Apportionment in Congress	By population	State equality	Great Compromise created the Senate and House
Method of election to Congress	By the people	By the states	House elected by the people; Senate elected by the state legislatures
Electing the executive (president)	By Congress	By the states	By the Electoral College
Who decides federal–state conflicts?	Some federal authority	State courts	State courts to decide*
	Position of the Slave States	**Position of the Nonslave States**	**Compromise**
Control over commerce	By the states	By Congress	By Congress, but with 20-year exemption for the importation of slaves
Counting slaves toward apportionment	Counted 1:1 like citizens	Not counted	Three-Fifths Compromise
	Position of the Federalists	**Position of the Antifederalists**	**Compromise**
Protection for individual rights[†]	Secured by state constitutions; national Bill of Rights not needed	National Bill of Rights needed	Bill of Rights passed by the 1st Congress; ratified by all states as of December 1791

*This was changed by the Judiciary Act of 1789, which provided for appeals from state to federal courts.

[†]This issue was raised but not resolved until after the convention.

be set against one another to counter each other's ambitions and prevent the tyranny of any single majority faction. This was to be accomplished through the "double protection" of the separation of powers within the national government in the form of checks and balances, and also by further dividing power across the levels of state and local governments.

Madison also argued that additional protection against majority tyranny would come from the "size principle." That is, the new nation would be a large and diverse republic in which majority interests would be less likely to organize and therefore less able to dominate. According to Madison, "Extend the sphere, and you take in a greater variety of parties and interests; you make it less probable that a majority of the whole will have a common motive to invade the rights of other citizens; or if such a common motive exists, it will be more difficult for all who feel it to discover their own strength, and to act in unison with each other."[11] This insight provides the basis for modern pluralism, a political theory that makes the same argument about the crosscutting interests of groups today.

pluralism
The idea that having a variety of parties and interests within a government will strengthen the system, ensuring that no group possesses total control.

The precise contours of Madison's solution still had to be hammered out at the convention, but the general principle pleased both the Antifederalists and the Federalists. State governments would maintain some autonomy, but the national government would become stronger than it had been under the Articles. The issue was striking the appropriate balance: none of the framers favored a pure populist majoritarian democracy, and few wanted to protect minority rights to the extent that the Articles had.

Small states versus large states

The question of the appropriate balance came to an immediate head in a debate between small-population and large-population states over representation in the national legislature. Under the Articles, every state had a single vote, but this did not seem fair to large states. They were pushing for representation based on population. This proposal, along with others that would strengthen the national government, was the Virginia Plan. The small states countered with the New Jersey Plan, which proposed maintaining equal representation for every state. Rhode Island, the smallest state, was so concerned about small-state power that it boycotted the convention. Tensions were running high; this issue appeared to have all the elements of a deal breaker, and there seemed to be no way to resolve the impasse.

Just as it appeared that the convention might grind to a halt before it really got started, Connecticut proposed what became known as the Great Compromise, or Connecticut Compromise. The plan suggested establishing a Congress with two houses: the Senate would have two senators from each state, and in the House of Representatives each state's number of representatives would be based on its population. Interestingly, Connecticut's population was ranked seventh of the 13 states (see What Do the Numbers Say?). It was in a perfect position to offer a compromise because it did not have strong vested interests in the plans offered by either the small states or the large states.

Legislative power versus executive power

An equally difficult challenge was how to divide power at the national level. Here the central issues revolved around the executive—the president. How much power should the president have relative to the legislative branch? (The courts also figured here, but they were less central to the discussions.) And how would the president be elected?

Limiting Presidential Power The delegates knew what they did not want: the king of England and his colonial governors were viewed as tramplers of liberty. But many delegates rejected outright the idea of a single executive because they believed it was impossible to have an executive who would not be oppressive. Edmund Randolph proposed a three-person executive for this reason, arguing that a single executive would be the "fetus of monarchy." The Virginia Plan envisioned a single executive who would share some legislative power with federal judges in a Council of Revision with the power to veto legislation passed by Congress (however, the veto could be overridden by a simple majority vote in Congress). The delegates finally agreed on the single executive because he would have the most "energy, dispatch, and responsibility for the office," but they constrained the president's power through the system

Virginia Plan

A plan proposed by the larger states during the Constitutional Convention that based representation in the national legislature on population. The plan also included a variety of other proposals to strengthen the national government.

New Jersey Plan

A plan that was in response to the Virginia Plan, in which smaller states at the Constitutional Convention proposed that each state should receive equal representation in the national legislature, regardless of size.

Great Compromise

A compromise between the large and small states, proposed by Connecticut, in which Congress would have two houses: a Senate with two legislators per state and a House of Representatives in which each state's representation would be based on population (also known as the Connecticut Compromise).

Connecticut's Pivotal Place at the Constitutional Convention

Though there were many disagreements over the details of America's new constitution, one of the most intense focused on how states would be represented in Congress, either allocating representatives equally or based on population. After other plans were considered and rejected, the Connecticut Compromise won out. But why Connecticut? What do the numbers say?

State Populations at the Time of the Constitutional Convention

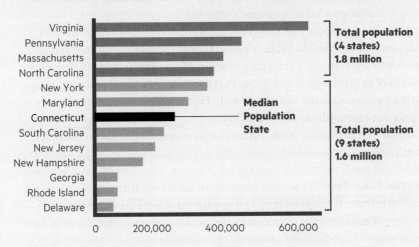

Votes at the Constitutional Convention

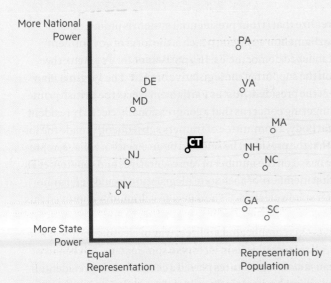

Source: Keith L. Doughterty and Jac C. Heckelman, "A Pivotal Voter from a Pivotal State: Roger Sherman at the Constitutional Convention," *American Political Science Review* 100:2 (May 2006): 298.

WHAT DO THE NUMBERS SAY?

At first glance, the Connecticut Compromise seems to make perfect sense: as the seventh of 13 states in terms of population, Connecticut was positioned to offer a compromise that would appeal to both large and small states. But it actually was much more complicated. First, Rhode Island did not attend the convention, so there was no true median state (with only 12 states at the convention, no one stood alone at the center). Second, given that each state had one vote at the convention, the smallest states could have easily outvoted the biggest ones and insisted on equal representation for each state.

Why didn't the smaller states impose their view? Two of the smaller states, Georgia and South Carolina, focused on their future growth, so they supported representation based on population, the Virginia Plan. But when other smaller states balked at their loss of power, the Connecticut Compromise was able to win the support of North Carolina (and Massachusetts's delegates were divided), so the compromise passed 5-4-1.

Despite this more complex picture, an analysis of all 569 votes at the Constitutional Convention clearly shows that Connecticut occupied a pivotal place at the convention. Connecticut was in the middle in terms of desire for representation based on population and in terms of desire for more state power. Connecticut's right in the center of this graph—no wonder they could broker a compromise!

Think about it

1. Looking at the graph "Votes at the Constitutional Convention," why do you think Connecticut was well positioned to find a compromise?

2. How do these graphs help us understand why the Virginia and New Jersey plans were in conflict and ultimately rejected?

of checks and balances. One significant power they granted to the executive was the veto. It could be overridden by Congress, but only with the support of two-thirds of both chambers. This requirement gave the president a significant role in the legislative process.

In addition to Hamilton, the other New Yorkers also favored a strong executive. This was probably because the governorship of New York closely resembled the type of executive that the Constitution envisioned. The governor of New York was elected by the people rather than by the legislature, served for three years, and was eligible for reelection. The office also had a legislative veto power and considerable control over appointments to politically controlled jobs. The arguments the New Yorkers made on behalf of the strong executive relied heavily on the philosophy of John Locke. Locke saw the general superiority of a government of laws created by legislatures, but he also saw the need for an executive with more flexible leadership powers, or what he called "prerogative powers." Legislatures are unable, Locke wrote, "to foresee, and so by laws to provide for all accidents and necessities." They also are, by virtue of their size and unwieldiness, too slow to alter and adapt the law in times of crisis, when the executive could step in to pursue policies in the public's interest.

Although there was support for this view, the Antifederalists were concerned that if such powers were viewed as open-ended they could give rise to the type of oppressive leader the framers were trying to avoid. Madison attempted to reassure the opponents of executive power, arguing that any prerogative powers would have to be clearly enumerated in the Constitution. In fact, the Constitution explicitly provides only one extraordinary executive power: the right to grant reprieves and pardons, which means that the president can forgive any crimes against the federal government.

Selecting the President The second contentious issue concerning the executive was the method of selecting a president. The way the president was elected incorporated the issues of majority rule and minority rights, state versus national power, and the nature of executive power itself. Would the president be elected by the nation as a whole, by the states, or by coalitions within Congress? If the state-level governments played a central role, would this mean that the president could not speak for national interests? If Congress elected the president, could the executive still provide a check on the legislative branch?

Most Americans do not realize that (1) our presidential system is unique and (2) we came close to having a parliamentary system, which is the form of government that exists in most other established democracies. In a **parliamentary system**, the executive branch depends on the support of the legislative branch. The Virginia Plan proposed that Congress elect the president, just as Parliament elects the British prime minister. However, facing lingering concerns that a congressionally elected president would be too beholden to that body, a committee of framers subsequently made the following recommendations: that the president be selected by an electoral college, representation in which would be based on the number of representatives and senators each state has in Congress, and that members of each state's legislature would determine the method for choosing their state's electors.[12] The delegates ultimately approved this recommendation.

Why did the delegates favor this complicated, indirect way of electing the president? As with good compromises, all sides could claim victory to some extent. Advocates of state power were happy because state legislatures played a central role in presidential elections; those who worried about the direct influence of the people liked the indirect manner of election; and proponents of strong executive power were satisfied that the president would not simply be an agent of Congress.

parliamentary system
A system of government in which legislative and executive power are closely joined. The legislature (parliament) selects the chief executive (prime minister) who forms the cabinet from members of the parliament.

However, the solution had its flaws and did not work out the way the framers intended. First, if the electoral college was supposed to provide an independent check on the voters it never played this role because the framers did not anticipate the quick emergence of political parties. Electors became agents of the parties, as they remain today, rather than independent actors who would use their judgment to pick the most qualified candidate for president. Second, the emergence of parties created a serious technical error in the Constitution: the provision that gave each elector two votes and elected the candidate with the most votes as president and the second-place finisher as vice president. With electors acting as agents of parties, they ended up casting one vote each for the presidential and vice-presidential candidate of their own party. This created a tie in the 1800 presidential election when Thomas Jefferson and Aaron Burr each received 73 electoral votes. The problem was fixed by the Twelfth Amendment, which required that electors cast separate ballots for president and vice president.

National power versus state and local power

Tensions over the balance of power cut across virtually every debate at the convention. The issues included presidential versus legislative power, whether the national government could supersede state laws, apportionment in the legislature, slavery, regulation of commerce and taxation, and the amending process. The overall compromise that addressed these tensions was the second of Madison's "double protections," the system of federalism, which divided power between autonomous levels of government that controlled different areas of policy.

Federalism is such an important topic that we devote the entire next chapter to it, but two brief points about it are important here. First, the Tenth Amendment, which was added as part of the Bill of Rights shortly after ratification, was a concession to the Antifederalists who were concerned that the national government would gain too much power in the new political system. The Tenth Amendment says: "The powers not delegated to the United States by the Constitution, nor prohibited by it to the States, are reserved to the States respectively, or to the people." This definition of **reserved powers** was viewed as setting outer limits on the reach of national power.

Between 1918 and 1937 and then again starting in the 1990s, the Supreme Court has frequently invoked the Tenth Amendment to nullify various laws passed by Congress as unconstitutional intrusions on the reserved powers of the states (see the discussion in Chapter 3 of the Supreme Court's recent preference for state-centered federalism). As noted in the chapter opener, the Tea Party has relied on the Tenth Amendment to support its arguments against national power. For example, Tea Partiers argue that the states and the private sector, not the national government, should have the primary responsibility for health care policy.

Second, the **national supremacy clause** of the Constitution (Article VI) says that any national law is the supreme law of the land and takes precedence over any state law that conflicts with it. This is especially important in areas where the national and state governments have overlapping responsibilities for policy.

Slave states versus nonslave states

Slavery was another nearly insurmountable issue for the delegates. Southern states would not agree to any provisions limiting slavery. Although the nonslave states

"

Yo.
The people are asking to hear my voice…
For the country is facing a difficult choice.
…And if you were to ask me who I'd promote…
Jefferson has my vote.

—*Hamilton,* the musical

A slave auction in Virginia. Slavery proved problematic at the Constitutional Convention: Would there be limits on the importation of slaves? How would runaway slaves be dealt with by nonslave states? And how would slaves be counted for the purposes of congressional representation?

opposed the practice, they were not willing to scuttle the entire Constitution by taking a principled stand. Even after these basic divisions had been recognized, many unresolved issues remained. Could the importation of slaves be restricted in the future? How would northern states deal with runaway slaves? Most important in terms of the politics of the issue, how would the slave population be counted for the purpose of slave states' representation in Congress?

The deals that the convention delegates cut on the issue of slavery illustrate the two most common forms of compromise: splitting the difference and logrolling (trading votes). Splitting the difference is familiar to anyone who has haggled over the price of a car or bargained for something at a flea market; you end up meeting halfway, or splitting the difference. Logrolling occurs when politicians trade votes for one another's pet projects.

The delegates went through similar negotiations over how slaves would be counted for purposes of states' congressional representation. The states had been through this debate once before, when they addressed the issue of taxation under the Articles of Confederation. At that point, the slave states had argued that slaves should not be counted because they did not receive the same benefits as citizens and were not the same burden to the government. Nonslave states had countered that slaves should be counted the same way as citizens when determining a state's fair share of the tax burden. The sides had reached a compromise by agreeing that each slave would count as three-fifths of a person for purposes of taxation. The arguments over the issue of representation became even more contentious at the Constitutional Convention, where the positions were reversed, with slave states arguing that slaves should be counted like everyone else for the purposes of determining the number of House representatives for each state. Once again, both sides managed to agree on the **Three-Fifths Compromise**.

The other two issues, the importation of slaves and dealing with runaway slaves, were handled by logrolling combined with an element of splitting the difference. Logrolling is more likely to occur than splitting the difference when the issue cannot be neatly divided. For example, northern states either would be obligated to return

Three-Fifths Compromise
The states' decision during the Constitutional Convention to count each slave as three-fifths of a person in a state's population for the purposes of determining the number of House members and the distribution of taxes.

runaway slaves to their southern owners or would not. There was no way to split the difference. On issues with no clear middle ground, opposing sides will look for other issues on which they can trade votes. The nonslave states wanted more national government control over commerce and trade than was provided under the Articles, a change that the slave states opposed. So a logroll—or vote trade—developed as a way to compromise the competing regional interests of slavery and regulation of commerce. Northern states agreed to return runaway slaves (the Fugitive Slave Clause), and southern states agreed to allow Congress to regulate commerce and tax imports with a simple majority vote (rather than the supermajority required under the Articles).

The importation of slaves was included as part of this logroll, along with some split-the-difference negotiating. Northern states wanted to allow future Congresses to ban the importation of slaves; southern states wanted to allow the importation of slaves to continue indefinitely, arguing that slavery was essential to produce their labor-intensive crops. After much negotiation among the states, the final language of the Article resulting from this part of the logroll prevented a constitutional amendment from banning the slave trade until 1808.[13]

From a modern perspective, it is difficult to understand how the framers could have taken such a purely political approach to the moral issue of slavery. Many of the delegates believed slavery was immoral, yet they were willing to negotiate for the southern states' support of the Constitution. Some southern delegates were apologetic about slavery, even as they argued for protecting their interests. Many constitutional scholars view the convention's treatment of slavery as its central failure. In fairness to the delegates, the issue of slavery could not be settled since the goal was to create a document that all states would support. However, the delegates' inability to resolve this issue meant that it would simmer below the surface for the next 70 years, finally boiling over into the bloodiest of all American wars, the Civil War.

The convention ended on a relatively harmonious note with Benjamin Franklin moving for adoption. Franklin's motion was worded ambiguously to allow those who still had reservations to sign the Constitution anyway. Franklin's motion was

📷

Union and Confederate troops clash in close combat in the Battle of Cold Harbor, Virginia, in June 1864. The inability of the framers to resolve the issue of slavery allowed tensions over the issue to grow throughout the early nineteenth century, culminating in the Civil War.

in the "following convenient form": "Done in Convention by the unanimous consent of the States present the 17th of September. . . . In Witness whereof we have hereunto subscribed our names." His clever wording meant that the signers were only bearing witness to the approval by the states and therefore could still, in good faith, oppose substantial parts of the document. Franklin's motion passed with 10 ayes, no nays, and one delegation divided. All but three of the remaining delegates signed.

★

CONTRAST THE ARGUMENTS OF THE FEDERALISTS WITH THOSE OF THE ANTIFEDERALISTS

Ratification

Article VII of the Constitution, which described the process for ratifying the document, was also designed to maximize its chance of success. Only nine states were needed to ratify, rather than the unanimity rule that had applied to changing the Articles of Confederation. Equally important, ratification votes would be taken in state conventions set up specifically for that purpose, bypassing the state legislatures, which would be more likely to resist some of the Constitution's state-federal power-sharing arrangements.

The near-unanimous approval at the Constitutional Convention's end masked the very strong opposition that remained. Many delegates simply left the convention when it became clear that things were not going their way (overall, 74 delegates were elected to go, 55 attended, and 39 signed the Constitution). Rhode Island sent no delegates and refused to appoint a ratification convention. More ominously, New York seemed dead set against the Constitution and Pennsylvania, Virginia, and Massachusetts were split. The ratifying conventions in each state subjected the Constitution to intense scrutiny, as attendees examined every sentence for possible objections. A national debate raged over the next nine months.

The Antifederalists' concerns

The Antifederalists were most worried about the role of the president, the transfer of power from the states to the national government, and the lack of specific guarantees of civil liberties. In short, they feared that the national government would become tyrannical. The doubts about the single central executive were expressed by Patrick Henry, a leading Antifederalist. Speaking to the Virginia ratifying convention, Henry was mocking in his indictment: "Your president may easily become a king. . . . There will be no checks, no real balances in this government."[14] Even Thomas Jefferson complained that the president would control the armed forces and could be reelected indefinitely.[15] State power and the ability to regulate commerce were also central concerns. States such as New York would lose substantial revenue if they could no longer charge tariffs on goods that came into their ports. Other states were concerned that they would pay a disproportionate share of national taxes.

The Antifederalists' foremost objection was to the lack of protections for civil liberties in the new political system. During the last week of the convention, Elbridge Gerry and George Mason offered a resolution "to prepare a Bill of Rights." However, the resolution was unanimously defeated by the state delegations. Some believed that the national government posed no threat to liberties, such as freedom of the press, because it did not have the power to restrict them in the first place. Others thought that because it would be impossible to enumerate all rights, it was better to

> **A lady asked Dr. [Benjamin] Franklin, "Well, Doctor, what have we got—a republic or a monarchy?"**
> **"A republic," replied the Doctor, "if you can keep it."**
>
> —**James McHenry,** *The Records of the Federal Convention of 1787*

list none at all. Federalists such as Roger Sherman argued that state constitutions, most of which protected freedom of speech, freedom of the press, right to a trial by jury, and other civil liberties, would be sufficient to protect liberty. However, many Antifederalists still wanted assurances that the *national* government would not trample their rights.

The Federalists' strategies

The Federalists counterattacked on several fronts. First, supporters of the Constitution gained the upper hand in the debate by claiming the term "federalist." It is a common tactic in debates to co-opt a strong point of the opposing side as a positive for your side. The opponents to the Constitution probably had a stronger claim than its supporters to being federalists—that is, those who favor and emphasize the autonomous power of the state governments. Today, for example, the Federalist Society is a conservative group organized around the principles of states' rights and limited government. By calling themselves Federalists, the supporters of the Constitution asserted that they were the true protectors of states' interests, which irritated the Antifederalists to no end. The Antifederalists also had the rhetorical disadvantage of having "anti" attached to their name, thereby being defined in terms of their opponents' position rather than their own. But the problem was more than just rhetorical: the Federalists pointed out that the Antifederalists did not have their own plan to solve the problems created by the Articles and therefore were cast as defenders of the status quo, which the Federalists viewed as unsustainable.

Second, the Federalists published the *Federalist Papers*. Although originally published in New York newspapers, they were widely read throughout the nation. The *Federalist Papers* were essentially one-sided arguments aimed at changing public opinion. The authors downplayed potentially unpopular aspects of the new system, such as the power of the president, while emphasizing points they knew would appeal to the

This political cartoon from 1788 depicts the erection of the "eleventh pillar of the great national dome" when New York became the eleventh state to ratify the Constitution, leaving only North Carolina and Rhode Island (shown as still wobbling in this cartoon) to ratify the document.

The CENTINEL. VOL IX

REDEUNT SATURNIA REGNA.

On the erection of the Eleventh PILLAR of the great National DOME, we beg leave most sincerely to felicitate "OUR DEAR COUNTRY."

Rise it will.

The foundation good—it may yet be SAVED.

The FEDERAL EDIFICE.

ELEVEN STARS, in quick succession rise—
ELEVEN COLUMNS strike our wond'ring eyes,
Soon o'er the whole, shall swell the beauteous DOME,
COLUMBIA's boast—and FREEDOM's hallow'd home.
Here shall the ARTS in glorious splendour shine!
And AGRICULTURE give her stores divine!
COMMERCE refin'd, dispense us more than gold,
And this new world, teach WISDOM to the old—
RELIGION here shall fix her blest abode,
Array'd in mildness, like its parent GOD!
JUSTICE and LAW, shall endless PEACE maintain,
And the "SATURNIAN AGE," return again.

opposition. Despite their biased arguments, the *Federalist Papers* are the best comprehensive discussion of the political theory underlying the Constitution and the framers' interpretations of many of its key provisions.

Third, the Federalists agreed that the new Congress's first order of business would be to add a **Bill of Rights** to the Constitution to protect individual rights and liberties. This promise was essential for securing the support of New York, Massachusetts, and Virginia. The ninth state, New Hampshire, ratified the Constitution on June 21, 1788, but New York and Virginia were still dragging their heels, and their support was viewed as necessary for the legitimacy of the United States, even if it technically was not needed. By the end of the summer, both Virginia and New York finally voted for ratification. Rhode Island and North Carolina refused to ratify until Congress made good on its promise of a Bill of Rights. The 1st Congress submitted 12 amendments to the states, and 10 were ratified by all the states as of December 15, 1791.

Bill of Rights
The first 10 amendments to the Constitution; they protect individual rights and liberties.

"Why Should I Care?"

Politicians today have a very difficult time compromising on issues like gun control, abortion rights, and even the proper levels of taxation and spending. At the Constitutional Convention, the framers had to struggle with fundamental issues such as executive power and state versus national power as well as incredibly divisive issues like slavery. The framers were facing uncertainty about the very survival of their new nation and the nearly impossible task of creating a new framework that would allow our nation to not only survive but also flourish. Yet the framers were able to arrive at workable compromises on all of these issues. Without compromise, our nation would not exist. When you hear a politician today say, "I am going to stick to my principles; I am not going to compromise," reflect on the fact that governing is not possible without compromise. "Compromise" is not a dirty word; it is an essential feature of politics.

The Constitution: a framework for government

The Constitution certainly has its flaws (some of which have been corrected through amendments), primarily its undemocratic qualities such as the indirect election of senators and the president, the compromises that suppressed the issue of slavery (indeed, the words "slave" and "slavery" do not appear in the Constitution), and the absence of any general statement about citizens' right to vote. However, given the delegates' political context and the various factions that had to be satisfied, the Constitution's accomplishments are substantial.

The document's longevity is testimony to the framers' foresight in crafting a flexible framework for government. Perhaps its most important feature is the system of separation of powers and checks and balances that prevent majority tyranny, while maintaining sufficient flexibility for decisive leadership during times of crisis (such as the Civil War, the Great Depression, and World War II). The system of checks and balances means that each branch of national government has certain exclusive powers, some shared powers, and the ability to check the other two branches (see How It Works: Checks and Balances).

> 99
>
> **The Constitution is the guide which I never will abandon.**
>
> **—George Washington**

Exclusive powers

The framers viewed Congress as the "first branch" of government and granted it significant exclusive powers. With the popularly elected House of Representatives and the Senate indirectly elected by state legislatures, Congress was designed to be both the voice of the people and an institution more removed from the people, with a significant role in domestic and foreign policy. Congress was given the power to raise revenue for the federal government through taxes and borrowing, regulate interstate and foreign commerce, coin money, establish post offices and roads, grant patents and copyrights, create the system of federal courts, declare war, "raise and support armies," make rules for the military, and create and maintain a navy. Most important is the so-called power of the purse—control over taxation and spending—given to Congress in Article I, Section 8, of the Constitution: "No money shall be drawn from the Treasury, but in consequence of appropriations made by law." Or, as Madison put it, "the legislative department alone has access to the pockets of the people."

Congress's exclusive powers take on additional significance through the **necessary and proper clause**, also known as the elastic clause. It gives Congress the flexibility to "make all Laws which shall be necessary and proper for carrying into Execution the foregoing Powers, and all other Powers vested by this Constitution in the Government of the United States, or in any Department or Officer thereof." This broad grant of power meant that Congress could pass laws related to any of its exclusive powers. For example, although the Constitution did not explicitly mention Congress's right to compel people to serve in the military, its power to enact a draft was clearly given by the necessary and proper clause, in conjunction with its power to "raise and support armies."

Congress's exclusive powers are more numerous and specific than the limited powers granted to the president. The president is the commander in chief of the armed forces and has power to receive ambassadors and foreign ministers and to issue pardons. The president's most important powers are contained in the executive powers clause that says: "The executive power shall be vested in a President of the

necessary and proper clause
Part of Article I, Section 8, of the Constitution that grants Congress the power to pass all laws related to its expressed powers; also known as the elastic clause.

How it works: in theory
Checks and Balances

In the Constitution, if one branch tries to assert too much power, the other branches have certain key powers that allow them to fight back and restore the balance. (In addition to the powers noted in the diagram, Congress can impeach the president and remove him or her from office.)

The president nominates judges.

The president can veto congressional legislation.

The Senate confirms the president's judicial nominations. Congress can impeach and remove judges from office.

Executive

Legislative

Judicial

The Senate approves presidential nominations, and Congress can pass laws over the president's veto.

The Court interprets the laws passed by Congress.

The Court interprets actions by the executive branch.

Checks and Balances in the War on Terror

Since shortly after the attacks of September 11, 2001, the president, acting on his power as commander in chief, authorized the Guantánamo Bay detention center in Cuba to be used as a place to detain, interrogate, and try prisoners related to the War on Terror. There have been allegations of human rights violations, including torture. The controversies and policies surrounding Guantánamo show how checks and balances work in practice.

So...

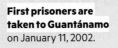

First prisoners are taken to Guantánamo on January 11, 2002.

He said...

President George W. Bush asserts that Guantánamo is **outside the legal jurisdiction** of the United States and that the prisoners held there do not have protections guaranteed to prisoners of war under the Geneva Convention.

But then...

The Supreme Court disagrees in *Hamdan v. Rumsfeld* on June 29, 2006, ruling that the detainees were entitled to basic legal rights and that the Geneva Convention did apply.

It's still a problem.

The detention center is increasingly controversial as Amnesty International, a human rights organization, calls it **"the gulag of our time,"** and in 2006, the United Nations urges the United States to close the facility.

New idea.

Two days after taking office, President Obama **signs an order to close the center** by the end of the year and to suspend all Guantánamo military commission hearings for 120 days.

Nope.

A week later, a military court judge **overturns the order** to suspend hearings at Guantánamo.

Sounds like a plan.

President Obama **wants to move Guantánamo prisoners** to a federal prison in Illinois.

Plan blocked.

A few months later, **Congress votes to block funds** needed for the transfer or release of prisoners held at the facility.

Sigh.

Going into the last year of President Obama's presidency, **more than 100 prisoners remain,** some of whom have been detained for 14 years without a trial.

Critical Thinking

1. **Why do you think it has been so difficult to close the detention center in Guantánamo?** Is it because of the issue of terrorism and national security? Or is it because of our system of checks and balances? Why?

2. **Do you think our system of checks and balances creates** too much gridlock, or is it an essential check on potential tyranny?

The president and the Senate share the appointment power to many federal offices: the president makes the nominations, and the Senate provides its "advice and consent." The nomination of Merrick Garland (pictured here at left) to the Supreme Court was stopped by Republican Senate leaders who decided to allow the next president to fill the vacancy on the Court.

United States of America" and in the directive to ensure "that the laws are faithfully executed." As we see later in the chapter, these Article II clauses impart most of the president's power.

The courts did not receive nearly as much attention in the Constitution as either Congress or the president. Alexander Hamilton argued in *Federalist 78* that the Supreme Court would be the "least dangerous branch," because it had "neither the power of the purse nor the sword." The most important positive powers that the framers gave the Supreme Court were lifetime tenure for justices in good behavior and relative independence from the other two branches. The critical negative power of judicial review, the ability to strike down the laws and actions of other branches, will be discussed later.

Shared powers

Along with dividing the exclusive powers between branches, checks and balances designate some shared powers. These are areas where no branch has exclusive control. For example, the president has the power to negotiate treaties and make appointments to the federal courts and other government offices, but these executive actions are to be undertaken with the "advice and consent" of the Senate, which means they were intended to be shared powers. In the twentieth century, these particular powers became executive centered, with the Senate providing almost no advice to the president and routinely giving its consent (often disapprovingly called rubber-stamping). However, the Senate can assert its shared power, as shown by the Senate's relatively recent blocking of several of President George W. Bush's and President Obama's lower-court nominees and Obama's nomination of Merrick Garland to the Supreme Court in 2016.

The war powers, which include decisions about when and how to use military force, were also intended to be shared but have become executive-dominated powers. After serious disagreements, the ultimate compromise that the framers reached shows checks and balances at work, with the president serving as the commander in chief of the armed forces and Congress having the power to declare war and to appropriate the funds to conduct a war. One other goal of the Founders in making the war powers a shared power was to ensure civilian control of the military. By providing a role for both Congress and the president, the Constitution made it more likely that this important democratic principle would be maintained. One critical event occurred before the Constitution was written when George Washington resigned his commission as commander in chief of the Continental Army. Congress had given Washington complete authority over conduct of the Revolutionary War, and many in Congress wanted him to continue to rule, almost as a king. Washington knew that it was critical for the new nation to have democratically elected leaders control the military. By resigning his commission, he made it clear that any future leadership role he would play (and it was widely assumed by the Founders that he would be the first president) would be as a civilian rather than a general.

Since very early in our nation's history, the president has taken a lead role in the war powers, making the decision to use military force. Presidents have authorized the use of American troops on hundreds of occasions, but Congress has declared war only five times. Of these, Congress debated the merits of entering only one war, the War of 1812. The other "declarations" recognized a state of war that already existed. (For example, after Japan bombed Pearl Harbor, Hawaii, in 1941, Congress's subsequent declaration of war formally recognized what everyone already knew.) As the 2003 invasion of Iraq demonstrated, if a president is intent on going to war Congress must go along or get out of the way.

This painting, which hangs in the Capitol rotunda, shows General George Washington resigning his commission as commander in chief of the Continental Army. This set the precedent that democratically elected officials would control the U.S. military.

Examples such as this are unusual. It would be impossible today for Congress to declare war without a willing commander in chief. However, since the Vietnam War Congress has tried to redress the imbalance in the war powers in other ways. In 1970, during the Vietnam War, Congress passed a resolution that prevented any funds from supporting ground troops in Laos or Cambodia (nations that bordered Vietnam). In 2013, Congress was strongly opposed to a military strike against Syria in response to its use of chemical weapons against its own people. A showdown with President Obama was averted when Syria agreed to allow weapons inspectors to destroy their chemical weapons stockpile. These examples show that although the president continues to dominate the war powers, Congress can assert its power when it has the will—just as it can by advising the president in treaty negotiations or by withholding approval of the president's nominees for appointed positions.

Congress alone has "the power of the purse" to fund government programs. Although President Obama ordered the "troop surge" in Afghanistan, Congress had to continue appropriating money to pay for the war.

Negative or checking powers

The last part of the system of checks and balances is the negative power that the branches have over one another. These powers are especially important to ensure that no single branch dominates the national government.

Congressional Checks Congress has two important negative checks on the other two branches: impeachment and the power of the purse. **Impeachment** is where the president, vice president, or other "officers of the United States" (including federal judges) can be removed for abuses of power—specifically, "Treason, Bribery, or other High Crimes or Misdemeanors." The framers placed this central check with Congress as part of the overall move toward centralizing power at the national level.

Through the **power of the purse**, Congress can punish executive agencies by freezing or cutting their funding or holding hearings on, investigations of, or audits of their operations to make sure money is being spent properly. Congress can also freeze judges' salaries to show displeasure with court decisions, and it has the power to limit the issues that federal courts can consider. Congress can also limit the discretion of judges in other ways, such as by setting federal sentencing guidelines that recommend a range of years in prison that should be served for various crimes. Even today, the system of checks and balances is not fixed in stone but evolves according to the changing political climate.

impeachment
A negative or checking power over the other branches that allows Congress to remove the president, the vice president, or other "officers of the United States" (including federal judges) for abuses of power.

power of the purse
The constitutional power of Congress to raise and spend money. Congress can use this as a negative or checking power over the other branches by freezing or cutting their funding.

The Constitution attempts to strike a balance between protecting our civil liberties from government intrusion and providing for a government strong enough to protect our national security. There has been much controversy around revelations that the National Security Administration (NSA) has used electronic surveillance to gather data about people living in the United States. Information about this program was leaked by Edward Snowden, a staffer at the NSA. #StopWatchingUs

judicial review
The Supreme Court's power to strike down a law or executive branch action that it finds unconstitutional.

Presidential Checks The framers placed important checks on congressional power as well, and the president's most important check on Congress is the veto. Again, there was very little agreement on this topic. The Antifederalists argued that it was "a political error of the greatest magnitude, to allow the executive power a negative, or in fact any kind of control over the proceedings of the legislature." But the Federalists worried that Congress would slowly strip away presidential powers and leave the president too weak. In the end, the Federalist view that the president needed some protections against the "depredations" of the legislature won the day. However, the veto has developed into a major policy-making tool for the president, which is probably broader than the check against "depredations" envisioned by the framers.

The president does not have any formal check on the courts other than the power to appoint judges. However, presidents have, at various times, found unconventional ways to try to influence the courts. For example, Franklin Delano Roosevelt tried to "pack the Court" by expanding the size of the Supreme Court with justices who would be sympathetic with his New Deal policies. More recently, George W. Bush attempted to expand the reach of executive power in the War on Terror by taking over some functions within the executive branch that the courts had previously performed. However, the Supreme Court struck down some of these policies as unconstitutional violations of defendants' due process rights. President Obama changed many of Bush's policies, such as harsh interrogation methods and excessive secrecy. But other Bush-era policies were either more difficult to change than Obama anticipated, such as the detainment of enemy combatants in the prison at Guantánamo Bay, or deemed necessary to fight terrorism, such as indefinite detention without trial for suspected terrorists who were arrested outside combat areas.[16] Critics claim that the expansion of executive power in order to fight terrorism has threatened the institutional balance of power by giving the president too much control over functions previously carried out by the courts.[17]

Judicial Review The Constitution did not provide the Supreme Court with any negative checks on the other two branches. Instead, the Court itself (in the landmark decision of *Marbury v. Madison* in 1803) established the practice of judicial review, the ability of the Supreme Court to strike down a law or an executive branch action as unconstitutional. According to Madison's notes, nine of the eleven framers who spoke on the topic clearly favored explicitly granting the Supreme Court the power of judicial review, but the issue was not resolved at the convention. In several states assertive courts had struck down state laws, and delegates from those states resisted giving an unelected national court similar power over the entire country. Although judicial review is not explicitly mentioned in the Constitution, supporters of the practice point to the supremacy clause, which states that the "Constitution, and the Laws of the United States which shall be made in Pursuance thereof . . . shall be the supreme Law of the Land."

As Chief Justice John Marshall argued in *Marbury v. Madison,* to enforce the Constitution as the supreme law of the land the Court must determine which laws are "in pursuance thereof." Critics of judicial review argue that the Constitution is supreme because it gains its legitimacy from the people and therefore elected officials—Congress and the president—should be the primary interpreters of the Constitution rather than the courts. This dispute may never be fully resolved, but Marshall's bold assertion of judicial review made the Supreme Court an equal partner in the system of separate powers and checks and balances rather than "the least dangerous branch" that the framers described.

If you remember anything from your elementary civics class it is probably some foggy memory of the system of checks and balances and separation of powers. But why is this so important? This institutional framework provides the basis for our government and explains the nature of political conflict and outcomes. When the government shuts down because of a dispute over spending or the Senate blocks the president's court nominees, this is because the president and Congress have different roles but can check each other's powers. Understanding checks and balances and separation of powers helps us be realistic about what government can do and shows us that all parts of the government are critical but not dominant in making policy and enforcing laws.

Is the Constitution a "living" document?

★

EXPLORE HOW THE MEANING OF THE CONSTITUTION HAS EVOLVED

Polls suggest that many Americans are unfamiliar with the Constitution's basic provisions. Indeed, a national poll found that only 31 percent could name all three branches of the U.S. government, while just as many could not identify even one; 12 percent believed there was a constitutional right to own a pet and 34 percent thought there was a right to own a home.[18] Even more disconcerting, another poll showed that 52 percent could name at least two members of Bart Simpson's family while only 28 percent could list more than one of their five First Amendment rights.[19] In the face of such public ignorance, can the Constitution provide the blueprint for modern democratic governance? If so, how has it remained relevant after more than 200 years? The answer to the first question, in our opinion, is clearly yes. Although the United States falls short on many measures of an ideal democracy, the Constitution remains relevant in part because it embodies many of the central values of American citizens: liberty and freedom, majority rule and minority rights, equal protection for all citizens under the laws, and a division of power across and within levels of government. The Constitution presents a list of substantive values, largely within the Bill of Rights, aimed at legally protecting certain individual rights that we still consider basic and necessary. The Constitution also sets out the institutional framework within which the government operates.

But these observations beg the question of *why* the Constitution remains relevant today. Why does this framework of government still work? How can the framers' values still be meaningful to us? There are at least three components of the Constitution that allow it to continue as a "living" document: the ambiguity in central passages that permits flexible interpretation, the amending process, and the document's own designation of multiple interpreters of the Constitution. These factors have allowed the Constitution to evolve with the changing values and norms of the nation (see the Take a Stand feature).

Ambiguity

The Constitution's inherent ambiguity is a characteristic that has kept the document relevant to this day. Key passages were written in very general language, which has allowed the Constitution to evolve along with changing norms, values, and political contexts.

> "
>
> The people made the Constitution, and the people can unmake it. It is the creature of their will, and lives only by their will.
>
> —**Justice John Marshall**

A Living Constitution?

Should the Constitution be viewed as a flexible framework or a document that has fixed meaning? The public is evenly split on this issue, with 49 percent saying that constitutional interpretation should be based on "what it means in current time" (the living Constitution approach) and 46 percent on "what it originally meant" (originalism). However, there is a deep partisan divide on this issue, with 70 percent of Democrats taking the living constitution approach and 69 percent of Republicans supporting originalism.[a]

There is a vigorous debate among justices of the Supreme Court as to whether the Constitution is a living document or should be interpreted more strictly according to the original intent of the framers.

The meaning of the Constitution doesn't change.

Justice Clarence Thomas is perhaps the strongest advocate of the originalist view. He wrote: "Let me put it this way; there are really only two ways to interpret the Constitution—try to discern as best we can what the framers intended or make it up."[b] Former chief justice William Rehnquist, although generally adhering to the originalist view, took a more nuanced approach. He favorably cites a 1920 Supreme Court opinion by Oliver Wendell Holmes: "When we are dealing with words that also are a constituent act, like the Constitution of the United States, we must realize that they have called into life a being the development of which could not have been foreseen completely by the most gifted of its begetters."[c] John Marshall in *McCulloch v. Maryland* also endorses this view, saying the Constitution was "intended to endure for ages to come, and consequently to be adapted to the various crises of human affairs." Rehnquist says that "scarcely anyone would disagree" with the idea that the Constitution was written broadly enough to allow principles such as the prohibition against illegal searches and seizures to apply to technologies, such as the telephone or the Internet, that could not have been envisioned by the framers.[d]

However, according to this view, the *meaning* of the Constitution cannot change with the times. Rehnquist writes that "mere change in public opinion since the adoption of the Constitution, unaccompanied by a constitutional amendment, should not change the meaning of the Constitution. A merely temporary majoritarian groundswell should not abrogate some individual liberty truly protected by the Constitution."[e] Therefore, recent rulings restricting the death penalty (which is clearly endorsed by the Constitution), expanding gay rights, or allowing a child to testify remotely against her sexual abuser rather than having to confront him directly in court (as guaranteed by the Sixth Amendment) would all be inconsistent with the originalist view. This view would also hold that anything other than relying on the meaning of the words of the Constitution allows justices to "legislate from the bench," which is undemocratic given that the judges are not elected.

The meaning of the Constitution changes with the times.

Proponents of a living constitution argue for a more flexible view. Justice Thurgood Marshall advocated a living constitution, noting that the framers "could not have imagined, nor would they have accepted, that the document they were drafting would one day be construed by a Supreme Court to which had been appointed a woman and the descendent of an African slave."[f] If the meaning of the Constitution is fixed, then the Court would have to uphold a state law allowing the death penalty for horse stealing, which was common during the Founding era. Executing horse thieves, or, more realistically, children and the mentally impaired (which was allowed in many states until 2005), is unacceptable in a modern society, even if it would be allowed by a strict reading of the Constitution.

Answering the question about how justices should interpret the Constitution ultimately depends on one's broader views of the proper role of the Court within a representative democracy. Should justices be constrained by the original meaning of the Constitution, or should that meaning evolve over time? Take a stand.

take a stand

1. If you were on the Supreme Court, would you adopt an originalist or a living constitution approach? Justify your position.
2. Based on the originalist view, should a state be allowed to execute whomever it wants to, including minors (or horse thieves)? Based on the living constitution approach, should limits be placed on justices to prevent them from "legislating from the bench"?

This ambiguity was a political necessity: not only were the framers aware that the document would need to survive for generations, but in many instances the language that they chose was simply the only wording that all the framers could agree on.

Three of the most important parts of the Constitution are also among its most ambiguous: the necessary and proper (or elastic) clause, the executive powers clause, and the commerce clause. As discussed earlier, the necessary and proper clause gives Congress the power to enact laws that are related to its enumerated powers, or those that are explicitly granted. But what does "necessary and proper" mean? For the most part, Congress gets to answer that question.

The executive powers clause is even more vague: Article II begins with the words "The executive Power shall be vested in a President of the United States of America." This sentence has served to justify a broad range of presidential actions because it does not define any boundaries for the "executive powers" it grants. The vague wording was necessary because the Constitutional Convention delegates could not agree on a definition of executive power. The wording also had the desirable consequence of making the clause flexible enough to serve the country both in times that require strong presidential action (such as the Civil War, the Great Depression, or World War II) and in times when the president was not as central (such as the "golden age of Congress" in the late nineteenth century).

Perhaps the best illustration of the importance of ambiguity in the Constitution is the commerce clause, which gives Congress "the power to regulate commerce . . . among the several States." What is "commerce" and what exactly does "among the states" mean? Different interpretations have reflected prevailing norms of the time. In the nineteenth century, when the national government was relatively weak and more power was held at the state level, the Supreme Court interpreted the clause to mean that Congress could not regulate commerce that was entirely within the boundaries of a single state (*intra*state, as opposed to *inter*state, commerce). Because manufacturing typically occurred within the boundaries of a given state, this ruling led to a distinction between manufacturing and commerce, which had significant implications. For example, Congress could not regulate working hours, worker safety, or child labor given that these were defined as part of manufacturing rather than commerce. In the New Deal era of the mid-1930s, the Court adopted a more expansive interpretation of the commerce clause that largely obliterated the distinction between intrastate and interstate commerce. This view was strengthened in the 1960s when the Supreme Court upheld a civil rights law that, among other things, prevented owners of hotels and restaurants from discriminating against African Americans. For nearly 60 years this interpretation held. More recently the Supreme Court has tightened the scope of Congress's powers to regulate commerce, but the clause still serves as the basis for most important national legislation. The commerce clause has been unchanged since 1789, but its ambiguous wording has been used to justify or restrict a varying array of legislation.

Changing the Constitution

The most obvious way that the Constitution keeps up with the times is by allowing for changes to its language. The framers broadly supported the idea behind Article V, which lays out the formal process for amending the Constitution: the people must control their own political system, which included the ability to change it through a regular, nonviolent process. George Washington called constitutional amendments "explicit and authentic acts," and Thomas Jefferson was adamant that each generation needed

executive powers clause
Part of Article II, Section 1, of the Constitution that states: "The executive Power shall be vested in a President of the United States of America." This broad statement has been used to justify many assertions of presidential power.

commerce clause
Part of Article I, Section 8, of the Constitution that gives Congress "the power to regulate Commerce . . . among the several States." The Supreme Court's interpretation of this clause has varied, but today it serves as the basis for much of Congress's legislation.

enumerated powers
Powers explicitly granted to Congress, the president, or the Supreme Court in the first three articles of the Constitution. Examples include Congress's power to "raise and support armies" and the president's power as commander in chief.

to have the power to change the Constitution. Toward the end of his life, he wrote in a letter to James Madison:

Some men look at constitutions with sanctimonious reverence, and deem them like the ark of the covenant, too sacred to be touched. They ascribe to the men of the preceding age a wisdom more than human, and suppose what they did to be beyond amendment. I knew that age well; I belonged to it and labored with it. . . . It was very like the present. . . . Let us not weakly believe that one generation is not as capable as another of taking care of itself.[20]

Proposal and Ratification Although there was strong consensus on including in the Constitution a set of provisions for amending it, there was no agreement on how this should be done. The Virginia Plan envisioned a relatively easy process of changing the Constitution "whensoever it shall seem necessary" by means of ratification by the people, whereas the New Jersey Plan proposed a central role for state governments. Madison suggested the plan that was eventually adopted, which once again accommodated both those who wanted a stronger national government and those who favored the states.

Article V describes the two steps necessary to change the Constitution: proposal and ratification. Congress may *propose* an amendment that has the approval of two-thirds of the members in both houses, or an amendment may be proposed by a national convention that has been called by two-thirds of the states' legislatures. In either case, the amendment must be *ratified* by three-fourths of the states' legislatures or state conventions (see Nuts & Bolts 2.3). A national convention has never been used to propose an amendment, and every amendment except for the Twenty-First, which repealed Prohibition, has been ratified by state legislatures rather than state conventions.

A Range of Amendments Amendments have ranged from fairly narrow, technical corrections of errors in the original document (Eleventh and Twelfth Amendments) to important topics such as the abolition of slavery (Thirteenth Amendment), mandating equal protection of the laws for all citizens (Fourteenth Amendment), providing for the popular election of senators (Seventeenth Amendment), giving blacks and then women the right to vote (Fifteenth and Nineteenth Amendments), and allowing a national income tax (Sixteenth Amendment). Potential constitutional amendments have addressed many other issues, with more than 10,000 proposed; of those, 33 were

📷

Amending the Constitution is difficult and can be controversial. Some amendments that are widely accepted today, like the Nineteenth Amendment giving women the right to vote, were intensely debated prior to their ratification.

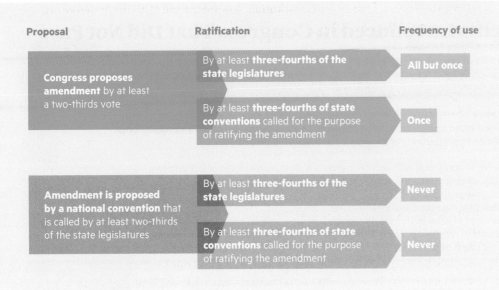

Proposal	Ratification	Frequency of use
Congress proposes amendment by at least a two-thirds vote	By at least **three-fourths of the state legislatures**	All but once
	By at least **three-fourths of state conventions** called for the purpose of ratifying the amendment	Once
Amendment is proposed by a national convention that is called by at least two-thirds of the state legislatures	By at least **three-fourths of the state legislatures**	Never
	By at least **three-fourths of state conventions** called for the purpose of ratifying the amendment	Never

Amending the Constitution

This flowchart shows how amendments to the Constitution can be proposed and ratified and the frequency with which each method has been used. Interestingly, the president is not a part of the formal process of amending the Constitution.

sent to the states and 27 have made it through the amending process (the first 10 came at once in the Bill of Rights). Table 2.1 shows several amendments that were introduced but not ratified.

Multiple interpreters

The final way that the Constitution maintains its relevance is through changing views of the document by multiple interpreters. As we pointed out in the previous discussion of the commerce clause, there have been significant changes in the way the Constitution structures the policy-making process, even though the pertinent text of the Constitution has not changed.[21] This point is best understood by examining the concept of implied powers—that is, powers that are not explicitly stated in the Constitution but can be inferred from an enumerated power. The Supreme Court often defines the boundaries of implied powers, but Congress, the president, and the public can also play key roles.

Three of the earliest examples of implied powers show the president, the Supreme Court, and Congress each interpreting the Constitution and contributing to its evolving meaning. The first involved the question of how active the president should be in stating national foreign policy principles. In issuing his famous proclamation of neutrality in 1793, George Washington unilaterally set forth a national foreign policy, even though the president's power to do so is not explicitly stated in the Constitution. Alexander Hamilton defended the presidential power to make such a proclamation as implied in both the executive powers clause and the president's explicitly granted powers in the area of foreign policy (receiving ambassadors, negotiating treaties, and serving as commander in chief). Thomas Jefferson, in contrast, thought it was a terrible idea for presidents to have that kind of power. He preferred that such general policy statements be left to Congress.

The Supreme Court made its mark on the notion of implied powers in a landmark case involving the creation of a national bank. In *McCulloch v. Maryland* (1819), the Court ruled that the federal government had the power to create a national bank and denied the state of Maryland the right to tax a branch of that bank. The Court said it was

implied powers
Powers supported by the Constitution that are not expressly stated in it.

TABLE
2.1

Amendments Introduced in Congress That Did Not Pass

Many proposed constitutional amendments have almost no chance of passing. Indeed, most of those listed here did not even make it to the floor of the House or Senate for a vote. Why do you think a member of Congress would propose an amendment that he or she knew would fail?

114th Congress (2015–2016)	Require that the rights extended by the Constitution be granted only to natural persons (not corporations). Repeal the Sixteenth Amendment (income tax).
113th Congress (2013–2014)	No treaty, executive order, or agreement with another nation can diminish the rights of U.S. citizens. All laws that apply to U.S. citizens must apply equally to U.S. senators and representatives.
112th Congress (2011–2012)	Impose 12-year term limits for the House and Senate. Amend the First Amendment to allow limitations on federal campaign contributions and expenditures. Protect the right of parents to raise and educate their children without interference from government. Require that the federal budget be balanced.

Sources: The U.S. Constitution Online: Some Proposed Amendments, www.usconstitution.net (accessed 3/22/12); http://thomas.loc.gov (accessed 2/21/16).

The Eighth Amendment's ban on "cruel and unusual punishments" is generally viewed as excluding capital punishment, but the execution of juveniles and the mentally impaired has been found unconstitutional. This picture shows the electric chair in the Southern Ohio Correctional Facility in Lucasville.

not necessary for the Constitution to expressly grant Congress the power to create the bank; rather, it was implied in Congress's power over financial matters and from the necessary and proper clause of the Constitution.

Congress got into the act with an early debate over the president's implied power to remove appointed officials. The Constitution clearly gives the president the power to make appointments to cabinet positions and other top executive branch offices, but it is silent on how these people can be removed. This was one of the most difficult issues in the 1st Congress, and members spent more than a month debating the topic. The record of the debate is the most thorough examination of implied powers ever conducted in Congress. However, Congress ended up not taking any action on the issue, which left the president's removal power implicit in the Constitution.

Issues concerning implied powers continue to surface. The president's appointment powers have recently evolved as the Senate has played a much more aggressive role in providing its "advice and consent" on presidential nominations to the federal courts. As we explore in Chapter 14, in the past 20 years the Senate has blocked court appointments at a significantly higher rate than it did in the first half of the twentieth century. The relevant language in the Constitution is the same, yet the Senate's understanding of its role in this important process has changed. President Obama's use of executive powers to go around Congress when they declined to act also demonstrates the ambiguous nature of constitutional powers. Obama's action on EPA rules concerning carbon emissions and immigration policy were viewed as either appropriate and necessary executive action or "constitutional overreach."

Public opinion and social norms also influence the prevailing interpretation of the Constitution, as is evident in the evolving meanings of capital punishment (the death penalty) and freedom of speech. When the Constitution was written, capital punishment was broadly accepted, even for horse thieves. The framers were only concerned that people not be "deprived of life, liberty, or property without the due process of law." Therefore, the prohibition in the Eighth Amendment against "cruel and unusual punishments" certainly did not mean to the framers that the death penalty was unconstitutional. However, in 1972 the Supreme Court struck down capital punishment as unconstitutional because it was being applied arbitrarily.[22] Subsequently, after procedural changes were made, the Court once again upheld the practice. However, the Court has since decided that capital punishment for a mentally impaired man constituted cruel and unusual punishment—a decision that reflects modern sensibilities but not the thinking of the framers. Similarly, the text of the First Amendment protections for freedom of speech has never changed, but the Supreme Court has been willing to uphold significant limitations on free speech, especially in wartime. When external threats are less severe, the Court has been more tolerant of controversial speech.

The line between a new interpretation of the Constitution and constitutional change is difficult to define. Clearly, not every new direction taken by the Court or new interpretation of the constitutional roles of the president or Congress is comparable to a constitutional amendment. In one respect, a constitutional amendment is much more permanent than a new interpretation by the Court. For example, the Supreme Court could not unilaterally decide that 18- to 20-year-olds, women, and African Americans no longer have the right to vote. Constitutional amendments expanded the right to vote to include these groups, and only further amendments could either expand or restrict the right to vote. However, gradual changes in constitutional interpretation are probably just as important as the amending process in explaining the Constitution's ability to keep pace with the times. For example, although the Civil War amendments produced lasting and significant changes in the Constitution, during the New Deal shifts in constitutional interpretation helped establish a huge growth in national power without changing a single word of the document.

"Why Should I Care?"

One of the most remarkable things about the Constitution is its longevity. While there are intense debates about whether a "living Constitution" is a good thing, there is no doubt its ability to change with the times, whether because of its amending process, multiple interpreters, or ambiguity, has helped make it the oldest constitution in the world. People may joke that the Constitution isn't relevant anymore, but it shapes the boundaries for all of today's policy debates and institutional struggles.

Conclusion

The debate between Tea Party supporters and opponents outlined in the introduction illustrates many of the themes of this chapter: the conflictual nature of politics established by the Constitution, multiple interpreters, and ambiguous language. The separation of powers and the system of checks and balances in our political system divide power to protect against majority tyranny. To Tea Party supporters, we have strayed too far from the limited government roots of the Founding. Their opponents claim that the Constitution centralized power in the national government while moving away from the state-centered Articles of Confederation. Well, which side is right? The rather unsatisfying answer is that both are correct. The Founders *did* create a system of limited government that was intended to protect individual liberty from government tyranny, but at the same time the Founders wanted a strong and effective government that could overcome the limitations of state-centered government. So clearly, a return to founding principles does not mean a return to states' rights; that would be a return to the principles of the Articles of Confederation. But equally clear is that the Founders were concerned about unchecked government power.

Congress, the president, and the Supreme Court all must interpret the Constitution in the normal course of fulfilling their institutional roles. But as the Tea Party debate shows, members of the public can differ in their interpretation of the Constitution as well. It is refreshing to see the Constitution thrust to the fore in congressional and presidential candidate debates. Maybe with enough attention, those public-opinion polls showing that Americans are more familiar with the Three Stooges than with the three branches of government can be reversed. If Americans are more informed about the Constitution, they can become even more significant interpreters of the Constitution.

Finally, the general and ambiguous language of the Constitution means that both supporters and opponents of the Tea Party can stake a claim to having views that are informed by the Constitution. When a Tea Party advocate claims that the Federal Reserve is unconstitutional because it is not specifically mentioned in the document, the other side can point out that if that logic is used, then the air force is certainly unconstitutional as well (the Constitution mentions Congress's power to support the army and navy but obviously not the air force). Furthermore, Tea Party opponents would say the commerce clause and the necessary and proper clause give Congress all the power it needs.

A leading constitutional scholar, Walter Murphy, addressed the relevance issue this way: "The ideals it enshrines, the processes it prescribes, and the actions it legitimizes must either help to change its citizenry or at a minimum reflect their current values. If a constitution does not articulate, at least in general terms, the ideals that form or will re-form its people and express the political character they have . . . , it will soon be replaced or atrophy."[23] The Constitution's ability to change with the times and reflect its citizens' values has enabled it to remain relevant and important today. Its flexibility and general language means that there will never be definitive answers to the conflict over its meaning, but it ensures that these debates will be enduring and meaningful.

STUDY GUIDE

The historical context of the Constitution

Describe the historical circumstances that led to the Constitutional Convention of 1787. (Pages 29–35)

Summary

The U.S. Constitution was shaped by historical events preceding its creation, particularly the period of British rule over the colonies, the Revolutionary War, and the states' experience under the Articles of Confederation. Under British rule, the colonies were relatively independent of one another, and the framers sought to create a strong nation while still maintaining the autonomy of the states in the system. The framers based the Constitution on three key principles: the rejection of a monarchy, popular control of the government, and a limited government that protected against tyranny.

Key terms

Articles of Confederation (p. 29)
limited government (p. 29)
Shays's Rebellion (p. 32)
monarchy (p. 32)
republicanism (p. 32)

"consent of the governed" (p. 33)
natural rights (p. 33)
Federalists (p. 35)
Antifederalists (p. 35)

Practice Quiz Questions

1. **How were members of Congress selected under the Articles of Confederation?**
   a. by the state governor
   b. by the state legislature
   c. by the state supreme court
   d. by popular election
   e. by random lot

2. **What power did the president have under the Articles of Confederation?**
   a. power to raise an army
   b. power to veto congressional legislation
   c. power to negotiate foreign agreements
   d. power to nominate federal judges
   e. There was no president under the Articles of Confederation.

3. **Who is the philosopher who argued that without government life would be "nasty, brutish, and short"?**
   a. Thomas Hobbes
   b. John Locke
   c. Baron de Montesquieu
   d. Thomas Paine
   e. Thomas Jefferson

4. **At the American Founding, what is the best way to describe the economic inequality among classes and the economic diversity among regions?**
   a. high inequality/ high diversity
   b. high inequality/ low diversity
   c. low inequality/ high diversity
   d. low inequality/ low diversity

The politics of compromise at the Constitutional Convention

Analyze the major issues debated by the framers of the Constitution. (Pages 35–44)

Summary

Although the framers of the Constitution agreed that the Articles of Confederation needed to be changed, there was little consensus otherwise. The Federalists and Antifederalists clashed on several issues, though the most important were (1) balancing majority rule with minority rights, (2) allocating power between large and small states, (3) allocating power between the legislature and executive, (4) allocating power between the national government and the states, and (5) determining how to handle slavery.

Key terms

pluralism (p. 37)
Virginia Plan (p. 38)
New Jersey Plan (p. 38)
Great Compromise (p. 38)

parliamentary system (p. 40)
reserved powers (p. 41)
national supremacy clause (p. 41)
Three-Fifths Compromise (p. 42)

Practice Quiz Questions

5. **Madison argued that the best way to prevent the tyranny of factions was to _____.**
   a. outlaw political parties
   b. establish a strong national government
   c. have various groups compete against one another in the government
   d. establish strong local governments
   e. try to ensure that all people were equal

6. **The Great Compromise provided solutions to which issue?**
   a. balancing majority rule with minority rights
   b. allocating power between big and small states
   c. allocating power between the legislature and executive
   d. allocating power between national and state governments
   e. determining how to handle slavery

7. **How are executives chosen in most other established democracies?**
   a. by popular election
   b. by electoral college
   c. through selection by the judiciary
   d. through selection by the legislature
   e. by the United Nations

8. **The outcome of the Three-Fifths Compromise was that each slave counted for three-fifths of a person for the purposes of _____ and _____.**
   a. voting; taxation
   b. congressional representation; taxation
   c. voting; congressional representation
   d. taxation; congressional appropriations
   e. congressional representation; agricultural subsidies

Ratification

Contrast the arguments of the Federalists with those of the Antifederalists. (Pages 44–46)

Summary

After the Constitution was written and approved at the Constitutional Convention, it still needed to be ratified by nine states. The Constitution was primarily criticized by the Antifederalists, which gave way to a lengthy public debate over the merits of the proposed framework. Ultimately, to win over the necessary support in the states the framers had to include the Bill of Rights, which was tailored to protect the rights of states and individuals from the national government.

Key term

Bill of Rights (p. 46)

Practice Quiz Questions

9. **What group was concerned about the Constitution's provisions for the strength of the president and the lack of specific guarantees of civil liberties?**
   a. Tories
   b. Unionists
   c. Federalists
   d. Antifederalists
   e. Free Soilers

10. **A series of arguments originally published in New York newspapers supported the Constitution and outlined the political theory behind it. What are these assembled works called?**
    a. *Pickwick Papers*
    b. *Federalist Papers*
    c. *Antifederalist Papers*
    d. *Common Sense*
    e. *The Second Treatise of Government*

The Constitution: a framework for government

Outline the major provisions of the Constitution. (Pages 47–53)

Summary

The defining feature of the Constitution is its separation of powers while still maintaining flexibility for leadership in times of crisis. The system of checks and balances gives each branch of the federal government some explicit powers, some shared powers, and some ability to limit the power of the other two branches of government.

Key terms

necessary and proper clause (p. 47) **power of the purse** (p. 51)
impeachment (p. 51) **judicial review** (p. 52)

Practice Quiz Questions

11. **The "necessary and proper" clause gives flexibility to which part of government?**
    a. the president
    b. the Supreme Court
    c. the bureaucracy
    d. the Congress
    e. interest groups

12. **Which branch has the fewest explicit powers?**
    a. the president
    b. the Supreme Court
    c. the bureaucracy
    d. the Congress
    e. the people

13. **Which of the following negative powers does the president enjoy?**
    a. the power to veto legislation
    b. the power to freeze judicial salaries
    c. the power to review the constitutionality of a law
    d. the power to impeach federal justices
    e. the power to dissolve Congress and call new elections

Is the Constitution a "living" document?

Explore how the meaning of the Constitution has evolved.
(Pages 53–59)

Summary

The Constitution is more than 200 years old, yet it still provides a blueprint for modern governance. It has maintained its relevance due to its ambiguity on several key passages, its ability to be amended rather than entirely rewritten, and its designation of multiple interpreters of the Constitution.

Key terms

executive powers clause (p. 55)   **enumerated powers** (p. 55)

commerce clause (p. 55)   **implied powers** (p. 57)

Practice Quiz Questions

14. **Which of the following clauses, central to congressional activity, has been interpreted differently over time though the wording has stayed the same?**

    a. establishment clause

    b. commerce clause

    c. enumerated powers clause

    d. executive powers clause

    e. prerogative powers clause

15. **Which part of government often defines the boundaries of implied powers?**

    a. the president

    b. the Supreme Court

    c. the bureaucracy

    d. the Congress

    e. the people

Suggested Reading

Allen, Danielle. *Our Declaration: A Reading of the Declaration of Independence in Defense of Equality*. New York: W. W. Norton, 2014.

Amar, Akhil Reed. *America's Unwritten Constitution: The Precedents and Principles We Live By*. New York: Basic Books, 2012.

Currie, David P. *The Constitution of the United States: A Primer for the People*, 2nd ed. Chicago: University of Chicago Press, 2000.

Dahl, Robert A. *How Democratic Is the American Constitution?* New Haven, CT: Yale University Press, 2001.

Davis, Sue. *Corwin and Peltason's Understanding the Constitution*, 17th ed. Boston: Wadsworth, 2008.

Hamilton, Alexander, James Madison, and John Jay. *The Federalist Papers*. 1788. Reprint, 2nd ed., edited by Roy P. Fairfield. Baltimore, MD: Johns Hopkins University Press, 1981.

Ketcham, Ralph. *The Anti-Federalist Papers and the Constitutional Convention Debates*. New York: Signet Classics, 2003.

Rossiter, Clinton. *1787: The Grand Convention*. New York: Macmillan, 1966.

Strauss, David. *The Living Constitution*. New York: Oxford University Press, 2010.

Sunstein, Cass R. *Designing Democracy: What Constitutions Do*. New York: Oxford University Press, 2001.

Wood, Gordon S. *The Creation of the American Republic*. New York: W. W. Norton, 1969.

3

Federalism

States or the federal government: who's got the power?

Following the passage of the 2010 Affordable Care Act (ACA), which is often referred to as "Obamacare,"[1] 26 states sued the national government over the new law. Intended to provide health care coverage to more than 30 million Americans who were uninsured, the law was viewed by the attorneys general from these states as an unconstitutional overreach of federal power. David Rivkin, one of the attorneys who filed the suit on behalf of the states, said, "This is one of the most important Constitutional challenges in history.... The states' sovereign authority is being trammeled upon by the federal government."[2] Michael Boldin, executive director of the Tenth Amendment Center, argued that the lawsuit showed "that state level resistance to federal power is not just an old idea relegated to history books. It's something that's alive and well right now."[3]

The Supreme Court largely upheld the ACA in 2012, but the Court agreed with the states on one important point: it ruled that the expansion of Medicaid, which would provide health care for an additional 17 million low-income Americans, was unconstitutionally coercive in requiring states to expand Medicaid or lose all their federal funding for the existing Medicaid program. States could still choose to accept the federal funding to expand Medicaid, but they would not lose their other Medicaid funding if they opted out of the expansion.[4]

However, the battle between the national government and the states did not end with the Court's ruling. Nineteen states decided not to accept the federal incentives to expand Medicaid, leaving 4.3 million poor Americans without health insurance.[5] Thirty-four states opted not to run the health insurance exchanges, requiring the federal government to do it for them (entirely, or at least in part). A few states have actively tried to obstruct implementation of the law by forbidding state employees to do anything to help that is not specifically required by the law.[6]

Some of these disputes continued to work their way up to the Supreme Court. In 2015, the Court ruled that federal subsidies to purchase insurance applied to all 50 states, despite language in the law that said subsidies would only apply in an "exchange established by the State." If the Court had followed a narrow interpretation of the legislative language, 6.4 million Americans would have lost their insurance and likely created a "death spiral" for the ACA. In the majority opinion

📷

Should the government require all Americans to have health insurance? While individual Americans disagreed about this question, the states and the federal government also disagreed about the states' role in implementing the Affordable Care Act.

Chief Justice John Roberts wrote: "Congress passed the Affordable Care Act to improve health insurance markets, not to destroy them." By deferring to Congress's broad legislative intent, the Supreme Court gave a huge victory to supporters of national power over state power. However, now that Republicans have unified control of national government, they will likely try to "repeal and replace" Obamacare, which will probably include returning more power to the states.

The conflict triggered by the ACA is a great example of the tensions that exist over how power is distributed between the states and the national government. What are the responsibilities of the states and what is the domain of the national government? What happens when levels of government disagree on a policy? Can the national government simply force the states to do something? Is this how federalism works?

federalism
The division of power across the local, state, and national governments.

sovereign power
The supreme power of an independent state to regulate its internal affairs without foreign interference.

What is federalism and why does it matter?

Federalism is a form of government that divides sovereign power across at least two political units. Dividing **sovereign power** simply means that each unit of government (in the U.S. context, the national and state governments) has some degree of authority and autonomy. As discussed in Chapter 2, this division of power across levels of government is central to the system of separated powers in the United States. Dividing power across levels of government seems a simple concept, but as we will see later in this chapter, the political battles over *how* that power is divided have been intense.

In practical terms, federalism is about intergovernmental relations: How do the different levels of government interact and how is power divided? But even that may seem a little abstract. Why does federalism matter? On a broad range of issues, the level of government that dictates policy can make a real difference. The conflict over health care reform is an obvious current example, but other policies include whether the national government can prevent states from allowing marijuana use for medical and recreational purposes, from allowing "aid in dying" (or what opponents to the practice label "assisted suicides"), from discriminating against employees based on age or disability, or from fighting national immigration laws. These questions involve defining the disputed boundaries between what the states and national government are allowed to do. Much of U.S. history has been rooted in this struggle to define American federalism.

The relationship between the national government and the states also involves cooperation. After unprecedented flash flooding devastated South Carolina in October 2015, FEMA partnered with state officials to provide relief at outposts like this one. @FEMA

Levels of government and their degrees of autonomy

A distinguishing feature of federalism is that each level of government has some degree of autonomy from the other levels—that is, each level can carry out some policies without interference from the others. In the United States, this means that the national and state governments have distinct powers and responsibilities (see Nuts & Bolts 3.1). The national government, for example, is responsible for national defense and foreign policy. State and local governments have primary responsibility for conducting elections and promoting public safety, or police powers. In other areas, such as transportation, the different levels of government have concurrent powers—that is, they share responsibilities. The national government has also taken on additional responsibilities through implied powers that are inferred from the powers explicitly granted in the Constitution (see Chapter 2 and the later discussion in this chapter).

Local governments—cities, towns, school districts, and counties—are not autonomous units of government. They are creatures of the state government. Thus, state governments create local governments and control the types of activities they can engage in by specifying in the state charter either what local governments can do or only what

police powers
The power to enforce laws and provide for public safety.

concurrent powers
Responsibilities for particular policy areas, such as transportation, that are shared by federal, state, and local governments.

National and State Responsibilities

National Government Powers	State Government Powers	Concurrent Powers
Print money	Issue licenses	Collect taxes
Regulate interstate commerce and international trade	Regulate intrastate (within the state) businesses	Build roads
Make treaties and conduct foreign policy	Conduct elections	Borrow money
Declare war	Establish local governments	Establish courts
Provide an army and navy	Ratify amendments to the Constitution	Make and enforce laws
Establish post offices	Promote public health and safety	Charter banks and corporations
Make laws necessary and proper to carry out these powers	May exert powers the Constitution does not delegate to the national government or does not prohibit the states from using	Spend money for the general welfare; take private property for public purposes, with just compensation

Powers Denied to the National Government	Powers Denied to State Governments
May not violate the Bill of Rights	May not enter into treaties with other countries
May not impose export taxes among states	May not print money
May not use money from the Treasury without an appropriation from Congress	May not tax imports or exports
May not change state boundaries	May not interfere with contracts
	May not suspend a person's rights without due process

Source: GPO Source Access: Guide to the U.S. Government, http://bensguide.gpo.gov/3-5/government/federalism.html (accessed 12/5/11).

they cannot do (which would allow them to do anything not specifically prohibited in the charter). Despite this lack of autonomy, local governments play an important role in providing public education, police and fire departments, and land use policies. They also raise money through property taxes, user fees, and, in some cases, local sales taxes. But, overall, because of their lack of autonomy, local governments do not directly share power within our federal system with the state and national governments.

A comparative perspective

It is useful to compare U.S. federalism with forms of government in other countries. Just because a nation is composed of states does not mean that it is a federal system. The key factor is the autonomy of the political subunits. The United Kingdom, for example, is made up of England, Scotland, Wales, and Northern Ireland. In 1998, the British Parliament created a new Scottish government and gave it authority in a broad range of areas. However, Parliament retained the right to unilaterally dissolve the Scottish government; therefore, the subunit (Scotland) is not autonomous (a September 2014 referendum rejected independence for Scotland by a 55–45 margin). This type of government in which power is centralized within the national government is a **unitary government**. Unitary governments are the most common in the modern world (about 80 percent); other examples include Israel, Italy, France, Japan, and Sweden. Although federalism is not as common, Australia, Austria, Canada, Germany, and Switzerland, among others, share this form of government with the United States.

At the opposite end of the spectrum is a **confederal government**, in which the states have most of the power and often can even veto the actions of the central government. This was the first type of government in the United States under the Articles of Confederation. Because so many problems are associated with having such a weak national government (see Chapter 2), few modern examples exist. The Commonwealth of Independent States (CIS), which formed in 1991 after the breakup of the former Soviet Union, has had some success in coordinating the economic activity and security needs of 12 independent states.[7] Over time, however, rifts among the member states have created problems, and today the CIS is viewed as largely ineffective.

Although true confederations are rare, **intergovernmental organizations** have proliferated in recent decades. Member nations have created over 1,200 multilateral organizations in an effort to coordinate their policies on, for example, economic activity, security, or environmental protection. The United Nations (UN), the International Monetary Fund (IMF), and the North Atlantic Treaty Organization (NATO) are important examples. The European Union (EU) is an intergovernmental organization that began as a loose confederation, but it is becoming more federalist in its decision-making process and structure. The EU's relative success, compared with the failure of the CIS, can be explained in part by this move toward a more federal structure, whereas the CIS maintained its confederal status.

unitary government
A system in which the national, centralized government holds ultimate authority. It is the most common form of government in the world.

confederal government
A form of government in which states hold power over a limited national government.

intergovernmental organizations
Organizations that seek to coordinate policy across member nations.

★

EXPLAIN WHAT THE CONSTITUTION SAYS ABOUT FEDERALISM

Balancing national and state power in the Constitution

Although the Founders wanted a national government that was stronger than it had been under the Articles of Confederation, they also wanted to preserve states' autonomy. These goals are reflected in different parts of the Constitution, which provides ample evidence for advocates of both state-centered and nation-centered federalism. This nation-centered position appears in the document's preamble, which begins: "We the People of the United States," whereas the Articles of Confederation began with the words: "We the undersigned delegates of the States." The Constitution's phrasing emphasizes the nation as a whole over the separate states. The competing perspectives of nation- and state-centered federalism is a lens through which we can examine the evolving conceptions of federalism and the current conflict over intergovernmental power.

A strong national government

The Founders wanted a strong national government to provide national security and a healthy and efficient economy, and so they included various powers in the Constitution that supported the nation-centered perspective. In terms of national security, as we saw in Chapter 2, Congress was granted the power to raise and support armies, declare war, and "suppress Insurrections and repel Invasion," while the president, as commander in chief of the armed forces, would oversee the conduct of war. Congress's power to regulate interstate commerce promoted economic efficiency and centralized an important economic power at the national level, and many restrictions on state power had similar effects. States were *prohibited* from entering into "any Treaty, Alliance, or Confederation" or keeping troops or "Ships of War" during peacetime. They also could not coin money or impose duties on imports or exports (see Article I, Section 10). These provisions in the Constitution ensured that states would not interfere with the smooth operation of interstate commerce or create problems for national defense. Imagine, for example, what would happen if Oklahoma had the power to tax oil produced in other states or if California decided to create its own army. This would create inefficiencies and potential dangers for the rest of the country.

The necessary and proper clause (Article I, Section 8) was another broad grant of power to the national government: it gave Congress the power "[t]o make all Laws which shall be necessary and proper for carrying into Execution the foregoing Powers." Similarly, the national supremacy clause (Article VI) says that the Constitution and all laws and treaties that are made under the Constitution shall be the "supreme Law of the Land" and that "the Judges in every State shall be bound thereby, any Thing

📷

Jim Obergefell, the plaintiff in the *Obergefell v. Hodges* Supreme Court case that legalized same-sex marriage nationwide, is backed by supporters of the ruling on the steps of the Texas capitol during a rally on June 29, 2015, in Austin. This ruling shows the power of the supremacy clause, as it struck down laws in 14 states. #LoveWins #Obergefell

in the Constitution or Laws of any State to the Contrary notwithstanding." This is perhaps the clearest statement of the nation-centered focus of the Constitution. If any state law or constitution conflicts with national law or the Constitution, the national perspective wins. Thus, the laws passed by states to limit implementation of the ACA had no effect after the Supreme Court upheld the central parts of the national law. The only way to change the law would be at the national level.

State powers and limits on national power

Despite the Founders' nation-centered bias, many parts of the Constitution also address state powers and limits on national power. Article II gives the states the power to choose electors for the electoral college, and Article V grants the states a central role in the process of amending the Constitution. Three-fourths of the states must ratify any constitutional amendment (either through conventions or their state legislatures, as specified by Congress), but the states can also bypass Congress in proposing amendments if two-thirds of the states call for a Constitutional Convention. This latter route to amending the Constitution has never been used, but the Founders clearly wanted to provide an additional check on national power.

There are also limitations on Congress's authority to regulate interstate commerce. For example, it cannot favor one state over another in regulating commerce and it cannot impose a tax on any good that is shipped from one state to another. Also, Congress could not prohibit slavery until 1808, but it was allowed to impose a duty of up to $10 per slave (which would be $280 in 2016).

While Article I of the Constitution enumerates many specific powers for Congress, the list of state powers is much shorter. One could interpret this as more evidence for the nation-centered perspective, but at the time of the Founding the default position was to keep most power at the state level. Therefore, the federal powers that were exceptions to this rule had to be clearly specified and state governments received authority over all other matters. The Tenth Amendment supports this view: "The powers not delegated to the United States by the Constitution, nor prohibited by it to the states, are reserved to the states respectively, or to the people."

The Eleventh Amendment, the first one passed after the Bill of Rights, was another important affirmation of state sovereignty. Antifederalists were concerned that the part of Article III that gave the Supreme Court authority over cases involving a "State and Citizens of another State" would undermine state sovereignty by giving the Court too much power over state laws. Federalists assured them this would not happen, but the Supreme Court ruled in *Chisholm v. Georgia* (1793) that citizens of one state could sue the government of another state. The majority opinion ridiculed the "haughty notions of state independence, state sovereignty, and state supremacy." The states struck back by adopting the Eleventh Amendment, which made such lawsuits unconstitutional. Although the Supreme Court lost this skirmish over state power, it continued to serve as the umpire in disputes between the national and state governments.

Clauses that favor both perspectives

Article IV of the Constitution has elements that favor both the state-centered and the nation-centered perspectives. For example, its **full faith and credit clause** specifies that states must respect one another's laws, granting citizens the "Full Faith and Credit" of their home state's laws if they go to another state. At the same time, however, the article's **privileges and immunities clause** says that citizens of each state are "entitled to

full faith and credit clause
Part of Article IV of the Constitution requiring that each state's laws be honored by the other states. For example, a legal marriage in one state must be recognized across state lines.

privileges and immunities clause
Part of Article IV of the Constitution requiring that states must treat nonstate residents within their borders as they would treat their own residents. This was meant to promote commerce and travel between states.

all Privileges and Immunities" of citizens in the other states, which means that states must treat visitors from other states the same as their own residents. This part of the Constitution favors a nation-centered perspective because it was intended to promote free travel and economic activity among the states.

There are many examples of the full faith and credit clause at work today. If you have a New York driver's license and are traveling to California, you do not need to stop at every state line to get a new license; each state will honor your New York license. Similarly, a legal marriage in one state must be honored by another state. Article IV has also fueled the ongoing controversy over same-sex marriage. In 1996, after courts in Hawaii gave couples in same-sex marriages most of the same legal rights as those in marriages between a man and a woman, many states passed laws saying they would not have to honor same-sex marriages. Congress passed the Defense of Marriage Act (DOMA) in 1996, which said that states would not have to recognize same-sex marriages. But in 2013 the Supreme Court struck down part of this law that denied federal benefits to same-sex couples[8] and then in 2015 the Court ruled that marriage is a fundamental right that cannot be denied by the states (see Chapter 5 for a discussion of these important cases).[9]

We can also cite examples of the privileges and immunities clause at work in a modern context. For example, states may not deny welfare benefits to new residents or deny police protection to visitors even though they do not pay state taxes. For example, a 1992 law in California limited the cash welfare benefit for new residents to the same level of benefits that they had been receiving in the state from which they moved. The law was intended to save California's government some money and also to discourage people from moving to California simply to get the higher benefit—this was particularly an issue because California's cash benefit for a mother and one child was $456 a month in 1992, but in the neighboring state of Arizona it was only $275.[10] The Supreme Court ruled that the California state law violated the privileges and immunities clause and the right to travel freely between the states.

But states are allowed to make some distinctions between residents and nonresidents. For example, states do not have to permit nonresidents to vote in state elections, and public colleges and universities may charge out-of-state residents higher tuition than in-state residents. Therefore, the privileges and immunities clause cuts both ways on the question of the balance of power: it allows the states to determine and uphold these laws autonomously, but it also emphasizes that national citizenship is more important than state citizenship.

"Why Should I Care?"

Why is it important to understand the Constitution's role in federalism? The Constitution sets the boundaries for the battles over state and federal power. For example, no state can decide to print its own currency, and the U.S. government cannot take over the public schools. But within those broad boundaries, the balance between national and state power at any given point in history is a political decision, the product of choices made by elected leaders and the courts. The struggle over the implementation of the ACA was a perfect example: the national government passed the law, the Supreme Court upheld most of it and struck down part of it, and the states implemented the law with varying levels of cooperation and resistance. This meant that you would be able to stay on your parents' health insurance until you are 26 (part of the national law that was upheld), but once you had to buy your own insurance, the process of getting signed up would vary depending on which state you live in.

The evolving concept of federalism

The nature of federalism has changed as the relative positions of the national and state governments have evolved. In the first century of our nation's history, the national government played a relatively limited role and the boundaries between the levels of government were distinct. As the national government took on more power in the twentieth century, intergovernmental relations became more cooperative and the boundaries less distinct. Even within this more cooperative framework, federalism remains a source of conflict within our political system as the levels of government share lawmaking authority.

The early years

As the United States gained its footing, clashes between the advocates of state-centered and nation-centered federalism turned into a partisan struggle. The Federalists—the party of George Washington, John Adams, and Alexander Hamilton—controlled the new government for its first 12 years and favored strong national power. Their opponents, the Democratic-Republicans, led by Thomas Jefferson and James Madison, favored state power.

Establishing National Supremacy The first confrontation came when the Federalists established a national bank in 1791, over Jefferson's objections. This controversy did not come to a head until Congress chartered the second national bank in 1816. At that time, the state of Maryland, which was controlled by the Democratic-Republicans, tried to tax the National Bank's Baltimore branch out of existence, but the head cashier of the bank refused to pay the tax and the case eventually ended up at the Supreme Court. The Court had to decide whether Congress had the power to create the bank and, if it did, whether Maryland had the right to tax the bank.

In the landmark decision *McCulloch v. Maryland* (1819), the Court ruled in favor of the national government on both counts. In deciding whether Congress could create the bank, the Court held that even though the word "bank" does not appear in the Constitution, Congress's power to create one is implied through its relevant enumerated powers—such as the power to coin money, levy taxes, and borrow money. The Court also ruled that Maryland did not have the right to tax the bank because of the Constitution's national supremacy clause. Both the concept of implied powers and the validation of national supremacy were critical for establishing the centrality of the national government.

A few years later, the Supreme Court decided another case that cemented Congress's power to act based on the commerce clause in the Constitution. In *Gibbons v. Ogden* (1824), the Supreme Court held that Congress has broad power to regulate interstate commerce and struck down a New York law that had granted a monopoly to a private company operating steamboats on the Hudson River between New York and New Jersey. By granting this monopoly, the ruling stated, New York was interfering with interstate commerce.

The Emergence of States' Rights At the same time, many states, especially in the South, pushed for broader states' rights on issues such as civil liberties (in response to a law passed in 1798 that made it illegal to criticize the government), tariffs, and slavery. John Calhoun, a South Carolina senator, used the term "nullification" to refer

states' rights
The idea that states are entitled to a certain amount of self-government, free of federal government intervention. This became a central issue in the period leading up to the Civil War.

In the early 1800s, the Supreme Court confirmed the national government's right to regulate commerce between the states. The state of New York granted a monopoly to a ferry company serving ports in New York and New Jersey, but this was found to interfere with interstate commerce and was therefore subject to federal intervention.

to a state's right to ignore a law passed by Congress if the state believed the law was unconstitutional (for example, Calhoun urged South Carolina to ignore a tariff law passed by Congress in 1832). The states' rights perspective was at the center of the dispute between southern and northern states over slavery, and it ultimately led to the secession of the Confederate states and subsequently to the Civil War. The stakes were enormous in the battles over federalism: about 528,000 people died in that bloodiest of American wars.[11] As Abraham Lincoln forcefully argued, concepts such as nullification and states' rights, when taken to their logical extremes, were too divisive to be allowed to stand. If states could ignore national laws, the basis of the United States would fall apart.

Dual federalism

The ideas of states' rights and nullification did not produce the Civil War by themselves. The Supreme Court's infamous *Dred Scott* decision lent fuel to the fire, but before explaining the significance of that case we will look at some key players in the evolution of the Court's approach to federalism. In this section, we will discuss the system of dual federalism, which defined intergovernmental relations for nearly the first 150 years of our nation's history. The Supreme Court's narrow interpretation of the Fourteenth Amendment and the commerce clause greatly limited the power of the national government in this period (see Table 3.1).

The Marshall Court versus the Taney Court The early to mid-nineteenth century saw incredible stability in the leadership of the Court, because only two chief justices served during this time—John Marshall from 1801 to 1835 and Roger Taney from 1835 to 1864. However, these men had very different ideas about federalism. Marshall was a Federalist who opposed states' rights, whereas Taney was a supporter of states' rights. A series of decisions under Marshall's leadership secured the place of the national government within our federal system. But in the years that followed, Taney was able to limit the reach of the national government through his vision of federalism, which is known as dual federalism.

TABLE
3.1

Early Landmark Supreme Court Decisions on Federalism

Case	Holding and Significance for States' Rights	Direction of the Decision
Chisholm v. Georgia (1793)	Held that citizens of one state could sue another state; led to the Eleventh Amendment, which prohibited such lawsuits.	Less state power
McCulloch v. Maryland (1819)	Upheld the national government's right to create a bank and reaffirmed the idea of "national supremacy."	Less state power
Gibbons v. Ogden (1824)	Held that Congress, rather than the states, has broad power to regulate interstate commerce.	Less state power
Barron v. Baltimore (1833)	Endorsed a notion of "dual federalism" in which the rights of a U.S. citizen under the Bill of Rights did not apply to that same person under state law.	More state power
Dred Scott v. Sandford (1857)	Sided with southern states' view that slaves were property and ruled that the Missouri Compromise violated the Fifth Amendment, because making slavery illegal in some states deprived slave owners of property. Contributed to the start of the Civil War.	More state power
National Labor Relations Board v. Jones and Laughlin Steel Corporation (1937)	Upheld the National Labor Relations Act of 1935 as consistent with Congress's commerce clause powers, reversing the Court's more narrow interpretation of that clause.	Less state power

dual federalism
The form of federalism favored by Chief Justice Roger Taney, in which national and state governments are seen as distinct entities providing separate services. This model limits the power of the national government.

Under **dual federalism,** the national and state governments were viewed as distinct, with little overlap in their activities or the services they provided. In this view, the national government's activities are confined to powers strictly enumerated in the Constitution, despite the necessary and proper clause and the implied powers endorsed in *McCulloch v. Maryland*. Although Taney fully developed the idea of dual federalism, one decision toward the end of Marshall's tenure endorsed a notion of "dual citizenship" in which an individual's rights as a U.S. citizen under the Bill of Rights did not apply to the same person under state law. That decision, *Barron v. Baltimore* (1833), held that a man whose wharf in the Baltimore harbor had been ruined by the city's dumping of sand and gravel could not sue the city for violating the Fifth Amendment's prohibition of taking property without due process. The Court ruled that the Fifth Amendment applied only to the U.S. Congress and not to state and local governments, which is a core principle of dual federalism.

Dred Scott and Civil War The state-centered views of the Taney Court also produced a tragic decision, *Dred Scott v. Sandford* (1857). Dred Scott was a slave who had lived for many years with his owner in the free Wisconsin Territory but was living in Missouri, a slave state, when his master died. Scott petitioned for his freedom under the Missouri Compromise, which said that slavery was illegal in any free state. The majority decision held that slaves were not citizens but private property and that therefore the Missouri Compromise violated the Fifth Amendment because it deprived people (slave owners) of property without the due process of law. This unfortunate decision contributed to the

Civil War, which started four years later, because it indicated that there could not be a political solution to the problem of slavery.

The Civil War ended the dispute over slavery, but it did not resolve basic questions about the balance of power between the national and state governments. At the end of the Civil War, the Constitution was amended to ensure that the Union's views on states' rights were the law of the land. The Civil War amendments banned slavery (Thirteenth Amendment), prohibited states from denying citizens due process or equal protection of the laws (Fourteenth Amendment), and gave newly freed male slaves the right to vote (Fifteenth Amendment). The Fourteenth Amendment was the most important in terms of federalism because it was the constitutional basis for many of the civil rights laws passed by Congress during Reconstruction. The Civil War fundamentally changed the way Americans thought about the relationship between the national government and the states: before the war people said "the United States *are*..." but after the war they said "the United States *is*...," highlighting the feeling that the United States was a unified nation, not merely a loose collection of states.

The Supreme Court and Limited National Government The assertion of power by Congress during Reconstruction was short-lived, as the Supreme Court soon stepped in again to limit the power of the national government. In 1873, the Court reinforced the notion of dual federalism, ruling that the Fourteenth Amendment did not change the balance of power between the national and state governments despite its clear language aimed at state action. Endorsing the notion of dual citizenship, the Court ruled that the Fourteenth Amendment right to due process and equal treatment under the law applied to individuals' rights only as citizens of the United States, not to their state citizenship.[12] By extension, freedom of speech, freedom of the press, and the other liberties protected in the Bill of Rights applied only to laws passed by Congress, not to state laws. This distinction between state and national citizenship sounds odd today, partly because the Fourteenth Amendment has long been viewed as the basis for ensuring that states do not violate basic rights.

In 1883, the Court overturned the 1875 Civil Rights Act, which had guaranteed equal treatment in public accommodations. The Court argued that the Fourteenth Amendment did not give Congress the power to regulate private conduct, such as whether a white restaurant owner had to serve a black customer; it affected only the conduct of state governments.[13] This narrow view of the Fourteenth Amendment left the national government powerless to prevent southern states from implementing state and local laws that led to complete segregation of blacks and whites in the South (called Jim Crow laws) and the denial of many basic rights to blacks after northern troops left the South at the end of Reconstruction.

The other area in which the Supreme Court limited the reach of the national government concerned Congress's authority to regulate the economy through its commerce clause powers. In a series of cases in the late nineteenth and early twentieth centuries, the Supreme Court endorsed a view of laissez-faire—French for "leave alone"—capitalism aimed at protecting business from regulation by the national government. To this end, the Court defined clear boundaries between *inter*state and *intra*state commerce, ruling that Congress could not regulate any economic activity that occurred *within* a state (intrastate). The Supreme Court allowed some national legislation that was connected to interstate commerce, such as limiting monopolies through the Sherman Antitrust Act (1890). However, when the national government tried to use this act to break up a cartel of four sugar companies that controlled 98 percent of the nation's sugar production the Court ruled that Congress did not have this power.

According to the Court's decision, the commerce clause dealt with the transportation of goods, not their manufacture, and the sugar in question was made within a

After the Supreme Court struck down the 1875 Civil Rights Act, southern states were free to impose Jim Crow laws. These state and local laws led to complete racial segregation, even for public drinking fountains.

single state. Even if the sugar was sold throughout the country, this was "incidental" to its manufacture.[14] On the same grounds, the Court struck down attempts by Congress to regulate child labor.[15] In some instances, the Court's laissez-faire perspective led the justices to strike down state laws, as in a case that ruled unconstitutional a New York law limiting the working hours of bakers to no more than 60 hours a week or 10 hours a day.[16] Therefore, the limits that the Court placed on Congress during this antiregulation phase did not necessarily tip the balance to the state governments. Rather, big business was the winner over both national and state governments.

Cooperative federalism

From the early years of the twentieth century through the 1930s, a new era of American federalism emerged. The first step was taking the election of U.S. senators away from state legislatures and providing for their direct election in the Seventeenth Amendment. This change was prompted by the Progressives' desire to shift power away from corrupt state legislatures.[17] The national government became much more involved in activities that were formerly reserved for the states, such as education, transportation, civil rights, agriculture, social welfare, and management–labor relations. At first, the Supreme Court resisted this broader reach of national power, clinging to its nineteenth-century conception of dual federalism.[18] But as commerce became more national, the distinction between interstate and intrastate commerce, and between manufacture and transportation, became increasingly difficult to sustain. Starting in 1937 with the landmark ruling *National Labor Relations Board v. Jones and Laughlin Steel Corporation*, the Supreme Court largely discarded these distinctions and gave Congress far more latitude in shaping economic and social policy for the nation.[19]

Shifting National–State Relations The type of federalism that emerged in the Progressive Era of the early twentieth century and blossomed in the late 1930s is called cooperative federalism, or "marble cake" federalism, as opposed to the "layer cake"

cooperative federalism
A form of federalism in which national and state governments work together to provide services efficiently. This form emerged in the late 1930s, representing a profound shift toward less concrete boundaries of responsibility in national–state relations.

model of dual federalism.[20] As the image of a marble cake suggests, the boundaries of state and national responsibilities are less well defined than they are under dual federalism. With the increasing industrialization and urbanization of the late 1930s and 1940s, more complex problems arose that could not be solved at one level of government. The Great Depression made it painfully clear that states did not have the resources necessary to address major economic crises. Cooperative federalism adopted a more practical focus on intergovernmental relations and how to efficiently provide services. State and local governments maintained a level of influence as the implementers of national programs, but the national government played an enhanced role as the initiator of key policies.

"Cooperative federalism" accurately describes this important shift in national–state relations in the first half of the twentieth century, but it does not begin to capture the complexity of modern federalism. The marble cake metaphor falls short in one important way: the lines of authority and patterns of cooperation are not as messy as implied by the gooey flow of chocolate through white cake. Instead, the 1960s metaphor of **picket fence federalism** is a better description of cooperative federalism in action. As the How It Works graphic shows, each picket of the fence represents a different policy area and the horizontal boards that hold the pickets together represent the different levels of government. This is a much more orderly image than the marble cake provides, and it illustrates important implications about how policy is made across levels of government.

The most important point to be drawn from this analogy is that activity within the cooperative federal system occurs *within* pickets of the fence—that is, within policy areas. Policy makers within a given policy area will have more in common with others in that area (even if they are at different levels of government) than they do with people who work in different areas (even if they are at the same level of government). For example, someone working in a state's Department of Natural Resources will have more contact with people working in local park programs and the national Department of the Interior than with people who also work at the state level but who focus on, say, transportation policy.

Cooperative federalism, then, is likely to emerge within policy areas rather than across them. This may create problems for the chief executives who are trying to run the show (mayors, governors, the president), as rivalries develop among policy areas competing for funds. Also, contact within policy areas is not always cooperative. (Think of detective shows in which the FBI arrives to investigate a local crime and pulls rank on the town sheriff, provoking resentment from local law-enforcement officials.) This is the inefficient side of picket fence federalism in action. But overall, this version of federalism provides great opportunities for coordination and the development of expertise within policy areas.

Franklin Delano Roosevelt's New Deal shifted more power than ever to the national government. Through major new programs to address the Great Depression, such as the Works Progress Administration construction projects pictured here, the federal government expanded its reach into areas that had been primarily the responsibility of state and local governments.

picket fence federalism
A more refined and realistic form of cooperative federalism in which policy makers within a particular policy area work together across the levels of government.

Why is it important to understand the history of federalism? You might think that the Civil War ended the debates over nation-centered versus state-centered federalism (in favor of the national government), but disputes today over immigration, health care, welfare, and education policy all revolve around the balance of power between the levels of government. State legislatures that talk about ignoring the Affordable Care Act today are invoking the same arguments used by advocates of states' rights in the 1830s and 1840s concerning tariffs and slavery.

"Why Should I Care?"

Versions of Federalism

Version 1:
Layer Cake Federalism

1789–1937

No interactions between the levels of government.

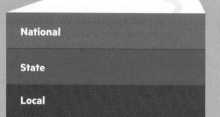

Version 2:
Marble Cake Federalism

1937–today

Interactions between the levels of government are common.

Version 3:
Picket Fence Federalism

1960s–today

Horizontal boards represent different levels of government, and the pickets are policy areas within which coordination happens across those levels.

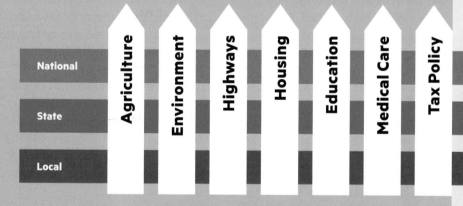

National

State

Local

Agriculture Environment Highways Housing Education Medical Care Tax Policy

Version 4:
Coercive Federalism

1970s–today

National government uses regulations, mandates, and conditions to pressure states to fall into line with national policy goals.

National

Regulations
National government provides new policy goals.

State   Local

Incentives
National government pressures or incentivizes state and local governments to act according to new goals.

Federalism and Environmental Policy

This is who carries out environmental policy in...

The National Government:
Environmental Protection Agency (EPA), Department of the Interior, Department of Energy

The State Government:
State Department of Natural Resources, State Park Service, State Environmental Protection Agencies

The Local Government:
City park system, city and county oversight boards for land use policy and zoning

Environmental policy shows contemporary federalism in action. As you can see on the right, all levels of government combine to effect environmental policy (exemplifying picket fence federalism). Also, the national government provides both rules and incentives for state and local governments to change their environmental policies (exemplifying coercive federalism).

Congress passed new acts.

Over the last few decades, Congress has passed the **Coastal Zone Management Act**, the **Clean Water Act**, the **Endangered Species Act**, and the **Clean Air Act**.

What does that mean?

These have all provided states and localities with **federal regulations and mandates.**

Stricter rules.

In 2015, the EPA set **new tougher standards** for ozone and proposed stricter limits on greenhouse gases.

Also...

The federal government **provides many incentives** designed to preserve the environment.

Cool bonus.

These include **tax credits** for electric cars, biodiesel and hydrogen fuel cells, and home improvements that increase energy efficiency.

Good deal.

In 2015, the EPA introduced a Clean Energy Incentive Program to promote expansion of renewable energy and energy efficiency. **States receive emission credits** for the clean energy they produce.

❓ Critical Thinking

1. **Which do you think is a more effective tool** to change environmental policy—the "stick" of regulation or the "carrot" of incentives? Why?

2. **Should the government provide tax credits and other incentives** for things like electric cars and alternative energy, or leave such things up to the free market?

In short:

The federal government **imposes new rules** on **state** and **local governments** and **provides incentives** to follow these new rules and goals. Goals such as: **increased energy efficiency and independence**

Federalism today

Federalism today is a complex mix of all the elements our nation's political system has experienced in the past. Our current system is predominantly characterized by cooperative federalism, but it has retained strong elements of national supremacy, dual federalism, and states' rights. Therefore, rather than categorizing types of federalism into neat time periods, the following discussion characterizes the dominant tendency within each period, keeping in mind that competing versions of federalism have always been just below the surface (see Nuts & Bolts 3.2). In the past 20 years, the competing versions are so evident that this period could be considered the "era of balanced federalism."[21]

Cooperative federalism lives on: fiscal federalism

fiscal federalism
A form of federalism in which federal funds are allocated to the lower levels of government through transfer payments or grants.

The cooperative relationship between the national and state governments is rooted in the system of transfer payments, or grants, from the national government to lower levels of government. This is called fiscal federalism. However, just because money flows from Washington, D.C., does not mean that cooperation by the recipients follows. Depending on how the money is transferred, the national government can either help local and state governments achieve their own goals or use its fiscal power to impose its will. This may sound familiar. When your parents let you use the car or lent you $50,

◆

The Evolution of Federalism

Type of Federalism	Period	Characteristics
Dual federalism (layer cake)	1789–1937	The national and state governments were viewed as very distinct with little overlap in their activities or the services they provided. Within this period, federalism could have been state centered or nation centered, but relations between levels of government were limited.
Cooperative federalism (marble cake)	1937–present	This indicates greater cooperation and collaboration between the levels of government.
Fiscal federalism	1937–present	This system of transfer payments or grants from the national government to lower-level governments involves varying degrees of national control over how the money is spent: categorical grants give the national government a great deal of control whereas block grants involve less national control.
Picket fence federalism	1961–present	This version of cooperative federalism emphasizes that policy makers within a given policy area have more in common with others in their area at different levels of government than with people at the same level of government who work on different issues.
New Federalism	1969–present	New Federalism attempts to shift power to the states by consolidating categorical grants into block grants and giving the states authority over programs such as welfare.
Coercive federalism	1970s–present	This involves federal preemptions of state and local authority and unfunded mandates on state and local governments to force the states to change their policies to match national goals or policies established by Congress.

did they expect something in return—such as help with yard work or other chores—or was it "no strings attached"? Even in the era of dual federalism this type of issue arose between different levels of government, but it happened far less frequently then because the national government provided very little aid to the states.

Grants in Aid Today, most aid to the states comes in one of two forms. Categorical grants are for specific purposes—they have strings attached—and therefore we discuss them in the section on coercive federalism. Block grants are financial aid to states for use within a specific policy area, but within that area the states have discretion on how to spend the money. Advocates of cooperative federalism promoted block grants as the best way for the levels of government to work together to solve problems: the national government identified problem areas and then provided money to the states to help solve them. Between 1966, when the first block grant was created, and 1994, 23 block grants were established.[22] For example, Community Development Block Grants were started in 1974 to help state and local governments revitalize their communities; such grants may support ongoing programs or help with large capital expenditures, such as building a waste treatment plant or a highway. Since the 1970s, grants to the states as a proportion of the size of the national economy (gross domestic product, or GDP) have been relatively constant, whereas the rate of state and local spending has continued to inch up (see What Do the Numbers Say?). Even including those that were part of the 2009 stimulus package, grants to the states were only 4 percent of GDP in 2009.

New Federalism New Federalism, the idea of giving states more control over programs, was started during Richard Nixon's presidency and then revived by Ronald Reagan in the 1980s. In his 1981 inaugural address, Reagan emphasized, "All of us need to be reminded that the federal government did not create the states. The states created the federal government." This classic statement of the states' rights position is similar to the Antifederalists' position at the Constitutional Convention.

Reagan's goal of returning more power to the states involved consolidating 77 categorical grants into 9 general block grants that gave local politicians more control over how money was spent. This change reflected the belief that because state and local politicians were closer to the people they would know better how to spend the money. Nonetheless, the increase in state control came with a 25 percent cut in the amount of federal money granted to the states.

The next phase of New Federalism came when Republicans won control of Congress in 1994. Working with President Clinton, a moderate Democrat, the Republican-controlled Congress passed several pieces of significant legislation that shifted power toward the states. In 1996, the Personal Responsibility and Work Opportunity Act reformed welfare by creating a block grant to the states, Temporary Assistance to Needy Families (TANF), to replace the largest nationally administered welfare program. Another law, the 1996 Prison Litigation Reform Act, ended federal court supervision of state and local prison systems. And the Unfunded Mandate Reform Act of 1995 made it more difficult for Congress to impose unfunded mandates on the states; it required a separate vote on mandates that imposed costs of more than $50 million, and it required a Congressional Budget Office estimate of exactly how much such mandates would cost the states. Although this law could not prevent unfunded mandates, Republicans hoped that bringing more attention to the practice would create political pressure against such policies.

The shift from categorical grants to block grants was an important part of New Federalism after Reagan, but it has not substantially affected the balance of power between the national and state governments. In fact, the amount of money going to the states through block grants has been surpassed by categorical grants since 1982. We will explore the reason for this later, but for now, suffice it to say that Congress prefers categorical grants because they give Congress more control over how the money is spent.

categorical grants
Federal aid to state or local governments that is provided for a specific purpose, such as a mass-transit program within the transportation budget or a school lunch program within the education budget.

block grants
Federal aid provided to a state government to be spent within a certain policy area, but the state can decide how to spend the money within that area.

unfunded mandates
Federal laws that require the states to do certain things but do not provide state governments with funding to implement these policies.

Federal and State/Local Government Spending

Advocates for smaller government often make the argument that spending in Washington is out of control and that state and local governments should have more power. What do the numbers say? What are the trends in state and local spending as a share of the total economy compared to federal spending?

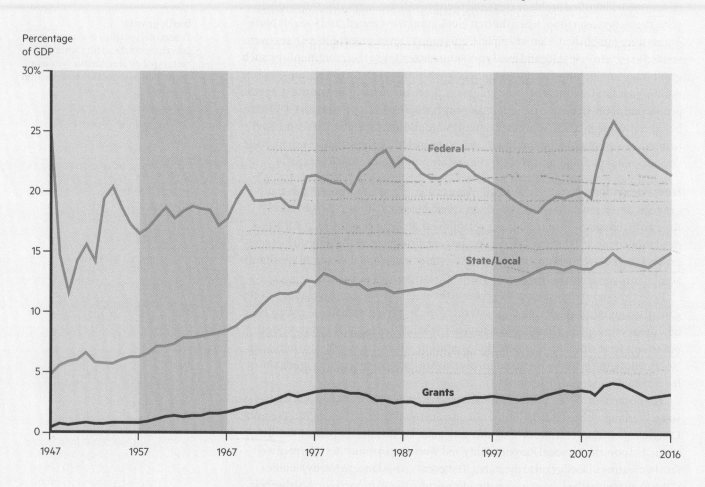

Percentage of GDP

Think about it

- How much is the federal government helping the states in terms of grants? Has this greatly increased? What does this say about the debates between nation-centered and state-centered federalism?
- Should the national government provide more grants to state and local governments to help even out inequalities and address national problems, or leave decisions about funding up to the states?
- What determines the appropriate level of government for spending on a given policy?

Source: 2012 Statistical Abstract of the United States, Table 4.31, and the Bureau of Economic Analysis, "Government Current Receipts and Expenditures" (accessed 5/31/16).

The rise of coercive federalism

Despite the overall shift toward cooperative federalism, strong overtones of national government supremacy remain. Three important characteristics of American politics in the past 60 years have reinforced the role of the national government: (1) reliance on the national government in times of crisis and war; (2) the "rights revolution" of the 1950s and 1960s, as well as the Great Society programs of the 1960s; and (3) the rise of coercive federalism.

Crisis and War Reliance on the national government in times of crisis and war has always been a characteristic of American politics. Even in the 1800s, during the period of dual federalism and strong state power, the national government's strong actions were needed during the Civil War to hold the nation together. More recently, following the terrorist attacks on September 11, 2001, most Americans expected the national government to improve national security and retaliate for the attacks. Even Republicans, who normally oppose increasing the size of government, largely supported President Bush's proposal to create a cabinet-level Department of Homeland Security. Policy responses to the major crises of the twentieth century (the Great Depression's New Deal policies, the massive mobilization for World War II), as well as the response to the banking meltdown of 2008–2009, also dramatically shifted the balance of power toward Washington.

The "Rights Revolution" and Great Society Programs The "rights revolution" created by the Supreme Court, as well as Lyndon Johnson's Great Society programs, contributed to increased national control over state policies. Landmark Court decisions thrust the national government into policy areas that had typically been reserved to the states. In the school desegregation and busing cases of the 1950s and 1960s, for example, the Court upheld the national goal of promoting racial equality and fighting discrimination over the earlier norm of local control of school districts.[23] The "one person, one vote" decisions, which required that the populations of legislative districts be equalized when district lines were redrawn, put the federal courts at the center of another policy area that had always been left to the states.[24] The rights revolution also applied to police powers, another area of traditional state control, including protection against self-incrimination and preventing illegally obtained evidence from being used in a criminal trial.[25]

📷

With the No Child Left Behind Act, the Bush administration increased the national government's power over education. This law was replaced by the Every Student Succeeds Act in 2015, which provides more flexibility to states to meet the needs of their students. #NCLB #edreform

These Court actions were paralleled by a burst of legislation that tackled civil rights, education, the environment, medical care for the poor, and housing. These so-called Great Society policies gave the national government much more leverage over policy areas previously controlled by state and local governments. For example, after passage of the 1965 Voting Rights Act federal marshals were sent to the South to make sure that African Americans were allowed to vote. Another part of this act required some state and local governments to submit changes in their electoral practices, including the boundaries of voting districts, to the Justice Department to make sure they did not have a discriminatory impact. But in 2013, the Court effectively overturned this part of the law by striking down the formula that determined which state and local governments were covered by the act.[26]

In the 1960s, the national government also expanded its reach through a large increase in categorical grants, which the states sorely needed even though the monies came with strings attached. For example, the 1964 Civil Rights Act required nondiscrimination as a condition for receiving any kind of federal grants. The Elementary and Secondary Education Act of 1965 gave the federal government heightened control over public education by attaching certain conditions to federal grant money.

Other Shifts toward National Supremacy Categorical grants aimed at a broad national goal have also reinforced national supremacy in recent decades—for example, requiring a state to set the legal drinking age to 21 before granting it federal highway funds. This policy direction from Washington is part of a trend known as **coercive federalism**. This practice involves the use of federal regulations, mandates, or conditions to force or entice the states to change their policies to match national goals or policies established by Congress. The Clean Air and Clean Water Acts, the Americans with Disabilities Act (ADA) (which promotes making public buildings and commercial facilities more accessible to those with disabilities), and the Motor Voter Act (which requires states to provide voter registration services at motor vehicle departments) are all laws that forced states to change their policies. The laws most objectionable to the states are unfunded mandates, which require states to do certain things but carry no federal money to pay for them.

Along with these mandates, federal preemption is another method of coercive federalism. Derived from the Constitution's national supremacy clause, **federal preemptions** impose national priorities on the states. Many preemptions also include unfunded mandates, making the state and local governments pick up the tab for policies that the national government wants them to implement. The U.S. Conference of Mayors has identified 10 federal mandates that consume 11 percent of city budgets, and the National Association of Counties estimates that 12 mandates account for 12 percent of county budgets.[27] Many of the most expensive mandates are environmental laws aimed at goals that a majority of Americans share. However, state and local governments complain that they should not have to shoulder so much of the burden.[28] These are among the most controversial assertions of national power because they impose such high costs on state and local governments.

The presidency of George W. Bush provided strong evidence of this shift toward national power. Beyond the centralization of power associated with fighting terrorism, Bush pushed the national government into areas that previously had been dominated by the states—for example, imposing significant mandates and preemptions in education testing, sales tax collection, emergency management, infrastructure, and election administration. This is particularly noteworthy because it happened at a time when Republicans, who have traditionally supported states' rights, largely controlled the presidency and Congress.[29]

President Obama continued the shift toward national power with one of the most active domestic policy agendas since the New Deal of the 1930s. A $787 billion

coercive federalism
A form of federalism in which the federal government pressures the states to change their policies by using regulations, mandates, and conditions (often involving threats to withdraw federal funding).

federal preemptions
Impositions of national priorities on the states through national legislation that is based on the Constitution's supremacy clause.

economic stimulus package of tax cuts and spending designed to address the financial
collapse of 2008–2009, a $938 billion health care reform law, efforts to prop up and
stimulate the battered housing industry, strengthened regulations of finance and
banking, and an expanded jobs program were all on the agenda in Obama's first term.
His objectives for the second term were more modest given the persistence of budget
deficits and split-party control of government. But Obama still pushed for comprehensive immigration reform, action on climate change, and job creation. When Congress
wouldn't work with the president, he increasingly relied on executive orders to implement a more limited agenda (for example, on immigration and climate change). This
was not popular with Republicans in Congress, who saw it as presidential overreach.
Health care reform has been especially controversial, as many state governments see
the law as an unwarranted expansion of federal power. This view was supported by the
Supreme Court's ruling that states could not be coerced by the federal government into
expanding their Medicaid coverage. This Court decision means that there are limits on
the scope of coercive federalism. Although the overall impact of national health care
reform has centralized more power at the national level, states remain very important
in this period of "balanced federalism," as the next section will demonstrate.

The states fight back

Most Americans support the national policies that have been imposed on the states:
racial equality, clean air and water, a fair legal process, safer highways, and equal
access to the voting booth. At the same time, there has always been strong support for
state and local governments. In fact, in most national surveys Americans typically
say that they trust state and local governments more than the national government
and they believe their tax dollars are spent more efficiently at the lower levels of government. Indeed, the shift in public opinion toward favoring national power after the
September 11 terrorist attacks was temporary, and it appears that state and local governments quickly reasserted their position as the more trusted level of government.
For example, a Gallup poll taken late in 2015 showed that 70 percent of Americans trust
their local government "a great deal or a fair amount" to "handle local problems," compared with 58 percent who trust their state government to handle state problems and 38
percent who trust the national government to handle domestic problems.[30]

States appear to be reversing their traditional role of resisting change and protecting the status quo. In recent years, states have taken the lead on environmental policy, refusing to accept national pollution standards that are too lenient or the lack of national action on issues such as global warming. Many policies to address climate change—including the development of renewable energy sources, carbon emissions limits, and carbon cap-and-trade programs—have been advocated at the state level. States have been out in front on fighting electronic waste, mercury emissions, and air pollution more generally.[31] States have also taken a lead role in health care policy, immigration, same-sex marriage, and stem-cell research.

Nonetheless, the willingness of the states to fight back in recent years has not always been for progressive causes. Indeed, with the Republican gains in the 2010 elections and the influence of the Tea Party, many states have been attempting to curb national power and protect their more conservative policies in a broad range of areas, including land use, gun control, immigration, and health care. For example, Kansas and Montana passed laws holding that federal gun laws do not apply to guns that are manufactured in their states (and making it a felony to try to enforce those laws).[32] Many of these state laws will not stand up in federal court. Indeed, the Montana gun law has already been struck down. But the laws are clearly a reflection of state frustration with assertions of federal power.

Competitive Federalism States have one important advantage over the national government when it comes to experimenting with new policies: their numbers. There are 50 states potentially trying a mix of different policies—another reason that advocates of state-centered federalism see the states as the proper repository of government power. In this view, such a mix of policies produces competitive federalism—competition among states to provide the best policies to attract businesses, create jobs, and maintain a healthy social fabric. Supporters point out that competitive federalism is also a check on tyranny because people will "vote with their feet"—that is, move to a different state—if they do not like a given state's policies. One advocate of this view argues that it "disciplines government and forces the states to compete for the citizens' business, talents, and assets," which makes government act more like a free market.[33]

But competitive federalism can also create a "race to the bottom" as states compete in a negative way. Cass Sunstein, of Harvard Law School, points out that when states compete for businesses and jobs they may do so by eliminating more environmental or occupational regulations than would be desirable. Likewise, a priority to keep taxes low may lead to cuts in benefits to those who can least afford it, such as welfare or Medicaid recipients.[34]

There is no doubt that competition among states provides citizens with a broad range of choices about the type of government they prefer. Choices by different state leaders about tax policies, levels of support for public schools and parks, and regulation of business all provide a range of options for businesses in deciding where to locate or expand, and to citizens considering a move. Because different citizens prefer different policies, this is generally viewed as an overall advantage to American democracy.

Fighting for states' rights: the role of the modern Supreme Court

Just as the Supreme Court played a central role in defining the boundaries of dual federalism in the nineteenth and early twentieth centuries and in opening the door to a more nation-centered cooperative federalism in the late 1930s, today's Court is once again reshaping federalism. But this time the move is decidedly in the direction of state power.

competitive federalism
A form of federalism in which states compete to attract businesses and jobs through the policies they adopt.

>

Crucial to understanding federalism in modern day America is the concept of mobility, or "the ability to vote with your feet." If you don't support the death penalty and citizens packing a pistol—don't come to Texas. If you don't like medicinal marijuana and gay marriage, don't move to California.

—**Rick Perry,** former Texas governor

The Tenth Amendment On paper, it seems that the Tenth Amendment would be at the center of any resurgence of state power because it ensures that all powers not delegated to the national government are reserved to the states or to the people. In practice, however, the amendment has had little significance except during the early 1930s and quite recently.

Forty years ago, a leading text on the Constitution said that the Tenth Amendment "does not alter the distribution of power between the national and state governments. It adds nothing to the Constitution."[35] To understand why, consider the following example. State and local governments have always controlled their own public schools. Thus, public education is a power reserved to the states under the Tenth Amendment. However, a state law concerning public education is void if it conflicts with the Constitution—as racial segregation conflicted with the equal protection clause of the Fourteenth Amendment—or with a national law that is based on an enumerated power. For example, a state could not compel an 18-year-old to attend school if the student had been drafted to serve in the army. Under the Tenth Amendment, the constitutionally enumerated national power to "raise and support armies" would trump the reserved state power to support public education.

This view was validated as recently as 1985 when the Court ruled that Congress had the power to impose a national minimum wage law on state governments, even if this was an area of traditional state power.[36] How times change! With the appointment of three conservative justices between 1986 and 1991 who favored a stronger role for the states, the Court started to limit Congress's reach. One technique was to require that Congress provide an unambiguous statement of its intent to overrule state authority. For example, the Court ruled that the Missouri constitution, which requires state judges to retire by age 70, did not violate the Age Discrimination in Employment Act because Congress did not make its intentions "unmistakably clear in the language of the statute."[37]

The Fourteenth Amendment The Fourteenth Amendment was intended to give the national government broad control over the potentially discriminatory laws of southern states after the Civil War. Section 1 guarantees that no state shall make or enforce any law depriving any person of "life, liberty, or property, without due process of law" or denying any person the "equal protection of the laws," and Section 5 empowers Congress "to enforce" those guarantees by "appropriate legislation."

The Supreme Court narrowly interpreted the Fourteenth Amendment in the late nineteenth century, severely limiting Congress's ability to affect state policy. However, throughout most of the twentieth century the Court interpreted Section 5 to give Congress broad discretion to pass legislation to remedy bad state laws. For example, discriminatory application of literacy tests prevented millions of African Americans from voting in the South before the Voting Rights Act was passed in 1965. As part of the federalism revolution of the 1990s, the Court started to chip away at Congress's Fourteenth Amendment powers.

In one important case in 1997, the Supreme Court struck down the Religious Freedom Restoration Act as an overly broad attempt to curtail state-sponsored harassment based on religion. This case established a new standard to justify remedial legislation—that is, national legislation that fixes discriminatory state law—under Section 5, saying: "There must be a congruence and proportionality between the injury to be prevented or remedied and the means adopted to that end."[38] Two applications of this logic also applied to the Eleventh Amendment, which originally was interpreted to mean that residents of any state could not sue other (non-home-state) state governments. More recently, the Supreme Court has expanded the reach of the Eleventh Amendment through the concept of states' sovereign immunity. States are now immune from a much broader range of lawsuits in state and federal court (see Table 3.2 for some examples). In one application of the new standard for remedial legislation, the Court ruled that the Age Discrimination in Employment Act of 1967 could not be applied to state

remedial legislation
National laws that address discriminatory state laws. Authority for such legislation comes from Section 5 of the Fourteenth Amendment.

states' sovereign immunity
Based on the Eleventh Amendment, immunity that prevents state governments from being sued by private parties in federal court unless the state consents to the suit.

employees because it was not "appropriate legislation."[39] The Supreme Court also struck down the portion of the ADA that applied to the states, saying: "States are not required . . . to make special accommodations for the disabled."[40]

In 2013 the Court demonstrated that it would uphold states' rights even when the issue concerned race. In striking down an important part of the Voting Rights Act, the Court established a new principle of "equal sovereignty" in saying that Congress had placed an unfair burden on the states.[41] The key point here is that laws passed by Congress cannot violate a state's sovereignty in a broad range of cases.

The Commerce Clause Another category of cases leading to more state power concerns the commerce clause of the Constitution. The first Court case to limit Congress's commerce powers since the New Deal of the 1930s came in 1995. The case involved the Gun-Free School Zones Act of 1990, which Congress passed in response to the increase in school shootings around the nation. The law made it a federal offense to have a gun

TABLE 3.2 Recent Important Supreme Court Decisions on Federalism

Case	Holding and Significance for States' Rights	Direction of the Decision
Gregory v. Ashcroft (1991)	The Missouri constitution's requirement that state judges retire by age 70 did not violate the Age Discrimination in Employment Act.	More state power
United States v. Lopez (1995)	Carrying a gun in a school did not fall within "interstate commerce"; thus, Congress could not prohibit the possession of guns on school property.	More state power
Seminole Tribe v. Florida (1996)	The Court used the Eleventh Amendment to strengthen states' sovereign immunity, ruling that Congress could not compel a state to negotiate with Native American tribes about gaming and casinos.	More state power
City of Boerne v. Flores (1997)	The Court struck down the Religious Freedom Restoration Act as an overly broad attempt to curtail the state-sponsored harassment of religion, saying that national legislation aimed at remedying states' discrimination must be "congruent and proportional" to the harm.	More state power
United States v. Morrison (2000)	The Court struck down part of the Violence Against Women Act, saying that Congress did not have the power under the commerce clause to provide a national remedy for gender-based crimes.	More state power
Alabama v. Garrett (2001)	The Court struck down the portion of the ADA that applied to the states, saying that state governments are not required to make special accommodations for the disabled.	More state power
Nevada Department of Human Resources v. Hibbs (2003)	The Court upheld Congress's power to apply the 1993 Family Leave Act to state employees as "appropriate legislation" under Section 5 of the Fourteenth Amendment.	Less state power
United States v. Bond (2011)	The Court upheld an individual's right to challenge the constitutionality of a federal law under the Tenth Amendment.	More state power
National Federation of Independent Business v. Sebelius (2012)	The Court upheld most provisions of the ACA but struck down the expansion of Medicaid as an unconstitutional use of coercive federalism (states could voluntarily take the additional funding to cover the expansion, but they would not lose existing funds if they opted out).	Mixed
United States v. Windsor (2013)	The Court held that Section 3 of DOMA was unconstitutional because it denied federal benefits to same-sex couples who were legally married under state law.	More state power
Shelby County v. Holder (2013)	The Court struck down Section 4 of the Voting Rights Act on the grounds that it violated the "equal sovereignty" of the states.	More state power

within 1,000 feet of a school. Congress assumed that it had the power to pass this legislation, given the Court's expansive interpretation of the commerce clause over the previous 55 years, even though it concerned a traditional area of state power. Although it was a stretch to claim that carrying a gun in or around a school was related to interstate commerce, Congress might have been able to demonstrate the point by showing that most guns are made in one state and sold in another (thus commercially crossing state lines), that crime affects the economy and commerce, and that the quality of education, which is also crucial to the economy, is harmed if students and teachers are worrying about guns in their schools. However, members of Congress did not present this evidence because they did not think it was necessary.

Alfonso Lopez, a senior at Edison High School in San Antonio, Texas, was arrested for carrying a concealed .38-caliber handgun with five bullets in it. Attorneys for Lopez moved to dismiss the charges, arguing that the law was unconstitutional because carrying a gun in a school could not be regulated as "interstate commerce." The Court agreed in *United States v. Lopez*,[42] and the ruling was widely viewed as a warning shot over Congress's bow. If Congress wanted to encroach on the states' turf in the future, it would have to demonstrate that the law in question was a legitimate exercise of the commerce clause powers.

Congress learned its lesson. The next time it passed legislation that affected law enforcement at the state level, it was careful to document the impact on interstate commerce. The Violence Against Women Act was passed in 1994 with strong bipartisan support after weeks of testimony and thousands of pages of evidence were entered into the record showing the links between violence against women and commerce. Despite the evidence Congress presented, the Supreme Court ruled that Congress did not have the power under the commerce clause to make a national law that gave victims of gender-motivated violence the right to sue their attackers in federal court (the Court struck down only that part of the law, however; the program funding remained unaffected and was reauthorized in 2013).[43]

The significance of this line of federalism cases is enormous. Not only has the Supreme Court set new limits on Congress's ability to address national problems

The Lopez decision struck down the 1990 Gun-Free School Zones Act, ruling that Congress did not have the power to forbid people to carry guns near schools. After the shooting of 12 students and one teacher at Columbine High School in Jefferson County, Colorado, on April 20, 1999, there were renewed calls nationwide for strengthening gun control laws.

(the "congruence and proportionality" test), but it has also clearly stated that the Court alone will determine which rights warrant protection by Congress. The cases have also shown how polarized the Court has become on some of these contentious issues. Nearly all of the cases mentioned here were decided by 5–4 margins, with intense and persistent dissents. In many instances, the dissenters took the unusual step of reading their opinions from the bench.

Many constitutional experts see these rulings as an important shift of power from the national government to the states. However, it is important to recognize that the Court does not consistently rule against Congress; it often rules against the states because of broader constitutional principles or general public consensus behind a specific issue. For example, the Court has struck down state laws limiting gay rights as a violation of the equal protection clause of the Fourteenth Amendment,[44] it ruled that the death penalty for those younger than 18 and the "mentally retarded" is "cruel and unusual punishment" and thus prohibited by the Eighth Amendment,[45] it upheld Congress's power to regulate marijuana over state laws that had allowed its medical use.[46] And although the Court rejected the commerce clause as the constitutional justification for national health care reform, it did uphold the ACA based on Congress's taxing power.[47]

Based on these cases, some would argue that the shift in power toward the states has been relatively marginal. Furthermore, the national government still has the upper hand in the balance of power and has many tools at its disposal to blunt the impact of a Court decision. First, Congress can pass new laws to clarify its legislative intent and overturn any of the Court cases that involved statutory interpretation. Second, Congress can use its financial power to impose its will on the states, as it did with raising the drinking age. So, for example, Congress could pass a law saying that before a state could receive money from the federal government related to the relevant law it had to agree to abide by the ADA or the Age Discrimination in Employment Act. However, as noted earlier, there are new limits on budgetary coercion. In the health care reform case, the Court ruled that the threat to withhold Medicaid funds was a "gun to the head" of states,[48] meaning states did not have a real choice. This was the first time the Court limited Congress's coercive budgetary power over the states, and the boundaries of the new limits will have to be decided in future cases.

"Why Should I Care?"

Why is it important to understand federalism today? The nature of the relationship between the national government and the states has a huge impact on most policy issues today. Sometimes the national government can force states to implement policies (coercive federalism), like when states raised their drinking ages to 21 so they wouldn't lose federal highway money. The national government may also entice states (fiscal federalism) to do things they might not otherwise do, like expanding alternative energy programs.

★

ANALYZE THE ARGUMENTS FOR AND AGAINST A STRONG FEDERAL GOVERNMENT

Assessing federalism

From Madison's "double security," which protects individual liberty, to states as the "laboratories of democracy" in policy innovation, there is much to recommend federalism as a cornerstone of our political system. However, there are disadvantages as well, such as inefficiency in the policy process and inequality in policy outcomes. This section will assess the advantages, disadvantages, and ideological complexities of federalism.

Ideological complexities

Issues concerning federalism often seem to break down along traditional liberal and conservative lines. Liberals generally favor strong national power to fight discrimination against women, minorities, disabled people, gay men and lesbians, and the elderly, and they push for progressive national policies on issues such as protecting the environment, providing national health care, and supporting the poor. Conservatives, in contrast, tend to favor limited intrusion from the national government and allowing the states to decide their own mix of social welfare and regulatory policies, including how aggressively they will protect various groups from discrimination.

However, assessing federalism is not so simple. In recent years the tables have turned, and in many cases liberals are suddenly arguing for states' rights while conservatives are advocating the virtues of uniform national laws. On a broad range of new issues, such as medical use of marijuana, gay rights, cloning, and aid in dying, state governments are passing socially liberal legislation (see the Take a Stand feature).[49] And the Court's earlier, state-centered rulings give it little precedent for striking down these laws. The Court's conservative justices will have to either continue applying its state-centered federalism and uphold these liberal state laws or strike them down on ideological grounds, which would undermine the Court's credibility.

Advantages of a strong role for the states

In addition to pointing out the ideological complexities of federalism, any assessment of federalism today must consider the advantages and disadvantages for our political system. The advantages of a strong role for the states can be summarized in four main points: (1) states can be laboratories of democracy, (2) state and local government is closer to the people, (3) states provide more access to the political system, and (4) states provide an important check on national power.

The first point refers to the role that states play as the source of policy diversity and innovation. If many states are trying to solve problems creatively, their efforts can complement those of the national government. Successful policies first adopted at the state level often percolate up to the national level. Consider welfare reform. Many states had great success in helping people get off welfare by providing worker training, education assistance, health benefits, and child care. The national government decided that states were doing a better job than the federal government was and, through the TANF block grant mentioned earlier, devolved welfare funding and responsibility to the states. Health care and environmental policy, especially on climate change, are other areas in which states have innovated.

Second, government that is closer to the people encourages participation in the political process and is responsive to their needs. Local politicians know better what their constituents want than further-removed national politicians do. If the voters want higher taxes to pay for more public benefits, such as public parks and better schools, they can enact these changes at the state and local levels. On the other hand, if they prefer lower taxes and fewer services, local politicians can be responsive to those desires. There is strong evidence that "statehouse democracy" is at work: more liberal states enact more liberal policies and conservative states have more conservative policies. State policy is also responsive to state public opinion across different policy areas.[50] In addition, local government provides a broad range of opportunities for direct involvement in politics, from working on local political campaigns to attending school board or city council meetings. When citizens are able to directly affect policies, they are more likely to get involved in the political process.

Medical Marijuana and Aid in Dying

Should Congress be able to tell a state that it cannot allow the use of medical marijuana? Can the U.S. attorney general interpret a congressional law as a prohibition of aid in dying? The debate over the balance of state and national power has grown increasingly complicated in the past several years. The courts have played a larger but inconsistent role, and issues of states' rights have increasingly cut across normal ideological and partisan divisions. Since the mid-1990s, the Supreme Court has played a central role in the shift of power to the states, but two cases involving medical marijuana (*Gonzales v. Raich*, 2005) and aid in dying—or assisted suicide, as it was called at the time of the decision (*Gonzales v. Oregon*, 2006)—show how the typical debate between national and state power can change when a moral dimension is introduced.

In both cases, state voters supported liberal policies. In 1996, California voters passed the Compassionate Use Act, by 56 to 44 percent. This law allowed seriously ill Californians, typically AIDS and cancer patients, to use marijuana as part of their medical treatment with the permission of a doctor. Oregon voters approved the Death with Dignity Act twice, the second time by a margin of 60 to 40 percent. This law allows physicians to prescribe a lethal drug dose for terminally ill patients who wish to end their lives. Both of these states' laws were challenged in federal court in classic confrontations between the states' rights and national power perspectives. Surprisingly, the Supreme Court ruled against medical marijuana and in favor of assisted suicide. (This summary oversimplifies the legal arguments, but these were the bottom-line outcomes.) How would you have ruled?

The states should decide these issues.

Unlike many of the cases discussed in this chapter, the states' rights position in these cases represented the liberal perspective, rather than the conservative position typically associated with state-centered federalism. Social liberals tended to support both the medical marijuana law and the assisted suicide law. However, if you examine these cases in terms of the question of federal versus state power, the traditional liberal and conservative perspectives are reversed: conservatives tend to favor state power, but that would put them on the socially liberal side of these issues. That is, if you support this side of the issue, you would be a states' rights conservative and a social liberal.

Congress should be able to tell the states what to do.

If you endorse this side of the debate, that Congress should have the power to regulate medical marijuana and assisted

📷 Federal drug enforcement agents raid a medical marijuana club.

suicide, you would be taking the socially conservative and national-power liberal position. In sorting out which side you take, you should consider which is more important to you—taking a consistent position on state versus national power or just figuring out which specific policy you support, regardless of whether the national or state government gets to call the shots.

As it turns out, the Court wasn't consistent on the question of federalism: in the medical marijuana case, the Court upheld Congress's power to regulate the medical use of marijuana under the Controlled Substances Act. But in the assisted suicide case, the Court said that under that same congressional law the U.S. attorney general did not have the power to limit the drugs that doctors in Oregon could prescribe for aid in dying.

Despite the Court's endorsement of Congress's power to regulate medical marijuana, the actual situation is more complex because of the evolving federal position on enforcing the law. Initially, the Obama administration said it would not enforce the federal law in states that had legalized or decriminalized medical marijuana. But then the Drug Enforcement Administration (DEA) shifted course, cracking down on large medical marijuana dispensaries, saying that the drug had become widely available for recreational use, not just medical use. Congress responded in 2014 by passing a law denying funds to the DEA to crack down on dispensaries.[a] However, the DEA continues to enforce federal law in the eight states that have legalized all uses of marijuana. The struggle between the national and state governments is likely to continue on this issue in the foreseeable future.

take a stand

1. As a matter of policy, should doctors be able to prescribe marijuana to alleviate pain? Should they be able to prescribe lethal drugs to terminally ill patients?

2. Do you tend to support a state-centered or nation-centered perspective on federalism? Now revisit your answers to question 1. Are your positions more consistent with your views on federalism or with your policy concerns?

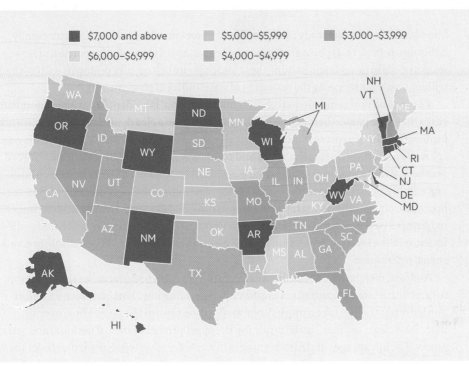

$7,000 and above $5,000–$5,999 $3,000–$3,999
$6,000–$6,999 $4,000–$4,999

FIGURE 3.1

State Spending per Person

Spending per person varies dramatically by state. What are some of the advantages and disadvantages of living in a low-spending state or in a high-spending state? What type of state would you rather live in? Why?

Source: State and Local Government Finance Data Query System, http://slfdqs. taxpolicycenter.org (accessed 10/17/16).

Third, our federalist system provides more potential paths to address problems. For example, the court system allows citizens to pursue complaints under state or federal law. Likewise, cooperative federalism can draw on the strengths of different levels of government to solve problems. A local government may recognize a need and respond to it more quickly than the national government, but if additional resources are needed to address the problem the municipality may be able to turn to the state or national government for help.

Finally, federalism can provide a check on national tyranny. Competitive federalism ensures that Americans have a broad range of social policies, levels of taxation and regulation, and public services to choose from (see Figure 3.1). When people "vote with their feet" by deciding whether to move and where to live, they encourage healthy competition among states that would be impossible under a unitary government.

In the debate over health care reform and the Affordable Care Act, supporters of nationalized health care argued the federal government could do a better job than the patchwork of state policies to ensure that all Americans receive sufficient care. #ACA #Obamacare

Disadvantages of too much state power

A balanced assessment of state and national power must acknowledge that there are problems with a federalist system that gives too much power to the states. The disadvantages include unequal distribution of resources across the states, unequal protection for civil rights, and competitive federalism that produces a "race to the bottom." Also, one puzzle (which we will explore in other chapters) is that more people vote in national elections than in state and local elections. Turnout at the local level is often ridiculously low. If people support local government so strongly, why aren't they more interested?

The resource problem becomes more acute when dealing with national-level problems that are intractable at the local or state level. For example, pollution spills across state lines, and the deteriorating public infrastructure, like the highway system, crosses state boundaries. In fact, one study estimated that 26 percent of U.S. bridges are structurally deficient or obsolete, 15 percent of highways are in need of repair, and 25 percent of mass transit needs to be updated. Solving these and other infrastructure problems will cost $2.2 trillion, vastly outstripping the resources of state and local governments.[51]

The second problem, unequal civil rights protection, is evident in various federalism cases that have passed before the Supreme Court. These clearly show that states are not uniformly willing to protect the civil liberties and civil rights of their citizens. This was critically important during the 1950s and 1960s when the national government forced southern states to end segregation and passed laws outlawing discrimination in housing, employment, transportation, and voting. The Supreme Court recently stepped in to provide equal rights to marry, but states vary a great deal in terms of antidiscrimination laws based on sexual orientation. Without national laws, there will be large differences in the levels of protection against discrimination based on age, disability, and sexual orientation.

And last, competitive federalism can create a "race to the bottom" as states attempt to lure businesses by keeping taxes and social spending low. This can place an unfair burden on states that take a more generous position toward the poor. Thus, overall, there is no clear "winner" in determining the appropriate balance of national and state power. The advantages and disadvantages of our federal system ensure that federalism will always remain a central source of conflict in the policy-making process as the various levels of government fight it out.

Conclusion

Alexis de Tocqueville, a French observer of American politics in the early nineteenth century, noted the tendency of democratic governments to centralize. This is especially true during wartime or times of crisis, as in the aftermath of the September 11 terrorist attacks, but it is also true during normal political times.

The health care reform example at the beginning of the chapter also illustrates the incentive to govern from Washington, D.C., rather than from the states. In the case of the ACA, passing a single piece of legislation was a much more efficient way to provide health insurance for more than 30 million Americans than was attempting to get each state to pass similar legislation. This scenario occurs again and again across a broad range of issues and creates a powerful centralizing force. Within that general pattern of government centralization, however, there have been lengthy periods when states' rights held sway over the national government. And even when laws are passed at the national level, states often play a vital role in their implementation, as with the ACA.

But this evolving balance of power between the national government and the states obscures a broader reality of federalism: we are citizens of several levels of government simultaneously. Martha Derthick, a leading scholar of American federalism, says that the basic question of federalism involves choices about how many communities we will be.[53] If you asked most people in our nation about their primary geopolitical community, they would probably not say, "I am a Montanan" or "I am an Arizonan." Most people would likely say, "I am an American." Yet, we have strong attachments to our local communities and state identities. Most Texans would not be caught dead wearing a Styrofoam cheesehead hat, but thousands of football fans in Green Bay, Wisconsin, regularly don the funny-looking things to watch their beloved Packers. We are members of multiple communities, a fact that has had an indelible impact on our political system.

One of the strengths of federalism is that it allows regional diversity to flourish. Green Bay Packers fans proudly wear their cheesehead hats at Lambeau Field, showing that what passes for normal behavior in one part of the country would be viewed differently in other areas. #PackersNation

STUDY GUIDE

What is federalism and why does it matter?

Define federalism and explain its significance.
(Pages 66–68)

Summary

A federal system simultaneously allocates power to both the state and federal government, whereas a confederal system gives power only to the states, and a unitary government gives power only to the federal government.

Key terms

federalism (p. 66)
sovereign power (p. 66)
police powers (p. 67)
concurrent powers (p. 67)

unitary government (p. 68)
confederal government (p. 68)
intergovernmental organizations (p. 68)

Practice Quiz Questions

1. **What system of government did the Articles of Confederation establish?**
   a. unitary
   b. federal
   c. confederal
   d. monarchy
   e. dictatorship

2. **Which is an example of a concurrent power?**
   a. printing money
   b. building roads
   c. conducting elections
   d. declaring war
   e. establishing post offices

Balancing national and state power in the Constitution

Explain what the Constitution says about federalism.
(Pages 68–71)

Summary

Although the state governments have considerable power in our system, the Founders disproportionately favored the federal government in the Constitution, so that the federal government's interests superseded those of the states in the event of a conflict.

Key terms

full faith and credit clause (p. 70)
privileges and immunities clause (p. 70)

Practice Quiz Questions

3. **States' rights are protected in which of the following constitutional provisions?**
   a. the Ninth Amendment
   b. the Tenth Amendment
   c. Article I of the Constitution
   d. Article III of the Constitution
   e. the First Amendment

4. **Which of the following would be best explained by the Tenth Amendment?**
   a. Congress increasing the minimum wage to $10 an hour
   b. the California state legislature declaring it was going to create its own navy
   c. state and local control over education policy
   d. the Supreme Court's recent decisions in same-sex marriage cases
   e. the Environmental Protection Agency passing a new regulation on carbon emissions that applies to all 50 states

The evolving concept of federalism

Trace the major shifts in state and federal government power over time. (Pages 72–79)

Summary

The relationship between the state and federal governments has changed dramatically over time. Whereas the federal and state governments traditionally operated with little interaction under the era of dual federalism, the trend over the past 80 years has been one of increasing federal interaction with state governments to address particular policy areas.

Key terms

states' rights (p. 72)
dual federalism (p. 74)

cooperative federalism (p. 76)
picket fence federalism (p. 77)

5. **Which analogy best describes the federalism arrangement today?**
   a. layer cake federalism
   b. marble cake federalism
   c. picket fence federalism
   d. gumbo federalism
   e. dual federalism

6. **Which case bolstered the federal government's power over the states?**
   a. *Barron v. Baltimore*
   b. *McCulloch v. Maryland*
   c. *Dred Scott v. Sanford*
   d. *Mapp v. Ohio*
   e. *Shelby County v. Holder*

7. **When did the federal government begin cooperating with the states on policy goals?**
   a. 1890s
   b. 1930s
   c. 1950s
   d. 1970s
   e. 1990s

Federalism today

Describe the major trends and debates in federalism today. (Pages 80–90)

Summary

Today's federal structure offers a complex mix of all previous components of federalism: some elements of national supremacy combine with states' rights for a varied federal landscape. Although the federal and state governments still exercise cooperative federalism to achieve joint policy goals, the federal government has also utilized coercive federalism to impose federal priorities on the states without offering compensation.

Key terms

fiscal federalism (p. 80)
categorical grants (p. 81)
block grants (p. 81)
unfunded mandates (p. 81)
coercive federalism (p. 84)
federal preemptions (p. 84)
competitive federalism (p. 86)
remedial legislation (p. 87)
states' sovereign immunity (p. 87)

8. **Which form of revenue sharing is given to the states by the federal government with explicit conditions on how it is to be allocated?**
   a. block grants
   b. categorical grants
   c. general revenue sharing
   d. federal mandates
   e. tax refunds

9. **Ronald Reagan's plans to increase states' rights led to an increase in _____.**
   a. block grants
   b. categorical grants
   c. federal taxes
   d. federal mandates
   e. state taxes

10. **The imposition of national priorities on the states through congressional legislation and imposition of the national supremacy clause is called _____.**
    a. cooperative federalism
    b. dual federalism
    c. competitive federalism
    d. federal preemption
    e. remedial legislation

11. **A state would usually challenge the constitutionality of a federal law under which of the amendments listed below?**
    a. Eighth Amendment
    b. Tenth Amendment
    c. Thirteenth Amendment
    d. Fourteenth Amendment
    e. First Amendment

12. **The Eleventh Amendment's protections of state sovereign immunity guarantee that _____.**
    a. residents of one state cannot sue the government of another state
    b. state governments cannot commit a legal wrong
    c. ambassadors from foreign countries cannot be detained by state governments
    d. state governments can sue the federal government
    e. state governments cannot be sued by anybody

13. **The Court has recently overturned a number of congressional laws rooted in the _____.**
    a. national supremacy clause
    b. reserve clause
    c. establishment clause
    d. commerce clause
    e. free exercise clause

Assessing federalism

Analyze the arguments for and against a strong federal government. (Pages 90–94)

Summary

Although conservatives have traditionally advocated for states' rights and liberals generally prefer a stronger national government, contemporary issues do not always fit neatly in this scheme. There are several reasons that strong state governments are beneficial for our country, such as the proximity of state and local governments to the citizens; however, there are also some drawbacks to the federal system, such as the vastly disproportionate distribution of resources across states.

Practice Quiz Questions

14. **Conservatives favor strong _____ rights on same-sex marriage and strong _____ rights on providing health care.**

    a. states'; states'

    b. states'; federal government

    c. federal government; states'

    d. federal government; federal government

    e. individual; federal government

15. **Which of the following is a drawback to strong state power?**

    a. State governments are often innovators on policy solutions.

    b. State governments give citizens more access to politicians than does the national government.

    c. State governments give citizens several paths to pursue policy reform.

    d. State governments give different civil rights protections to their citizens.

    e. States have an equal distribution of resources.

Suggested Reading

Banks, Christopher P., and John C. Blakeman. *The U.S. Supreme Court and New Federalism: From the Rehnquist to the Roberts Court.* Lanhan, MD: Rowman & Littlefield, 2012.

Beer, Samuel. *To Make a Nation: The Rediscovery of American Federalism.* Cambridge, MA: Harvard University Press, 1993.

Conlan, Timothy. *From New Federalism to Devolution: Twenty-Five Years of Intergovernmental Reform.* Washington, DC: Brookings Institution, 1998.

Derthick, Martha. *Keeping the Compound Republic: Essays on American Federalism.* Washington, DC: Brookings Institution, 2001.

Elkins, Stanley, and Eric McKitrick. *The Age of Federalism: The Early American Republic, 1788-1800.* New York: Oxford University Press, 1993.

Grodzins, Martin. *The American System: A New View of Government in the United States.* Chicago: Rand McNally, 1966.

LaCroix, Alison L. *The Ideological Origins of American Federalism.* Cambridge, MA: Harvard University Press, 2010.

Manna, Paul. *School's In: Federalism and the National Education Agenda.* Washington, DC: Georgetown University Press, 2006.

McDonald, Forrest. *States' Rights and the Union: Imperium in Imperio, 1776-1876.* Lawrence: University Press of Kansas, 2000.

Nagel, Robert F. *The Implosion of American Federalism.* New York: Oxford University Press, 2001.

Peterson, Paul E. *The Price of Federalism.* Washington, DC: Brookings Institution, 1995.

Posner, Paul L. *The Politics of Unfunded Mandates: Whither Federalism?* Washington, DC: Georgetown University Press, 1998.

Scheberle, Denise. *Federalism and Environmental Policy: Trust and the Politics of Implementation*, 2nd ed. Washington, DC: Georgetown University Press, 2004.

4

Civil Liberties

It's a free country . . . right?

The constitutional protections for religious freedom are clear and strong: "Congress shall make no law respecting an establishment of religion, or prohibiting the free exercise thereof." But what happens when one person's religious beliefs collide with another person's constitutional right? Shortly after the Supreme Court upheld the constitutionality of same-sex marriage for all Americans, a county clerk in Rowan County, Kentucky, Kim Davis, refused to provide marriage licenses to same-sex couples because of her religious beliefs. Davis described herself as a "soldier for Christ" and said, "I am confident that God is in control of all of this!"

The issue came to a head when a district court judge, David Bunning, appointed to the bench by President George W. Bush, sentenced Davis to jail for five days, saying that public officials are not allowed to pick which laws and court orders they obey: "We expect at the end of the day for the court's orders to be complied with. That's how things work here in America."[1] After she got out of jail, Davis continued to refuse to put her name on the marriage licenses but did issue them. Late in 2015, the newly elected governor, Matt Bevin, issued an executive order saying the county clerks did not have to put their names on the licenses. Governor Bevin issued his order "to ensure that the sincerely held religious beliefs of all Kentuckians are honored."[2] However, same-sex couples were able to be married.

In general, religious beliefs do not provide legal grounds for discrimination. For example, a religious belief that women should not work outside the home would not provide the basis for refusing to hire a woman. The same applies to discrimination based on race, ethnicity, or sexual orientation. However, the Supreme Court recently ruled that a "closely held" private corporation could not be forced to provide contraception to women under the Affordable Care Act if there was a "less restrictive" means available to have the insurance provide it. This was the first time that a corporation, Hobby Lobby, was given First Amendment protections based on the religious beliefs of the owners of the corporation. Family Research Council president Tony Perkins said, "The Supreme Court has delivered one of the most significant victories for religious freedom in our generation."[3] The American Civil Liberties Union had a very different view, saying:

📷

Should freedom of religious expression be protected even when acting on those views means discriminating against someone else? In general, discrimination based on religious views is not allowed, but Rowan County Clerk of Courts Kim Davis served time in jail for contempt of court after refusing a court order to issue marriage licenses to same-sex couples.

"This is a deeply troubling decision. For the first time, the highest court in the country has said that business owners can use their religious beliefs to deny their employees a benefit that they are guaranteed by law."[4] This is fundamentally a clash of whose rights are at stake—the owners of the corporation with their specific religious beliefs or the employees who want their health insurance to pay for contraception.

Is this how civil liberties work? Unfortunately, yes, it is messy and complicated figuring out what our liberties and freedoms actually mean. Even central freedoms such as the freedom of speech, the press, and religious practices are subject to limitations if there are threats to national security or public safety or if these freedoms conflict with another fundamental right (such as the right to marry). Simply put, civil liberties are not absolute. So how should political actors draw the lines between protected behavior and actions that may be regulated? People say that America is a free country, but are there limits to those freedoms?

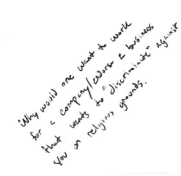

★
DEFINE WHAT WE MEAN BY CIVIL LIBERTIES

civil liberties
Basic political freedoms that protect citizens from governmental abuses of power.

Defining civil liberties

The terms "civil rights" and "civil liberties" are often used interchangeably, but there are important differences (see Nuts & Bolts 4.1). To oversimplify a bit, civil liberties are about freedom and civil rights are about equality. Given that civil liberties are rooted in the Bill of Rights, it might have been less confusing if it had been called the "Bill of Liberties." (This distinction is discussed further in Chapter 5.)

Civil liberties are deeply rooted in our key idea that politics is conflictual and involves trade-offs. When the Supreme Court rules on civil liberties cases, it must balance an individual's freedom with government interests and the public good. In some cases, the Court must not only balance these interests but also "draw a line" between permissible and illegal conduct concerning a specific liberty.

Balancing interests

Civil liberties must be balanced against competing interests, because when it comes to our freedoms there are no absolutes. The trade-off between civil liberties and national security in the "war on terrorism" illustrates this point. Many Americans were

○
NUTS & BOLTS 4.1

Distinguishing Civil Liberties from Civil Rights

Civil Liberties	Civil Rights
Basic freedoms and liberties	Protection from discrimination
Rooted in the Bill of Rights and the "due process" protection of the Fourteenth Amendment	Rooted in laws and the "equal protection" clause of the Fourteenth Amendment
Primarily restrict what the government can do to you ("*Congress* shall make no law . . . abridging the freedom of speech")	Protect you from discrimination both by the government and by individuals

concerned that our civil liberties were being eroded upon discovering that the government was conducting surveillance of U.S. citizens without court orders, including collecting data from millions of phone calls and e-mail messages; had condoned the abuse of Iraqi prisoners; and was applying a process in which suspected terrorists were arrested in the United States and taken to foreign countries that are less protective of civil liberties—Egypt, Syria, Jordan, and Morocco—to be interrogated through torture.[5] Despite these concerns, even the strongest critic of state-sponsored torture would have to admit that, in some instances, it might be justified. For example, if a nuclear device were set to detonate in Manhattan in three hours few would insist on protecting the civil liberties of someone who knew where the bomb was hidden. Once we recognize that our freedoms are not absolute, it becomes a question of how they are balanced against other interests, such as national security.

Other interests that compete with civil liberties include public safety and public health. For example, members of some Christian fundamentalist churches regularly handle dangerous snakes in their services, but many states and cities have laws against "the handling of poisonous reptiles in such manner as to endanger the public health, safety, and welfare." These conflicting interests collided in a 1947 case in which members of a church in North Carolina were each fined $50 for handling a poisonous copperhead snake in a church service. They appealed all the way to the North Carolina Supreme Court, arguing that the local ordinance "impinges on the freedom of religious worship." The court rejected this view, saying that "public safety is superior to religious practice."[6] In 2013, Tennessee Wildlife Resource Agency officials cited a minister for keeping 53 poisonous snakes and using them in services (an estimated 125 churches still handle snakes, despite the laws). But Reverend Andrew Hamblin, co-star of the National Geographic Channel reality show *Snake Salvation,* was acquitted by a grand jury and will not be indicted. A couple of months later, his co-star Reverend Jamie Coots died after being bitten by a rattlesnake in his church and refusing treatment.[7] Similarly, in some states the Amish are forced to place reflective "slow-moving vehicle" triangles on their horse-drawn carriages, even if it violates their religious beliefs, because of the paramount concern for public safety (see the How It Works graphic in this chapter).[8] Yet the Amish are not forced to send their children to public schools despite a state law requiring all children to attend school through age 16. The Court said this law presented "a very real threat of undermining the Amish community and religious practice as it exists today."[9]

📷

How can conflicts be resolved between civil liberties and other legitimate interests, such as public safety and public health? Sometimes freedom is forced to give way. Courts have upheld bans on the religious practice of snake handling and laws requiring the Amish to display reflective triangles when driving slow-moving buggies on public roads, despite religious objections to doing so.

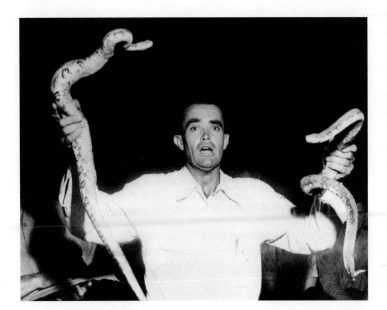

How it works: in theory
The First Amendment

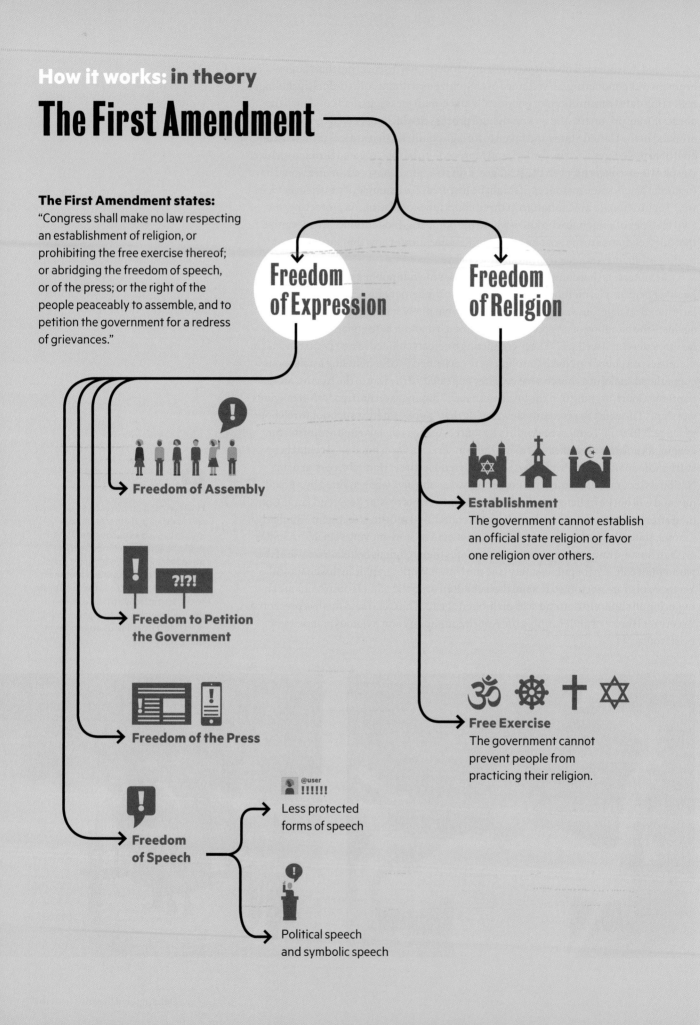

The First Amendment states:
"Congress shall make no law respecting an establishment of religion, or prohibiting the free exercise thereof; or abridging the freedom of speech, or of the press; or the right of the people peaceably to assemble, and to petition the government for a redress of grievances."

Freedom of Expression

Freedom of Assembly

Freedom to Petition the Government

Freedom of the Press

Freedom of Speech

@user
!!!!!!
Less protected forms of speech

Political speech and symbolic speech

Freedom of Religion

Establishment
The government cannot establish an official state religion or favor one religion over others.

Free Exercise
The government cannot prevent people from practicing their religion.

Balancing Interests and Drawing Lines: Government and Religion

While the different branches of the First Amendment on the opposite page are an accurate representation of the various aspects of our religious and expressive freedoms, in practice, the implementation of these civil liberties is more complicated.

Free Exercise:

When she refused...

When county clerk Kim Davis **refused to issue marriage licenses to same-sex couples,**

They said no.

the court ruled that her religious convictions **did not allow her to discriminate.**

Here's why.

In cases like these, **courts must balance religious freedom against other state interests,** such as freedom from discrimination.

Establishment Clause:

Banned.

Since 1962 the Supreme Court has **banned school prayer as a violation of the establishment clause.**

What about...?

But does the separation of church and state also apply to town board members who **start their meetings with a prayer?** In 2014, the Court decided by a 5–4 vote that it did not.

It's tough.

The establishment clause often asks courts to **draw lines between what type of religious conduct is allowed** and what would be considered an "excessive entanglement" between church and state.

❓ Critical Thinking

1. **Balancing interests can be tricky. Consider these two scenarios** in which competing interests are in play: Company policy restricts employees from wearing political T-shirts or buttons at work. A pharmacist denies birth control pills to a customer for religious reasons. Which (if either) do you think should be allowed? Why did you select the one(s) you did?

2. **Drawing lines for a given civil liberty** can also be difficult. What if Kim Davis, instead of refusing to issue marriage licenses to same-sex couples, wore a necklace with a large crucifix at work? Should that be allowed? Or, consider a different scenario: Should Congress be able to start its sessions with a prayer? Reference the First Amendment and its interpretations in your answer.

In some cases, the free exercise and establishment clauses are in tension with one another. For example, while the establishment clause prohibits school-sponsored prayer, the free exercise clause guarantees that any student can pray at any time in school on their own, **as long as they are not bothering others.**

These decisions show that balancing interests is never a simple process but involves deciding whether a specific civil liberty or some competing public interest is more compelling in a specific case.

Drawing lines

Along with balancing competing interests, court rulings draw the lines defining the limits of permissible conduct by the government or an individual in the context of a specific civil liberty. For example, despite the First Amendment protection of freedom of speech, it is obvious that some speech cannot be permitted. The classic example is falsely yelling "fire!" in a crowded theater. Therefore, the courts must interpret the law to draw the line between protected speech and impermissible speech.

The same applies to other civil liberties, such as the establishment of religion, freedom of the press, freedom from illegal searches, or other due process rights. For example, the First Amendment prohibits the government from establishing an official religion, which the Court has carefully interpreted over the years to avoid "excessive entanglement" between any religion and the government. On these grounds, government-sponsored prayer in public schools has been banned since the early 1960s. But sometimes it is difficult to draw the line between acceptable and impermissible government involvement concerning religion in schools. One such ruling allowed taxpayer subsidies to fund parochial schools for buying books but not maps. (This odd hairsplitting led the late senator Daniel Patrick Moynihan to quip, "What about atlases?"[10]) Another difficult issue is the Fourth Amendment prohibition against "unreasonable searches and seizures" and the role of drug-sniffing dogs. Here the line drawing involves deciding whether a sniff is a search and, if so, under what circumstances it is reasonable (see the Take a Stand feature in this chapter). Search and seizure cases also involve balancing interests: in this case, the individual freedoms of the target of police action and the broader interests in public order and security.

★

EXPLAIN WHY THE BILL OF RIGHTS WAS ADDED TO THE CONSTITUTION AND HOW IT CAME TO APPLY TO THE STATES

The origins of civil liberties

Courts define the boundaries of civil liberties, but the other branches of government and the public often get involved as well. The earliest debates during the American Founding illustrate the broad public involvement concerning the basic questions of how our civil liberties would be defined: Should government be limited by an explicit statement of individual liberties? Would these limitations apply to the state governments or just the national government? How should these freedoms evolve as our society changes?

Origins of the Bill of Rights

The original Constitution provided only limited protection of civil liberties: a guarantee of habeas corpus rights (a protection against illegal incarceration) and a prohibition of bills of attainder (legislation punishing someone for a crime without the benefit of a trial) and ex post facto laws (laws that retroactively change the legal consequences of some behavior). There were a few attempts to include a broader statement of civil liberties, including one by George Mason and Elbridge Gerry five days before the Constitutional Convention adjourned. But their motion to appoint a committee to draft a bill of

Drug-Sniffing Dogs: An Illegal Search?

In 2013, the Supreme Court was presented with the case of Joelis Jardines, whom police suspected of growing marijuana inside his Miami home based on an anonymous tip. Police went to the home with a trained drug-detection dog. On the front porch, the dog gave a positive signal indicating the presence of drugs. The police returned with a search warrant, found a marijuana-growing operation, and arrested Jardines. However, the Florida Supreme Court threw out the evidence, arguing it was an illegal search. The case then made its way to the U.S. Supreme Court, which was faced with this question: Should drug-sniffing dogs be allowed outside a home without a warrant? More broadly, in the context of rapidly changing technology, what is the public's "reasonable expectation" for privacy? Take a stand.

A drug-sniffing dog is no more invasive than the surveillance technologies we encounter every day.
The Court has ruled that police do not need a search warrant to have drug-sniffing dogs search luggage at an airport or a car that has been stopped for a traffic violation unrelated to drugs. Lower courts have also ruled that sniffs are not considered searches in a hotel hallway, at a school locker, outside a passenger train's sleeper compartments, or outside an apartment door. Is a sniff outside someone's home any more invasive?

It might not seem that way, especially when you consider the reach of new surveillance methods that are on the horizon. Other technologies that are becoming more common or will be used soon include RFIDs (radio frequency identifications), which are the size of a grain of rice and transmit information wirelessly through radio waves; facial recognition software and iris scanners; "smart dust devices"—tiny wireless micromechanical sensors—that can detect light and movement; and drones, which have primarily been used for military purposes but also have vast potential for tracking suspects in any situation.

Warrantless surveillance of somebody's home crosses a line.
Lower courts have been split on whether drug-sniffing dogs may be used outside a home without a warrant, due, in part, to a Supreme Court precedent giving homes stronger Fourth Amendment protection than cars, lockers, or other areas. For example, in 2001 the Court ruled that police needed a warrant to use a thermal-imaging device outside a home when trying to detect marijuana that was believed to be growing under heat lamps inside.

The U.S. Supreme Court ultimately agreed in the Jardines case, saying that there is a general expectation that anyone may come onto a front porch as long as the uninvited person simply knocks and then leaves if there is no answer. The majority opinion wryly noted: "Complying with the terms of that traditional invitation does not require fine-grained legal knowledge; it is generally managed without incident by the Nation's Girl Scouts and trick-or-treaters." But, they continued, "introducing a trained police dog to explore the area around the home in hopes of discovering incriminating evidence is something else. There is no customary invitation to do *that*."[a]

Federal agents use a drug-sniffing dog to inspect a car.

New and future technologies continue to complicate the question of just what is "reasonable." Justice Alito raised this question in oral arguments in a Supreme Court case involving a GPS tracking device. He said, "Technology is changing people's expectations of privacy.... Maybe 10 years from now 90 percent of the population will be using social networking sites and they will have on average 500 friends and they will have allowed their friends to monitor their location 24 hours a day, 365 days a year, through the use of their cell phones. Then—what would the expectation of privacy be then?"[b]

take a stand

1. If you had to decide the case of the drug-sniffing dog, how would you have ruled? Do you think that homes should have stronger privacy expectations than cars or school lockers? Even when it concerns illegal drugs?

2. How would you answer Justice Alito's question about the expectation of privacy in an era of rapidly changing technology? When should law-enforcement officials have to get a warrant to monitor our behavior?

rights was rejected. Charles Pinckney and Gerry also tried to add a provision to protect the freedom of the press, but that too was rejected.[11]

Mason and Gerry opposed ratification of the Constitution, partly because it did not include a bill of rights, and many Antifederalists echoed this view. In a letter to James Madison, Thomas Jefferson predicted that four states would withhold ratification until a bill of rights was added.[12] Some states ratified the Constitution but urged Congress to draft specific protections for individuals' and states' rights from federal action (they believed protection of civil liberties from state actions should reside in state constitutions). In other states, the Antifederalists who lost the ratification battle continued making their case to the public and Congress. One of the most famous arguments came from the Antifederalists of Pennsylvania, who claimed that a bill of rights was needed to "fundamentally establish those unalienable and personal rights of men, without the full, free, and secure enjoyment of which there can be no liberty, and over which it is not necessary for a good government to have the control."[13] Their statement went on to outline many of those civil liberties that ultimately became the basis for the Bill of Rights.

Madison and other supporters of the Constitution agreed that the first Congress would take up the issue, despite their reservations that a Bill of Rights could lead the people into falsely believing that it was an exhaustive list of all of their rights. State conventions submitted 124 amendments for consideration. That list was whittled down to 17 by the House and then to 12 by the Senate. This even dozen was approved by the House and sent to the states, which in 1791 ratified the 10 amendments that became the Bill of Rights (see Nuts & Bolts 4.2).[14]

Despite the profound significance of the Bill of Rights, one point limited its reach: it applied only to the national government and not the states. For example, the First

The Bill of Rights: A Statement of Our Civil Liberties

NUTS & BOLTS 4.2

First Amendment	Freedom of religion, speech, press, and assembly; the separation of church and state; and the right to petition the government.
Second Amendment	Right to bear arms.
Third Amendment	Protection against the forced quartering of troops in one's home.
Fourth Amendment	Protection from unreasonable searches and seizures; requirement of "probable cause" for search warrants.
Fifth Amendment	Protection from forced self-incrimination or double jeopardy (being tried twice for the same crime); no person can be deprived of life, liberty, or property without due process of law; private property cannot be taken for public use without just compensation; and no person can be tried for a serious crime without the indictment of a grand jury.
Sixth Amendment	Right of the accused to a speedy and public trial by an impartial jury, to an attorney, to confront witnesses, to a compulsory process for obtaining witnesses in his or her favor, and to counsel in all felony cases.
Seventh Amendment	Right to a trial by jury in civil cases involving common law.
Eighth Amendment	Protection from excessive bail, excessive fines, and cruel and unusual punishment.
Ninth Amendment	The enumeration of specific rights in the Constitution shall not be construed to deny other rights retained by the people. This has been interpreted to include a general right to privacy and other fundamental rights.
Tenth Amendment	Powers not delegated by the Constitution to the national government, nor prohibited by it to the states, are reserved to the states or to the people.

Amendment says that "*Congress* shall make no law" infringing on freedom of religion, speech, and the press, among others. Madison submitted another amendment, which he characterized as "the most valuable of the whole list," requiring states to protect some civil liberties: "The equal rights of conscience, the freedom of speech or of the press, and the right of trial by jury in criminal cases shall not be infringed by any State."[15] But Antifederalists feared another power grab by the Federalists in limiting states' rights, so the proposed amendment was voted down in Congress. This decision proved consequential, because the national government was quite weak for the first half of our nation's history. Given that states exercised as much or more power over people's lives than did the national government, it would have been more important for the Bill of Rights to limit the reach of the state governments rather than that of the federal government, but this did not occur. Thus, the Bill of Rights played a surprisingly small role for more than a century. The Supreme Court used it only once before 1866 to invalidate a federal action—in the infamous *Dred Scott* case that contributed to the Civil War.

Selective incorporation and the Fourteenth Amendment

The significance of the Bill of Rights increased somewhat with the ratification of the Fourteenth Amendment in 1868. It was one of the three Civil War amendments that attempted to guarantee equal rights to the newly freed slaves. (The other two Civil War amendments were the Thirteenth, which abolished slavery, and the Fifteenth, which gave male former slaves the right to vote.) Northern politicians were concerned that southerners would deny basic rights to the former slaves, so the sweeping language of the Fourteenth Amendment was adopted. Section 1 of the Fourteenth Amendment says:

> *All persons born or naturalized in the United States, and subject to the jurisdiction thereof, are citizens of the United States and of the State wherein they reside. No State shall make or enforce any law which shall abridge the privileges or immunities of citizens of the United States; nor shall any State deprive any person of life, liberty, or property, without due process of law; nor deny to any person within its jurisdiction the equal protection of the laws.*

This language was intended to make sure that states would not deny newly freed slaves the full protection of the law.[16] The due process clause, which forbids any state from denying "life, liberty, or property, without due process of law," led to an especially important expansion of civil liberties because the similar clause of the Fifth Amendment had previously been interpreted by the Court to apply only to the federal government.

Evolving Interpretations by the Supreme Court Despite the clear language of the amendment saying that "no State shall make or enforce any law," in its first opportunity to interpret the Fourteenth Amendment in 1873 the Court continued to rule in favor of protecting states from national government actions only, embracing the "dual citizenship" idea set forth in *Barron v. Baltimore* (the 1833 case ruling that the Fifth Amendment's protection of property from being taken by the government without compensation only applied to the federal government, not to state governments).[17] Over the next 50 years, a minority of justices tried mightily to strengthen the power of the Fourteenth Amendment and use it to protect civil liberties against state government action. The first step was an 1897 case in which the Court ruled that the Fourteenth Amendment's due process clause forbade the state of Illinois from taking

Civil War amendments
The Thirteenth, Fourteenth, and Fifteenth Amendments to the Constitution, which abolished slavery and granted civil liberties and voting rights to freed slaves after the Civil War.

due process clause
Part of the Fourteenth Amendment that forbids states from denying "life, liberty, or property" to any person without due process of law. (A nearly identical clause in the Fifth Amendment applies only to the national government.)

private property without just compensation. However, the decision did not specifically mention the Fifth Amendment's compensation clause.[18] The next step came in a self-incrimination case in which a state judge gave the jury instructions that included references to the fact that the accused did not take the stand in his defense. The Supreme Court upheld his conviction but said: "It is possible that some of the personal rights safeguarded in the first eight amendments against National action may also be safeguarded against state action, because a denial of them would be a denial of the due process of law."[19] Thus, in both the property and self-incrimination cases, the Supreme Court started to use the Fourteenth Amendment to prohibit state governments from violating individual rights—but without specific reference to the Bill of Rights.

This progression culminated in the 1925 case *Gitlow v. New York*. Here the Court said for the first time that the Fourteenth Amendment incorporated one of the amendments in the Bill of Rights (provisions protecting freedom of speech and freedom of the press) and applied it to the states. The case involved Benjamin Gitlow, a radical socialist convicted under New York's Criminal Anarchy Act of 1902 for advocating the overthrow of the government. The Court upheld his conviction, arguing that his writings were the "language of direct incitement," but also warned state governments that there were limits on such suppression of speech.[20]

Applying Civil Liberties to the States Slowly over the next 50 years, most civil liberties covered in the Bill of Rights were applied to the states on a right-by-right, case-by-case basis through the Fourteenth Amendment. However, this process of selective incorporation was not smooth and incremental. Rather, it progressed in surges with flurries of activity in the 1930s and the 1960s (see Table 4.1). As a result, the Bill of Rights has evolved from only protecting people from national government actions during the early nineteenth century to a robust set of protections for freedom and liberty that limit national, state, and local government actions today.

selective incorporation
The process through which the civil liberties granted in the Bill of Rights were applied to the states on a case-by-case basis through the Fourteenth Amendment.

"Why Should I Care?"

Today the Bill of Rights is one of the most revered and important parts of the Constitution. But it didn't start out that way. Initially, the Bill of Rights only applied to the national government, not the states. But through the Fourteenth Amendment and the process of selective incorporation, the Supreme Court has gradually applied the Bill of Rights to the states. While all levels of government must respect our civil liberties today, there are many unresolved areas in terms of balancing interests and drawing lines. Do religious beliefs allow a county clerk to deny a marriage license to a same-sex couple? How do we balance our freedom of speech or freedom from illegal searches with the need for national security? These are central questions in today's politics.

DESCRIBE THE FIRST AMENDMENT RIGHTS RELATED TO FREEDOM OF RELIGION

Freedom of religion

The First Amendment's ringing words are the most famous statement of personal freedoms in the Constitution: "Congress shall make no law respecting an establishment of religion, or prohibiting the free exercise thereof; or abridging the freedom of speech, or of the press; or the right of the people peaceably to assemble, and to petition the Government for a redress of grievances." (The How It Works graphic illustrates how much is packed into this one amendment.)

Selective Incorporation

TABLE
4.1

The process of applying the Bill of Rights to the states progressed in two stages. The first, coming in the 1920s and 1930s, applied the First Amendment to the states; the second came a few decades later and involved criminal defendants' rights.

Amendment	Issue	Case
First Amendment	Freedom of speech	*Gitlow v. New York* (1925)
	Freedom of the press	*Near v. Minnesota* (1931)
	Freedom of assembly	*De Jonge v. Oregon* (1937)
	Right to petition the government	*Hague v. CIO* (1939)
	Free exercise of religion	*Hamilton v. Regents of the University of California* (1934); *Cantwell v. Connecticut* (1940)
	Separation of church and state	*Everson v. Board of Education of Ewing Township* (1947)
Second Amendment	Right to bear arms	*McDonald v. Chicago* (2010)
Fourth Amendment	Protection from unreasonable search and seizure	*Wolf v. Colorado* (1949); *Mapp v. Ohio* (1961)*
Fifth Amendment	Protection from forced self-incrimination	*Malloy v. Hogan* (1964)
	Protection from double jeopardy	*Benton v. Maryland* (1969)
Sixth Amendment	Right to a public trial	*In re Oliver* 333 U.S. 257 (1948)
	Right to a fair trial and an attorney in death-penalty cases	*Powell v. Alabama* (1932)
	Right to an attorney in all felony cases	*Gideon v. Wainwright* (1963)
	Right to an attorney in cases involving jail time	*Argersinger v. Hamlin* (1972)
	Right to a jury trial in a criminal case	*Duncan v. Louisiana* (1968)
	Right to cross-examine a witness	*Pointer v. Texas* (1965)
	Right to compel the testimony of witnesses who are vital for the defendant's case	*Washington v. Texas* (1967)
Eighth Amendment	Protection from cruel and unusual punishment	*Robinson v. California* (1962)[†]
	Protection from excessive bail	*Schilb v. Kuebel* (1971)[‡]
Ninth Amendment	Right to privacy and other nonenumerated, fundamental rights	*Griswold v. Connecticut* (1965)[§]

Not Incorporated

Third Amendment	Prohibition against the quartering of troops in private homes	
Fifth Amendment	Right to indictment by a grand jury	
Seventh Amendment	Right to a jury trial in a civil case	
Eighth Amendment	Prohibition against excessive fines	

* *Wolf v. Colorado* applied the Fourth Amendment to the states (which meant that states could not engage in unreasonable searches and seizures); *Mapp v. Ohio* applied the exclusionary rule to the states (which excludes the use in a trial of illegally obtained evidence).

[†] Some sources list *Louisiana ex rel. Francis v. Resweber* (1947) as the first case that incorporated the Eighth Amendment. While the decision mentioned the Fifth and Eighth Amendments in the context of the due process clause of the Fourteenth Amendment, this argument was not included in the majority opinion that upheld as constitutional the bizarre double electrocution of prisoner Willie Francis (the electric chair malfunctioned on the first attempt but was successful on the second attempt; see Abraham and Perry, *Freedom and the Court*, pp. 71–72).

[‡] Justice Blackmun "assumed" in this case that "the Eighth Amendment's proscription of excessive bail [applies] to the states through the Fourteenth Amendment," but later decisions did not seem to share this view. However, Justices Stevens and O'Connor agreed with Blackmun's view in *Browning-Ferris v. Kelco Disposal* (1989). Some sources argue that the excessive bail clause of the Eighth Amendment is unincorporated.

[§] Justice Goldberg argued for explicit incorporation of the Ninth Amendment in a concurring opinion joined by Justices Warren and Brennan. The opinion of the Court referred more generally to a privacy right rooted in five amendments, including the Ninth, but did not explicitly argue for incorporation.

establishment clause
Part of the First Amendment that states "Congress shall make no law respecting an establishment of religion," which has been interpreted to mean that Congress cannot sponsor or favor any religion.

free exercise clause
Part of the First Amendment that states that Congress cannot prohibit or interfere with the practice of religion.

> **The number, the industry, and the morality of the Priesthood, & the devotion of the people have been manifestly increased by the total separation of the Church from the State.**
>
> **—James Madison**

Can a cross be displayed on federal land? The Supreme Court has ruled that religious displays on government property must be part of larger, secular displays. This cross on federal land in the Mojave Desert was covered up after it became controversial. Now it looks like a sign.

The First Amendment has two parts that deal with religion: the establishment clause, which has been interpreted to mean that Congress cannot sponsor or endorse any particular religion, and the free exercise clause, which has been interpreted to mean that Congress cannot interfere with the practice of religion unless there are important secular reasons for doing so. To simplify only slightly, the former says that Congress should not help religion and the latter that it should not hurt religion. The establishment clause is primarily concerned with drawing lines. For example, does a prayer at a public high school football game or a Nativity scene on government property constitute state sponsorship of religion? The free exercise clause has more to do with balancing interests. Recall the earlier examples of balancing public safety concerns against snake handling in religious services and the use of Amish buggies on highways.

The combination of the establishment and free exercise clauses results in a general policy of noninterference and government neutrality toward religion. As Thomas Jefferson put it in 1802, the First Amendment provides a "wall of eternal separation between church and state." This language continues to be cited in Court cases in which religion and politics intersect.[21] Since both areas carry great moral weight and emotional charge, it's no wonder that vehement debates continue over the appropriateness of the saying "In God We Trust" on our currency, of the White House Christmas tree, and of whether evolution and "intelligent design" should be taught in the public schools. The boundaries of religious expression remain difficult to draw, as the case of Kim Davis and same-sex marriage demonstrated.

The establishment clause and separation of church and state

Determining the boundaries between church and state—the central issue of the establishment clause—is very difficult. As a leading text on civil liberties puts it, the words of the establishment clause—"Congress shall make no law respecting an establishment of religion"—are commanding and clear, but their meaning is entirely unclear. What does the clause allow or forbid?[22] We know that the Founders did not want an official state religion and did not want the government to favor one religion over another, but beyond that it's hard to say. Jefferson's "wall of eternal separation" comment has been used in Court decisions that prohibit state aid for religious activities, but lately the Court has been moving toward a more "accommodationist" perspective that sometimes allows religious activity in public institutions.

School Prayer The prohibition of prayer in public schools has become the most controversial establishment clause issue. It exploded onto the political scene in 1962 when the Court ruled in *Engel v. Vitale*[23] that the following prayer, written by the New York Board of State Regents and read every day in the state's public schools, violated the separation of church and state: "Almighty God, we acknowledge our dependence upon Thee, and we beg Thy blessing upon us, our parents, our teachers, and our country." Banning the prayer caused a huge public outcry protesting the perceived attack on religion.

Over the next 50 years, Congress repeatedly tried, unsuccessfully, to amend the Constitution to allow school prayer. Meanwhile, the Court continued to take a hard line on school-sponsored prayer. In 1985, the Court struck down the practice of observing a one-minute moment of silence for "meditation or voluntary prayer" in the Alabama public schools.[24] More recently, the Court said that benedictions or prayers at public school graduations and a school policy that allowed an elected student representative to lead a prayer at a high school football game also violated the establishment clause. The former established a strong "coercion test" that prohibited prayers that may appear to be voluntary (students are not required to attend their high school graduation) but in effect are compulsory.[25] Yet the Court has upheld the practice of opening every session of Congress with a prayer, has let stand without comment a lower-court ruling that allowed a prayer that was planned and led by students (rather than being school policy) at a high school graduation, and most recently in 2014 upheld prayers by voluntary chaplains for town board meetings in Greece, New York.[26] The latter case was especially significant because the town meetings included residents, unlike the previously approved legislative prayers that were intended for the elected leaders.

Aid to Religious Organizations The Court has had an even more difficult time coming up with principles to govern aid to religious organizations, either directly, through tax dollars, or indirectly, through the use of public space. One early attempt was known as the **Lemon test**, after one of the parties in a 1971 case involving government support for religious schools (*Lemon v. Kurtzman*). This case said that a practice violated the establishment clause if it (1) did not have a "secular legislative purpose," (2) either advanced or inhibited religion, or (3) fostered "an excessive government entanglement with religion."[27] The third part of the test was later found open to interpretation by lower courts and therefore led to conflicting rulings.

The Court started to move away from the Lemon test in a 1984 case involving a crèche owned by the city of Pawtucket, Rhode Island, and displayed in a park owned by a nonprofit corporation. The Court allowed the Nativity display, saying: "The Constitution does not require complete separation of church and state; it affirmatively mandates accommodation, not merely tolerance, of all religions, and forbids hostility toward any."[28] This "endorsement test" simply says that government action is unconstitutional if a "reasonable observer" would think that the action either endorses or disapproves of religion. Later rulings upheld similar religious displays, especially if they conformed to what observers have labeled the "three plastic animals rule"—if the baby Jesus is surrounded by Rudolph the red-nosed reindeer and other secular symbols, the overall display is considered sufficiently nonreligious to pass constitutional muster.[29]

The Court has also applied the accommodationist perspective to funding for religious schools by looking more favorably on providing tax dollars to students' families to subsidize tuition costs rather than funding parochial schools directly. For example, a 2002 case upheld an Ohio school voucher program that distributed scholarships to needy students so they could attend the Cleveland school of their choice, including private, religious schools. The Court said the program did not violate the establishment clause because it allowed students and their families "to exercise genuine choice among options public and private, secular and religious."[30] Critics of the decision pointed out that 96 percent of the students participating in the scholarship program were enrolled in religiously affiliated schools, which amounted to state sponsorship of religious education, something that the Court had not previously allowed. In 2011, the Court expanded taxpayer support for religious education when it upheld an Arizona law that provides state tax credits for contributions to organizations that provide tuition for religious schools.[31] The Court has also ruled that it is acceptable to use federal funds to buy computers and other educational equipment to be used in public and private schools for "secular, neutral, and nonideological programs"[32] and tax dollars for a sign language interpreter for a deaf student who attended a parochial school.[33]

The free exercise clause

While the freedom of belief is absolute, freedom of religious conduct cannot be unrestricted. That is, you can believe whatever you want without government interference,

Lemon test
The Supreme Court uses this test, established in *Lemon v. Kurtzman*, to determine whether a practice violates the First Amendment's establishment clause.

but if you *act* on those beliefs the government may regulate your behavior. And while the government has restricted religious conduct in dozens of cases, the freedom of religion has been among the most consistently protected civil liberties.

There is one prominent example of the Court restricting the free exercise of religion but then quickly correcting its error. This 1940 case concerned the children in a Jehovah's Witness family who were kicked out of a public school in Minersville, Pennsylvania, for refusing to recite the Pledge of Allegiance.[34] The children cited Exodus 20:3, "you shall have no other Gods before Me," in explaining why they refused to recite the pledge and salute the flag. The Court surprised the experts by siding with the school—until, three years later, the justices reversed course and ruled that the school could not force anyone to say the pledge, especially when it served no important government interest, such as protecting public safety.[35]

Demonstrators rally outside of the U.S. Supreme Court during oral arguments in the 2014 Hobby Lobby case. The court ruled that a for-profit corporation may exclude contraceptives from their employees' health insurance, which is otherwise entitled by federal law, based on the religious objections of the corporation's owners. #TeamLife

Hundreds of cases have come before the Court in the area of the free exercise of religion.[36] Here are some examples of the questions they addressed: May Amish parents be forced to send their children to schools beyond the eighth grade? (No.) May religion serve as the basis for attaining "conscientious objector" status and avoiding the draft? (Generally yes, but with many qualifications.) Is animal sacrifice as part of a religious ceremony protected by the First Amendment? (Generally yes.) May Mormons have multiple wives? (No.) May people be forced to work on Friday night and Saturday if those are their days of worship? (No.) Does the First Amendment protect distributing religious leaflets on public streets? And religious meetings in public parks? (Yes, for both, but the latter is subject to "time, manner, and place" restrictions.) May religious dress be regulated? (Generally not, but in some contexts, such as the military, yes.) Are all prison inmates entitled to hold religious services (apparently yes, but this is still an open question) and grow short beards? (Yes.) Are religious organizations subject to child labor laws? (Yes.) Whew! Keep in mind that this list is by no means exhaustive.

One case had broad implications that defined the general basis for government restrictions of religious expression. The Court ruled that the state of Oregon had not violated the free exercise clause in denying unemployment benefits to the plaintiffs in the case, who were fired for using peyote as part of a religious ceremony. The broader significance of the ruling came with the Court's announcement of a new interpretation of the free exercise clause: the government does not need a "compelling interest" in regulating a particular behavior to justify a law that limits a religious practice.[37] In other words, after this decision it would be easier for the government to limit the exercise of religion because the Court would no longer require a "compelling" reason for the restrictions but rather demonstration that it was a "neutral law of general applicability."

Congress responded by passing the Religious Freedom Restoration Act (RFRA) in 1993, reinstating the need to demonstrate a "compelling state interest" before limiting religious freedoms; the act also specified exceptions to the Controlled Substances Act to allow the use of peyote in religious ceremonies. After several cases and congressional actions, the Court made it clear that it would have the final word in deciding when a compelling interest is required in order to limit religious practice.[38] The Court relied on this standard in the controversial 2014 case discussed in the chapter opener involving the family-owned Hobby Lobby stores.[39]

Would you, or do you, send your children to religious schools? Should the government pay for it? If you attend a public college or university, should it be allowed to organize a prayer before a football or basketball game? These questions, and more, are at the heart of the controversies around religious freedoms—one of the most deeply personal freedoms debated today.

"Why Should I Care?"

★

DESCRIBE THE MAJOR FIRST AMENDMENT RIGHTS RELATED TO FREEDOM OF SPEECH

Freedom of speech, assembly, and the press

As we noted earlier, defining the scope of our civil liberties depends on balancing interests and drawing lines. This is especially true of the First Amendment's freedom of speech, which can be envisioned on a continuum from most to least protected types of speech based on the Supreme Court cases that have tested their limits.

Generally protected expression

Any time you attend a religious service or a political rally, post a Tweet, write a blog post or letter to the editor, or express a political idea, you are being protected by the First Amendment. However, the nature of this protection is continually evolving due to political forces and shifting constitutional interpretations. For much of our nation's history, freedom of speech and freedom of the press were not strongly protected. Only recently have the courts developed a complex continuum ranging from strongly protected political speech to less-protected speech.

Standards for Protection The basis for the continuum of protected speech is rooted in the content of the speech. The Supreme Court has interpreted the law to mean that content-based regulation of speech is not permissible (unless it falls into one of the categories of exceptions we outline later). For example, the Court struck down a local ordinance that banned picketing outside of schools except for labor picketing.[40] This

strict scrutiny
The highest level of scrutiny the courts can use when determining whether a law is constitutional. To meet this standard, the law or policy must be shown to serve a "compelling state interest" or goal, it must be narrowly tailored to achieve that goal, and it must be the least restrictive means of achieving that goal.

intermediate scrutiny
The middle level of scrutiny the courts can use when determining whether a law is constitutional. To meet this standard, the law or policy must further an important government interest in a way that is "substantially related" to that interest and must use means that are a close fit to the government's goal and not substantially broader than is necessary to accomplish that goal, and the policy must be "content neutral."

clear and present danger test
Established in *Schenck v. United States,* this test allowed the government to restrict certain types of speech deemed dangerous.

ordinance was content-based regulation because it favored one form of speech (from labor unions) over others. Such regulation is subject to the strict scrutiny standard of judicial review, which means the regulation must be narrowly tailored so that it is the least restrictive on an individual's fundamental right to free speech and the government must demonstrate a compelling state interest to curtail the speech. In most cases, such strict scrutiny by the courts means that the speech will be protected and the regulation will be struck down. If a regulation is content neutral and does not favor any given viewpoint over another, then it is subject to the less demanding intermediate scrutiny standard. This means that the government must only demonstrate a substantial interest in curtailing the speech, the interest must be unrelated to the content of the speech, and there must be alternative opportunities for communication.[41]

Political Speech Freedom of speech got off to a rocky start when Congress passed the Alien and Sedition Acts in 1798. The controversial Sedition Act made it a crime to "write, print, utter or publish . . . any false, scandalous and malicious writing or writings against the government of the United States." Supporters of the four acts claimed they were necessary to strengthen the national government in response to the French Revolution, but in reality they were an attempt by the governing Federalist Party to neutralize the opposition—the Democratic-Republican Party. As many as 25 people, mostly newspaper editors, were tried under the law and 10 were jailed, including Benjamin Franklin's grandson. The outcry against the laws helped Thomas Jefferson to win the presidential election in 1800. Jefferson pardoned the convicted editors, Congress repealed one of the acts in 1802, and the other acts were allowed to expire before the Supreme Court had a chance to rule that they were unconstitutional.

World War I prompted the harshest crackdowns on free speech since the Sedition Act of 1798. The most important case from this period involved the general secretary of the Socialist Party, Charles Schenck, who opposed U.S. involvement in the war. He had printed a leaflet urging young men to resist the draft. Schenck was arrested under the Espionage Act of 1917, which prohibited "interfering with military or naval operations," including the draft. He appealed all the way to the Supreme Court, arguing that the First Amendment permitted him to protest the war and to urge others to resist the draft, but the Court sustained his conviction, noting that free speech is not an absolute right:

> The most stringent protection of free speech would not protect a man in falsely shouting fire in a theatre and causing a panic. . . . The question in every case is whether the words used are used in such circumstances and are of such a nature as to create a clear and present danger that they will bring about the substantive evils that Congress has a right to prevent.[42]

This clear and present danger test meant that the government could suppress speech it deemed dangerous (in this instance, preventing the government from fighting the war). However, critics of the decision argue that Schenck's actions were not dangerous for the country and should have been allowed.[43]

Justice Oliver Wendell Holmes, author of the *Schenck* decision and the clear and present danger test, had a change of heart and dissented in a case later that year that upheld the conviction of six anarchists who supported the cause of the Bolsheviks in Russia. In one of the most famous statements of the importance of the freedom of speech, he touted the "free trade in ideas," saying, "The best test of truth is the power of the thought to get itself accepted in the competition of the market. . . . [W]e should be eternally vigilant against attempts to check the expression of opinion that we loathe and believe to be fraught with death."[44] This notion of the marketplace of ideas in which good ideas triumph over bad is still central to modern defenses of the First Amendment.

Over the next several decades, the Court struggled to draw the line between dangerous speech and words that were simply unpopular. During the Red Scare of the late 1940s and early 1950s the hunt for communists in government was led by Senator Joe McCarthy, and the Court had many opportunities to defend unpopular speech; but for the most part it declined to do so. For example, in 1951 the Court upheld the conviction of 11 members of the Communist Party under the Smith Act, which banned the advocacy of force or violence against the United States.[45]

Then, in 1969, the Court established a strong protection for free speech that still holds today. This case involved a leader of the Ku Klux Klan who made a threatening speech at a cross-burning rally that was subsequently shown on television. Twelve hooded figures were shown, many with weapons. The speech said that "revengence [*sic*]" might be taken if "our president, our Congress, our Supreme Court continues to suppress the white, Caucasian race." It continued, "We are marching on Congress July the Fourth, four hundred thousand strong." The Klan leader was convicted under the Ohio law banning "sabotage, violence, or unlawful methods of terrorism as a means of accomplishing industrial or political reform," but the Court unanimously reversed his conviction, arguing that threatening speech could not be suppressed just because it sounded dangerous. Specifically, the direct incitement test holds that speech is protected "except where such advocacy is directed to inciting or producing imminent lawless action and is likely to incite or produce such action."[46] Under this standard, most, if not all, of the sedition convictions during World War I and the Red Scare would have been overturned.

Perhaps that strongest example of protecting unpopular speech comes from the case of the Westboro Baptist Church (WBC). Since 2005, members of the WBC have protested at hundreds of funerals of members of the armed services who were killed in Iraq and Afghanistan. However, these are not typical antiwar protests. Instead, the protesters claim that the troops' deaths were God's punishment for "the homosexual lifestyle of soul-damning, nation-destroying filth." The church and its members have drawn strong reactions and counterprotests for their confrontational approach at the military funerals, including their use of signs that say "God Hates Fags," "Thank God for Dead Soldiers," "God Killed Your Sons," and "God Hates America." Critics, including many veterans groups and attorneys general from 48 states, argue that the protests should

> "
> **Restriction of free thought and free speech is the most dangerous of all subversions. It is the one un-American act that could most easily defeat us.**
> —**Supreme Court Justice William O. Douglas,** 1952

direct incitement test
Established in *Brandenburg v. Ohio*, this test protects threatening speech under the First Amendment unless that speech aims to and is likely to cause imminent "lawless action."

Should free speech be protected even when the ideas are offensive? The Supreme Court ruled that the Westboro Baptist Church had a right to protest at military funerals, even though many Americans found the arguments and approach of the church members deeply offensive.

not be considered protected speech under the First Amendment. The Veterans of Foreign Wars issued a statement saying: "In a time of profound grief and emotional vulnerability, these personal attacks are an affront of the most egregious kind." However, in 2011 the Supreme Court ruled 8–1 that the WBC's protests were protected speech.[47]

Symbolic Speech The use of signs, symbols, or other unspoken acts or methods to communicate in a political manner—symbolic speech—enjoys many of the same protections as regular speech. For example, during the Vietnam War the Court protected the right of a war protester to wear an American flag patch sewn on the seat of his pants,[48] high school students' right to wear an armband to protest the war,[49] and an individual's right to tape a peace symbol on the flag and fly it upside down outside an apartment window.[50] Lower courts had convicted these protesters under state laws that protected the American flag or under a school policy that prohibited wearing armbands to protest the Vietnam War. In the flag desecration case involving the peace symbol, the Court stated that protected "speech" need not be verbal: "there can be little doubt that appellant communicated through the use of symbols."[51]

A 1989 case provided the strongest protection for symbolic speech yet. The case involved a man who burned a flag outside the 1984 Republican national convention in Texas, chanting along with other protesters, "America the red, white, and blue, we spit on you. You stand for plunder, you will go under." The Court refrained from critiquing the jingle, but its 5–4 decision overturned the man's conviction under Texas's flag desecration law on the grounds that symbolic political speech is protected by the First Amendment.[52] In response to this unpopular decision, Congress passed the Flag Protection Act of 1989, which the Court also struck down as an unconstitutional infringement on political expression.[53] Congress then attempted to pass a constitutional amendment to overturn the Court decision; the House passed the amendment six times between 1995 and 2005 with the necessary two-thirds vote, but each time the measure failed by a narrow margin in the Senate (by just one vote in 2006).

Although the Court has protected flag burning and other forms of symbolic speech, there are limits, especially when the symbolic speech conflicts with another substantial governmental interest. Here the critical test is whether the action can be regulated for important reasons unrelated to ideas. If so, then the "intermediate scrutiny" standard

DID YOU KNOW?

75%

of black Americans and 25 percent of white Americans view the Confederate battle flag primarily as a symbol of racism.
Source: ORC International

The American flag is a popular target for protesters: it has been spat upon, shredded, turned into underwear, and burned. Here, protesters burn a U.S. flag as they march through downtown Washington, D.C., following the Ferguson, Missouri, grand jury's decision not to indict Officer Darren Wilson for the shooting death of Michael Brown. #BlackLivesMatter #Ferguson

will apply. For example, Vietnam War protesters who burned their draft cards were not protected by the First Amendment because their actions interfered with Congress's constitutional authority to "raise and support" armies and the purpose of the draft was not to suppress speech.[54] The Court also ruled in 2015 that states may ban the use of the Confederate battle flag on state vanity plates. The Sons of Confederate Veterans argued that the battle flag honored their southern heritage, but the state of Texas said it was offensive.[55]

Money as Speech Spending money in political campaigns may also be protected by the First Amendment since it provides the means for more-conventional types of political speech. Here the central question is whether the government can control campaign contributions and spending for a broader public purpose such as controlling corruption, or whether such laws violate the First Amendment rights of candidates or their supporters. You probably have heard the old saying "Money talks," which implies that money is speech. Given the importance of advertising in modern campaigns, limitations on raising and spending money could limit the ability of candidates and groups to reach voters with their message. The Court has walked a tightrope on this one, balancing the public interest in honest and ethical elections and the First Amendment rights of candidates and their advocates. The Court has upheld individual candidates' right to spend their own money in federal elections, but presidential candidates give up that right if they accept federal campaign funds (taxpayers' money) in a presidential election. Also, candidates in federal elections are subject to limits on the types and size of contributions they can receive and they must report all contributions and spending to the Federal Election Commission.[56]

The Bipartisan Campaign Reform Act, which went into effect for the 2004 elections, included a "Millionaires' Amendment" that lifted restrictions on campaign contributions for candidates whose opponents spent more than $350,000 of their own money in the election. This attempt to level the campaign finance playing field was struck down by the Supreme Court in 2008 as a violation of wealthy candidates' First Amendment rights.[57] In 2010 the Court also extended First Amendment rights to corporations and labor unions that want to spend money on campaign ads, and in 2014 it struck down the aggregate (collective) limits placed on individual contributions to candidates and parties (these cases are discussed in more detail in Chapter 9).[58] However, the Court upheld a ban on unlimited "soft money" contributions because they were seen by the Court as the type of contribution with the most potential for corruption.[59]

Student fees as a form of symbolic speech came up in a case in 2000 involving student activity fees at the University of Wisconsin. A group of students argued that they should not have to pay fees to fund groups whose activities they opposed, including a student environmental group, a gay and bisexual student center, a community legal office, an AIDS support network, a campus women's center, and the Wisconsin Student Public Interest Research Group. The Court ruled that mandatory student fees could continue to support the full range of groups as long as the process for allocating money was "viewpoint neutral." The Court also said that student referendums that could add or cut money for specific groups violated viewpoint neutrality. The potential for the majority to censor unpopular views was unacceptable to the Court, since "the whole theory of viewpoint neutrality is that minority views are treated with the same respect as are majority views."[60]

Hate Speech Whether or not freedom of speech should apply to hate speech has been a controversial issue both on college campuses and in society generally. Do people have a right to say things that are offensive or abusive, especially in terms of race, gender, and sexual orientation? By the mid-1990s, more than 350 public colleges and universities said no by regulating some forms of hate speech.[61] One example was a speech code

hate speech
Expression that is offensive or abusive, particularly in terms of race, gender, or sexual orientation. It is currently protected under the First Amendment.

adopted at the University of Michigan that prohibited "any behavior, verbal or physical, that stigmatizes or victimizes an individual on the basis of race, ethnicity, religion, sex, sexual orientation, creed, national origin, ancestry, age, marital status, handicap, or Vietnam veteran status" and "creates an intimidating, hostile, or demeaning environment for educational pursuits, employment or participation in University-sponsored extra-curricular activities."[62]

Many of these speech codes were struck down in federal court, but late in 2015 the issue resurfaced on many college campuses. At Yale University, controversy erupted over the response of a residential college faculty administrator, Erika Christakis, to an e-mail students received cautioning them not to wear Halloween costumes that could be racially or culturally insensitive. Christakis wrote that universities no longer allowed students to be "a little bit inappropriate or provocative or, yes, offensive."[63] She resigned a few weeks later saying, " . . . the current climate at Yale is not, in my view, conducive to the civil dialogue and open inquiry required to solve our urgent societal problems."[64] The president at the University of Missouri also resigned after students, including the football team, said that he was racially insensitive and not open to their demands for a more inclusive and supportive environment on campus. President Obama weighed in on this issue largely on the free speech side, saying college students shouldn't be "coddled and protected from different points of view."[65]

Another significant issue combines the topics of symbolic speech and hate speech. Can a person who burned a cross on a black family's lawn be convicted under a city ordinance that prohibited conduct in St. Paul, Minnesota, that "arous[ed] anger, alarm, or resentment in others on the basis of race, color, creed, religion, or gender"? Or is the ordinance an unconstitutional limit on First Amendment rights? The Court said the cross burner could be punished for arson, terrorism, trespassing, or other violations of the law, but he could not be convicted under this ordinance because it was overly broad and vague. The Court said: "Let there be no mistake about our belief that burning a cross in someone's front yard is reprehensible. But St. Paul has sufficient means at its disposal to prevent such behavior without adding the First Amendment to the fire."[66] The city ordinance was unconstitutional because it took selective aim at a disfavored message; it constituted "viewpoint discrimination." However, the Court has since upheld more carefully worded bans of cross burning. Eleven years after the St. Paul case, the Court ruled that Virginia could prohibit cross burning if there was intent to intimidate. The Court also noted that the law was content neutral because it did not engage in viewpoint discrimination: any burning of a cross in a threatening context was illegal.[67]

Internet hate speech has become increasingly controversial in recent years. Cyberbullying, some of which was done on social media like Myspace, Twitter, and Facebook, precipitated several suicides. In 2013, Facebook cracked down on offensive content that glorified violence against women, such as pages with headlines like "Violently Raping Your Friend Just for Laughs."[68] Facebook's "community standards" have a more restrictive definition of hate speech than is allowed by the direct incitement test. While Facebook makes a distinction between humor and serious speech, they "do not permit individuals or groups to attack others based on their race, ethnicity, national origin, religion, sex, gender, sexual orientation, disability or medical condition."[69] This led law professor Jeffrey Rosen to conclude "today, lawyers at Google, YouTube, Facebook, and Twitter have more power over who can speak and who can be heard than any president, judge, or monarch."[70] This may sound like hyperbole, but he is right: corporations are not restricted by the First Amendment (which, after all, says "*Congress* shall make no law . . ."). So if Facebook and other social media want to restrict hate speech, they can. Although free speech advocates are concerned about restrictions on Internet hate speech, civil rights groups such as the Anti-Defamation League, the Leadership Conference on Civil Rights, and the National Organization for Women all support the move. Early in 2014, a bill was proposed by 13 House Democrats that would mandate a study of how the Internet, cell phones, television, and radio are used to advocate and encourage violent acts and the commission of crimes of hate.[71]

Freedom of Assembly The right to assemble peaceably has been consistently protected by the Supreme Court.[72] Perhaps the most famous freedom of assembly case involved a neo-Nazi group that wanted to march in Skokie, a suburb of Chicago that had 70,000 residents, nearly 60 percent of whom were Jewish, including many Holocaust survivors. The village passed ordinances that effectively banned the group from marching, arguing that residents would be so upset by the Nazi marchers that they might become violent. But the lower courts did not accept this argument, ruling that if "the audience is so offended by the ideas being expressed that it becomes disorderly and attempts to silence the speaker, it is the duty of the police to attempt to protect the speaker, not to silence his speech."[73] Otherwise, the right to assemble would be restricted by a "heckler's veto." The Court elaborated on this responsibility to protect expressions of unpopular views by striking down another town's ordinance that allowed them to charge a higher permit fee to groups whose march would likely require more police protection.[74]

Are laws banning hate speech constitutional? Sometimes yes, but the threshold is relatively high. These Ku Klux Klan members are free to hold rallies, preach racism and xenophobia, and burn crosses, as long as they do not directly incite violence or display an "intent to intimidate."

While broad protection is provided for peaceable assemblies, governments may regulate the time, manner, and place of expression as long as these regulations do not favor certain groups or messages over others. For example, anti-abortion protesters were not allowed to picket a doctor's home in Brookfield, Wisconsin. The Court ruled that the ordinance banning all residential picketing was content neutral and that there was a government interest in preserving the "sanctity of the home, the one retreat to which men and women can repair to escape from the tribulations of their daily pursuits."[75] "Time, manner, and place" restrictions also may be invoked for practical reasons. If the Ku Klux Klan planned to hold a march around a football stadium on the day of a game, the city council could deny them a permit and could suggest that they choose another day that would not interfere with game day activities. The legal standard for these regulations is that they are "reasonable." For example, in 2014 the Court ruled that a Massachusetts state law creating a 35-foot buffer zone around entrances to abortion clinics violated the First Amendment. While the buffer zone was content neutral, it was unreasonable because it was more restrictive than necessary to allow access to the clinics. While the "reasonableness" standard is vague, it allows the courts to balance the right to assemble against other practical considerations.

Freedom of the Press The task of balancing interests is central to many First Amendment cases involving freedom of the press. Which is more important, the First Amendment freedom of the press to disclose details about current events or the Sixth Amendment right to a fair trial, which may require keeping important information out of the public eye? When do national security concerns prevail over journalists' right to keep citizens informed? The general issue here is prior restraint, the government's right to prevent the media from publishing something.

Prior restraint has never been clearly defined by the Court, but several landmark cases have set a very high bar for applying it. In 1971, the Pentagon Papers case involved disclosure of parts of the top-secret report on internal planning for the Vietnam War. This incredibly divided case had nine separate written opinions! In a 6–3 decision the Court said that the government could not prevent the publication of the Pentagon Papers, but at least five justices supported the view that, under some circumstances, the government could use prior restraint—although they could not agree on the standard.[76] For some of the justices, a crucial consideration was the Pentagon Papers' revelation that the U.S. government had lied about its involvement in and the progress of the Vietnam War. Justice Hugo Black noted the importance of this point, saying, "Only a free and unrestrained press can effectively expose deception in government."[77]

Prior restraint has taken on new significance in the War on Terror. The media, especially the *New York Times*, skirmished with the Bush administration over publishing stories on various classified programs, including taking suspected terrorists to foreign countries and torturing them, domestic surveillance, and the Terrorist Finance Tracking Program, which monitors all large financial transactions in the international banking system. The debate over restraining the media heated up in 2010, when WikiLeaks released a classified video of an air strike in Baghdad showing U.S. pilots mistakenly firing on two Reuters reporters and more than 91,000 classified battlefield incident reports from Iraq and Afghanistan and U.S. State Department cables. All of these documents had been leaked to them by U.S. Army Private First Class Bradley Manning. This

prior restraint
A limit on freedom of the press that allows the government to prohibit the media from publishing certain materials.

Bradley Manning (center), whose job in the U.S. military gave him access to classified information, downloaded thousands of classified videos, diplomatic cables, reports, and other information and gave them to the website WikiLeaks.

sensational leaking ratcheted up the stakes, and some members of Congress called the leaks treason and urged for prosecution (Manning was tried and convicted in a military court for violations of the Espionage Act and for copying and releasing classified information).

The forms of expression discussed in this section—speech, assembly, and press—all have strong protections based on the First Amendment. The strongest protections are for content-based expression—that is, if a regulation is trying to limit *what* can be said, the Court applies the strict scrutiny standard and usually strikes down the regulation. However, there are exceptions, such as speech that directly incites an imminent danger. If the regulation is content neutral and does not favor one viewpoint over another, then it is easier to uphold. But even then, the government must have a substantial reason for limiting expression.

Less-protected speech and publications

Some forms of speech do not warrant the same level of protection as political speech because they do not contribute to public debate or express ideas that have important social value. Four categories of speech may be more easily regulated by the government than political speech: fighting words, slander and libel, commercial speech, and obscenity.

Fighting Words Governments may regulate fighting words, "which by their very utterance inflict injury or tend to incite an immediate breach of the peace."[78] Such laws must be narrowly written; it is not acceptable to ban all foul language, and the prohibited speech must target a single person rather than a group. Moreover, the question of whether certain words provoke a backlash depends on the reaction of the targeted person. Inflammatory words directed at Archbishop Emeritus Desmond Tutu would not be fighting words because he would turn the other cheek, whereas the same words yelled at musician Kanye West or actor Alec Baldwin *would* be fighting words because they would probably deck you. The Court has further clarified the test, based on "what persons of common intelligence would understand to be words likely to cause an average addressee to fight."[79] While this is a more objective test than the previous subjective standard, the fighting words doctrine has still been difficult to apply.

Slander and Libel A more extensive line of cases prohibiting speech concerns slander, spoken false statements that damage someone's reputation, and libel, written statements that do the same thing. As in many areas of First Amendment law, it is difficult to draw the line between permissible speech and slander or libel. The current legal standard distinguishes between speech about a public figure, such as a politician or celebrity, and about a regular person. In short, public figures must have much thicker skin than the average person because it is much more difficult for them to prove libel. A public figure has to demonstrate that the defamatory statement was made with "actual malice" and "with knowledge that it was false or with reckless disregard of whether it was false or not."[80]

One of the most famous libel cases was brought against *Hustler* magazine by the Reverend Jerry Falwell, a famous televangelist and political activist. Falwell sued *Hustler* for libel and emotional distress after the magazine published a parody of a liquor advertisement depicting him in a "drunken incestuous rendezvous with his mother in an outhouse" (this quote is from the Supreme Court case).[81] The lower court said that the parody wasn't believable, so *Hustler* couldn't be sued for libel, but they awarded Falwell damages for emotional distress. The Court overturned this decision, saying

"

The freedom of the press is one of the greatest bulwarks of liberty, and can never be restrained but by despotic governments.

—George Mason

fighting words
Forms of expression that "by their very utterance" can incite violence. These can be regulated by the government but are often difficult to define.

slander
Spoken false statements that damage a person's reputation. They can be regulated by the government but are often difficult to distinguish from permissible speech.

libel
Written false statements that damage a person's reputation. They can be regulated by the government but are often difficult to distinguish from permissible speech.

that public figures and public officials have to put up with such things and compared the parody to outrageous political cartoons, which have always been protected by the First Amendment.

Commercial Speech Commercial speech, which mostly refers to advertising, has evolved from having almost no protection under the First Amendment to enjoying quite strong protection. One early case involved a business owner who distributed leaflets to advertise rides on his submarine, which was docked in New York City. Under city ordinances, leafleting was permitted only if it was devoted to "information or a public protest," but not for a commercial purpose. The plaintiff changed the leaflet to have his advertisement on one side and a statement protesting a city policy on the other side (clever guy!). He was arrested anyway, and the Supreme Court upheld his conviction, saying that the city council had the right to regulate the distribution of leaflets.[82]

The Court became much more sympathetic to commercial speech in the 1970s when it struck down a law against advertising prescription drug prices and a law prohibiting placing newspaper racks on city streets to distribute commercial publications such as real estate guides.[83] The key decision in 1980 established a test that is still central today: the government may regulate commercial speech if it concerns an illegal activity, if the advertisement is misleading, or if regulating speech directly advances a substantial government interest and the regulation is not excessive. In practice, this test means that commercial speech can be regulated but that the government has to have a very good reason to do it. Even public health concerns have not been allowed to override commercial speech rights. For example, the Court struck down a Massachusetts regulation that limited the content of advertisements aimed at children (the ban on R. J. Reynolds's Joe Camel character is the classic example) in a manner that was more restrictive than federal law.[84]

Obscenity One area in which the press has never experienced complete freedom involves the publication of pornography and material considered obscene. The difficulty arises in deciding where to draw the line. Nearly everyone would agree that child pornography should not be published[85] and that pornography should not be available to minors. However, beyond these points there is not much consensus. For

Joe Camel peddles his wares on a New York City billboard. Commercial speech, as a general category, is not as strongly protected by the First Amendment as political speech, but advertising can be limited by the government only in specific circumstances.

example, some people are offended by nude paintings in art museums, while others enjoy watching hard-core X-rated movies.

Defining obscenity has proven difficult for the courts. In an often-quoted moment of frustration, Justice Potter Stewart wrote that he could not define obscenity, but "I know it when I see it."[86] In its first attempt, the Court ruled that a particular publication could be banned if an "average person, applying contemporary community standards," would find that the material appeals to prurient interests and is "utterly without redeeming social importance."[87] This standard proved unworkable because lower courts differed in their interpretation. The Court took another stab at it in 1973 in a case that gave rise to the **Miller test**, which is still applied today.[88] The test has three standards that must all be met in order for material to be banned as obscene: (1) it appeals to prurient interests, (2) it is "patently offensive," and (3) the work as a whole lacks serious literary, artistic, political, or scientific value. The Court also clarified that *local* community standards were to apply rather than a single national standard, reasoning that what passes for obscenity in Sioux City, Iowa, probably would be considered pretty tame in Las Vegas.

Congress and the president also have tried to control the dissemination of what they consider to be obscene. In general, they take a more conservative approach: they seek legislation to limit obscenity. In contrast, the Court focuses on whether certain speech is protected. Furthermore, the Court tends to rein in Congress and the president when they try to limit obscene speech.

Recent efforts have focused on the Internet as a pornography medium. Congress passed the Communications Decency Act in 1996, which criminalized the use of any computer network to display "indecent" material unless the provider could offer an effective way of screening out potential users under age 18. The Court struck down the law in 1997 because it was overly vague and because limiting access to websites based on age is technically impossible. This ruling gives the Internet the same free speech protection as print.[89] But Congress wasn't going to give up without a fight. In 1998, it enacted the Child Online Protection Act, which prohibited commercial websites from distributing material that is "harmful to minors," using the language of the Miller test to specify what this means. The law bounced around in the federal courts for six years, twice making it to the Supreme Court, which ultimately struck it down.[90]

In 2009, the Supreme Court addressed an area of the law that it had not touched for more than 30 years: regulating vulgar language that does not rise to the level of obscenity on broadcast television and radio (but not on cable or other paid-subscription services, which are not regulated as to language). In 1978, the Court had ruled that the Federal Communications Commission (FCC) had the power to regulate indecent language, but the FCC had always interpreted that power to only cover repeated use of vulgar words.[91] After the use of vulgar words by Bono during the 2003 Golden Globe Awards and by Cher and Nicole Richie during the 2002 and 2003 Billboard Music Awards, the FCC announced that it would no longer tolerate even "isolated uses of sexual and excretory words."

Fox Television challenged this new rule, but in 2009 the Supreme Court upheld the ban on "fleeting expletives" as "entirely rational" under existing law, while taking a swipe at the "foul-mouthed glitteratae from Hollywood."[92] The Court also ruled the following week that the FCC had not acted capriciously in fining CBS $550,000 for Janet Jackson's infamous "wardrobe malfunction" at the 2004 Super Bowl.[93] However, after sending the cases back to the lower courts and another round of appeals the Supreme Court ruled that television networks had not been given "fair notice" about the changed policy on fleeting expletives, and therefore the regulations were unconstitutionally vague and the networks could not be fined. The Court also let stand a lower-court ruling that voided the fine against CBS on similar grounds.[94] But the Court did not address the broader constitutional questions, holding open the possibility of stronger First Amendment protections for broadcast radio and television in the future.

Miller test
Established in *Miller v. California*, this three-part test is used by the Supreme Court to determine whether speech meets the criteria for obscenity. If so, it can be restricted by the government.

Two more-recent cases made clear that violence in published material could not be regulated in the same way as sexual content. In 2010, the Court struck down a federal law that criminalized depictions "in which a living animal is intentionally maimed, mutilated, tortured, wounded, or killed." The law focused on "crush videos," which show the torture and killing of helpless animals, but also included dog fighting and other forms of animal cruelty. In striking down the law, the Court said the First Amendment protected such depictions, even if the underlying behavior itself could be illegal.[95] In 2011, the Court struck down a California law that banned the sale of violent video games to children, saying: "Like the protected books, plays and movies that preceded them, video games communicate ideas—and even social messages—through many familiar literary devices (such as characters, dialogue, plot and music) and through features distinctive to the medium (such as the player's interaction with the virtual world). That suffices to confer First Amendment protection."[96]

★

EXPLORE WHY THE SECOND AMENDMENT'S MEANING ON GUN RIGHTS IS OFTEN DEBATED

The right to bear arms

Until recently, the right to bear arms was the only civil liberty that the Supreme Court had played a relatively minor role in defining. Between 1791 and 2007, the Court issued only four rulings directly pertaining to the Second Amendment. The federal courts had always interpreted the Second Amendment's awkward phrasing—"A well regulated Militia, being necessary to the security of a free State, the right of the people to keep and bear Arms, shall not be infringed"—as a right to bear arms within the context of serving in a militia, rather than as an individual right to own a gun.

Although legal conflict over gun ownership has intensified only recently, battles over guns have always been intense in the broader political realm.[97] Interest groups such as the National Rifle Association have long asserted that the Second Amendment guarantees an individual right to bear arms. Critics of this view emphasize the first clause of the amendment and point to the frequent mention of state militias in congressional debates at the time the Bill of Rights was adopted. They argue that the Second Amendment was adopted to reassure Antifederalist advocates of states' rights that state militias, not a national standing army, would provide national security. In this view, the national armed forces and the National Guard have made the Second Amendment obsolete.

Before the Court's recent entry into this debate, Congress and state and local lawmakers had largely defined gun ownership and gun carrying rights, creating significant variation among the states. Wyoming and Montana have virtually no restrictions on gun ownership, for example, whereas California and Connecticut have many. At the national level, Congress tends to respond to crime waves or high-profile assassinations by passing new gun control laws. The broadest one, the Gun Control Act of 1968, was passed in the wake of the assassinations of Robert F. Kennedy and Martin Luther King Jr. The law sets standards for gun dealers, bans the sale of weapons through the mail, and restricts the sale of new machine guns, among other provisions.

Following the assassination attempt on President Reagan in 1981, the push for stronger gun control laws intensified. Spearheading this effort was Sarah Brady, whose husband, James Brady (Reagan's press secretary), was shot and disabled in the assassination attempt. It took nearly 13 years for the campaign to bear fruit, but in 1993 Congress passed and President Clinton signed the Brady Bill, which mandates a background check and a five-day waiting period for any handgun purchase.

But not all gun tragedies lead to more gun control. In 2014 and 2015 there were 610 mass shootings, defined as incidents in which at least four people were killed or injured, not counting the shooter. By the FBI's definition—at least three people killed—there were 86 mass shootings in those two years, including those in San Bernardino, California, Charleston, South Carolina, and Roseburg, Oregon. In the deadliest mass shooting by a single gunman, 49 people were killed and 53 injured in June 2016 at an Orlando, Florida, nightclub. While in the past three years 41 states passed new "smart gun" laws, 19 states strengthened laws concerning mental health and gun ownership, and 5 passed laws restricting ownership of assault weapons, there were 12 states that expanded the places in which guns may be carried.[98] In 2008, a landmark Supreme Court ruling recognized for the first time an individual right to bear arms for self-defense and hunting.[99] The decision struck down the District of Columbia's ban on handguns, while noting that state and local governments could enforce ownership restrictions, such as preventing felons or the mentally impaired from buying guns. The Court did not apply the Second Amendment to the states in this decision, but it did so two years later in striking down a gun control ordinance in Chicago, while reaffirming the ownership restrictions noted in the Washington, D.C., case.[100] The dissenters in both strongly divided 5–4 decisions lamented the Court's activism in reopening a legal question considered settled for 70 years (in 32 instances since a 1939 Court ruling, appeals courts had affirmed the focus on a collective right—in the context of a militia—rather than an individual right to bear arms, and recognized an individual right only twice).[101]

Given the strong public support for gun ownership—there are about 300 million privately owned guns in the United States—and the Supreme Court's endorsement of an individual right to bear arms, stronger gun control at the national level is highly unlikely (especially given the unsuccessful pushes after the shootings at Sandy Hook Elementary

📷

While the Constitution guarantees the individual right to bear arms (as shown by the woman taking target practice), the shootings at Umpqua Community College in Roseburg, Oregon, shocked the nation. In response, college students organized a demonstration on Capitol Hill urging Congress to vote on gun reform. #SecondAmendment #2A #GunControl #GunSense

💡

DID YOU KNOW?

33,304

people were killed by guns in the United States in 2014 (the most recent year with complete data). About 60 percent of these deaths were from suicides.
Source: U.S. Centers for Disease Control

School in 2012 and Orlando, Florida, in 2016). Early in 2016 President Obama issued an executive order requiring all gun sales to be through federally licensed dealers who would conduct background checks.[102] In addition to this limited executive action, extensive litigation will be necessary to define the acceptable boundaries of gun control and which state and local restrictions will be allowed to stand. To this point, the verdicts have been mixed, with some lower courts upholding limitations on gun ownership (such as prohibiting felons from owning guns), while other lower courts have struck them down. Almost all challenges to gun laws in criminal cases, however, have been unsuccessful.[103]

★

DESCRIBE THE PROTECTIONS PROVIDED FOR PEOPLE ACCUSED OF A CRIME

due process rights
The idea that laws and legal proceedings must be fair. The Constitution guarantees that the government cannot take away a person's "life, liberty, or property, without due process of law." Other specific due process rights are found in the Fourth, Fifth, Sixth, and Eighth Amendments, such as protection from self-incrimination and freedom from illegal searches.

Law, order, and the rights of criminal defendants

Every advanced democracy protects the rights of people who have been accused of a crime. In the United States, the due process rights of the Fourth, Fifth, Sixth, and Eighth Amendments include the right to a fair trial, the right to consult a lawyer, freedom from self-incrimination, the right to know what crime you are accused of, the right to confront the accuser in court, and freedom from unreasonable police searches.

It is difficult to apply the abstract principles of due process to concrete situations in a way that protects civil liberties without jeopardizing order. The Fifth and Fourteenth Amendments specify that life, liberty, and property may not be denied "without due process of law." In general, this language refers to *procedural* restrictions on what government can do and is based on the idea of fairness and justice. The difficulty comes in defining what is fair or just.

The difference between abstract principles of due process and their specific application also raises difficult *political* questions. Most people endorse the principle of "due process of law" and general ideas such as requiring that police legally obtain any evidence used in court. However, when the Supreme Court applies these principles to protect the rights of criminal defendants there is a public outcry that too many suspects are going free on "legal technicalities," such as having to inform a suspect of his or her right to talk to an attorney before being questioned by the police. Elected politicians are very vulnerable to such public pressure and have a strong incentive to be "tough on crime," while the courts are left to decide whether a specific case involves a legal technicality or a fundamental civil liberty. The first aspect of due process, discussed next, is a perfect example of the political and legal difficulty of defining and applying due process rights: the Fourth Amendment protection against *unreasonable* searches and seizures.

The Fourth Amendment: unreasonable searches and seizures

The Fourth Amendment says: "The right of the people to be secure in their persons, houses, papers, and effects, against unreasonable searches and seizures, shall not be violated." Defining "unreasonable" puts us back in the familiar position of drawing lines and balancing interests.

Over the years, the Supreme Court has provided strong protections against searches within a person's physical space, typically defined as his or her home. With the introduction of new technology—first telephones and wiretapping, then more sophisticated listening and searching devices—the Court has had to confront a broad array of complicated questions. It has attempted to achieve a balance between privacy and security by requiring the courts to approve search warrants, yet continuing to carve out limited exceptions to this general rule.

Searches and Warrants Under most circumstances, a law-enforcement official seeking a search warrant must provide the court with "personal knowledge" of a "probable cause" of specific criminal activity and must outline the evidence that is the target of the search. Broad, general "fishing expeditions" for evidence are not allowed.

School officials must also balance the constitutional rights of students against the need to maintain discipline. But school searches may be permitted with a weaker "reasonable suspicion"; this is because the courts have viewed the schools as "in loco parentis" (that is, as playing the role of surrogate parents for the students). In 1985, the Court ruled in favor of a school official who discovered two girls smoking in a school bathroom and, in searching the purse of one of the girls for cigarettes, found marijuana, a pipe, rolling papers, plastic bags, and enough cash to suggest that the girl was selling marijuana. Yet, in other cases, the Court ruled that there are limits to searches by school officials and that students have the right to privacy. For example, in 2003 school administrators in Safford, Arizona, responding to a tip that a student was in possession of prescription-strength ibuprofen pills, subjected 13-year-old Savana Redding to a strip search. After searching her backpack and outer clothing and finding nothing, the police told Savana "to pull her bra out and to the side and shake it, and to pull out the elastic on her underpants, thus exposing her breasts and pelvic area to some degree." The Court ruled that this search violated her Fourth Amendment rights because "the content of the suspicion failed to match the degree of intrusion."[104]

Police searches inherently involve a clash between public safety and an individual's private freedom from government intrusions. These issues came to the fore with the passage of the Patriot Act of 2001 after the terrorist attacks of September 11. (The official name of this law is the USA PATRIOT Act, which includes an acronym for "Uniting and Strengthening America by Providing Appropriate Tools Required to Intercept and Obstruct Terrorism.") Several of the most controversial parts of the act strengthen police surveillance powers; make it easier to conduct "sneak and peek" searches (the police enter a home with a warrant, look for evidence, and do not inform the suspect that they searched his or her home until months later); broaden Internet surveillance; increase the government's access to individuals' library, banking, and medical records; and permit roving wiretaps for suspected terrorists.

Most police searches conducted without warrants occur because suspects consent to being searched. Officers are not required to tell a suspect that he or she may say no or request a warrant. Here are examples of other instances in which the Court will allow a warrantless search:

· Conducting a search at the time of a legal arrest that "is confined to the immediate vicinity of the arrest."
· Collecting evidence that was not included in the search warrant but is out in the open and in plain view.
· Using a police roadblock to search for information about a crime, to check for illegal immigrants or contraband at borders, or to conduct sobriety checks (but not for random drug searches or license checks), as long as the roadblock stops all drivers.
· Searching containers in cars if the officer has probable cause to suspect criminal activity.
· Searching passengers and the passenger area of a car if the driver has been stopped for a traffic offense (because people in automobiles do not have the same Fourth Amendment protections as people do in their homes).

Law enforcement officials may conduct searches in schools if they have "reasonable suspicion" of illegal activity.

- Searching an area where the officer thinks there is either a crime in progress or an "armed and dangerous" suspect.
- Searching school lockers, with probable cause.
- Searching for weapons and/or to prevent the destruction of evidence.[105]

Strip searches after an arrest and before the suspect is put in jail were upheld in 2012 by the Supreme Court even when there was no suspicion of illegal substances. The dissenting justices argued that "the humiliation of a visual strip-search" after being "arrested for driving with a noisy muffler, failing to use a turn signal and riding a bicycle without an audible bell" should not be allowed under the Fourth Amendment.[106]

In 2013, the Court ruled that a DNA swab of an arrested suspect is simply for identification and therefore is no more intrusive than a photograph or fingerprint. The late Justice Scalia, a strong defender of privacy rights, wrote in his dissent: "I doubt that the proud men who wrote the charter of our liberties would have been so eager to open their mouths for royal inspection."[107] Scalia argued that DNA evidence could be used to identify the arrestee as a suspect in an unrelated crime and therefore a swab should be taken only if there is probable cause that another crime has also been committed.

The Court has generally made it easier for law-enforcement officials to conduct searches without warrants, but two important decisions in the other direction were a 2014 case that required a warrant to search cell phones of people who had been arrested[108] and a 2012 case that required a warrant to place a GPS tracking device on a vehicle. In the latter case, the FBI suspected Antoine Jones of selling cocaine, so agents placed a tracking device on his vehicle without a warrant, monitored his movements for four weeks, and then used the evidence to convict him. Jones was sentenced to life in prison. While the Court required a warrant in this specific case, the basis for the majority's decision was fairly narrow: the placement of the device was a "physical trespass," and the lengthy monitoring of his movement constituted an illegal search.[109] Remote tracking without physical trespass or shorter-term monitoring with a GPS device without a warrant may be acceptable to the Court. Additional cases will be required to sort this out.

A second set of cases determines what to do if the police obtain evidence illegally. Here the need to balance security and privacy becomes concrete. Either the evidence is excluded from a criminal trial to protect privacy rights or it is allowed to support the conviction of the suspect.

The Exclusionary Rule In 1961, the Fourth Amendment was incorporated (applied to the states through the Fourteenth Amendment) in a case, *Mapp v. Ohio*. This case established for all courts the **exclusionary rule**, which says that illegally or unconstitutionally obtained evidence cannot be used in a criminal trial. Previously, the rule had applied only at the national level.[110]

In the landmark case, police broke into Dollree Mapp's residence without a warrant, looking for a suspect thought to be hiding in the house. The officers did not find him, but they did find illegal pornographic material, and Mapp was convicted of possessing it. Mapp's lawyer tried to defend her on First Amendment grounds, claiming she had the right to own the pornography, but instead the Court used the opportunity to apply the Fourth Amendment to the states. The Court threw out Mapp's conviction because the police did not have a search warrant, arguing that applying the Fourth Amendment only to the national government and not the states didn't make any sense: Why should a state's attorney be able to use illegally obtained evidence while a federal prosecutor could not? The justices ruled that for the exclusionary rule to deter illegal searches and seizures it must apply to law enforcement at both state and national levels.

Can the police search your home without a warrant? After Dollree Mapp was arrested for possession of pornographic material, the case made its way to the Supreme Court and the search was ruled unconstitutional. This case established the exclusionary rule for evidence that is obtained without a warrant.

exclusionary rule
The principle that illegally or unconstitutionally acquired evidence cannot be used in a criminal trial.

Subsequently, the Supreme Court began weakening the exclusionary rule. For example, the Court established a "good faith exception" to the exclusionary rule, allowing evidence to be used as long as the officer believed that he or she had conducted a legal search. In the specific case, the officer had a warrant with the wrong address.[111] Yet another case established an "independent source" exception allowing the use of evidence that was initially obtained in an illegal search but subsequently acquired with a valid warrant. A major new exception was established in 2016 when the Court ruled that drugs found during a search in which an officer stopped a person with no probable cause are admissible as evidence if there was an outstanding arrest warrant for the suspect (in this case for a traffic offense) at the time of the search. Justice Sotomayor pointed out in her dissent that there are 7.8 million outstanding warrants, mostly for traffic and parking violations, which means that this new exception has far-reaching consequences: "The mere existence of a warrant not only gives an officer legal cause to arrest and search a person, it also forgives an officer who, with no knowledge of the warrant at all, unlawfully stops that person on a whim or hunch."[112] The bottom line is that the exclusionary rule remains in effect, but in the last several decades the courts have eased the conditions in which prosecutors can use evidence obtained under questionable circumstances.

Drug Testing Another area of Fourth Amendment law concerns drug testing. The clause granting people the right "to be secure in their persons" certainly seems to cover drug testing. However, the courts have long recognized the right of private companies to test their employees for illegal drugs. Moreover, in professional sports testing for performance-enhancing drugs is increasingly common. Lance Armstrong was stripped of his seven Tour de France titles after admitting in 2013 to doping, and Major League Baseball has struggled to rein in steroid and human growth hormone use by many of its players, including stars such as Ryan Braun, Miguel Tejada, and Alex Rodriguez, who was banned from the entire 2014 season for his use of performance-enhancing drugs.

What about drug testing by the state? The Court has upheld random drug testing for high school athletes and mandatory drug testing for any junior high or high school students involved in extracurricular activities.[113] In the case of athletes, proponents of the policy asserted that safety concerns should preclude a 260-pound lineman or a pitcher with a 90-mile-per-hour fastball from using drugs. However, the same arguments could not be made for members of the choir, band, debate club, social dance, or the chess club, so this decision to include all extracurricular activities was a particularly strong endorsement of schools' antidrug policies.

The Court has also upheld drug testing of public employees, with one exception. It struck down a Georgia law that would have required all candidates for state office to pass a drug test within 30 days of announcing a run for office because candidates are not public employees.[114] Rather than appealing to the courts, former senator Ernest Hollings of South Carolina had a different approach to avoid drug testing. When his opponent, Representative Tommy Hartnett, challenged him to take a drug test, the senator shot back, "I'll take a drug test if you take an IQ test."

The Post–September 11 Politics of Domestic Surveillance The debate over the trade-off between civil liberties and security intensified in 2005 when a White House–approved domestic surveillance program was revealed. At the center of this controversy is the NSA, which was created during the Korean War in 1952 by President Harry Truman. The agency was initially kept so secret that for many years the government even denied its existence. Insiders joked that the "NSA" stood for "No Such Agency." Today the NSA is responsible for surveillance to protect national security, whereas the FBI is in charge of spying related to criminal activity and the Central Intelligence Agency (CIA) oversees foreign intelligence gathering. Since the terrorist attacks of September 11, 2001, the NSA has been monitoring the phone calls and Internet usage of many U.S. citizens who have had contact with suspected terrorists overseas. These calls were intercepted without the approval of the Foreign Intelligence Surveillance Court (FISC), which was created by Congress in 1978 under the Foreign Intelligence Surveillance Act (FISA) specifically for approving requests for the interception of calls. The NSA was also found to be creating a database of every phone call made within the borders of the United States. Phone companies AT&T, Verizon, and BellSouth reportedly turned over records of millions of customers' phone calls to the government.[115] In 2013, classified information revealed by Edward Snowden showed that the NSA had been monitoring the phone calls of German chancellor Angela Merkel and other leaders of allied countries. Outrage over these practices prompted President Obama to outline important changes to how information would be gathered and stored.

Critics warn that phone surveillance may be the tip of the iceberg, because the government may be monitoring travel, credit card, and banking records more widely than we think. Government agencies have previously skirted the restrictions in the Privacy Act of 1974 and the Fourth Amendment by purchasing this information from businesses, since the Privacy Act requires disclosure of how the government is using personal information only when the government itself collects the data. The Justice Department spent $19 million in 2005 to purchase commercially gathered data about American citizens, according to a report by the Government Accountability Office. These data are then used to search for suspicious patterns of behavior in a process known as data mining.[116]

The debate over domestic surveillance has generated intense disagreement. At one extreme, critics conjure up images of George Orwell's classic novel *1984*, in which Big Brother, a reclusive totalitarian ruler, watches the characters' every move. Critics see the surveillance as a threat to civil liberties and to our system of checks and balances and separation of powers. They believe that when the executive branch refuses to obtain warrants through the FISA court to conduct surveillance it is taking on too

The Director of National Intelligence testified at a congressional hearing on possible changes to the FISA as protesters in the background called for an end to government surveillance.

much power without consulting the other branches of government. But supporters of the program argue that getting a court order may take too long, jeopardizing the surveillance necessary to protect the country. Congress tried to strike a balance between these two positions when it enacted the FISA Amendments Act of 2008. This law continued the ban on monitoring the purely domestic communications of Americans without a court order, gave the government authority to intercept international communications, and provided legal immunity to the telecommunications companies that had cooperated in the original wiretapping program. However, the *New York Times* revealed that the NSA had still been engaged in "overcollection" of domestic communication between Americans under the new law, including an attempt to wiretap a member of Congress without a court order. Although the Obama administration vowed to stop purely domestic surveillance without a court order, technical problems make it difficult to distinguish between communications made within the United States and overseas.[117]

The Fifth Amendment

Miranda Rights and Self-Incrimination The familiar phrase "I plead the Fifth" has been part of our criminal justice system since the Bill of Rights was ratified, ensuring that a suspect cannot be compelled to provide court testimony that would cause him or her to be prosecuted for a crime. However, what about outside a court of law? If a police officer coerces a confession out of a suspect, does that amount to self-incrimination?

Coercive police interrogations were allowed until a landmark case in 1966. Ernesto Miranda had been convicted in an Arizona court of kidnapping and rape, on the basis of a confession extracted after two hours of questioning in which he was not read his rights. The Court overturned the conviction, saying that a police interrogation "is inherently intimidating" and in these circumstances "no statement obtained from the defendant can truly be the product of his free choice."[118] To ensure that a confession is truly a free choice, the Court came up with the well-known **Miranda rights**.

Miranda rights
The list of civil liberties described in the Fifth Amendment that must be read to a suspect before anything the suspect says can be used in a trial.

This is a typical example of the Miranda warning card that police officers carry with them and read to every suspect after an arrest.

```
DEFENDANT                          LOCATION

       SPECIFIC WARNING REGARDING INTERROGATIONS

  1. YOU HAVE THE RIGHT TO REMAIN SILENT.

  2. ANYTHING YOU SAY CAN AND WILL BE USED AGAINST YOU IN A COURT
     OF LAW.

  3. YOU HAVE THE RIGHT TO TALK TO A LAWYER AND HAVE HIM PRESENT
     WITH YOU WHILE YOU ARE BEING QUESTIONED.

  4. IF YOU CANNOT AFFORD TO HIRE A LAWYER ONE WILL BE APPOINTED
     TO REPRESENT YOU BEFORE ANY QUESTIONING, IF YOU WISH ONE.

  SIGNATURE OF DEFENDANT                    DATE

  WITNESS                                   TIME

  [ ] REFUSED SIGNATURE    SAN FRANCISCO POLICE DEPARTMENT    PR.9.1.4
```

If police do not read a suspect these rights, nothing the suspect says can be used in court.

The Court has carved out exceptions to the Miranda rights requirement because the public has viewed the practice as "coddling criminals" and letting too many people go free on legal technicalities. In one case, police failed to read a suspect his Miranda rights until after frisking him, finding an empty holster, and asking him where his gun was. The suspect led police to a gun. The lower court dismissed the charges because the gun had been used as incriminating evidence in the trial, but the Supreme Court reinstated the conviction because "concern for public safety must be paramount to adherence to the literal language of the *Miranda* rule."[119]

Although the Court has been willing to carve out limited exceptions to the Miranda rule, in 2000 the Court rejected Congress's attempt to overturn *Miranda* by designating all voluntary confessions as legally admissible evidence. The Court ruled that it, and not Congress, has the power to determine constitutional protections for criminal defendants. The justices also affirmed their intent to protect the Miranda rule, saying: "*Miranda* has become embedded in routine police practice to the point where the warnings have become part of our national culture."[120]

Double Jeopardy Another Fifth Amendment right for defendants is protection against being tried more than once for a particular crime. This is known as double jeopardy because the suspect is "twice put in jeopardy of life or limb" for a single offense. This prohibition was extended to the states in 1969.[121] But prosecutors can exploit two loopholes in this civil liberty: (1) a suspect may be tried in federal court and state court for the same crime, and (2) if a suspect is found innocent of one set of *criminal* charges brought by the state he or she may still be found guilty of the same or closely related offenses based on *civil* charges brought by a private individual.

Usually these loopholes are exploited only in high-profile cases in which there is public or political pressure to get a conviction. For example, in 1992 four Los Angeles police officers were acquitted of beating Rodney King, a driver they had chased for speeding. Before the trial, a bystander's video of the beating had been widely broadcast; subsequently, at news of the police officers' acquittal massive and destructive riots broke out that lasted three days. Responding to political pressure, President George H. W. Bush urged federal prosecutors to retry the officers not for the *criminal* use of excessive force but for violating Rodney King's *civil* rights. (Two were ultimately found guilty, and two were acquitted.)

Property Rights The final part of the Fifth Amendment is at the heart of a hot legal debate over property rights. The clause says "nor shall private property be taken for public use, without just compensation." For most of American history, this civil liberty has been noncontroversial. When the government needs private property for a public use such as building a highway or a park, it may force a property owner to sell at a fair market value in a practice known as eminent domain.

A new, controversial interpretation of the Fifth Amendment's "takings" clause, however, has attempted to expand the principle of just compensation to cover not only "physical takings" but also "regulatory takings." For example, if the Endangered Species Act protects an animal whose habitat is on your land, you would not be able to develop that property. Thus, its market value would probably be lower than if the endangered species did not live on your land. Therefore, the argument goes, because of this law the government has "taken" some of the value of your land by legally protecting the species, so it should compensate you for your loss.

One key Court case decided that if a regulation "deprives a property owner of all beneficial use of his property" the owner must receive compensation. This case

double jeopardy
Being tried twice for the same crime. This is prevented by the Fifth Amendment.

involved a man who bought two residential lots on the Isle of Palms, a South Carolina barrier island. His plan was to build single-family homes on the lots, but shortly after his purchase the state legislature enacted a law banning "permanent habitable structures" on this part of the barrier islands to prevent further erosion and destruction of the vulnerable land. The owner sued in state court and won a large monetary judgment, and the Supreme Court upheld this ruling.[122]

This issue became even more controversial after a case involving a development project in New London, Connecticut. A working-class neighborhood was sold to a private developer to build a waterfront hotel, office space, and higher-end housing, but a homeowner sued the city to stop the development. The Court supported the local government, saying that "promoting economic development is a traditional and long accepted function of government," so a "plausible public use" is satisfied. Justice O'Connor wrote a strong dissent, saying that the "specter of condemnation hangs over all property. Nothing is to prevent the State from replacing any Motel 6 with a Ritz-Carlton, any home with a shopping mall, or any farm with a factory."[123] In reaction to this decision, between 2005 and 2011 legislation or constitutional amendments have been passed in 42 states restricting the use of eminent domain for economic development.[124]

The Sixth Amendment: the right to legal counsel and a jury trial

When it comes to criminal law, the right to an attorney is one of the key civil liberties, because the legal system is too complicated for a layperson to navigate. However, at one time, poor people accused of a felony were forced to defend themselves in court if they could not afford a lawyer (except in cases involving the death penalty, for which the state would provide a lawyer).[125] This changed in 1963 with the celebrated case of *Gideon v. Wainwright*. Clarence Gideon was accused of breaking into a pool hall and stealing beer, wine, and money. He could not afford an attorney, so he tried to defend himself. He did a pretty good job—calling witnesses, cross-examining the prosecutor's witnesses, and providing a good summary argument. However, he was convicted and sentenced to five years in jail, based largely on the testimony of the person who turned out to be the guilty party. The Court unanimously overturned Gideon's conviction, saying: "In our adversary system of criminal justice, any person hauled into court who is too poor to hire a lawyer cannot be assured a fair trial unless counsel is provided for him."[126]

Unlike the exclusionary rule and the protection against self-incrimination, the right to an attorney has been strengthened over time, through both legislation and subsequent Court rulings. One year after *Gideon*, Congress passed the Criminal Justice Act, which provided better legal representation for criminal defendants in federal court; within two years, 23 states had taken similar action. The Court has defined a general right to *effective* counsel (although the bar is set considerably low in terms of defining "effective") and more recently mandated that defense attorneys must conduct any reasonable investigation into possible lines of defense when presenting evidence that could help the defendant.[127]

The Sixth Amendment also protects an individual's right to a speedy and public trial by an impartial jury in criminal cases. The Court affirmed the right to a speedy trial in 1967,[128] and today under the Federal Speedy Trial Act a trial must begin within 70 days of the defendant's arrest or first appearance in court. This law was strengthened by a 2006 Court decision stating that a defendant may not waive the right to a speedy trial.[129] The most important legal disputes over the "impartial jury" issue concern the process

The fight against terrorism has raised controversial questions about due process rights. After the United States killed Anwar al-Awlaki—an Al Qaeda leader living in Yemen, and a U.S. citizen—critics argued that his due process rights, such as the right to a fair trial, had been violated.

of jury selection and peremptory challenges, in which lawyers from each side may eliminate certain people from the jury pool without providing any reason. The Court has ruled that race and gender may not be the basis for a peremptory challenge.[130]

The Eighth Amendment: cruel and unusual punishment

The Founders would be surprised by the intense debates over whether the Eighth Amendment prohibition against "cruel and unusual punishments" applies to the death penalty. Clearly, the death penalty was accepted in their time (even stealing a horse was a capital offense!), and the language of the Constitution reflects that. Both the Fifth and Fourteenth Amendments say that a person may not be deprived of "life, liberty, or property, without due process of law," which implies that someone *could* be deprived of life as long as the state follows due process. The death penalty continues to be supported by many people in the United States, with 31 states allowing capital punishment. However, there is a clear overall trend away from the death penalty. Seven U.S. states have abolished the death penalty since 2007 (and four more states have moratoriums on the death penalty imposed by their governors, but Nebraska reinstated the death penalty by state referendum in 2016) and dozens of other countries have done so in recent years. There were 28 executions in the United States in 2015, which is the second-lowest number since 1991 and well below the peak of 98 in 1999.[131] A botched execution in Oklahoma in 2014, in which Clayton Lockett writhed and gasped for nearly 30 minutes when one of the lines filled with the lethal drugs failed, led to renewed calls for abolishing the death penalty.[132]

Supreme Court Rulings on the Death Penalty The Supreme Court remained silent on the issue of the death penalty for nearly two centuries. But in 1972 the Court ruled that the death penalty was unconstitutional because the process of applying it was too inconsistent. Congress and 35 states rushed to make their laws compliant with the Court decision. The typical fix was to say more explicitly which crimes were punishable by death and to make capital sentencing a two-step process: first the determination of guilt or innocence and then a sentencing phase if the suspect was found guilty. Four years later, the Court approved these changes and allowed states to bring back the death penalty.[133]

While never again challenging the constitutionality of the death penalty, the Supreme Court has been chipping away at its edges for two decades. The Court has struck down state laws that mandated the death penalty in murder cases and a law requiring a death sentence for rape. It has also prohibited the execution of insane prisoners and abolished the death penalty for the "mentally retarded"—although the Court left it to the states to define who is "mentally retarded" and struck down Florida's strict IQ cutoff as too rigid in defining mental stability. The Court has also prohibited the death penalty for juveniles under the age of 18 and for child rapists.[134]

These death-penalty cases have shown that the Court responds to public opinion and political change (this is sometimes called the living Constitution perspective, as discussed in Chapters 2 and 14). In his opinion in the juvenile death-penalty case, Justice Anthony Kennedy noted that 30 states forbid the death penalty for offenders younger than age 18, which was an increase of 5 states from 1989, when the Court had upheld the juvenile death penalty. Similarly, the number of states banning the death penalty for the mentally impaired grew from 14 in 1989 (when the practice was upheld) to 25 in 2002 (when it was struck down).

DID YOU KNOW?

337

people have been exonerated post-conviction in the United States based on DNA evidence, out of 1,700 total exonerations. Twenty of those served time on death row and 16 more had been convicted of capital offenses.

Source: The Innocence Project

Privacy rights

You may be surprised to learn that the word "privacy" does not appear in the Constitution. Privacy rights were first developed in a 1965 case that questioned the constitutionality of an 1879 Connecticut law against using birth control. Estelle Griswold, the director of Planned Parenthood in Connecticut, was arrested nine days after opening a clinic that dispensed contraceptives. She was fined $100 and appealed her conviction. Although she lost in state court, she appealed all the way to the Supreme Court, which overturned her conviction.[135]

In a very fractured decision (there were six different opinions), the Court agreed that the law was outdated, but the justices agreed on little else. Even the justices who based their opinions on an implied constitutional right to privacy cited various constitutional roots. Justice William O. Douglas found privacy implicit in the First Amendment right of association, the Third Amendment's protection against the quartering of troops, the Fourth Amendment's prohibition against unreasonable searches and seizures, the Fifth Amendment's protection against self-incrimination, and the Ninth Amendment's catchall statement "The enumeration in the Constitution, of certain rights, shall not be construed to deny or disparage others retained by the people." These all seem like reasonable grounds for implicit privacy rights except the First Amendment right of association—since the Founders clearly meant political association, not an association with your spouse in bed.

The *Griswold v. Connecticut* case was significant for establishing the constitutional basis for a right to privacy, but the dissenters in the case were concerned about where this right would lead. Justice Black warned that privacy "is a broad, abstract and ambiguous concept" that can be shrunk or expanded in subsequent decisions. He said that Douglas's argument "require[d] judges to determine what is or is not constitutional on the basis of their own appraisal of what laws are unwise or unnecessary. The power to make such decisions is of course that of a legislative body. Surely it has to be admitted that no provision of the Constitution specifically gives such blanket power to courts to exercise such a supervisory veto over the wisdom and value of legislative policies and to hold unconstitutional those laws which they believe to be unwise or dangerous."[136]

Abortion rights

Justice Black's prediction came true eight years later in *Roe v. Wade*, the landmark ruling that struck down laws in 46 states that limited abortion. Twelve of those states allowed abortions for pregnancies due to rape or incest, to protect the life of the mother, and in cases of severe fetal handicap. The much-criticized trimester analysis in the *Roe* ruling said that states could not limit abortions in the first trimester; in the second trimester, states could regulate abortions in the interests of the health of the mother; and in the third trimester, states could forbid all abortions except those necessary to protect the health or life of the mother. The justices cited a constitutional basis for abortion rights in the general right to privacy outlined in *Griswold*; the concept of "personal liberty" in the Fourteenth Amendment's due process clause; and the "rights reserved to the people" in the Ninth Amendment.[137]

Subsequent decisions have upheld *Roe* but endorsed state restrictions on abortion, such as requiring parental consent, a waiting period, or counseling sessions aimed at convincing the woman not to have an abortion (see the What Do the Numbers Say? feature for more on restrictions currently in effect). Most significantly, *Roe*'s trimester analysis has been replaced by a focus on the viability of the fetus. When the fetus would

privacy rights
Liberties protected by several amendments in the Bill of Rights that shield certain personal aspects of citizens' lives from governmental interference, such as the Fourth Amendment's protection against unreasonable searches and seizures.

Abortion Rights Today

The Court's 1973 decision in *Roe v. Wade* made abortion legal throughout the United States. How do abortion rights look today? What do the numbers say?

Source: Guttmacher Institute, *State Policies in Brief*, "An Overview of Abortion Laws," October 1, 2016, www.guttmacher.org (accessed 10/17/16).

Think about it

1. Which states have the most restrictive policies concerning access to abortions?

2. How do you think waiting periods and parental notification affect the number of abortions in a state? What about the number of abortions nationwide?

Parental Consent Laws for Abortions for Minors

■ No parental notification or consent laws
■ One or both parents must consent
■ One or both parents must be informed
■ Both parental consent and notification required
■ Parental consent or notification laws blocked

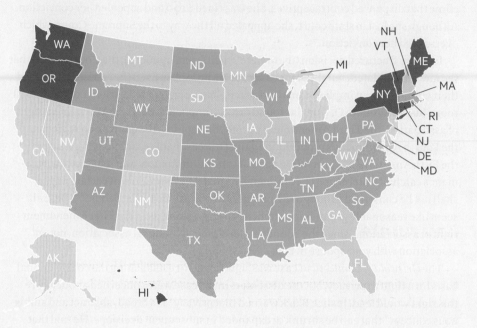

Pre-Abortion Mandatory Waiting Period Laws

■ No mandatory waiting period
■ Waiting period of less than 24 hours
■ Waiting period of 24 hours or more
■ Waiting period law blocked

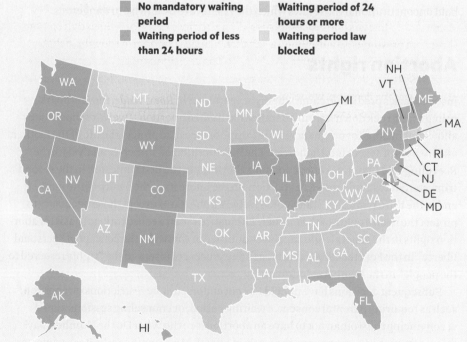

be viable (generally at 22 or 23 weeks), states can ban abortions "except where it is necessary, in appropriate medical judgment, for the preservation of the life or health of the mother."[138] Laws passed in 2013 by Arkansas and North Dakota limiting abortions as soon as a fetal heartbeat can be detected (as early as 6 weeks) were struck down by federal courts, but laws in nine states now ban abortions at 20 weeks, in apparent contradiction with *Roe v. Wade*.

Since *Roe*, most political action concerning abortion has been in the courts, but that could change if the Supreme Court overturns the decision. Opponents of abortion are hoping that *Roe* will be overturned, which would shift the politics of abortion back to state legislatures and make it an even more contested political issue. One effort to challenge *Roe* was a "personhood amendment" to the Mississippi constitution that defined life beginning at conception. But the amendment was soundly defeated in a statewide vote in 2011.[139] The pace of state restrictions on abortions accelerated from 2011 to 2013, with more than 200 limitations on abortion services. In 2013, 22 states enacted 70 new restrictions, including a requirement that abortion doctors have admitting privileges at local hospitals—which would close up to one-third of abortion clinics in affected states.[140] In 2016, the Supreme Court struck down the latter as an "undue burden" on the right to an abortion.[141]

Gay rights

Gay rights have typically been thought of more as a civil right (that is, freedom from discrimination) than a civil liberty, so these issues will be discussed in the next chapter. In 1986, the Court had ruled in *Bowers v. Hardwick* that there was no privacy protection or fundamental right for consenting adults to engage in homosexual sodomy.[142] But in 2003, in *Lawrence v. Texas*, the Court established very broad privacy rights for sexual behavior. The case involved two Houston men, John Geddes Lawrence and Tyron Garner, who were prosecuted for same-sex sodomy after police entered Lawrence's apartment—upon receiving a false tip about an armed man—and found the two having sex. Under Texas law, sodomy was illegal for gays but not for heterosexuals. In a landmark 6–3 ruling, the Supreme Court said that the liberty guaranteed by the Fourteenth Amendment's due process clause allows homosexuals to have sexual relations: "Freedom presumes an autonomy of self that includes freedom of thought, belief, expression, and certain intimate conduct."[143] The decision explicitly overturned *Bowers v. Hardwick* and five members of the majority signed onto the broad "due process" reasoning of the decision, while Justice O'Connor wrote a concurring opinion in which she agreed that the Texas law was unconstitutional but on narrower grounds. With the broader due process logic, a total of 13 state laws that banned sodomy were struck down.

Tyron Garner and John Geddes Lawrence after the Supreme Court decision in *Lawrence v. Texas* in 2003 established broad privacy rights for sexual behavior (including homosexual behavior).

Privacy might not seem important. You may think you'll never be accused of a crime or have your privacy invaded or questioned by the government. Indeed, many people think, "I have nothing to hide, so it is fine if the NSA monitors e-mail and Internet traffic to keep tabs on suspected terrorists." What if your e-mail revealed that you had a serious medical or mental health condition? What if the NSA paid special attention to you because of tweets you posted criticizing a government policy? Knowing your rights and how those rights apply to everyone—both criminals and innocent people—will help you make informed decisions about which policies to support.

"Why Should I Care?"

Conclusion

You exercise your civil liberties every day, whether speaking in public, going to church, being searched at an airport, participating in a political demonstration, writing or reading an article in your school newspaper, or being free from illegal police searches in your home. Because civil liberties are defined as those things the government *cannot* do to you, defining civil liberties is a political process. Often this process is confined to the courts, but for many issues—including free speech, freedom of the press, pornography, criminal rights, abortion, and gun control—it takes place in the broader political world, where defining civil liberties involves balancing competing ideals and interests and drawing lines by interpreting and applying the law. For example, debates over how to balance national security and civil liberties—whether newspapers should publish stories about classified government programs that may threaten civil liberties, or if government surveillance powers should be strengthened to fight terrorism—will rage for years.

Other cases, such as the protests at military funerals or protecting the due process rights of suspected criminals and terrorists, illustrate how difficult and politically unpopular it can be to protect our freedoms and liberty. Nearly everyone would agree that the behavior of the members of Westboro Baptist Church is completely outrageous. But protecting the freedom of speech is easy if you agree with what is being spoken. It becomes much more difficult if the freedom is manifest in filth directed at the families of fallen soldiers, protects the rights of Nazis to march in Skokie, or defends a person accused of a heinous crime.

Finally, the chapter opener on religious freedom revealed that even cherished liberties often must be balanced against other policy goals. A county clerk's religious freedom does not mean she may deny a same-sex couple the right to marry and religious beliefs may not be used to deny someone health care (however, employers in small family-held companies may have stronger protections for their religious beliefs). Many of the earliest settlers fled to our nation because of religious persecution, yet serious debates about excluding Muslims from the United States were part of the 2016 presidential campaign. As with all political questions, the evolving nature of our civil liberties is sure to generate more political conflict. But that process affirms the essence of our political system.

STUDY GUIDE

Defining civil liberties

Define what we mean by *civil liberties*. (Pages 100–104)

Summary

Civil liberties are the protections that individuals receive from the government. These are not absolute rights, however, as individual freedoms can become at odds with the public good and government interests. The courts often play the deciding role in determining where to draw the line between individual rights and public safety.

Key term
civil liberties (p. 100)

Practice Quiz Questions

1. **Civil liberties are rooted in what document?**
   a. the Declaration of Independence
   b. the *Federalist Papers*
   c. the Magna Carta
   d. the Bill of Rights
   e. Article I of the Constitution

2. **Why are civil liberties not absolute?**
   a. Equality for a group under the law is hard to define.
   b. Individual freedoms may conflict with the public good.
   c. Laws are often outdated and don't characterize modern society.
   d. The Bill of Rights protections were intentionally weakened by Antifederalists.
   e. The Supreme Court generally decides not to hear cases concerning civil liberties.

The origins of civil liberties

Explain why the Bill of Rights was added to the Constitution and how it came to apply to the states. (Pages 104–108)

Summary

The Bill of Rights, which lists individual protections from the federal government, was included in the Constitution in response to demands from the Antifederalists, who feared a strong national government. For most of the nineteenth century, these individual freedoms were only guaranteed from the *federal* government and did not extend to protections from *state* governments. With the ratification of the Fourteenth Amendment and the process of selective incorporation, federal freedoms have been gradually extended to the state level.

Key terms
Civil War amendments (p. 107)   selective incorporation
due process clause (p. 107)   (p. 108)

Practice Quiz Questions

3. **The inclusion of the Bill of Rights in the Constitution reflects the _____ concerns that the federal government would be too _____.**
   a. Antifederalists'; strong
   b. Antifederalists'; weak
   c. Federalists'; strong
   d. Federalists'; weak
   e. president's; strong

4. **The Bill of Rights originally protected individuals from which level of government?**
   a. all levels of American government
   b. state governments
   c. local governments
   d. federal government
   e. the bureaucracy

5. **Which amendment has been used as the basis for selective incorporation?**
   a. the Eighth Amendment
   b. the Fourteenth Amendment
   c. the Tenth Amendment
   d. the Nineteenth Amendment
   e. the Fifth Amendment

Freedom of religion

Describe the First Amendment rights related to freedom of religion. (Pages 108–113)

Summary

Religious freedoms are defined by two clauses in the First Amendment: the establishment clause and the free exercise clause. Together, they do not allow the government to do anything to benefit any particular religion, nor do they allow the government to hinder religious practice without adequate justification. As is often the case, the Court has struggled to define exactly what constitutes "excessive government entanglement" in religion.

Key terms

establishment clause (p. 110)   Lemon test (p. 111)
free exercise clause (p. 110)

Practice Quiz Questions

6. **The establishment clause is invoked under which of the following circumstances?**
   a. allowing "conscientious objectors" to avoid the military draft
   b. outlawing polygamy
   c. prohibiting prayer in public schools
   d. allowing the Amish to keep children home from school after the eighth grade
   e. banning the handling of snakes in church services

7. **Which test does the Supreme Court use to establish whether there has been "excessive government entanglement in religion"?**
   a. Lemon test
   b. Kreutz test
   c. Miller test
   d. Meyer test
   e. Brandenburg test

Freedom of speech, assembly, and the press

Describe the major First Amendment rights related to freedom of speech. (Pages 113–124)

Summary

The Supreme Court's attempt to balance individual freedoms and public good is reflected in the scope of protections guaranteed by the First Amendment. The Court generally prioritizes protecting individual rights to political speech, hate speech, symbolic speech, the freedom to assemble, and the freedom of the press unless under extreme circumstances (such as speech that directly incites violence). By contrast, the Court regularly places a lower priority on, and affords less protection to, fighting words, slander, libel, and commercial speech.

Key terms

strict scrutiny (p. 114)
intermediate scrutiny (p. 114)
clear and present danger test (p. 114)
direct incitement test (p. 115)
symbolic speech (p. 116)
hate speech (p. 117)

prior restraint (p. 120)
fighting words (p. 121)
slander (p. 121)
libel (p. 121)
commercial speech (p. 122)
Miller test (p. 123)

Practice Quiz Questions

8. **Which test does the Court use to determine if speech is considered dangerous and should not be legally protected?**
   a. Lemon test
   b. clear and present danger test
   c. Miller test
   d. direct incitement test
   e. the balancing test

9. **Flag burning is an example of _____ that is currently _____ under the First Amendment.**
   a. symbolic speech; protected
   b. symbolic speech; not protected
   c. hate speech; protected
   d. hate speech; not protected
   e. offensive slander; not protected

The right to bear arms

Explore why the Second Amendment's meaning on gun rights is often debated. (Pages 124–126)

Summary

The Supreme Court has done little to define what freedoms are established in the Second Amendment, largely preferring to allow the national, state, and local governments to make their own laws. The majority of public sentiment appears in favor of continued gun ownership, and limitations on Second Amendment rights appear unlikely.

Practice Quiz Question

10. **What is the best summary of the current position of the Supreme Court on the Second Amendment?**
    a. The Court has upheld most gun control laws, both at the state and national level, arguing that there is no individual right to own guns.
    b. The Court has upheld most gun control laws at the state level but struck down federal gun control laws, arguing that the Second Amendment only applies to Congress.
    c. The Court has struck down some state and national limitations on gun ownership, arguing that the Second Amendment protects an individual right to bear arms.
    d. The Court has struck down all state and national limitations on gun ownership, arguing that the Second Amendment protects an individual right to bear arms.
    e. The Court has refused to take a general position on the individual right to bear arms.

Law, order, and the rights of criminal defendants

Describe the protections provided for people accused of a crime. (Pages 126–134)

Summary

The Fourth, Fifth, Sixth, and Eighth Amendments provide protections to individuals accused of a crime, known as due process rights. Interpreting these general due process rights in specific cases is difficult, however, because specific standards of fairness and justice are very hard to define.

Key terms

due process rights (p. 126)   Miranda rights (p. 131)

exclusionary rule (p. 128)   double jeopardy (p. 132)

Practice Quiz Questions

11. Protections from unreasonable searches and seizures are guaranteed by which constitutional amendment?

a. the Third Amendment

b. the Fourth Amendment

c. the Fifth Amendment

d. the Seventh Amendment

e. the Eighth Amendment

12. The Miranda rights are protections that primarily fall under which constitutional amendment?

a. the Third Amendment

b. the Fourth Amendment

c. the Fifth Amendment

d. the Seventh Amendment

e. the Eighth Amendment

13. In 1972, the Supreme Court banned the death penalty for what reason?

a. It deprived individuals of their rights to "life, liberty, or property."

b. It was cruel and unusual.

c. It was being inconsistently applied and violated the due process of law.

d. It was racially biased.

e. It was inconsistent with international law.

Privacy rights

Explain why the rights associated with privacy are often controversial. (Pages 135–137)

Summary

The term "privacy rights" is not found in the Constitution—rather, it was established in a 1965 Supreme Court case—but it may be implied in several amendments in the Bill of Rights. The right to privacy is controversial because of the lack of explicit language in the Constitution and the lack of consensus on exactly what the right to privacy means.

Key term

privacy rights (p. 135)

Practice Quiz Questions

14. Which of the following freedoms guaranteed in the Bill of Rights is thought to imply a right to privacy?

a. right to bear arms

b. right to refuse to quarter soldiers

c. right to secure legal counsel

d. right to request a jury trial

e. freedom of speech

15. In what case did the Supreme Court first establish the right to privacy?

a. *Roe v. Wade*

b. *Lawrence v. Texas*

c. *Griswold v. Connecticut*

d. *Gonzales v. Oregon*

e. *Lemon v. Kurtzman*

Suggested Reading

Abraham, Henry J., and Barbara A. Perry. *Freedom and the Court: Civil Rights and Liberties in the United States*, 8th ed. Lawrence: University Press of Kansas, 2003.

Amar, Akhil Reed. *The Bill of Rights*. New Haven, CT: Yale University Press, 1998.

Bondenhamer, David J., and James W. Ely, eds. *The Bill of Rights in Modern America*. Bloomington: Indiana University Press, 2008.

Lewis, Anthony. *Gideon's Trumpet*. New York: Random House, 1964.

Moynihan, Daniel Patrick. *Secrecy: The American Experience*. New Haven, CT: Yale University Press, 1998.

Posner, Richard A. *Not a Suicide Pact: The Constitution in a Time of National Emergency*. New York: Oxford University Press, 2006.

Pritchett, C. Herman. *Constitutional Civil Liberties*. Englewood Cliffs, NJ: Prentice Hall, 1984.

Schweber, Howard. *Speech, Conduct, and the First Amendment*. New York: Peter Lang, 2003.

Walker, Samuel. *Presidents and Civil Liberties from Wilson to Obama: A Story of Poor Custodians*. New York: Cambridge University Press, 2014.

5

Civil Rights

You can't discriminate against me ... right?

Joe Arpaio, of Phoenix, Arizona, is the self-described "toughest sheriff in America." He was also the target of a four-year investigation by the U.S. Justice Department of discriminatory practices in the enforcement of immigration laws. He is either a hero or villain, depending on one's views concerning illegal immigration. His supporters see him as a courageous and tireless fighter who is enforcing the law that the federal government seems incapable or unwilling to enforce. His critics see him as a bigoted publicity hound who abuses the civil rights of people who are nonwhite.

In a lawsuit brought by the Justice Department, the brief concluded: "As a result of the pattern or practice of unlawful discrimination, Latinos in Maricopa County are systematically denied their constitutional rights."[1] The expert who conducted the analysis noted that Latino drivers were four to nine times more likely to be stopped than non-Latino drivers, calling this practice "the most egregious racial profiling he had ever seen."[2] Sheriff's deputies would use minor traffic violations, such as failure to signal a lane change, to pull over Latinos and ask for their documents. One incident that drew international attention was a neighborhood sweep of a town of about 6,000 Yaqui Indians and Latinos outside of Phoenix. Over a period of two days, more than 100 deputies conducted hundreds of searches, netting nine undocumented immigrants. Residents have sued the county, and one critical report said: "The community was so scarred by the event that families are still terrified to leave their homes when they see the sheriff's patrol cars."[3] This case was settled in 2015 and Arpaio agreed to stop the raid. In a separate federal case, district court judge Murray Snow issued two injunctions barring the sheriff's office from continuing the pattern of discrimination and establishing an elaborate system of monitoring and reporting to make sure the abuse did not continue.[4] Sheriff Arpaio defended his office, saying, "We don't racially profile, I don't care what everybody says," while his deputy called the court order "ludicrous crap."[5] In 2016, Judge Snow found Arpaio in civil contempt of court and in October 2016 federal prosecutors charged Arpaio with criminal contempt of court for ignoring those injunctions.[6] In November, his constituents voted him out of office.

Enforcing immigration law is an extremely conflictual issue. Hard-liners on immigration, such as Sheriff Arpaio, see illegal immigrants as a threat to the

★

**CHAPTER
GOALS**

Describe the historical struggles
groups have faced in winning
civil rights.
pages 145–151

Analyze inequality among racial,
ethnic, and social groups today.
pages 152–158

Explain the approaches used to
bring about change in civil rights
policies.
pages 158–179

Examine affirmative action and
other ongoing civil rights issues.
pages 179–185

Joe Arpaio, former sheriff of Maricopa
County (which includes Phoenix),
Arizona, argued that strong measures
were necessary to discourage illegal
immigration. Here, Arpaio stands in front of
Maricopa County jail the day the County's
controversial measures went into effect.

country and want to make securing our borders the top priority of immigration policy (while deporting all illegal immigrants). The alternative perspective emphasizes controlling illegal immigration, while protecting the civil rights of citizens and legal residents, and providing a path to citizenship for illegal residents who are productive and law-abiding. It would seem that such a conflictual issue would not be very amenable to compromise. Indeed, both President Bush and President Obama tried and failed to enact comprehensive immigration reform. Frustrated with Congress's inactivity on the DREAM Act, which would have given legal status to young immigrants who came to the United States as children, Obama took steps in June 2012 to halt the deportation of "dreamers" and then in April 2014 he issued an executive order aimed at curbing deportations.[7] This order was struck down by the Supreme Court in June 2016. The issue was prominent throughout the presidential campaign, as Donald Trump promised to build a wall between Mexico and the United States (and make Mexico pay for it) and to deport all 12 million illegal residents in the United States. President Trump has since backed away from the latter pledge and the fate of the wall is in question. Any reform that secures our borders while protecting the civil rights of law-abiding people will involve compromise.

The concept of civil rights encompasses much more than immigration policy. Indeed, civil rights are one of the best examples of the idea that politics is everywhere: policies concerning discrimination in the workplace and in housing and against women, minorities, gays, and the disabled affect millions of Americans every day. To see how civil rights may affect you, consider the following scenarios:

- Scenario 1: You are driving home one night with a few of your friends after a party. It is late at night, but you have not had anything to drink and you are following all traffic laws. Your heart sinks as you see the flashing lights of a squad car signaling you to pull over. As the police officer approaches your car, you wonder if you have been pulled over because you and your friends are African Americans driving in an all-white neighborhood. Have your civil rights been violated? Change the scene to a car full of white teenagers with all the other facts the same. Can an officer pull them over just because he or she thinks that teenagers are more likely to be engaging in criminal activity than older people?
- Scenario 2: You are a 21-year-old Asian-American woman applying for your first job out of college. After being turned down for a job at an engineering firm, you suspect that you didn't get the job because you are a woman and because management thought that you would not fit in with the "good ol' boy" atmosphere of the firm. Have your civil rights been violated?
- Scenario 3: You and your gay partner are told that "your kind" are not welcome in the apartment complex that you wanted to live in. Should you call a lawyer?
- Scenario 4: You are a white male graduating from high school. You have just received a letter of rejection from the college that was first on your list. You are very disappointed, but then you get angry when a friend tells you that one of your classmates got into the same school even though he had virtually the same grades as you and his SAT scores were a bit lower. Your friend says that it is probably because of the school's affirmative action policy—the classmate who was accepted is Latino. Are you a victim of "reverse discrimination"? Have your civil rights been violated?

All of these scenarios would seem to be civil rights violations. However, some are, some are not, and some depend on additional considerations (we will return to these examples in the chapter's conclusion). What is discrimination? When is discrimination legal, and when isn't it? How are civil rights in the United States defined today?

The context of civil rights

★
DESCRIBE THE HISTORICAL STRUGGLES GROUPS HAVE FACED IN WINNING CIVIL RIGHTS

In general, civil rights are rights that guarantee individuals freedom from discrimination. In the United States, individuals' civil rights are monitored by the U.S. Commission on Civil Rights, a bipartisan, independent, federal commission that was established by the 1957 Civil Rights Act.[8] The commission's mission is to "appraise federal laws and policies," investigate complaints, and collect information regarding citizens who are "being deprived of their right to vote" or who are being discriminated against or denied the "equal protection of the laws under the Constitution because of race, color, religion, sex, age, disability, or national origin." It investigates government actions, such as allegations of racial discrimination in elections, and discriminatory actions of individuals in the workplace, commerce, housing, and education.

This definition seems straightforward enough, but confusion may arise when comparing the terms "civil rights" and "civil liberties." They are often used interchangeably, but there are important differences. "Civil liberties" refers to the freedoms guaranteed in the Bill of Rights, such as the freedom of speech, religious expression, and the press, as well as the due process protection of the Fourteenth Amendment. In contrast, civil rights protect all persons from discrimination and are rooted in laws and the equal protection clause of the Fourteenth Amendment. Moreover, civil liberties primarily limit what the government can do to you ("*Congress* shall make no law … abridging the freedom of speech"), whereas civil rights protect you from discrimination both by the government and by individuals. As noted in the previous chapter, to oversimplify, civil liberties are about freedom and civil rights are about equality.

Neither civil liberties nor civil rights figured prominently at the Constitutional Convention. Equality is not even mentioned in the Constitution or the Bill of Rights. However, equality was very much on the Founders' minds, as is evident in this ringing passage from the Declaration of Independence: "We hold these truths to be self evident, that all men are created equal, that they are endowed by their Creator with certain unalienable rights, that among these are life, liberty, and the pursuit of happiness." Despite the broad language, this was a limited conception of equality. The reference to "men" was intentional: women had no political or economic rights in the late eighteenth century. Similarly, equality did not apply to slaves or to Native Americans. Even propertyless white men did not have full political rights until several decades after the Constitution was ratified. Equality and civil rights in the United States have been a continually evolving work in progress.

African Americans

From the early nineteenth century and the movement for the abolition of slavery until the mid-twentieth century and the civil rights movement, the central focus of civil rights was on the experiences of African Americans. Other groups received attention more gradually. Starting in the mid-nineteenth century women began their fight for equal rights, and over the next century the civil rights movement expanded to include other groups such as Native Americans, Latinos, and Asian Americans. Most recently, attention has turned to the elderly, the disabled, and LGBTQs (lesbian, gay, bisexual, transgender, queer/questioning people). The most divisive civil rights issue with the greatest long-term impact, however, has been slavery and its legacy.

Slavery and Its Impact Slavery was part of the American economy from nearly the beginning of the nation's history. Dutch traders brought 20 slaves to Jamestown,

civil rights
Rights that guarantee individuals freedom from discrimination. These rights are generally grounded in the equal protection clause of the Fourteenth Amendment and more specifically laid out in laws passed by Congress, such as the 1964 Civil Rights Act.

Slavery was part of the American economy from the 1600s until it was abolished by the Thirteenth Amendment in 1865. The system of slavery in the South created a highly unequal society in which African Americans were denied virtually all rights. Abolitionists worked to undermine and abolish slavery. Harriet Tubman was instrumental in the success of the Underground Railroad, which brought countless slaves to freedom.

> **A house divided against itself cannot stand. I believe this government cannot endure permanently half-slave and half-free.**
>
> — President Abraham Lincoln

Virginia, in 1619, a year before the Puritans landed at Plymouth Rock. It is impossible to overstate the importance of slaves to the southern economy. The 1860 census shows that there were 2.3 million slaves in the Deep South, constituting 47 percent of its population, and there were nearly 4 million slaves in the South overall. The economic benefits of slavery for the owners were clear. By 1860, the per capita income for whites in the South was $3,978; in the North, it was $2,040. The South had only 30 percent of the nation's free population, but it had 60 percent of the wealthiest men.[9]

Abolitionists worked to rid the nation of slavery as its importance to the South grew, setting the nation on a collision course that would not be resolved until the Civil War. The Founders largely ducked the issue (see Chapter 2), and subsequent legislatures and courts did not come any closer to resolving the impasse between the North and South over slavery. The Missouri Compromise of 1820, which limited the expansion of slavery and kept the overall balance between slave states and free states, eased tensions for a while, but the issue persisted. Slave owners became increasingly frustrated with the success of the Underground Railroad, which helped some slaves escape to the North. The debate over admitting California as a free state or a slave state (or making it half-free and half-slave) threatened to split the nation once again. Southern states agreed to admit California as a free state, but only if Congress passed the Fugitive Slave Act, which required northern states to treat escaped slaves as property and return them to their owners. Soon after, Congress enacted the Compromise of 1850, which overturned the Missouri Compromise and allowed each new state to decide for itself whether to be a slave state or a free state.

All possibility of further compromise on the issue ended with the misguided *Dred Scott v. Sandford* decision in 1857. The Supreme Court ruled that states could not be prevented from allowing slavery. It also held that slaves were property rather than citizens and, as such, had no legal rights. But believing that slavery was in jeopardy when Abraham Lincoln won the presidency in 1860, the southern states seceded from the Union and formed the Confederacy.

The outcome of the Civil War restored national unity and ended slavery, but the price was very high. About 528,000 Americans died in the war, with an astonishingly high casualty rate (25 percent).[10] After the war, Republicans moved quickly to ensure that the changes accomplished by the war could not easily be undone: they promptly adopted the Civil War amendments to the Constitution. The Thirteenth Amendment banned slavery, the Fourteenth guaranteed that states could not deny newly freed slaves the equal protection of the laws and provided citizenship to anyone born in the United States, and the Fifteenth gave African-American men the right to vote. These amendments were ratified within five years of the war, although southern states resisted giving freed slaves and their descendants "equal protection of the laws" over the next 100 years.

Voting Rights During Reconstruction (1866–1877), blacks in the South gained political power through institutions such as the Freedmen's Bureau and the Union League. With the protection of the occupying northern army, blacks were able to vote and even hold public office. When federal troops withdrew and the Republican Party abandoned the South, however, blacks were almost completely disenfranchised (denied the right to vote) through the imposition of residency requirements, poll taxes, literacy tests, the grandfather clause (which permitted those who had voted before the war and their descendants to vote even if they did not meet current voting requirements), physical intimidation, and other forms of disqualification. Later the practice known as the "white primary" allowed only whites to vote in Democratic primary elections and, given that the Republican Party did not exist in most southern states, blacks were effectively disenfranchised. Although most of these provisions claimed to be race neutral, their impact fell disproportionately on black voters. For example, the grandfather clause enabled illiterate whites (but not illiterate blacks) to avoid the literacy test.[11] Many states also had "understanding" or "good character" exceptions to the literacy tests, which gave election officials substantial discretion over who would be allowed to vote.

The collective impact of these obstacles virtually eliminated black voting. For example, only 6 percent of blacks were registered to vote in Mississippi in 1890 and only 2 percent were registered in Alabama in 1906. After the last post-Reconstruction black congressman left the House in 1901, 72 years passed before another African American represented a southern district in Congress. In Mississippi, one county in 1947 had 13,000 blacks who were eligible to vote, but only 6 were actually registered. Despite the constitutional guarantees of the Fourteenth and Fifteenth Amendments, blacks had little access to the political system in the South and they had little success in winning office at any level in the rest of the nation.[12]

Jim Crow The social and economic position of blacks in the South followed a path similar to their political fortunes. Soon after the Civil War ended, sympathetic Republicans passed the Civil Rights Acts of 1866 and 1875, which aimed to outlaw segregation and provide equal opportunity for blacks. However, there were no enforcement provisions and when Reconstruction ended in 1877 the southern states enacted "black codes," or Jim Crow laws, that led to complete segregation of the races. Then, in 1883, the Supreme Court ruled that the 1875 Civil Rights Act was unconstitutional because Congress did not have the power to forbid racial discrimination in private businesses. Southern states interpreted this decision as a signal that the national government was unconcerned about protecting the rights of blacks.

Jim Crow laws forbade interracial marriage and mandated the complete separation of the races in neighborhoods, hotels, apartments, hospitals, schools, and restrooms, at drinking fountains, and in restaurants, elevators, and even cemetery plots. In cases where it would have been inconvenient to completely separate the races, as in public transportation, blacks had to sit in the back of the bus or in separate cars on the train and give up their seats to whites if asked. The Supreme Court validated these practices in *Plessy v. Ferguson* (1896) in establishing the "separate but equal" doctrine, officially permitting segregation as long as blacks had equal facilities.

Senator Hiram Revels, the first African American to serve in the U.S. Congress, represented Mississippi in 1870 and 1871.

In the first several decades after Reconstruction, the rest of the nation mostly ignored the status of blacks, because 90 percent of all African Americans lived in the South. But blacks' northward migration to urban areas throughout the first half of the twentieth century transformed the nation's demographic profile and its racial politics. America's "race problem" was no longer a southern problem. Although conditions for blacks were generally better outside the South, they still faced discrimination and lived largely segregated lives throughout the nation. In World Wars I and II, black soldiers fought and died for their country in segregated units. Professional sports teams were segregated, and black musicians and artists could not perform in many of the nation's leading theaters. Moreover, blacks largely were hired for the lowest-paying menial jobs.

Progress began in the 1940s. The Supreme Court struck down the white primary in 1944, Jackie Robinson broke the color line in Major League Baseball in 1947, and President Harry Truman issued an executive order integrating the U.S. armed services in 1948. Then came the landmark decision *Brown v. Board of Education* (1954), which rejected the "separate but equal" doctrine, followed by *Brown II* (1955), which ordered that public schools be desegregated "with all deliberate speed." These events set the stage for the growing success of the civil rights movement, discussed later in this chapter.

Native Americans, Latinos, and Asian Americans

The legacy of slavery and racial segregation in the South has been the dominant focus of U.S. civil rights policies, but many other groups have also fought for equal rights. Native Americans were the first group to come in contact with the European immigrants. Although initial relations between the Native Americans and the European settlers were good in many places, the settlers' appetite for more land and their insensitivity to Native-American culture soon led to continual conflict. Native Americans were systematically pushed from their land and placed on reservations. The most infamous example was the removal of 46,000 members of the "Five Civilized Tribes" from the southeastern United States following the enactment of the Indian Removal Act in 1830. Thousands of Native Americans died on the Trail of Tears on their way to reservations in Oklahoma.[13] Native Americans had no political rights; indeed, through much of the nineteenth century the U.S. government considered them "savages" to be eliminated. They did not gain the universal right to vote until 1924, just after women and well after black men. Although the U.S. government signed treaties with Native-American tribes that recognized them as sovereign nations (not as foreign nations but as "domestic dependent nations"),[14] in practice the government ignored most of the agreements. Only in recent decades has the government started to uphold its obligations, although compliance remains spotty. Native Americans have struggled to maintain their cultural history and autonomy in the face of widespread poverty and unemployment.

Latinos have also struggled for political and economic equality. The early history of Latinos in the United States is rooted in the Mexican-American War (1846–1848) and the conquest by the United States of the territory that today makes up most of the southwestern states. Since that time, Mexicans have resided in large numbers in the Southwest. Although Latinos had long experienced prejudice and discrimination, one of their first major political successes was Cesar Chavez's effort to organize farmworkers in the 1960s and 1970s. He established the United Farm Workers Union

In the 1960s and 1970s, Cesar Chavez and the United Farm Workers Union successfully organized mostly Mexican-American farmworkers, first in California and then in other parts of the country. Here, Chavez speaks to a group in Texas.

and forced growers to bargain with 50,000 mostly Mexican-American fieldworkers in California and Florida. Although many Mexican Americans have roots that go back hundreds of years, a majority of Latinos have been in the United States for less than two generations. Consequently, they have become a political force only recently, despite the fact that they now are the nation's largest minority.

Latinos' relative lack of political clout when compared with that of African Americans can be explained by two factors: (1) Latinos vote at a much lower rate than African Americans because many have language barriers and about one-third of Latinos are not U.S. citizens and therefore cannot vote in national elections, and (2) unlike African Americans, Latinos are a relatively diverse group politically, including people from many Latin American nations. Most Latino voters are loyal to the Democratic Party, but a majority of Cuban Americans are Republicans. Although this diversity means that Latino voters do not speak with one voice, it brings opportunity for increased political clout in the future. The diversity of partisan attachments among Latinos and their relatively low levels of political involvement mean that both parties are eager to attract them as new voters. In 2016, Donald Trump surprised many experts by winning a higher percentage of the Latino vote (29 percent) than Mitt Romney did in 2012 (27 percent).

Asian Americans experienced discrimination beginning with their arrival in the United States in the nineteenth century. The first wave of Chinese immigrants came with the 1848 California gold rush. Initially, foreign miners, including the Chinese, were able to stake out their claims along with Americans. But by 1850, when the easy-to-find gold was gone, Americans tried to drive out the Chinese through violence and the Foreign Miners Tax. Subsequently, Chinese immigrants played a crucial role in building the intercontinental railroad between 1865 and 1869. Yet, because they were given the most dangerous jobs, many lost their lives. After the railroad was completed, Chinese workers returned to the West Coast, where they experienced increasing discrimination and violence. Following several race riots, Congress passed the Chinese Exclusion Act of 1882, which prevented Chinese already in the United States from becoming U.S. citizens—although the Supreme Court later granted their American-born children automatic citizenship under the Fourteenth Amendment.[15] The Chinese Exclusion Act also barred virtually all immigration from China—the first time in U.S. history that a specific ethnic group was singled out in this way. During World War II, more than 110,000 Japanese were placed in internment camps. Despite the internment being upheld by the Supreme Court at the time, a 1980 congressional commission determined that it was a "grave injustice" motivated by "racial prejudice, war hysteria and the failure of political leadership." Eight years later, President Ronald Reagan signed into law the Civil Liberties Act, which paid more than $1.6 billion in reparations to the survivors of the camps and their heirs.[16] In recent decades, a much broader range of Asians have emigrated to the United States, including Koreans, Filipinos, Hmong, Vietnamese, and Asian Indians. This variation in national heritage, culture, and language means that Asian Americans are quite diverse in their political views, partisan affiliation, and voting patterns.

Women and civil rights

On the eve of the United States' declaration of independence in 1776, John Adams's wife, Abigail, advised him not to "put such unlimited power in the hands of the husbands. Remember, all men would be tyrants if they could.... If particular care and attention is not paid to the ladies, we ... will not hold ourselves bound by any laws in which we have no voice or representation."[17] John Adams did not listen to his wife. The Constitution did not give women the right to vote, and they were not guaranteed that civil right until the Nineteenth Amendment was ratified in 1920—although 16 states had allowed women to

protectionism
The idea under which some people have tried to rationalize discriminatory policies by claiming that some groups, like women or African Americans, should be denied certain rights for their own safety or well-being.

vote before then. Until the early twentieth century, women in most parts of the country could not hold office, serve on juries, bring lawsuits in their own name, own property, or serve as legal guardians for their children. A woman's identity was so closely tied to her husband that if she married a noncitizen she automatically gave up her citizenship!

The rationale for these policies was called protectionism. The argument was that women were too frail to compete in the business world and needed to be protected by men. This reasoning served in many court cases to deny women equal rights. For example, in 1869 Myra Bradwell requested admission to the Illinois bar to practice law. She was the first woman to graduate from law school in Illinois and the editor of *Chicago Legal News* and held all the qualifications to be a lawyer in the state except for one—she was a woman. Her request was denied, and she sued all the way to the Supreme Court. In 1873, the Court ruled that the prohibition against women lawyers did not violate the Fourteenth Amendment's privileges and immunities clause because there was no constitutional right to be an attorney. If the Court had stopped there, the decision would have been unremarkable for its time. But Justice Joseph Bradley went on to provide a classic example of protectionism:[18]

> The civil law as well as nature itself has always recognized a wide difference in the respective spheres and destinies to man and woman. Man is, or should be, women's protector and defender. The natural and proper timidity and delicacy which belongs to the female sex evidently unfits it for many of the occupations of civil life. The constitution of the family organization which is founded in the divine ordinance, as well as the nature of things, indicates the domestic sphere as that which properly belongs to the domains and functions of womanhood.[18]

While protectionist sentiment on the Court had waned by the mid-twentieth century, as recently as 1961 the Court upheld a Florida law that automatically exempted women but not men from compulsory jury duty. The case involved a woman who killed her husband with a baseball bat after he admitted that he was having an affair and wanted to end the marriage. The woman argued that her conviction by an all-male jury violated her Fourteenth Amendment guarantee of "equal protection of the laws" and that a jury panel containing some women would have been more sympathetic to her "temporary insanity" defense. The Court rejected this argument, ruling that the Florida law excluding women from jury duty was reasonable because "despite the enlightened emancipation of women from the restrictions and protections of bygone years, and their entry into many parts of community life formerly considered to be reserved to men, woman still is regarded as the center of home and family life."[19] Apparently, it was unthinkable to the all-male Court that a man might have to stay home from work and take care of the kids while his wife served on a jury. Later in this chapter, we will describe how the Supreme Court has moved away from this discriminatory position and rejected protectionist thinking.

Gays and lesbians

The most recent group in the struggle for civil rights is the LGBTQ community. For most of American history, gays and lesbians lived secret lives and were subject to abuse and discrimination if they openly acknowledged their sexual preferences. The critical moment that spurred the gay rights movement occurred on June 28, 1969, during a routine police raid on the Stonewall Inn in New York City.[20] (Police often raided gay bars to harass patrons and selectively enforce liquor laws.) This time, rather than submitting to the arrests, the customers fought back, throwing stones and beer bottles, breaking windows, and starting small fires. A crowd of several hundred

The protectionist view that women are weaker and unfit for some occupations was one reason women were excluded from the military for most of the nation's history. Pictured here are 1st Lt. Shaye Haver and Capt. Kristen Griest, the first female graduates of the U.S. Army's rigorous Ranger School at Fort Benning, Georgia.

In 2016, President Obama designated the historic site of the Stonewall uprising in New York City as a national monument to honor the LGBTQ equality movement.

people gathered, and the fighting raged for three nights. The Stonewall Rebellion galvanized the gay community by demonstrating the power of collective action.

Since Stonewall, the gay rights movement has made steady progress through a combination of political mobilization and protest, legislative action, and legal action. Public support for gay rights has increased dramatically in recent years. Between two-thirds and three-fourths of Americans (depending on the poll) agree with the national policy established in 2011 that gays may openly serve in the military, whereas a majority of Americans opposed this policy when it was first proposed by President Clinton in 1993. Between 55 and 62 percent of Americans support same-sex marriage in recent polls, whereas only 35 to 40 percent held that view in 2009. More than 60 percent believe that same-sex couples should be able to adopt children, 81 percent think that businesses should not be able to discriminate against gays and lesbians, and 63 percent believe that same-sex couples should be entitled to the same benefits as heterosexual couples (whereas only 32 percent think they should not).[21] In May 2012, President Obama endorsed same-sex marriage for the first time, completing his gradual evolution on the issue. In 2015, the Supreme Court ruled that same-sex marriage is legal in all 50 states (we will discuss this and other issues concerning gay and lesbian rights later in the chapter).[22]

"Why Should I Care?"

Why does this history matter for politics today? First, the effects of slavery and Jim Crow laws are still quite evident: legal racial segregation ended 50 years ago, but its legacy—especially evident in the difference that exists in the relative quality of education available to most whites and blacks—remains. Second, active discrimination based on race, gender, and sexual orientation is still evident in our society. Given the importance of race in the everyday lives of millions of Americans and in gaining an understanding of American politics, a grasp of the history that got us to where we are today is an important starting point.

The racial divide today

The racial divide today begins with the unequal treatment of racial minorities, women, gays, and lesbians and is rooted in a gulf that remains between the objective condition of minorities and that of whites as well as between the political views that they hold. Although substantial progress has been made in bridging that gulf, inequalities in political, social, and economic conditions remain.

Discriminatory treatment

Discrimination is much more common today than many people realize. The Equal Employment Opportunity Commission (EEOC) filed an average of 96,000 charges of employment discrimination each year in the past five years,[23] while the National Fair Housing Alliance reports an average of 27,000 cases of housing discrimination a year.[24] The Justice Department has won dozens of lawsuits against banks and mortgage lenders who engage in discriminatory practices, winning settlements totaling several hundred million dollars in 2015.[25]

The experience of a former graduate student in our department who is white and whose wife is black puts a human face on these statistics. The couple wanted to rent a bigger apartment, so they searched the want ads and made appointments to see some apartments. One landlord told them to meet him in front of the apartment at a specific time. They waited where they were told, but the landlord didn't show up. Later they remembered seeing a car that slowed down and almost stopped but then sped away. They wondered if this was a case of a "drive-by landlord"—one who checks out potential tenants' race from a distance; if they are not white, he or she skips the appointment and tells them it is rented if they ask. This is exactly what happened. This couple called the landlord, asked what had happened, and were told that the apartment was already rented. To check their suspicions, they had some friends ask about the apartment, and the friends were told it was available. Their friends (both white) made an appointment to meet the landlord, and this time the same car pulled up and stopped. The landlord showed them the apartment and was very friendly. The next day, the graduate student filed a racial discrimination lawsuit.

These types of stories, ranging from irritating and demeaning to a serious violation of the law, are familiar to nearly every racial minority, woman, and gay person in the United States. Consider the well-dressed businessman who cannot get a cab in a major city because he is black, the woman who is sexually harassed by her boss but hesitates to say anything for fear of losing her job, the teenage Latino who is shadowed in the music store by a clerk, the Arab American who endures taunts about her head covering, or the lesbian couple who cannot find an apartment. Such anecdotal evidence, as well as extensive government data and academic research, indicates continuing discrimination in our society, despite significant progress in the past generation.

Differences in voting access

The United States has a long history of discriminating against racial and ethnic minorities in the election process. Although African Americans voted at a rate that was quite similar to that of whites in presidential elections from 2008–2016, their turnout was somewhat lower than that of whites in midterm elections and other racial and ethnic minorities have generally lower turnouts (see Figure 5.1). Much of the difference in

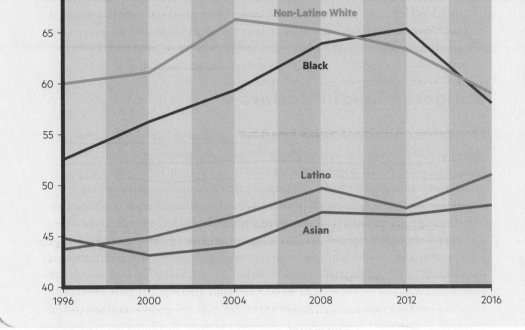

FIGURE
5.1

Turnout in Presidential Elections by Race

Turnout among African Americans has risen steadily over the last 20 years, while turnout of other groups has remained relatively flat. What do you think accounts for these trends? What could state governments do to increase voter turnout?

Source: The Diversifying Electorate—Voting Rates by Race and Hispanic Origin in 2012 (and Other Recent Elections), from Current Population Survey, www.census.gov (accessed 5/19/14); 2016 data aggregated by author from various sources.

voter turnout can be accounted for by education and income, but there still are practices and institutions that specifically depress minority-voter turnout. And many of these deterrents are intentional. The National Association for the Advancement of Colored People (NAACP), the U.S. Commission on Civil Rights, and the Brennan Center for Justice have all documented such practices in elections going back to 2000, including moving and reducing the number of polling places in areas with predominantly minority voters, changing from district-based to at-large elections (citywide or countywide elections in which there is often a mix of minority and white voters), using voter challenges to target minority voters, redistricting to dilute minority voting power, withholding information about registration and voting procedures from blacks, and "causing or taking advantage of Election Day irregularities."[26]

There are other state practices that are not specifically aimed at minority voters but that have a disproportionate impact on them. For example, in the 2008 election three states removed voters' names from the voting rolls if there wasn't an identical match between the name the voter used when registering to vote and the name as it appeared in another state database (often the database of driver's license information). Seven states purged the names of people who had committed felonies from the voting registration lists, which often produced false matches to people with the same names who had not committed a crime. Fourteen states engaged in voter intimidation and deceptive practices. Moreover, several states used technical barriers to voter registration and voting, limited access to voter registration services at social services offices (even though such access was required by federal law), and used poorly designed ballots that were especially confusing to less educated or older voters.[27]

In 2016, there were 17 changes in state laws that restricted access to voting, including requiring a photo ID to vote (which has a disproportionate impact on minorities because they are less likely to have a photo ID), requiring proof of citizenship before someone is allowed to vote, cutbacks in early voting days and times, and making it more difficult to register people to vote. In addition, as we will discuss later, in 2013 the Supreme Court struck down an important part of the Voting Rights Act, making it easier for the nine

Despite the removal of most formal barriers to voting, Latinos are less likely to vote and participate in politics than whites, blacks, and Asian Americans. Latino advocacy groups like Mi Familia Vota work to engage and register voters in their local communities.

states that had been covered by this provision of the law to implement discriminatory practices. In early 2016, there were lawsuits in 11 states challenging limits on early voting and strict voter ID laws. Those supporting voting rights won at least partial victories in eight states, and cases were still pending in three states. Also, several states passed laws to automatically register voters and restore the right to vote for those with past criminal convictions.[28]

Socioeconomic indicators

The racial divide is also evident in social and economic terms. Nearly three times as many black families are below the poverty line as white families: 24.1 percent compared with 9.1 percent in 2015. The poverty rate of 21.4 percent for Hispanic families in 2015 was similar to that of black families. While white median household income (that is, income from wages, salaries, interest, and disability and unemployment payments) was $62,950 in 2015, black median household income was $36,898 (58.6 percent of white family income) and Hispanic median household income was $45,145 (71.7 percent of white family income).[29] Moreover, the gap in overall wealth is much more dramatic. The average white household has more than six times the assets of the typical nonwhite family. In 2013, the median household net worth (that is, the sum of all assets, including houses, cars, and stock) was $142,000 for whites and $18,100 for nonwhites.[30] Poverty is not distributed equally throughout the United States but rather is concentrated in areas where the minority population is the highest (see Figure 5.2).

Other indicators show similar patterns. The rate of black adult male unemployment has been about twice as high as that of white adult male unemployment for the past 45 years. In September 2016, the unemployment rate among blacks was 8.3 percent, compared with 4.4 percent for whites and 6.4 percent for Latinos.[31] Moreover, 38.6 percent of black children lived in two-parent households in 2015, compared with 74.9 percent of white children and 67 percent of Latino children.[32] Also, blacks are significantly more likely than whites to be victimized by crime. African Americans are nearly seven times as likely to be murdered as whites.[33]

On every measure of health—life expectancy, infectious diseases, infant mortality, cancer rates, heart disease, and strokes—the gaps between whites and blacks are large and, in some cases, increasing. For example, life expectancy for blacks is about four years shorter than for whites (74.5 years for blacks compared with 78.8 years for whites), the infant mortality rate is more than double for blacks (13.31 deaths per 1,000 live births compared with 5.62 deaths per 1,000 live births for whites), and maternal mortality is more than triple (35.6 deaths per 100,000 births for black women compared with 11.7 deaths per 100,000 births for white women). Similar gaps also exist for incidences of cancer, diabetes, strokes, and heart attacks in blacks and whites.[34]

While social scientists continue to debate the causes of the racial disparities in health outcomes, an increasing body of evidence indicates that at least some of the gap is caused by government policies and business-related decisions. Broadly labeled "environmental racism," these practices mean that minority groups are much more likely to live in areas affected by pollution, toxic waste, and hazardous chemical sites.[35] One of the most extreme examples of this, uncovered in late 2015 and early 2016, involved the public water supply in Flint, Michigan. In 2014, to save money, the city switched the water supply from Lake Huron to the Flint River. Residents of the poor, majority-black city soon reported discolored, foul-looking water, but their complaints were ignored by city and state officials. After researchers demonstrated levels of lead in the water that far exceeded safe levels, 6,000 to 12,000 residents had elevated levels of lead in their blood and experienced serious health issues. President Obama declared

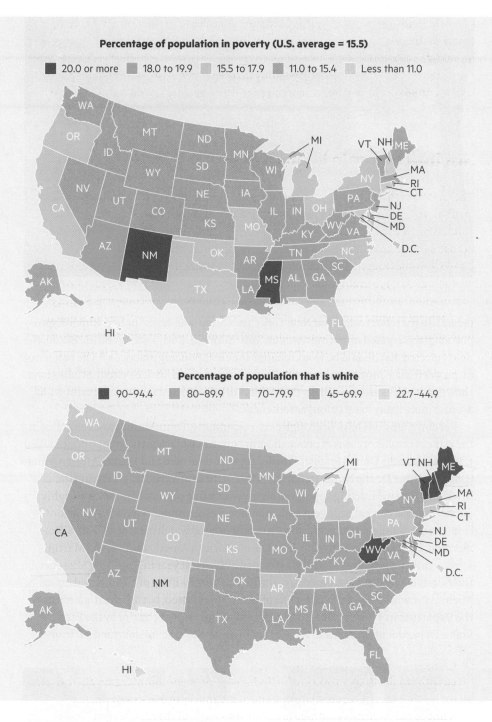

Percentage of population in poverty (U.S. average = 15.5)

■ 20.0 or more ■ 18.0 to 19.9 ■ 15.5 to 17.9 ■ 11.0 to 15.4 ■ Less than 11.0

Percentage of population that is white

■ 90–94.4 ■ 80–89.9 ■ 70–79.9 ■ 45–69.9 ■ 22.7–44.9

FIGURE 5.2

Poverty and Race, 2014

Carefully examine these maps. What is the relationship between poverty and the minority population? How do you think these patterns might affect the politics of civil rights policies aimed at reducing discrimination in the workplace or housing?

Sources: Poverty data from U.S. Census Bureau, 2014 American Community Survey, www.census.gov/acs; race data from U.S. Census Bureau, *2012 Statistical Abstract*, Population Table 18, "Resident Population by Hispanic Origin and State: 2010," www.census.gov (accessed 11/3/12).

the city a disaster area and aid was provided in early 2016, but permanent damage had already been done.[36]

Criminal justice and hate crimes

The greatest disparity between racial minorities and whites may be in the criminal justice system. Racial profiling subjects many innocent blacks to intrusive searches. Nick Cannon, the rapper and host of *America's Got Talent*, has complained about constantly being stopped for "driving while black." He said, "Now in L.A. I get pulled over like once a week. Honestly, I think it's because I'm a black man in a nice car."[37] In 2013, a

There have been dozens of high-profile cases in recent years of police officers shooting unarmed black men. Michael Slager, a North Charleston, South Carolina, police officer, is shown here shooting Walter Scott following a traffic stop for a broken brake light.

federal district court ruled that New York City's "stop-and-frisk" policy, which disproportionately targeted minorities, was unconstitutional. Early in 2014, Bill de Blasio, the newly elected mayor, said he would change the city's policing practices.[38] The pattern of disproportionate profiling also occurs later in the criminal justice system. Studies have shown that blacks are more likely than whites to be convicted for the same crimes and are also more likely to serve longer sentences.[39]

Recently, tensions have been high between minority communities and the police in the wake of dozens of cases of police shooting unarmed black men. In 2015, police killed 1,139 people in the United States; of those, 223 were unarmed and 75 were African Americans (see What Do the Numbers Say?).[40] Most of these involved tragic circumstances in which police were acting appropriately given existing protocol. But several highly publicized cases reveal negligent and, in some cases, criminal behavior by police officers. In 2013, following the acquittal of a neighborhood watch member, George Zimmerman, for shooting an unarmed 17-year-old African American, Trayvon Martin, a group called Black Lives Matter was formed.[41] The next year in Ferguson, Missouri, thousands of protesters gathered to call attention to the killing of an unarmed man, Michael Brown, by a police officer. The officer was acquitted, but an investigation by the Department of Justice found patterns of discriminatory behavior by the Ferguson Police Department. In 2015 and 2016, other high-profile cases of unarmed African

Dylann Roof is shown here after his arrest for shooting and killing nine people during a prayer service in a church in Charleston, South Carolina. A mourner outside the church is overcome with grief.

People Killed by Police in 2015, by Race

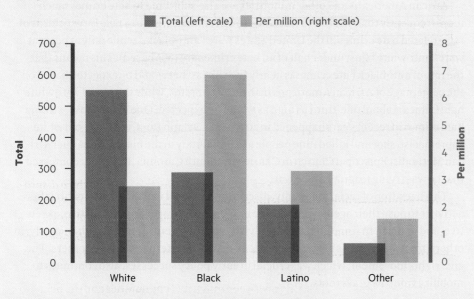

Legend: Total (left scale) | Per million (right scale)

Categories: White, Black, Latino, Other

Unarmed People Killed by Police in 2015, by Race

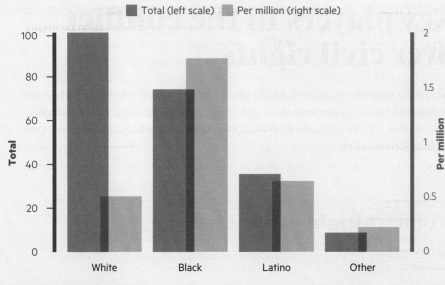

Legend: Total (left scale) | Per million (right scale)

Categories: White, Black, Latino, Other

Racial Inequality in Law Enforcement

Recent events in Ferguson, Missouri, Baltimore, Maryland, and Staten Island, New York, among other places have touched off a nationwide debate about fairness in law enforcement. Do racial inequalities exist in law enforcement? What do the numbers say?

Source: "The Counted: People Killed by Police in the US," *The Guardian*, www.theguardian.com/us-news/ng-interactive/2015/jun/01/the-counted- police-killings-us-database# (accessed 8/15/16).

Think about it

- For all victims (total and unarmed), what racial category had the highest number of deaths? What racial category had the highest number per million people? What do you think accounts for this difference?
- Is there a greater racial disparity in the first chart that shows all people killed by police, or the second chart that shows unarmed people?
- What, if anything, surprises you about these numbers? Why?

Americans being killed by officers happened in Cleveland, Baltimore, Chicago, Staten Island, Baton Rouge, and Minneapolis–St. Paul. One case in North Charleston, South Carolina, led to the officer being charged with murder. Following a daytime traffic stop for a broken taillight, Officer Michael Slager shot Walter Scott in the back eight times from 15 to 20 feet away as Scott was running away, and lied about what happened to cover up his crime. A bystander's video showed the murder and led to his arrest. Slager's trial was underway as this edition went to press (November 2016).

African Americans and other minorities are also subjected to hate crimes much more frequently than whites.[42] According to FBI statistics, in 2014 nearly two-thirds of race-related hate crimes in the United States were "anti-black," while only 23 percent were "anti-white" (just under half of all hate crimes are race based). This means that the rate of anti-black hate crimes is nearly five times what would be expected based on the percentage of African Americans in the United States, while the rate of anti-white hate crimes is about one-third as high as would be expected. One of the most extreme hate crimes in recent years happened in 2015 when Dylann Roof, a 21-year-old white supremacist, shot and killed nine people at a Bible study in the historic Emanuel African Methodist Episcopal Church in Charleston, South Carolina. Roof later confessed that he was trying to ignite a race war.

This backdrop of racial inequality, discrimination, and violence drives civil rights activists to push their agenda in the three branches of government: legislative, executive, and judicial. In some instances, activists work in several arenas simultaneously; in others, they seek redress in one arena after exhausting alternatives in the others. The civil rights movement, which was crucial in early policy successes, also continues to mobilize from the grass roots.

★

EXPLAIN THE APPROACHES USED TO BRING ABOUT CHANGE IN CIVIL RIGHTS POLICIES

Key players in the conflict over civil rights

Our civil rights policies are produced by several key players. First, the public becomes involved through social movements to put pressure on the political system to change. But Congress, the president, and the courts all also exert their own influence on policies that define civil rights.

FIGURE 5.3

Women's Rights Time Line

First women's rights convention held in Seneca Falls, New York.	Territory of Wyoming gives women the right to vote.	Congress requires equal pay for equal work for federal employees (but not for private sector workers).	The Nineteenth Amendment gives women the right to vote.	Equal Pay Act requires equal pay for equal work.	Title VII of the Civil Rights Act bars employment discrimination based on race, sex, and other grounds.
1848	1869	1872	1920	1963	1964

Social movements

From the early women's rights movement and abolitionists of the nineteenth century to the gay rights and civil rights movements of the mid-twentieth century, activists have pressured the political system to change civil rights policies. Through collective action, these social movements have made sure that such controversial issues remained on the policy agenda.

Women started to push for the right to vote at a convention in 1848 at Seneca Falls, New York. Subsequently, a constitutional amendment to give women the right to vote was regularly introduced in Congress between 1878 and 1913 but never was passed, despite the efforts of women such as Susan B. Anthony and Elizabeth Cady Stanton. After a parallel movement at the state level had some success, the Nineteenth Amendment, giving women the right to vote, was finally passed in 1919 and ratified in 1920 (see Figure 5.3).

The civil rights movement of the 1950s and 1960s, aimed at ending segregation and guaranteeing equal political and social rights for blacks, is the most famous example of a successful social movement (see Figure 5.4). Although the *Brown v. Board of Education* decision, which struck down segregation in public schools, gave the movement a boost, most southern blacks saw little change in their daily lives. As white school boards and local governments resisted integration, black leaders became convinced that the courts would not effect change because of resistance to their decisions. The only way to change the laws was to get the public, both black and white, to demand change.

The spark came on December 1, 1955, in Montgomery, Alabama, when a woman named Rosa Parks refused to give up her seat on a bus to a white person, as she was required to do by law. Parks is often described as a seamstress who was tired after a long day's work and simply did not want to give up her seat. That is true, but there is more to the story. Local civil rights leaders had been waiting for years for an opportunity to boycott the local bus company because of its segregation policy. They needed a perfect test case—someone who would help draw attention to the cause.

Rosa Parks was just that person. She was a well-educated, law-abiding citizen who had been active in local civil rights organizations. In her book, *My Story*, Parks says: "I was . . . no more tired than I usually was at the end of a working day. . . . No, the only tired I was, was tired of giving in."[43] When she was arrested for refusing to give up her seat, local civil rights leaders organized a boycott of the bus company that lasted more than a year. Whites in Montgomery tried to stop the boycott. The police arrested and fined blacks who had arranged a car pool system to get to work: people waiting for a car to

Four African-American college students protest at a whites-only lunch counter in Greensboro, North Carolina. These sit-ins spread throughout the South in 1960 as civil rights activists were able to put pressure through their nonviolent protests on businesses to integrate.

Griswold v. Connecticut legalizes the use of contraceptives by married couples.	Federal affirmative action policies are extended to women by an executive order.	Title IX of the Education Amendments of 1972 requires equal access to programs for men and women in higher education.	*Roe v. Wade* establishes a constitutional right to abortion.	Thirty-five states ratify the Equal Rights Amendment, passed by Congress in 1971–1972, falling three states short of the number needed to add the amendment to the Constitution.	Lilly Ledbetter Fair Pay Act makes it easier to sue for gender-based pay discrimination.
1965	**1967**	**1972**	**1973**	**1982**	**2009**

FIGURE
5.4

African American Civil Rights Time Line

Government Action

May 17
U.S. Supreme Court rules segregated schools are unconstitutional in the *Brown v. Board of Education* decision.

September 9
The Federal Civil Rights Act prohibits discrimination.

September 23
President Eisenhower sends troops to escort black students into a white high school in Little Rock, Arkansas.

1954   1957

Social Movement

December 1
Rosa Parks is arrested for refusing to move to the back of a bus in Montgomery, Alabama.

February 1
Black college students, refused service at a lunch counter in Greensboro, North Carolina, launch a sit-in.

May 4
Freedom Riders test a Supreme Court decision that integrated interstate bus travel, sparking violence.

1955   1960   1961

Source: Adapted from "Key Moments in Civil Rights History," *Ann Arbor News*, January 11, 2004, www.mlive.com

---

pick them up were arrested for loitering, and car pool drivers were arrested for lacking appropriate insurance or having too many people in their car. Martin Luther King Jr. was elected leader of the bus boycott, and he was subjected to harassment and violence—his house was firebombed, and he was arrested several times. Finally, a federal district court ruled that Montgomery's segregation policy was unconstitutional and the Supreme Court upheld the ruling.

Nonviolent Protest On February 1, 1960, four black students in Greensboro, North Carolina, went to a segregated lunch counter at a local Woolworth's and asked to be served. They sat there for an hour without being served and had to leave when the store closed. When 20 students returned the next day, national wire services picked up the story. Within two weeks, the sit-ins had spread to 11 cities. In some cases, the students were met with violence; in others, they were simply arrested. However, the students continued to respond with passive resistance, and new waves of protesters replaced those who had been arrested. The Student Nonviolent Coordinating Committee (SNCC) was created to coordinate the protests. The Greensboro Woolworth's was integrated on July 26, 1961, but the protests continued in other cities. By August 1961, the sit-ins had 70,000 participants and there had been 3,000 arrests.[44] The sit-ins marked an important shift in the tactics of the civil rights movement: away from the

July 2
President Johnson signs the Civil Rights Act.

August 6
The Federal Voting Rights Act prohibits denying anyone the vote on the basis of color or race.

1964

1965

• • • • • • • • **April 16**
Martin Luther King Jr. writes his "Letter from the Birmingham Jail," defending nonviolent civil disobedience against unjust laws.

• • • • • • • • **August 28**
Martin Luther King Jr. delivers his "I Have a Dream" speech at the March on Washington.

• • • • **September 15**
Four girls are killed when a Baptist church in Birmingham, Alabama, is bombed.

June 21
Three civil rights workers are murdered outside Philadelphia, Mississippi.

• • • • **February 21**
Malcolm X is shot and killed in New York.

• • • • **March 7**
Six hundred voting rights marchers are attacked by police with clubs and whips on the Edmund Pettus Bridge outside Selma, Alabama. On March 21, about 3,200 marchers head out again on a four-day march to Montgomery in support of voting rights.

April 4
Martin Luther King Jr. is slain in Memphis, Tennessee.

1963

1964

1965

1968

court-based approach and toward the nonviolent civil disobedience approach that had been successful in Montgomery.

Also during this period, the Freedom Riders were working to get President Kennedy to enforce two Supreme Court decisions that banned segregation in interstate travel, including at bus terminals, in waiting rooms, in restaurants, and in other public facilities related to interstate travel.[45] On May 4, 1961, a group of whites and blacks boarded two buses in Washington, D.C., headed for New Orleans. The whites and blacks sat together and went into segregated areas of bus stations. The trip was uneventful until Rock Hill, South Carolina, where several Freedom Riders were beaten. Then, in Anniston, Alabama, one bus had its tires slashed and was firebombed. The Freedom Riders were beaten as they fled the burning bus. A second group encountered an angry mob at the bus station in Birmingham and was severely beaten with baseball bats and iron pipes. When it became clear that police protection would not be forthcoming, the Freedom Riders abandoned the trip and regrouped in Nashville. After much internal debate, they decided to continue the rides.

Following more violence in Montgomery, President Kennedy intervened and his brother Robert Kennedy, the attorney general, worked out a deal: the Freedom Riders would receive police protection, federal troops would not intervene, and they would face the local courts upon their arrest for "disturbing the peace." The Freedom Rides

Left, a 15-year-old civil rights demonstrator, defying an anti-parade ordinance, is attacked by a police dog in Birmingham, Alabama, on May 3, 1963. Reaction against this police brutality helped spur Congress and the president to enact civil rights legislation. Three months later, civil rights leader Martin Luther King Jr. (right) waves to supporters from the steps of the Lincoln Memorial in Washington, D.C. The March on Washington drew an estimated 250,000 people who heard King deliver his famous "I Have a Dream" speech.

continued throughout the summer. They successfully drew national attention to the continuing resistance in the South to desegregation rulings, forced the Kennedy administration to take a stand on this issue, and led to a stronger Interstate Commerce Commission ruling banning segregation in interstate travel.[46]

The next significant events occurred in Birmingham, Alabama, in 1963. Birmingham had more racial violence than any southern city, with 18 unsolved bombings of black churches and homes in a six-year period. The city had closed its parks and golf courses rather than integrate them, and there was no progress on integrating the local schools. A leading supporter of integration had been castrated to intimidate other blacks who might advocate integration. The city's police chief, "Bull" Connor, was a strong segregationist who had allowed the attacks on the Freedom Riders. During a peaceful protest in April 1963, Martin Luther King Jr. and many others were arrested. While in solitary confinement, King wrote his now-famous "Letter from the Birmingham Jail," an eloquent statement of the principles of nonviolent civil disobedience.

The letter was a response to white religious leaders who had told King in a newspaper ad that his actions were "unwise and untimely" and that "when rights are consistently denied, a cause should be pressed in the courts and in negotiations among local leaders, and not in the streets." King responded with a justification for civil disobedience, writing that everyone had an obligation to follow just laws but an equal obligation to break unjust laws.

King also laid out the four steps of nonviolent campaigns: (1) collection of the facts to determine whether injustices are alive; (2) negotiation with white leaders to change the injustices; (3) self-purification, which involved training to make sure that the civil rights protesters would be able to endure the abuse that they would receive; and (4) direct action (for example, sit-ins and marches) to create the environment in which change could occur, but always in a nonviolent manner. By following these steps, civil rights protesters ensured that their social movement would draw attention to their cause while turning public opinion against their opponents' violent tactics.

Following King's release from jail, the situation escalated. The protest leaders decided to use children in the next round of demonstrations. After more than 1,000 children were arrested and the jails were overflowing, the police turned fire hoses and police dogs on children who were trying to continue their march. Media coverage of the incident turned the tide of public opinion in favor of the marchers as the country expressed outrage over the violence in Birmingham. Similar protests occurred throughout the South, with more than 1,000 actions in over 100 different southern cities and more than 20,000 people arrested throughout the summer. The demonstration culminated in August 1963, when 250,000 people participated in the March on

Washington. King delivered his famous "I Have a Dream" speech and civil rights leaders pressured congressional leaders to pass civil rights legislation.

Protest Today After King's and others' nonviolent protests produced significant successes, mass protest became the preferred tool of many other social movements for civil rights and other causes. Vietnam War protesters marched on Washington by the hundreds of thousands in the late 1960s and early 1970s. The women's rights, gay rights, and environmental movements have staged many mass demonstrations in Washington and other major cities.

Most recently, large-scale demonstrations against Wall Street and international organizations, such as the International Monetary Fund and the World Trade Organization, have swept the nation. The Occupy Wall Street movement, which started in September 2011, spread to more than 1,500 cities in 82 nations. Rooted in the nonviolent protests of the civil rights era, protesters occupied public spaces to make their views known. The Occupy movement's slogan, "We are the 99%," drew attention to income inequality and helped set the tone for the 2012 presidential election. Conservative activists, such as those in the pro-life movement, have also used nonviolent protests, sit-ins, and mass demonstrations. Protests against President Obama's policies early in 2009 evolved into the Tea Party movement (evoking the Boston Tea Party of the American Revolution). Rooted in opposition to high taxes and activist government, the Tea Party movement organized protests on Tax Day (April 15, 2009) that drew more than 300,000 people in 346 cities.[47] The legacy of the civil rights movement has been not only to help change unjust laws but also to provide a new tool for political action across a broad range of policy areas.

This tool has evolved in the most recent period to combine the power of social media and mass protest. #BlackLivesMatter started in 2013 on social media, but expanded in 2014–2016 to organize mass protests against police killings in many cities across the country.

The courts

The Supreme Court has played an important role in defining civil rights. In the mid-twentieth century, the justices moved away from the "separate but equal" doctrine, required the desegregation of public schools, and upheld landmark civil rights legislation passed by Congress. More recently, they have expanded civil rights for women and the LGBTQ community, but they also have endorsed a color-blind position that some see as a movement away from protecting civil rights.

Challenging "Separate but Equal" in Education In the 1930s, the NAACP, which was established to fight for equal rights for black people, started a concerted effort to nibble away at the "separate but equal" doctrine. Rather than tackling segregation head-on, the NAACP challenged an aspect of segregation that would be familiar to the Supreme Court justices: the ways in which states kept blacks out of all-white law schools. Another strategy was to challenge admission practices in law schools outside the Deep South to demonstrate that segregation was not just a "southern problem" and to raise the chances for compliance with favorable Court decisions. A young NAACP attorney named Thurgood Marshall (who later became the first African-American Supreme Court justice) argued that the University of Maryland's practice of sending black students to out-of-state law schools rather than admitting them to the university's all-white law school violated the black students' civil rights. (The state gave black students a $200 scholarship, which did not cover the costs of

Busing students from one school district to another in the interest of desegregation has been controversial since the 1960s. In 2007, the Supreme Court invalidated voluntary desegregation plans in Louisville and Seattle school districts.

tuition and travel and was not available to all black students who wanted to attend law school.) The circuit court and subsequently the Maryland appeals court in 1936 rejected this arrangement and ordered that black students be admitted to the University of Maryland law school.[48]

Over the next 15 years, a series of successful lawsuits slowly chipped away at the idea of "separate but equal." After these victories, there was a debate within the NAACP whether to continue the case-by-case approach against the "separate but equal" doctrine or to directly challenge the principle itself. The latter approach was risky because it was unclear if the Court was ready to take this bold step and because defeat in the Court would set back the movement. However, the signals increasingly indicated that the Supreme Court was ready to strike down the "separate but equal" doctrine. In addition to the law school cases, in 1948 the Court ruled that "restrictive covenants"—clauses in real estate contracts that prevented a property owner from selling to an African American—could not be enforced by state or local courts because of the Fourteenth Amendment's prohibition against a state denying blacks the "equal protection of the laws."

This application of the Fourteenth Amendment was expanded in the landmark ruling *Brown v. Board of Education*. The case arrived on the Court's docket in 1951, was postponed for argument until after the 1952 election, and then was re-argued in December 1953. The ruling was postponed for so long because the Court was keenly aware of the firestorm that would ensue. In its unanimous decision, the Court ruled: "In the field of public education, the doctrine of separate but equal has no place. Separate educational facilities are inherently unequal, depriving the plaintiffs of the equal protection of the laws. Segregated facilities may generate in black children a feeling of inferiority that may affect their hearts and minds in a way unlikely ever to be undone."[49] The case was significant not only because it required all public schools in the United States to desegregate but also because it used the equal protection clause of the Fourteenth Amendment in a way that had potentially far-reaching consequences.

Nonetheless, the decision was limited by focusing on segregation in schools rather than segregation more generally and by focusing on the psychological damage done to black schoolchildren because of segregation rather than on the broader claim that racial classification itself was not allowed by the Constitution. Chief Justice Earl Warren wanted a unanimous vote and knew that two justices would not support a broader ruling that would overturn *Plessy v. Ferguson* and rule segregation unconstitutional in all contexts. Even if segregation in other public places still was legal, the *Brown* ruling provided an important boost to the civil rights movement.

The Push to Desegregate Schools In 1955, *Brown v. Board of Education II* addressed the implementation of desegregation and required the states to "desegregate with all deliberate speed."[50] The odd choice of words, "all deliberate speed," was read as a signal by southerners that they could take their time with desegregation. The phrase does seem to be contradictory: being deliberate does not usually involve being speedy. Southern states engaged in "massive resistance" to the desegregation order, as articulated by Harry F. Byrd, the segregationist senator from Virginia. In some cases, they even closed public schools rather than integrate them—and then reopened the schools as "private" segregated schools for which the white students received government vouchers. However, Maryland, Kentucky, Tennessee, Missouri, and the District of Columbia desegregated their schools within two years.

Eight years after *Brown I*, little had changed in the Deep South: fewer than 1 percent of black children attended school with white children.[51] Through the 1960s, the courts had to battle against continued resistance to integrate. In 1971, the Court shifted its focus from **de jure** segregation (segregation mandated by law) to **de facto** segregation (segregation that existed because of segregated housing patterns) and approved school busing as a tool to integrate schools.[52] This approach was extremely controversial. The Court almost immediately limited the application of busing by ruling in a Detroit case that busing could not go beyond the boundaries of a city's school district—that is, students did not have to be bused from suburbs to cities unless it could be shown that the school district's lines were drawn in an intentionally discriminatory way.[53] This rule encouraged "white flight" from the cities to the suburbs in response to court-ordered busing.

In 2007, in perhaps the most important decision on race in education since *Brown*, the Court invalidated voluntary desegregation plans implemented by public school districts in Seattle and Louisville. Both districts set goals for racial diversity and denied assignment requests if they tipped the racial balance above or below certain thresholds. In a ringing endorsement of the color-blind approach, the majority opinion said: "The way to stop discrimination on the basis of race is to stop discriminating on the basis of race." In this case, the discrimination was against white students who wanted to be in schools with few minority students, rather than black students who wanted to be in integrated schools.[54]

Expanding Civil Rights Other significant rulings in the 1960s struck down state laws that forbade interracial marriages (16 states had such laws), upheld all significant parts of the Civil Rights Act, and upheld and expanded the scope of the Voting Rights Act (VRA). In central cases, the justices ruled that Congress had the power to eliminate segregation in public places, such as restaurants and hotels, under the commerce clause of the Constitution.

The first case involved a hotel in Atlanta that was close to an interstate highway, advertised extensively on the highway, and had a clientele that was about 75 percent from out of state. The Court ruled that this establishment was clearly engaging in interstate commerce, so Congress had the right to regulate it.[55] In the second case, "almost all, if not all," of the patrons of Ollie's Barbecue in Birmingham, Alabama, were local. However, the Court pointed out that meat purchased for the restaurant came from out of state and this constituted 46 percent of the total amount spent on supplies. Therefore, the practice of segregation would place significant burdens on "the interstate flow of food and upon the movement of products generally."[56]

The next important area of cases was in employment law. In 1971, the Court ruled that employment tests, such as written exams or general aptitude tests, that are not related to job performance and that discriminate against blacks violate the 1964 Civil Rights Act.[57] This **disparate impact standard** of discrimination meant that if the employment practice had a bad *effect* on a racial group it didn't matter whether

de jure
Relating to actions or circumstances that occur "by law," such as the legally enforced segregation of schools in the American South before the 1960s.

de facto
Relating to actions or circumstances that occur outside the law or "by fact," such as the segregation of schools that resulted from housing patterns and other factors rather than from laws.

DID YOU KNOW?

75%

of African-American students and 79 percent of Latino students attend schools that are majority minority.
Source: *U.S. News & World Report*

disparate impact standard
The idea that discrimination exists if a practice has a negative effect on a specific group, whether or not this effect was intentional.

Race-Related Discrimination as Defined by the Equal Employment Opportunity Commission

Race/Color Discrimination

Race discrimination involves treating someone (an applicant or employee) unfavorably because he/she is of a certain race or because of personal characteristics associated with race (such as hair texture, skin color, or certain facial features). Color discrimination involves treating someone unfavorably because of skin color complexion. . . . Discrimination can occur when the victim and the person who inflicted the discrimination are the same race or color.

Race/Color Discrimination and Work Situations

The law forbids discrimination when it comes to any aspect of employment, including hiring, firing, pay, job assignments, promotions, layoff, training, fringe benefits, and any other term or condition of employment.

Race/Color Discrimination and Harassment

It is unlawful to harass a person because of that person's race or color. Harassment can include, for example, racial slurs, offensive or derogatory remarks about a person's race or color, or the display of racially offensive symbols. Although the law doesn't prohibit simple teasing, offhand comments, or isolated incidents that are not very serious, harassment is illegal when it is so frequent or severe that it creates a hostile or offensive work environment or when it results in an adverse employment decision (such as the victim being fired or demoted). The harasser can be the victim's supervisor, a supervisor in another area, a coworker, or someone who is not an employee of the employer, such as a client or customer.

Race/Color Discrimination and Employment Policies/Practices

An employment policy or practice that applies to everyone, regardless of race or color, can be illegal if it has a negative impact on the employment of people of a particular race or color and is not job-related and necessary to the operation of the business.

Source: U.S. Equal Employment Opportunity Commission, "Race/Color Discrimination," www.eeoc.gov (accessed 10/4/12).

or not the discrimination was *intended*. The Supreme Court and Congress have gone back and forth in defining this concept, but it is still important in workplace discrimination suits. (See Nuts & Bolts 5.1 for the legal definition of race-based workplace discrimination.)

The Color-Blind Court and Judicial Activism Recently, the Supreme Court has been gradually imposing a "color-blind jurisprudence" over a range of issues. One significant area was the 1992 racial redistricting in which 15 new U.S. House districts were drawn to help elect African Americans and 10 new districts were drawn to help elect Latino members. The resulting dramatic change in the number of minorities in Congress (an increase greater than 50 percent) was rooted in the 1982 amendments to the VRA. Instead of mandating a fair *process*, this law and subsequent interpretation by the Supreme Court mandated that minorities be able to "elect representatives of their choice" when their numbers and configuration permit. As a result, the legislative redistricting process now had to avoid discriminatory *results* rather than being concerned only with discriminatory *intent*.

However, in a series of decisions starting with the 1993 landmark case *Shaw v. Reno*, the Supreme Court's adherence to a color-blind jurisprudence has thrown the constitutionality of black-majority districts into doubt. The Court has ruled that black-majority districts are legal as long as they are "done right,"[58] but it has consistently held that if race is the predominant factor in drawing district lines the districts are unconstitutional because they violate the equal protection clause of the Fourteenth Amendment. Based on this reasoning, black-majority districts in North Carolina, Georgia, Louisiana, Virginia, Texas, and Florida were found to be unconstitutional. In the most recent case, in 2001, the Court upheld the re-drawn 12th District in North Carolina, which no longer was a black-majority district, arguing that when race and partisanship are so intertwined—as they are when 90 percent of African Americans vote for a Democratic candidate—plaintiffs cannot assume that African Americans were placed together for racial reasons. This ruling opens the door for a greater consideration of race than had been allowed in the previous cases. However, racial redistricting remains an unsettled area of the law.[59]

The Court also struck down an important part of the 1965 VRA in a 2013 ruling. This case concerned the "coverage formula" that determines which states have to get approval from the Justice Department before implementing changes in an election law or practice (such as redistricting or moving the location of a polling place). This "preclearance" provision of the law was viewed as one of the best ways to stop discriminatory voting practices because it could prevent them before they were implemented, rather than having to wait until they went into effect. The Court ruled that the coverage formula was an unconstitutional burden on the covered states and was a violation of the Tenth Amendment.[60]

The racial redistricting and voting rights cases illustrate that the Supreme Court is increasingly activist in civil rights. It is generally unwilling to defer to any other branch of government that disagrees with its view of discrimination and equal protection (see Chapter 14 for a discussion of judicial activism). In some periods, judicial activism may serve to further civil rights, as in the 1950s and 1960s, or to limit them, as in the recent period.

Women's Rights The Supreme Court has also been central in shaping women's civil rights. Until relatively recently, the Court did not apply the Constitution to women, despite the Fourteenth Amendment's language that states may not deny any *person* the equal protection of the laws. Apparently, women were not regarded as people when it came to political and economic rights in the nineteenth and early twentieth centuries. These protectionist notions were finally rejected in three cases between 1971 and 1976, when the Court made it much more difficult for states to treat men and women differently.

The first case involved an Idaho state law that gave a man priority over a woman when they were otherwise equally entitled to execute a person's estate. This law was justified on the "reasonable" grounds that it reduced the state courts' workload by having an automatic rule that would limit challenges. But the Court ruled that the law was arbitrary, did not meet the "reasonableness" test, and therefore violated the woman's equal protection rights under the Fourteenth Amendment.[61] The second case involved a female air force officer who wanted to count her husband as a dependent for purposes of health and housing benefits. Under the law at the time, a military man could automatically count his wife as a dependent, but a woman could claim her husband only if she brought in more than half the family income. The Court struck down this practice, saying protectionist laws, "in practical effect, put women not on a pedestal, but in a cage."[62]

These two cases relied on the rational basis test for discrimination between men and women. Along with the strict scrutiny test (see Chapter 4), it allowed the Fourteenth Amendment to be applied differently to particular categories of people. Under the rational basis test, states could discriminate against a group of people as long as

rational basis test
The use of evidence to suggest that differences in the behavior of two groups can rationalize unequal treatment of these groups.

there was a "rational basis" for that state law. Today, for example, states can pass drinking laws that only allow those who are 21 and older to drink on the grounds that traffic fatalities will be lower with that drinking age rather than a law that allows 18-year-olds to drink.

The strict scrutiny test gave racial minorities the strongest protection as the "suspect classification" under the Fourteenth Amendment. This test stipulated that there must be a "compelling state interest" to discriminate among people if race is involved. The suspect classification was first used in a case involving the internment of Japanese Americans during World War II. It is one of the few instances in which racial classification has survived strict scrutiny. In a controversial ruling, the Court said that the internment camps were justified on national security grounds.[63]

In 1976, the Court established a third test, the intermediate scrutiny test (see Chapter 4), in a case involving the drinking age. In the early 1970s, some states had a lower drinking age for women than for men on the "rational basis" that 18- to 20-year-old women are more mature than men of that age (states argued that women were less likely to be drunk drivers and less likely to abuse alcohol than men). The new intermediate scrutiny standard meant that the government's policy must be "substantially related" to an "important government objective" to justify the unequal treatment of men and women, so the law was struck down.[64]

The intermediate scrutiny test gives women stronger protections than the reasonable basis test, but it is not as strong as strict scrutiny (see How It Works: Civil Rights). To use the legal jargon, the gender distinction would have to serve an "important government objective," but not a "compelling state interest," in order to withstand intermediate scrutiny.

In many instances, as with the Idaho case, the rights of women were strengthened by the new standard of equal protection. However, in other instances women may actually be more restricted by being treated the same as men. For example, in the drinking age case, instead of dropping the drinking age for men to 18, states raised the age for women to 21. Similarly, the Court struck down an Alabama divorce law in which husbands but not wives could be ordered to pay alimony.[65] Arguably, women would have been better off in these two specific instances under the old discriminatory laws (because they could drink at 18 instead of 21 and did not have to pay alimony in some states). However, the more aggressive application of the Fourteenth Amendment for women was an important step in providing them with the equal protection of the laws, as clearly shown in a Court decision that struck down the Virginia Military Institute's (VMI's) male-only admission policy. The majority opinion stated that VMI violated the Fourteenth Amendment's equal protection clause because it failed to show an "exceedingly persuasive justification" for its sex-biased admissions policy.[66]

Two other areas where the Supreme Court helped advance women's rights were affirmative action and protection against sexual harassment. In 1987, the Court approved affirmative action in a case involving a woman who was promoted over a man despite the fact that he had scored slightly higher than she did on a test. The Court ruled that this was acceptable to make up for past discrimination.[67] And in 1993 the Court made it easier to sue employers for sexual harassment, saying that a woman did not have to reach the point of a nervous breakdown before claiming that she was being harassed; it was enough to demonstrate a pattern of "repeated and unwanted" behavior that created a "hostile workplace environment."[68] Later rulings stated that if a single act is flagrant the conduct did not have to be repeated to create a hostile environment.

More recently, Lilly Ledbetter sued Goodyear Tire & Rubber Company because she had received lower pay than men doing the same work over a 20-year period, which she claimed was gender discrimination. However, the Court rejected her claim, saying that she did not meet the time limit required by the law, as the discrimination must

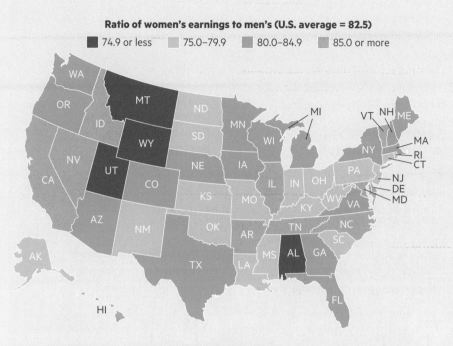

Ratio of women's earnings to men's (U.S. average = 82.5)

74.9 or less   75.0–79.9   80.0–84.9   85.0 or more

Sources: Data from "Highlight of Women's Earnings in 2014," *BLA Reports*, U.S. Bureau of Labor Statistics, November 2015, Table 3, p.26, www.bls.gov (accessed 1/29/16); map taken from U.S. Bureau of Labor Statistics, "Women's Earnings in Texas—2014," Chart 3 (accessed 1/29/16).

FIGURE 5.5

Women's Earnings as a Percentage of Men's Earnings, 2014

There is a substantial difference between women's and men's earnings in the United States. What could account for this variation? How much do you think it has to do with levels of discrimination and how much with differences in the nature of the jobs that men and women hold?

have occurred within 180 days of the claim (this overturned the long-standing policy of the EEOC, which held that each new paycheck restarted the 180-day clock as a new act of discrimination).[69] Dissenters pointed out that pay discrimination usually occurs in small increments over long periods, so it would be impossible to recognize unequal pay within 180 days of an initial paycheck. Furthermore, workers do not have access to information about fellow workers' pay, so it would be almost impossible to meet the standard set by the Court. Congress restored the old standard in January 2009 by passing the Lilly Ledbetter Fair Pay Act. But as Figure 5.5 shows, significant pay disparities between men and women remain throughout much of the United States. Early in 2016, President Obama issued an executive order requiring companies to report to the federal government what they pay employees by race, gender, and ethnicity. He said, "Women are not getting the fair shot that we believe every single American deserves."[70]

The largest sexual discrimination lawsuit in the nation's history was filed in 2001 against Walmart on behalf of 1.5 million women who had worked at Walmart since 1998. Among other things, the plaintiffs alleged the following:

- Over objections from a female executive, senior management regularly referred to female store employees as "little Janie Qs" and "girls."
- A Sam's Club (Walmart's warehouse retail chain) manager in California told another woman that she should "doll up" to get promoted.
- Managers have repeatedly told female employees that men "need to be paid more than women because they have families to support."
- A male manager in South Carolina told a female employee that "God made Adam first, so women would always be second to men."
- A female personnel manager in Florida was told by her manager that men were paid more than women because "men are here to make a career and women aren't. Retail is for housewives who just need to earn extra money."[71]

Civil Rights

**Cases Involving
"Suspect Classification"**
(race, ethnicity, creed,
or national origin)

Strict Scrutiny Test

1. Is unequal treatment
justified by a **"compelling
state interest"**?

yes **no**

↓

**discrimination
is illegal**

↓

2. Is unequal treatment
the **"least restrictive"** option?

yes **no**

↓

**discrimination
is illegal**

Very few cases meet
this standard.

**Cases Involving Sex
or Gender Equality**

Intermediate
Scrutiny Test

1. Is the discriminatory policy
"substantially related" to an
"important government objective"?

yes **no**

↓

**discrimination
is illegal**

↓

2. Is the discrimination
not substantially broader than
it needs to be to protect the important
government interest?

yes **no**

↓

**discrimination
is illegal**

Some discrimination based
on gender is permitted, but
this test is harder to pass
than the rational basis test
applied to gender cases in
the past.

**Cases Involving Age,
Economic Status,
or Other Criteria**

Rational
Basis Test

1. Is the law **rationally related
to furthering** a legitimate
government interest?

yes **no**

↓

**discrimination
is illegal**

↓

2. Does the policy avoid
**"arbitrary, capricious, or
deliberate"** discrimination?

yes **no**

↓

**discrimination
is illegal**

This is the easiest hurdle
for a law or policy to pass.

→ **discrimination
is legal** ←

Evaluating Discrimination Cases

Strict Scrutiny Test

Intermediate Scrutiny Test

Rational Basis Test

Case 1:

The University of Michigan Law School's "holistic" race-conscious admissions policy is designed to promote diversity.

Case 2:

The University of Michigan's more rigid race-conscious undergraduate admissions policy was designed to promote diversity.

Case 1:

A California state law says that men—but not women—can be guilty of statutory rape.

Case 2:

The Virginia Military Institute maintained a male-only admissions policy.

Case 1:

States have a 21-year-old drinking age that applies equally to men and women.

Case 2:

An Oklahoma law allowed 18- to 20-year-old women—but not men—to buy 3.2% beer.

The Court asked...

1. Is unequal treatment justified by a "compelling state interest"?
2. Is unequal treatment the "least restrictive" option?

The Court asked...

1. Is the discriminatory policy "substantially related" to an "important government objective"?
2. Is the discrimination not substantially broader than it needs to be to to protect the important government interest?

The Court asked...

1. Is the law rationally related to furthering a legitimate government interest?
2. Does the policy avoid "arbitrary, capricious, or deliberate" discrimination?

The Court said...

In Case 1, discrimination is OK. In *Grutter v. Bollinger* (2003), the Court ruled that the state's interest in **racial diversity in higher education was compelling,** and that this specific admissions policy was narrowly tailored. This was affirmed in *Fisher v. Univ. of Texas* (2016).

In Case 2, discrimination is not OK. In *Gratz v. Bollinger* (2003), the Court **struck down Michigan's undergraduate admissions policy** for not being narrowly tailored.

The Court said...

In Case 1, discrimination is OK. In *Michael M. v. Superior Court* (1981), the Court found that the state had a **strong interest in preventing illegitimate pregnancy** and in punishing only the participant who, by nature, suffers few of the consequences of his conduct.

In Case 2, discrimination is not OK. In *United States v. Virginia* (1996), the Court **struck down the Virginia Military Institute's policy** as a violation of the equal protection clause of the Fourteenth Amendment.

The Court said...

In Case 1, discrimination is OK. Various state supreme courts have upheld these laws on the rational basis that **the laws may prevent drunk driving among 18- to 20-year-olds.**

In Case 2, discrimination is not OK. In *Craig v. Boren* (1976), the Court **struck down this law,** rejecting the rational basis that Oklahoma had claimed and instead applying intermediate scrutiny.

❓ Critical Thinking

1. **Is it easier for the government to discriminate against** someone based on age or race? Why?

2. **What is the standard used by the Court if the state wants** to make distinctions between people based on race? Under what circumstances and in what scenarios is discrimination based on race legal?

Demonstrators rallied in support of the female workers who had filed a sexual discrimination lawsuit against Walmart. Betty Dukes (the lead plaintiff in the case) and a class of 1.6 million women who worked for Walmart filed a class-action suit against Walmart, claiming that Walmart paid men more than women and favored men over women when deciding on promotions. In 2011, the Supreme Court ruled in favor of Walmart, saying that women would have to prove discrimination individually rather than in a class-action lawsuit.

But in 2011 the Court ruled that the class-action lawsuit was not valid because there was no "convincing proof of a companywide discriminatory pay and promotion policy." That is, women would have to prove discrimination individually, not as a group. Civil rights experts said this was the "death knell" for class-action lawsuits seeking monetary damages for discrimination.[72]

Gay Rights The Supreme Court has a similarly mixed record on gay rights. The Court's decisions in early cases were not supportive of gay rights. One of the first cases concerned Georgia's law banning sodomy. As we have discussed in Chapter 4, the Supreme Court ruled in *Bowers v. Hardwick* (1986) that homosexual behavior was not protected by the Constitution and that state laws banning it could be justified under the most lenient rational basis test.[73]

After cases where it sidestepped the issue, the Court first endorsed civil rights for gays in 1996. Here the Court struck down an amendment to the Colorado state constitution that would have prevented gays from suing for discrimination in employment or housing. The Court said that the state amendment violated gays' equal protection rights because it "withdrew from homosexuals, but no others, specific legal protection from the injuries caused by discrimination."[74] The Court rejected the state's "reasonable basis" arguments and came close to putting gays in the "suspect classification" that has been restricted to racial and ethnic minorities.

An important ruling came in 2003 in a case involving two Houston men. As we have discussed in Chapter 4, John Geddes Lawrence and Tyron Garner were prosecuted for same-sex sodomy (which was illegal in Texas) after police found them having sex in Lawrence's apartment. The Supreme Court ruled in a historic 6–3 decision that the due process clause of the Fourteenth Amendment guarantees freedom of not only thought, belief, and expression but also certain intimate conduct (including homosexual relations). This reasoning is rooted in the substantive due process doctrine that underlies constitutional protections for birth control, abortion, and decisions about how to raise one's children.

The decision overturned *Bowers v. Hardwick*, and the majority opinion had harsh words for that decision, saying it "was not correct when it was decided, and it is not correct today." Five members of the majority signed on to the broad "due process"

substantive due process doctrine
One interpretation of the due process clause of the Fourteenth Amendment; in this view the Supreme Court has the power to overturn laws that infringe on individual liberties.

reasoning of the decision, rather than the narrower reasoning in Justice O'Connor's concurring opinion, in which she said that the decision should apply only to the four states that treated gays differently (that is, banning sodomy for homosexuals but not for heterosexuals). With the broader due process logic, a total of 13 state laws that banned sodomy were struck down. Justice Scalia wrote a strong dissent, saying that the decision was "the product of a court that has largely signed on to the so-called homosexual agenda" and warned that the ruling "will have far-reaching implications beyond this case." He predicted that the ruling would serve as the basis for constitutional protections for same-sex marriage.[75]

The Supreme Court issued two important rulings on same-sex marriage in 2013. The first case was a narrow ruling that reinstated same-sex marriage in California but did not affect any other state. The second case was a more far-reaching decision that struck down part of the Defense of Marriage Act (DOMA) as a violation of the Fifth Amendment's due process clause. The majority opinion said that the federal government cannot deny benefits to same-sex couples who are legally married under state law. The gradual movement toward endorsing same-sex marriage culminated in 2015 in the landmark ruling *Obergefell v. Hodges*, which legalized same-sex marriage in all 50 states.[76] (For more on the Supreme Court's ruling in this case, see How It Works: The Court System in Chapter 14.) The 5-4 ruling said that the fundamental right to marry is guaranteed by both the due process clause and the equal protection clause of the Fourteenth Amendment.

This section demonstrates that the courts can be both a strong advocate of and an impediment to civil rights. In general, however, the courts have a limited *independent* impact on policy. That is, as the school desegregation cases clearly demonstrate, the courts must rely on the other branches of government to carry out their decisions.

Congress

Congress has provided the basis for today's protection of civil rights through a series of laws that were enacted starting in the 1960s. Applying to racial and ethnic minorities and to women, these laws attempted to ensure that there is a "level playing field" of equal opportunity.

Key Early Legislation The bedrock of equal protection that exists today stems from landmark legislation passed by Congress in the 1960s—the 1964 Civil Rights Act, the 1965 VRA, and the 1968 Fair Housing Act. President Kennedy was slow to seek civil rights legislation for fear of alienating southern Democrats. The events in Birmingham prompted him to act, but he was assassinated before the legislation was passed. President Lyndon Johnson, a former segregationist, helped push through the Civil Rights Act when he became president. The act barred discrimination in employment based on race, sex, religion, or national origin; banned segregation in public places; and established the EEOC as the enforcement agency for the legislation. One of the southern opponents of the legislation inserted the language referring to sex, thinking that it would defeat the bill (assuming, perhaps, that there would be a majority coalition of male chauvinists and segregationists), but it became law anyway.

The VRA of 1965 eliminated direct obstacles to minority voting in the South, such as discriminatory literacy tests and other voter registration tests, and also provided the means to enforce the law: federal marshals were charged with overseeing elections in the South. After its passage, President Johnson hailed the VRA as a "triumph for

DID YOU KNOW?

66.2%

of African Americans voted in 2012 compared with 64.1 percent of whites (but African-American turnout was slightly lower than whites' turnout in 2016).
Source: Pew Research Center

freedom as huge as any ever won on any battlefield."[77] The VRA, which is often cited as one of the most significant pieces of civil rights legislation in our nation's history,[78] precipitated an explosion in black political participation in the South. The most dramatic gains came in Mississippi, where black registration increased from 6.7 percent before the VRA to 59.8 percent in 1967. As one political scientist noted, "The act simply overwhelmed the major bulwarks of the disenfranchising system. In the seven states originally covered, black registration increased from 29.3 percent in March 1965, to 56.6 percent in 1971–1972; the gap between black and white registration rates narrowed from 44.1 percentage points to 11.2."[79]

The last piece of landmark legislation, the Fair Housing Act of 1968, barred discrimination in the rental or sale of a home based on race, sex, religion, and national origin. Important amendments to the law enacted in 1988 added disability and familial status (having children under age 18), provided new administrative enforcement mechanisms, and expanded Justice Department jurisdiction to bring suit on behalf of victims in federal district courts.[80]

There have been many other amendments to civil rights laws since the 1960s. Most important were the 1975 amendments to the VRA that extended coverage of many of the law's provisions to language minorities (that is, guaranteeing that registration and voting materials would be made available to voters in their native language in certain districts with large numbers of citizens who are not proficient in English); the 1982 VRA amendments, which extended important provisions of the law for 25 years and made it easier to bring a lawsuit under the act; the 1991 Civil Rights Act; and the 2006 extension of the VRA for another 25 years. The 1991 law overruled or altered parts of 12 Supreme Court decisions that had eroded the intent of Congress when it passed the civil rights legislation. It expanded earlier legislation and increased the costs to employers for intentional, illegal discrimination.

Protections for Women Women have also received extensive protection through legislation. As noted, Title VII of the Civil Rights Act, which barred discrimination based on gender, was almost an accidental part of the bill (it was included by an opponent to the legislation). Indeed, the first executive director of the EEOC would not enforce the gender part of the law because it was a "fluke." In 1966, the National Organization for Women (NOW) was formed to push for enforcement of the law. Its members convinced President Johnson to sign an executive order that eliminated sex discrimination in federal agencies and among federal contractors, but the order was difficult to enforce. Finally, in 1970, the EEOC started enforcing the law. Before long, one-third of all civil rights cases involved sex discrimination, and those numbers have remained high in recent years (see Figure 5.6).

Congress passed the next piece of important legislation for women in 1972: Title IX of the Education Amendments, which prohibits sex discrimination in institutions that receive federal funds. The law has had the greatest impact in women's sports. In the 1960s and 1970s, opportunities for women to play sports in college or high school were extremely limited. Very few women's scholarships were available at the college level, and budgets for women's sports were tiny compared with the budgets for men's sports. Although it took nearly 30 years to reach parity between men and women, most universities are now in compliance with Title IX. Nonetheless, the law has its critics. Many men's sports, such as baseball, tennis, wrestling, and gymnastics, were cut at universities that had to bring the number of male and female student athletes into rough parity. Critics argued that such cuts were unfair, especially given that the interest in women's sports was not as high. Defenders of the law argue that the gap in interest in women's and men's sports will not change until there is equal opportunity. There is some evidence to support that claim, as interest is increasing in professional women's

soccer with the NWSL (National Women's Soccer League) and professional women's basketball with the WNBA (Women's National Basketball Association), as well as in well-established women's professional sports such as golf and tennis.

Another significant effort during this period was the failed Equal Rights Amendment. The amendment was approved by Congress in 1972 and was sent to the states for ratification. Its wording was simple: "Equality of rights under the law shall not be denied or abridged by the United States or any state on account of sex." Many states passed it within months, but the process lost momentum and after seven years (the deadline set by Congress for ratification by the states) the amendment fell three states short of the required 38 states required for adoption. The amendment received a three-year extension from Congress, but it still did not get the additional three states.

In 1994, Congress passed the Violence against Women Act, which allowed women who were the victims of physical abuse and violence to sue in federal court and provided funding for investigating and prosecuting violent crimes against women, for helping the victims of such crimes, and for prevention programs. In 2000, part of the law was overturned by the Supreme Court, which ruled that Congress had exceeded its powers under the commerce clause.[81] Nonetheless, the funding provisions of the act were reauthorized and expanded by Congress in 2000, 2005, and then 2013.

Protections for the Disabled and for Gay Rights Yet another important piece of civil rights legislation was the 1990 Americans with Disabilities Act, which provided strong federal protections for the 45 million disabled Americans to prevent workplace discrimination and to provide access to public facilities. This law produced curb cuts in sidewalks, access for wheelchairs on public buses and trains, special seating in sports stadiums, and many other changes that make the daily lives of the disabled a little easier and that provide them with an equal opportunity to participate more fully in society.[82]

Congress's track record in protecting gay rights has not been as strong. In fact, most of the steps taken by Congress have been to restrict rather than expand gay rights.

FIGURE
5.6

Discrimination Cases Filed with the Equal Employment Opportunity Commission, 2015

Discrimination based on race and color, and discrimination based on sex, are the two types most frequently reported, but there is a significant amount of discrimination based on age and disability as well. What types of discrimination do you think would be most likely to go unreported?

Note: Percentages do not sum to 100 because complaints may be filed in more than one category.

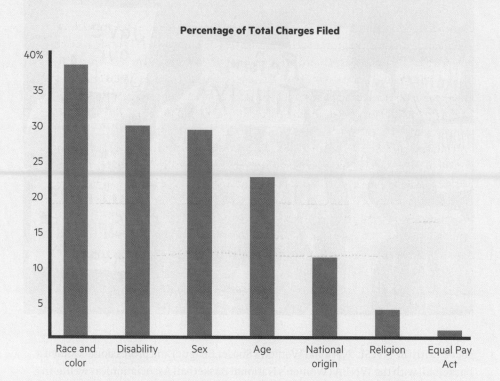

Percentage of Total Charges Filed

Source: U.S. Equal Employment Opportunity Commission, "Charge Statistics," http://eeoc.gov (accessed 3/9/16).

In 1996, Congress passed DOMA to avert the possibility that some liberal states such as Hawaii would allow gay marriage. This act defined marriage as only between a man and woman and barred couples in same-sex marriages from receiving federal insurance or Social Security spousal benefits and from filing joint federal tax returns. Nonetheless, as we have noted, the part of the law depriving same-sex spouses of federal benefits was struck down by the Supreme Court in 2013 and the entire law was overturned in 2015.

In what may represent a change of course, in October 2009 Congress passed the Matthew Shepard and James Byrd Jr. Hate Crimes Prevention Act. This legislation expanded the previous hate-crime laws based on race, color, religion, or national origin to include attacks based on a victim's sexual orientation, gender identity, or mental or physical disability. The law also lifted a requirement that a victim had to be attacked while engaged in a federally protected activity, such as attending school, for it to be a federal hate crime. In signing the bill, President Obama said, "After more than a decade of opposition and delay, we've passed inclusive hate-crimes legislation to help protect our citizens from violence based on what they look like, who they love, how they pray or who they are."[83] The law commemorates the horrific murders of James Byrd Jr., who in 1998 was dragged behind a pickup truck by white supremacists for three miles until his head and right arm were severed, and Matthew Shepard, a gay teenager who in 1998 was beaten by two men, tied to a fence, and left to die. Also, the Employment Non-Discrimination Act, which would prohibit discrimination in employment based on sexual orientation, has been proposed in nearly every Congress since 1994. A version of the bill passed the House in 2007 but died in the Senate.

The president

The civil rights movement has benefited greatly from presidential action, such as President Truman's integration of the armed services in 1948 and President Eisenhower's use of the National Guard to enforce a court order to integrate Central High School in Little Rock, Arkansas, in 1957. Executive orders by President Kennedy in 1961 and President Johnson in 1965 established affirmative action, and in 1969 Richard Nixon expanded the "goals and numerical ranges" for hiring minorities in the federal government.

The most significant unilateral action taken by a president in the area of civil rights for gays was President Clinton's effort to end the ban on gays in the military. Clinton was surprised by the strength of the opposition to his plan, so he ended up crafting a compromise policy of "don't ask, don't tell," which pleased no one. Under this policy, the military would stop actively searching for and discharging gays from the military ranks and recruits would not need to reveal their sexual orientation. But if the military did find out (without conducting an investigation) that a person was gay, he or she still could be disciplined or discharged.

You do not take a person who, for years, has been hobbled by chains and liberate him, bring him up to the starting line of a race and then say "you are free to compete with all the others," and still just believe that you have been completely fair.

—President Lyndon Johnson on affirmative action

The controversial "don't ask, don't tell" policy of the U.S. military had prevented gay men and lesbians from serving openly in the armed forces. Congress passed the Don't Ask, Don't Tell Repeal Act of 2010, which went into effect on September 20, 2011. Once gays and lesbians in the military did not have to hide their sexual affiliation, they were free to marry in states that permitted same-sex marriage. #DADT

During the 2008 campaign, President Obama promised to repeal "don't ask, don't tell." Several attempts to change the policy toward gays in the military were stopped by Republican filibusters in 2010, but Congress finally passed the Don't Ask, Don't Tell Repeal Act of 2010 in December and it went into effect on September 20, 2011. Minutes after the new policy was in place, navy lieutenant Gary Ross and his longtime partner were married in Vermont and Ross became the first openly gay married person in the military.[84]

The low priority that recent presidential candidates have given to civil rights policy more generally means that it is less likely that significant and dramatic change will come from unilateral action by the president. Instead, attention to civil rights concerns in the executive branch has primarily been in two areas since 1993: racial diversity in presidential appointments and use of the bully pulpit to promote racial concerns and interests.

President Obama had a diverse cabinet in terms of race and gender since the beginning of his presidency, exemplified by his first-term cabinet, shown here.

President Bill Clinton was active in both areas. In 1992, as a candidate, Clinton promised a government that "looks like America." His cabinet, subcabinet, and judicial appointments achieved the greatest gender and racial balance of any in history. Fourteen percent of Clinton's first-year presidential appointments were African American (compared with 12 percent of the country's population in 1992), 6 percent were Latino (compared with 9.5 percent of the country's population), and the percentages of Asian Americans and Native Americans who were appointed were identical to their proportions in the population. Clinton delivered an administration that "looked like us." And even though the proportion of women appointees—27 percent—was well short of the proportion of women in the population, it still was a record high. Clinton also used the bully pulpit to advocate a civil rights agenda. Most significant was his effort to promote a "National Conversation on Race," which helped focus national attention on many of the problems faced by minorities.

President George W. Bush did not achieve the same level of diversity in his appointments as had Clinton, but his administration was more diverse than the administrations of other Republican presidents had been. His initial 19 cabinet and cabinet-rank appointments included 15 men and 4 women, of whom 6 were members of racial minorities. The rhetoric that surrounded these appointments, however, was not couched in terms of affirmative action but rather merit. Critics argued that gender and race played a central role in these decisions, just as they had with Clinton, even if the rhetoric had a different tone. Despite the different approach, Bush made serious overtures to minorities, especially Latinos, in his effort to expand the Republican Party base.

While the long-term impact of the Obama presidency on the civil rights movement remains to be seen, the historical significance of his successful campaign as a minority candidate is clear. At the 2008 Democratic National Convention, some African-American delegates openly wept as Obama accepted the party's nomination. Many delegates had not expected that they would live to see an African American become a strong contender for the presidency. Obama's nominations for his cabinet and cabinet-level offices consisted of a diverse group of 14 men and 7 women, with 7 of them members of racial minorities. Eric Holder was the first African American to serve as attorney general, and Sonia Sotomayor is the first Latina on the Supreme Court.

💡

DID YOU KNOW?

Women working full time earn

$0.78

compared to every dollar earned by men.
Source: WhiteHouse.gov

Obama also nominated Elena Kagan to the Supreme Court, putting three women on the Court for the first time. Obama's second-term team was similar, consisting of 14 men and 8 women, 6 of them racial minorities.

In his first term, Obama tried to downplay race and diversity concerns. Indeed, some observers argue that Obama's presidency signaled the beginning of a "post-racial politics" that places less emphasis on race and devotes more attention to issues that concern all Americans, such as the economy, education, and health care. However, Obama himself rejects this view. In Obama's second term, he used the bully pulpit to draw more attention to women's issues, such as rape on college campuses and equal pay, used executive action on immigration policy to limit deportations of young adults who were brought to the United States as children, called attention to racial disparities in the criminal justice system, and was president when the Supreme Court recognized same-sex marriage as a fundamental right. Donald Trump was elected with racially divisive positions, such as building a wall with Mexico and deporting 12 million illegal residents. In his election night victory speech he emphasized the importance of representing all Americans and uniting the country. It will be interesting to watch how his administration deals with these seemingly divergent viewpoints.

Civil rights issues today

★

EXAMINE AFFIRMATIVE ACTION AND OTHER ONGOING CIVIL RIGHTS ISSUES

There is vigorous debate over the likely direction of the civil rights movement in the twenty-first century. There are three main perspectives. The first group, whose views are articulated by such scholars as Stephan Thernstrom of Harvard University and Abigail Thernstrom of the Manhattan Institute, has suggested that our nation must "move beyond race." This group argues that on many social and economic indicators the gap between blacks and whites has narrowed and that public opposition to race-based policies indicates the need for a new approach. The Supreme Court has largely endorsed this view by implementing a color-blind jurisprudence over a broad range of issues. The second group is represented by traditional civil rights activists and groups such as the Congressional Black Caucus and the NAACP; it argues that the civil rights movement must continue to fight for equal opportunity by enforcing existing law and pushing for equality of outcomes by protecting and expanding affirmative action programs and other policies that address racial inequality. These first two groups share the goal of racial equality and integration but differ on how much progress we have made and how to make further progress. A final group does not support the goal of integration; instead, activists such as Louis Farrakhan and the Nation of Islam argue for African-American self-sufficiency and separation. They believe that

African Americans can never gain equality within what they see as the repressive, white-dominated economic and political system.

Most civil rights advocates endorse the second view. They argue that it would be a mistake to conclude that the work of the civil rights movement is complete. They point to the resegregation of public schools, persistent gaps between whites and racial minorities in health and economic status, racial profiling, hate crimes, a backlash against immigrant groups, and continuing discrimination in employment and housing. At the same time, this group rejects calls for racial separation as shortsighted and self-defeating.

The other two groups would argue that although the traditional civil rights agenda made important contributions to racial equality, further progress will require a different approach. Advocates of the color-blind approach prefer to stop making distinctions between people based on race. They want to use government policies to make sure there is no overt discrimination and to provide equal opportunity for all, and then let merit decide outcomes. The segregationists have given up on the civil rights agenda and believe that minorities can achieve success only on their own. Debates among advocates of these three views play out over a broad range of issues, several of which are outlined in the last section of this chapter.

Affirmative action

The Civil Rights Act of 1964 ensured that, at least on paper, all Americans would enjoy equality of opportunity. But even after the act was passed, blacks continued to lag behind whites in socioeconomic status; there was still a substantial gap between the equality of opportunity and the equality of outcomes. In an important speech at Howard University in 1965, President Johnson outlined his argument for affirmative action, saying, "This is the next and the more profound stage of the battle for civil rights.... We seek not just legal equity but human ability, not just equality as a right and a theory but equality as a fact and equality as a result.... To this end equal opportunity is essential, but not enough, not enough."[85] Later that year, Johnson attempted to move closer to equality of outcomes by issuing an executive order requiring all federal agencies and government contractors to submit written proposals to provide an equal opportunity for employment of blacks, women, Asian Americans, and Native Americans within various job categories and to outline programs to achieve those goals. The policy was expanded under President Nixon, and throughout the 1970s and 1980s affirmative action programs grew in the private sector, higher education, and government contracting. Through such programs, employers and universities gave special opportunities to minorities and women, either to make up for past discrimination or to pursue the general goals of diversity.

Affirmative action takes many forms. The most passive type involves extra effort to recruit women and minorities for employment or college admission by placing ads in newspapers and magazines, visiting inner-city schools, or sending out targeted mailings. A more active form involves including race or gender as a "plus factor" in the admissions or hiring decisions. That is, from a pool of qualified candidates a minority applicant may receive an advantage over white applicants. (Women generally do not receive special consideration in admissions decisions, but gender may be a "plus factor" in some employment decisions; in fact, many selective schools have been quietly applying affirmative action for men because more highly qualified women apply than men.) The strongest form of affirmative action is the use of quotas—strict numerical targets to hire or admit a specific number of applicants from underrepresented groups.

Affirmative action has been a controversial policy. Polls indicate that minorities are much more supportive of the practice than are whites. Many whites view it as "preferential treatment" and "reverse discrimination." A majority of whites support passive forms of affirmative action, such as "education programs to assist minorities in competing for college admissions," but draw the line at preferences, even when they are intended to make up for past discrimination.[86] This backlash has spilled over into state politics. California passed Proposition 209 in 1996, which banned the consideration of "race, sex, color, ethnicity or national origin" in public employment, public education, or public contracting.[87] Voters have passed similar laws in nine other states.

The Supreme Court has helped define the boundaries of this policy debate. The earliest cases concerning affirmative action in employment upheld preferential treatment and rigid quotas when the policies were necessary to make up for past discrimination. The cases involved a worker training program that set aside 50 percent of the positions for blacks, a labor union that was required to hire enough minorities to get its nonwhite membership to 29.23 percent, and a state police force that was required to promote one black officer for every white even if there was a smaller pool of blacks who were eligible for promotion.[88] In each instance, there had been a previous pattern of discrimination and exclusion.

The Court moved in a more color-blind direction in an important reverse-discrimination employment case in 2009. In that case, 17 white firefighters and 1 Hispanic firefighter sued the city of New Haven, Connecticut, for throwing out the results of a test that would have been used to promote them. The city tried to ignore the results of the test because no African-American firefighters would have qualified for promotion and the city feared a "disparate impact" lawsuit. However, the Court ruled that the exam did appear to be "job related and consistent with business necessity" (as required by Section VII of the Civil Rights Act) and that unless the city could provide a "strong basis in evidence" that it would have been sued it had to consider the results of the exam.[89]

The landmark decision for affirmative action in higher education was *Regents of the University of California v. Bakke* (1978).[90] Allan Bakke, a white student, sued when he was denied admission to medical school at the University of California, Davis, in successive years. Bakke's test scores and GPA were significantly higher than those of some minority students who were admitted under the school's affirmative action program. Under that program, 16 of the 100 slots in the entering class were reserved for minority or disadvantaged students. The Supreme Court agreed with Bakke that rigid racial quotas were unconstitutional but allowed race to be used in admissions decisions as a "plus factor" to promote diversity in the student body. This standard was largely unquestioned until 1996, when the Fifth Circuit Court of Appeals held that it was unconstitutional to consider race in law school admissions at the University of Texas. In 2000, the Ninth Circuit Court of Appeals in Seattle, however, reached the opposite conclusion and ruled that race could be considered in admissions to promote educational diversity.[91]

In 2003, the Court affirmed *Bakke*, saying that the University of Michigan law school's "holistic approach" that considered race as one of the factors in the admission decision was acceptable but that the more rigid approach for undergraduate admissions at Michigan, which automatically gave minority students 20 of the 100 points needed to guarantee admission, was unacceptable.[92] This was the first time that a majority of the Court clearly stated that "student body diversity is a compelling state interest that can justify the use of race in university admissions."[93] In 2006, voters in Michigan passed Proposal 2, an initiative to make it illegal for state bodies to consider race in admissions and hiring decisions; this policy was upheld by the Supreme Court in 2014.[94] This means that states will be able to decide whether to consider affirmative

action in higher education because the policy is neither prohibited nor required by the Constitution.

In 2008, the University of Texas at Austin was sued by a white student who claimed she was a victim of reverse discrimination. Texas had achieved a racially diverse student body by giving admission to the top 10 percent of every graduating high school class (in recent years, this policy was changed to the top 7 percent). This approach worked since most high schools in Texas were still segregated. In 2013, the Court affirmed that diversity could be a legitimate goal for the state but that the appeals court that upheld the admissions policy had failed to apply the strict scrutiny standard. The case was therefore sent back to the appeals court, which upheld Texas's affirmative action policy in July 2014. In June 2016, the Court affirmed that decision by a 4–3 vote.[95] For more on affirmative action in college admissions, see the Take a Stand feature.

Multicultural issues

A host of issues involving the multicultural, multiracial nature of American society will become more important as whites cease to constitute the majority of the population by mid-century. Two key issues are English as the country's official language and immigration reform.

Decisions to establish English as the official language in many states have had wide-reaching consequences. For example, the Supreme Court upheld an Alabama state law requiring that the state driver's license test be conducted only in English. A Mexican emigrant, Martha Sandoval, sued under Title VI of the 1964 Civil Rights Act, claiming that the Alabama law had had a disparate impact on non-English-speaking residents. However, the Court held in *Alexander v. Sandoval* (2001) that individuals may not sue federally funded state agencies over policies that have a discriminatory

Affirmative Action in College Admissions

Since 1978, the Supreme Court has endorsed the idea of race as a "plus factor" in college admissions while rejecting the idea of strict quotas or point systems. This approach was affirmed in a 2003 case involving the University of Michigan's law school, but many Court-watchers believed that affirmative action would be struck down in the 2016 case *Fisher v. University of Texas, Austin*.[a] Instead, Justice Kennedy sided with the liberals and upheld the practice.

UT Austin's college admissions process has two parts. First, anyone in the top 10 percent of a Texas public high school is guaranteed admission to UT (in recent years this has been closer to the top 8 percent). Because most high schools in Texas are somewhat segregated by race, the 10 percent plan automatically creates diversity for the entering class. Second, the remaining 25 percent of in-state students are admitted by a "holistic" program that evaluates their entire record and includes race as a "plus factor." It was this second part that Abigail Fisher challenged after being denied admission to UT. The legal question that the Court had to decide was whether the university's affirmative action program violated the equal protection clause of the Fourteenth Amendment and civil rights laws barring discrimination on the basis of race or could it be justified as serving a "compelling state interest" under the strict scrutiny standard.

Diversity deserves consideration.

Advocates of affirmative action argue that a diverse student body promotes viewpoint diversity that is essential to learning. Having racial diversity in the student body is likely to produce more viewpoint diversity in classroom

Students protest outside the Supreme Court in support of diversity at the University of Texas.

discussions than would occur with a mostly white student body. The majority opinion in the Texas case also argued that a more diverse student body leads to "the destruction of stereotypes," promotes "cross-racial understanding," and prepares students "for an increasingly diverse work force and society." Furthermore, proponents argue, the courts are not the proper place to decide these issues. Instead, as with the complex and highly charged topic of racial redistricting, the political branches of government are where these decisions should be made. The Court endorsed this position of judicial restraint in a 2014 case involving a ban on affirmative action in Michigan.[b]

The Court argued that the Texas approach was "narrowly tailored" to serve the compelling state interest of viewpoint diversity because the 10 percent plan, by itself, did not produce the desired level of diversity and would create perverse incentives. Justice Kennedy wrote, "Percentage plans encourage parents to keep their children in low-performing segregated schools, and discourage students from taking challenging classes that might lower their grade point averages."

Affirmative action is just another kind of discrimination.

Opponents reply that supporters of affirmative action have not provided convincing evidence that racial diversity in colleges has any beneficial effects. They also argue that "viewpoint diversity" arguments assume that members of all racial minorities think alike, drawing a comparison to racial profiling in law enforcement. It is just as offensive, they say, that an admissions committee thinks that one black student has the same views as another black student as it is that a police officer may pull over a black teenage male just because he fits a certain criminal profile.

Opponents also argue that affirmative action amounts to "reverse discrimination" and that any racial classification is harmful. Justice Alito's scathing dissent in the Texas case said, "[. . .] U.T. has never provided any coherent explanation for its asserted need to discriminate on the basis of race, and [. . .] U.T.'s position relies on a series of unsupported and noxious racial assumptions." Alito also argued that concepts such as viewpoint diversity and "cross-cultural understanding" are "slippery" and difficult to analyze systematically.

The Texas case will not be the end of the debate concerning affirmative action in higher education. A pending suit challenges Harvard University's affirmative action program as discriminating against Asian Americans. If you had to rule on the Texas case, how would you have decided? Take a stand.

take a stand

1. To what extent should race be used as a "plus factor" to promote racial diversity and viewpoint diversity, if at all? Is the "top 10 percent" plan a better approach?

2. Think of your own experiences in high school and college. Has racial diversity contributed to viewpoint diversity?

effect on minorities under Title VI. This decision has had far-reaching consequences for the use of the Civil Rights Act to fight patterns of discrimination. Two areas that have been affected are education policy (for example, civil rights advocates have challenged the use of standardized testing because of its disparate impact on minorities) and environmental policy (lawsuits brought under Title VI have alleged "environmental racism" in decisions to place hazardous waste dumps in predominantly minority areas).

The second key issue, immigration, regained center stage in the wake of the September 11 terrorist attacks. At that time, some people saw immigration as a threat that must be curtailed. The government made it clear that it would not engage in racial profiling of Arab Americans—for example, subjecting them to stricter screening at airports—but many commentators argued that such profiling would be justified, and there was at least anecdotal evidence of an increase in discrimination against people of Middle Eastern descent. After the terrorist attacks in Paris and San Bernardino, California, in 2016 the debate in the presidential campaign shifted to a strongly anti-immigrant tone. Donald Trump proposed preventing all Muslims from entering the United States until we could make sure there was not a terrorist threat. Other Republican presidential candidates endorsed the idea of preventing all emigrants from Syria, who were flooding into Europe, from entering the United States, but Hillary Clinton strongly resisted this idea, pointing out that the United States is a nation of immigrants and that precautions can be taken to make sure that terrorists do not slip into the country.

Over the past two decades, immigration has been central in many political debates. The intensity of that debate increased in 2010 when Arizona enacted an anti-immigration law that requires local law-enforcement officials to check the immigration status of a person in a "lawful stop, detention, or arrest" if there is a "reasonable suspicion" that the person is an illegal alien. The law also requires immigrants to always carry papers verifying their immigration status and bans people without proper documents from seeking work in public places. The chapter opener noted some of the violations in civil rights that occurred when local law-enforcement officials started enforcing this law. States with similar laws include South Carolina, Alabama, Utah, Georgia, and Indiana. Arizona governor Jan Brewer said, "Decades of federal inaction and misguided policy have created a dangerous and unacceptable situation, and states deserve clarity from the Court in terms of what role they have in fighting illegal immigration."[96] Opponents of the law argue that it requires illegal racial profiling and that the federal government has the sole responsibility for deciding immigration law.

The Supreme Court struck down three of the four main provisions of the law, citing the supremacy clause of the Constitution. This decision meant that Congress, not the states, determines immigration law when the two laws conflict. The Court upheld the controversial "show me your papers" part of the law, saying that the state was simply enforcing the federal law. However, the Court indicated that the law must be applied in a race-neutral way and could be struck down if there was clear evidence of racial profiling.[97] Several months later, a federal district court judge cleared the way for implementation of the "show me your papers" law, saying that the Supreme Court wanted to see actual evidence of discrimination rather than speculation that the law could have a discriminatory effect.[98]

As noted in the introduction, the immigration system is widely viewed as broken and in need of reform. However, neither President Bush nor President Obama was able to get Congress to approve his proposal to provide a "path to citizenship" for undocumented immigrants. Americans are in favor of reform, but their level of support varies depending on the wording of the question. In 2015, a Gallup poll showed that 65 percent of those surveyed said that the government should "allow illegal immigrants to remain

Border patrol agents detain undocumented immigrants apprehended near the Mexican border outside McAllen, Texas. Illegal immigration continues to be a hot-button issue in national electoral and legislative politics.

in the United States and become U.S. citizens but only if they meet certain requirements"; another 14 percent said illegal immigrants should be able to stay without applying for citizenship, while only 19 percent said they should have to leave the United States. A Pew poll also taken in 2015 showed that 51 percent of Americans think "immigrants today strengthen our country because of their hard work and talents" while 14 percent believe "immigrants today are a burden on our country because they take our jobs, housing and health care."[99] In 2015, President Obama used executive orders to implement part of his immigration policy (concerning the deportation of young adults who were brought to the United States illegally by their parents and the parents of children who are citizens). The Supreme Court deadlocked 4–4 in a June 2016 case, upholding the lower court's ruling that struck down the executive order. More than 4 million immigrants had to await the results of the election. President Trump has vowed to cancel this program, but it is less clear that he will be able to implement the massive deportation program that he endorsed during the campaign.

The debates over affirmative action, English as the country's official language, and immigration reform clearly illustrate the conflictual nature of civil rights policy. However, history has shown that when public opinion strongly supports a given application of civil rights—for example, the integration of African Americans in the South in the 1960s and, more recently, allowing gays to openly serve in the military and recognizing same-sex marriage—public policy soon reflects those views. Although it is impossible to say when there will be comprehensive immigration reform that includes a path to citizenship, policy appears to be headed in that direction, given the trends in public opinion.

Conclusion

Enforcing civil rights means providing equal protection of the law to individuals and groups that are discriminated against, which may include noncitizens and illegal immigrants. Figuring out exactly when an individual's civil rights have been violated can be tricky. When does a routine traffic stop by a police officer turn into racial profiling?

To help figure that out, we now can answer the questions about possible civil rights violations that introduced this chapter:

- Scenario 1: On the one hand, the African-American teenagers who were pulled over by the police may or may not have had their civil rights violated, depending on the laws in their state. In Massachusetts, for example, it is prohibited to consider the "race, gender, national or ethnic origin of members of the public in deciding to detain a person or stop a motor vehicle" except in "suspect specific incidents."[100] On the other hand, in the scenario in which the police pulled over white teenagers the traffic stop would have been acceptable as long as there had been "probable cause" to justify the stop.
- Scenario 2: The Asian-American woman who did not get the job could certainly talk to a lawyer about filing a "disparate impact" discrimination suit. Under the 1991 Civil Rights Act, the employer would have the burden of proof to show that she was not a victim of the good ol' boy network.
- Scenario 3: The gay couple who could not rent the apartment because of their sexual orientation might have a basis for a civil rights lawsuit based on the Fourteenth Amendment. But this would depend on where they lived, given that there is no federal protection against discrimination against gay men and lesbians (and the Supreme Court has not applied the Fourteenth Amendment in this context).
- Scenario 4: Court decisions concerning affirmative action at the University of Michigan and the University of Texas show that the white student who was not admitted to the university of his choice would just have to take his lumps, as long as the affirmative action program considered race as a general "plus factor" rather than assigning more or fewer points for it (and the practice was allowed by his state).

This review of civil rights in the United States has highlighted only some of the most important issues, but a significant agenda remains. The civil rights movement will continue to use the multiple avenues of the legislative, executive, and judicial branches to secure equal rights for all Americans. Although this process may take many years, history demonstrates that when public opinion becomes more supportive of diversity and stronger civil rights our political institutions support the views of the people.

STUDY GUIDE

The context of civil rights

Describe the historical struggles groups have faced in winning civil rights. (Pages 145–151)

Summary

Civil rights are protections from discrimination both by the government and by individuals and are rooted in laws and the equal protection clause of the Fourteenth Amendment. The concept of equality has evolved over time, with protections now for the LGBTQ community, women, African Americans, Native Americans, Asian Americans, and Latinos. Despite our attempts to live in a color-blind society, awareness of race still influences many people's opinions and behavior.

Key terms

civil rights (p. 145)
disenfranchised (p. 147)
grandfather clause (p. 147)
Jim Crow laws (p. 147)

"separate but equal" doctrine (p. 147)
protectionism (p. 150)

Practice Quiz Questions

1. **The distinction between civil rights and civil liberties is that civil rights _____ while civil liberties _____.**
   a. protect against discrimination; are guaranteed in the Bill of Rights
   b. are guaranteed in the Bill of Rights; protect against discrimination
   c. are guaranteed in the Bill of Rights; limit what the government can do to you
   d. limit what the government can do to you; protect against discrimination
   e. limit what the government can do to you; are guaranteed in the Bill of Rights

2. **The Missouri Compromise _____.**
   a. ruled that people held as slaves are not protected by the Constitution
   b. established that three-fifths of the slaves could count in a state's population
   c. limited the expansion of slavery while maintaining the balance of slave states
   d. gave slaves the right to vote
   e. ended slavery in the South

3. ***Plessy v. Ferguson* established _____.**
   a. the legitimacy of poll taxes
   b. the "separate but equal" doctrine
   c. that Jim Crow laws were illegal
   d. the process of desegregation in the South
   e. the legality of slavery

4. **The principle of _____ was used in many court cases to deny women equal rights.**
   a. matriarchy
   b. "separate but equal"
   c. sectionalism
   d. misandry
   e. protectionism

5. **Early in the nation's history, civil rights activism was focused on _____.**
   a. women
   b. gays and lesbians
   c. African Americans
   d. Latinos
   e. Native Americans

The racial divide today

Analyze inequality among racial, ethnic, and social groups today. (Pages 152–158)

Summary

Beyond the unequal treatment of racial minorities, women, and LGBTQ individuals, inequalities in political, social, and economic conditions also persist. Whites are able to participate in politics at a higher rate, enjoy a better standard of living, and avoid prejudice in the criminal justice system.

Practice Quiz Questions

6. ***Most* of the differences in voter turnout among whites relative to racial minorities can be accounted for by _____.**
   a. contemporary Jim Crow laws
   b. voter purge lists
   c. voter ID laws
   d. poll taxes
   e. education and income

7. **The gaps between whites and blacks on health measures are _____ and in many cases _____.**
   a. large; decreasing
   b. large; increasing
   c. small; decreasing
   d. small; increasing
   e. small; staying the same

8. **In economic terms, the average Hispanic family is _____ .**
    a. better off than the average white family from the same area
    b. likely to have more assets than the average white family
    c. roughly equal with the average white family
    d. worse off than the average white family
    e. more likely than any other group to be poor

Key players in the conflict over civil rights

Explain the approaches used to bring about change in civil rights policies. (Pages 158–179)

Summary

Depending on the political context, each branch of government has played a role in the expansion of civil rights. Moreover, federalism has played a role in this process. Although the state governments often lagged behind the federal government in African Americans' civil rights, they have been on the forefront in protecting the rights of gays and lesbians.

Key terms

de jure (p. 165)
de facto (p. 165)
disparate impact standard (p. 165)
rational basis test (p. 167)
substantive due process doctrine (p. 172)

Practice Quiz Questions

9. **Early in the civil rights movement (before the 1960s), which branch provided most of the successes?**
    a. state governments
    b. Congress
    c. the presidency
    d. the bureaucracy
    e. the Supreme Court

10. **The difference between de facto segregation and de jure segregation is that de facto segregation _____ , while de jure segregation _____ .**
    a. is the result of circumstances; is mandated by law
    b. is mandated by law; is the result of circumstances
    c. applies to racial minorities; applies to women
    d. applies to women; applies to racial minorities
    e. applies to all groups; applies to racial minorities

11. **The strongest protection as the "suspect classification" applies which test?**
    a. rational basis
    b. strict scrutiny
    c. intermediate scrutiny
    d. privileged interest
    e. disparate impact

12. **The VRA _____ .**
    a. established "majority-minority" districts
    b. established compulsory voter registration for African Americans
    c. eliminated direct obstacles to minority voting in the South
    d. barred discrimination in the rental or sale of a home
    e. reduced participation by African Americans in the South

13. **Relative to the protection of individuals with disabilities, Congress's track record in protecting gay rights is _____ .**
    a. stronger
    b. about the same
    c. weaker
    d. nonexistent
    e. more focused on job discrimination

Civil rights issues today

Examine affirmative action and other ongoing civil rights issues. (Pages 179–185)

Summary

The public is divided on the appropriateness of civil rights policies, with some groups preferring a "color-blind" and some groups preferring a "color-conscious" approach. Furthermore, the debates over issues such as affirmative action, immigration reform, and establishing English as the official language in many states indicate the level of conflict over civil rights policy. Nonetheless, when public opinion does strongly support the application of civil rights in a particular arena policy makers generally respond to these views.

Practice Quiz Questions

14. **The Supreme Court's implementation of "color-blind jurisprudence" fits the agenda of those who argue _____ .**
    a. that the gap between blacks and whites has narrowed
    b. that the civil rights movement needs to continue to fight for equal opportunity
    c. that African Americans need to be separate and fully self-sufficient
    d. that equality of outcomes is important
    e. that the gap between blacks and whites has widened

15. **What did the case *Regents of the University of California v. Bakke* establish?**

    a. that race could play no role in the college admissions process

    b. that gender could play no role in the college admissions process

    c. that strict racial quotas in the admissions process were legal

    d. that race could be used as a "plus factor" in the admissions process

    e. that gender could be used as a "plus factor" in the admissions process

---

Suggested Reading

Berman, Ari. *Give Us the Ballot: The Modern Struggle for Voting Rights in America*. New York: Farrar, Straus and Giroux, 2015.

Canon, David T. *Race, Redistricting, and Representation: The Unintended Consequences of Black-Majority Districts*. Chicago: University of Chicago Press, 1999.

Dawson, Michael C. *Behind the Mule: Race and Class in African-American Politics*. Princeton, NJ: Princeton University Press, 1994.

Hochschild, Jennifer L., Vesla M. Weaver, and Traci R. Burch. *Creating a New Racial Order: How Immigration, Multiracialism, Genomics, and the Young Can Remake Race in America*. Princeton, NJ: Princeton University Press, 2012.

Katznelson, Ira. *When Affirmative Action Was White: An Untold History of Racial Inequality in Twentieth-Century America*. New York: W. W. Norton, 2005.

Kennedy, Randall. *For Discrimination: Race, Affirmative Action, and the Law*. New York: Vintage Books, 2015.

Kousser, J. Morgan. *Colorblind Injustice: Minority Voting Rights and the Undoing of the Second Reconstruction*. Chapel Hill: University of North Carolina Press, 1999.

Tate, Katherine. *Black Lawmaking in the U.S. Congress from Carter to Obama*. Ann Arbor: University of Michigan Press, 2014.

Thernstrom, Stephan, and Abigail Thernstrom. *America in Black and White: One Nation, Indivisible—Race in Modern America*. New York: Simon and Schuster, 1997.

6

Public Opinion

Do politicians listen to the people? Should they?

At first glance, it seems clear that Americans demand stricter controls on gun ownership. Even before the Orlando shooting in June 2016, polls showed that strong majorities favored background checks for gun purchasers, prohibiting people on the federal "no fly" list from purchasing guns, and constructing a federal database of gun owners. At the same time, however, no observer of Washington politics believed that these measures had any chance of becoming law. This discrepancy between apparent citizen demands and policy outcomes suggested to some that House members and senators feared that a vote for gun control would prompt the National Rifle Association and other groups to run campaign ads against them. If so, wasn't this a case of politicians not listening to the people and instead giving in to the pressure of a well-funded special interest group?

Before we blame elected officials, we need to examine public opinion itself. What does it mean when someone expresses a political opinion—for example, support for a gun control proposal or disapproval of the president's performance? Where do these sentiments come from? Are they long held or fleeting? Are these sentiments real, in the sense that they reflect judgments that shape a person's behavior, or are they just something that a person says without really believing it? Candidates, political parties, journalists, and political scientists take thousands of polls to determine who is likely to vote; what sorts of arguments, slogans, and platforms would appeal to these voters; and which policies are in demand by the electorate. Yet some evidence suggests that most Americans make up answers to poll questions or treat surveys as an opportunity to make a joke. (One 2015 poll found that Republican presidential candidates were rated less favorably than the Terminator, the shark from the movie *Jaws*, and the character Voldemort from the Harry Potter series.)[1] Another found that a quarter of Republican citizens agreed that President Obama might be the Antichrist.[2]

★

CHAPTER GOALS

Define *public opinion* and explain why it matters in American politics.
pages 192–197

Explain how people form political attitudes and opinions.
pages 197–201

Describe basic survey methods and potential issues affecting accuracy.
pages 202–211

Present findings on what Americans think about government and why it matters.
pages 211–219

📷

Many Americans have attended or seen pictures of memorials to victims of gun violence. Strong majorities favor some limits on gun ownership. Why, then, have such proposals failed to be enacted? #WeAreOrlando #PulseOrlando

Are Americans poorly informed about politics? One survey found that more Americans could identify characters on *The Simpsons* than could list which liberties the Bill of Rights guarantees, and another found most respondents unable to name any Supreme Court justices. #SCOTUS

Some research indicates that the public often has no firm opinions about government policy and that people are easily swayed by candidates, advocacy groups, or the media and may respond inconsistently to questions that ask the same thing but are worded differently. If such studies are correct, how do we know what people think? And how should we expect politicians to react? How does public opinion work?

⭐
DEFINE *PUBLIC OPINION* AND EXPLAIN WHY IT MATTERS IN AMERICAN POLITICS

public opinion
Citizens' views on politics and government actions.

What is public opinion?

Public opinion describes what the population thinks about politics and government—what government should be doing, evaluations of what government *is* doing, and judgments about elected officials and others who participate in the political process, as well as the wider set of beliefs that shape these opinions.

Public opinion matters for three reasons. First, citizens' political actions—including voting, contributing to campaigns, writing letters to senators, and other kinds of activism—are driven by their opinions.[3] For example, as we discuss in more detail in Chapter 8, party identification shapes voting decisions. A voter who thinks of him- or herself as a Democrat is more likely to vote for Democratic candidates than a voter who identifies as a Republican.[4] Therefore, if we want to understand an individual's behavior or analyze broader political outcomes, such as who wins an election or the fate of a legislative proposal, we need good data on public opinion.

Second, examining public opinion helps explain the behavior of candidates, political parties, and other political actors. Later chapters (particularly Chapter 9 and Chapter 11) show a strong link between citizens' opinions and candidates' campaign strategies and their actions in office. Politicians look to public opinion to determine what citizens want them to do and how satisfied citizens are with their behavior in office. For example, in Chapter 11 we see how congressional representatives are reluctant to cast votes that are inconsistent with their constituents' preferences, especially on issues that constituents consider important. Therefore, to explain a legislator's votes you need to begin with his or her constituents' opinions.

Third, because public opinion is a key to understanding what motivates both citizens and political officials, it can shed light on the reasons for specific policy outcomes. For example, changes in the policy mood—the public's demand for new policies—are linked to changes in government spending.[5] When people want government to do more,

❝
Whoever can change public opinion can change the government.

—President Abraham Lincoln

Politicians read public opinion polls closely to gauge whether their behavior will anger or please constituents. Few politicians always follow survey results—but virtually none would agree with Calvin's father that polls should be ignored entirely.

spending increases more rapidly; when people want government to do less, spending goes down (or increases more slowly).

There are different kinds of opinion

Modern theories of public opinion distinguish between two types of opinions: opinions that are preformed as well as opinions that are formed on the spot as needed. The first kind of opinions are broad expressions, such as how a person thinks about politics, what a citizen wants from government, or principles that apply across a range of issues. These kinds of beliefs typically form early in life and remain stable over time. Some of these beliefs are obviously political, such as party identification, liberal or conservative ideology, and judgments about whether elected officials lose touch with citizens. Others, such as beliefs about homosexuality or religion, may seem irrelevant to politics, but their presence on the questionnaire illustrates an important finding: Americans' political opinions are shaped by a wide range of beliefs and ideas, including some that are not inherently political.

Liberal or conservative ideology is a good example of a stable opinion: the best way to predict an American's ideology at age 40 is to assume it will match his or her ideology at age 20. The same is true for party identification. However, even these typically stable opinions sometimes change in response to events. In a later section, we will look more closely at how such opinions form and why they change.

Many Opinions Are Latent The most important thing to understand about public opinion is that although ideology and party identification are largely consistent over time, they are exceptions to the rule.[6] The average person does not maintain a set of fully formed opinions on all political topics, such as evaluations of all the candidates for state or local office or assessments of the entire range of government programs. Instead, most Americans' political judgments are latent opinions: they are constructed only as needed, such as when answering a survey question or deciding on Election Day how to vote. For example, when most people are asked about climate change they probably do not have a specific response in mind simply because they have not thought much about the question. They might have, at best, some vague ideas about the subject. Their opinions become concrete only when they are asked about them.

People who follow politics closely have more preformed opinions than the average American, whose interest in politics is relatively low. But very few people are so well informed that they have ready opinions on a wide range of political and policy questions. Moreover, even when people do form opinions in advance, they may not remember every factor that influenced their opinions. Thus, an individual may identify as a liberal or a conservative or as a supporter of a particular party but may be unable to explain the reasons behind these ideological leanings.[7]

liberal or conservative ideology
A way of describing political beliefs in terms of a position on the spectrum running from liberal to moderate to conservative.

latent opinion
An opinion formed on the spot, when it is needed (as distinct from a deeply held opinion that is stable over time).

A person's ideological perspective is relatively stable over time. People who have a conservative ideology generally oppose increasing government spending and taxes.

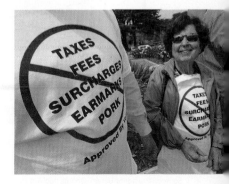

How people form opinions

When people form opinions on the spot, they are based on *considerations*, the pieces of relevant information—such as ideology, party identification, religious beliefs, recent events, and personal circumstances—that come to mind when the opinion is requested.[8] The process of forming an opinion usually is not thorough or systematic, since most people don't take into account everything they know about the issue.[9] Rather, they only use considerations that come to mind immediately.[10] Highly informed people who follow politics use this process, as do those with low levels of political interest and knowledge.[11]

Consider how people decide whether they approve of the job the president is doing. Surveys on this topic typically ask respondents whether they approve or disapprove of the president's performance, although the questions' wording can vary. Responses are in part driven by the state of the economy—people are more likely to approve of the president if they hold positive views of economic conditions. Approval is also more likely if a respondent shares the president's party identification. These patterns are seen in Figure 6.1, which shows approval and disapproval percentages for President Obama through 2016. After an initial bounce in his first year in office, Obama's approval rating has hovered between 40 and 50 percent, for most of his presidency. Events such as Obama's reelection in 2012, the troubled rollout of Obamacare in 2013, and revelations in 2014 about NSA surveillance of American citizens generated smaller, temporary moves up or down in Obama's popularity—these events were used as considerations, but only for short periods of time. Finally, as signs of economic recovery became stronger in 2016, Obama's approval rating moved to over 50 percent.

Many studies of public opinion support the idea that most people form opinions on the spot using a wide range of considerations. Consider the following findings: Attitudes about immigration are shaped by evaluations of the state of the economy.[12]

FIGURE 6.1

Approval Ratings for President Obama

President Barack Obama had high approval ratings (around 80 percent approval) in October 2009, but after a steady decline his ratings leveled off in February 2010 (with about 45 percent approval and 45 percent disapproval) and remained fairly level for the rest of his presidency. What factors account for fluctuations in presidential approval?

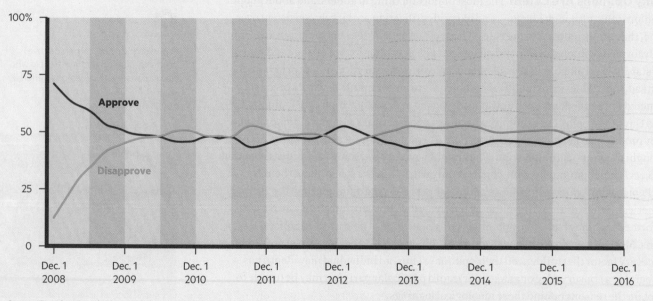

Source: "President Barack Obama Job Approval," https://elections.huffingtonpost.com/pollster/obama-job-approval (accessed 10/18/16).

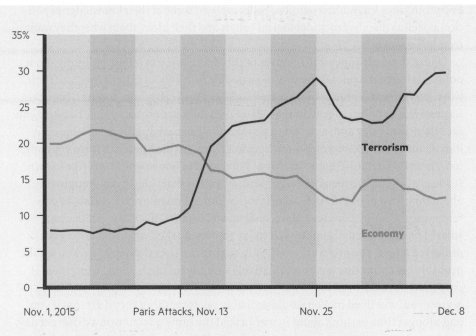

35%

30

25

20

15

10

5

0

Nov. 1, 2015   Paris Attacks, Nov. 13   Nov. 25   Dec. 8

Terrorism

Economy

Source: Reuters, "Most Important Problem Facing US," http://polling.reuters.com (accessed 12/2/15).

FIGURE 6.2

Views on Terrorism before and after Paris Attacks

Opinions are sensitive to recent events; when asked to name the most important problem facing the United States today, the percentage of respondents who answered "terrorism" increased sharply after the 2015 attacks in Paris, France. Rahm Emanuel (President Obama's first Chief of Staff) once said, "You never let a serious crisis go to waste." Based on this argument, how would a politician respond to the Paris attacks?

People judge government spending proposals differently depending on whether a Republican or a Democrat made the proposal, using their own party identification as a consideration.[13] Evaluations of affirmative action programs vary depending on whether the survey question reminds respondents that their own personal economic well-being may be hurt by these programs.[14] Voters' party identification and ideology influence their evaluations of candidates.[15] Individuals' willingness to allow protests and other expressions of opinions they disagree with depends on their belief in tolerance.[16] And if people feel obligated to help others in need, they are more likely to support government programs that benefit the poor.[17]

Sometimes competing or contradictory considerations influence the opinion-formation process. In the case of abortion laws, many people believe in protecting human life but also in allowing women to make their own medical decisions.[18] When a survey asks people who hold both beliefs for their opinion about abortion laws, their response will depend on which consideration comes to mind and seems most relevant when they are answering the question. Opinions about other morally complex issues such as right-to-die legislation, or about race-related issues such as affirmative action, also often involve competing considerations.[19]

Events can influence considerations. Consider Figure 6.2, which shows Reuters poll data from surveys conducted in the weeks before and after the November 2015 ISIS terrorist attacks against civilians in Paris, France. As you see, the percentage of Americans who saw terrorism as the most important problem jumped upward in the week after the attack from about 10 percent to about 30 percent, moving ahead of the percentage who saw the economy as the most important problem.

Personal knowledge and considerations

Most Americans form legitimate, meaningful opinions when they are needed. Though these people don't usually seek out new information or take account of everything they know, their opinions reflect at least some of their knowledge of politics, as well as their bedrock ideological beliefs and their ideas about what they want from government.

One of the most appealing features of this description of public opinions about politics is that it resembles the way most people think about other aspects of their lives. Do you prefer blue or black jeans? Coke or Pepsi? Hip-hop, country, or rock? Lattes, regular coffee, decaf, or tea? These decisions are probably easy because you face them every day and, as a result, you are likely to have highly accessible opinions about which option you prefer. You don't have to think much to form your opinion. Now consider a different question: What kind of house would you like to own? If you are in your late teens or early twenties, you probably have not thought much about this. New or old? Ranch, split-level, colonial, bungalow, Victorian, or contemporary? Granite counters, slate, quartz, or Corian? Oil, gas, or electric heat—or solar? The list is virtually endless. If today someone asked you to describe your preferred house, you probably could only begin to answer the question. You would probably base your response on a relatively small set of ideas, using a few mental snapshots of your image of the perfect house and relying on your impressions of the houses you have lived in. You would probably say something very different if you had a longer time to think about it, were asked the same question on a different day, or were asked at a time when you were actually in the market for a house—or after you already owned one.

This is exactly how most Americans form their opinions about politics. When people are asked for an opinion on a political question they know little about, they base their response on a few general, simple considerations. A question about gun control may call to mind a recent school shooting, the respondents' love for hunting (or their dislike of venison), an armed robbery of a nearby store, or even their views on President Trump's performance in office. These considerations may not lead to the most well-thought-out answer, but they may be all that many people use to form their opinions.

This description of how most people think about politics explains why public outrage about mass shootings does not translate into congressional action on new gun control legislation. Support for gun control generally increases in the days after a mass shooting, as events provide a strong consideration for opinion formation. However, in the weeks or months that follow a shooting public support fades. People revert to using other considerations (such as partisanship) to form opinions about gun control and eventually public opinion looks essentially the same as it did before the shooting took place.[20] Politicians are just as aware as political scientists are of how most people respond to events, and are not likely to pay attention to a change in public opinion unless it is sustained over time.

Thinking about opinions in terms of considerations implies that it is impossible to measure public opinion once and for all. Even if nothing major happens—no big events, new proposals, or other high-profile political activity—opinions may change as people call up different considerations for one reason or another. Such variation does not mean that people are indecisive or that they do not understand what they are being asked. Rather, it reflects the reality of how the average person thinks and develops opinions.

Images of confrontation between pro-choice and pro-life protesters may conceal the more nuanced considerations that underlie most Americans' opinions about abortion. A majority of Americans believe that the decision to have an abortion should be left up to the woman but are uncomfortable allowing unrestricted access to the procedure. #ProChoice #ProLife

In a democracy, elected officials stay in office by keeping their constituents happy. As a result, knowing what public opinion looks like—what citizens believe, what they want government to do—helps us to understand the choices elected officials make. New policy initiatives such as stricter gun control laws are unlikely to be enacted in the absence of strong, sustained public support. Conversely, even controversial proposals such as Obamacare can be enacted over strong opposition, as long as there are enough enthusiastic supporters. In both ways, public opinion both motivates and constrains elected officials. And understanding what goes into people's opinions—whether they are deep and well considered or shallow and formed in the moment—can help you evaluate claims by politicians and the media, and better predict which policies are likely to be enacted and which will fail.

Where do opinions come from?

This section describes the sources of public opinion. Some influences come from early life experiences, such as exposure to the beliefs of parents, relatives, or teachers; others result from later life events. Politicians also play a critical role in the opinion-formation process.

★

EXPLAIN HOW PEOPLE FORM POLITICAL ATTITUDES AND OPINIONS

Socialization: families and communities

Theories of political socialization show that many people's political opinions start with what they learned from their parents. These principles include a liberal or conservative ideology, level of trust in others, and class, racial, and ethnic identity.[21] There is also a high correlation between both the party identification and the liberal or conservative ideology of parents and those of their children.[22] Even some personality traits that develop early in life appear to shape political behavior: people who have high agreeableness, for example, are more likely to favor policies that help the disadvantaged.[23] These principles are not necessarily permanent; in fact, people sometimes respond to events by modifying their opinions, even those developed early in life. Even so, for many people, ideas learned during childhood continue to shape their political opinions throughout their lives.[24]

Beyond these influences, research finds broader aspects of socialization that shape political opinions. People are socialized by their communities, the people they interact with while growing up, such as neighbors, teachers, clergy, and others.[25] Support for democracy as a system of government and for American political institutions is higher for individuals who take a civics class in high school.[26] Growing up in a homogeneous community, one where many people share the same cultural, ethnic, or political beliefs, increases adults' sense of civic duty—their belief that voting or other forms of political participation are important social obligations.[27] Volunteering in community organizations as a child also shapes political beliefs and participation in later life.[28] Engaging in political activity as a teenager, such as volunteering in a presidential campaign, generates higher levels of political interest as an adult; it also strengthens the belief that people should care about politics and participate in political activities.[29]

political socialization
The process by which an individual's political opinions are shaped by other people and the surrounding culture.

In general, children tend to adopt their parents' ideology and party affiliation. Former president George H. W. Bush and his sons, former president George W. Bush and former governor of Florida (and presidential candidate) Jeb Bush, are all Republicans.

Events

Although socialization often influences individuals' fairly stable core beliefs, public opinion is not fixed. All kinds of events—from everyday interactions to traumatic, life-changing disasters—can capture people's attention and force them to revise their understanding of politics and the role of government. For example, though an individual's initial partisan affiliation likely reflects his or her parents' leanings, this starting point will change in response to subsequent events such as who runs for office, what platforms they campaign on, and their performance in office.[30]

Some events that shape beliefs are specific, individual experiences. For example, someone who believes that he or she managed to get a college degree only because of government grants and guaranteed student loans might favor a large, activist government that provides a range of benefits to its citizens. And individuals' support for same-sex marriage is strongly influenced by the number of people they know who are gay or lesbian.[31] Beliefs are also shaped by major national or world events. Scholars have shown that after the September 11 terrorist attacks many citizens became more willing to restrict civil liberties to reduce the chances of future attacks.[32] Support for restrictions increased soon after the September 11 attacks and remained elevated even 15 years later, suggesting a long-term change in public opinion.[33]

Events hold a similar sway over other opinions, such as presidential approval, which is driven by factors such as changes in the economy. Presidents are more likely to have high approval ratings when economic growth is high and inflation and unemployment are low, whereas their approval ratings fall when growth is negative and unemployment and inflation are high. A president's popularity is also affected by scandals involving his or her administration. For example, the slight dip in President Obama's popularity during 2013 was in part due to revelations about NSA monitoring of Americans' cell phone conversations.

Some events have a greater impact on public opinion than others, and some people are more likely than others to change their views. Political scientist John Zaller has shown that opinion changes generated by an event or some other new information are more likely when an individual considers the event or information to be important and when it is unfamiliar. In such cases, the individual does not have a set of preexisting principles or other considerations with which to interpret the event or information. Changes in opinions are also more likely for people who do not have strong beliefs than they are for people who hold strong opinions.[34]

Group identity

Individuals' opinions are also influenced by social categories or groups, such as gender, race, income, and education level. Political scientists refer to these differences in opinion as *cohort effects*. These characteristics might shape opinions in three ways. First, people learn about politics from the people around them. Therefore, those who live in the same region or who were born in the same era might have common beliefs because they experienced the same historical events at similar points in their lives or learned political viewpoints from one another. In the United States, opinions on many issues are highly correlated with the state or region where a person grew up. For example, until the 1970s relatively few native white southerners identified with the Republican Party.[35] Even today, native white southerners tend to have distinctly different attitudes about many issues (such as less support for affirmative action policies and less support for same-sex marriage) and hold different attitudes (such as lower support for government involvement in creating racial equality) from people of color and people from other regions of the country.[36]

In some cases group identity is a function of age. Changes in attitudes about same-sex marriage over the last decade illustrate this phenomenon as shown in Figure 6.3. The figure shows that overall support for allowing gay and lesbian couples to marry (or allowing civil unions) has doubled in the last decade. Moreover, while opinions have shifted in all age cohorts, younger Americans are much more likely to express support than are older Americans—in part because they are much more likely to know someone who is gay or a lesbian and in part because they are likely to have other characteristics that predispose them to favor same-sex marriage, such as not being a regular churchgoer.

Although events such as wars, economic upheavals, and major policy changes certainly influence public opinion, research shows that most Americans acquire some political opinions early in life from parents, friends, teachers, and others in their community. #Trump2016

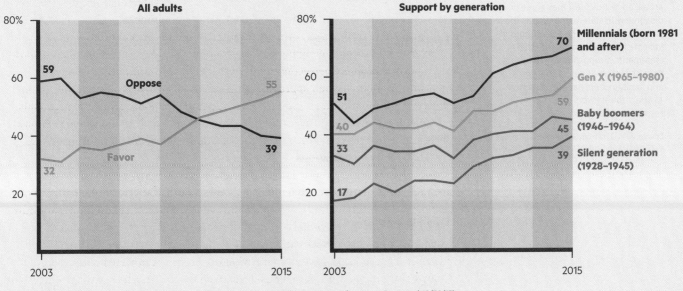

Attitudes about Same-Sex Marriage

FIGURE 6.3

Recently, support for same-sex marriage has grown. What do these graphs tell us about the influence of group identity on public opinion? Is support for same-sex marriage likely to increase or decrease in the future? Why?

All adults

Oppose 59 → 39
Favor 32 → 55

Support by generation

Millennials (born 1981 and after) 70
Gen X (1965–1980) 59
Baby boomers (1946–1964) 45
Silent generation (1928–1945) 39

51, 40, 33, 17 (2003) → 2015

Source: Pew Research Center, "Changing Attitudes on Gay Marriage," July 29, 2015, www.pewforum.org (accessed 10/30/15).

Individuals also may rely on others who "look like" them as a source of opinions. Political scientists Donald Green, Bradley Palmquist, and Eric Schickler, for example, argue that group identities shape partisanship: when people are trying to decide between being a Republican or a Democrat, they think about which demographic groups are associated with each party and pick the party that has more members from the groups they think they are a part of.[37]

One reason for looking at group variations in public opinion is that candidates and political consultants often formulate their campaign strategies in terms of groups. For example, analyses of the three previous presidential elections show that Obama's and Hillary Clinton's electoral strategies were shaped by the goal of attracting support from young Americans, African Americans, Hispanics, and women.[38]

Table 6.1 includes data on the variation in opinions across different groups of Americans, as measured in the General Social Survey (GSS). The table shows group differences on three broad questions: hiring preferences for African Americans, access to abortions, and free speech. There are sharp differences among groups on some questions. For example, people of different education levels respond very differently to both questions about abortion and free speech—however, education has little to do with opinions about affirmative action. Moreover, even with these differences across groups, political scientists Jack Citrin and David O. Sears have found that most people think of themselves as Americans rather than as part of an ethnic, racial, or age-based group.[39]

These data indicate that group characteristics can be important predictors of some of an individual's opinions, but they are not the whole story.[40] Americans' opinions are

TABLE 6.1

The Importance of Groups

The General Social Survey (GSS) has been conducted since 1972 to assess the opinions of Americans on certain key issues. Those who take the surveys are asked to indicate if they agree or disagree with statements such as those shown in the table. The percentages indicate those who agree with the statements. Group differences based on such factors as gender, age, race, and family income have been shown to affect the answers given by the respondents.

Source: 2014 Data from General Social Survey 1972–2014, Cumulative Datafile, Survey Documentation and Analysis (SDA) at UC Berkeley, http://sda.berkeley.edu (accessed 10/30/15).

		"Favor preferences in hiring blacks" (percentage who strongly support or support)	"Abortions OK if woman wants one for any reason" (percentage who agree)	"OK to allow anti-American Muslim cleric to speak" (percentage who agree)
Gender	Male	18.5%	47.1%	49.1%
	Female	18.8	43.5	36.6
Age	18–30	25.1	49.4	39.2
	31–40	13.6	42.3	41.3
	41–55	20.8	40.3	46.3
	56–89	16.1	45.2	41.4
Education	Less than High School	28.1	21.8	26.3
	High School	17.9	40.8	39.0
	Bachelor's Degree	17.2	61.9	58.9
	Advanced Degree	22.2	58.9	58.8
Race	White	12.2	46.5	50.0
	African-American	38.9	46.7	30.9
	Hispanic	23.9	34.5	26.2
	Other	30.1	62.0	31.1
Family Income	Low	25.0	35.6	30.6
	Lower Middle	21.0	42.5	40.9
	Higher Middle	10.9	45.7	44.0
	High	17.3	57.9	55.7

also a product of their socialization and life experiences. People's group characteristics may tell us something about their opinions on some issues but reveal little about their thoughts on other issues.

Politicians and other political actors

Opinions and changes in opinion are also subject to influence by politicians and other political actors including political parties and party leaders; interest groups; and leaders of religious, civic, and other large organizations. In part, this link exists because Americans look to these individuals for information based on their presumed expertise. For example, if you do not know what to think about immigration reform or gun control you might seek out someone who appears to know more about the issues than you do. If that person's opinions seem reasonable, you might adopt them as your own.[41] Of course, people do not search haphazardly for advice; they only take account of an expert's opinions when they generally agree with the expert, perhaps because they are both conservatives or Democrats or because the individual has some other basis for thinking their preferences are alike. Thus, during the general election, Donald Trump's claims that the electoral process was rigged against him contributed to his supporters' high levels of distrust of government.

Politicians and other political actors also work to shape public opinion. Political scientists Lawrence R. Jacobs and Robert Y. Shapiro argue that politicians describe proposals through arguments and images designed to tap the public's strong opinions, with the goal of winning support for these proposals.[42] Although President Obama and his staff expended much time and effort to promote health care reform, giving dozens of public speeches, holding rallies, and briefing legislators, opponents of the proposal were able to shape the opinions of many Americans by making dire pronouncements about what the proposal might do. While health care reform was eventually passed into law in April 2010, these opposition efforts turned majority public support into a dead heat at the time of enactment. However, in the years after enactment, as none of these dire predictions have come true, support for Obamacare gradually increased, confirming that the success of efforts to shape public opinion depends on facts as well as argument.[43]

In sum, public opinion at the individual level is driven by many factors, most notably life experiences, including current events as we perceive them. In the case of gun control, for example, beliefs are likely to depend on individuals' background—whether they own a gun, hunt, or know someone who does; their political beliefs, including how tolerant they are of government regulation of individual behavior; as well as horrific events involving guns. Thus, although public opinion may shift somewhat in response to events like the Orlando shooting, such events are only one factor that shapes opinion. As a result, even though an event may be momentous, the shift in opinion may be quite small.

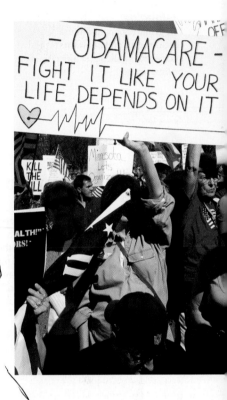

Politicians on both sides of the debate tried to influence public opinion about health care reform. While Obama and the Democrats sought to convince Americans that the new plan was necessary, opponents played up the possible disadvantages, with references to costs, "death panels," and bureaucratic incompetence. #ACA #Obamacare

How people form opinions matters because understanding what people say about politics on the news, or in the classroom, or around the dinner table depends on where they are coming from. Perhaps an important event has shaped their opinion, maybe their parents or connection to a social or generational group has influenced them, or maybe a combination of all of these and more. Knowing what's behind someone's opinions and arguments on an issue can help you decide how you feel about that issue and whether or not that argument carries weight.

"Why Should I Care?"

Measuring public opinion

For the most part, information about public opinion comes from mass surveys—in-person or phone interviews with hundreds or thousands of individuals. The aim of a mass survey is to measure the attitudes of a particular population or group of people, such as the residents of a particular congressional district, evangelicals, senior citizens, or even the entire adult population in America (see How It Works: Measuring What a Nation of 320 Million Thinks: A Checklist). For large groups such as these, it would be impossible to survey everyone. So surveys typically involve samples of between a few hundred and several thousand individuals. One of the principal attractions of mass surveys is that they can, in theory, provide very accurate estimates of public opinion for a large population (such as a state or even the entire United States) using relatively small samples. This property of surveys is detailed in Nuts & Bolts 6.1. For example, although polls taken early in a presidential campaign (such as a year in advance of the election) are poor predictors of the ultimate outcome on Election Day, polls taken at the

mass survey
A way to measure public opinion by interviewing a large sample of the population.

population
The group of people whom a researcher or pollster wants to study, such as evangelicals, senior citizens, or Americans.

NUTS & BOLTS 6.1

Sampling Error in Mass Surveys

The sampling error in a survey (the predicted difference between the average opinion expressed by survey respondents and the average opinion in the population, sometimes called the *margin of error*) using a random sample depends on the sample size. Sampling error is large for small samples of around 200 or fewer but decreases rapidly as sample size increases.

The graph shows how the sampling error for a random sample decreases as sample size increases. For example, in surveys with 1,000 respondents the sampling error is 3 percent, meaning that 95 percent of the time the results of a 1,000-person survey will fall within the range of 3 percentage points above or below the actual percentage in the population who hold a particular opinion surveyed. If the sample size was increased to 5,000 people, the sampling error would decline to 1.4 percent.

Sampling errors need to be taken into account in interpreting what a poll says about public opinion. For example, a June 2016 YouGov poll of 1,300 Americans found that 66 percent gave an unfavorable rating of Donald Trump, and 33 percent rated him favorably. Because the difference in the percentages (33 points) exceeds the sampling error (about 2.5 points), it is reasonable to conclude that, at the time the poll was conducted, more Americans saw Trump unfavorably than favorably.

In contrast, suppose the poll found a narrow 51 to 49 percent split slightly favoring approval. Because the difference in support is smaller than the sampling error, it would be a mistake to conclude that the majority of Americans have a favorable opinion of Trump. Even though more people in the sample express this opinion, there is a good chance that the opposite is true in the overall population.

You don't need to calculate sampling errors to make sense of political polls—just keep two things in mind. First, large samples (1,000 or more) are much more likely to provide accurate information about population opinions than small ones (fewer than 500). Second, be cautious when you read about small differences in survey responses, as these patterns are unlikely to hold true in the entire population.

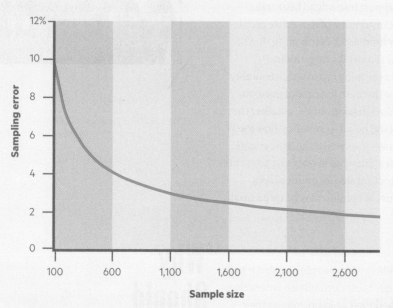

Sample size

sampling error
The predicted difference between the average opinion expressed by survey respondents and the average opinion in the population, sometimes called the *margin of error*. Increasing the number of respondents lowers the sampling error.

beginning of the official presidential race, when both parties' nominees are known, can provide very good predictions of who will win the election and how many votes he or she will receive.[44]

An alternate technique for measuring public opinion uses focus groups, which are small groups of people interviewed in a group setting. Focus groups allow respondents to answer questions in their own words rather than being restricted to a few options in a survey question, and they can provide deep insights into why people hold the opinions they do. Candidates sometimes use focus groups to test campaign appeals or fine-tune their messages. However, because of their small size, focus groups cannot be used to draw conclusions about public opinion across the entire country.

Large-scale surveys such as the American National Election Study (ANES), which is conducted every election year (typically both before and after the general election), use various types of questions to measure citizens' opinions. In presidential election years, participants in the ANES are first asked whether they voted for president. If they say they did, they are asked which candidate they voted for: a major-party candidate (for example, Hillary Clinton or Donald Trump in 2016), an independent candidate, or some other candidate.

Another kind of survey question measures people's preferences using an *issue scale*. For a range of topics, two opposing statements are given and respondents are asked to agree with the one that comes closest to their views, including options in the middle of the two extremes. As we discuss later, on questions such as these, most Americans pick positions in the middle of these scales.

A typical survey like the GSS or the ANES will ask about a hundred questions related to issues and candidates, along with additional questions that elicit personal information such as a respondent's age, education, marital status, and other factors. Some surveys conducted by media sources, candidates, or political parties are shorter, focusing on voter evaluations of the candidates and the reasons for these evaluations. In the main, the length of a survey reflects the fact that people have limited attention spans, so there is a trade-off between learning more about each respondent's opinions and getting him or her to agree to be surveyed in the first place (shorter surveys can also be less expensive).

An important development in recent years is the use of techniques to combine different surveys into a more powerful measure of public opinion. These techniques weigh data from different polls based on their accuracy in previous elections and combine state- and national-level results to generate predictions—thus, if a poll finds that candidate A is ahead in state 1 and polls have found that the winner in state 1 will also win state 2, then the results from state 1 will be used to predict the result in state 2. These techniques generate powerful predictions of election returns—for example, Nate Silver of FiveThirtyEight.com was able to correctly predict the winner of 49 out of 50 states in the 2008 and 2012 presidential elections and came the closest of all political analysts in predicting Trump's upset victory in 2016.

Problems in measuring public opinion

Although measuring public opinion might seem an easy task—just find some people and ask them questions!—it is actually very complicated. The problems begin with determining and gathering an appropriate, representative sample of subjects. These difficulties are compounded by issues pertaining to the wording of the questions and

sample
Within a population, the group of people surveyed in order to gauge the whole population's opinion. Researchers use samples because it would be impossible to interview the entire population.

DID YOU KNOW?

45

state- and national-level polls of the presidential race were released in the last two weeks of the 2016 campaign.
Source: Pollster.com

"

On average, people should be more skeptical when they see numbers. They should be more willing to play around with the data themselves.

—**Nate Silver,** FiveThirtyEight.com

DID YOU KNOW?

90%

of people contacted by phone to participate in a political survey either don't answer or refuse to participate.
Source: Pew Research Center

Measuring What a Nation of 320 Million Thinks: A Checklist

✓ **A Random Sample:**
Were the people who participated in the survey selected randomly, such that any member of the population had an equal chance of being selected?

✓ **Sample Size:**
How many people do researchers need to survey to know what 320 million Americans think? Major national surveys usually use a sample of 1,000–2,000 respondents.

± 2%

✓ **Sampling Error:**
For a group of any size (even 320 million), 95 percent of the time a survey of 1,000 randomly selected respondents will measure the average opinion in a population within 2 percentage points. Reputable surveys will usually give the sampling error (sometimes also called "margin of error").

✓ **Question Wording:**
Did the way the question was worded influence the results? Scientific surveys try to phrase questions in a neutral way, but even in reputable polls, differences in question wording can influence answers.

✓ **Reliable Respondents:** Respondents often give socially acceptable answers rather than truthful ones—or invent opinions on the spot. Is there a reason to think people may not have answered a survey honestly and thoughtfully?

Surveying the 2016 Elections: Two Approaches

To illustrate how these requirements for good survey design play out in real life, we examine how two well-known polling organizations, the Pew Research Center and Rasmussen Reports, designed polls to measure presidential preference during the 2016 campaign.

Rasmussen Reports

Land-line only.

A random sample: Use a **land-line-only sample.**

Sample size: Survey the **first person who answers the phone.**

Adjust results.

Sampling error: If there are more Democrats in your sample than you expect, **adjust your results** to reduce support for Clinton.

Use a script to call.

Reliable respondents: Use a computer script, and only call once. Do the survey in a **short time period (hours).**

Pew Research Center

Include cell phones.

A random sample: Generate a **random sample of Americans,** including people who only have cell phones.

Sample size: When you call a residence, only **talk to the person who's in your sample.**

Don't adjust results.

Sampling error: If the partisan divide in the sample is not what you expect, **treat it as a finding**—people may be changing their party ID.

Use a person to call.

Reliable respondents: Use a live interviewer, and call back people you miss the first time. **Implement the survey over several days.**

Outcome

Rasmussen data are incomplete...

A random sample: Rasmussen misses **people who only use cell phones** (many of whom are younger and are Democrats).

Sample size: Rasmussen is **biased toward people likely to answer the phone.** These people tend to be older and include more men than average.

and assume nothing has changed.

Sampling error: Adjusting for partisan-ship **assumes that no changes in party ID have occurred** since the last election.

Reliable respondents: Rasmussen tactic **lowers response rate.** Rasmussen tactic makes poll results sensitive to short-term events.

Pew is more reliable.

Pew's results were generally regarded as more reliable than Rasmussen's—and ultimately **made more accurate predictions about the 2016 results.** Furthermore, Rasmussen kept its data largely private, while Pew released its question-naire. This made Pew's survey verifiable and provided an opportunity for further analysis.

Critical Thinking

1. **When evaluating these two polling organizations, how would you respond to someone who said he still** preferred Rasmussen's polls because they correctly predicted the outcome of a Senate race in his state in 2014?

2. **Which kinds of respondents are likely to be put off by polls** that the computer scripts? How might this affect the findings of the survey?

further complicated by the very nature of public opinion itself. Consequently, survey results must be read carefully, taking into account who is being surveyed, when they are being surveyed, what opinions people are being asked about, and what mechanism is used to ask survey questions.

Issues with Survey Methods Building a random sample of individuals is not an easy task. One tactic is to choose households at random from census data and send interviewers out for face-to-face meetings or to contact people by telephone using random digit dialing, which allows surveyors to find people who have unlisted phone numbers or who only use a cell phone. In theory, each of these techniques produces a random sample, but in practice, they both may deviate from this ideal. Face-to-face interviews of people in their homes during work hours won't include adults who work during the day and are not home. Even with phone surveys, many people refuse to participate. Pollsters must adjust their survey results to account for these and other potential biases. Sometimes these corrections can introduce new errors. For example, in the 2016 presidential race, attempts to account for likely voters appear to have led to underestimates of support for Donald Trump, the ultimate winner.

To keep costs down, many organizations use Internet polling, in which volunteer respondents log on to a website to participate in a survey, or robo-polls, in which a computer program phones people and interviews them. Although these techniques are less expensive, there are often doubts about the quality of the samples they produce.[45] (*Push polls*, in which a campaign uses biased survey questions as a way of driving support away from an opponent, are not legitimate polls because they are not designed to measure opinion—they are designed to shape it and are a form of negative campaigning; see Chapter 9.)

The wording of questions can also influence survey results. Table 6.2 shows different questions asked to measure opinions about providing citizenship to illegal aliens. As you can see, support depends on the requirements that people would need to fulfill in order to become citizens. As a result, support for immigration reform is much higher in the top three polls than in the bottom three. These issues shouldn't make you suspicious that pollsters are trying to skew their findings—rather, it shows just how hard it is to accurately measure opinions. (See Take a Stand for more on public opinion on immigration.)

Unreliable Respondents Another problem with surveys is that people are sometimes reluctant to reveal their opinions. Rather than speaking truthfully, they often give socially acceptable answers or answers that they believe the interviewers want to hear. In the case of voter turnout in elections, up to one-fourth of respondents who say they voted when surveyed actually did not vote at all.[46] Political scientists refer to this behavior as the social desirability bias, meaning that people answering survey questions were less willing to admit to actions or express opinions, such as racial prejudice, that they believed their neighbors or society at large would disapprove of.[47] In 2016, a small percentage of poll respondents, labeled "shy Trump voters," refused to express their true support for candidate Donald Trump.

Pollsters use various techniques to address this problem. One approach is to ask questions in multiple ways; another is to verify answers whenever possible, such as checking with county boards of elections to see if respondents who said they voted had actually gone to the polls. When there is concern that respondents will try to hide their prejudices, pollsters sometimes frame a question in terms of the entire country rather than the respondent's own beliefs. For example, during the 2008 and 2016 presidential primaries, rather than asking respondents whether they were willing to vote for a

random sample
A subsection of a population chosen to participate in a survey through a selection process in which every member of the population has an equal chance of being chosen. This kind of sampling improves the accuracy of public opinion data.

The Impact of Question Wording on Opinions

TABLE
6.2

How questions are worded can affect survey results. These surveys all ask about immigration reform but differ in the number of requirements that noncitizens would have to satisfy. In light of how the responses to survey questions are shaped by the precise wording of these questions, what sort of question would you ask if your goal was to show that Americans favored immigration reform? What if you wanted to show high levels of opposition?

% Support or Favor	Question	Pollster	Poll Date
81	Here are some questions about how the U.S. government should treat illegal immigrants who have **been in the country for a number of years, hold a job, speak English and are willing to pay any back taxes they owe**. Would you favor or oppose a bill that allowed immigrants to stay in this country rather than being deported and eventually allow them to apply for U.S. citizenship?	CNN/ORC	2/2/2014
78	Do you favor or oppose allowing illegal immigrants to remain in the country and eventually qualify for U.S. citizenship, **as long as they meet certain requirements like paying back taxes, learning English, and passing a background check**?	Fox News	4/22/2013
77	Would you favor or oppose providing a path to citizenship for illegal immigrants in the United States if they met certain requirements including a **waiting period, paying fines and back taxes, passing criminal background checks, and learning English**?	CBS News	10/21/2013
51	The U.S. Senate is considering an immigration bill that would attempt to **increase border security and create a path to citizenship for many immigrants who are in this country without permission** from the U.S. government. Based on what you have read or heard about this bill, do you favor or oppose it?	CNN/ORC	6/13/2013
46	As you may know, the U.S. Senate passed an immigration law that includes **a path to citizenship for undocumented immigrants now living in the United States and stricter border control at a cost of $46 billion**. Do you support or oppose this proposal?	*Post*/ABC	7/21/2013
46	Congress is debating changing immigration laws. Do you support or oppose a revision of immigration policies that would provide a **path to citizenship for 11 million undocumented immigrants in the United States**?	Bloomberg	6/3/2013

Source: Scott Clemet, "Immigration Reform Is Super Popular. Here's Why Congress Isn't Listening," *Washington Post*, July 2, 2014 (accessed 11/2/15).

women candidate (such as Democrat Hillary Clinton), some pollsters posed the question indirectly, asking whether a respondent believed that the country was ready for a woman president. Another tactic is to ask respondents for a different kind of evaluation—rather than asking whether you like or dislike candidates, ask whether you would sit down for a beer (or coffee) with them.

It is also the case that surveys can be designed to elicit controversial or attention-grabbing responses. In the case of the "Obama is the Antichrist" poll mentioned at the beginning of the chapter, the survey question began with "Some people have argued that…," a phrase that when used in a survey can produce higher levels of respondent agreement regardless of what is being asked.[48] Before political scientists believed this survey finding, they would want to see the question asked in different ways, at different times, with survey samples constructed in different ways. Again, the problem is not that pollsters are dishonest or inept—the problem is that public opinion is often difficult to measure.

Because poll results play such an important role in media coverage and public discussions about politics, questions are often raised about the assumptions and corrections that pollsters use to account for all of these issues. During the 2016 presidential campaign, many Republican politicians and observers argued that polls showing a narrow but significant lead for Democrat Hillary Clinton over Republican Donald Trump were the product of inaccurate assumptions about turnout and party identification—some even argued that pollsters were deliberately skewing their findings so as to bolster support for Clinton. While Trump won the election, this outcome does not imply that pollsters altered their surveys to hurt his chances. Rather, it points to the difficulty of accurately surveying the American people, and how we should be reluctant to over-interpret survey results.

The Accuracy of Public Opinion As previously noted, early theories of public opinion held that the average American's views about politics were incomplete at best and wildly inaccurate at worst. Modern theories have revised these conclusions. It is true that many Americans have significant gaps in factual information, such as which party controls the House or the Senate.[49] Americans also routinely overestimate the amount of federal money spent on government programs such as foreign aid. However, rather than reflecting ignorance, these misperceptions often result from poor survey design or participants' misinterpretation of survey questions.

In some cases, we see inaccurate or outlandish survey returns because some respondents don't take surveys seriously. They agree to participate but are not interested in explaining their beliefs to a stranger. Faced with a long list of questions, they give quick, thoughtless responses so as to end the interview as quickly as possible. Misperceptions may also result when respondents form opinions on the basis of whatever considerations come to mind. This strategy causes many respondents to exclude important pieces of information from their opinion-formation process.

Consider claims about Obamacare. A 2015 poll asked people whether health care spending by the federal government was higher or lower than estimates made at the time the program was enacted in 2010. Forty-two percent said spending was higher, 40 percent did not know—and only 5 percent of respondents gave the correct answer, that spending was less than expected.[50]

How can these findings be squared with our earlier statement that Americans generally hold opinions that have some basis in reality? For one thing, many respondents probably had not thought about these questions in detail—and it's likely that only very few knew anything about health care costs in the first place. When asked for an opinion as part of a survey, respondents had no time to do research or think things through. One possibility is that people used partisan considerations: Obama supporters (Democrats) said they didn't know, while Obama opponents (Republicans) said costs were higher than expected. If so, the responses say more about partisanship and attitudes toward President Obama than the cost of Obamacare.

Incomplete or inaccurate responses to survey questions may also reflect respondents' unwillingness to admit they don't know about something. There is good evidence that survey participants sometimes make up responses to avoid appearing ill informed.[51] Thus, when asked about death panels and health care reform respondents might affirm that a link existed even if they know little or nothing about the situation. In the main, people are more likely to express sensible, thoughtful, and accurate opinions when asked about an issue or question that they have personal experience with—for example, whether their own spending on health care had increased, rather than their assessment of Obamacare.

Should Politicians Follow the Polls?

Elected officials in America work hard to cast votes and take other actions that their constituents will like. At first glance, this behavior seems easy. All a politician needs to do is take a poll, measure public opinion in his or her state or district, and comply with the demands expressed in the survey responses. The problem is, poll results need interpretation. As we saw in Table 6.2, small differences in question wording can produce very different responses, or public opinion can remain vague, despite the polls. As a result, even if representatives want to follow constituent opinion, they may decide that they don't really know enough about these opinions to decide what they should do.

Imagine that a survey on immigration was conducted in your congressional district, asking voters if they favored allowing illegal immigrants to stay in the country or if people here illegally should be deported as soon as possible. Suppose that the poll results indicate strong support for one of the two options and that you yourself have no strong feelings about illegal immigrants. The decision you face is: Should you demand that Congress enact immigration reform consistent with the poll results or should you quietly ask that immigration reform be kept off the agenda?

Follow the poll.

Elected officials often have strong incentives to do what constituents demand—in this case, to push for immigration reform measures that are consistent with the demands expressed in the poll. By this logic, if most constituents want immigrants to gain legal status then you'd ask for a reform proposal that made legal status possible. Conversely, if the poll indicated that most constituents favored deportation you would push for legislation that funded a program to achieve this goal. Doing so would allow you to claim some credit for the specifics of the bill, as well as for your vote, which in theory would please most of your constituents and increase your chances of reelection.

Stay quiet.

As we discuss throughout the chapter, poll results are highly sensitive to question wording, timing, and other factors, making it hard to interpret even seemingly clear findings. Suppose, for example, the poll indicates support for allowing illegal immigrants to gain legal status. However, the survey did not ask about any of the conditions described in Table 6.2: whether legal status would require learning English,

holding a stable job, paying back taxes, or other conditions. Even though none of these conditions were in the question, most of your constituents probably had some of them in mind when they thought about how they wanted to answer the question. In other words, even if nothing changes, your constituents' support of immigration reform depends on what the reforms look like.

The situation is no easier if your poll indicates support for deportation. Would the government search for illegals to deport or just deport people they happen to find? What would happen to children whose parents entered the country illegally but who were born in the United States and are therefore citizens? For some respondents, the solution is a nationwide house-to-house search, with children deported with their parents. But others would reject a deportation process that did either of these things. So here again, the poll results, one-sided as they are, don't provide you with foolproof guidance about how to vote.

📷 Americans in both parties agree on the need for immigration reform but differ as to what they think the new immigration policies should be.

take a stand

1. Suppose you are a politician who feels that changes in immigration policy are needed but is faced with the quandary described above. Would you do nothing, so as to avoid alienating your constituency, or would you force a policy change and accept the political consequence—possible removal from office?

2. What poll questions would you use to get a clearer picture of public opinion on immigration?

Moreover, opinions about health care proposals are subject to influence by politicians and others. Over the last five years, Republicans in Congress have tried to repeal Obamacare nearly fifty times and Republican pundits have described the program in highly negative terms. It's no wonder, then, that Republican survey respondents select negative responses when asked about Obamacare—after all, that's all they've been hearing from the political figures they listen to and trust.

Finally, many supposed facts are actually "contested truths," meaning that even if people move beyond considerations to develop beliefs in a systematic way, they may nevertheless disagree.[52] For example, it is a fact that the unemployment rate almost doubled during George W. Bush's presidency and fell by over a third during President Obama's years in office.[53] Do these changes mean that Obama was a better steward of the economy than Bush? Bush's presidency began at the end of the 1990s tech boom that produced strong economic growth, while Obama took office during the most severe economic downturn since the Great Depression. People can easily arrive at different conclusions depending on how they account for these starting points.

Such problems do not arise in all areas of public opinion. Studies show that respondents' ability to express specific opinions, as well as the accuracy of their opinions, rises if the survey questions have something to do with their everyday life.[54] Thus, average Americans would be more likely to have an accurate sense of the state of the economy or their personal economic condition than of the military situation in Syria or the Ukraine. Everyday life gives us information about the economy; we learn about Syria or the Ukraine only if we take time to gather information. These effects are magnified insofar as the respondent considers the economy the more salient issue of the two.

How useful are surveys?

By now, CNN's disclaimer about the limits of mass surveys should not be much of a surprise. Survey results are most likely to be accurate when they are based on a simple, easily understood question about a topic familiar to the people being surveyed—such as the choice between two candidates, measured close to an election—and when the survey designers have worked to account for all of the problems discussed here. Under these conditions, with samples of 1,000 voters or more, poll results are generally within 3 or 4 percentage points of the true, population values.[55] You can be even more confident if multiple surveys addressing the same topic in different ways and at different times produce similar findings. However, if a single survey asks about a complex, unfamiliar topic—replacing the income tax with a national sales tax or determining whom to blame for a policy failure—then the results may not provide much insight into public opinion.

Surveys taken after an event—for example, a survey on gun control taken immediately after a school shooting—are generally not a good guide to public opinion. The problem is not that people are being insincere or thoughtless. Rather, it is because respondents' opinions are colored by the recent tragedy—but only in the short term. Over the next days, weeks, or months, opinions are likely to return to what they were before the event. Thus, polls taken in the wake of a powerful event may not be a good guide to what people might demand from government in light of what has happened, nor may they reflect how people might react a year later given government inaction. The same is true of polls taken well in advance of the time when the public actually has to act on their preferences—for example, a poll about the 2016 presidential election taken a year before the election, when most people know almost nothing about the candidates and have not even begun to think about their choice. Under these conditions, poll results tell us almost nothing about what people will ultimately do.

What Americans think about politics

In this section, we describe American public opinion, including people's ideological beliefs and what they think of the federal government. These opinions drive overall support for government action and serve as the basis for opinions on more specific policy questions. So, to understand what America's national government does and why, we have to determine what Americans ask of it.

Ideological polarization

We begin by examining liberal and conservative ideology and party identification to see whether historical data show evidence of polarization. Are there fewer moderates and more strong liberals and conservatives today than a generation ago? The What Do the Numbers Say? feature shows two kinds of survey data: responses to a question measuring ideology (liberal-moderate-conservative), and a question that taps a respondent's party identification (Republican-Independent-Democrat). The trends show no evidence of **ideological polarization**. It is hard to look at these data and think in terms of sharp divisions.

Looking more closely at opinion polarization, the third part of the What Do the Numbers Say? feature divides the electorate into eight groups based on answers to questions that tap important principles, from foreign policy to domestic issues, civil liberties, and morality. Principles such as these are a kind of consideration—they form the basis for opinions that people express in surveys or act on when they vote or engage in other political behavior. The figure shows, first, that only about a third of the electorate (Steadfast Conservatives, Business Conservatives, and Solid Liberals) hold consistent ideological beliefs—meaning that they generally give one kind of answer (conservative or liberal) when asked questions that tap their underlying principles. Even then, the data show that there are two broad groups of conservatives, one focused more on social issues, the other oriented more toward Wall Street

ideological polarization
The effect on public opinion when many citizens move away from moderate positions and toward either end of the political spectrum, identifying themselves as either liberals or conservatives.

Are the American People Polarized?

Many commentators describe politics in America as highly conflictual, with most Americans holding either liberal or conservative points of view and identifying with one of the two major parties. Is polarization as strong as these commentators think? What do the numbers say?

Sources: Data from General Social Survey 1972–2014, Cumulative Datafile, Survey Documentation and Analysis (SDA) at UC Berkeley, http://sda.berkeley.edu (accessed 11/5/15); Pew Research Center, "Trends in Party Identification, 1939–2014," April 5, 2015, www.people-press.org (accessed 11/5/15); Pew Research Center, "Beyond Red vs. Blue: The Political Typology," June 26, 2014, www.people-press.org (accessed 12/9/15).

Think about it

- According to the top figure, how have levels of polarization changed since the 1970s?
- What does the political typology reveal about divisions within each political party?

Liberal or Conservative Ideology in America

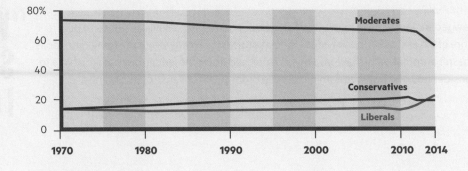

Party Identification in America

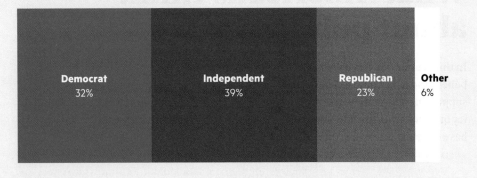

Political Typology

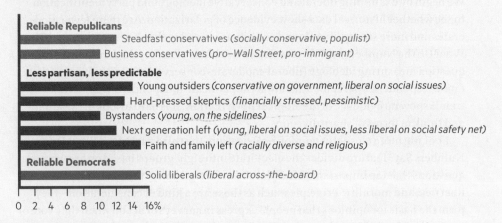

and pro-immigration reform. Moreover, most people fall into one of the intermediate groups, meaning that they express a mix of liberal and conservative issue positions.

While these data confirm that Americans disagree on important policy questions, they argue against the conception of a polarized America, with a large group of secular liberals opposing another large group of religious conservatives, with few people in the middle. Public opinion is much more complex. Most people could be labeled as liberals or as conservatives, secular or religious, depending on which issues they are asked about. Thus, even though people say they are liberals (or conservatives), this response does not mean that they hold liberal (or conservative) preferences on all issues. In addition, self-professed moderates may hold relatively extreme preferences on certain policy questions. Thus, understanding what Americans think and what they want from government often requires data on specific policy questions rather than broad judgments about the liberal or conservative nature of American public opinion.

Evaluations of government and officeholders

Another set of opinions that are important in American politics addresses how people view their government: How well or poorly do they think the government is doing? Do they trust the government? How do they evaluate individual politicians? These opinions matter for several reasons. Citizens' judgments about the government's overall performance may shape their evaluations of specific policies, especially if they do not know much about the policies.[56] Evaluations of specific policies may also be shaped by how much a citizen trusts the government; more trust brings higher evaluations.[57] Trust in government and overall evaluations might also influence a citizen's willingness to vote for incumbent congressional representatives or for a president seeking reelection.[58] In fact, the chances that someone voted for Donald Trump in 2016 were much higher given low trust in government.

The top graph in Figure 6.4 reveals that the average American is fairly disenchanted with the government. As of 2015, a majority believes that government is not run for the benefit of all the people and that government programs are usually wasteful and inefficient. These beliefs have not changed much over the last generation.

This impression of a disenchanted and disapproving public is reinforced by the second graph, which generally shows declining levels of trust in government since the 1960s. Within this overall trend, trust generally increases given a strong economy (the mid-1980s and mid-1990s) and declines during economic hard times (the mid-2000s to now) As noted earlier, many scholars have argued that low levels of trust make it harder for elected officials to enact new policies, especially those that require large expenditures.[59] On a more profound level, some scholars argue that low levels of trust raise questions about the future of democracy in America.[60] How can we say that American democracy is a good or popular form of government when so many people are unhappy with the performance of elected officials and bureaucrats and so few people trust the government?

Interestingly, low trust in government does not preclude people from approving of specific government programs and activities. Figure 6.5 shows that a majority of Americans give positive evaluations of a wide range of government programs, suggesting that the downward trend in trust is not the result of people being increasingly unhappy with what government actually does.

Trust in government reached a low point during the mid-1970s. The decline partly reflected the economic downturn and conflict over the Vietnam War, but opinions were also shaped by the discovery that President Richard Nixon lied about the Watergate scandal. Here, Nixon resigns from office to avoid impeachment.

FIGURE
6.4

What Do Americans Think about Government?

A significant percentage of Americans have always been distrustful and disparaging of the federal government—and the percentage of people holding such views has increased markedly in the last generation. Does the perception that government is wasteful and inefficient make it easier or harder to enact new policies? How might the decline in trust explain the rise of the Tea Party organization and candidates like Donald Trump and Bernie Sanders?

Source: Pew Research Center, "A Wider Ideological Gap Between More and Less Educated Adults," April 26, 2016, www. people-press.org (accessed 8/24/16); Pew Research Center, "Beyond Distrust: How Americans View Their Government," August 25, 2016, www.people-press.org (accessed 8/25/16).

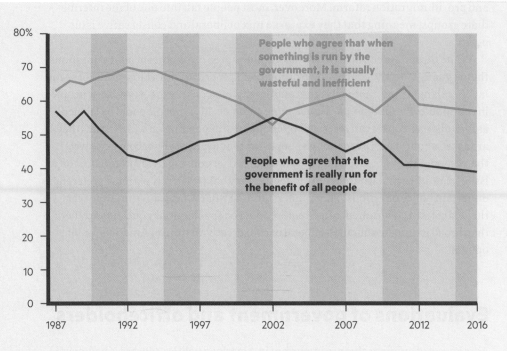

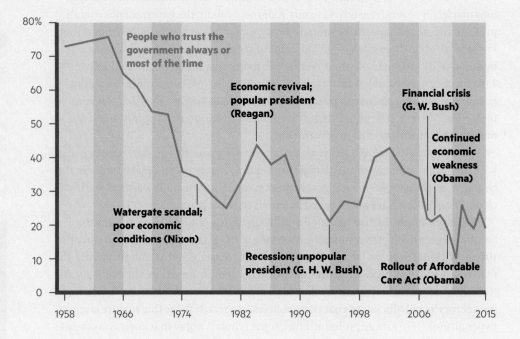

A second response is that although Americans don't like the government in general, they tend to be far more satisfied with their own representatives in Washington (see Chapter 11). One possibility is that putting a human face on government by asking about specific individuals in office improves respondents' opinions because it calls to mind different considerations. Asking about "the government" may call to mind a vast

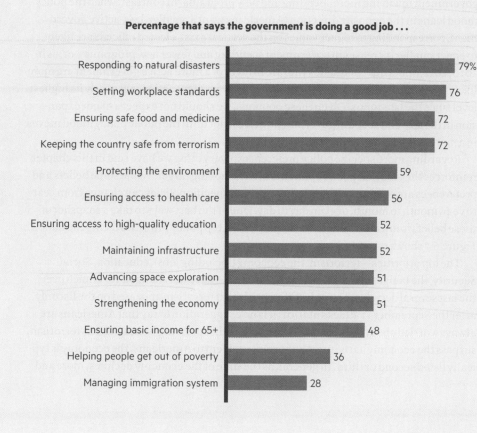

Percentage that says the government is doing a good job . . .

Category	Percentage
Responding to natural disasters	79%
Setting workplace standards	76
Ensuring safe food and medicine	72
Keeping the country safe from terrorism	72
Protecting the environment	59
Ensuring access to health care	56
Ensuring access to high-quality education	52
Maintaining infrastructure	52
Advancing space exploration	51
Strengthening the economy	51
Ensuring basic income for 65+	48
Helping people get out of poverty	36
Managing immigration system	28

FIGURE 6.5

Measuring American Public Opinion: Is the Government Doing a Good Job?

How is it that Americans disapprove of government overall, but give relatively high ratings in many specific areas?

Source: Pew Research Center, "Beyond Distrust: How Americans View Their Government," November 23, 2015, www.people-press.org (accessed 12/5/15).

room of bureaucrats pushing paperwork from one desk to another, whereas asking about "your representative" may lead people to think of someone working on their behalf.

Survey respondents may also be responding to trust questions in ways we do not expect. In particular, in an era of polarized parties considerations such as perceptions of the economy and the president may dominate trust responses as well as questions about government efficiency and effectiveness. If so, the decline in trust may say more about the nature of contemporary politics than it does about citizens' confidence in their government.

Policy preferences

In a diverse country of more than 320 million, people care about a wide range of government policies. One useful measure of Americans' policy preferences is the **policy mood**, mentioned earlier, which captures the public's collective demands for government action on domestic policies.[61] Policy mood measures are constructed from surveys that ask about opinions on a wide range of policy questions.[62]

Changes in the policy mood in America have led to changes in defense spending, environmental policy, and civil rights policies, among others—and have influenced elections (see Figure 6.6).[63] When the policy mood leans in an activist direction (Americans want government to do more, corresponding to lower values on the vertical axis), such as in the early 1960s, conditions are ripe for an expansion of the federal

policy mood
The level of public support for expanding the government's role in society; whether the public wants government action on a specific issue.

government involving more spending and new programs. In contrast, when the policy mood leans in the opposite direction (Americans want a smaller, less-active government, corresponding to higher values on the vertical axis), elected officials are likely to enact smaller increases in government spending and fewer new programs—or, as in 2010, 2012, and 2014, candidates who are in favor of a more active government are more likely to be defeated. At present, opposition to government action is at nearly its highest level since the late 1980s. Given these opinions, we should not expect a major expansion in the size and scope of government, at least not until the public policy mood moves in a more activist direction.

Regarding more specific policy preferences, everything we have said in this chapter reinforces the idea that public opinion is often a moving target. While some beliefs and preferences are stable over time, opinions about specific policies can change from year to year, month to month, or even day to day. One of the best ways to take a snapshot of these beliefs is to ask citizens what they see as the top policy priorities facing the nation. Figure 6.7 shows responses to a 2015 survey.

The top priorities—terrorism, the economy (including jobs), education, Social Security, the budget deficit, and health care costs—have not changed very much over the last several decades. The only difference is that terrorism appeared on the list only after the September 11 attacks in 2001. It is no exaggeration to say that Americans are always worried about the economy. Even when other pressing issues, such as terrorism, surpass the economy as the most important problem to Americans, the economy is typically listed second or third. In general, as the state of the economy declines, more and

FIGURE 6.6

Policy Mood

Surveys assess the public's policy mood by asking questions about specific policy questions such as levels of taxation and government spending and the role of government. The level of conservatism (for example, support for smaller, less-active government) was at a high in 1952 and 1980. Could you have used the policy mood prior to the election to predict the outcomes of the 2012 presidential and 2012 and 2014 congressional elections?

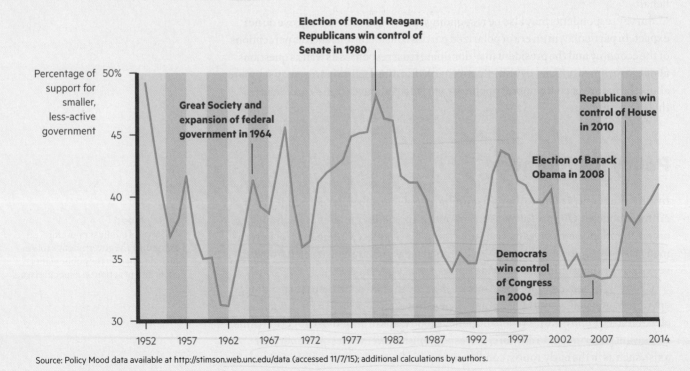

Source: Policy Mood data available at http://stimson.web.unc.edu/data (accessed 11/7/15); additional calculations by authors.

more people rate the economy as their greatest concern. Moreover, the percentage of people who make reference to their personal economic concerns—for example, unemployment or worries about retirement—also increases.

These policy priorities frame contemporary political debates and divide the political parties. Think about what Republicans and Democrats in Washington argue about: how best to fight terrorism and secure the United States from attack, how to increase economic growth and reduce the unemployment rate, and what the government's role should be in providing health care and making sure that Americans have secure retirements. In a very fundamental way, then, this list confirms that American politicians are intimately connected to their constituents—the issues that politicians debate and legislate on are the ones that many people care about.

The list of policy priorities also explains government inaction on some issues. For example, only 38 percent of Americans see global warming as a top policy priority—and gun control doesn't even appear on the list. Thus, the fact that Congress has not legislated on either of these issues in recent years is actually consistent with public opinion. For better or worse, the average American has other priorities for government action.

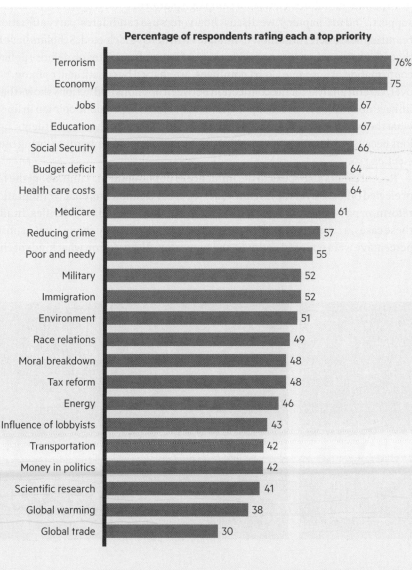

Percentage of respondents rating each a top priority

Issue	Percentage
Terrorism	76%
Economy	75
Jobs	67
Education	67
Social Security	66
Budget deficit	64
Health care costs	64
Medicare	61
Reducing crime	57
Poor and needy	55
Military	52
Immigration	52
Environment	51
Race relations	49
Moral breakdown	48
Tax reform	48
Energy	46
Influence of lobbyists	43
Transportation	42
Money in politics	42
Scientific research	41
Global warming	38
Global trade	30

FIGURE 6.7

The American Public's Policy Priorities, 2015

Given this data on policy priorities, what legislation will likely be proposed by incoming president Donald Trump?

Source: Pew Research Center, "Public's Policy Priorities for 2015," www.people-press.org (accessed 11/7/15).

Public Opinion Is Relevant We can say with confidence that public opinion remains highly relevant in American politics today. One key piece of evidence is the amount of time and effort politicians, journalists, and political scientists spend trying to find out what Americans think. Of course, it is easy to find examples in which the political process appears to ignore public opinion in cases in which policy has stayed the same despite a majority supporting change. In other cases, new policies have been enacted even though a majority preferred the status quo. But these examples do not mean that public opinion is irrelevant—just that the policy-making process is complex. It is not always possible to please a majority of citizens. Politicians' willingness to do so depends on whether the majority is organized into interest groups, how much they care about the issue (and the intensity of the opposition), and, most important, the details of their preferences.

Public Opinion Can Influence Government Despite all the difficulties described, public opinion exerts a conspicuous influence in widespread areas of government. We mention this broad influence repeatedly throughout this book. In Chapter 11, we describe how legislators endeavor to determine what their constituents want and how their constituents will respond to different actions. In Chapter 9, we see how voters use retrospective evaluations to form opinions about whom to vote for and how candidates incorporate the public's views into campaign platforms that will attract widespread support. And in Chapter 8, we discuss how voters use candidates' party affiliations like brand names to determine how candidates will behave if elected. Scholars have found that congressional actions on a wide range of issues, from votes on defense policy to the confirmation of Supreme Court nominees, are shaped by constituent opinion.[64] Moreover, careful analysis of the connection between opinions and actions shows that this linkage does not exist because politicians are able to shape public opinion in line with what they want to do; rather, politicians behave in line with their constituents' opinions because to do otherwise would place the politicians in jeopardy of losing the next election.[65]

Recent events also speak to the influence of public opinion. Think about the failure of elected officials over the last few years to repeal Obamacare, enact immigration reform, or pass new limits on the ownership of handguns and assault rifles. In all of these cases, a significant portion of Americans wanted policy change, but a substantial percentage were opposed and even the supporters disagreed on what kinds of changes

Public opinion influences government at election time, when voters' opinions about incumbent politicians and the party in power influence voters' decisions at the polls. In 2016, voters' evaluations of President Obama were an important influence on the election outcome.

were best. Congressional inaction on these measures does not reflect a willful ignorance of public opinion. Rather, it reflects the lack of a public consensus about what government should do. Inaction on these issues is exactly what we should expect if public opinion is real and relevant to what happens in politics.

"Why Should I Care?"

Political scientists and pollsters spend so much time trying to measure public opinion because it shapes election outcomes and policy changes in Washington. If you want to know what the federal government is going to do over the next four years, spend some time trying to determine what people want.

Conclusion

Public opinion is real, and it matters. Americans have ideas about what they want government to do, and they use these ideas to guide their political choices. While Americans disagree about many issues, they also do agree about some issues—which provides areas in which compromise is possible. In a country as large and diverse as the United States, disagreement over government policy is inevitable. However, as we have shown in this chapter, disagreement does not make compromise impossible—and it does not support the idea that Americans are engaged in a culture war. In many areas people disagree, but their opinions reflect a willingness to accept compromise.

The roles of public opinion in shaping the policy response to mass shootings, immigration reform, the budget deficit, or any of the other policy questions we have discussed in this chapter are all examples of how much public opinion matters in American politics. The average American is not an expert on government policies and knows relatively little about possible alternatives. But even a small amount of information is enough to inform beliefs about what policies should be enacted. Moreover, politicians generally take care to behave in accordance with these demands, which may even make them backtrack on positions or votes they have previously taken or made if they believe the public mood has changed. And the changes in the last few years in government policy, politicians' statements, and election outcomes all reflect such changes in the policy mood.

Likewise, very few Americans are experts about gay rights, health care reform, or immigration reform. Their responses to questions about these issues may vary from day to day, but most Americans know enough to decide what they want government to do about these problems—and to act on these opinions. Politicians, in turn, take public opinion very seriously, as it provides the yardstick that measures citizens' judgments of their behavior in office.

Gun control is an example of all of these phenomena. Even after a mass shooting, Americans are divided on the need for making it harder to own or carry a handgun and on whether ownership of assault weapons should be banned. Even in areas where there is some consensus, such as regulating gun ownership by people judged to be mentally ill, people disagree as to how an individual's mental health would be evaluated. In light of all of these factors, Congress's inability to enact gun control legislation makes sense. The problem is not that legislators are ignoring Americans' opinions. Rather, the problem is that different groups are demanding different things. In the absence of agreement among at least a majority of Americans about how government policy should change, it is no surprise that policy stays the same.

STUDY GUIDE

What is public opinion?

Define *public opinion* and explain why it matters in American politics. (Pages 192–197)

Summary

What the population thinks about politics and government matters for three reasons: people's political actions are driven by their opinions; there is a strong linkage between people's opinions and political actors' behavior; and public opinion helps us understand how specific policy outcomes are achieved. Although early research was skeptical that people held meaningful opinions, current research shows that people do have real and meaningful policy positions.

Key terms

public opinion (p. 192)   latent opinion (p. 193)
liberal or conservative ideology
(p. 193)

Practice Quiz Questions

1. **What does it mean that most political judgments are latent opinions?**
    a. Most Americans have preformed opinions.
    b. Most Americans have well-thought-out reasons for preferring a policy.
    c. Most Americans do not have any meaningful political attitudes.
    d. Most Americans form their opinions only as needed.
    e. Most opinions are not accurate.

2. **Which of the following is *not* true regarding considerations?**
    a. Well-informed and poorly informed people use them in forming opinions.
    b. Opinions on morally complex issues do not involve considerations.
    c. Political events can become considerations.
    d. They may be contradictory.
    e. Party identification is often used in considerations.

Where do opinions come from?

Explain how people form political attitudes and opinions. (Pages 197–201)

Summary

Political opinions are influenced by a number of factors. The belief systems of parents and relatives influence our opinions early on, and our social groups influence our perspectives later in life. Personal events such as attending college or moving to a new city may also influence how we think about politics, as do national events such as the attacks on September 11, 2001. Even debates among political elites and party leaders shape our political attitudes.

Key term

political socialization (p. 197)

Practice Quiz Questions

3. **The theory of political socialization says that people's opinions are influenced first by _____.**
    a. what they learned from their parents
    b. the way political parties change over time
    c. genetic and biological factors
    d. their personality traits
    e. politicians

4. **An event or some other new information is most likely to change an individual's opinion when _____.**
    a. the individual is highly informed about the issue
    b. the individual holds strong opinions
    c. the individual is strongly partisan
    d. the individual does not have a set of preexisting principles with which to interpret the event
    e. the individual does not watch the news

5. **The idea that individuals will rely on others who "look like" them for opinions relates to _____**
    a. party identification
    b. political socialization
    c. group identity
    d. political events
    e. generational effects

6. **Which phrase best completes the following statement regarding the sources of public opinion? "Politicians and other political actors work to _____ public opinion."**
    a. respond to
    b. ignore
    c. disregard
    d. stabilize
    e. shape

Measuring public opinion

Describe basic survey methods and potential issues affecting accuracy. (Pages 202–211)

Summary

While most information on public opinion comes from mass surveys where thousands of people respond, some information comes from focus groups where small groups of people are interviewed together. Despite a number of limitations, most research on public opinion focuses on mass surveys, as they can be used to draw broad conclusions about the country.

Key terms
mass survey (p. 202)   sample (p. 203)
population (p. 202)   random sample (p. 206)
sampling error (p. 202)

Practice Quiz Questions

7. **Why are focus groups helpful in understanding public opinion?**

    a. They provide deep insights into why people hold the views that they do.

    b. They provide a representative sample of the population.

    c. They use a small number of respondents to draw conclusions about the country.

    d. It is impossible to understand someone's partisanship based on a survey.

    e. They restrict respondents to a few answer choices.

8. **Which of the following is *not* a random sampling technique?**

    a. random digit dialing

    b. face-to-face interviewing

    c. Internet polling

    d. push polls

    e. robo-polling

9. **Why is it important to get a large random survey sample?**

    a. to keep costs down

    b. to provide deep insights into why people hold their opinions

    c. to help candidates fine-tune their campaign messages

    d. to be able to generalize about the broad population

    e. to prevent question wording from biasing survey results

10. **Suppose a survey of Americans' attitudes about NSA surveillance of cell phone records reveals that the level of opposition to surveillance varies with how the question is phrased. What is the best explanation for this variation?**

    a. People don't take surveys seriously.

    b. People are afraid to express truthful opinions on surveys.

    c. Changes in the wording of questions call to mind different considerations.

    d. Changes in in the wording of questions make people suspicious.

    e. Few people can respond in a rational way to survey questions.

What Americans think about politics

Present findings on what Americans think about government and why it matters. (Pages 211–219)

Summary

As a whole, the American electorate is ideologically moderate, with relatively little ideological polarization. Paradoxically, although trust in the government has declined steadily since the 1960s, people are still generally happy with their own representatives in Washington, D.C., and low trust in government does not preclude Americans from approving of specific government programs and activities. While it can be difficult to determine exactly what the American public wants, public opinion is still quite relevant in American politics. Government policy and congressional outcomes are responsive to changes in public mood, and most policy decisions (and arguments) reflect the priorities of a majority of Americans.

Key terms
ideological polarization (p. 211)   policy mood (p. 215)

Practice Quiz Questions

11. **In the 1970s, the majority of Americans identified themselves as ideologically _____; in the 2000s, most Americans identified themselves as _____.**

    a. moderate; conservative

    b. moderate; moderate

    c. moderate; liberal

    d. conservative; moderate

    e. conservative; conservative

12. **What is policy mood?**

    a. public support for Congress

    b. presidential approval rating

    c. trust in government

    d. public demand for government action on domestic policies

    e. public demand for government action on international policies

13. **Which policy area is always near the top of Americans' concerns?**

    a. economic conditions

    b. health care

    c. same-sex marriage

    d. immigration

    e. the environment

14. **Americans generally _____ of the government and generally _____ of their own representatives.**

    a. approve; approve

    b. approve; disapprove

    c. disapprove; approve

    d. disapprove; disapprove

15. When the government enacts policies even though a majority of Americans prefer the status quo, it serves as evidence that _____.

   a. public opinion is irrelevant

   b. the policy-making process is complex

   c. politicians don't listen to what their constituents want

   d. the government is not trustworthy

   e. public opinion is stable

Suggested Reading

Alvarez, R. Michael, and John Brehm. *Hard Choices, Easy Answers.* Princeton, NJ: Princeton University Press, 2002.

Campbell, David. *Why We Vote: How Schools and Communities Shape Our Civic Life.* Princeton, NJ: Princeton University Press, 2006.

Carmines, Edward G., and James A. Stimson. *Issue Evolution: Race and the Transformation of American Politics.* Princeton, NJ: Princeton University Press, 1990.

Delli Carpini, Michael X., and Scott Keeter. *What Americans Know about Politics and Why It Matters.* New Haven, CT: Yale University Press, 1997.

Druckman, James N., and Lawrence P. Jacobs. *Who Governs? Presidents, Public Opinion, and Manipulation.* Chicago: University of Chicago Press, 2015.

Green, Donald P., Bradley Palmquist, and Eric Schickler. *Partisan Hearts and Minds.* New Haven, CT: Yale University Press, 2002.

Hetherington, Mark, and Thomas Rudolph. *Why Washington Won't Work: Polarization, Political Trust, and the Governing Crisis.* Chicago: University of Chicago Press, 2015.

Hibbing, John R., and Elizabeth Theiss-Morse. *Congress as Public Enemy: Public Attitudes toward American Political Institutions.* New York: Cambridge University Press, 1995.

Jacobs, Lawrence R., and Robert Y. Shapiro. *Politicians Don't Pander: Political Manipulation and the Loss of Democratic Responsiveness.* Chicago: University of Chicago Press, 2000.

Lodge, Milton, and Charles Taber. *The Rationalizing Voter.* New York: Cambridge University Press, 2013.

Marcus, George E., John L. Sullivan, Elizabeth Theiss-Morse, and Sandra L. Wood. *With Malice toward Some: How People Make Civil Liberties Judgments.* New York: Cambridge University Press, 1995.

Peffley, Mark, and Jon Hurwitz. *Justice in America: The Separate Realities of Blacks and Whites.* New York: Cambridge University Press, 2010.

Zaller, John. *The Nature and Origins of Mass Opinion.* New York: Cambridge University Press, 1992.

7

The Media

Do the media make us more informed?

During the 2016 presidential campaign, reporters needing a story could always count on Donald Trump. His campaign began with a speech that labeled Mexican immigrants as drug dealers, criminals, rapists—"and some, I assume, are good people." Over the course of the primary and general-election campaign, Trump frequently lobbed insults at his opponents, but also at various media outlets, both political parties, a wide range of current and past Republican and Democratic elected officials, foreign leaders, and even magician Penn Jillette—calling them clowns, lightweights, pathetic, stupid, low-energy, crazy, crooked, losers, haters, dishonest, broken down, boring, frauds, puppets, kooky, dopey, and hypocrites.

From the beginning of his campaign, Trump's willingness to say outrageous things also made it easy to write campaign stories that people wanted to read—not a small thing for reporters faced with daily deadlines. But in focusing on Trump and his antics, reporters were helping him to connect with Americans and get his message across. Admittedly, Trump attracted considerable public support from the moment he announced his candidacy, so there is no reason to think that his victory was the product of overly favorable media coverage. But in focusing on Trump, reporters had less time to follow other candidates. Would different coverage have led to a different Republican nominee, or a different general-election outcome?

Decisions by reporters and editors about what to publish are especially important because media coverage is the primary mechanism through which Americans learn about politics and public policy.[1] For democracy to work, citizens need to know something about candidates and have a sense of which policy options are consistent with their own goals. Not everyone has to be an expert, but people have to meet a minimum standard of knowing which direction they would like government policy to go and which candidates would work toward this goal if elected.

★
CHAPTER GOALS

Describe the role of the media in American politics and how people get political information.
pages 226–232

Explain how politicians use the media to achieve their goals.
pages 233–236

Explain how the media influence how people think about politics.
pages 236–243

Assess whether the media fulfill their role in American democracy.
pages 244–247

📷

Reporters in need of a story could always rely on U.S. Republican presidential candidate Donald Trump to say something they could write a story around. But did media coverage of Trump provide voters with the information they needed to assess whether he would be a good president?
@realDonaldTrump

Many critics blame the media for gaps in Americans' political knowledge, low levels of civic engagement, and distrust of the federal government.[2] These observers want media coverage that gives Americans a detailed appreciation of the policy questions facing elected officials and that holds elected officials accountable for their campaign promises and behavior in office, and want sound, substantiated coverage instead of outrage, scandals, failures, and poll results.[3] Why do the media fail to fulfill this important role in American politics?

Not only does the content of many news stories influence politics, but political processes and outcomes also influence the news industry. Coverage is shaped by federal regulations that affect what journalists can print or broadcast, as well as by the structure and ownership of media corporations, most of which need to make a profit to survive. These political influences on the media can, in turn, affect how Americans view officeholders, candidates, and events.

In this chapter, we ask whether the media's coverage of candidate and now president Donald Trump is the exception or the rule. That is, do the media avoid the often-dull complexities of American politics in favor of scandals, insults, and attention-grabbing headlines? Is this how the media work? And if so, why? Along the way, we will also consider whether the media are biased, describe how Americans gather information about politics, and show how the Internet's evolution into a major source of political information has changed both the traditional media business and what Americans know about politics.

★

DESCRIBE THE ROLE OF THE MEDIA IN AMERICAN POLITICS AND HOW PEOPLE GET POLITICAL INFORMATION

mass media
Sources that provide information to the average citizen, such as newspapers, television networks, radio stations, podcasts, and websites.

Political media today

This section describes the mass media, the many sources of political information available to Americans, and how people use (or don't use) this information. The development of the Internet over the last generation has dramatically increased the number of media sources and the range of information available to the average American. With this change, it is less important to describe each source and what kinds of information they can (and cannot) provide. In contemporary America, there are so many sources and so much information that Americans can become experts on virtually any aspect of politics or public policy—if they are willing to search for information and put together what they find.

Historical overview: how did we get here?

The role of the media as an information source and the controversy over how the media report about politics are nothing new. Since the Founding, politicians have understood that Americans learn about politics largely from the media, have complained about coverage, and sought to influence both the media's selection of stories and the way they report on them.

The Media as Watchdog and Business From the beginnings of the United States, mass media has served as a reporter of political events and as a watchdog, keeping track of what politicians are doing and offering insight about their policy successes and failures. During the Revolutionary War, many newspapers chronicled the conflict; after the war, while politicians negotiated over the size and scope of the new federal government, newspapers became a venue for debates over different plans.[4] At the same time that the media cover politics, politicians try to shape this coverage to their advantage. During the ratification of the Constitution, Alexander Hamilton, John Jay, and James Madison helped pro-ratification forces in New York by publishing (under a pseudonym) a series of articles in local newspapers.[5] And in 1798 Congress and President John Adams enacted the Alien and Sedition Acts, which made it a crime to publish articles that criticized the president or Congress.[6] While these press restrictions were later repealed or allowed to expire, they serve as a reminder of the conflictual relationship between politicians and reporters and that the American media have never been free of government regulation.

Long before the Internet, the media's role as watchdog expanded because of changes in technology. In 1833, the *New York Sun* began selling papers for a penny a copy rather than the standard price of six cents. The price reduction, which was facilitated by cheaper, faster printing presses, made the newspaper available to the mass public for the first time, and this increase in circulation made it possible, even with the lower price, to hire larger staffs of reporters.[7] The development of the telegraph also aided newspapers by enabling reporters on assignment throughout the country to quickly send stories back home for publication. Many of the new publications were unabashedly partisan. For example, the *New York Tribune* was strongly antislavery. By 1860, the *Tribune*'s circulation was larger than that of any other newspaper in the world and its articles "helped to add fuel to the fires of slavery and sectionalism that divided North and South."[8] At the other extreme, the *New York Times* was transformed in the 1800s into a nonpartisan paper with the goals of journalistic impartiality, accuracy, and complete coverage of events—its motto to the present day is "All the News That's Fit to Print."[9]

The media's role as a watchdog has always been constrained by the need to attract a paying audience in order to stay in business—as well as the gains to be had from running a profit-making business. The period after the Civil War saw the beginning of yellow journalism, reporting that appealed to a wider audience by using bold headlines, illustrations, and sensational stories (the name came from the yellow paper it was printed on). And during the 1920s hundreds of small, local radio stations appeared, along with some larger stations that could broadcast nationwide, eventually leading to the development of networks, that is, groups of local radio (and, later, television) stations owned by one company that broadcast a common set of programs. While these new electronic sources made more information available to Americans, many of them were developed not as watchdogs but as highly profitable enterprises that delivered entertainment as well as news to citizens, and monetized their audience by selling radio or television time to advertisers.[10]

Regulating the Media Federal regulation of the news media was driven by the fact that many media sources are profit-seeking businesses—as well as concerns over the media's potential to shape public opinion. For example, the Federal Communications Commission (FCC) regulates the broadcast media, such as radio stations, as well as broadcast and cable television. Until very recently, a central concern of the FCC was that one company or organization might buy enough stations to dominate the airwaves in an area and become a monopoly, offering only one set of programs or point of view. For many years, FCC regulations limited the number of radio and television stations a company could own in a community and the total nationwide audience that a company's television stations could reach.[11] The FCC also created the equal time provision, which says that if a radio or television station gives air time to a candidate outside its news coverage—such as during an entertainment show or a cooking program—it has

Yellow journalism emphasized sensational stories and bold headlines, but also made information about contemporary politics available to a wider audience.

yellow journalism
A style of newspaper reporting popular in the late 1800s that featured sensationalized stories, bold headlines, and illustrations to increase readership.

Federal Communications Commission (FCC)
A government agency created in 1934 to regulate American radio stations and later expanded to regulate television, wireless communications technologies, and other broadcast media.

broadcast media
Communications technologies, such as television and radio, that transmit information over airwaves.

equal time provision
An FCC regulation requiring broadcast media to provide equal air time on any non-news programming to all candidates running for an office.

to give an equivalent amount of time to other candidates running for the same office. For example, when presidential candidate Donald Trump hosted *Saturday Night Live* in November 2015 the television network (NBC) that broadcast the program had to give free television time (in the form of free advertising slots) to other presidential candidates.

Deregulation The FCC's limits on ownership and content have been eliminated because of the development of new communications technologies such as cable television, satellite television, and the Internet. The logic is that with so many sources of information, if one broadcaster ignores a candidate, an issue, or a viewpoint citizens could still find out what they wanted to know from another source. Pressure for deregulation also came from the owners of media companies, who wanted to buy more television, radio, and cable stations, as well as from book and magazine publishers, Internet service providers, and newspapers.[12]

These regulatory changes have shaped the current media landscape in two ways. First, concentration: many media companies own multiple media sources in a town or community. For example, ClearChannel Communications owns multiple AM and FM radio stations in more than 30 cities. The second trend is cross-ownership, which involves one company owning several different kinds of media outlets, often in the same community. The Tribune Company in Chicago owns the WGN radio station, the WGN television station, and the *Chicago Tribune* daily newspaper. These trends have given rise to media conglomerates, companies that control a wide range of news sources.[13] Nuts & Bolts 7.1 shows the diverse holdings of one such company, News Corp/21st Century Fox.

media conglomerates
Companies that control a large number of media sources across several types of media outlets.

Media sources in the twenty-first century

Over the last two decades, the Internet has become a major and often dominant information source for information about American politics. Most U.S. newspapers, magazines, television networks, radio stations, and cable stations offer free or (increasingly)

Holdings of News Corp/21st Century Fox

News Corp/21st Century Fox* is an example of a media conglomerate, a company that controls a variety of media outlets throughout the world. It owns cable television networks, television and radio stations, newspapers, movie-production companies, magazines, and even sports teams. This structure allows the company to rebroadcast or reprint stories in different outlets and thus operate more efficiently, but opponents are concerned that conglomerates might expand to control most—or even all—of the sources that are available to the average citizen, making it impossible to access alternate points of view.

Fox Television Stations	Film Companies	Books and Magazines
31 U.S. stations	21st Century Fox Fox Searchlight Pictures Fox Television Studios Blue Sky Studios 11 other film companies	45 book publishers (including HarperCollins) worldwide 3 magazines

Satellite and Cable Holdings	Newspapers	Other Holdings
Fox News Channel More than 60 other cable channels in and outside the United States 6 satellite television channels	*New York Post* *Wall Street Journal* 3 UK newspapers 19 Australian newspapers 30 local U.S. newspapers	AmericanIdol.com Over 50 news and entertainment websites Many other businesses

*These two companies were created in 2013 by dividing the operations of the News Corporation. However, the founder of the News Corporation, Rupert Murdoch, is the chairman and CEO of 21st Century Fox and the executive chairman of News Corp, and his family trust still holds a controlling interest in both corporations.

paid access to all of their content via websites and mobile apps. There are also many Internet-only sites that offer a combination of rumor, inside information, and deep analysis of American politics. Some, such as Politico, Vox, and FiveThirtyEight, have paid staff and report on a wide range of topics. Others have a narrower focus: SCOTUS-blog (the Supreme Court of the United States blog) analyzes Supreme Court decisions, judicial nominations, and other legal questions.[14] Other blogs, such as The Monkey Cage (now affiliated with the *Washington Post*) and the Mischiefs of Faction (now part of Vox), use political science research to explain contemporary American politics.[15] And many websites, some run by ordinary citizens, provide their own insights and information about American politics. Finally, even Facebook offers news about politics through its news feed and trending stories menu.

The creation of the Internet, along with increases in the number of mainstream media sources, has dramatically increased the amount of information about politics that is available to the average American. Imagine yourself in the late 1940s. Suppose you wanted to learn about President Truman's State of the Union address. If you couldn't go to Washington to hear it in person, where could you have gotten information about the speech? If you lived in a big city, the speech would probably be covered in the next day's newspaper. If you lived in a small town, your local paper might or might not run the story. If it didn't, you would need a subscription to either a big-city paper (which would arrive a week after the fact) or a weekly or monthly news magazine or you would need to have access to a radio that could pick up a station broadcasting the speech.

DID YOU KNOW?

65%

of American adults use Facebook, and about half of these people say they get their news from Facebook.
Source: Pew Research Center

"Viral" is not the same thing
as "true."

—Kevin Drum,
Mother Jones magazine

Across the world, from Black
Live Matter protests to citizens
documenting the scene after the Paris
attacks, the Internet makes it easy
for ordinary citizens to share political
information and report on political
events as they happen.
#BlackLivesMatter #PorteOuverte

Now consider the modern era in which major political events saturate the media. Suppose it's a day in early 2016, right before the Iowa Caucuses, and you want to know what Donald Trump said during a campaign appearance yesterday. You can tune in to one of the four major television networks, numerous cable news channels, public television stations, or radio stations or watch video clips on many websites. Most television stations will feature pundits' commentaries on the race and will interview prominent politicians and commentators. Jimmy Fallon and other late-night hosts will probably make jokes about Trump and the other candidates on television, and John Oliver will skewer them on his Sunday show. Tomorrow the race will be front-page news and larger papers will publish the full text of Trump's speech. Countless Internet sites will offer information and analyses. And you will be able to watch a video of the speech on You-Tube and many other sites. The point is, there are many places to get information; you would have to work to avoid them.

The Internet has created more opportunities for homegrown media, allowing a would-be citizen journalist or subject expert to easily set up a website, Facebook page, YouTube channel, or some other way to present information. Such reporting has the potential to shape elections or at least to distract politicians from their desired message. During the last month of the 2016 presidential election, someone sent the *Washington Post* outtakes from a 2005 episode of *Access Hollywood* in which Donald Trump discussed "kissing, groping, and trying to have sex with women" (in the *Post*'s terms). After the story became public, many other women came forward to claim that Trump had sexually harassed or sexually assaulted them. Of course, Trump won the election—but these revelations cost him significant support from women voters.

The Internet has also made new kinds of political information available to the average citizen. For example, the Center for Responsive Politics offers a searchable database of contributions to candidates and political organizations.[16] Many sites, including FiveThirtyEight.com and Pollster.com, collect and analyze public opinion surveys, including presidential election polls.[17] Other websites offer less useful but entertaining political information. The Internet also creates new opportunities for interaction between citizens, reporters, and government officials. Many reporters and politicians host live online chat sessions, allowing people to ask follow-up questions about published stories, or interact with their audience through a variety of social media sites, including Facebook, Twitter, and reddit.

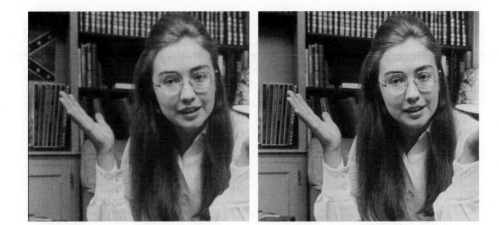

While there is much more information available today than a generation ago, these sources are constantly in flux. Websites and Web pages come and go. Even well-established media sources can quickly change. For example, recent years have seen sizable declines in magazine and newspaper readership. Companies that once owned newspapers in Chicago, Philadelphia, and Minneapolis have gone bankrupt, whereas several major U.S. cities, including Seattle, Birmingham, and New Orleans, have a hometown daily newspaper that appears in print form. Other newspapers have cut foreign bureaus, reduced their staff, and thinned the amount of news in every edition.[18] At the same time, the major television networks as well as cable television sources have also seen declines in viewership.

In addition, some of the vast quantity of information on the Internet is of questionable reliability. For example, it is easy to find fake photographs showing Hillary Clinton with the Confederate flag on her bookshelf. Some websites identify these pictures as the fabrications that they are, but others do not. In a world where websites come and go and where citizens often do not take the time to investigate what they see or read, false information may easily be accepted as true.

Where do people get political information?

While there is a vast amount of information available about politics, very few Americans make it a priority to be well informed about politics—which would require them to systematically consult a range of different sources.

Rather, most Americans acquire political information accidentally through a process known as the **by-product theory**.[19] That is, they read a newspaper's sports pages and glance at front-page stories along the way. They watch television and catch a few minutes of the news. They read a story on Facebook or an Internet news site because the title looks interesting. Only sometimes do they actually seek out media coverage of politics.

Even so, there are some systematic differences in media use according to an individual's ideological beliefs. Table 7.1 shows the top-10 most-used media sources for people who are consistent liberals, people who are consistent conservatives, and people whose beliefs are a mix of conservative and liberal beliefs.

Clearly, there are some sharp differences between liberals and conservatives: liberals and people with mixed beliefs are most likely to get information from National Public Radio (NPR), network and cable news channels, and other sites such as that of the *New York Times*, while conservatives rely on one television channel, Fox News, and various talk radio and online conservative websites. Even with these

by-product theory
The idea that many Americans acquire political information unintentionally rather than by seeking it out.

💡

DID YOU KNOW?

The weekly audience for Rush Limbaugh's program, the top conservative talk radio show, is

13 million

The top liberal program has an audience of only 2 million.
Source: *Talkers Magazine*

TABLE
7.1

Top-10 Media Sources for Different Ideological Groups

Consistent Liberal	Mixed	Consistent Conservative
NPR	Facebook	Fox News
CNN	CNN	*The Sean Hannity Show*
Facebook	ABC News	*The Rush Limbaugh Show*
MSNBC	NBC News	Facebook
NBC News	Fox News	*The Glenn Beck Program*
PBS	CBS News	TheBlaze
The Daily Show	Yahoo News	ABC News
BBC	Google News	CBS News
ABC News	MSNBC	NBC News
New York Times	YouTube	CNN

> **"**
> All I know is just what I read in the papers, and that's an alibi for my ignorance.
>
> —Will Rogers

differences in media usage, there is considerable overlap: for example, regardless of beliefs, news presented on Facebook is a popular source for everyone. And there is some overlap in other sources: the network news sites and CNN are on all three lists. One final difference between liberal and conservative sources is the number of talk radio shows on the top-10 list for conservatives—there are no equivalents on the liberals' list.

The question raised by Table 7.1 is whether the differences in issue positions and policy demands of liberals and conservatives in America are driven by the differences in media sources—do some people demand liberal policies because they listen to NPR, while others demand conservative policies because they listen to Rush Limbaugh? The answer is almost surely no. As we discuss in Chapter 6, people aren't liberal or conservative because of the stories they listen to, watch, or read—their beliefs run much deeper than that. Moreover, the fact that most Americans gather political information as a by-product of everyday life means that they are exposed to many different sources. A liberal might listen to NPR every day (just as a conservative might listen to Rush Limbaugh every day), but both sides hear, read, or watch sources such as network news—and their dislike (or affinity) for a particular politician or policy may be informed by media coverage but is not the result of it.

"Why Should I Care?"

It's important to have a clear and accurate understanding of today's media sources. If you're looking for someone to blame for Americans' lack of knowledge about politics, the mass media is not a good candidate. While most sources fall short in one way or another, there is a wealth of information available, most of it for free. But most people never search for political information and ignore much of what they encounter. Journalists can do the most effective reporting possible—providing in-depth, balanced coverage of critical events—but unless people take time to read or view that coverage, they will remain uninformed.

How do politicians use the media? How do the media use politicians?

While the media and politicians are often thought of as adversaries, with a watchdog press making sure the public knows what politicians are doing, the fact is that each side has something to offer the other. Reporters want to write stories that attract public attention, so they need information on what is happening inside the government, preferably information that is given only to them. Politicians in turn want media coverage that highlights their achievements, which ideally will build public support and secure their election (or reelection). Bureaucrats want favorable attention for their programs, and interest groups want publicity to further their causes. Thus, coverage of American politics reflects trade-offs between reporters who want complete, accurate information and sources who want favorable coverage.

Politicians' media strategies

One way politicians try to shape citizen perceptions is to run campaign ads on television, in newspapers, and on websites. As we discuss in Chapter 9, candidates running for federal office generally spend about 80 to 90 percent of their budget on advertising. Candidates also target these ads to reach groups of likely supporters. A conservative Republican might try to buy advertising slots during a broadcast of a NASCAR event, knowing that people who are interested in NASCAR tend to vote Republican. These ads are an example of the by-product theory in action; people don't watch NASCAR to learn about politicians, but watching the broadcast means they will be exposed to the candidate's messages.

Politicians and others in government try to influence coverage by providing select information to reporters. Sometimes they hold press conferences where they take questions from the media. Other times they speak to single reporters or to a group **on background** or **off the record**, meaning that the reporter can use the information but cannot attribute it to the politician by name. These efforts are sometimes trial balloons, where politicians release details of a new proposal to gauge public reaction without committing themselves. Other times politicians might reveal some details of a negotiation or conflict with the hope of producing media coverage that puts their role in a favorable light.

Some scholars argue that elected officials use the media to shape public opinion, doling out information to reward reporters who write stories that support the officials' points of view.[20] To some extent this argument is true: much of the information reporters use to write their stories comes from political appointees, bureaucrats, elected officials, and party leaders.[21] Reporters who are known to be writing stories that are critical of a government program or a political leader may find that some people refuse to talk to them. However, while there is no doubt that elected officials would like to receive sympathetic media coverage and are sometimes successful, news reports on American politics reflect a multitude of sources and information. One politician's attempt to shape coverage by talking or remaining silent may be negated by another's efforts to promote a different point of view, with the same reporter or a different one.

Besides talking with the media, politicians also hold events aimed at securing favorable press coverage or appear at an event that the press is likely to cover. For example,

on background or **off the record**
Comments a politician makes to the press on the condition that they can be reported only if they are not attributed to that politician.

99

You don't tell us how to stage the news, and we won't tell you how to cover it.

—Larry Speakes, press secretary to President Ronald Reagan

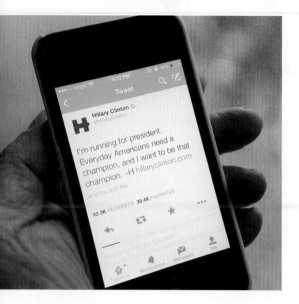

Information and coverage of important events become instantaneously available through Internet sources like Twitter feeds and blogs. For instance, Clinton's campaign announcement was followed by commentary and analysis. @HillaryClinton #I'mWithHer

during the summer of 2015, six months before the Iowa Caucuses met to begin selecting presidential nominees, all of the Republican and Democratic candidates for president made a point of visiting the Iowa State Fair, where they shook hands, ate some local specialties (from pork chops to fried Snickers bars), and in general tried to attract as much media attention as they could. (Donald Trump even used his private helicopter to give rides to fair attendees.) By attending the fair, candidates were trying to get their names and their pictures in local newspapers and on local television and thereby increase their name recognition. Such coverage might also help persuade Iowa voters that a candidate shared their views on the issues.

Similarly, potential presidential candidates often appear on television talk shows as a way of increasing name recognition and gaining some free advertising. Studies have shown that viewing a candidate in such a relaxed, nonconfrontational setting can help persuade opponents that a candidate is worth a second look.[22] Many candidates use social media to attract attention to their campaigns. Most notably, Donald Trump used Twitter frequently throughout the nomination and general-election campaigns to attack his opponents, rebut attacks against him, and highlight polls with favorable results.

Like all campaign strategies, however, candidates' attempts to shape media coverage work only some of the time. While Trump was able to generate a great deal of media coverage of his Tweets, campaign events, and even his record as a businessman some of his tweets, including criticism of Khizr and Ghazala Khan, Gold Star parents who spoke at the 2016 Democratic National Convention, clearly cost him some support. Candidate strategies can also backfire, such as when the campaign of another Republican presidential candidate, Ben Carson, allowed a reporter from the *New York Times* to interview Carson's foreign policy advisers, only to find that the story focused on Carson's lack of knowledge about international affairs and the difficulty of teaching him enough about foreign policy to be a credible candidate.[23] Candidates such as Carson, who are relative newcomers to politics, sometimes believe they can control the media, getting reporters to focus on subjects that only show the candidate in a favorable light. The reality is that stories about a politician's mistakes, gaffes, and embarrassing pasts often attract sizable audiences and politicians have little control over reporters who want to use this material.[24]

The pressures on reporters

The proliferation of media sources has increased competition among reporters to find interesting stories and report on them. Reporters who refuse to use information that a politician has provided on grounds that they may be giving free advertising to the politician or the policies he or she champions may find that the politician refuses to talk with them in the future. Moreover, the rise of the Internet has increased the demand for new stories and updates of old ones. Even if reporters covering Congress think that nothing important is happening on a given day, they may be forced to write a story just to have something new on their newspaper's Web page.

Because of these demands, reporters are forced to rely on their sources, people inside government who provide them with documents, inside information, and the details of negotiations. This process is often called **leaking** to denote the fact that sources are revealing information that is not supposed to be public knowledge. Reporters covering important or controversial stories often promise their sources that they will remain anonymous in any coverage based on the information they provide. These assurances

leaking
The practice of someone in government providing nonpublic information to a reporter, with the aim of generating press coverage favorable to the leaker's aims.

The publication of thousands of government documents, including some sensitive reports and communications, raised new questions about press freedom and national security. Here, demonstrators protest government surveillance and thank Edward Snowden for his revelations. @Snowden

are an important factor in the decision to leak information, especially classified information. However, these assurances are not absolute. Reporters and their editors can, under certain circumstances, be compelled by a court to reveal the sources for their stories. Although some states have shield laws that allow reporters to refuse to name their sources, there is no such law at the federal level. As a result, federal prosecutors can ask a judge to force journalists to name their sources, on the grounds that the source's identity is fundamental to the prosecutor's case. If the judge agrees, the reporter can be jailed for contempt for an indefinite period unless he or she provides the information.

Reporters also face legal hurdles as they research stories. Notwithstanding the freedom of the press guaranteed in the Bill of Rights, reporters are subject to legal limitations, including the clear and present danger test and prior restraint. If the government can convince a judge that publication of a particular story would lead to immediate harm to a person or persons, a judge can halt publication. But the clear and present danger test sets the bar extremely high for stopping publication of a story. As we discussed in Chapter 4, most attempts to prevent publication have been unsuccessful.

To appreciate the issues surrounding classified information and prior restraint, consider the case of Edward Snowden. While working as a contractor for America's NSA, Snowden downloaded a collection of files that documented the NSA's surveillance activities, including the collection of data on Americans' phone calls overseas and the monitoring of foreign politicians' cell phones. In 2012, Snowden approached several major publications across the world, including the *Washington Post*, to offer access to these documents. After several months of negotiation, the *Post* would not agree to all of Snowden's conditions—among other things, he wanted certain documents to be published in their entirety, while the *Post* wanted to hold back some classified information.[25] Snowden then came to an agreement with a British newspaper, the *Guardian*, which has gradually made the documents public, although he also allowed the *Post* to publish some of the documents.

The *Post*'s refusal to accept Snowden's demands was the product of several months of discussions with the U.S. government over what information could be released without harming national security or placing confidential sources in jeopardy. Although some government officials mentioned the possibility of invoking the prior restraint prohibition, no attempts were made to do so. In any case, even if the *Post* could be deterred from publication the information would soon appear in stories published by other outlets.

The Snowden episode illustrates how government officials work to deter leaks or influence the media's coverage of a story without resorting to prior restraint. First, there are laws prohibiting the disclosure of classified information. The Obama administration, in particular, worked to prosecute government employees who leak classified information to reporters.[26] Newspapers can also face prosecution. The *Post* sat on the Snowden documents for several months, publishing only when it was rumored that the *Guardian* planned to release its own story. Even then, *Post* reporters and editors agreed to keep certain information out of their stories.

Why do reporters and publishers restrain their stories? Sometimes they agree with the government that keeping secrets is in the national interest. For example, for several years mainstream media voluntarily decided not to run stories about secret American bases in Saudi Arabia from which drone missions were being flown over Iran and other countries. (Ultimately the information was revealed in a *Wired* magazine story.[27]) Other times reporters are rewarded for cooperating—they may get information about another government policy or be promised future access to officials. Alternately, reporters may be coerced to back down from a story through the threat of losing future access to people in government or of even going to jail.

In the main, these constraints apply only to mainstream organizations and their reporters. Groups that are anonymous or which operate outside the United States can violate these laws and norms with impunity. Thus, when the WikiLeaks group released e-mails and documents they had obtained from the Democratic National Committee, the Clinton campaign, and the Gmail account of Clinton campaign chair John Podesta, there was no way for these groups (or the government) to initiate legal action or otherwise prevent publication.

Thus, the shaping of the news can also affect the way that the media report about politics. Politicians will try to shape media coverage in ways that show them winning and their opponents losing and to depict their opponents as ill-advised and scandal ridden. Given the multitude of media sources, it is not hard for a politician to find a reporter who is willing to write exactly what that politician wants, either because the reporter believes the information is true or because he or she wants to attract an audience or to gain the politician's trust.

"Why Should I Care?"

Understanding the relationship between politicians and the media is critical for evaluating the quality and accuracy of the political news you see and read. Because journalists are constrained in what they can learn about and what they can report, there is no guarantee that any one media source will be able to publish a full and complete account of a political event or outcome. Under these conditions, the only way to be well informed about politics is to consult multiple sources and remember that politicians and media members both have agendas. Sometimes those agendas are similar, but often politicians and the media want different things.

★

EXPLAIN HOW THE MEDIA INFLUENCE HOW PEOPLE THINK ABOUT POLITICS

How do the media shape politics?

The study of media effects explores whether exposure to media coverage of politics changes what people think or do. There is considerable evidence that media coverage influences its audience—in simple terms, much of what Americans know about politics comes from stories they read, watch, or listen to. In part, media effects arise because people exposed to stories that describe a particular event learn new facts as a result of their exposure. However, some of the impact of media coverage stems not from what such stories contain but from how they present information or even whether a story is reported at all (see How It Works: How News Makes It to the Public).[28]

media effects
The influence of media coverage on average citizens' opinions and actions.

The impact of media coverage

Many studies have found that exposure to political coverage changes what citizens know: at the most basic level, people who watch, read, or listen to more coverage about politics know more than people with less exposure.[29] What people learn can shape the demands they place on politicians.[30] However, at least part of this effect arises because of underlying interest: people who are interested in politics know more in the first place and, because of their interest, watch more media coverage of events as they happen. Moreover, because people can pick and choose which coverage to watch, read, or listen to, what they learn from the media tends to reinforce their preexisting beliefs. That is, a conservative might listen to Sean Hannity, while a liberal would opt for watching MSNBC. Both people may learn something from the coverage, but the most likely result is that they will only grow more certain in their opinions.[31] Finally, changes caused by media coverage are usually (but not always) short-lived, which is consistent with our discussion in Chapter 6 of how public opinion is shaped by events.

Given this evidence on media effects, one of the central questions is whether reporters and editors have a discernable bias: That is, do their decisions about which events to report on and how they report on them reflect a conscious effort to shape public opinion in a liberal, conservative, or other direction? Surveys of the American electorate have found a hostile media effect: Democrats generally think the media favor Republicans, whereas Republicans have the opposite belief. That is, everyone seems to think that the media are biased against the candidates and policies they prefer.[32] Conservative critics point to surveys that show that most reporters identify themselves as liberals. Liberal critics respond that most pundits, especially on talk radio, offer conservative points of view—and many media sources are owned by large corporations, which could lead to underreporting of some stories, such as those offering a favorable portrayal of labor unions.[33]

hostile media
The tendency of people to see neutral media coverage of an event as biased against their point of view.

Republican presidential candidate Donald Trump being interviewed by George Stephanopoulos, a so-called "liberal" media person. Some critics of media coverage claim that a liberal interviewer would not be able to do an impartial interview of a conservative candidate (or vice versa).

How News Makes It to the Public

Editor assigns reporter to cover a particular story or event.

Filtering
Editor decides which stories are important and will attract an audience.

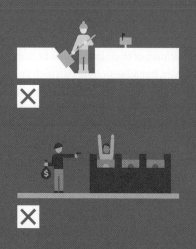

Reporter gathers information and prepares a story.

Framing
Reporter's story includes the overall argument and other information that shapes what the audience learns.

Priming
By describing events using some words or phrases and omitting others, the reporter has additional influence over what the audience learns.

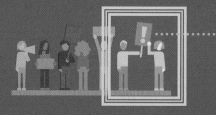

The people have a point!

Chaos in the streets!

Editor revises story, decides on length, content, and placement.

Filtering, Framing, and Priming
Decision about where, when, and how to carry the story gives an additional opportunity for filtering. In addition, the editor can make changes to a story that involve framing, and priming.

The Media's Coverage of Hillary Clinton's E-Mail Server

During her tenure as secretary of state, 2016 Democratic presidential candidate Hillary Clinton did not use a State Department e-mail address and secure government server for official business; rather, she used a private e-mail address to send or receive **over 60,000 e-mails**, with messages stored on a server in her home in New York. The way the media covered this situation shows framing, filtering, and priming in action.

Filtering
It's not a story...

Anyone who received a message from Clinton during her tenure as secretary of State knew about her e-mail practices...

until it is!

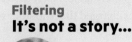

but media coverage began only **after conservative groups filed Freedom of Information Act requests** to gain access to Clinton's e-mails.

Framing
The background:

Some news stories focused on policies that require federal employees and appointees to use **government e-mail addresses for all official business...**

It's complicated.

but others noted that this restriction was **not in place at the time** Clinton was Secretary of State.

Priming
She told secrets...

Some news stories emphasized the fact that some of **Clinton's e-mails contained classified or secret information...**

but it wasn't her fault.

while others added that in all cases the information **was not classified at the time** Clinton sent these messages.

Filtering, Framing, and Priming
More trouble? No, in the clear!

In the immediate aftermath of the FBI's decision to not bring charges against Clinton, **news stories used sharply different combinations of filters and frames**: one focused on FBI Director James Comey's logic for finding that Clinton's actions did not fit the standard for criminal activity, while the other emphasized Comey's sharp criticism of Clinton's behavior. During the last weeks of the campaign, when Comey reopened then reclosed the investigation, some stories used a new frame. One centered on the possible political motivations for these actions and dysfunction inside the FBI.

❓ Critical Thinking

1. **Of the three media effects** (filtering, framing, and priming), which is the easiest one for citizens to detect? Which one is the hardest?

2. **Do a Web search for** "Clinton email server". In the first two articles you see, find all the instances of filtering, priming, and framing. Do you think these articles provide a balanced picture of the events? Why or why not?

It is easy to find examples of suspicious decisions by reporters and their editors that suggest some sort of overt bias in coverage. In the fall of 2013, a host on the Saturday edition of the Fox News program *Fox & Friends* discussed the closure of the World War II Memorial in Washington, D.C., due to a government shutdown, reporting that President Obama had done nothing to keep the memorial open but stating that at the same time Obama donated some of his own money to support a museum of Muslim culture. In fact, the story about Obama's donation came from a satirical website and was completely false. Fox retracted the story, saying they had made an honest mistake, but critics charged that the story reflected an anti-Obama bias by Fox reporters and editors.[34]

Many journalists and commentators admit that they take an ideological or partisan perspective. Talk show hosts Sean Hannity and Rush Limbaugh, for example, describe themselves as strong conservatives. And many commentators on the Fox News Channel make no secret of their conservative viewpoint—as do liberal commentators on MSNBC. Similarly, the political news magazine the *Nation* describes itself as "a weekly journal of left/liberal opinion, covering national and international affairs as well as the arts."[35] These journalists' and organizations' points of view are well known and easy to identify. Some people might even find the bias useful. A liberal, for example, could use the *Nation*'s endorsements as a guide as to which candidates to support, and a conservative might listen to Rush Limbaugh to get similar information.

It is also no surprise that politicians complain about media coverage: the stakes for them are very high. For example, during the final weeks of the 2016 election, Donald Trump's campaign wanted more attention paid to their claims about the need for trade reform and their claims that Hillary Clinton was a corrupt politician, instead of the media's focus on several harassment claims against Trump and his poor performance in the presidential debates. While Trump's campaign argued that media coverage was biased against their candidate, the simpler explanation for their anger is that they wanted Trump to win, and that a fair accounting of the campaign (which is what the mainstream media provided, by and large) would be harmful to their candidate.

In fact, while it is easy to find media coverage of politics that is incomplete or cases where reporters made predictions that later turned out to be false, it is hard to find cases of systematic bias in media coverage. For example, in the fall of 2015 Republican candidate Ben Carson complained that reporters were spending too much time searching for inconsistencies and exaggerations in his autobiography, arguing that they had not scrutinized President Obama or Democratic candidate Hillary Clinton in the same way.[36] Yet it is easy to find exhaustive media coverage of similar issues in Obama's and Clinton's autobiographies. You may think that the media were making too much of Carson's past—but it is hard to say that they gave a free pass to Obama, Clinton, or other candidates.

It is also hard to find a scholarly study that presents strong evidence of systematic media bias in a liberal or conservative direction. Part of the problem is that it is hard to measure media bias. For example, one study found that when the Fox News Network began broadcasting in a community, voting for Republican candidates in the next election increased significantly.[37] Does this mean that some viewers became pro-Republican after listening to allegedly pro-Republican broadcasts on Fox News? Perhaps, but the study did not directly measure the behavior of individuals in these communities, so there was no way to be sure that new Republican supporters were actually Fox News viewers. Even if they were, it may be that watching Fox News had no effect on voting but that Fox News executives were looking for communities that were trending Republican when deciding which new markets to enter. Untangling these effects is difficult, and if media bias were as pronounced as some critics claim it would likely be easier to measure.

Filtering and framing

Compared with overt bias, filtering and framing could produce subtler but stronger impacts on public opinion. **Filtering** (also called *agenda-setting*) results from journalists' and editors' decisions about which stories to report. "**Framing**" refers to how the description or presentation of a story, including the details, explanations, and context, changes the reaction people have to the information. Space and time limitations mean that some filtering is inevitable as reporters and editors decide which stories to cover. Similar decisions about what to report and how to present the information lead to framing effects. Even if everyone in the political media adhered to the highest standards of accuracy, these influences would still exist.

The concept of filtering is illustrated by Project Censored's annual list of Top Censored Stories.[38] The group's list for 2014 included stories about rising sea levels, government surveillance of cell phone conversations, and deforestation of northern Canada. The group's point is not that the government forces reporters to keep quiet; it claims that reporters and their editors decide against covering these stories, sometimes for self-serving reasons, such as beliefs about what their audience wants to see or read. The impact of filtering is also apparent in cases of government inaction. Figure 7.1 shows media coverage (number of stories) of gun control legislation following a mass shooting at Sandy Hook Elementary School in Newtown, Connecticut, in December 2013.

The graph shows that after a sharp spike in stories following the shooting and coverage of President Obama's legislative proposals the topic gradually disappeared from coverage, with smaller, temporary spikes after the failure of a Senate gun control bill and a subsequent shooting at the Washington Navy Yard. To a large extent, the drop in media coverage mirrors public opinion—as Americans move on from thinking about mass shooting, media attention shifts with them. Whether sustained media attention would have galvanized public opinion behind stricter gun control laws is an open

filtering
The influence on public opinion that results from journalists' and editors' decisions about which of many potential news stories to report.

framing
The influence on public opinion caused by the way a story is presented or covered, including the details, explanations, and context offered in the report.

FIGURE 7.1

Gun Control Stories per Week, December 2012 to December 2013

Press attention to gun control spikes upward after a mass shooting, then fades as reporters move to other stories. How does this pattern help opponents of gun control legislation to preserve the status quo?

Source: Danny Hayes, "Why It's So Hard to Pass Gun Control Laws (in One Graph)," *Washington Post*, August 26, 2015, www.washingtonpost.com/blogs/monkey-cage (accessed 11/21/15).

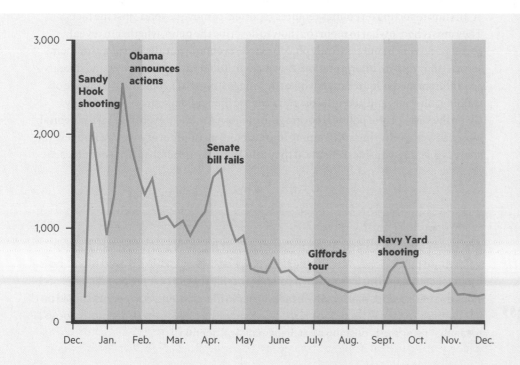

question. But if one effect of media coverage is to raise public awareness of an issue, people are not going to be aware of an issue the media ignore.

Reporting on violent crime in America shows clear framing effects. Many stories during the summer of 2015 reported on sharp increases in homicide rates in cities such as Chicago, St. Louis, and Baltimore, suggesting a nationwide problem.[39] However, almost as many cities saw homicide rates decline as those that saw an increase. (See the What Do the Numbers Say? feature.) Moreover, for the nation as a whole, homicide rates have been dropping for the last two decades. Adding data on nationwide crime rates to a story on murders in three cities doesn't change the facts about what's happening there, but it does suggest that these events are not proof of a larger national trend.

The way a story is reported—which information is included in an article or which images are used—makes a big difference in what people learn from it. Stories that focus on cases of violent crime suggest an epidemic of murders, rapes, and assault, but actual data on crime rates paint a very different picture.

In sum, reporting on politics requires reporters to move beyond "just the facts." They must choose what to report on, how to describe the news, whether to reveal secrets, and which sources to rely on. Moreover, events do not always speak for themselves—they require interpretation. As we saw in Table 7.1, conservatives and liberals see different media sources as trustworthy, suggesting that people are well aware of framing, filtering, and potential bias and choose their media sources accordingly. Given the vast array of political coverage in modern America, even if we take potential biases as well as filtering and framing into account, virtually everyone can find several sources that they consider reliable, if they take the time to search for those sources.[40]

"Why Should I Care?"

Americans often demand that journalists give "just the facts and all the facts" about politics and public policy. Most of the time, however, what looks like biased reporting is a journalist trying to make sense of a complex world. The act of reporting requires decisions on which stories matter, which facts deserve mention, and how events should be interpreted. To say that you don't like how a journalist resolves these decisions doesn't mean that he or she is pushing a particular political agenda.

A Nationwide Murder Epidemic?

Numerous articles published in late 2015 and early 2016 raised alarms about a sharp increase in homicides in large U.S. metropolitan areas, citing data from cities like Baltimore (138 homicides in 2014 to 215 in 2015). But homicide rates in any city can vary sharply from year to year simply because homicide is a fairly rare crime. As a result, drawing conclusions about the entire country requires aggregating data across a large number of cities. What do the numbers say about the media's coverage of violent crime?

Yearly change in rate of homicides per 100,000 people in the 50 largest U.S. cities

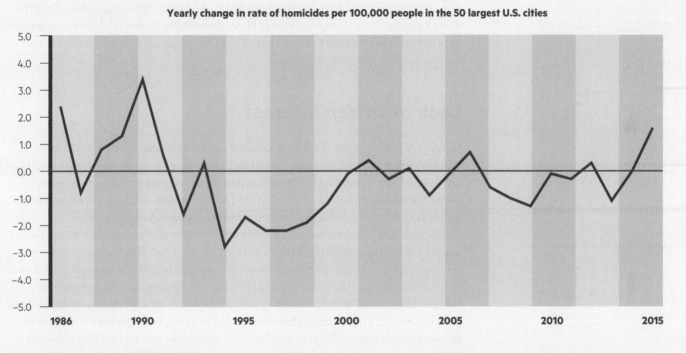

Source: Max Ehrenfreund and Denise Lu, "More People Were Killed Last Year Than in 2014, and No One's Sure Why," *The Washington Post*, January 26, 2016, www.washingtonpost.com/graphics/national/2015-homicides (accessed 6/30/16).

Think about it

- Does the data on percent change in homicide rates across the 50 largest U.S. cities confirm or dispute the conclusion of a sharp increase in homicides in 2015?
- One of the principle arguments in this chapter about media coverage is that there is a tendency to describe everything as a major crisis—in this case, to focus on increased homicide rates in a small number of cities, but ignore the small overall change. Why is it so hard for reporters to provide the whole picture to their audiences?

Do the media work?

In a democracy, the media's role is to provide citizens with information about politicians, government actions, and policy debates. It is easy to argue that the media are falling down on the job: surveys taken in 2015 showed that a majority of Americans believe that crime is on the rise, that illegal immigration from Mexico is increasing, that the cost of Obamacare exceeds estimates, and that 25 percent of federal spending is on foreign aid. All of these statements are false (in fact, foreign aid spending is about 2 percent of the budget).

Claims of ideological bias do not explain these shortcomings. The central finding of the political science literature on media effects is that, in the main, systematic bias is hard to find. Media sources did not highlight Donald Trump's propensity to insult his opponents in the presidential race because reporters and editors are hard-core liberals (or Democrats) who wanted to destroy Trump's chances of getting elected. If nothing else, many of the same sources also published numerous unflattering stories about the other Republican and Democratic candidates, from Republican Ted Cruz's poor standing among his Senate colleagues to Democrat Hillary Clinton's use of a private e-mail server while she was secretary of state.

Lack of citizen interest

In part, the media's apparent failure to create a well-informed citizenry is driven by a lack of citizen interest. As we discussed in Chapter 6, the average American has a low-to-moderate interest in politics and only a small percentage of Americans care enough to take the time and effort to become well informed. Everyone else learns about politics as a by-product of other things they do throughout the day.

The lack of citizen interest is one reason why the increased amount of information available on the Internet has not produced a better-informed citizenry: while information is available, average Americans make little attempt to find and understand it. Even if they tried, finding information, sifting through conflicting sources, and assessing the credibility of different accounts is a difficult task even for experts. For example, suppose you wanted to learn more about the conflict in Syria. A Google search in late 2015 of the terms "America," "Syria," and "war" returned over 100 million Web pages, ranging from reports on America's military strategy to pictures of Syrian refugees. Thus, the problem is not in finding information but in deciding which of the millions of pages available will help you learn about the conflict.

In short, despite the Internet's wealth of information, there is no guarantee that people will sit down, search for what they want or need to know, distinguish truth from falsehood, and assemble their findings into coherent conclusions. In fact, rather than creating a uniformly well-informed citizenry, the availability of information on the Internet may exacerbate the "knowledge gap" we saw in Chapter 6, where a small percentage of Americans are extremely well informed about politics, whereas the vast majority of the public may simply throw up their hands and make no attempt to become better informed.[41]

Market forces

Another influence on media coverage is competition for an audience. Mass media sources have always tried to get as large an audience as possible in order to generate

Many Americans, attracted by clickbait headlines and dramatic storylines, now get the bulk of their political news from nontraditional online sources like Buzzfeed.

profits and stay in business, but the expansion of the Internet and the increased availability of free information have increased competitive pressures.[42] In part, these pressures have had positive effects for consumers: newspapers, for example, have put their content online and moved from publishing once per day to continually producing new stories and updates. Television stations have placed their video content online as well, including footage that was never used in broadcasts, so that people can watch at any time.

One downside of audience pressures is that they lead reporters to search for stories—any story—to have something new to offer their audience, who otherwise will be in danger of going somewhere else. For example, most theories of elections show that polls taken during the early days of a political campaign are almost irrelevant. Early on most people know very little about the candidates, so a well-known figure such as Donald Trump may attract support simply because people know his name. But because reporters need something to write about, they may focus on a new poll even though they are well aware that the poll's findings about each candidate's support are almost meaningless.

More generally, audience pressures lead reporters to focus on standing out and making their stories simple and dramatic in order to catch the attention of a distracted audience. Stories that say "nothing much happened today in the presidential campaign" or "today's events are hard to explain but almost surely will not affect who wins the election" will lose out to reports that cast events in simple, life-and-death terms. For example, during the summer of 2015 many news stories described the use of a private e-mail server by Democratic candidate Hillary Clinton when she was secretary of state, with speculation about whether the server had been hacked by Russian or Chinese agents, whether Clinton had erased e-mails to avoid scrutiny, and whether she would face criminal charges for having the server or for using it to transmit classified information. Many stories argued that the revelations would doom Clinton's presidential campaign. However, while the issue attracted considerable attention during the primary and general-election campaign, Clinton's defeat had more to do with economic uncertainty than with her e-mail accounts. (See the How It Works feature earlier in this chapter.)

> The bias of the mainstream media is toward sensationalism, conflict, and laziness.
>
> —Jon Stewart

Grading the Media's Coverage of the 2016 Presidential Debates

Millions of Americans watched the 2016 presidential debates. After all three debates, the vast majority of media accounts described these events as clear victories for Democrat Hillary Clinton. The Trump campaign argued that these analyses were biased, citing a number of polls where the overwhelming percentage of respondents said that Trump had won all three debates, and complaining that the moderators shifted the debate away from topics that would highlight Clinton's shortcomings as a candidate. While the campaign's polling claims can be dismissed (the only polls that showed Trump winning the debates were those that broke many of the rules for good polling discussed in Chapter 6, including allowing anyone to participate, and allowing multiple votes), the deeper question is whether the media did a good job of using their debate coverage to help provide Americans with the information they needed to determine which candidate they should vote for in light of their interests.

Media coverage fell short.

One problem with virtually all of the pre- and post-debate coverage was its emphasis on the campaign horserace—what each candidate had to do in order to mobilize their supporters and convert opponents. Before the third debate, for example, one focus was on how Donald Trump would address sexual harassment complaints against him; after the debate, a great deal of attention was paid to his categorical denials as well as his refusal to commit to accepting the results of the election. Relatively little attention was paid to the candidates' statements on Supreme Court appointments or their plans for reducing the federal debt—both important issues that they were asked about during the debate. Media coverage also overlooked the fact that many important issues that divide Americans, such as climate change or LGBTQ rights, were given very little attention throughout all three debates. Even if someone watched debate coverage from all of the major TV networks and print outlets, they would learn more about what Clinton and Trump "needed to do" to prevail on Election Day (and who succeeded and failed at these tasks) rather than learning about how the candidates would act as president.

Media coverage was as good as it could be.

Complaints about media coverage of presidential debates miss a crucial point: the media doesn't determine the format of the debates or how candidates respond to questions. As a result,

Rows of journalists prepare to cover the second presidential debate at Washington University in St. Louis. Did the media provide debate watchers with the information they needed to judge which candidate they should vote for?

there's no way for the media to ensure that debates provide a comprehensive overview of each candidate's positions and background—they are limited to reporting on what happened. It would make little sense for commentators to try to guess at how candidates would respond to questions that were not asked—in fact, doing so would be a clear example of moving beyond reporting to interpreting and even inventing. With regard to the emphasis on the horserace in debate coverage, while this claim is largely true, it reflects an argument made elsewhere in this chapter, that media coverage of politics reflects the demands of their audience. Are people more likely to watch a debate focused on policy details or on the horserace?

The Trump campaign's complaints that debate coverage favored Clinton are also suspect. Anyone who watched the debates heard Clinton respond to questions about her use of a nonsecure e-mail server, the grants made by the Clinton Foundation, or the failures of American foreign policy while Clinton was secretary of state. Her answers were extensively discussed in post-debate coverage. In this sense, the Trump campaign's complaints have more to do with the media's reporting on Trump's poor performance during all three debates than with a lack of attention to Clinton.

Did the media do its job in reporting on the 2016 presidential debates? Take a stand.

take a stand

1. Do you think coverage of the debates should have focused more on the candidates' policy plans or on their inflammatory or evasive statements? Why or why not?

2. Why do you think so many people watched the 2016 presidential debates? Do you think they learned what they set out to learn?

3. Does the media televise and report on debates to make profits or to inform the public? Does their coverage help with one or the other, both, or neither?

These effects are nothing new.[43] For decades, scholars have documented the rise of **attack journalism**, where journalists focus on scandal, government failures, and politicians' personal failings.[44] Other researchers have argued that campaign coverage overemphasizes the **horse race** aspects, such as which candidates are ahead and which are falling behind, rather than offering a complete description of each candidate's promises and an analysis of how he or she is likely to behave in office.[45] Similarly, coverage of debates over public policy often focuses on personalities and predictions about who is likely to achieve his or her goals, not the details of what the policies include. Media coverage of politics also emphasizes **soft news** (stories that are sensational or entertaining) over **hard news** (stories that focus on important issues and emphasize facts and figures).[46] The media also often give disproportionate coverage to events that are more likely to be recognized by the average American—for example, while American media gave extensive coverage of the November 2015 ISIL attacks in Paris, there was much less coverage of terrorist attacks in Lebanon and in Mali that happened at the same time and caused similar levels of casualties.[47]

Why do journalists ignore details and emphasize scandal? Describing the media as an information source for citizens makes sense in terms of how American politics works, but this description does not capture the sometimes contradictory incentives that journalists face. They may feel the need to demonstrate their independence from politicians and government interests and perhaps counter or prevent claims of media bias. And this may lead to aggressive questioning of elected officials and cynical stories about the political process.[48] But again, reporters and their editors are in a competitive business to attract a paying audience.[49] Most American media outlets are for-profit enterprises. Because they need to produce coverage that attracts an audience, they often seek to create stories that consumers want. So if the media focus on Hillary Clinton's hair—or Donald Trump's—it is because these stories find a ready audience.

Even if reporters for major news outlets tried to explain how our democratic government works or the complexity of most policy questions, it is unlikely that citizens would respond favorably. There are sources available that work this way. The nightly television program *PBS Newshour* has a reputation for producing thoughtful, in-depth stories about politics and policy. The same is true for the magazine *National Journal*. But the audience for these sources is minuscule, confirming that most people would prefer soft news, cynicism, and scandals to hard news, policy details, and sober analysis.

Thus, complaints about how the media cover American politics are to a large extent misdirected. The media give Americans the coverage they want. If the average citizen wants to become an expert on politics and public policy, the necessary information is surely available. But few people are interested in seeking that degree of understanding. For most Americans, the media's coverage of politics as a sports event is enough to keep us satisfied, even as we complain about a lack of details and an emphasis on scandal. (Read the Take a Stand feature to see how these constraints affect the questions reporters ask in a presidential debate.)

attack journalism
A type of increasingly popular media coverage focused on political scandals and controversies, which causes a negative public opinion of political figures.

horse race
A description of the type of election coverage that focuses more on poll results and speculation about a likely winner than on substantive differences between the candidates.

soft news
Media coverage that aims to entertain or shock, often through sensationalized reporting or by focusing on a candidate or politician's personality.

hard news
Media coverage focused on facts and important issues surrounding a campaign.

Reporters compete for an audience—that's how they stay in business. That means that stories you consider important (or that really are important) may not get media attention because they're too hard to explain or because people aren't interested. The only way to get more detailed, thoughtful political coverage is for Americans to start demanding it.

"Why Should I Care?"

Conclusion

News media are the primary source of public information about American politics and policy. The considerable controversy about how well the media fulfill this role reflects both the importance of the task and the interest many people have in the shaping of political coverage. Coverage of Donald Trump's presidential campaign illustrates the causes and consequences of media coverage. In running story after story about Trump's insults and bombast or the protests that occurred during his rallies, media sources were largely responding to public demand for dramatic coverage. Americans might be better informed if the media ignored sensational stories and focused on the details of public policy, but lurid stories help attract and keep the audience that media companies need to stay in business. Americans will get different media coverage when they alter how they search for information and when they value sources that emphasize details and complexity over scandals and drama.

The average American consults only a tiny fraction of the information provided by the media. Americans tend to learn about politics as a by-product of other activities and focus on exciting stories regardless of their importance. This process can lead people to some peculiar conclusions, even about well-reported events. Such shortcomings do not constitute an indictment of the news media or of the average American. For most policy questions, for example, even a small amount of research using different sources would produce a detailed understanding about the pros and cons of different options and the political forces aligning for and against change. We cannot blame people for refusing to become well informed, but at the same time we cannot blame the media for citizens' refusal to consider what is placed before them.

STUDY GUIDE

Political media today

Describe the role of media in American politics and how people get political information. (Pages 226–232)

Summary

The media have been the primary sources of political information in America since the Founding, though the forms of media have changed considerably over time. While the term "media" traditionally referred only to print sources, technological advances have allowed political information to be spread through radio, television, and the Internet. The creation of the Internet and the proliferation of media sources more generally have drastically increased the amount of information about politics that is available to the average American.

Key terms

mass media (p. 226)

yellow journalism (p. 227)

Federal Communications Commission (FCC) (p. 227)

broadcast media (p. 227)

equal time provision (p. 227)

media conglomerates (p. 228)

by-product theory (p. 231)

Practice Quiz Questions

1. The deregulation of the media has resulted in _____ .
   a. increasing enforcement of the equal time provision
   b. increasing enforcement of the fair play doctrine
   c. increasing use of the Internet
   d. increasing scrutiny of media concentration
   e. increasing frequency of cross-ownership

2. Which is the result of the decreased barriers to publication on the Internet?
   a. Few opportunities exist for citizens to interact with reporters or government officials.
   b. People with no official connection to politics can have a significant influence on elections.
   c. The accuracy of political information has improved.
   d. Few average citizens report on events as they happen.
   e. Like-minded political supporters have difficulty organizing and staying informed on issues.

3. Why hasn't the Internet increased citizens' political knowledge?
   a. It can be hard to find political news on the Internet.
   b. Most people do not have access to the Internet.
   c. Most people read content from a wide range of balanced media sources.
   d. Most people fail to systematically search for information about politics.
   e. Search engines don't include political topics.

4. What is the by-product theory of political information?
   a. Local media sources often rely on major sources for their national news coverage.
   b. Most Americans learn about politics accidentally.
   c. Reporters often learn about a political story while working on a different story.
   d. Bloggers typically do not produce news; rather, they comment on news gathered secondhand.
   e. News coverage often influences policy decisions.

How do politicians use the media? How do the media use politicians?

Explain how politicians use the media to achieve their goals. (Pages 233–236)

Summary

Coverage of politics requires that the reporter, on the one hand, make a trade-off between cultivating sources with favorable stories and providing complete and accurate information. Politicians, on the other hand, want favorable media coverage that highlights their achievements. One of the best ways reporters can cover political events is to get information "off the record." To maintain this information resource, the confidentiality of sources must be protected, although reporters can be compelled to reveal them in court.

Key terms

on background or off the record (p. 233)

leaking (p. 234)

Practice Quiz Questions

5. Shield laws _____ .
   a. allow editors to protect their reporters from vengeful politicians
   b. allow politicians to protect reporters who provide favorable coverage
   c. protect politicians from slander
   d. allow reporters to protect confidential sources
   e. protect reporters from being sued for slander

6. **Why are elected officials often able to successfully demand that journalists give favorable coverage of events and actions?**

    a. Elected officials can throw the journalists in jail.

    b. The fairness doctrine requires that journalists publish what elected officials tell them.

    c. Journalists defer to elected officials because they need the information that elected officials can provide.

    d. Journalists are constrained by the equal time provision included in federal law.

    e. Media consolidation has increased the power of elected officials.

7. **Prior restraint of reporting on government policy is _____ .**

    a. relatively rare because the constitutional guarantees of a free press are very strong

    b. relatively rare because reporters are afraid of having to pay large fines

    c. common because of media consolidation

    d. common in the post–September 11 era

    e. ruled as illegal by the Supreme Court

How do the media shape politics?

Explain how the media influence how people think about politics. (Pages 236–243)

Summary

Much of what Americans know about politics comes not only from the stories that they are exposed to in the news but also from the way these stories are presented (or if stories are reported at all). Potential media bias, filtering, and framing all may influence the type and scope of information that reporters choose to disseminate. In particular, the effects of filtering and framing are simply unavoidable given limited resources.

Key terms
media effects (p. 237)   filtering (p. 241)

hostile media (p. 237)   framing (p. 241)

Practice Quiz Questions

8. **"Filtering" the news refers to _____ .**

    a. the media's attempts to frame public opinion

    b. sources' attempts to remain confidential

    c. newspaper editors determining which stories to report

    d. politicians attempting to influence coverage by providing select information

    e. reporters' choices to delay a story

9. **Space and time limitations mean that some _____ is inevitable.**

    a. filtering

    b. adjudicating

    c. pandering

    d. systematic bias

    e. soft news

10. **Why do reporters move beyond "just the facts" reporting?**

    a. Politicians are corrupt, and people need to know about it.

    b. Americans don't realize the media are not always objective.

    c. Readers have already interpreted the news themselves.

    d. Politics is complicated and often requires some interpretation.

    e. Reporters have a strong personal bias and can't write strictly factual stories.

11. **What is one problem with research on media bias?**

    a. Few scholars are interested in studying media bias.

    b. It is difficult to measure bias.

    c. No journalist will admit that bias exists.

    d. There's little chance that media sources are biased.

    e. There are not enough media sources to create a sample.

Do the media work?

Assess whether the media fulfill their role in American democracy. (Pages 244–247)

Summary

In a democracy, the media's job is to provide citizens with information about politicians, government action, and policy debates. Although the media often fall short of this ideal, there are many reasons for this failure, including market forces and lack of citizen interest.

Key terms
attack journalism (p. 247)   soft news (p. 247)

horse race (p. 247)   hard news (p. 247)

Practice Quiz Questions

12. **Which is an example of "soft news"?**

    a. CNN's coverage of a White House press conference

    b. ABC's coverage of the president's State of the Union address

    c. NPR's report on the details of the debt-ceiling debate

    d. CBS's coverage of election results

    e. MSNBC's story about a member of Congress posting risqué photos of himself to his Twitter account

13. Which of the following statements best characterizes soft news?

a. Soft news stories sell far better than hard news stories.

b. Journalists aren't interested in writing hard news and would prefer to write soft news pieces.

c. Hard news and policy analysis articles tend to sell better than soft news.

d. Most citizens have several sources of hard news and they have to search to find soft news stories.

e. Soft news was popular in the past but is now declining.

14. Which of the following would increase the amount of hard news reporting on politics and public policy?

a. Mandating that reporters covering American politics have degrees in political science

b. The rise of new publications that focus on scandals, electoral horse races, and human interest stories

c. Changes in the kinds of stories demanded by the electorate

d. Repeal of the fairness doctrine

e. Increased media concentration and consolidation

Suggested Reading

Baum, Matthew A. *Soft News Goes to War: Public Opinion and American Foreign Policy in the New Media Age*. Princeton, NJ: Princeton University Press, 2003.

Bennett, W. Lance, and Shanto Iyengar. "A New Era of Minimal Effects? The Changing Foundations of Political Communication," *Journal of Communication* 58 (2008): 707–31.

Brader, Ted. *Campaigning for Hearts and Minds: How Emotional Appeals in Political Ads Work*. Chicago: University of Chicago Press, 2006.

Davenport, Christian. *Media Bias, Perspective, and State Repression: The Black Panther Party*. New York: Cambridge University Press, 2010.

Druckman, Jamie. "Media Effects in Politics." In *Oxford Bibliographies Online: Political Science*, ed. Rick Valelly. New York: Oxford University Press, 2012.

Iyengar, Shanto. *Media Politics: A Citizen's Guide*. New York: W. W. Norton, 2016.

Ladd, Jonathan M. *Why Americans Hate the Media and How It Matters*. Princeton, NJ: Princeton University Press, 2012.

Mutz, Diana. "Effects of 'in Your Face' Television Discourse on Perceptions of a Legitimate Opposition." *American Political Science Review* 101 (2007): 621–36.

Norris, Pippa. *A Virtuous Circle? Political Communications in Post-Industrial Democracies*. New York: Cambridge University Press, 2000.

Prior, Markus. *Post-Broadcast Democracy: How Media Choice Increases Inequality in Political Involvement and Polarizes Elections*. New York: Cambridge University Press, 2007.

8

Political Parties

How do political parties organize American politics?

Anyone paying attention during the 2016 elections might easily conclude that American political parties were beset with internal conflicts and subordinate to candidates and officeholders. Citizens' confidence in the two parties was at an all-time low. Both parties had contentious presidential nomination contests, complete with charges that party leaders were biased and that the rules were rigged. While Democrats ultimately united behind their general-election nominee, Hillary Clinton, many Republicans refused to endorse or campaign with their party's nominee, Donald Trump. Republican Senate Majority Leader Mitch McConnell refused to say anything about Trump, and Speaker of the House of Representatives Paul Ryan told his colleagues in the Republican caucus that he would focus on helping them get reelected, ignoring requests by Republican National Committee Chair Reince Priebus for Ryan to get involved in the presidential campaign. After the election, Republican members of Congress congratulated Trump on his victory, but refused to commit to enacting his agenda.

Though parties appear fractured, unpopular, and leaderless, political scientists argue that parties play a critical role in American politics. Decades of public opinion research have shown that most Americans have a long-term attachment to one of the major parties and that this attachment shapes whom they vote for and how they interpret events. One of the best explanations of the modern presidential nomination process, *The Party Decides*, argues that endorsements from politicians and party officials are essential to a nominee's success.[1] And a key theory that scholars use to explain the legislative process says that parties are the key players in the legislative process.

This chapter explains the complex role of American political parties. Political parties embody some of the most fundamental conflicts that underlie American politics. Political parties help shape the way Americans think about candidates, policies, and vote decisions. Political parties also impact elections by recruiting candidates, paying for campaign ads, and mobilizing supporters. After elections, the winning party's candidates implement their vision, while the losers try to derail these efforts and develop an alternative vision that will attract support. In so doing, parties unify and mobilize disparate groups, simplify the choices that voters face, and bring efficiency and coherence to government policy making.

Define *political parties* and show how American political parties and party systems have evolved over time.
pages 254–257

Describe the main characteristics of American parties as organizations, in the government, and in the electorate.
pages 258–268

Explain the important functions parties perform in the political system.
pages 268–279

Evaluate the benefits and possible problems of the American party system.
pages 279–282

📷

At first glance, it may seem that American political parties exercise control over the candidates running for their nominations, as is the case here, with Donald Trump displaying his signed pledge to support the party's eventual presidential nominee. The reality is quite different: Trump won the nomination over the objections of many party leaders, and several of the candidates who lost to Trump repudiated their pledges by publicly refusing to support Trump in the general election.

Although American political parties often have an impact on elections and policy, the same organizations can sometimes seem inept, irrelevant, and paralyzed by conflict. Our task in this chapter is to explain this variation using two of our main themes—conflict is natural and the rules of the political games matter. While American political parties are the product of disagreements about what government should do, these differences can sometimes split politicians and activists within an established party organization—making it all but impossible for these individuals to work together. Why—and when—do parties matter?

What are political parties and where did today's parties come from?

Political parties are organizations that run candidates for political office and coordinate the actions of officials elected under the party banner. Looking around the world, we find many different kinds of parties. In many western European countries, the major political parties have millions of dues-paying members and party leaders control what their elected officials do. In contrast, in many new democracies candidates run as representatives of a party, but party leaders have no control over what candidates say during the campaign or how they act in office.

America's major political parties, the Republican Party and the Democratic Party, lie somewhere between these extremes. Rather than being unified organizations with party leaders at the top, candidates and party workers in the middle, and citizen-members at the bottom, American political parties are decentralized, each one a loose network of organizations, groups, and individuals who share a party label but are under no obligation to work together.[2] The **party organization** is the structure of national, state, and local parties, including party leaders and workers. The **party in government** is made up of the politicians who were elected as candidates of the party. And the **party in the electorate** includes all the citizens who identify with the party. For example, the Speaker of the House of Representatives, Paul Ryan, is the leader of Republican House members, but he works independently of the party's national organization, the RNC; neither one is in charge of the other. In fact, Ryan waited only until just before the Republican National Convention to endorse Donald Trump, and avoided talking about Trump during the campaign. Ryan is also not in charge of other Republican groups in Congress, such as the Freedom Caucus (a group of conservative Republicans)—and although Caucus members may be somewhat sympathetic to Ryan's arguments, they are under no obligation to do what he asks. Similarly, the RNC cannot command state and local Republican Party organizations to take some actions and not others. Moreover, while many Americans think of themselves as members of a political party, someone who identifies with the Republican Party is not obligated to work for or give money to the party or to vote for its candidates. As you will see, organization matters: the fact that American political parties are split into three parts has important implications for what they do and for their impact on the nation's politics.

History of American political parties

The Republican and Democratic parties have existed for a long time—the Republicans since 1854 and the Democrats since the early 1800s. This section shows that, at

party organization
A specific political party's leaders and workers at the national, state, and local levels.

party in government
The group of officeholders who belong to a specific political party and were elected as candidates of that party.

party in the electorate
The group of citizens who identify with a specific political party.

different points in history American political parties have looked and acted very differently from the way they do today. These differences help to explain the structure and behavior of modern parties.

Political scientists use the term "**party system**" to describe periods of time in which the major parties' names, their groups of supporters, and the issues dividing them have all been constant. As Table 8.1 shows, there have been six party systems in America.[3] For each party system, the table gives the names of the two major parties, indicates which party dominated (won the most presidential elections or controlled Congress), and describes the principal issues dividing the parties.

The Evolution of American Political Parties Political parties formed soon after the Founding of the United States. The first American parties, the Federalists and the Democratic-Republicans, were primarily parties in government. The first parties consisted of like-minded legislators: Federalists wanted a strong central government and a national bank, and they favored assumption of state war debts by the national government; Democratic-Republicans took the opposite positions based on their preference for concentrating power at the state level. These political parties were quite different from their modern counterparts. In particular, there were no national party organizations, few citizens thought of themselves as party members, and candidates for office did not campaign as representatives of a party.

For two decades, the two parties were more or less evenly matched in Congress, although the Federalists did not win a presidential contest after 1800. However, during

American political parties have three largely separate components: the party organization, represented here by Donna Brazile, interim chair of the DNC; the party in government, represented by House Minority Leader Nancy Pelosi (D-CA) and House Minority Whip Steny Hoyer (D-MD); and the party in the electorate, exemplified by the crowd at a rally for Hillary Clinton. #DNC @TheDemocrats

party system
Periods in which the names of the major political parties, their supporters, and the issues dividing them have remained relatively stable.

American Party Systems

TABLE 8.1

There have been six party systems in the United States since 1789.

Party System	Major Parties (dominant party in boldface)	Key Issues
First (1789–1828)	Federalists, Democratic-Republicans (neither party was dominant)	Location of the capital, financial issues (e.g., national bank)
Second (1829–1856)	**Democrats**, Whigs	Tariffs (farmers vs. merchants), slavery
Third (1857–1896)	Democrats, **Republicans**	Slavery (pre–Civil War), Reconstruction (post–Civil War), industrialization
Fourth (1897–1932)	Democrats, **Republicans**	Industrialization, immigration
Fifth (1933–1968)	**Democrats**, Republicans	Size and scope of the federal government
Sixth (1969–present)	Democrats, Republicans (neither party is dominant)	Size and scope of the federal government, civil rights, social issues, foreign policy

party principle
The idea that a political party exists as an organization distinct from its elected officials or party leaders.

spoils system
The practice of rewarding party supporters with benefits like federal government positions.

There's no evidence from decades of Pew Research surveys that public opinion, in the aggregate, is more extreme now than in the past. But what has changed—and pretty dramatically—is the growing tendency of people to sort themselves into political parties based on their ideological differences.

—Pew Research Center

The Tammany Hall political machine, depicted here as a rotund version of one of its leaders, William "Boss" Tweed, controlled New York City politics for most of the nineteenth and early twentieth centuries. Its strategy was "honest graft," rewarding party workers, contributors, and voters for their efforts to keep the machine's candidates in office.

"THAT'S WHAT'S THE MATTER."
s Tweed. "As long as I count the Votes, what are you going to do about it? say?"

the 1814 elections the Federalist Party lost most of its congressional seats because many Federalist legislators had opposed the War of 1812 and supported a politically unpopular pay raise for members of Congress.[4] These defeats led to the demise of the Federalist Party and the start of the Era of Good Feelings, when there was only one political party, the Democratic-Republican Party. Following the election of President Andrew Jackson in 1828, this party became known as the Democratic Party. At the same time, another new party, the Whig Party, was formed and the second party system came into existence.

The new Democratic Party cultivated electoral support by building organizations to mobilize citizens and bind them to the party. The party also implemented the party principle, the idea that a party is not just a group of elected officials but an organization that exists apart from its candidates, and the spoils system, whereby party workers were rewarded with benefits such as federal jobs.[5]

In the 1840s, the issue of slavery split the second party system. Most Democratic politicians either supported slavery outright or wanted to avoid debating the issue.[6] The Whig Party was split between politicians who agreed with the Democrats and the abolitionists, who wanted to end slavery. Ultimately, antislavery Whigs left the party and formed the Republican Party, which also attracted antislavery Democrats, and the Whig Party soon ceased to exist. These changes initiated the third party system, in which the country was divided into a largely Republican Northeast, a largely Democratic South, and politically split Midwestern and border states.[7]

These developments illustrate that political parties exist only because elites, politicians, party leaders, and activists want them to. The Republican Party was created by people who wanted to abolish slavery, but many other politicians subsequently joined the party because of ambition: these politicians believed that their chances of winning political office were higher as Republicans than as Whigs or Democrats.

After the Civil War, the Republicans and Democrats remained the two prominent national parties. They were divided over the size and scope of the federal government, questioning whether the federal government should help farmers and rural residents or inhabitants of rapidly expanding cities and whether it should regulate America's rapidly growing industrial base. Democrats built a coalition of rural and urban voters by proposing a larger, more active federal government, as well as other policies that would help both groups. These strategies demonstrate how American political parties adapt to societal changes and subsequently reflect the basic political divisions.

The fifth party system was born out of the Great Depression, the worldwide economic collapse that led to the unemployment of millions of people. Many Republicans argued that conditions would improve over time and that government intervention would do little good, whereas Democrats proposed new programs that would help people in need and spur economic growth. The Democratic landslide in the 1932 election led to the New Deal, a series of federal programs proposed by President Franklin Delano Roosevelt and enacted by Congress to stimulate the national economy, help needy people, and impose a variety of new regulations. Debate over the New Deal brought together the New Deal coalition of African Americans, Catholics, Jews, union members, and white southerners, who became strong supporters of Democratic candidates over the next generation.[8] This transformation established the basic division between the parties that exists to the present day: Democrats generally favor a large federal government that takes an active role in managing the economy and regulating behavior, and Republicans believe that many such programs should be provided by state and local governments or not provided at all.

The move from the fifth to the sixth party system was marked by the introduction of new political questions and debates that divided the parties.[9] Beginning in the late 1940s, many Democratic candidates and party leaders, particularly outside the South, came out against the "separate but equal" system of racial discrimination in southern states and in favor of programs designed to ensure equal opportunity for minority citizens. Then, during the 1960s, many Democratic politicians argued for expanding the role of the federal government in health care, antipoverty programs, and education. Most Republicans opposed these initiatives, although a significant portion did not. At the same time, these new issues also began to divide American citizens and organized groups.[10]

These developments produced a gradual but significant shift in the groups that identified with each party. White southerners and some Catholics moved to the Republican Party, and minorities, particularly African Americans, started identifying more strongly as Democrats. Democrats also gained supporters in New England and West Coast states. By the late 1980s, all three elements of the Republican and Democratic parties (organization, government, and electorate) were much more like-minded than they had been a generation earlier.

The sixth party system also brought changes in party organizations. Both the Republican and Democratic parties increased their involvement in recruiting, training, conducting fund-raising, and campaigning for their party's congressional and presidential candidates in an effort to elect like-minded colleagues who would vote with them to enact their preferred policies.[11] At the same time, disagreements between congressional Republicans and Democrats increased, making it harder to find common ground in many policy areas.

Realignments Each party system is separated from the next by a realignment, a change in one or more of the factors that define a party system, including the issues that divide the parties, the nature and function of the party organizations, the composition of the party coalitions, and the specifics of government policy. In most cases, a realignment begins with the emergence of a new question or issue debate that captures the attention of large numbers of ordinary citizens, activists, and politicians.[12] To spur a realignment, the issue has to be *cross-cutting*, meaning that within each party coalition there are people who disagree on what government should do.

A realignment between the fifth party system (1933–1968) and the sixth (1969–present) produced the division between modern-day Republicans and Democrats.[13] Parties in the fifth party system were primarily divided by their positions on the appropriate size of the federal government. In the sixth party system, new issues such as civil rights emerged to divide the parties and their supporters. By the 1980s, the changes in party coalitions and election outcomes were apparent, with control of Congress and the presidency divided between the two parties. Republicans gained House and Senate seats in southern states, and Democrats gained seats in the Northeast, West, and Southwest.[14] After the 2016 elections, Republicans controlled only one Senate seat in the Northeast, while there are only three Democratic senators in the South (two in Virginia).

Debate over Roosevelt's New Deal programs established the basic divide between Democrats and Republicans that continues to this day: in the main, Democrats favor a larger federal government that takes an active role in managing the economy; Republicans prefer a smaller federal government and fewer programs and regulations.

THIS IS ONE RABBIT THAT NEVER FAILED ME!

SPENDING

OLD RELIABLE!

realignment
A change in the size or composition of the party coalitions or in the nature of the issues that divide the parties. Realignments typically occur within an election cycle or two, but they can also occur gradually over the course of a decade or longer.

Looking at American political parties today, you might think that Democratic and Republican parties have been around forever, that they are evenly split in party identifiers and officeholders, and that their main disagreement has always concerned the size and scope of government. None of these ideas is true. Moreover, the changes over time in the Republican and Democratic parties illustrate how these organizations adapt to shifts in public opinion. Thus, American political parties may look very different 10 years from now than they do today.

"Why Should I Care?"

American political parties today

We've seen that, from the beginning, political parties have been a central feature of American politics. The next steps are to examine the different aspects (the party organization, the party in government, and the party in the electorate) of American political parties, describe the role they play in elections and in government, and compare their behavior in practice with the job description presented earlier in the chapter.

The party organization

national committee
An American political party's principal organization, comprising party representatives from each state.

The principal body in each party organization is the **national committee**, which consists of representatives from state party organizations, usually one man and one woman per state. The state party organizations in turn are made up of professional staff plus thousands of party organizations at the county, city, and town levels. The job of these organizations is to run the party's day-to-day operations, recruit candidates and supporters, raise money for future campaigns, and work to build a consensus on major issues. (Of course, other groups in the party, as well as individual politicians, carry out similar tasks at the same time and not always in agreement with the national or state committees.)

Both parties also include a number of *constituency groups* (the Democrats' term) or *teams* (the Republicans' term). These organizations within the party work to attract the support of demographic groups—such as African Americans, Hispanics, people with strong religious beliefs, senior citizens, women, and many others—who are considered likely to share the party's issue concerns and to assist in fund-raising.[15] In some cases, these organizations also attempt to win over groups typically identified with the other party. For example, African Americans have long been strong supporters of Democratic candidates. Accordingly, the Democratic Party has a constituency group that informs African Americans about the party's candidates and works to convince these citizens to vote on Election Day. The Republican Party's corresponding constituency team works toward the opposite goal, trying to convince African Americans that Republican policies and candidates would better serve their interests.

Each party organization also includes groups designed to build support for, or coordinate the efforts of, particular individuals or politicians. These groups include the Democratic and the Republican Governors' Associations, the Young Democrats, the Young Republicans, and more-specialized groups such as the Republican Lawyers' Organization or the DLC, an organization of moderate Democratic politicians.[16] The parties use their college and youth organizations to motivate politically minded students to work for the party and its candidates. Groups such as the Governors' Associations and the DLC hold meetings where elected officials discuss solutions to common problems and try to formulate joint strategies. People who work for a party organization perform a wide range of tasks, from recruiting candidates and formulating political strategies to mobilizing citizens, conducting fund-raising, filling out campaign finance reports, researching opposing candidates and parties, and developing websites for the party and its candidates.

political action committee (PAC)
An interest group or a division of an interest group that can raise money to contribute to campaigns or to spend on ads in support of candidates. The amount a PAC can receive from each of its donors and the amount it can spend on federal electioneering are strictly limited.

527 organization
A tax-exempt group formed primarily to influence elections through voter mobilization efforts and to issue ads that do not directly endorse or oppose a candidate. Unlike PACs, 527 organizations are not subject to contribution limits and spending caps.

Other Allied Groups Many other groups, such as **political action committees (PACs)** or **527 organizations**, labor unions, and other interest groups and organizations, are loosely affiliated with one of the major parties. For example, the organization

Party organizations at the local level coordinate support for the party's candidates, but they don't necessarily have to follow the lead of the national party organization.

MoveOn.org typically supports Democratic candidates. Similar organizations on the Republican side include the Club for Growth, Americans for Prosperity, Crossroads GPS, and many evangelical groups. Most groups that use the "Tea Party" label to describe themselves generally have some connection to the national or local Republican Party.[17] Many of these organizations take advantage of a loophole in a provision of the IRS code to legally solicit large, anonymous donations from corporate and individual contributors. Although these groups often favor one party over the other, they are not part of the party organization and do not always agree with the party's positions or support its candidates—in fact, many have to operate independently of the parties and their candidates to preserve their tax-exempt status. (For more details on campaign finance, see Chapter 9 and Chapter 10.)

As this description suggests, the party organization has a fluid structure rather than a rigid hierarchy.[18] Individuals and groups work with a party's leaders and candidates when they share the same goals, but unless they are paid party employees they are under no obligation to do so (even paid party workers can, of course, quit rather than work for a candidate or a cause they oppose).

Party Brand Names The Republican and Democratic Party organizations have well-established "brand names." Because the parties stand for different things, in terms of both their preferred government policies and their ideological leanings, the party names themselves become a shorthand way of providing information to voters about the parties' candidates.[19] Hearing the term "Democrat" or "Republican" calls to mind ideas about what kinds of positions the members of each party support, what kinds of candidates each party runs, and how these candidates will probably vote if they are elected to office. Citizens can use these brand names as a cue to decide whom to vote for in an election. (See Chapter 9 for more information on voting cues.)

Figure 8.1 shows the most fundamental difference in Democratic and Republican brand names: currently Democrats are the more liberal party in America, while Republicans are more conservative. As you see, the Democratic Party distribution is dominated by liberal identifiers, while the Republican distribution is dominated by conservatives—although there is still some overlap in the middle, meaning that both parties claim some moderates. Research by many scholars confirms the description of the parties included in the excerpt from the Pew Research Center: that the current parties are much more homogeneous than a generation ago, with liberals much more likely to be Democrats and conservatives more likely to be Republicans.

FIGURE 8.1

The Parties in the Electorate

This graph shows the current ideological differences between people who identify with the Democratic and Republican parties. The blue area shows the distribution of Democrats, and the red plot shows the same distribution for Republicans. This confirms that modern American political parties are polarized (the median, or average, Democrat is a liberal, while the median, or average, Republican is a conservative) and homogeneous (most Democrats are liberal or liberal-leaning, while most Republicans are conservative or conservative-leaning). How might these differences affect the kinds of candidates who compete for each party's nomination and the positions they take during campaigns?

Source: Pew Research Center, "Ideological Polarization in the American Public." June 12, 2014, www.people-press.org (accessed 12/20/15).

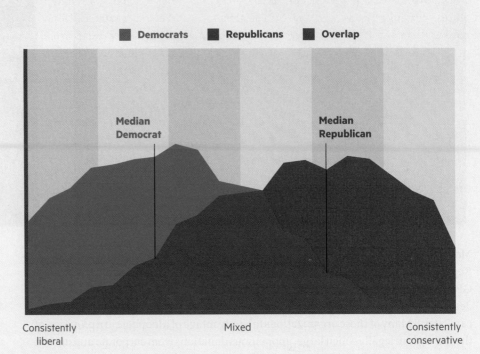

■ Democrats ■ Republicans ■ Overlap

Median Democrat

Median Republican

Consistently liberal — Mixed — Consistently conservative

> "
> I am not a member of an organized political party. I am a Democrat.
>
> —Will Rogers

Limits of the Party Organization The critical thing to understand about the Democratic and Republican party organizations is that they are not hierarchies. No one person or group in charge determines what either organization does—which often makes them look disorganized, as the Will Rogers quote indicates. Because the RNC and DNC are organized in the same way, we can consider the example of Donna Brazile, the chair of the DNC as of the 2016 election. She has some influence over who works at the DNC. However, the party organization's issue positions are set not by Brazile's employees but by DNC members from all 50 states. The individual committee members are appointed by their state party organizations, so they do not owe their jobs to Brazile—in fact, they can remove *her* from office if they like. If Brazile and the committee disagree, she can't force the committee members to do what she wants. For example, during the 2016 Democratic primary campaign DNC members who supported Bernie Sanders complained about Brazile's predecessor, Debbie Wasserman Schultz, claiming that the decision to limit the number of debates favored her preferred candidate, Hillary Clinton. They may have been right, but the fact is that Wasserman Schultz could implement this policy only if she had majority support from other DNC members.

The national party organization is also unable to force state and local parties to share its positions on issues or comply with other requests. State and local parties make their own decisions about state- and local-level candidates and issue positions. The national committee can ask nicely, cajole, or even threaten to withhold funds. But if a state party organization, an independent group, or even an individual candidate disagrees with the national committee, there's little the national committee can do to force compliance. For example, Republican leaders could not prevent Tea Party candidates from running in 2014 primaries against two incumbent senators, Pat Roberts of Kansas and Thad Cochran of Mississippi, or deter Donald Trump's candidacy in 2016.

The party in government

The party in government consists of elected officials holding national, state, and local offices who took office as candidates of a particular party. They are the public face of the party, somewhat like the players on a sports team. Although players are only one part of a sports franchise—along with owners, coaches, trainers, and support staff—the players' identities are what most people call to mind when they think of the team. Because the party in government is made up of officeholders, it has a direct impact on government policy. Members of the party organization can recruit candidates, write platforms, and pay for campaign ads, but only those who win elections—the party in government—serve as members of Congress or as executive officials and actually propose, debate, vote on, and sign the legislation that determines what government does.

Caucuses and Conferences In the House and Senate, the Democratic and Republican parties are organized around working groups called a **caucus** (Democrats) or a **conference** (Republicans). The party caucus or conference serves as a forum for debate, compromise, and strategizing among a party's elected officials. Under unified government (when the same party controls Congress and the presidency) these discussions focus on finding common ground within the party—such as the negotiations that led to the enactment of Obamacare in 2010 without any support from Republicans. Under divided government or when a party is in the minority, the focus changes to finding opportunities to work with the other party, or strategizing on how to block the other party's initiatives.

Each party's caucus or conference meets to decide legislative committee assignments, leadership positions on committees, and leadership positions within the caucus or conference.[20] Caucus or conference leaders also serve as spokespeople for their respective parties, particularly when the president is from the other party. The party in government also contains groups that recruit and support candidates for political office, the Democratic Congressional Campaign Committee (DCCC), the Democratic Senatorial Campaign Committee (DSCC), the National Republican Congressional Committee (NRCC), and the National Republican Senatorial Committee (NRSC).

Polarization and Ideological Diversity The modern Congress is polarized: in both the House and the Senate, Republicans and Democrats hold different views on government policy (see What Do the Numbers Say? on p. 263). Figure 8.2 compares legislators on the basis of their ideology, or their general feelings about government policy, as measured by a liberal–conservative scale. The data reflect two House sessions: the 83rd House of 60 years ago (elected in 1952) and the 114th House (elected in 2014).

These graphs tell us two things. First, over the last 60 years the magnitude of ideological differences between the parties in Congress has increased. In the 83rd House there was some overlap between the positions of Democrats and Republicans, but it had disappeared by the 114th House.[21] Of course, because Democrats and Republicans in Congress often disagree does not mean that compromise is impossible—just that the differences that must be bridged are that much wider.

Second, Figure 8.2 reveals that both parties in government include a mixture of ideologies, not a uniform consensus opinion. In the graph depicting the 83rd House, for example, Democrats vary from the relatively liberal left end of the axis to the moderate (middle) and even somewhat conservative right end. Democrats in the 114th House were, on average, more liberal than their colleagues were in the 83rd, but a range of ideologies was still represented in the Democratic Caucus. The same is true for Republicans, who leaned in the conservative direction in both the 83rd and the 114th Houses.

The ideological diversity within each party in government can create situations in which a caucus or conference is divided on a policy question. Compromise within a

caucus (congressional)
The organization of Democrats within the House and Senate that meets to discuss and debate the party's positions on various issues in order to reach a consensus and to assign leadership positions.

conference
The organization of Republicans within the House and Senate that meets to discuss and debate the party's positions on various issues in order to reach a consensus and to assign leadership positions.

FIGURE 8.2

Ideology of the Parties in Government: 83rd House and 114th House

Over the last several decades, ideological differences between Democrats and Republicans in Congress have increased significantly. However, even in the 114th House both parties still included a wide range of views. In light of these data, would you expect more or less partisan conflict in the modern Congress than there was in the early 1950s? According to these data, would you expect House members in each party to agree on what policies to pursue?

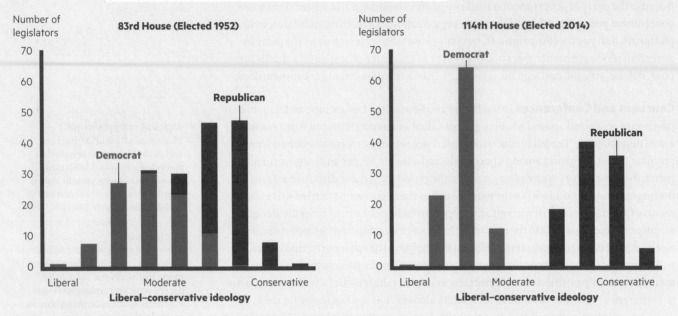

Source: "Constant Space DW-NOMINATE Scores," December 19, 2015, http://voteview.com (accessed 1/19/16).

party caucus is not inevitable—even though legislators share a party label, they may not be able to find common ground. In the last few years, congressional Democrats have been divided on issues such as regulation of banks and other financial issues, while divisions on the Republican side arose on issues of immigration policy as well as spending levels and the federal debt limit.[22]

The party in the electorate

The party in the electorate consists of citizens who identify with a particular political party. Most Americans say they are either Democrats or Republicans, although the percentage has declined over the last two generations. Party identification (party ID) is a critical variable in understanding votes and other forms of political participation.

Party ID Party ID is different from formal membership in a political party. Although the Republicans and the Democrats have websites where people can sign up to receive e-mail alerts and to contribute online to party causes, joining a party does not give a citizen any direct influence over what the party does. Rather, the party leaders and the candidates themselves make the day-to-day decisions. These individuals often heed citizens' demands, but there is no requirement that they do so. Real participation in party operations is open to citizens who become activists by working for a party organization or one of its candidates. Activists' contributions vary from stuffing envelopes to helping out with a phone bank, being a delegate to a party convention, attending campaign rallies, or campaigning door-to-door.

party identification (party ID)
A citizen's loyalty to a specific political party.

DID YOU KNOW?

7%

of Americans say they worked for a political candidate or issue campaign during the last year.

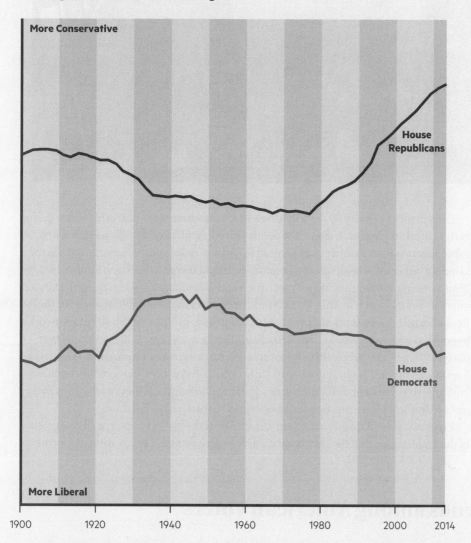
Are the Parties More Polarized than Ever?

For the last twenty years, it seems as though all the news about political parties has been about conflict and stalemate. It seems as though political campaigns are increasingly negative, compromise on issues is rare, and Republicans and Democrats have divided into camps that are never likely to agree on anything. Is this trend new? What do the numbers say?

Ideological Polarization in Congress

More Conservative

House Republicans

House Democrats

More Liberal

1900 1920 1940 1960 1980 2000 2014

Think about it

- This graph uses voting behavior to measure the average ideology (liberal–conservative) of House Democrats and Republicans.
  Since the 1980s, have Republicans gotten more conservative, have Democrats become more liberal, or both?
- How might these changes make it harder for members of the contemporary Congress to enact major changes in government policy?
  What is more likely: compromise or gridlock?

Activist volunteers undertake most of the one-on-one efforts to mobilize support for a party and its candidates.

Early theories of party ID described it as a deep attachment to a party that was acquired early in life from parents, friends, and political events and was generally unaffected by subsequent events.[23] Further work showed that party ID does not necessarily remain the same but rather involves continuing evaluation that takes account of new information.[24] Thus, when people say they identify with the Republican Party they are saying that, based on what they have seen in American politics, they prefer the positions suggested by the Republicans' brand name and how Republicans behave in office. At the same time, work by political scientists Donald Green, Bradley Palmquist, and Eric Schickler shows that party ID shapes how people think about politics and react to new information. Thus, when Republicans argue for sending troops to fight ISIS in Syria while Democrats focus on aiding Syrian refugees, the difference is not what they know but how they react to the same pieces of information—a response that is shaped by their party affiliation.

Figure 8.3 gives data on party ID in America over the last 75 years. The first segment of the graph shows that the Democratic Party had a considerable advantage in terms

FIGURE 8.3   **Party ID Trends among American Voters**

In terms of party ID, the parties have moved from rough parity in the late 1930s and 1940s to a period of Democratic advantage that lasted from the 1950s to the 1980s. Beginning in 2003, Democrats appeared to be opening up another advantage, although this change has eroded in recent years. What events might have caused these changes in party ID?

Source: Pew Research Center, "A Deep Dive into Party Affiliation," April 7, 2015, www.people-press.org (accessed 12/20/15).

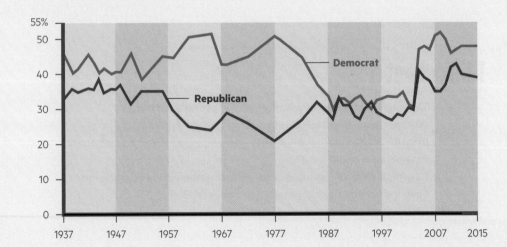

of the number of citizens identifying with the party from the late 1930s until the late 1980s. During the 1970s, nearly half of adults identified with the Democratic Party and only about 20 percent identified with the Republicans. During the 1990s, the percentage of Democratic identifiers decreased significantly and the percentage of Republican identifiers increased slightly, to the point that in 2002 the parties had roughly the same percentage of identifiers.[25] But beginning in 2003, the Democrats again opened up a significant advantage in terms of identifiers, although the difference has largely disappeared in recent years. The two lines in Figure 8.3 do not add up to 100 percent, and the difference represents the percentage of independent voters who do not identify with either party. Just like the percentages of Republican and Democratic identifiers, the percentage of Independents fluctuates over time.

Independents Some early analyses concluded that Independents were unaffiliated with a party because they were in the process of shifting their identification from one party to the other.[26] Others saw Independents as evidence that more and more people regard the parties as irrelevant to their view of politics and their voting decisions.[27] The rise in the number of Independents was also seen as an indication that Americans were becoming more politically savvy—learning more about candidates and not always blindly voting for the same party.[28]

More-recent work has modified these findings. Most Independents actually have some weak attachment to one of the major political parties—in fact, some scholars refer to Independents as "closet partisans," people who have party ties but who simply don't admit that they do.[29] Independents are not necessarily better informed about candidates, parties, or government policy than party identifiers. However, they are much less likely to get involved in political activity beyond voting, such as contributing to or working for a candidate or party.[30]

With a closer look at voting decisions, Figure 8.4 shows how Democrats, Republicans, and Independents voted in the 2016 presidential election ("closet partisan" Independents are grouped with the party they actually affiliate with). This figure shows that

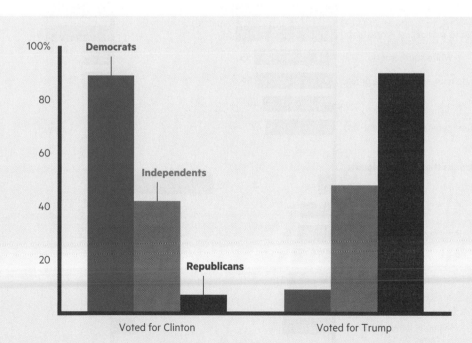

Source: Data compiled from CNN Exit Poll, www.cnn.com/election/results/exit-polls/national/president (accessed 11/9/16).

FIGURE 8.4

The Impact of Party ID on Voting Decisions in the 2016 Presidential Election

Americans are much more likely to vote for candidates who share their party affiliation. What does this relationship tell us about the impact of campaign events (including speeches, debates, and gaffes) on voting decisions?

if you are trying to predict how someone will vote, the most important thing to know is his or her party ID.[31] Almost 90 percent of Democrats voted for Hillary Clinton, the Democratic nominee, and about the same percentage of Republicans voted for Donald Trump. Trump's victory was due to his slightly higher margin among independents.

Party Coalitions Data on party IDs enable scholars to study **party coalitions**—that is, groups of citizens who identify with each party. Figure 8.5 shows the contemporary Democratic and Republican party coalitions. As you can see, some groups are disproportionately likely to identify as Democrats (African Americans), some are disproportionately likely to identify as Republicans (white evangelicals), and other groups have no clear party favorite (people born in 1945 and earlier). Again, these coalitions have shifted over time. For example, the Republican advantage among white southerners and white evangelical Protestants has existed only since the 1980s.[32]

The Republican and Democratic Party coalitions differ systematically in terms of their policy preferences—what they want government to do—as shown in Figure 8.6. This indicates the extent to which they disagree about the relative importance of issues like providing health insurance to the uninsured, dealing with global warming, and

party coalitions
The groups that identify with a political party, usually described in demographic terms such as African-American Democrats or evangelical Republicans.

FIGURE 8.5

The Party Coalitions

Many groups, such as African Americans and white evangelicals, are much more likely to affiliate with one party than the other. What are the implications of these differences for the positions taken by each party's candidates?

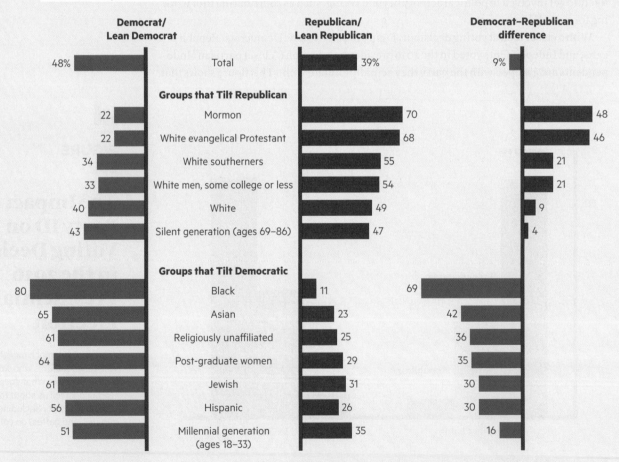

Source: Pew Research Center, "A Deep Dive into Party Affiliation," April 7, 2015, www.people-press.org (accessed 12/20/15).

strengthening the military. On only a few issues—for example, reducing crime or dealing with lobbyists—are the percentages of those in both parties who consider the matter a priority nearly the same. These data demonstrate that party labels are meaningful: if you know someone is a Republican (or a Democrat), this information tells you something about what that person probably wants government to do, and how he or she will likely vote in the next election. These differences also create opportunities

Democrats' and Republicans' Top Priorities

FIGURE 8.6

The Republican and Democratic Party coalitions have different priorities on many issues, ranging from environmental protection to deficit reduction—and on a few issues their differences are small, such as reforming the tax system and reducing the influence of lobbyists. Do these differences make sense in light of each party's "brand name"?

Percentage considering each as a "top priority"

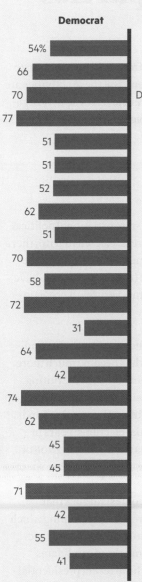

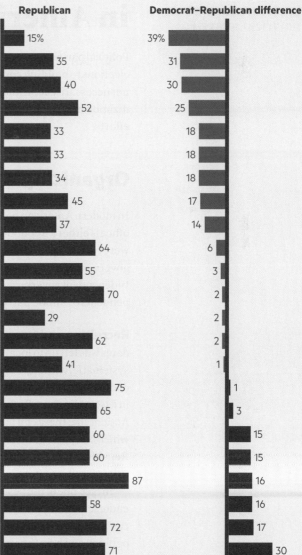

	Democrat	Republican	Democrat–Republican difference
Dealing with global warming	54%	15%	39%
Protecting the environment	66	35	31
Dealing with problems of poor and needy	70	40	30
Improving the educational system	77	52	25
Supporting scientific research	51	33	18
Dealing with role of money in politics	51	33	18
Improving roads, bridges, and transit	52	34	18
Addressing race relations	62	45	17
Dealing with nation's energy problem	51	37	14
Reducing health care costs	70	64	6
Making Medicare system sound	58	55	3
Improving the job situation	72	70	2
Dealing with global trade issues	31	29	2
Reducing crime	64	62	2
Reducing the influence of lobbyists	42	41	1
Strengthening the nation's economy	74	75	1
Making Social Security system sound	62	65	3
Reforming the nation's tax system	45	60	15
Dealing with issue of immigration	45	60	15
Defending country from terrorism	71	87	16
Dealing with moral breakdown	42	58	16
Reducing the budget deficit	55	72	17
Strengthening the U.S. military	41	71	30

Source: Pew Research Center, "Public's Policy Priorities Reflect Changing Conditions at Home and Abroad," January 15, 2015, www.people-press.org (accessed 12/20/15).

for **issue ownership**: candidates from a party tend to concentrate their campaigns on issues that are priorities for members of their party in the electorate and ignore issues that their party in the electorate considers unimportant.[33]

"Why Should I Care?"

Knowing that someone is a Democrat or a Republican tells you a lot about the issues he or she cares about, whether he or she will like or dislike different candidates, and whom he or she will vote for in an election. Taken together, information about the kinds of people who identify with each party tells you a lot about the kinds of candidates who will run under the party banner and the platforms they will campaign on.

★

EXPLAIN THE IMPORTANT FUNCTIONS PARTIES PERFORM IN THE POLITICAL SYSTEM

The role of political parties in American politics

Political parties play an important role in American politics, from helping to organize elections to building consensus across branches of government. But these activities are not necessarily coordinated. Candidates and groups at different levels of a party organization may work together, refuse to cooperate, or even actively oppose one another's efforts.

Organizing elections

In modern American politics, virtually everyone elected to a state or national political office is either a Republican or a Democrat. In the 115th Congress, elected in 2016, there were two Independent senators and no Independent House members. Similarly, the governors of 48 states were either Democrats or Republicans (Alaska and Maine have Independent governors) and of more than 7,300 state legislators very few were Independents or minor-party candidates.

Recruiting and Nominating Candidates Historically, the recruitment of candidates was left up to local party organizations. But the process has become much more systematic, with state and national party leaders playing a central role in recruiting, endorsing, and contributing to candidates—and often promising those candidates help in assembling a staff, organizing a campaign, and raising additional campaign funds.[34] Actions like these can have a profound impact on congressional elections; years in which one party gains significant congressional seats (such as Democrats in 2008 or Republicans in 2010) are in part the result of one party having disproportionate success in its recruiting efforts.

In fact, one of the best theories of presidential nomination contests argues that endorsements by party leaders and elected officials play a key role in determining which candidate emerges as the nominee.[35] Endorsements enhance a candidate's name recognition and help to persuade undecided voters and contributors about candidates' electability and their ability to deliver on campaign promises. In all recent presidential nomination contests except 2016, the winning candidate was the one who gathered the most endorsements from party leaders, elected officials, and other notables. This theory was one of the main reasons why most political scientists thought that Donald Trump was unlikely to be the Republican nominee in 2016. While he led in the polls for several months, he received almost no endorsements from party leaders or elected officials. Conversely, one reason why Hillary Clinton was seen as the inevitable Democratic nominee was the large number of endorsements she garnered from Democratic Party leaders.[36]

Party leaders also play an active role in recruiting candidates for House and Senate seats. When a Senate seat opened up in Florida because of Marco Rubio's presidential run in 2016, Republican national leaders encouraged Florida Lieutenant Governor Carlos Lopez-Cantera to enter the race, and discouraged other potential candidates, such as Representative David Jolly. These decisions reflected a simple political logic: party leaders believed that Lopez-Cantera would have a better chance of winning the general election given Florida's large Hispanic vote. In addition, party leaders were angry at Jolly because he had criticized the party's fund-raising efforts during an interview on the CBS investigative reporting show *60 Minutes*. After Rubio withdrew from the presidential race and party leaders convinced him to seek another Senate term, both Lopez-Cantera and Jolly exited the campaign.

For all of these efforts, however, parties and their leaders do not control who runs in House, Senate, or presidential races (see the Take a Stand feature). In most states, candidates for these offices are selected in a **primary election** or a **caucus**, in which they compete for a particular party's spot on the ballot. (About two-thirds of the states use some type of primary election while the rest use caucuses to select candidates; see Nuts & Bolts 8.1 for a further explanation of the different ways that the parties select candidates.) Most notably, Donald Trump won the 2016 Republican presidential nomination by virtue of his victories in the party's primaries and caucuses over the objections of many party leaders. Trump's victory demonstrates that party endorsements, while significant, are not the only factor in shaping nomination contests.

Running as a major party's congressional nominee, as opposed to running as an Independent, is almost always the easiest way to get on the general-election ballot. Some states give the Republican and Democratic nominees an automatic spot on the ballot. Even in states that don't automatically allocate ballot slots this way, the

primary election
A ballot vote in which citizens select a party's nominee for the general election.

caucus (electoral)
A local meeting in which party members select a party's nominee for the general election.

Types of Primaries and Caucuses

NUTS
& BOLTS
8.1

Primary Election	An election in which voters choose the major-party nominees for political office, who subsequently compete in a general election.
Closed primary	A primary election system in which only registered party members can vote in their party's primary.
Nonpartisan primary	A primary election system in which candidates from both parties are listed on the same primary ballot. Following a nonpartisan primary, the two candidates who receive the most votes in the primary compete in the general election, even if they are from the same party.
Open primary	A primary election system in which any registered voter can participate in either party's primary, regardless of the voter's party affiliation.
Semi-closed primary	A primary election system where voters registered as party members must vote in their party's primary, but registered Independents can vote in either party's primary.
Caucus Election	A series of local meetings at which registered voters select a particular candidate's supporters as delegates who will vote for the candidate in a later, state-level convention. (In national elections, the state-convention delegates select delegates to the national convention.) Caucuses are used in some states to select delegates to the major parties' presidential nominating conventions. Some states' caucuses are open to members of any party, while others are closed.

Should Parties Choose Their Candidates?

One of the facts of life for the leaders of the Democratic and Republican parties is that they cannot determine who runs as their party's candidate for political office. They can encourage some candidates to run and attempt to discourage others by endorsing their favorites and funneling money, staff support, and other forms of assistance to the candidates they prefer. But in the end, congressional candidates get on the ballot by winning a primary or a vote at a state party convention; presidential candidates compete in a series of primaries and caucuses. Is this system a good one?

Let the party decide.

Many scholars have argued that letting parties choose their candidates increases the chances of getting experienced, talented candidates on the ballot.[a] After all, party leaders probably know more than the average voter about who would make a good candidate or elected official. Plus, party leaders have a strong incentive to find good candidates and convince them to run: their party's influence over government policy increases with the number of people they can elect to political office. And finally, in states that have no party registration or day-of-election registration giving the nomination power to party leaders would ensure that a group of outsiders could not hijack a party primary to nominate a candidate who disagreed with a party's platform or who was unqualified to serve in office.

While cases of outright hijacking of party nominations are fairly rare, political parties don't always get the nominees their leaders want and party leaders cannot force candidates out of a race. In the 2016 election cycle, for example, many Republican Party leaders believed that Donald Trump was not the party's strongest nominee. Trump gained the nomination over their objections by winning the party's caucus and primary contests.

Let the people decide.

One argument in favor of giving the nomination power to the people is that party leaders have not always shown good judgment in picking either electable or qualified candidates. Many of the same Republican leaders who opposed Trump had supported party nominees John McCain in 2008 and Mitt Romney in 2012, both of whom went on to lose in the general-election contest. This track record suggests that party leaders are far from infallible.

The second argument for letting the people decide hinges on a judgment about whose wishes should prevail in nomination contests: the people who make up the party in the electorate or the people in the party organization. What right does the party organization have to select nominees, given that support from the party in the electorate (their contributions and votes in elections) is essential for electoral success? Moreover, shouldn't voters have a say in determining what their electoral choices look like? If party leaders choose, voters may not like any of the options put before them.

Why, then, do voters in America get to pick party nominees in primaries? Direct primaries were introduced in American politics during the late 1800s and early 1900s.[b] The goal was explicit: reform-minded party activists wanted to take the choice of nominees out of the hands of party leaders and give it to the electorate, with the assumption that voters should be able to influence the choice of candidates for the general election. Moreover, reformers believed that this goal outweighed the expertise held by party leaders.

Here is the trade-off: If party leaders select nominees, they would likely choose electable candidates who share the policy goals held by party leaders. If voters choose nominees, they can pick whomever they want, using whatever criteria they like—but there is no guarantee that these candidates will be skilled general-election campaigners or effective in office.

In the end, some groups must be given control over the selection of a party's nominees. Should this power be given to party leaders or to the people? Take a stand.

📷 Both political parties organize a series of candidate debates during their presidential nomination contests, giving candidates a chance to present themselves before a national audience.

take a stand

1. One reform proposal would increase the importance of the parties as sources of campaign funds. Would this change have made much of a difference in the 2016 Republican presidential contest?

2. What kind of nomination procedure would be favored by insurgent groups such as the various Tea Party organizations?

requirements for the major parties to get a candidate on the ballot are much less oner-ous than those for minor parties and Independents. For example, in California a party and its candidates automatically qualify for a position on the ballot if any of the party's candidates for statewide office received more than 2 percent of the vote in the previous election. In contrast, Independent candidates need to file petitions with more than 150,000 signatures to get on the ballot without a major-party label—an expensive, time-consuming task.[38] These advantages help explain why virtually all prominent candidates for Congress and the presidency run as Democrats or Republicans.

National parties also manage the nomination process for presidential candidates. This process involves a series of primaries and caucuses held over a six-month period beginning in January of a presidential election year. The type of election (primary or caucus) and its date are determined by state legislatures, although national party committees can limit the allowable dates, using their control over seating delegates at the party conventions to motivate compliance. Voters in these primaries and cau-cuses don't directly select the parties' nominees. Instead, citizens' votes are used to determine how many of each candidate's supporters become delegates to the party's national **nominating convention**, where delegates vote to choose the party's presi-dential and vice-presidential nominees. The national party organizations determine how many delegates each state sends to the convention based on factors such as state population, the number of votes the party's candidate received in each state in the last presidential election, and the number of House members and senators from the party that each state elected (see How It Works: Nominating Presidential Candidates).

Campaign Assistance One of the most visible ways that the political parties support candidates is by contributing to and spending money on campaign activities. By and large, federal law mandates that these funds be spent by the organization that raised them—the national party, for example, is limited in the amount of money it can contrib-ute to congressional and presidential candidates or to state party organizations. As we will discuss in Chapter 9, however, party organizations that raise campaign funds can use them to help candidates get elected through independent expenditures—running their own ads in a candidate's district or state.

Figure 8.7 shows the amount of money raised by the top groups within the Repub-lican and Democratic parties for the 2016 election (through November 4). The final figures show that the parties and their various committees raised over a billion dollars. The DNC and RNC raised the most money, but the congressional campaign commit-tees also raised significant sums. Congressional Democratic committees outraised their Republican counterparts. And congressional leaders raised almost $50 million for the campaigns of their colleagues.[39]

Along with supplying campaign funds, party organizations give candidates other assistance, ranging from offering campaign advice (including which issues to empha-size, how to deal with the press, and the like) to conducting polls. Party organizations at all levels also undertake get-out-the-vote activities, encouraging supporters to get to the polls. In the last few elections, Democrats have been more effective than Repub-licans. In the 2016 election, Republican candidate Donald Trump's campaign was almost completely reliant on the Republican Party's mobilization efforts, while Demo-crat Hillary Clinton's campaign used a combination of campaign and party resources. In the end, however, the Democratic operation did not prevent turnout from declining (compared to 2012) among key groups such as African Americans and Latinos.

Party Platforms The **party platform** is a set of promises explaining what candidates from the party will do if elected. The most visible party platform is the one approved at each party's presidential nominating convention, but the party organizations in the House and Senate also release platforms, as do other groups in the major parties. Party

nominating convention
A meeting held by each party every four years at which states' delegates select the party's presidential and vice-presidential nominees and approve the party platform.

party platform
A set of objectives outlining the party's issue positions and priorities. Candidates are not required to support their party's platform.

Nominating Presidential Candidates

Primaries and caucuses...

Closed Primaries
Only voters registered with party vote

Open Primaries
Open to voters from any political party and Independents

Caucus or Local Convention
Party members meet in groups to select delegates

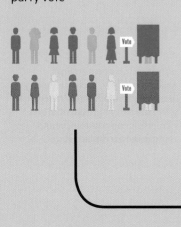

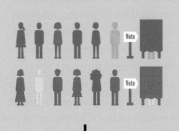

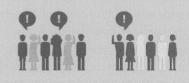

are used to select delegates...

Republican Party
States can award all delegates to the winning candidate

or award delegates proportionally.

Democratic Party
The state's delegates are divided proportionally.

who attend national nominating conventions.

Delegates from all states attend the national convention, where they vote for the party's presidential and vice-presidential nominees based on the primary and caucus results. Superdelegates—important party leaders—also vote at the convention.

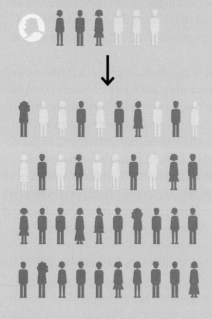

The Nomination of Donald Trump for President, 2016

While Donald Trump was the clear winner in the 2016 Republican presidential nomination contest, his campaign benefitted from the rules used in some of the early contests, particularly the use of primary elections rather than caucuses and the use of winner-take-all rules for delegate allocation.

☐ Winner-take-all delegate allocation
☐ Proportional delegate allocation
% Percentage of popular vote won
ᵢ Delegates allocated

		Trump	Rubio	Cruz	Kasich	Caucus/ Primary	Winner Take All?
Feb. 1	Iowa	24%	23%	28%	2%	Caucus	NO
Feb. 9	New Hampshire	35%	12%	11%	16%	Primary	NO
Feb. 20	South Carolina	33%	23%	23%	8%	Primary	YES
Feb. 23	Nevada	46%	24%	21%	4%	Caucus	NO
Mar. 1	Alabama	43%	19%	21%	4%	Primary	NO
	Alaska	34%	15%	36%	4%	Caucus	NO
	Arkansas	33%	25%	31%	4%	Primary	NO
	Georgia	39%	24%	24%	6%	Primary	NO
	Massachusetts	49%	18%	10%	18%	Primary	NO
	Minnesota	21%	37%	29%	6%	Caucus	NO
	Oklahoma	28%	26%	34%	4%	Primary	NO
	Tennessee	39%	21%	24%	5%	Primary	NO
	Texas	27%	19%	44%	4%	Primary	NO
	Vermont	33%	19%	10%	30%	Primary	NO
	Virginia	35%	32%	17%	9%	Primary	NO
Total delegates		**340**	**116**	**230**	**27**		

Note: Colorado has been omitted because its caucus did not allocate delegates.
Source: Data compiled by the authors.

❓ Critical Thinking

1. **Which states used winner-take-all rules in 2016?** How much did Trump benefit from this rule in the early primaries? If there were more winner-take-all states, which candidate(s) would have done better? Which would have done worse?

2. **One argument about caucuses is that they allow** lesser-known candidates (such as John Kasich) to build support. Did this rule hold for Kasich in 2016?

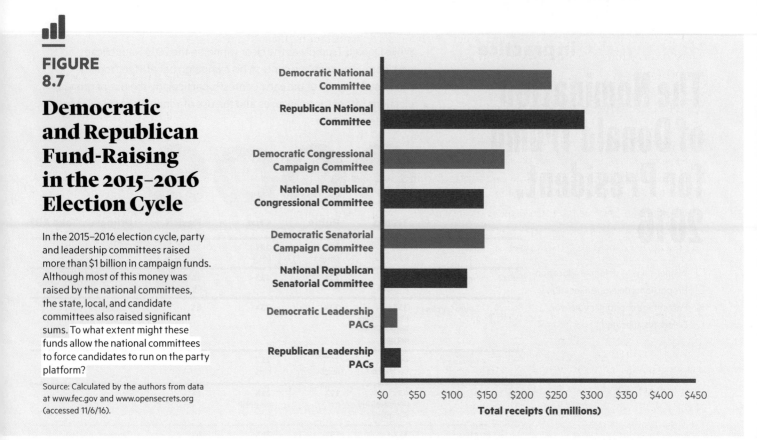

FIGURE 8.7

Democratic and Republican Fund-Raising in the 2015–2016 Election Cycle

In the 2015–2016 election cycle, party and leadership committees raised more than $1 billion in campaign funds. Although most of this money was raised by the national committees, the state, local, and candidate committees also raised significant sums. To what extent might these funds allow the national committees to force candidates to run on the party platform?

Source: Calculated by the authors from data at www.fec.gov and www.opensecrets.org (accessed 11/6/16).

platforms generally reflect the brand name differences between the parties discussed earlier. For example, in the case of abortion rights, the 2016 Republican presidential platform favored a total ban on abortions, while the Democratic presidential platform expressed support for a woman's right to choose, meaning that abortion would be legal under a wider range of conditions.

In theory, party platforms describe differences between the major parties, capture each party's diagnosis of the problems facing the country, and give the party's plan for solving those problems. In this way, party platforms give citizens an easy way to evaluate candidates. However, candidates are not obligated to support their party's platform

One of the most important ways parties help candidates is by raising money to fund campaigns. In 2012, the DNC raised nearly a billion dollars to help reelect President Obama and to support other Democratic candidates. The RNC raised a similar amount. #DNC #RNC

and many take divergent stances on some issues. For example, notwithstanding the consistently strong pro-choice position on abortion in the Democratic Party's presidential platforms over the last generation, some Democratic members of Congress, such as Illinois representative Dan Lipinski, promised to vote to restrict abortions—a position closer to the Republican platform.[40] For some of these candidates, this position reflected personal or religious beliefs; for others, it was driven by the desire to reflect the opinion of voters in their district or state.

Despite these exceptions, party platforms are important documents. Political scientist John Geering's research shows that platforms provide a general guide for voters about the issues and issue positions that separate the major parties. Platforms indicate what sorts of policies winning candidates are likely to vote for if elected—and while some candidates may ignore or run against their party's platform, most candidates will support the platform because they agree with it or because they believe it is popular with their constituents.[41]

Cooperation in government

Particularly in recent years, as Republicans and Democrats in Congress have polarized, the majority- and minority-party caucuses have taken on larger roles in efforts to set legislative priorities, formulate compromise proposals, and work to enact these proposals on the floor of the House and Senate. Political scientists refer to this phenomenon as conditional party government. As a result, understanding what happens in Congress (or what doesn't) requires information about what the parties in Congress are trying to do.

Agenda-Setting Throughout the year, the parties in government meet to devise strategies for legislative action—that is, to set agendas. What proposals should they offer, and in what order should these proposals be considered? Should the parties try to make a deal with the president or with legislators from the other party? For example, after the 2008 election Democratic congressional leaders met with President-elect Barack Obama and his staff to discuss priorities for the 2009–2010 legislative term, including climate change legislation, health care reform, and an economic stimulus package. Some of these efforts were highly successful. Less than a month after Obama took office, Congress passed a $787 billion stimulus plan, which Democrats passed with no Republican support in the House and only three Republican votes in the Senate. Congress enacted landmark health care reform legislation with no Republican votes a year later.

Similarly, when Republicans gained control of the House after the 2010 midterms (and the Senate after 2014), the House and Senate Republicans used their powers to schedule repeated votes on repealing Obamacare, block votes on gun control measures, and delay consideration of Obama's nominees to federal judgeships and cabinet positions, including Obama's 2016 Supreme Court nominee, Merrick Garland.

Yet the party in government can act collectively this way only when its members can agree on what they want. Such agreement is not always possible or may require extensive negotiation and compromise. Even with unified Republican control of Congress and the presidency after the 2016 election, disagreements within the party on issues such as trade, immigration reform, and infrastructure spending may delay or deter legislative action.

Coordination Political parties play an important role in coordinating the actions taken in different branches of government. Such coordination is extremely important for enacting new laws, because unless supporters in Congress can amass a two-thirds

Within the government, politicians from the same party work together to develop an agenda and try to get it enacted. Here, President Obama meets with Democratic leaders from the Senate.

Parties don't exert total control over their members. Republican Party leaders could not stop then–freshman senator Ted Cruz (R-TX) from filibustering for 23 hours in an attempt to stop a budget compromise.
@TedCruz

majority to override a veto they need the president's support. Similarly, the president needs congressional support to enact the proposals he or she favors. To these ends, the president routinely meets with congressional leaders from his or her party and occasionally meets with the entire caucus or conference. Various members of the president's staff also meet with House and Senate members to present the president's proposals and to hear what members of Congress from both parties want to enact.

During 2009, President Obama held many meetings with Democratic members of Congress to lobby them to support his proposals for health care reform. Although many congressional Democrats supported Obama's proposals, enactment was nearly derailed by several Democratic representatives and senators who demanded amendments to restrict government payment for abortions. The president opposed these efforts but was powerless to stop them. In fact, getting the last few votes needed for enactment required Obama to promise to issue an executive order that had essentially the same effect as the proposed amendments.

Coordination can also occur between caucuses or conferences in the House and Senate. At the same time that President Obama and Democrats in Congress were negotiating over health care reform, congressional Republicans were devising strategies for delaying and defeating these proposals. Although Republican efforts did not prevent the enactment of reform legislation, the strong opposition of the Republicans required the president and congressional leaders to accept many changes favored by moderate and conservative Democrats in order to enact the legislation without Republican support.

Such coordination efforts require real work and compromise since party leaders in the House and the Senate do not have authority over each other or over the elected members of their party. Nor can the president order a House member or senator to do anything, even if the legislator is from the president's own party. In 2010, for example, President Obama and congressional leaders needed the votes of several anti-abortion Democrats, including Congressman Bart Stupak, to pass health care legislation through the House of Representatives. The congressional leaders and the president held repeated meetings with Stupak and his allies, offering various promises and enticements to secure their votes. Ultimately, these legislators voted for the proposal, but neither the president nor party leaders could have forced them to support it.

Accountability One of the most important functions political parties play in a democracy is to give citizens identifiable groups to reward or punish for government action or inaction. Using the ballot box, voters will reward and punish elected officials, often based on their party affiliation and on the behavior of that party's members in office. In this way, the electorate uses the party system to hold officials accountable for outcomes such as the state of the economy or America's relations with other nations.

During periods of **unified government**, when one party holds majorities in both the House and the Senate *and* controls the presidency that party has enough votes to enact policies in Congress and a good chance of having them signed into law by the president. During times of **divided government**, when one party controls Congress but not the presidency or when different parties control the House and Senate, the president's party is considered the party in power.

Focusing on parties makes it easy for a citizen to issue rewards and punishments. Thus, for example, if the economy is doing well people can reward the party in power by voting for its candidates. But if the economy is doing poorly or if people feel that government is wasting tax money or enacting bad policies they can punish the party in power by voting for candidates from the party that is currently out of power. When citizens behave this way, they strengthen the incentive for elected officials from the party in power to work together to develop policies that address voters' concerns—on the premise that if they do voters will reward them with another term in office. Consider the 2010 midterm elections, when many Americans voted against Democratic candidates because of poor economic conditions. Although Democrats lost seats in both the House and the Senate, most Democratic incumbents were still returned to office. Why? Some were elected from states or districts dominated by Democratic identifiers. But many others were reelected because they campaigned on a platform of changing policy or because of their efforts to help local businesses, saying in effect, "Instead of punishing me for my party affiliation, reward me for working on your behalf."

In the end, reelecting members of the party in power despite a poor economy or other troubles makes sense given how American political parties are organized and their lack of control over individual officeholders. Of course, insofar as incumbent members of the party in power present themselves as loyal party members and cast votes in accordance with the wishes of party leaders they will increase the chances that their constituents will take account of their party label when casting their votes—which will help them get reelected in good times but will increase the chances of defeat when conditions turn against their party.

unified government
A situation in which one party holds a majority of seats in the House and Senate and the president is a member of that same party.

divided government
A situation in which the House, Senate, and presidency are not controlled by the same party—for example, when Democrats hold the majority of House and Senate seats and the president is a Republican.

Minor parties

So far, this chapter has focused on the major American political parties, the Republicans and the Democrats, and paid less attention to other party organizations. The reason is that minor political parties in America are *so* minor that they are generally not significant players on the political stage. Many such parties exist, but few run candidates in more than a handful of races and very few minor-party candidates win political office. Few Americans identify with minor parties, and most of these parties exist for only a relatively short period.

Even so, you may think we are giving minor parties too little attention. Consider Ralph Nader, who ran as the Green Party nominee for president in 2000, winning almost 5 percent of the vote. In some states, the number of votes Nader received exceeded the margin separating Democrat Al Gore from Republican George Bush. In particular, in Florida, where Bush won by only a few hundred votes after a disputed recount, Nader received almost 100,000 votes. These votes would have been enough to swing the state, and the election, to Gore.

However, the outcome of Nader's 2000 presidential campaign doesn't so much highlight the importance of minor parties as it illustrates the closeness of the 2000 presidential election. If Nader had not run, Gore might have received enough additional support to win. But given that Bush's margin of victory in Florida was so small, any number of seemingly minor events (a polling station closing early or rain in some areas and sunshine in others) could have changed the outcome.

Effects on Election Outcomes Minor parties did not play a decisive role in the 2016 presidential election, but in several swing states (for example, Florida, Pennsylvania, Wisconsin, and Michigan) they received more votes than the margin of difference between Donald Trump and Hillary Clinton. The most successful were the Green Party (1.4 million votes) and the Libertarian Party (over 4 million votes). In all, minor parties won about 6.5 million votes in the 2016 presidential race, about 4.5 percent of the total.

Even in terms of lower offices, minor-party candidates typically attract only meager support. While the Libertarian Party claims to have over a dozen officeholders, many of these officials held unelected positions such as seats on county planning boards or ran unopposed for relatively minor offices such as justice of the peace.[42]

Looking back in history, some minor-party candidates for president have attracted a substantial percentage of citizens' votes. George Wallace ran as the candidate of the American Independent Party in 1968, receiving about 13 percent of the popular vote nationwide. Ross Perot, the Reform Party candidate for president in 1996, won 8.4 percent of the popular vote. Perot also ran as an Independent in 1992, winning 18.2 percent of the popular vote.

Unique Issues Facing Minor Parties The differences between major and minor political parties in contemporary American politics grow even more substantial when considered in terms other than election outcomes. For most minor parties, the party in government does not exist, as few of their candidates win office. Many minor parties have virtually no organization beyond a small party headquarters and a website. Some minor parties, such as the Green Party, the Libertarian Party, and the Reform Party, have local chapters that meet on a regular basis. But these modest efforts pale in comparison with the nationwide network of offices, thousands of workers, and hundreds of millions of dollars deployed by Republican and Democratic Party organizations.

Research shows that people vote for minor-party candidates because they find these candidates' positions more attractive than those of the major parties and also because they believe that neither major party can govern effectively.[43] In 2016, for example, Libertarian presidential candidate Gary Johnson advocated withdrawal of American troops from Afghanistan, as well as deep cuts in defense spending. To vote for Johnson, a citizen would have had to like Johnson's positions on issues and believe that neither of the major parties could effectively address these problems.

The issues and issue positions taken by minor parties and their candidates are almost always very different from those espoused by the major parties. The Constitution Party, for example, advocates an end to government civil service regulations; a ban on compulsory school attendance laws; withdrawal of the United States from the UN and all international trade agreements; abolishing foreign aid, the income tax, the Internal Revenue Service, and all federal welfare programs; and repealing all campaign finance legislation, the Endangered Species Act, and federal firearms regulations.

📷

Minor-party presidential candidates, such as Ralph Nader in 2000, sometimes attract considerable press attention because of their distinctive, often-extreme policy preferences—but they rarely affect election outcomes. Nader ran again, as an Independent, in 2004 and 2008.

votenader.com

These positions are extreme, not in the sense of being silly or dangerous but in the sense that relatively few Americans agree with them.

The basic structure of the American political system also works against minor political parties. This principle is summed up by **Duverger's Law**, which states that in a democracy that has **single-member districts** and **plurality voting** there will be only two political parties that are able to elect a significant number of candidates to political office, which is the case in contemporary America. Given these electoral institutions (see Chapter 9), many people consider a vote for a minor-party candidate to be a wasted vote, as there is no chance that the candidate will win office. As a result, well-qualified candidates are driven to affiliate with one of the major political parties because they know that running as a minor-party nominee will put them at a considerable disadvantage. These decisions reinforce citizens' expectations that minor-party candidates have no chance of winning elections and that a vote for them is a wasted vote. Although there is no evidence that the Founders wanted to choose electoral institutions that made it hard for minor parties and their candidates, there is no doubt that the rules of the American electoral game have these effects.

Duverger's Law
The principle that in a democracy with single-member districts and plurality voting only two parties' candidates will have a realistic chance of winning political office, as in the United States.

single-member district
An electoral system in which every elected official represents a geographically defined area, such as a state or congressional district, and each area elects one representative.

plurality voting
A voting system in which the candidate who receives the most votes within a geographic area wins the election, regardless of whether that candidate wins a majority (more than half) of the votes.

You may dislike political parties or party leaders in Congress, but the fact is, the parties are key players in congressional policy making and in negotiations between Congress and the president. If you are trying to decide whether a new program (or nominee) has a chance of being approved, one of the first things you need to consider is whether the party caucuses in the House and Senate (particularly the majority-party caucuses) are in favor or opposed.

"Why Should I Care?"

What kind of democracy do American political parties create?

★
EVALUATE THE BENEFITS AND POSSIBLE PROBLEMS OF THE AMERICAN PARTY SYSTEM

Parties help political activists, party leaders, and citizens who identify with the party to pursue their policy goals by focusing collective efforts on electing people who share their priorities. For politicians, parties provide ballot access, a brand name, campaign assistance, and a group of like-minded colleagues with whom they can coordinate, compromise, and strategize. For citizens, political parties provide information and a means of holding specific individuals accountable for what government does.

The question of whether political parties are good or bad for democracy depends on how individual party members and officials carry out these tasks. Political parties can help democracy by filling the ballot with well-qualified candidates, helping them get elected, offering citizens clear choices about government policies, informing citizens about platforms and candidates, motivating citizens to vote, and helping elected officials enact the party platform. The problem is that the people who make up American political parties are not primarily interested in democracy; they are interested in their own careers, policy goals, and winning political office. These goals often lead them away from actions that would improve American democracy.

Recruiting good candidates

One of the most important things the Republican and Democratic parties can do for democracy is to recruit candidates for national political offices who can run effective campaigns and uphold their elected positions. After all, a voter's choices are limited to the people on the ballot. If good candidates decide against running or are prevented from doing so, citizens will be dissatisfied no matter who wins the election.

As we discussed, the Republican and Democratic parties work to find good candidates and to persuade them to run. However, the potential candidates have to decide for themselves whether their chances of winning justify the enormous investment of time and money needed to run a campaign. When a party is unpopular, the best potential candidates may decide to wait until the next election to run, leaving the already disadvantaged party with a less competitive set of candidates.[44] Even when recruitment is not a problem, party leaders have only limited control over the nomination process. As Donald Trump's candidacy illustrates, party leaders could not prevent Trump from running, from dominating press coverage at the expense of other, more viable candidates, and from saying things that drove some important groups away from the party and its candidates.

Of course, Trump won the election, indicating that party leaders misread the situation. Even so, insofar as party leaders are experienced politicians with deep knowledge of public opinion and political institutions, their lack of control over the nomination process can lead to unfavorable outcomes.

Working together in campaigns

Parties can also work to simplify voters' choices by trying to get candidates to emphasize the same issues or to take similar issue positions. That way, citizens know that when they vote for, say, a Democrat they are getting someone whose policy positions are likely to differ from those held by a Republican. The problem is that members of the party organization and the party in government do not always agree. Sometimes the differences within the parties reflect genuine differences of opinion. Other times candidates are trying to match the preferences of citizens in their state or district. Either way, the simple fact is that political parties in America generally speak with many voices, not one.

Why don't party leaders simply order their candidates to support the party platform or to work together in campaigns? As we have discussed, party leaders actually have very little power over candidates.[45] They can't kick a candidate off the ballot, because candidates win the nomination in a primary election or caucus, not through party appointment. Even though parties have a lot of campaign money to dispense, their contributions typically make up only a fraction of what a candidate spends on a campaign. And incumbent candidates, who generally hold an advantage over challengers when seeking reelection, are even less beholden to party leaders. Even if party leaders could somehow prevent an incumbent from running for reelection, they would have to find another candidate to take the incumbent's place, which would mean losing the incumbent's popularity and reputation and reducing the party's chances of holding the seat.

Working together in office

Because candidates are not required to support their party's platform, there is no guarantee that they will be able to work together with other members of the party in office. Sometimes, as with the Democrats and the economic stimulus plan, the members of a party can come together fairly easily. However, there are also many examples of issues that can split a party wide open, such as health care reform (for the Democrats) or immigration reform (for the Republicans). Sometimes party members can compromise on their differences, as in the case of Democrats' positions on health care reform, but sometimes compromise may be impossible, as in the case of Republicans' immigration proposals. And of course, even if the members of a party can find common ground, they may fail at building the bipartisan coalitions that are often necessary to enact major legislation, such as in the case of deficit-reduction proposals. Even when compromise is reached, the time spent negotiating means that members have less time to scrutinize the details of budgets and policy proposals. For this reason, one recent study argued that the party caucuses are "too weak to govern."[46] Or, as former Senate Majority Leader Howard Baker's quote illustrates, party leaders may do a good job in determining what their colleagues want but be unable to persuade them to support a proposal that they are inclined to oppose.

The fact that American political parties are ideologically diverse means that elected members of the party may not agree on spending, policy, or anything else. In that sense, voters can't expect that putting one party in power will result in specific policy changes. Instead, policy outcomes depend on how (and whether) individual officeholders from the party can resolve their differences. Institutions such as the party caucuses or conferences provide a forum in which elected officials can meet and seek common ground, but there is no guarantee that they will find acceptable compromises.

Moreover, concerted action by members of a party in government may be aimed at political rather than policy goals. For example, during the last several years Republicans in the House and Senate uniformly opposed many Democratic initiatives. Moreover, legislators from both parties failed to find common ground around proposals to cut the deficit, enact new controls on firearms, reform immigration law, or make changes to the ACA. For many legislators, opposition was based on policy concerns. But for others, their opposition reflected a political calculation—that this strategy was their party's best bet for gaining seats in the 2016 elections. In this way, American political parties can work against the enactment of effective responses to public problems and increase, rather than decrease, the amount of conflict in American politics.

Providing accountability

As we discussed earlier, a party serves as an accountability mechanism that gives citizens an identifiable group to reward when policies work well and to punish when policies fail. However, individual legislators also work to build a reputation with voters that is independent of their party label. They are happy to emphasize their party affiliation when it brings them support, but they choose not to mention it when the party is associated with unpopular policies or outcomes. Republican legislators, for example, highlighted their party ID in the 2002 and 2004 elections, as a relatively high percentage of voters held the party in high regard.[47] However, by 2006, with voter evaluations of the party and President Bush at all-time lows, many Republican candidates deemphasized their connection to the party.[48] Even in the 2016 election, many Democratic and Republican congressional candidates emphasized their connections to constituents and tried to stay as far away as possible from their party's unpopular nominee.

When politicians work to secure their own political future in this way, they make it harder for voters to use party labels to decide who should be rewarded and who should be punished for government performance. The result is that legislators are held accountable for their own performance in office, such as how they voted—but no one in Congress is accountable for large-scale outcomes such as the state of the economy

In 2016, Representative Stephanie Murphy (D-FL) defeated 12-term Republican incumbent John Mica on the strength of a campaign that emphasized Mica's support for Donald Trump's views on women's health and gun policy.

or for foreign policy. Of course, some voters hold legislators accountable based on whether they are members of the party in power, which is why Republicans lost House and Senate seats in 2006 and 2008 and Democrats lost seats in 2010. Even so, most Republicans and Democrats in Congress managed to survive these elections, suggesting that party-based accountability is rather weak in contemporary American politics.

Citizens' behavior

As we have seen, most Americans identify as either Republican or Democrat and many citizens use party labels to cue their voting decisions. However, citizens are under no obligation to give money or time to the party they identify with or to any of its candidates. They don't have to vote for its candidates or even vote at all. All these actions would strengthen party organizations, but citizens do not have to take them even if the citizens strongly identify with a party.

Here again, citizens are free to choose how to participate in American politics, including the option of not participating. But many of the things citizens do—such as not contributing to campaigns or party organizations, splitting their votes between candidates from different parties in the general election, or ignoring party affiliation in their retrospective evaluations—weaken party organizations and make it harder for them to operate as a team to enact policies and oversee the bureaucracy.

Conclusion

American political parties help organize elections, unify disparate social groups, simplify the choices facing voters, and build compromises around party members' shared concerns—all with the goals of winning elections and setting government policy. However, recent events demonstrate that the success of political parties depends on whether individual party members—candidates, citizens, and party leaders—are willing to take the actions necessary to achieve electoral and policy goals. In recent years, congressional Republicans have campaigned on a platform of making substantial changes in the size and scope of the federal government. However, their apparent consensus disappeared once they were in office, as legislators disagreed on which programs should be cut, constituents demanded that their favorite programs be saved, and party leaders worried that taking a hard line would lead to electoral defeat. Ultimately, the party's budget-cutting goals were not achieved. Similarly, Trump's victory masks deep disagreements within the current Republican Party in government.

Of course, these difficulties do not reflect a problem with the Republican Party per se. The Democrats' success at enacting Obamacare and other significant proposals in Obama's first term masked significant differences of opinion among the Democratic Party's elected officials, activists, and citizen supporters. And Hillary Clinton's loss in the 2016 election will no doubt push Democrats to examine weaknesses in their party's message. They will have to decide how much to compromise with—or block—President Trump as he tries to enact his policy agenda. As we have seen, parties try to find a way to bridge such differences in order for members to act together to accomplish common goals. However, the parties' ability to bring people together is not absolute. Individual party members respond to constituents, party leaders, and public opinion in many ways, sometimes taking actions in line with party goals and other times acting in ways that help themselves and that defy the party.

STUDY GUIDE

What are political parties and where did today's parties come from?

Define *political parties* and show how American political parties and party systems have evolved over time. (Pages 254–257)

Summary

Political parties are organizations that run candidates for political office and coordinate the actions of officials elected under the party banner. Here in the United States, parties are relatively decentralized, putting forth a loose configuration of candidates who share a party label but don't necessarily work together. The parties are composed of three semiautonomous units: the party organization, the party in government, and the party in the electorate. Political parties are a central feature of American politics, although they look and act very differently today than they have in the past. Political scientists use the term "party system" to refer to a period of party stability; in all, there have been six different party systems in the country's history. Party systems are broken up by realignments, which occur when some of the defining factors of the party system are changed or specified and rifts in the group develop because of these changes.

Key terms

party organization (p. 254)

party in government (p. 254)

party in the electorate (p. 254)

party system (p. 255)

party principle (p. 256)

spoils system (p. 256)

realignment (p. 257)

Practice Quiz Questions

1. **Which statement best characterizes the American political parties?**

   a. Parties in the electorate pay dues to the party organization; leaders in the party organization tell elected officials what to do.

   b. Candidates run as representatives of the party; leaders have no influence on how candidates campaign or govern.

   c. Candidates are generally autonomous of the party organization, although they do receive support from the party organization.

   d. Parties help candidates only after they are elected.

   e. Parties handle 90 percent of fund-raising for candidates.

2. **Which were the first well-known parties in the United States?**

   a. Federalists and Democratic-Republicans

   b. Democrats and Republicans

   c. Whigs and Federalists

   d. Democrats and Whigs

   e. Whigs and Republicans

3. **The idea that a party is not just a group but an organization that exists apart from its candidate is called the _____.**

   a. party system

   b. spoils system

   c. conditional party government

   d. party ID

   e. party principle

American political parties today

Describe the main characteristics of American parties as organizations, in the government, and in the electorate. (Pages 258–268)

Summary

The modern party is composed of three parts. The party organization is a loosely defined group of individuals and organizations that are focused on supporting political candidates when they share the same policy goals. The party in government consists of elected officials who are the members of a particular party. The party in the electorate consists of citizens who identify with a particular political party.

Key terms

national committee (p. 258)

political action committee (PAC) (p. 258)

527 organization (p. 258)

caucus (congressional) (p. 261)

conference (p. 261)

party identification (party ID) (p. 262)

party coalitions (p. 266)

issue ownership (p. 268)

Practice Quiz Questions

4. **The Democratic and Republican party organizations _____ hierarchical; they are _____ to force state and local parties to share their positions on issues.**

   a. are not; able

   b. are not; unable

   c. are; able

   d. are; unable

   e. are; sometimes able

5. **A group of elected officials of the same party who come together to organize and strategize is called a _____.**
   a. cabal
   b. conditional party government
   c. primary
   d. PAC
   e. caucus

6. **The modern Congress is _____; the distance between the parties has _____ over the past 60 years.**
   a. polarized; increased
   b. polarized; stayed the same
   c. not polarized; decreased
   d. not polarized; stayed the same
   e. not polarized; increased

7. **What has recent analysis of political Independents concluded?**
   a. They are in the process of changing parties.
   b. More and more people regard parties as irrelevant.
   c. Americans are politically savvy and do not blindly follow party lines.
   d. The number of Independents has grown substantially in the past 20 years.
   e. Independents are not better informed on candidates, parties, or policy.

The role of political parties in American politics

Explain the important functions parties perform in the political system. (Pages 268–279)

Summary

Political parties serve two major roles in the political system. First, they contest elections by recruiting and nominating candidates and supporting candidate campaigns. Second, they facilitate cooperation in government by providing a framework for agenda-setting, coordination, and accountability among members of the same party. There are many different minor political parties, and while they rarely make a significant impact on the political stage, they do occasionally influence election outcomes. The two big issues facing minor parties are that their platforms do not appeal to a large portion of Americans and that the electoral system makes it hard for minor parties to win elections.

Key terms

primary election (p. 269)
caucus (electoral) (p. 269)
nominating convention (p. 271)
party platform (p. 271)
unified government (p. 277)

divided government (p. 277)
Duverger's Law (p. 279)
single-member district (p. 279)
plurality voting (p. 279)

Practice Quiz Questions

8. **Which is *not* one of the ways political party organizations support candidates?**
   a. by controlling who runs in House and Senate races
   b. by contributing money to campaign activities
   c. by offering advice on how to deal with the press
   d. by organizing get-out-the-vote activities
   e. by offering advice on which issues to emphasize

9. **Why do most candidates support their party platforms?**
   a. because candidates are required to support the platforms
   b. because all candidates vote on the platforms that are written
   c. because candidates get kicked out of the party for not doing so
   d. because both major parties' platforms are essentially the same
   e. because most candidates and their constituents generally agree with the platform

10. **Which of the following options best defines the theory of conditional party government?**
    "As policy differences between the parties in government _____, the parties in government will be _____ important in helping legislators develop policy plans and strategies."
    a. increase; less
    b. increase; more
    c. decrease; less
    d. decrease; more
    e. decrease; equally

11. **When the president, House, and Senate are controlled by the same party, this is called:**
    a. party in government
    b. responsible party government
    c. unified government
    d. divided government
    e. conditional party government

12. **The principle that single-member districts and plurality voting will support only two political parties is _____.**
    a. Condorcet's theorem
    b. Pascal's paradox
    c. Duverger's Law
    d. Fermat's theorem
    e. conditional party government

What kind of democracy do American political parties create?

Evaluate the benefits and possible problems of the American party system. (Pages 279–282)

Summary

Political parties do a number of things that are important to facilitate good democracy: they generally recruit good candidates, simplify voters' choices, encourage candidates to work together in office, and provide a mechanism for holding politicians accountable. Nonetheless, there are limits to the extent to which parties are able to achieve these goals, partially due to the fact that the people who make up the parties are primarily interested in their own careers.

Practice Quiz Question

13. **Which feature of political parties is undermined by legislators who build a reputation with voters independent of the party label?**

    a. the recruitment of good candidates

    b. the provision of ballot access

    c. the simplification of voter choices

    d. the encouragement of policy cooperation

    e. the provision of electoral accountability

14. **All of the following are reasons why members of a party in government might find it difficult to work together to enact new government programs except:**

    a. Constituents from different districts might demand different policies.

    b. Members might disagree about the desirability of different policy changes.

    c. The party's National Committee might fail to write an acceptable party platform.

    d. Enacting legislation might require votes from members of the other party.

    e. Members might be focused on getting reelected.

Suggested Reading

Aldrich, John. *Why Parties?*, 2nd ed. Chicago: University of Chicago Press, 2014.

Bartels, Larry M. *Unequal Democracy: The Political Economy of the New Gilded Age*. New York: Russell Sage Foundation, 2008.

Carmines, Edward G., and James A. Stimson. *Issue Evolution: Race and the Transformation of American Politics*. Princeton, NJ: Princeton University Press, 1989.

Cohen, Marty, David Karol, Hans Noel, and John Zaller. *The Party Decides: Presidential Nominations before and after Reform*. Chicago: University of Chicago Press, 2008.

Cox, Gary, and Mathew McCubbins. *Setting the Agenda: Party Government in the U.S. House of Representatives*. New York: Cambridge University Press, 2005.

Fiorina, Morris. *Retrospective Voting in American National Elections*. New Haven, CT: Yale University Press, 1981.

Green, Donald, Bradley Palmquist, and Eric Schickler. *Partisan Hearts and Minds*. New Haven, CT: Yale University Press, 2004.

Noel, Hans. *Political Ideologies and Political Parties in America*. New York: Cambridge University Press, 2014.

Polsby, Nelson. *Consequences of Party Reform*. New York: Oxford University Press, 1983.

Rohde, David. *Parties and Leaders in the Post-reform House*. Chicago: University of Chicago Press, 1991.

Schattschneider, E. E. *Party Government*. New York: McGraw-Hill, 1942.

9

Elections

Who wins? Who loses?
And why?

Every two years, Americans elect 435 House members and 33 or so senators; every four years, we elect a president. Out of these many separate contests, a few races attract disproportionate interest because they provide insights into what voters are thinking, because they reveal the usefulness of different campaign strategies, or simply because of what's at stake. In 2016, the election to watch was the battle for the presidency, Republican Donald Trump versus Democrat Hillary Clinton. It is hard to imagine a starker choice: Trump, the political newcomer who had never held elected office or served in government, against Clinton, the Washington insider and the first female general-election presidential candidate; Trump's promise to "make America great again" with a combination of tax cuts, renegotiating trade deals, more military spending, and threats of mass deportation against Clinton's platform of increasing funding for a wide range of initiatives, from curing Alzheimer's to helping displaced workers, and putting government squarely on the side of LGBTQ equality, disability rights, racial justice, and preventing gun violence. Regardless of what you think of these candidates and their promises, it is clear that this election mattered. Over the next four years (and beyond), America will be a different place with Donald Trump in the White House than if Hillary Clinton had won.

The 2016 presidential elections are also a good example of the central themes of this text. Candidates compete for political office, offering the people distinct, competing visions of what the federal government should do—from what the tax code should look like, to how the government should spend the tax money it collects, to what regulations the government should impose on individuals and corporations. These considerations mattered even in 2016, when Donald Trump's qualifications, temperament, and behavior toward women became central issues in the campaign.

American elections are also about rules. The fact that Donald Trump won the Republican nomination reflects his popularity with Republican primary voters but also the way the party chooses its candidate. Moreover, Trump won the general election by winning a majority of votes in the electoral college

★
CHAPTER
GOALS

Present the major rules and procedures of American elections.
pages 288–299

Describe the features, strategies, and funding of campaigns for federal office.
pages 299–314

Explain the key factors that influence voters' choices.
pages 315–319

Analyze the issues and outcomes in the 2016 election.
pages 320–326

📷
The 2016 presidential election between Secretary of State Hillary Clinton and billionaire businessman Donald Trump reflected the country's deep divisions over policy, race, gender, class, and even geography. And this election showed how electoral rules and processes—even when things seem unique and unpredictable— can greatly affect the outcome.

(awarded by winning the most votes in different states), despite losing the popular vote to Clinton. More generally, candidates in American elections are elected for different periods of time to represent districts, states, or the entire nation—places that vary tremendously in terms of what constituents want from government. A variety of rules determine who runs, who votes, and how candidates campaign. Even ballot layouts and how votes are cast and counted vary across states. Elections also differ in the amount of media coverage they receive, the level of involvement of political parties and other organizations, and how much attention citizens pay to the contests. All these aspects of the election process—who runs, how candidates campaign, and how voters respond—shape who wins and who loses, what happens in Washington, and ultimately the policies that affect people's everyday lives. Why do some candidates win and others lose—and why do these outcomes matter in American politics?

★

PRESENT THE MAJOR RULES AND PROCEDURES OF AMERICAN ELECTIONS

incumbent
A politician running for reelection to the office he or she currently holds.

How do American elections work?

The American political system is a representative democracy: Americans do not make policy choices themselves, but they vote for individuals who make these choices on their behalf. This section describes the rules and procedures that define American national elections.

Functions of elections

Our working assumption for explaining the rules and processes of elections as well as the behavior of candidates and voters is that they are tied directly to what elections do: selecting representatives, giving citizens the ability to influence the direction of government policy, and providing citizens with the opportunity to reward and punish officeholders seeking reelection. We will discuss each of these functions in turn.

Selecting Representatives The most visible function of American national elections is the selection of officeholders: members of the House and Senate and the president and vice president. Candidates can be **incumbents** or challengers. America has a representative democracy, which means that by voting in elections Americans have an indirect effect on government policy. Although citizens do not make policy choices themselves, they determine which individuals get to make these choices. In this way, elections are supposed to connect citizen preferences and government actions.

Shaping Policy The fundamental choice in an election is between two or more candidates running for some political office—a seat in the House or the Senate or the presidency. But elections also involve a choice between candidates' policy platforms, the set of things they promise to do if elected. By investigating candidates' platforms, citizens learn about the range of options for government policy. Moreover, their voting decisions determine who gets to make choices about future government policy, and thereby shape government policy itself. This description is particularly true for the 2016 Senate elections, where Trump's victory and Republican victories in House and Senate elections gave Republicans unified control of the federal government.

Promoting Accountability The election process also creates a way to hold incumbents accountable. When citizens choose between voting for an incumbent or a challenger, they can make a retrospective evaluation. They consider the incumbent's performance, asking, "Has he [or she] done a good job on the issues I care about?"[1] Citizens who answer yes typically vote for the incumbent, and those who answer no typically vote for the challenger.

Retrospective evaluations are significant because they make incumbents responsive to their constituents' demands.[2] If elected officials anticipate that some constituents will make retrospective evaluations, they will try to take actions that these constituents will like. If incumbents ignore the possibility of voters' retrospective evaluations, they may be removed from office in the next election. Retrospective evaluations can also form the basis for prospective judgments—voters' beliefs about how the country will fare if different candidates win. This provides an additional reason for incumbents to be responsive to citizens' demands.

Two stages of elections

House and Senate candidates running for office face a two-step procedure. First, if the prospective candidates want to run on behalf of a political party they must win the party's nomination in a primary election. If the would-be candidates want to run as Independents, they need to gather signatures on a petition to secure a spot on the ballot. Different states hold either **open primaries**, **semi-closed primaries**, or **closed primaries**, and state law sets the timing of these elections. A few states hold single primaries, where there is one election involving candidates from both parties, with the top two finalists (regardless of party) receiving nominations to the general election.

The second step in the election process is the **general election**, which is held throughout the nation on the first Tuesday after the first Monday in November. Federal law designates this day as Election Day. General elections determine who wins elected positions in government. The offices at stake vary depending on the year. Presidential elections occur every four years (2008, 2012, 2016, ...). In a presidential election year, Americans elect the entire House of Representatives, one-third of the Senate, and a

Though incumbents fared very well in 2016's congressional elections, some still lost, like Nevada Republican Crescent Hardy.

open primary
A primary election in which any registered voter can participate in the contest, regardless of party affiliation.

semi-closed primary
A primary where anyone who is a registered member of the party or registered as an Independent can vote.

closed primary
A primary election in which only registered members of a particular political party can vote.

general election
The election in which voters cast ballots for House members, senators, and (every four years) a president and vice president.

Americans vote in all sorts of places, including libraries, fire stations, schools, private homes, and sometimes churches, as shown in this photo of a polling station in the 2016 South Carolina primary.

president and vice president. During midterm elections (2006, 2010, 2014, ...), there is no presidential contest, but the entire House and a third of the Senate are up for election.

The Constitution limits voting rights to American citizens who are at least 18 years old. There are also numerous restrictions on voter eligibility that vary across states, including residency requirements (usually 30 days) and whether people convicted of a major crime can vote. A recent development in American elections is an increase in the practice of no-excuse absentee voting as well as early voting, or casting a general-election vote prior to Election Day.[3] Voters in Oregon vote entirely by mail, and almost all votes in Washington State were cast by mail. Across the nation in 2016, more than a third of votes were cast before Election Day and many campaigns distributed absentee ballots to would-be supporters. These changes have had only a modest impact on voter turnout, perhaps because efforts by candidates and parties to encourage early voting have reduced resources allocated to mobilization efforts on Election Day.[4]

Constituencies: who chooses representatives?

Another critical feature of American elections is that officeholders are elected in single-member districts in which only the winner of the most votes takes office. (Although both of each state's senators represent the whole state, they are elected separately, usually in different years.) Senate candidates compete throughout the state; House candidates compete in congressional districts. In most states, congressional district lines are drawn by state legislatures. In a few states, nonpartisan commissions or committees of judges perform this function. Redistricting can happen at any time, but in general, district lines are revised after each census to make sure the boundary lines reflect shifts in population across and within states. (For details on redistricting, see Chapter 11.)

Because members of the House and Senate are elected from specific geographic areas, they often represent very different kinds of people. Their constituents differ in terms of age, race, income level, occupation, and political leaning, including party affiliation and ideology. Therefore, legislators from different areas of the country face highly diverse demands from their constituents, which often leads them to pursue very dissimilar kinds of policies.

For example, Democratic senator Charles Schumer, one of the senators from New York, represents a fairly liberal state where most people take some sort of pro-choice position on abortion rights, while Republican senator Richard Shelby is one of the senators from the conservative state of Alabama, where most voters have long been opposed to abortions. Suppose the Senate votes on a proposal to ban all abortions after the twelfth week of pregnancy. Shelby knows that most of his constituents would probably want him to vote for the proposal, and Schumer knows that most of his constituents would probably want him to vote against it. This example illustrates that congressional conflicts over policy often reflect differences in constituents' demands. Schumer and Shelby themselves may hold different views on abortion rights, but even if they agreed, their constituents' distinct demands would make it likely that as legislators they would vote differently.

Determining Who Wins Most House and Senate contests involve plurality voting: the candidate who gets the most votes wins. However, some states use majority voting, meaning that a candidate needs a majority (more than 50 percent of the vote) to win. If no candidate has a majority, a runoff election takes place between the top two finishers. Some candidates have lost runoff elections even though they received the most votes in the first contest.

The two-step process of primary and general elections can have a similar effect on the election's outcome. Sometimes the winner of a primary is not a party's best

plurality voting
A voting system in which the candidate who receives the most votes within a geographic area wins the election, regardless of whether that candidate wins a majority (more than half) of the votes.

majority voting
A voting system in which a candidate must win more than 50 percent of votes to win the election. If no candidate wins enough votes to take office, a runoff election is held between the top two vote-getters.

runoff election
Under a majority voting system, a second election held only if no candidate wins a majority of the votes in the first general election. Only the top two vote-getters in the first election compete in the runoff.

candidate for the general election. For example, in the 2016 presidential race, one of the principal arguments for choosing someone other than Hillary Clinton as the Democratic nominee (such as Senator Bernie Sanders, Vice President Joe Biden, or some other Democratic senator or governor) was that these candidates would have a better chance of winning the general election. While Clinton had many enthusiastic volunteers, a first-rate campaign organization, and considerable Washington experience as First Lady, senator, and secretary of state, she was also strongly disliked by a sizable fraction of the American electorate—partly because of her status as a Washington insider, and partly because of issues such as her use of a private e-mail server while secretary of state. In the end, despite beating Sanders in the primaries and discouraging other Democrats from entering the nomination contest, Clinton lost the general election to Donald Trump. Given the closeness of the 2016 election, another Democrat, someone who did not have Clinton's disadvantages, might well have gone on to defeat Trump.

The Ballot Americans vote using a variety of machines and ballot structures based on where they live. Over the last decade, electronic touch screen voting machines have replaced paper ballots and mechanical voting machines, usually with some sort of paper receipt to allow manual recounts. The nationwide change in voting technologies was driven by two concerns revealed in the 2000 Florida presidential election. One problem was that the race between Republican George Bush and Democrat Al Gore in Florida was extraordinarily close, so the winner would be determined by decisions made after Election Day by local election officials about which so-called spoiled ballots (paper ballots where a voter's choice was ambiguous) should be counted and which should not. (Moreover, the national presidential contest was close enough that Florida's winner would win the entire election.) The other problem the election revealed was that in at least one community, Palm Beach County, the ballot structure may have caused citizens to vote for Reform Party candidate Pat Buchanan when they thought they were voting for Democrat Al Gore. Analyses suggested that the butterfly ballot cost Gore several thousand Palm Beach County votes—enough to change the results of the election in Florida and thus the outcome of the 2000 presidential election.[5] We don't know whether ballots used in other counties and states favored Gore or some other candidates. But it is clear that choices about how ballots are structured can affect who wins elections. These events led to the passage of the Help America Vote Act of 2002, which provided funds to local communities to purchase new electronic voting machines. At the same time, political scientists have researched which ballot structures minimize the chances that individuals will vote for the wrong candidate, as well as how to ensure that electronic voting is free of fraud and mistakes.[6]

Ballot counting adds more complexities. Most states have laws that allow vote recounts if a race is sufficiently close (typically within 1 percent or less). Even when a

After Hillary Clinton lost her campaign for president, many Democrats wondered if Senator Bernie Sanders (I-VT) would have been a stronger general-election candidate.

Many different mechanisms are used to record votes in American elections, including paper keypunch ballots and computerized, electronic machines (left). The design of the infamous butterfly ballot (right), which was used in the 2000 presidential election to vote in Palm Beach County, Florida, inadvertently led some people who intended to vote for Democrat Al Gore to select Reform Party candidate Patrick Buchanan.

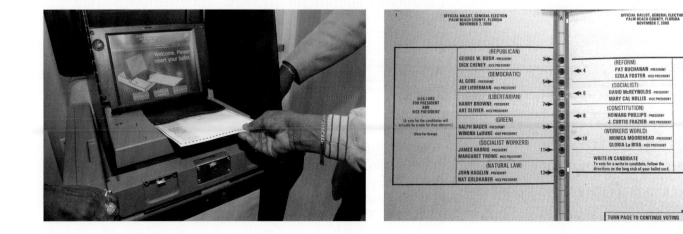

recount occurs, it may be impossible to definitively determine who won a particular election, as the rules that determine which ballots are valid are often open to interpretation. More significant is that when an election is close the question of which candidate wins may depend on how ballots are structured and votes are counted. The problem is not that election officials are dishonest; rather, close elections inherently tend to produce ambiguous outcomes.

Claims are often made that officials manipulate election rules to guarantee wins for their favored candidates. In some states, Republican state and local officials have enacted laws that require voters to verify their identity by showing polling officials an official form of identification such as a driver's license or a passport. The purported goal of these laws is to prevent voter fraud—one person voting under another's name, or casting multiple votes for the same candidate. However, there is almost no evidence of voter fraud in American elections. Moreover, voter ID laws create barriers to voting for individuals who lack an official ID—these individuals are generally poor and nonwhite, and disproportionately vote Democratic. While some supporters of voter ID laws may be sincerely concerned about preventing fraud, research shows that enacting these laws hurts Democratic candidates by lowering turnout from groups that are likely to support them.[7]

Presidential elections

Many of the rules governing elections, such as who is eligible to vote, are the same for both presidential and congressional elections. But presidential contests have several unique rules regarding how nominees are determined and how votes are counted. Moreover, the constitutional requirements for presidential candidates are also somewhat stricter than those for congressional candidates (see Nuts & Bolts 9.1).

The Nomination: Primaries and Caucuses Presidential nominees from the Democratic and Republican parties are determined by state-level primaries and caucuses over a five-month period beginning in January of an election year.[8] Voters in these elections select delegates to attend the nominating conventions that take place during the summer. There the delegates cast the votes that determine their party's presidential and vice-presidential nominees. The format of these elections, including their timing and the number of delegates selected per state, is determined on a state-by-state basis by the state and national party organizations.[9] In some states, each candidate preselects a list of delegates who will attend the convention if the candidate wins sufficient votes in the primary or caucus. In other states, delegates are chosen by party leaders after the actual primary or caucus takes place. In both cases, a candidate's principal goal is to win as many delegates as possible—and to select delegates who

primary
A ballot vote in which citizens select a party's nominee for the general election.

caucus
A local meeting in which party members select a party's nominee for the general election.

Constitutional Requirements for Candidates

Office	Minimum Age	Residency Requirement
President	35	Natural-born citizen (born in the United States or on U.S. territory, or child of citizen parent)
Senator	30	Resident of state; U.S. citizen for at least nine years
Representative	25	Resident of state; U.S. citizen for at least seven years

will be reliable supporters at the convention. Some states require delegates to vote for the candidate they are pledged to—at least for the first ballot at the party nominating convention. However, these laws have never been tested and it is not clear that they are enforceable.

The details of translating primary and caucus votes into convention delegates vary from state to state, but some general rules apply. All Democratic primaries and caucuses use **proportional allocation** to divide each state's delegate seats among the candidates; thus, if a candidate receives 40 percent of the votes in a state's primary the candidate gets roughly 40 percent of the convention delegates from that state. Some Republican contests use proportional allocation, but others use **winner-take-all**. In these, the candidate who receives the most votes gets all of the state's convention delegates. These rules can have a significant effect on candidates' campaign strategies and the outcome of the nomination process (see How It Works: Nominating Presidential Candidates in Chapter 8).

The order in which the primaries and caucuses in different states take place is important because many candidacies do not survive beyond the early contests.[10] Most presidential candidates pour everything they have into the first few elections. Candidates who do well attract financial contributions, campaign workers, endorsements, and additional media coverage, all of which enables them to move on to subsequent primaries or caucuses. Candidates who do poorly in the first contests face the problem identified by former congressman and presidential candidate Richard Gephardt: contributions and coverage dry up, leaving these candidates with no alternative but to drop out of the race. For example, a total of 17 candidates entered the race for the 2016 Republican presidential nomination. Five withdrew before any convention delegates were selected. By mid-March, two months into the process and six months before the convention where the nominee was actually selected, the race was down to only three candidates. Thus, the candidate who leads after the first several primaries and caucuses generally wins the nomination—as was the case for both Donald Trump and Hillary Clinton in 2016.[11] However, when the first few contests do not yield a clear favorite the race can continue until the last states have voted or even until the convention.

If a sitting president runs for reelection, as Barack Obama did in 2012, he typically faces little opposition for his party's general-election nomination—not because challengers defer to the president but because most presidents are popular enough among their own party's faithful supporters that they can win the nomination without too much trouble. Only presidents with particularly low approval ratings have faced serious opposition in their nomination bids.

Among the states, the presidential nomination process is always changing.[12] In 2016 many southern states held their primaries on the same day in early March (Super Tuesday). Others moved the date of their primary (Florida), moved from a primary to a caucus (Kentucky), or, on the Republican side, added a minimum number of votes a candidate needed to win any delegates. For many years, Iowa and New Hampshire held the first presidential nomination contests, with the Iowa Caucuses held a week before the New Hampshire primary. These states' position at the beginning of the process is largely a historical accident, but it is controversial. State party officials from other states often complain about the media attention given to these contests and their disproportionate influence in winnowing the candidate pool, but there is no consensus around an alternate schedule. As a result, the 2016 nomination process was roughly the same as in previous years, with Iowa and New Hampshire holding the initial contests in early February 2016, followed by a primary in South Carolina and a caucus in Nevada later in the month and the remaining contests beginning in March and continuing to June. One recent trend is regional primaries, where all of the states in a given area (such as southern states) hold their primaries or caucuses on the same date.

proportional allocation
During the presidential primaries, the practice of determining the number of convention delegates allotted to each candidate based on the percentage of the popular vote cast for each candidate. All Democratic primaries and caucuses use this system, as do some states' Republican primaries and caucuses.

winner-take-all
During the presidential primaries, the practice of assigning all of a given state's delegates to the candidate who receives the most popular votes. Some states' Republican primaries and caucuses use this system.

> **"**
>
> **Campaigns don't end—they run out of money.**
>
> —**Richard Gephardt,** former Speaker of the House and presidential candidate

Presidential campaign appearances almost always involve extensive print and electronic media coverage, reporting on virtually everything the candidates say or do.

❝

You win some, you lose some. And then there's that little-known third category.

—**Al Gore,** who lost the 2000 presidential vote in the electoral college despite winning the most votes on Election Day

electoral college
The body that votes to select America's president and vice president based on the popular vote in each state. Each candidate nominates a slate of electors who are selected to attend the meeting of the college if their candidate wins the most votes in a state or district.

One rule that distinguishes the parties' candidate selection process is that about one-fifth of the delegates to the Democratic convention are not supporters of a particular candidate nor have they been chosen to attend the convention based on primary and caucus results. Rather, they are elected officials and party officials whom their colleagues select to serve as superdelegates. Most are automatically seated at the convention regardless of primary and caucus results, and they are free to support any candidate for the nomination. By forcing candidates to court support from superdelegates, the party aims to ensure that the nominee is someone these officials believe can win the general election and whom they can work with if he or she is elected.[13] (Republicans give state party leaders automatic delegate slots at their convention, but the number of such delegates is a much smaller percentage than for Democrats.)

The National Convention Presidential nominating conventions happen late in the summer of an election year. Their main task is to select the party's presidential nominee, although usually the vote at the convention is a formality; in most recent contests, one candidate has emerged from the nomination process going into the convention with a clear majority of delegates and was able to win the nomination on the first ballot. To get the nomination, a candidate needs the support of a majority of the delegates. If no candidate receives a majority after the first round of voting at the convention, the voting continues until someone does.

After the convention delegates nominate a presidential candidate, they nominate a vice-presidential candidate. The presidential nominee gets to choose his or her running mate (generally before the convention), and the delegates almost always ratify this choice without much debate. Delegates also vote on the party platform, which describes what the party stands for and what kinds of policies its candidates will supposedly seek to enact if they are elected.

The final purpose of a convention is to attract public attention to the party and its nominees. Public figures give speeches during the evening sessions when all major television networks have live coverage. At some recent conventions, both parties have drawn press attention by recruiting speakers who support their political goals despite being associated with the opposing party.

Once presidential candidates are nominated, the general-election campaign officially begins—although it often unofficially starts much earlier, as soon as the presumptive nominees are known. We say more about presidential campaigns in a later section.

Counting Presidential Votes Even though in the voting booth you choose between the candidates by name, you actually don't vote directly for a presidential candidate. Rather, when you select your preferred candidate's name you are choosing that person's slate of pledged supporters from your state to serve as electors, who will then vote to elect the president.

The number of electors for each state equals the state's number of House members (which varies by state population) plus the state's number of senators (two per state). Altogether, the electors chosen by the citizens of each state constitute the **electoral college**, the body that formally selects the president. Small-population states, therefore, have few electoral votes—Delaware and Montana each have only 3—while the highest-population state, California, has 55 (see How It Works: The Electoral College). In most states, electoral votes are allocated on a winner-take-all basis: the candidate who receives the most votes from a given state's citizens gets all of that state's electoral votes. But two states, Maine and Nebraska, allocate most of

Electoral Votes and Swing States

Presidential campaigns focus their attention on states with high electoral votes and swing states, those where each candidate has a good chance of winning. In this box, we group states into categories based on their number of electoral votes and on whether one party always won the state in recent presidential elections.

	One Party Dominates in Recent Elections?	
Number of Electoral Votes	Yes (Not a Swing State)	No (Swing State)
3–5	D.C., Delaware, Alaska, Montana, North Dakota, South Dakota, Vermont, Wyoming, Hawaii, Maine, Rhode Island, Idaho, Nebraska, West Virginia	New Hampshire, New Mexico
6–10	Arkansas, Kansas, Utah, Connecticut, Oregon, Oklahoma, Kentucky, Louisiana, Alabama, South Carolina, Maryland, Mississippi, Missouri, Minnesota	Iowa, Nevada, Colorado, Wisconsin
More than 10	Massachusetts, Arizona, Tennessee, Washington, New Jersey, Georgia, Illinois, New York, Texas, California	Indiana, Virginia, North Carolina, Ohio, Florida, Michigan, Pennsylvania

their electoral votes at the congressional district level: in those states, the candidate who wins the most votes in each congressional district wins that district's single electoral vote. Then the remaining 2 electoral votes go to the candidate who gets the most votes statewide.[14]

The winner-take-all method of allocating most states' electoral votes makes candidates focus their attention on two kinds of states: high-population states with lots of electoral votes and so-called swing states where the contest is relatively close. It's better for a candidate to spend a day campaigning in California (55 electoral votes) than in Montana (3 electoral votes). However, if one candidate is sure to win a particular state both candidates will direct their efforts elsewhere. For example, during the final week of the campaign, Trump's campaign followed the strategy described in the How It Works feature, focusing on Florida, North Carolina, and key Rust Belt states including Pennsylvania, Michigan, and Wisconsin, with the Clinton campaign responding with increased advertising and rallies in Pennsylvania, North Carolina, and Florida.

Nuts & Bolts 9.2 divides states based on their electoral vote and whether they are swing states—defined as states that each party won at least once from 2004 to 2016. The table explains why both campaigns in 2016 spent so much time and campaign funds on states such as Ohio and Florida (swing states with a large number of electoral votes)—and why they largely ignored states such as Delaware (small state, one-party-dominates category).

After citizens' votes are counted in each state, the slates of electors meet in December in the state capitals. At their meetings, the electors almost always vote for the presidential candidate they have pledged to support. After the votes are certified by a joint session of Congress, the candidate who wins a majority of the nation's electoral votes (at least 270) is the new president. One peculiarity of the electoral college is that in most states it is legal for an elector to either (1) vote for a candidate he or she is not pledged to support or (2) abstain from voting.[15] Such events are uncommon for the simple reason that electors are selected by the presidential candidates with an eye toward reliable support.

In the 2000 presidential election, the popular vote was so close in Florida that individual ballots were examined to make sure every last vote was counted accurately before Florida's electoral votes were all given to the winner. In the end, all of Florida's electoral votes went to George W. Bush, giving him the additional electoral votes he needed to win the presidency.

The Electoral College

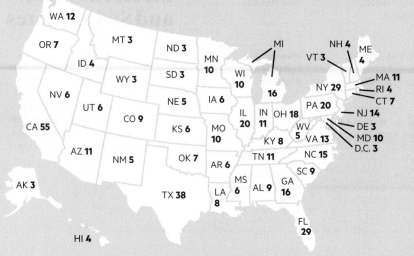

WA 12
OR 7
MT 3
ND 3
MN 10
MI
VT 3
NH 4
ME 4
ID 4
WI 10
NY 29
MA 11
RI 4
CT 7
WY 3
SD 3
16
PA 20
NV 6
NE 5
IA 6
IL 20
IN 11
OH 18
NJ 14
DE 3
MD 10
D.C. 3
UT 6
CO 9
KS 6
MO 10
WV 5
VA 13
CA 55
KY 8
NC 15
AZ 11
NM 5
OK 7
AR 6
TN 11
SC 9
AK 3
MS 6
AL 9
GA 16
TX 38
LA 8
HI 4
FL 29

Electoral Votes per State

The number of electors from each state equals the state's number of House members (which varies based on state population) plus the number of senators (two per state). Each elector has one vote in the electoral college.

Who Are the Electors?

Candidates to be electors are nominated by their political parties. They pledge to support a certain candidate if they are elected to the electoral college. When you cast your vote for a presidential candidate, you are in fact voting for the slate of potential electors who support that candidate.

Delaware ☐ ☑   Idaho ☑ ☐   Nebraska ☑ ☐   South Dakota ☐ ☑

Washington ☐ ☑   West Virginia ☑ ☐

California Popular Vote

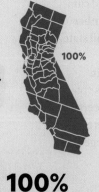

40%

60%

California Electoral Votes (55)

100%

100%
of electoral votes
go to winner

Winning a State

Most states give all of their electoral college votes to the candidate who wins the most votes in that state. So, even if a candidate only gets 51 percent of the vote in the state, his or her entire slate of electors is elected, and he or she gets all of the state's votes in the electoral college.

How it works: in practice

Donald Trump's Electoral College Strategy, 2016

Trump's campaign started by identifying "solid Republican" states—ones with a history of strong Republican support—which gave them a start of 164 electoral votes. Then, they focused on what campaign manager Kellyanne Conway called their "core four" states—ones they knew they needed in order to have a chance at victory: Florida, North Carolina, Ohio, and Iowa. This would bring them to 232 electoral votes. Where would they go to get the additional 38 electoral votes needed for victory?

■ Solid Republican States (164)
□ Core Four States (68)

164 + 68
232

Target the Rust Belt: *Michigan, Minnesota, Pennsylvania, and Wisconsin* These states have relatively weak economies and few minority voters.

MN **10**
WI **10**
MI **16**
PA **20**

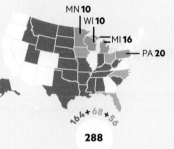

164 + 68 + 56
288

Hold off Growing Minority Populations: *Arizona, Georgia, Nevada, Colorado* Though Democrats hoped to win all these states because of their high minority populations, only Nevada and Colorado have been swing states in recent elections, and many people felt that Georgia and Arizona had been trending toward Democrats.

NV **6**
AZ **11**
CO **9**
GA **16**

164 + 68 + 42
274

Total Votes
306

2016 Results

Trump used **a combination of these strategies** to win 306 electoral votes, and the presidency.[†]

Trump's Final Winning Electoral College Map

AL **9**	IN **11**	MS **6**	OK **7**	WV **5**
AK **3**	IA **6**	MO **10**	PA **20**	WI **10**
AZ **11**	KS **6**	MT **3**	SC **9**	WY **3**
AR **6**	KY **8**	NE **5**	SD **3**	
FL **29**	LA **8**	NC **15**	TN **11**	
GA **16**	ME **1***	ND **3**	TX **38**	
ID **4**	MI **16**	OH **18**	UT **6**	

Critical Thinking

1. **Why didn't the Trump campaign** focus on some delegate-rich states like California and New York?

2. **In what state do you think the Trump campaign** spent the most money? Where do you think Trump made the most personal appearances? Why?

* Maine splits its electoral votes; Trump received 1, Clinton 3.

† Ultimately, Trump won the electoral college with 304 votes to Hillary Clinton's 227. Seven electors voted for someone other than their party's candidate.

If no candidate receives a majority of the electoral college votes, the members of the House of Representatives choose the winner. They follow a procedure in which the members from each state decide which candidate to support and then cast one collective vote per state, with the winner needing a majority of these state-level votes to win. This procedure has not been used since 1824, although it might be required if a third-party candidate wins a significant number of electoral votes or if a state's electors refuse to cast their votes.[16]

A presidential candidate can win the electoral college vote, and thus the election, without receiving a majority of the votes cast by citizens—one way this can happen is if a third-party candidate for president receives a substantial number of votes. Bill Clinton, for example, won a substantial electoral college majority in 1992 while receiving only 43 percent of the **popular vote**. This was because Ross Perot, running as a third-party candidate, received almost 19 percent of the national popular vote but not enough support in any one state to win **electoral votes**. Even in a race where no third-party candidate wins a significant percentage of the vote, the electoral college magnifies the winning candidate's vote percentage. Yet because of the way popular votes translate into electoral votes, even when there are only two candidates, a candidate can receive a majority of the electoral votes even though another candidate wins more popular votes (see Figure 9.1). As this figure shows, this outcome occurred in 2016 and

popular vote
The votes cast by citizens in an election.

electoral votes
Votes cast by members of the electoral college; after a presidential candidate wins the popular vote in a given state, that candidate's slate of electors casts electoral votes for the candidate on behalf of that state.

FIGURE 9.1

Popular Vote versus Electoral Vote Percentages, 2000–2016

Political scientists argue that the electoral college system tends to magnify the winning candidate's margin of victory. Do the data presented here support this view?

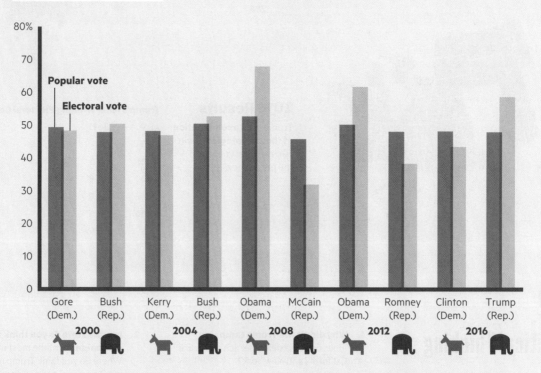

Sources: U.S. National Archives and Records Administration, www.archives.gov/federal-register/electoral-college/historical.html (accessed 11/12/12); 2016 data from CNN Presidential Results, www.cnn.com/election/results/president (accessed 11/16/16).

2000. Other presidents who won the electoral college vote but lost the popular vote were John Quincy Adams in 1824, Rutherford B. Hayes in 1876, and Benjamin Harrison in 1888.

American elections incorporate a complex set of laws, rules, and procedures. And these rules matter—the candidates who win under current rules might lose given other reasonable ways to conduct elections. Put another way, one key to winning elections (just like any other game of strategy) is to know the rules.

Electoral campaigns

This section explores the campaign process and what candidates do to convince people to vote for them on Election Day. Our emphasis is on things that candidates do regardless of the office they are running for, across the entire election cycle, the two-year period between general elections.

★

DESCRIBE THE FEATURES, STRATEGIES, AND FUNDING OF CAMPAIGNS FOR FEDERAL OFFICE

election cycle
The two-year period between general elections.

The "fundamentals"

Before talking about all the things candidates and their supporters do to shape election outcomes, it is crucial to understand that many important factors are beyond their control. Political scientists call these factors the *fundamentals*. In part, the fundamentals include the rules that govern elections, such as photo ID requirements for voting, which in turn shape voter turnout in ways that hurt some candidates (usually Democrats) and help others. Another fundamental is how many people in a candidate's district share his or her party ID. As we showed in Chapter 8, an individual's party ID is a strong influence on his or her voting decisions. Particularly in presidential elections, economic conditions also have a strong effect on who wins. As you see in the What Do the Numbers Say? feature, a stronger economy benefits incumbent presidents running for reelection (for example, Obama in 2012), while a weak economy hurts incumbents (Jimmy Carter in 1980) and their successors (Hillary Clinton in 2016).

The impact of party ID and economic conditions, along with many of the electoral rules we discussed earlier, illustrates another important fact about elections in America: many of the factors that shape election outcomes are out of the candidates' control. Candidates might like to think that they can convince people to vote for them regardless of circumstances. But the fundamentals tell us which candidates face an uphill fight or an easy ride—either because voters are well aware of these factors before the campaign begins or because campaigns are mechanisms by which voters become informed.[17] It may not be fair to reward or blame candidates for the state of the economy, as even presidents have only limited control over economic growth or unemployment levels. For better or worse, however, a significant fraction of American voters behave this way.[18]

Setting the stage

On the day after an election, candidates, party officials, and interest groups all start thinking about the next election cycle. They consider who won and who lost the election, which incumbents look like safe bets for reelection and which ones might be vulnerable, who might retire soon or run for another office in the next election, and whether the election returns reveal new information about what kinds of campaigns or issues might increase voter turnout or support.

These calculations also reflect the costs of running for office. Challengers for House and Senate seats know that a campaign will consume at least a year of their time and deplete their financial resources. Presidential campaigns require even more money and effort. If a potential challenger already holds elected office, such as a state legislator running for the House or a House member running for the Senate, that person may have to give up his or her current office to run for a new one.[19]

Party organizations and interest groups face similar constraints both in recruiting candidates and in discouraging some people from running. They do not have the funds to offer significant support to candidates in all 435 congressional districts, in 33 or 34 Senate races, and in a presidential contest.[20] So which races draw their attention? The answer depends on many factors, including how well incumbents did in the last election, how much money those who won have available for the next election, whether party affiliation in the state or district favors Republicans or Democrats (and by how much), and whether the newly elected officeholders are likely to run for reelection.

Party committees and candidates also consider the likelihood that incumbents might retire, thereby creating an open seat. In the run-up to the 2016 election, some senior citizen legislators such as Senate Minority Leader Harry Reid (D-NV, 77 years old) announced their retirement, as well as younger incumbents such as Dan Benishek (R-MI), who had pledged to serve only three terms. Open seats are of special interest to potential candidates and other political actors because incumbents generally hold an election advantage.[21] So, when a seat opens up, candidates from the party that does not control the seat know that they may have a better chance to win because they will not have to run against an incumbent. Consequently, the incumbent's party leaders have to recruit an especially strong candidate in order to hold the seat. Interest groups watch all these decisions with an eye toward deciding whom to endorse or support with campaign donations and advertisements.

Presidential campaigns work the same way. Virtually all first-term presidents run for reelection. Potential challengers in the opposing party study the results of the last election to see how many votes the president received and how this support was

open seat
An elected position for which there is no incumbent.

Each term, members of Congress decide whether to retire or run for another term. Rep. Dan Benishek (R-MI) announced his decision not to seek reelection in 2016 in late 2015, leaving his seat in the House open. Retirement decisions, which create open-seat races, are an opportunity for one party to gain seats from the other.

"The Fundamentals" and Presidential Elections

Vote Share for President's Party vs. Economic Growth

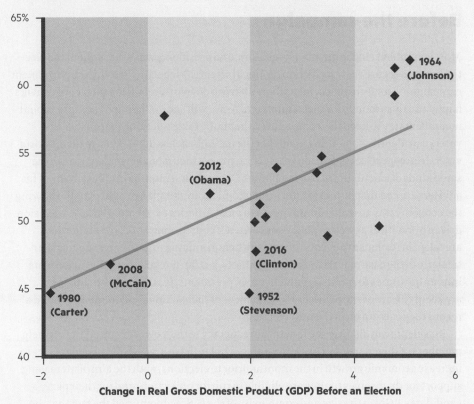

Political scientists argue that "the fundamentals" play a key role in American elections. For example, the state of the economy is thought to influence vote decisions in presidential elections—a strong economy benefits incumbent presidents or their successors. However, most candidates (and journalists) argue that the things candidates say and do during the campaign determine who wins and who loses. What do the numbers say?

To answer this question, let's examine this figure, which shows the relationship between presidential election outcomes (vote for the incumbent president or the candidate from their party) and economic conditions (the growth in real personal income in the year before the election).

Think about it

- Do incumbent presidents do better when the economy is strong than when it is weak?
- Candidates who lose, such as Clinton in 2016 or Romney in 2012, are criticized for running poor campaigns. Look at the data points that describe economic conditions in these elections and the percentage of the popular vote received by Obama in 2012 and Clinton in 2016. Given the state of the economy in these years, is there any evidence that Romney or Clinton did worse than you would expect?
- What signs are there in the chart that other factors besides "the fundamentals" might influence presidential election outcomes?

distributed across the states to determine their own chances of winning against the incumbent. Candidates in the president's party make the same calculations, although no sitting president in the twentieth century was denied renomination. Nonetheless, some presidents (Harry Truman in 1952, Lyndon Johnson in 1968) retired because their chances of being renominated were not good, while others (Gerald Ford in 1976, Jimmy Carter in 1980) faced tough primary contests.[22]

Before the campaign

Most incumbent House members, senators, and presidents work throughout the election cycle to secure their reelection. Political scientists label this activity the permanent campaign.[23] To stay in office, incumbents have to do two things: keep their constituents happy and raise money for their campaign. As we will see in Chapter 11, congressional incumbents try to keep their constituents happy by taking actions that ensure the voters can identify something good that the incumbent has done. This, in turn, boosts voters' retrospective evaluations at election time.[24] Incumbent presidents make the same kinds of calculations. During Barack Obama's first months in office, many of his advisers argued that he had to offer an economic stimulus plan in light of polls showing the economy was an overriding concern to most Americans. Obama did so—a decision driven by political as well as policy concerns. Of course, many presidential actions are taken in response to events rather than being initiated to gain voter support. Particularly in the case of wars and other conflicts, it is far-fetched to say that presidents initiate hostilities for political gain. Even so, presidents, just like other politicians, are keenly aware of the political consequences of their actions and the need to build a record they can run on in the next election.

Presidents can also use the federal bureaucracy to their own advantage and to help members of their party. For example, some scholars have argued that presidents try to increase economic growth in the months prior to elections, with the aim of increasing support for themselves (if they are eligible to run for reelection) and for their party's candidates.[25] Given the size and complexity of the U.S. economy and the fact that the independent Federal Reserve System controls monetary policy, it is unlikely that such efforts could have much success. Even so, out of a desire to stay in office and help their party's candidates it seems clear that presidents would want to be seen as having a positive impact on the economy.

Candidates for all offices, incumbents and challengers alike, also devote considerable time before the campaign to raising campaign funds. Fund-raising helps an incumbent in two ways.[26] First, it ensures that if the incumbent faces a strong opponent she or he will have enough money to run an aggressive campaign. Second, successful fund-raising deters opposition. Potential challengers are less likely to run against an incumbent if that individual is well funded with a sizable campaign war chest.[27]

The other thing candidates do before the campaign is build their campaign organization.[28] Just like fund-raising, the success or failure of these efforts is a signal of a candidate's prospects. If experienced, well-respected people agree to work in a candidate's campaign, observers conclude that the candidate's prospects for being elected are probably good.

Campaign Staff Skilled campaign consultants are among the most sought-after campaign staff. These consultants plan strategies, run public-opinion polls, assemble ads and buy television time, and talk with members of the media on the candidate's behalf, among other things. For many consultants, electioneering is a full-time, year-round

Most officeholders are always campaigning—traveling around their states or districts, talking with constituents, and explaining their actions in office—all in the hope of winning and keeping support for the next election. Here, Representative Beto O'Rourke (D-TX) meets with constituents on the Paso del Norte bridge, which crosses into the United States from Mexico. @RepBetoORourke

position. Many concentrate on electing candidates from one party, although some work for whoever will hire them.

Almost all campaigns have paid and volunteer staff, ranging from the dozen or so people who work for a typical House candidate to the thousands needed to run a major-party candidate's presidential campaign. Some campaign staff work full-time for an incumbent's campaign committee or are on the incumbent's congressional or presidential staff. With some exceptions for senior presidential staff, federal law prohibits government employees from engaging in campaign activities during work hours or with congressional resources.[29]

As a result, many congressional or presidential staffers take a leave of absence from their government jobs to work on their bosses' reelection campaigns during the last few months of the election cycle, then return to working for the government after the election—assuming the incumbent is reelected.

It's hard to separate what candidates do at election time from what they do between elections—incumbents are *always* campaigning, which is part of the reason they are so likely to win reelection. In many cases, incumbent House members and senators wind up running against poorly funded, inexperienced candidates because stronger challengers—seeing that the incumbent has been working hard to solidify a hold on the constituency—decide to wait until the incumbent retires, when they can run for the open seat. Thus, though incumbents are not automatically favored for reelection, they often win by large margins because of all the things they do while holding office in between elections.[30]

The general-election campaign

Officially, the general-election campaigns begin in early September. By then, both parties have chosen their presidential nominees and their congressional candidates. Interest groups, candidates, and party committees have raised most of the funds they will use or donate in the campaign. The race is on.

DID YOU KNOW?

The 2016 Clinton campaign had

200,000

volunteers and 4,000 paid staff (including people working in Democratic party organizations).

Candidates may gain media attention and name recognition by hosting campaign events alongside well-known "surrogates." Here, senator and former presidential candidate John McCain (R-AZ) speaks at an event supporting incumbent Senator Pat Toomey (R-PA).

Unlike in the early primary states, where candidates engage in "retail politics" by meeting more directly with voters, the presidential general-election campaigns emphasize wholesale politics. Here candidates contact voters indirectly, such as through media coverage and campaign advertising. At this point, presidential campaign events generally involve large numbers of citizens, or if they are smaller events or one-on-one encounters they are designed to generate media coverage and thereby reach a larger audience. In contrast, some campaigns for the House and even a few Senate races are more likely to practice retail politics, stressing direct contact with voters. At the same time, average citizens start to pay more attention to the various campaigns. This combination of increased voter attention and a shift in campaign tactics means that preelection polls can show sharp shifts in support for different candidates as the campaign gets under way.

Name Recognition One of the most fundamental campaign strategies, particularly in congressional campaigns, is to build name recognition. Since many citizens tend not to be well informed about congressional candidates, efforts to increase a candidate's name recognition in these races can deliver a few extra percentage points of support—enough to turn a close defeat into a victory. (Practically all voters can identify the major-party presidential candidates, so name recognition efforts are not as central to these elections.)

Getting Out the Vote A second basic strategy is mobilization. Turnout is not automatic: just because a citizen supports a candidate does not mean that he or she will actually vote. Candidates have to make sure that their supporters go to the polls and vote. Moreover, focusing on getting supporters to the polls (or making sure they have an absentee ballot) is a relatively efficient use of candidates' resources. Given that most people don't pay much attention to politics, it's much easier to get a supporter to go to the polls than it is to convert an opponent into a supporter.

GOTV ("get out the vote") or the ground game
A campaign's efforts to "get out the vote" or make sure their supporters vote on Election Day.

Campaign professionals refer to voter mobilization efforts as GOTV ("get out the vote") or the ground game.[31] Most campaigns for Congress or the presidency use extensive door-to-door canvassing, as well as phone banks and e-mail. Both Republican and Democratic campaigns use sophisticated databases, combining voter registration data with demographics to determine who their potential supporters are and how best to reach them and convince them to vote.[32] Sometimes these contacts are made through social media, but many campaigns still use volunteers to knock on doors and present their candidate's message to voters one at a time.

Sometimes candidates also try to decrease support and turnout for their opponent. One tactic is push polling, in which a candidate or a group that supports a candidate conducts a voter "survey," typically by phone, that isn't actually designed to measure opinions so much as to influence them. Campaigns use these so-called polls to spread false or misleading information about another candidate by including this (mis)information in questions posed to large numbers of citizens.[33]

Promises and Party Positions Another set of campaign decisions involves the candidate's campaign platform, which includes stances on issues and promises about how the candidate will act in office. Given that few voters are well informed about public policy or inclined to learn, candidates do not win elections by trying to educate the electorate or making complex promises. What works is making promises and taking positions that are simple and consistent with what the average voter believes, even if these beliefs are inconsistent with reality. For example, many people believe that interest groups

American presidential campaigns depend on thousands of paid and volunteer staff. Here, volunteers for Democratic candidate Hillary Clinton make phone calls to potential supporters from a Clinton campaign office in Newark, Ohio.

have too much power in Washington, although their influence is far less powerful than most Americans believe (see Chapter 10). Even so, many candidates accuse their opponents of being beholden to interest groups. These claims may be far-fetched, but they work well politically because they play to citizens' perceptions.

In writing their platform, candidates may be constrained by positions they have taken in the past or by their party affiliation. For one thing, candidates whose positions vary from one election to another or between the primary and general elections often lose support from voters who see the changes as a sign of manipulation.[34] Also, Chapter 8 showed that the parties have strong brand identities that lead many citizens to associate Democrats with liberal policies and Republicans with conservative ones. Candidates often find it difficult to make campaign promises that contradict these perceptions. For example, during the Republican nomination campaign Donald Trump pledged to expand Medicare and Social Security benefits. However, in light of past attempts by Republican officeholders to cut these programs, voters might be suspicious that Trump—himself a Republican—would carry out this pledge if elected. A candidate's positions are also influenced by demands from potential supporters. In a state or district with many conservative or Republican voters, opposition to Obamacare or to amnesty for undocumented immigrants might be a winning electoral strategy—just as support for these proposals would generally be helpful for candidates running in states or districts where most voters are moderate to liberal or Democrats.

The two-step electoral process in American elections also influences candidate positions. To win office, candidates have to campaign three times, first to build a staff and gain contributors and volunteers (the so-called silent primary or money primary), then in a primary to get on the ballot, and then in a general election. This process gives candidates an incentive to take relatively extreme policy positions—and encourages the entry of relatively extreme candidates. The reason is that party activists, contributors, and primary voters (the people whose support candidates need to attract in the first two steps) hold more extreme positions than voters in the general election. Thus, in the typical congressional district, Republican candidates win primaries by taking conservative positions, while Democratic candidates win primaries by upholding liberal views. However, a position or promise that attracts votes in a primary election might not work so well in the general election, or vice versa. For example, during the 2016

Democratic presidential nomination campaign, challenger Bernie Sanders attracted support by promising to expand government health insurance programs. While this promise was popular among Democratic activists, contributors, and primary voters and helped Sanders compete in a close race against Hillary Clinton for the nomination, it would likely have cost Sanders considerable support in the general election.

Table 9.1 lists part of the campaign platforms of the 2016 presidential candidates and shows the similarities and differences in eight issue areas that received considerable attention during the campaign. In all of these areas, Clinton and Trump offered sharply different ideas of what government should do, although in some cases (for example, the ISIL terrorist organization), one or both platforms did not offer policy details. The sharp differences between the platforms on most of the issues is somewhat uncommon—in most elections, there are a few areas where parties offer similar proposals, differing only in details.

Issues matter in American elections. A candidate's issue positions help to mobilize supporters and attract volunteers, activists, interest-group endorsements, and contributions. Issue positions also define what government will do differently depending on who gets elected. And as we see later in this chapter, some people vote based on candidates' issue positions. Even so, there is considerable evidence that many voters do not know much about candidates' issue positions, particularly for House and Senate races. As a result, when a candidate wins a race or a party wins seats across the country it is risky to read the outcome as a sign that the winners had the most popular set of issue positions.

Debates Candidates often contrast their own records or positions with those of opposing candidates or make claims designed to lower citizens' opinions of their opponents. Sometimes these interactions occur during a formal debate. Most congressional campaigns involve debates in front of an audience of likely voters, a group of reporters, or the editorial board of a local newspaper. Typically candidates take questions from reporters, although sometimes candidates question each other or answer questions from the audience.

TABLE 9.1

Presidential Candidates' Issue Positions (Selected), 2016

The table indicates where Hillary Clinton and Donald Trump stood on eight key issues in 2016 as the presidential election approached in November: immigration, health care, gun control, trade, climate change, Iran, fighting ISIL, and LGBTQ rights.

Source: Compiled by authors from news coverage and candidate websites.

Issue	Hillary Clinton	Donald Trump
Immigration	Comprehensive reform with path to citizenship for undocumented aliens	Build wall between United States and Mexico, increase deportations, ban refugees
Health Care	Improve Obamacare	Repeal Obamacare
Gun Control	Expand background check system	Repeal limits on gun ownership and carry
Trade	Generally supportive of free trade	Renegotiate agreements, limit trade
Climate Change	Address climate change, stress renewable energy	No action on climate change, withdraw from Kyoto treaty
Iran	Support Iran nuclear agreement	Repudiate Iran nuclear agreement
Fighting ISIL	Continue existing U.S. effort against ISIL	Expand effort against ISIL
LGBTQ Rights	End discrimination against LGBTQ individuals	Support law giving businesses right to refuse service to LGBTQ individuals

Presidential campaigns involve multiple debates during the primary and caucus season. During the months before the first primaries and caucuses, each party's candidates gather for many single-party debates using a variety of formats. During the general election, the Republican and Democratic nominees meet for several debates. (The number and format are negotiated by the campaigns and the Commission on Presidential Debates, a nonpartisan organization that coordinates the debates.)[35] The 2016 presidential campaign featured three debates between the presidential nominees and one between the vice-presidential nominees. The debates not only give candidates a chance to present themselves to the electorate but also offer valuable free exposure. Given a relatively uninterested electorate, candidates must figure out how to present themselves to voters in a way that captures their attention and gains their support. Thus, in the 2016 presidential election Republican Donald Trump positioned himself as a successful businessman who could manage the economy and an agent of change in Washington—a good fit to Trump's status as a political outsider, a good match to voters' concerns about the economy, and a way to turn his personal wealth into a campaign asset.

Campaign advertising: getting the word out

One of the realities of modern American electoral campaigns is that they are, for the most part, conducted indirectly—through social media, through news coverage of events, and (most important) through paid campaign advertising. Candidates, party committees, and interest groups spend more than several billion dollars during each election cycle on campaign-related activities by all candidates for federal office. Most of that money is spent on 30-second television spots. Campaign advertising is critical because, as we discussed in Chapter 7, candidates cannot assume that citizens will take the time to learn from other sources about the candidates, their qualifications, and their issue positions.

What Do the Ads Involve? Campaign advertising has evolved considerably over the last generation.[36] During the early years of television, many campaign ads consisted of speeches by candidates or endorsements from supporters and they ran several minutes in length. In the 1964 presidential race, Lyndon Johnson's campaign ran a

The "Daisy" ad from the 1964 presidential campaign interspersed images of a child in a field of flowers and footage of a nuclear detonation. It was broadcast only once but caused much controversy—and helped to crystallize doubts about Republican candidate Barry Goldwater.

TABLE
9.2

Campaign Advertising by Major Spenders in the 2016 Presidential Election

The table shows total spending and the total number of ads, as well as the percentage of positive ads, as paid for directly by the candidates, their parties, and Republican PACs and Democratic PACs.

	Organization	Spending (Millions)	Number of Ads	Positive Ads (%)
Candidates	Clinton campaign	$219	231,241	36
	Trump campaign	77	68,805	57
Parties	Republican National Committee	8.3	30,636	Mostly negative
	Democratic National Committee	1.8	475	Mostly negative
Republican Groups	National Rifle Association	9.4	9,236	Mostly negative
	Reform America	1.4	2,051	Mostly negative
	45 Committee	2.1	2,022	Mostly negative
Democratic Groups	Priorities USA Action	75	76,965	Mostly negative
	Next Gen	11	10,437	Mostly negative
	Service Employees Union	1	590	Mostly negative

Source: Calculated by authors from data available at Wesleyan Media Project, mediaproject.wesleyan.edu (accessed 11/7/16).

five-minute ad titled "Confessions of a Republican" that featured an actor talking about why he didn't want to vote for Republican presidential candidate Barry Goldwater.[37] Johnson's campaign also ran a one-minute ad titled "Peace Little Girl" (nicknamed "Daisy"), which featured a child holding a daisy and pulling its petals off as she counted them aloud one by one. In the background, a voice provided a parallel countdown to the detonation of a nuclear bomb. The ad ended as the television screen filled with the image of the mushroom cloud produced by the nuclear explosion.[38] The implication was that electing Goldwater would increase the chances of a future conflict involving nuclear weapons. The ad remains one of the most iconic pieces of campaign advertising.

Much like the "Daisy" ad, modern campaign ads are short, with arresting images that often use photomontages and bold text to engage a distracted citizenry. Content varies depending on who is running the ads. Table 9.2 gives data from campaign ads in the 2016 presidential general-election campaign from candidates, parties, and interest groups (the top three from each side are listed). These data reinforce our earlier discussion about the Trump campaign's spending disadvantage compared to the Clinton. The table also shows a striking difference in ad content: while the candidates ran a mix of positive and negative ads, ads run by political parties and interest groups were uniformly negative.

Going Negative Candidates and their supporters often try to raise doubts about their opponents by citing politically damaging statements or unpopular past behavior. In conducting opposition research, candidates and interest groups dig into an opponent's past for embarrassing incidents or personal indiscretions, either by the candidate or by a member of the candidate's family or staff. Examples in the 2016 campaign include sexual assault claims made against Donald Trump, as well as information suggesting he paid no federal income taxes over a 20-year period. In turn, Trump's campaign highlighted the fact that during Hillary Clinton's time as a public defender in Arkansas she defended a client accused of forcible rape.

The Internet also facilitates efforts to popularize damaging information. For example, in early October 2016, various media organizations released video of Donald Trump describing his pursuit of women in vulgar, disturbing terms—ending with the phrase "and when you're a star, they let you do it." While Trump later apologized and tried to explain his comments as "locker room talk," the availability of the video made it difficult for Trump to put the issue to rest. Trump's victory is even more notable in light of the negative publicity generated by media coverage of the video and its aftermath.

Candidates who are behind in the polls (or the organizations that support them) sometimes resort to attack ads, campaign ads that criticize the opponent. Many such ads stretch the truth (or break it outright), trying to get voters to stop and think—or to get the opposing candidate to spend time and money denying the ads' claims. One of Trump's central campaign themes was to emphasize the economic and security dangers facing America, then argue that he was the only candidate who could mitigate these dangers. Trump's strategy played an important role in motivating his core supporters to turn out on Election Day.

Do Campaign Ads Work? One critical question about campaign advertising is whether the ads work—whether they shape what people know or influence their voting decisions or other forms of participation. Some observers have complained that campaign ads depress voter turnout and reinforce citizens' negative perceptions of government.[39] Many of these arguments focus on attack ads or negative campaigning. Ads have portrayed candidates as evil blimps hovering over Washington, D.C., or even "demon sheep."[40] Such ads seek to catch voters' attention, to get them to focus on a race long enough to consider the candidates and their real messages. Studies of campaign advertising have shown that most of the time campaign ads fail at this task. Most citizens ignore the ad or remain unconvinced of its message. For example, during the 2016 presidential nomination campaign Republican Jeb Bush and groups supporting him spent millions on campaign ads, only to find that citizens simply did not want to vote for Bush regardless of how many ads his campaign ran. In the general election, Hillary Clinton lost despite vastly outspending Donald Trump on campaign ads.

Insofar as ads matter and Americans pay attention to politics, studies of campaign advertising suggest that Americans are reasonably thoughtful when assessing campaign ads. Evidence suggests that campaign advertising has several beneficial effects. Researchers have found that people who are exposed to campaign ads tend to be more interested in the campaign and to know more about the candidates.[41] Moreover, many campaign ads highlight real differences between the candidates and the parties.[42] Nonetheless, average citizens know that they cannot believe everything they see on television, so campaign advertising, if it does anything at all, captures their attention without necessarily changing their minds.[43]

With regard to negative campaigning, evidence suggests that attack ads often do not help the candidates who run them.[44] In fact, negative ads run by a candidate's campaign can backfire, driving away supporters and depressing turnout. As a result, candidates often rely on party committees and interest groups to run negative ads. Then the candidates themselves can run more positive ads (recall Table 9.2) and can try to disassociate themselves from the negative ads run by others.

In the 2016 presidential race, many of the ads aired by the Trump campaign and Republican groups criticized Hillary Clinton, focusing on what they deemed to be her corrupt political associations.

HILLARY CLINTON ONLY CARES ABOUT
POWER, MONEY AND HERSELF

PAID FOR BY DONALD J. TRUMP FOR PRESIDENT, INC., APPROVED BY DONALD J. TRUMP.

In the end, despite all the money and effort poured into campaign advertising, these messages must be designed to capture the attention of citizens whose interest in politics is minimal, delivering a message that can be understood without too much interpretation. In this way, campaign advertising reflects an old political belief, that most things candidates do in campaigns are wasted efforts that have little impact on the election. The problem is that candidates don't know which of their actions will amount to wasted efforts and which will help them win, so they try them all.

Campaign finance

"Campaign finance" refers to money collected for and spent on campaigns and elections by candidates, political parties, and other organizations and individuals. The **Federal Election Commission** is in charge of administering election laws, including the complex regulations pertaining to how campaigns can spend money. Changes in campaign finance rules, which were passed as the Bipartisan Campaign Reform Act (BCRA), took effect after the 2002 elections and have been modified by subsequent Supreme Court decisions, most notably *Citizens United v. Federal Election Commission* (2010) and *McCutcheon v. Federal Election Commission* (2013), which we describe later.

While campaign finance law is complex, most Americans believe the effects of campaign finance are simple: candidates cannot win without spending money, victory goes to the candidate with the larger budget, and, as a result, candidates listen to large donors and ignore average citizens. They also believe that elections cost too much. The reality is much more complex. Candidates need money to run effective campaigns (and particularly to pay for campaign advertising), but spending does not guarantee victory. And while candidates court large donors, they are even more obsessed with winning the support of ordinary citizens, because in the end elections are about votes, not money.

Types of Funding Organizations The limits on campaign contributions in the BCRA—also known as the McCain-Feingold Act—vary depending on whether contributions are made by an individual or a group and by the type of group, as shown in Table 9.3. But in a 5–4 ruling in *McCutcheon v. Federal Election Commission* in April 2014, the Supreme Court struck down limits on overall campaign contributions to candidates and PACs, which meant that donors could contribute to as many candidates and PACs as they liked. These contributions are called **hard money**, meaning funds that can be used to help elect or defeat a specific candidate (donations made during the primaries and general elections count separately).

Contributions that are not used to help a specific candidate are called **soft money** and are not subject to the limits imposed on hard money. A 527 organization (the number refers to a provision in IRS regulations) can raise unlimited soft money from individuals or corporations for voter mobilization and for issue advocacy, but these expenditures must not be coordinated with a candidate or a party. Ads by 527s cannot advocate the election or defeat of a particular candidate or political party.[45] Another type of organization, again described using the IRS code as a 501(c)(4), has been active in recent elections. The principal difference between 527s and 501(c)(4)s is that the latter type of organization does not have to disclose the names of its contributors. Chapter 10 looks more closely at PACs, 527s, and 501(c)(4)s.

PACs are groups that aim to elect or defeat particular candidates or political parties. A company or an organization can form a PAC and solicit contributions from employees or group members. As Table 9.3 shows, the amount PACs can give to each candidate

Federal Election Commission
The government agency that enforces and regulates election laws; made up of six presidential appointees, of whom no more than three can be members of the same party.

hard money
Donations that are used to help elect or defeat a specific candidate.

soft money
Contributions that can be used for voter mobilization or to promote a policy proposal or point of view as long as these efforts are not tied to supporting or opposing a particular candidate.

in an election is limited, but these limits pertain only to hard money. PACs can also form a 527, which can then accept unlimited amounts of soft money.

As discussed in Chapter 8, political party committees are entities within the Republican and Democratic parties. Both major parties have a national committee and a campaign committee in each house of Congress. Party committees are limited in the amount of hard money they can give to a candidate's campaign and in the amount they can spend on behalf of the candidate as a coordinated expenditure. But a party committee (and, after *Citizens United*, corporations and labor unions) can spend an unlimited amount in independent expenditures to elect a candidate or candidates. To be considered independent (not coordinated), expenditures must not be controlled, directed, or approved by any candidate's campaign. Independent expenditures can pay for campaign advertising, either to promote a party's candidate or to attack an opponent, but the candidate or candidates cannot be consulted on the specific messages.

Current law gives presidential candidates the ability to receive federal campaign funding for the primary and general-election campaign (in the primary, these are matching funds; in the general, they are a block grant). These federal funds are generated, in part, by money that taxpayers voluntarily allocate out of the taxes they pay to the federal government by checking off a particular box on their federal tax return form. Funds are also given to minor political parties if their candidate received more than 5 percent of the vote in the previous election. However, in order to accept federal funds, candidates must abide by overall spending limits (and, during the nomination, by state-by-state spending caps). During the last two presidential campaigns, all of the major candidates decided against accepting these funds during the nomination and general-election campaign, which meant that they were not bound by the spending caps (although individual contributors were still limited to the amounts shown in Table 9.3).

TABLE
9.3

Contribution Limits in the 2016 Elections

The BCRA of 2002 put into effect limits on how much individuals, organizations, and corporations could contribute to candidates' campaigns. The limits were changed based on Supreme Court decisions in 2010 and 2014. At present, although there are still limits on contributions that individuals and PACs can make to each individual candidate, there are no limits on total overall contributions to multiple candidates by individuals and PACs.

	Individual Candidates	National Party Committees	State, District, and Local Parties	PACs	Limit on Total Contributions
Individuals	$2,700	$33,400	$10,000 (combined limit)	$5,000	No limit
PACs	$5,000	$15,000	$5,000 (combined limit)	$5,000	No limit
National Party Committees	$5,000	No limit	No limit	$5,000	$45,400 to Senate candidate per campaign
State, District, and Local Party Committees	$5,000 (combined limit)	No limit	No limit	$5,000 (combined limit)	No limit

Source: Federal Election Commission, "Contribution Limits for 2015–2016," www.fec.gov (accessed 3/13/16).

The effects of money in politics

Campaign finance regulations reflect two simple truths. First, any limits on campaign activities involve balancing the right to free speech about candidates and issues with the idea that rich people or well-funded organizations should not be allowed to dominate what voters hear during the campaign. Second, an enormous amount of money is spent on American elections. Table 9.4 shows the amount raised by candidates, political parties, and others in 2014 and 2016. More than $3 billion was raised for the 2014 midterms, and over $5 billion in 2016, a presidential election year. Moreover, campaign spending is concentrated among a relatively small number of organizations with sizable electioneering budgets. In each of the last several election cycles, the largest organizations have spent hundreds of millions of dollars on contesting the election.

The principal concern about all this campaign cash is that the amount of money spent on candidates' campaigns might matter more than the candidates' qualifications or issue positions. That is, candidates—in particular, wealthy candidates who could self-fund their campaigns—could get elected regardless of how good a job they would do, simply because they had more money than competing candidates to pay for campaign ads, polls, a large staff, and mobilization efforts. Another concern is that individuals and organizations or corporations that can afford to make large contributions (or to fund their own electioneering efforts) might be able to dictate election outcomes or, by funding campaigns, garner a disproportionate amount of influence over the subsequent behavior of elected officials. In the main, these concerns affect soft money contributions and independent expenditures because the current law places no limits

Political action committees spend millions on campaign advertising. Often, their ads are highly negative. This one attacks Donald Trump for being homophobic in his rhetoric.

TABLE 9.4

Candidate, Party, and Interest-Group Election Fund-Raising, 2014–2016

Candidates and political parties raise and spend a great deal of money in their campaigns. Do these numbers help to explain the high reelection rates for members of Congress?

Source: Calculated by authors from data at www.opensecrets.org (accessed 11/6/16).

	2014	2016
Presidential Candidates		
Republican	—	$562,047,053
Democrat	—	$734,118,418
Congressional Candidates		
House incumbents	$614,461,886	$627,192,004
House challengers	$154,056,805	$135,688,346
House open-seat candidates	$188,948,198	$197,293,425
Senate incumbents	$330,229,985	$356,227,722
Senate challengers	$144,176,116	$177,561,478
Senate open-seat candidates	$140,150,238	$97,993,147
Political Parties		
Republicans	$574,483,784	$756,931,035
Democrats	$731,318,780	$985,956,892
Independent Expenditures	$781,690,240	$1,482,375,912
Totals	$3,659,516,032	$6,113,385,432

on how much soft money a party can collect, or on the size of a group's independent expenditures (see the Take a Stand feature). When you look at campaign finance data, the first thing you will see is that it is easy to find which individuals or organizations gave money to a candidate, political party, or other organization.[46] Thus, if you are worried that a particular organization is using campaign contributions to influence elected officials, you can learn which officeholders have received the group's donations. In fact, campaign finance records are so readily available that it is generally easy to identify fraudulent organizations.

However, the raw data do not always tell the whole story. For example, the total amount spent on electioneering represents the sum of all funding for the 435 House contests, 33 or 34 Senate races, a presidential election, and state and local races. Moreover, consider the cost of television advertising. Nearly 80 percent of campaign expenditures are for television time. In major media markets, a 30-second ad on a major television network can cost tens or hundreds of thousands of dollars.[47] Given that even House campaigns may run hundreds of ads and presidential campaigns generally run tens of thousands of ads, it is easy to see why campaign costs pile up so quickly.

There is little evidence that campaign contributions alter legislators' behavior or that contributors are rewarded with votes supporting their causes or favorable policies. Research suggests that most contributions are intended to help elect politicians whom contributors already like, with no expectation that these officials will do anything differently because they received a contribution.[48] Contributions may also help with access, getting the contributor an appointment to present arguments to a politician or his or her staff.[49] And yet people and organizations that generally contribute are already friendly with the politicians they support, and so the politicians would likely hear their arguments in any case.

It's also clear that having a lot of campaign cash doesn't make a candidate a winner—and winners don't always outspend their opponents. Consider the 2016 Republican presidential primaries: the campaigns of Jeb Bush, Chris Christie, and Marco Rubio had large budgets and the support of outside groups with deep pockets. Even so, they all lost. The winner of the election, Donald Trump, spent substantially less than his opponents in both the nomination and general-election campaigns. Of course, Trump entered the campaign with high levels of name recognition and his campaign message resonated with Republican primary voters. But that is exactly the point: victories aren't bought with campaign cash. Candidates need a base level of funding to hire staff, travel, and run some campaign ads. Beyond that point, success is a function of what candidates say and do, not the amount of contributions they receive or ads run on their behalf.[50]

"Why Should I Care?"

When you follow the news about political campaigns, pay attention to the money candidates raise (and spend), where they campaign (and to whom they appeal), the tone and message of their campaigns, and larger fundamentals, such as the strength of the economy. These factors can provide strong clues about who is likely to win (or lose). Remember, though, that politicians don't win elections just by spending a lot of money. Sometimes candidates win despite lower budgets. The other factors listed here and examined in this chapter often have stronger effects on the outcome than money alone.

Is There Too Much Money in Politics?

Campaign finance regulations place restrictions on what Americans can do to influence election outcomes—but should they? Suppose you are a wealthy person or the head of a corporation with deep pockets. Under current law, you and your corporation can only donate about $15,000 to a candidate's campaign; corporations have to form a PAC to do so and cannot pay for the contribution with business revenues. You can also form one of several types of organizations that can spend unlimited money to run campaign ads designed to help elect your preferred candidates or donate to an existing organization. Clearly, having money gives you options for participation in American elections that are not open to the average citizen. Is that a good thing?

It's a free country, and spending money on politics is part of that freedom.

Limits on campaign spending conflict with fundamental tenets of American democracy. The Bill of Rights states that Congress cannot abridge "freedom of speech, or of the press; or the right of the people peaceably to assemble, and to petition the Government for a redress of grievances." One interpretation of the First Amendment that has shaped recent Supreme Court decisions on campaign finance is that people should be free to spend whatever they want on contesting elections—excluding bribes, threats, and other illegal actions, of course. Also, given that campaign spending is no guarantee of electoral success, it is not clear that eliminating spending limits would give big donors control over election outcomes.

Another argument for eliminating limits on political activities is that with one exception (donations to 501[c][4] organizations), donors and political activists are required to file quarterly reports on their campaign activities. Therefore, other activists and even ordinary citizens would quickly learn of any large-scale attempts to manipulate election outcomes and could decide to work for the other side or simply vote against a big donor's preferred candidates.

Campaign contributions need to be constrained.

Even if there's no evidence that money buys elections, there is also no guarantee that under the right circumstances a big donation or ad campaign would not make the difference for one or more candidates. With this possibility in mind, it makes sense to place broad limits on campaign contributions and independent expenditures, to level the playing field between ordinary citizens and political activists with deep pockets.

Just because someone is rich shouldn't give him or her additional ways to influence election outcomes.

Moreover, while it is true that limiting campaign activities requires imposing limits on speech rights, limitations on civil liberties are nothing new. All of the individual rights set out in the Bill of Rights are limited in one way or the other. Even freedom of speech is limited in areas such as hate speech and statements that pose a clear and present danger. Imposing limits on campaign activities could be justified on grounds that maintaining free and fair elections is important enough to justify a modest limitation on what individuals and organizations can do to influence election outcomes.

📷 Does money equal speech or should campaign contributions be limited?

Because money for ads is a necessary component of a political campaign, the possibility remains that a rich donor could change election outcomes by giving large sums to challengers in congressional elections. And in close races, giving a candidate extra funds to increase his or her GOTV efforts or to run additional campaign ads might be enough to change the outcome.

Does the risk of allowing rich donors disproportionate power over elections outweigh the dangers associated with restricting their speech rights? Take a stand.

take a stand

1. Limits on individual campaign contributions guard against allowing wealthy people to dominate elections. What are some of the possible drawbacks of such regulations?

2. Under current law, corporations and unions (not just individuals) are allowed unlimited political expenditures as long as they are independent of a candidate's campaign organization. Why do you think independent expenditures are less regulated than direct contributions to campaigns?

How do voters decide?

All the electoral activities we have considered so far are directed at citizens: making sure they are registered to vote, influencing their voting decisions, and getting them to the polls. In this section, we examine how citizens respond to these influences. The first thing to understand is that the high level of attention, commitment, and energy exhibited by candidates and other campaign actors is not matched by ordinary citizens. We have seen throughout this chapter and others that politics is everywhere, and we have described elections as the primary mechanism citizens have to control the federal government. Even so, only a minority of citizens report high levels of interest in campaigns, many people know little about the candidates or the issues, and many people do not vote.[51]

Who votes, and why?

Politics is everywhere, but getting involved is your choice. Voting and other forms of political participation are optional. Surprisingly, even a strong preference between two candidates may not drive a citizen to the polls because each citizen's vote is just one of many.[52] The only time a vote "counts," in the sense that it changes the outcome, is when the other votes are split evenly so that one vote breaks the tie. Moreover, voting involves costs. Even if you don't learn about the candidates but vote anyway, you still have to get to the polls on Election Day. Thus, the **paradox of voting** is this: Why does anyone vote, given that voting is costly and the chances of affecting the outcome are small?

Figure 9.2 shows that, among Americans, the percentage of registered voters who actually voted has been, in recent presidential elections, around 60 percent, although actual turnout (votes as a percentage of the total adult population) has been closer to

Voting is costly in terms of time and effort. After registering and informing themselves about the election, voters have to take the time to go to the polls and possibly wait in line.

paradox of voting
The question of why citizens vote even though their individual votes stand little chance of changing the election outcome.

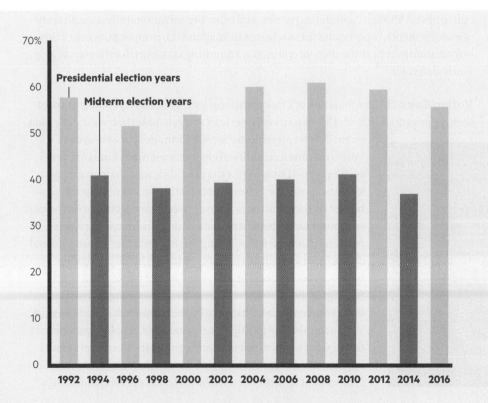

FIGURE 9.2

Turnout in Presidential and Midterm Elections, 1992–2016

The figure shows how turnout of registered voters varies both over time and between presidential and midterm elections. Why don't more people vote in midterm election years? Why don't more people vote in any given year?

Source: United States Election Project, www.election-project.org (accessed 11/9/16).

Presidential election years

Midterm election years

1992 1994 1996 1998 2000 2002 2004 2006 2008 2010 2012 2014 2016

DID YOU KNOW?

61.2%

Voter turnout for African Americans in the 2016 presidential election
Source: Calculated by author from exit polls and historical data.

issue voters
People who are well informed about their own policy preferences and knowledgeable about the candidates, and who use all of this information when they decide how to vote.

voting cues
Pieces of information about a candidate that are readily available, easy to interpret, and lead a citizen to decide to vote for a particular candidate.

During campaigns, candidates often seek to strengthen the perception that they share (or at least are sympathetic to) average Americans' beliefs and interests. Here, Hillary Clinton meets with voters over coffee and pastries at a campaign stop in Stone Ridge, Virginia.

50 percent.[53] As the figure shows, turnout is significantly higher in presidential elections than in midterm elections. Turnout is even lower in primaries and caucuses: in the 2016 presidential primaries, some states reported turnout exceeding 30 percent, which was regarded as unusually high. For caucuses, which require individuals to spend several hours voting, turnout is generally only a few percentage points.

In the main, turnout is higher for whites than for nonwhites (African Americans have been an exception in recent elections), for older Americans than for younger Americans, and for college graduates than for people with a high school education or less. Men and women, however, say they vote at roughly the same rate. Many factors explain variation in turnout. People who vote regularly are more likely to consider going to the polls as an obligation of citizenship, to feel guilty when they do not vote, and to think that the elections matter. In contrast, turnout is much lower among those who are angry with the government, think that government actions do not affect them, or think that voting will have no impact on government policy. Citizens who hold these beliefs are unlikely to care about the outcome of the election, are unlikely to feel guilty for abstaining, and are unlikely to see voting as an obligation.[54]

These findings demonstrate the importance of mobilization in elections. As we discussed earlier, many candidates for political office spend at least as much time trying to convince their supporters to vote as they do attempting to persuade others to become supporters in the first place. Because many Americans either do not vote or vote only sporadically, mobilization is a vital strategy for winning elections.

How do people vote?

Some people are highly interested in politics, collect all the information they can about the candidates, and vote based on this information; they are known as **issue voters**.[55] But most citizens are not interested enough in politics to spend their time that way, and they don't care enough about the details of politics to find out which candidates come closest to their preferences. Reliable information about candidates is also often difficult to find. Although candidates, parties, and other organizations produce a blizzard of endorsements, reports, and press releases throughout the campaign, much of this information may be difficult to interpret. It is a daunting task, even for the rare, highly motivated voter.

Voting Cues This combination of a lack of interest and the relatively complex task of seeking information leads the majority of American voters to base their voting decision on easily interpretable pieces of information, or **voting cues**.[56] Voters in American national elections use many kinds of cues, such as party ID (voting for the candidate who shares your party identification), the personal vote (voting for a candidate who has helped you get assistance from a government agency or has helped your community benefit from desirable government projects), personal characteristics (voting for the candidate whose personal characteristics such as age, race, gender, ethnicity, religious beliefs, or background match your own), or pocketbook voting (voting for the incumbent if the economy is strong and for the challenger otherwise, as illustrated by the quote from Ronald Reagan). Voters can also use multiple cues. Cues give people a low-cost way to cast what political scientist and campaign consultant Samuel Popkin called a reasonable vote—a vote that, more likely than not, is consistent with the voter's true preference among candidates.[57]

Studies have found that citizens who use cues and are politically well informed are more likely to cast a reasonable vote than those who use cues but are otherwise relatively politically ignorant. In essence, information helps people to select the right cue.[58]

The use of voting cues implies that a candidate's personal characteristics play a crucial role in voting decisions. For example, some people voted for Hillary Clinton because she was a woman, because of her political experience as first lady, senator, and secretary of state, or simply because she was a Democrat. Equally, some people voted for Donald Trump because of his career as a businessman or because he was the Republican nominee.

On the one hand, the role that cues play in voting decisions is one reason why "the fundamentals matter" in American elections. Because some people vote based on the state of the economy, incumbent presidents are good bets to win reelection when economic conditions are good and poor bets when the economy is in trouble. Similarly, because party ID is often used as a cue, candidates are more likely to win if their party affiliation is shared by the bulk of voters in their state or district. But the use of cues also implies that candidates (and campaigns) matter. For example, citizens may use a candidate's record in office to guide their vote decision, especially if the candidate makes this record a central theme in their campaign speeches and advertising. In fact, many campaign events and communication are designed to reinforce the impression that candidates share voters' concerns and values. For example, at several points during the campaign, Donald Trump tweeted pictures of his fast-food dinner on the campaign plane.

Moreover, because personal characteristics are used as a cue, some candidates have a better chance of winning than others, because they have one or more cues that citizens see as desirable. Table 9.5 offers some details on what kind of candidate characteristics attract voter support. On the one hand, many voters consider a candidate's military service, experience as a governor, or business experience as assets. On the

Are you better off than you were four years ago?

—**Ronald Reagan,** running for president against incumbent Jimmy Carter

TABLE 9.5

Candidate Traits and Voter Choice

Many Americans cast votes based on candidates' personal characteristics and background. What sorts of candidates are advantaged by this practice—and what sorts are disadvantaged?

Source: Pew Research Center, "For 2016 Hopefuls, Washington Experience Could Do More Harm than Good," May 19, 2014, www.people-press.org (accessed 3/5/16).

Likelihood of Supporting a Candidate Who . . .	More Likely	Less Likely	Wouldn't Matter
Has served in the military	43%	4%	53%
Has been a governor	33	6	59
Has been a business executive	33	13	53
Has Washington experience	21	17	48
Is a woman	19	6	71
Attended a prestigious university	19	6	74
Is an Evangelical Christian	21	17	58
Never held political office	9	52	37
Has used marijuana in the past	6	22	70
Is in his or her seventies	6	36	55
Is an atheist	5	53	41
Is gay or lesbian	5	37	66
Had an extramarital affair in the past	2	35	61

other hand, Americans tend not to vote for a candidate who is a known atheist, has had an extramarital affair, or is gay or lesbian. Of course, candidate information is only one of the things a voter considers and some cues override others—businessman Donald Trump won the Republican nomination despite having never been elected to political office, being 70 years old, and admitting to past extramarital affairs.

Who (usually) wins

All the strategies discussed so far are used to some extent in every election. However, in normal elections, when congressional reelection rates are high, voters generally use cues that focus on the candidates themselves, such as incumbency, partisanship, a personal connection to a candidate, the candidate's personal characteristics, or retrospective evaluations. This behavior is consistent with what Tip O'Neill, Speaker of the House from 1977 to 1987, meant when he said that "all politics is local": many congressional elections are independent, local contests in which a candidate's chances of winning depend on what voters think of the candidate in particular—not the president, Congress, or national issues. It also explains why electoral **coattails** are typically very weak in American elections and why so many Americans cast **split tickets** rather than **straight tickets**. In the main, voting decisions in presidential and congressional elections are made independently of each other.

"Wave" elections generally occur when a large number of voters vote against incumbents because of poor economic conditions, political scandal, or a costly, unpopular war. In 2006, many voters rated the war in Iraq as the most important issue and generally disapproved of how the war was being conducted.[59] And in 2010, economic concerns again returned to the fore, with many voters disapproving of economic conditions in general, as well as corporate bailouts, economic stimulus legislation, and health care reform. Under these conditions many voters look for someone to blame, focusing on members of Congress from the party in power. They then

---

coattails
The idea that a popular president can generate additional support for candidates affiliated with his or her party. Coattails are weak or nonexistent in most American elections.

split ticket
A ballot on which a voter selects candidates from more than one political party.

straight ticket
A ballot on which a voter selects candidates from only one political party.

FIGURE 9.3

Percentage of House Incumbents Reelected

The figure shows that, despite public dissatisfaction with Congress, incumbents still tend to be reelected in their respective districts. According to the chart, which congressional elections were wave elections? Which were normal elections?

Source: Calculated by the authors from election results.

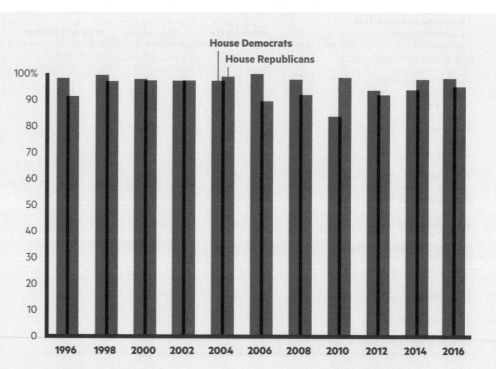

House Democrats
House Republicans

vote against these members, either as a protest vote, because they disapprove of their performance, or because they want to put different individuals in charge in the hope that new members will bring about improved conditions. Whether viewed in terms of voting against one party's incumbents or for the other party's challengers, these motivations lead to the same voting behavior; the difference is a matter of voters' attitudes and emphases.

Even in wave elections, reelection rates for members of Congress (the percentage of incumbents who successfully run for reelection) are generally high, as Figure 9.3 shows. Over the last generation, neither party has had a House reelection rate less than 80 percent; even in 2006, when 100 percent of Democratic House incumbents running for reelection won, the reelection rate for House Republican incumbents was almost 90 percent. In wave elections such as those in 2006 and 2010, one party's House reelection rate is significantly higher than that of the other party's; in normal elections such as the ones in 2000 and 2002, the House reelection rates are similar and approach 100 percent. Reelection rates for Senate incumbents are somewhat lower but show the same patterns.

Reelection rates for members of Congress are so high because the members work to insulate themselves from electoral challenges through tactics we discussed in this chapter and will discuss further in Chapter 11. They raise large sums of campaign cash well in advance of upcoming elections, use redistricting to give themselves a safe district populated by supporters, and enact pork-barrel legislation that provides government benefits and programs to their constituents. Even so, congressional incumbents are not necessarily safe from electoral defeat. Rather, their high reelection rates result from the actions they take every day, which are calculated to win favor with their constituents. In normal elections, these strategies are generally enough to ensure reelection. In nationalized elections, however, they are not enough to guarantee reelection for some legislators from the disadvantaged party, such as Democrats in 2010.

Despite the sequence of three wave elections in 2006, 2008, and 2010, wave elections are relatively rare. Most of the time, relatively few citizens are highly concerned about national issues or hold strong opinions about the president, Congress, or the overall state of the nation. Congressional incumbents also work hard to focus attention on the good things they have done for their constituents. And it is important to remember that even in wave elections some voters still use the incumbent-centered cues described earlier. In a wave election, voters don't suddenly become better informed about politics. Rather, some of them just switch to a different set of voting cues depending on the circumstances of the election.

"Why Should I Care?"

After each election, people look at the results and try to figure out what the election was about—why some candidates won and others lost. Before each election, would-be candidates wonder whether this is "the year" to run for office (you may be one of these candidates someday). The most important thing to understand is that there are no easy explanations and no guarantees. The problem is not that voters are fickle or clueless or that the rules are too complex. Rather, elections boil down to voters and the many different ways they decide how to vote. Knowing what is likely to influence voters can help you make predictions about who will win elections and thus what policies and issues government will tackle.

Understanding the 2016 election

The 2016 contest is an excellent example of how and why elections matter. When the campaigns began, it seemed as though several critical issues hung in the balance. America's next president would likely appoint at least one (and probably two or three) Supreme Court justices. This had the potential to change the ideological balance of the Court, making recent decisions on campaign finance, affirmative action, same-sex marriage, and abortion rights open for revision. Republican control of the presidency would make it easier to repeal President Obama's health care and financial reforms. All of Obama's executive orders, ranging from limits on deporting undocumented aliens to measures restoring commercial and diplomatic ties with Cuba, could be abolished by the new president on his or her first day in office. Finally, the next president—if they chose—could work to resolve policy gridlock in areas such as gun control, reducing the federal deficit, making changes to Social Security and Medicare, entitlement reform, and immigration law.

The first thing to understand about the 2016 elections is their uniqueness. For the first time in 50 years, a major party nominated a presidential candidate with no prior political experience, Republican Donald Trump. It is hard to think of another candidate in American politics who even comes close to Trump and his willingness to say completely outlandish things if doing so helped him to gain political advantage. Trump also ran a unique campaign, with limited advertising, a weak ground game, and a willingness to deviate from the standard Republican platform on issues such as trade, civil liberties, and foreign policy. Trump was the least popular major-party presidential nominee of all time, and many Republican elected officials and party leaders refused to support Trump in the general election.

Democrats in 2016 selected Hillary Clinton, a former First Lady, senator, and secretary of state, as their nominee. This choice was historic: Clinton was the first woman to lead a major-party presidential ticket in America. Notwithstanding this distinction, Clinton's popularity was only somewhat higher than Trump's. Clinton also faced a surprisingly strong challenge in the Democratic primaries from Senator Bernie Sanders, and was only narrowly ahead of Trump during most of the general-election campaign.

All of these factors make the 2016 election a crucial test of many of the theories we have offered throughout this text. How could Trump win the Republican nomination in light of our assertion that "the party decides"? How did Clinton win the nomination despite the many arguments made against her candidacy—or, why did Trump win despite his political baggage and under-financed campaign? You will see that for all its uniqueness, much of what happened in the 2016 election fits our description of how campaigns work and why some candidates win while others lose.

The path to 2016: the 2012 and 2014 elections

At first glance, the 2012 and 2014 elections were mirror-image contests: Democrat Barack Obama won reelection in 2012 and his party gained seats in both houses of Congress, but in 2014, Republicans regained control of the Senate and enlarged their House majority. These outcomes illustrate the essence of contemporary American politics: Americans are sharply divided on many issues, no party has an enduring advantage, and election outcomes hinge on factors such as the state of the economy, the number of seats each party has to defend, and the candidates that each party runs for office.

The 2012 Presidential and Congressional Elections The economy was the central issue in the 2012 campaign. Unemployment remained relatively high and economic growth was relatively low. At first glance, the data appeared to pose a serious threat to President Obama's reelection chances. But many Americans seemed to hold Obama only partially responsible for the economy, believing that he had inherited many of the problems from the previous administration, and gave him some credit for his economic stimulus legislation.

In the presidential race, Mitt Romney was the front-runner on the Republican side from the beginning of the nomination process, although he faced serious opposition for most of the primary season. Nonetheless, it was not a surprise that Romney won the nomination: he was an experienced candidate who had run for president in 2008 and had served as governor of Massachusetts from 2003 until 2007. His record as a businessman appealed to voters who thought that government should be run more efficiently. In contrast to Romney and the Republicans, President Obama won renomination with no significant opposition, as is usual for incumbent presidents.

Early in the general-election campaign, with most states squarely in one candidate's camp or the other, attention focused on nine swing states where neither candidate was significantly ahead: North Carolina, Ohio, Virginia, Florida, New Hampshire, Nevada, Wisconsin, Colorado, and Iowa. Most Americans had largely made up their minds fairly early in the campaign, and few were open to persuasion. Under these conditions, voter mobilization played a crucial role, and Obama's campaign was much better organized to get people to the polls, both for early voting and on Election Day. In the end, Obama defeated Romney by a slight margin in the popular vote and by a somewhat larger margin in the electoral college.

At the congressional level, many Republican candidates in 2012 ran on platforms emphasizing the need to reduce government spending and regulations, generally saying that they would make the repeal of President Obama's health care reforms a central priority if they were elected or reelected. Most Democrats either championed the health care reforms or, in swing districts and states, talked about them as little as possible. On Election Day, Democrats won one additional Senate seat (counting two Independents who were expected to caucus with the Democrats) and eight House seats.

The 2014 Congressional Elections On one level, the 2014 midterm election was among the least exciting in recent years. Various Tea Party organizations remained active, but had limited success in electing their preferred candidates. No single overarching issue, such as fears of an economic collapse or the costs of a protracted war in Iraq, informed voters' choices or debates between candidates. Many stories described 2014 as "an election about nothing," meaning that the issues motivating voters varied somewhat from state to state.

National conditions in 2014 favored the Republican Party and its candidates. President Obama's approval rating had declined steadily since his reelection, enough so that he did not campaign with many Democratic candidates to avoid hurting their election efforts. These factors, combined with fears about Ebola and the ISIL terrorist organization, contributed to a small but discernible advantage for Republican candidates in most areas of the country.

Democrats were also disadvantaged because they had more Senate seats to defend: of the 35 seats being contested, Democrats controlled 21 and Republicans only 15. More important, many of the Democratic seats were in states where the party was weak. These conditions, coupled with the Republican Party's success in helping their incumbents and strong challengers to win primaries and caucuses, meant that, even before the general-election campaign began, Republicans stood an excellent chance to gain control of the Senate. Control of the House was not at stake, as the 2010 and 2012

Elections matter, especially when they determine who controls the congressional agenda. Republican gains in the Senate in 2014 led to Mitch McConnell (R-KY) taking over as Senate Majority Leader.

elections had left relatively few vulnerable Democratic or Republican incumbents. In the end, the narrow Republican advantage translated into modest gains for the party in the House and larger gains in the Senate where Republicans gained nine seats and took control of the chamber with a 53 to 46 advantage over Democrats.

The 2016 elections: the nomination process

When Donald Trump entered the race for the Republican presidential nomination in the summer of 2015, many analysts (and some political scientists) argued that he would have little chance of winning. How could a twice-divorced political amateur, reality TV star with moderate positions on LGBTQ rights and a reputation for saying and doing controversial things, hope to win the nomination from a party dominated by social conservatives, much less a general election?

In retrospect, the conditions of the 2016 Republican nomination were ideal for a candidate like Trump. Seventeen candidates competed for the Republican nomination—many were current or former senators or governors, or had successful careers outside politics. However, none of the other candidates had the combination of organization, campaign funds, and voter appeal needed to claim the status of front-runner or gather endorsements from party leaders. Among these candidates, Trump stood out because of his preexisting high name recognition, his popularity among a large group of Republican primary voters, and his ability to largely self-fund a campaign. It is possible (but not certain) that Trump would have lost the nomination if party leaders had moved early in the process to unify behind one of the other challengers—but they did not. Trump went to the Republican Convention in July 2016 with solid support from Republican identifiers.

After the Republican Convention, there were clear signs that the general election was going to be an uphill fight. Trump had not built the large organization needed to run a national campaign or mobilize supports on Election Day. His campaign fund-raising lagged far behind Clinton's. Many Republican politicians (including many of Trump's former opponents) either skipped the Convention or came out against Trump. The central themes of the Convention, particularly Trump's vow to "make America great again," the focus on security, the depiction of Clinton and her fellow Democrats as corrupt and dangerous, and Trump's claim that "only I can fix" a troubled economy, nation, and world, were aimed at motivating Trump's core supporters rather than at converting wayward Republicans and independents.

On the Democratic side of the presidential race, many potential candidates decided against entering the race in 2016, believing that Hillary Clinton was likely to run, and would be the odds-on favorite if she did. Vice President Joe Biden considered running,

Donald Trump's victory in the 2016 presidential campaign was a shock to many, even his supporters.

but decided not to in the wake of his son's death from a brain tumor. Ultimately, the race boiled down to a contest between Clinton and Senator Bernie Sanders. At first, Sanders was not expected to present much of a challenge to Clinton, as he held relatively liberal positions on many issues and had spent most of his career in Congress as an independent, officially joining the Democratic Party at the same time that he announced his presidential campaign. However, while Clinton's center-left positions on many issues were well-suited to a general-election campaign, Sanders's positions were attractive to the more liberal Democratic base and to young voters. After a long, drawn-out, sometimes heated contest, Clinton won the Democratic nomination because of steadfast support from minority Democrats, because she was seen as more electable by many voters, and because of overwhelming support from Democratic party leaders.

In congressional elections, attention focused largely on Senate races, as Democrats needed to gain only five Senate seats to take majority control of the chamber (four if a Democrat won the presidency). In a reverse of 2014, the fundamentals in 2016 favored Democrats, who had only 10 seats to defend. Democrats also had considerable success in convincing good candidates to enter these Senate races and discouraging competitive primaries. In contrast, 22 Republican senators were up for reelection (plus two open seats), about a third in states won by Obama in 2012. However, Republican control of the House was thought to be largely secure, given their substantial 32-seat majority and a relatively low number of electorally vulnerable members on both sides.

Congressman David Jolly (R-FL) was one of only a handful of incumbents who lost their seats in 2016.

The 2016 general election

Trump's high point in the polls was immediately after the Republican Convention, when polling averages showed him drawing even with Clinton and perhaps even a little ahead. After that point in the campaign, these averages always showed Clinton in front, although the margin varied over the course of the campaign and some individual surveys produced results showing Trump with a narrow lead. Even so, the consistently high percentage of undecided voters, relatively large support for minor-party candidates, and Clinton's low popularity ratings suggested the race was far from over.

As we discussed earlier, there were clear differences between the presidential candidates on issues ranging from immigration reform to gun control. However, there was an even bigger difference in the candidates' diagnoses of what was needed to effect policy change in Washington. The message from Clinton's campaign was that partisan conflict reflects sincere differences of opinion, differences that often cannot be compromised. In contrast, Donald Trump argued that his management experience and deal-making talents gave him a unique ability to broker policy change, even given deep-set differences between Republicans and Democrats. Trump also referred to Clinton as "Crooked Hillary," arguing that because Clinton had worked as a senator and secretary of state, she was at least partly responsible for policy failures and gridlock in Washington. By mid-October Trump had lost significant support from independents and Republicans because of more than a dozen allegations of sexual harassment and assault, and because of his relatively poor performance during the three debates, where he seemed unprepared and unwilling to provide specifics of how he would implement his campaign promises. Trump also dropped in the polls because of many inflammatory statements, such as his refusal to commit to conceding the election if he lost.

In the last two weeks of the campaign, the polling gap between Trump and Clinton narrowed considerably, partly driven by a reopening of the FBI investigation into Clinton's use of a private e-mail server. (The investigation was closed on the weekend before the election.) While the Clinton campaign continued extensive campaign advertising, the Trump campaign ramped up spending in its own advertising effort.

Days before the election, most campaign experts expected Clinton to win, based on her narrow lead and the Democrats' expected advantage in early voting and Election Day mobilization.

However, on Election Day, Trump benefitted from significantly higher than expected turnout in rural communities, which helped him win recent Democratic strongholds of Michigan, Pennsylvania, and Wisconsin. And while Clinton received strong support from African-American, Latino, and younger voters (see Figure 9.4), lower than expected turnout from these groups cost Clinton support in the crucial swing states of North Carolina and Florida, especially in light of Trump's strong support from rural, white, and older voters. The results also show a much larger gender gap than in previous elections—women, especially those with a college degree, were much more likely to vote for Clinton over Trump. Clinton won more votes overall, but Trump prevailed in the electoral college (see Figure 9.5). Notably, Trump won the election despite receiving fewer votes than losing 2012 Republican candidate Mitt Romney—however, Clinton lost even more votes compared to Barack Obama in 2012. In congressional races, Democrats gained only two Senate seats, and five House seats.

What drove the election results? One important factor was turnout, especially the apparent failure of the Democrats' get-out-the-vote drive compared to the much more modest Republican effort. Trump did not improve on Mitt Romney's poor showing

FIGURE 9.4

Groups and Votes in the 2016 Election

This figure shows variation in group support for Democrats and Republicans in the 2016 elections. How did the positions and issues emphasized by candidates in the two parties create or strengthen these differences?

Source: CNN Exit Poll, www.cnn.com/election/results/exits-polls/national/house (accessed 11/9/16).

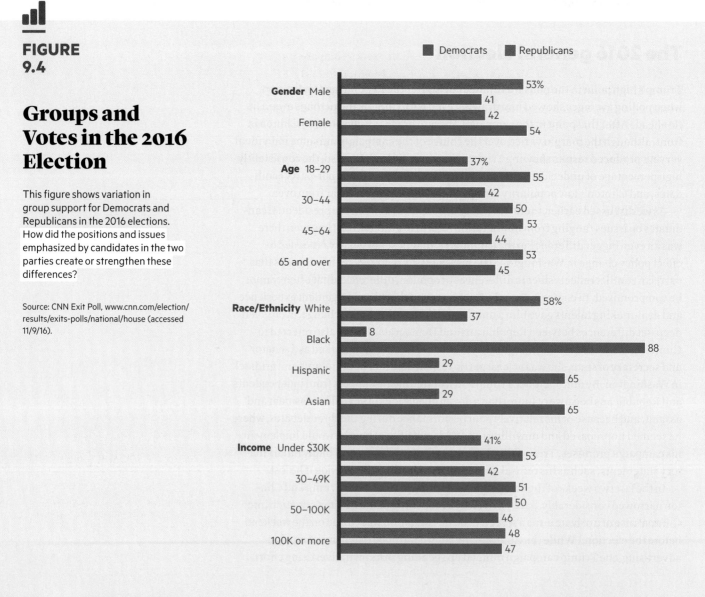

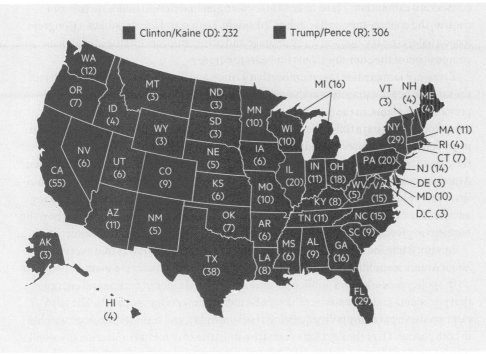

Clinton/Kaine (D): 232   Trump/Pence (R): 306

WA (12)
OR (7)
MT (3)
ND (3)
MN (10)
MI (16)
VT (3)
NH (4)
ME (4)
ID (4)
SD (3)
WI (10)
NY (29)
MA (11)
RI (4)
WY (3)
IA (6)
PA (20)
CT (7)
NV (6)
NE (5)
IN (11)
OH (18)
NJ (14)
CA (55)
UT (6)
CO (9)
KS (6)
MO (10)
KY (8)
WV (5)
VA (15)
DE (3)
MD (10)
D.C. (3)
AZ (11)
NM (5)
OK (7)
AR (6)
TN (11)
NC (15)
IL (20)
AK (3)
MS (6)
AL (9)
GA (16)
SC (9)
TX (38)
LA (8)
FL (29)
HI (4)

The 2016 Presidential Election: State-by-State

Note: Donald Trump won the electoral college with 304 votes to Hillary Clinton's 227. Seven electors voted for someone other than their party's candidate.

with minority voters in 2012, but lower turnout from these groups compared to 2012 and 2008 was a key factor in Clinton's defeat. In addition, Table 9.6 shows clear policy differences between Clinton and Trump supporters, especially on immigration reform and the economy. Vote decisions in 2016 were also highly correlated with evaluations of President Obama (people who were critical of Obama's presidency were more likely to vote for Trump), which makes sense given the importance of party identification in shaping presidential approval.

Consequences of the 2016 elections

The 2016 elections move America from divided government to unified Republican control of the presidency and Congress. At least for the next two years, this change should reduce the level of policy gridlock in Washington, and move policy in a firmly

TABLE
9.6

Issue	Position	Democrat	Republican
Illegal immigrants	Should be deported	17%	82%
	Offered legal status	61	37
Condition of the U.S. economy	Good	77	22
	Poor	34	63
Fight against ISIS	Going well	74	24
	Going badly	29	70
President Barack Obama	Approve	84	15
	Disapprove	9	88

Issues and Voting in the 2016 Election

Source: CNN Exit Poll, www.cnn.com/election/results/exit-polls/national/house (accessed 11/9/16).

Though Hillary Clinton fell short in her effort to become America's first female president, she was able to win over 64 million votes—more than any candidate besides Barack Obama.

conservative direction. Thus, instead of focusing on inaction on issues such as gun control, the country may well watch as President Trump and the Republican Congress loosen federal restrictions on gun purchase and ownership, or shift the ideological composition of the Supreme Court for years to come.

Even so, it is important to remember that Trump and his fellow Republicans will face the same policy constraints that shaped policy under the Obama administration and previous presidents. In the first weeks after his election, for example, Trump moved away from proposing a full-scale repeal of Obamacare, offering to keep in place popular provisions such as allowing children to remain on their parents' health insurance until they are 26. And while Trump vowed to destroy ISIL, the reality is that this goal has been America's policy for several years, and it is not clear what new initiatives Trump's administration could implement to achieve this goal. Finally, as a political outsider with many advisers from outside Washington, Trump is at a disadvantage in understanding how the bureaucracy works and the limits to his ability to force compliance with his directives.

In sum, while the easy prediction following the 2016 elections was that everything about American politics is about to change, the reality is that there are many constraints on the policy process, from public opinion to the limited amount of time and energy that presidents and their advisers have to formulate new policy proposals. The 2016 elections have put many policy questions back into play, and revealed ideological splits in both parties. Over the next four years (two until the 2018 midterm elections), we will watch how President Trump and the Republican Congress determine their agenda, arrive at compromises, and work to enact their policy proposals—working inside the rules and institutions that define American politics, and acting in light of the fundamental divisions in American society over the size and scope of the federal government.

Conclusion

Candidates in American national elections compete for different offices using a variety of rules that determine who can run for office, who can vote, and how ballots are counted and winners determined. Election outcomes are shaped by who runs for office and how they campaign, who decides to vote, and how they decide whom to support, but also by the rules that govern electoral competition. By taking these factors into account, we can explain why Donald Trump defeated Hillary Clinton in 2016—or why these candidates won their party's nominations rather than someone else.

It is easy to complain about American elections. Citizens are not experts about public policy. They often know little about the candidates running for office. Candidates sensationalize, attack, and dissemble rather than giving details about what they would do if elected. Even so, there are clear, systematic differences between Democratic and Republican candidates that translate into different government policies depending on who holds office. It matters that Trump was elected in 2016 and Republicans held onto control of the House and the Senate. Moreover, the criteria that average Americans use to make voting decisions reflect these differences. In addition, many examples of seemingly strange behavior in American elections make more sense once you examine them. It is understandable that so few Americans are issue voters and that many people decide to not vote. It also makes sense that candidates seeking the attention of distracted voters tend to emphasize sensationalism over sober discussion of policies, or that attack ads often succeed. The outcome of every election is the result of all these individual-level choices added together. In that sense, election outcomes reflect the preferences of the American people.

STUDY GUIDE

How do American elections work?

Present the major rules and procedures of American elections. (Pages 288–299)

Summary

Elections in America generally have two steps. Primary elections select candidates for each party, and general elections determine who wins the office. Some of the rules for presidential elections differ from other elections; notably, the electoral college system determines the winner of the general election.

Key terms

incumbent (p. 288)

open primary (p. 289)

semi-closed primary (p. 289)

closed primary (p. 289)

general election (p. 289)

plurality voting (p. 290)

majority voting (p. 290)

runoff election (p. 290)

primary (p. 292)

caucus (p. 292)

proportional allocation (p. 293)

winner-take-all (p. 293)

electoral college (p. 294)

popular vote (p. 298)

electoral votes (p. 298)

Practice Quiz Questions

1. **Runoff elections occur only in states that use _____.**
   a. majority voting
   b. primary elections
   c. plurality voting
   d. absentee ballots
   e. proportional allocation

2. **The recent trend in the presidential nomination process has been to _____.**
   a. schedule primary elections later in the process
   b. add so-called regional primaries
   c. replace primaries with caucuses
   d. break up primaries so that they are not held in the same region at the same time
   e. limit the influence of third-party candidates

3. **The winner-take-all method of allocating most states' electoral votes results in candidates focusing on _____ states and _____ states.**
   a. low-population; safe
   b. high-population; safe
   c. low-population; swing
   d. high-population; swing
   e. safe; swing

Electoral campaigns

Describe the features, strategies, and funding of campaigns for federal office. (Pages 299–314)

Summary

Party organizations and candidates begin preparing for the next election the day after the last election ends. They focus on fund-raising and determining which races are likely to be competitive. Incumbents work throughout the election cycle to maintain their good standing among the voters and secure their reelection bids. During a campaign, candidates work hard, particularly through the use of advertisements, to increase their name recognition and mobilize their supporters.

Key terms

election cycle (p. 299)

open seat (p. 300)

GOTV ("get out the vote") or the ground game (p. 304)

Federal Election Commission (p. 310)

hard money (p. 310)

soft money (p. 310)

Practice Quiz Questions

4. **An open-seat election is one where _____.**
   a. there is no challenger in the race
   b. there is no incumbent in the race
   c. an incumbent loses his/her seat due to redistricting
   d. an incumbent faces a challenger in his/her own primary
   e. an incumbent faces a challenger in the general election

5. **What effect does fund-raising have for incumbents?**
   a. It ensures the potential for an aggressive campaign, but it has no effect on opposition.
   b. It ensures the potential for an aggressive campaign, and it deters opposition.
   c. It ensures the potential for an aggressive campaign, and It encourages opposition.
   d. It has no effect on the potential for an aggressive campaign, but it does deter opposition.
   e. It has no effect on the potential for an aggressive campaign, nor does it deter opposition.

6. **"GOTV" and "ground game" refer to a candidate's attempts to _____.**
   a. boost name recognition
   b. mobilize supporters
   c. increase fund-raising
   d. deter opposition
   e. win endorsements

7. **Research shows that modern campaign ads are likely to _____.**
   a. change voters' minds
   b. feature speeches by the candidate
   c. have beneficial effects, such as informing voters
   d. run several minutes in length
   e. increase turnout

8. **What is soft money?**
   a. money that can be given directly to a candidate
   b. money that is given by members of the opposing party
   c. money that can be spent to mobilize voters for a specific candidate
   d. money that candidates spend to boost the party's reputation
   e. money that is not tied to a specific candidate

How do voters decide?

Explain the key factors that influence voters' choices. (Pages 315–319)

Summary

Despite the fact that politics is everywhere, ordinary voters don't pay much attention to politics. Turnout rates are modest, and people know relatively little about the candidates and their positions. While some voters are highly interested in politics and collect all the information they can about the candidates, most voters make their decision based on voting cues. Most elections are determined by local-level politics, but occasionally national issues come to the fore.

Key terms

paradox of voting (p. 315)   coattails (p. 318)
issue voters (p. 316)   split ticket (p. 318)
voting cues (p. 316)   straight ticket (p. 318)

Practice Quiz Questions

9. **What is the paradox of voting?**
   a. Voting is costly, and the chances of affecting the election outcome are small.
   b. Voting is costly, and approval for government is high.
   c. Voting is easy, and the chances of affecting the election outcome are large.

   d. Voting is easy, but informing yourself about the candidates takes time.
   e. Approval for government is low, but voter turnout rates are high.

10. **Voters who rely on voting cues to determine their voting choice are _____.**
    a. likely to cast a reasonable vote, regardless of their information level
    b. unlikely to cast a reasonable vote, regardless of their information level
    c. likely to cast a reasonable vote, and more so if they are informed
    d. unlikely to cast a reasonable vote, and less so if they are informed
    e. neither more nor less likely to cast a reasonable vote than voters who ignore cues

11. **Weak coattails and split tickets serve as indicators that _____.**
    a. most voters don't know anything about the candidates
    b. most elections are determined by local issues
    c. most elections are determined by national issues
    d. most voters use political parties as their dominant voting cue
    e. most voters use incumbency as their dominant voting cue

Understanding the 2016 election

Analyze the issues and outcomes in the 2016 election. (Pages 320–326)

Summary

The 2016 elections were a significant victory for Republicans: they held on to majorities in the House and Senate, and the presidential election was won by the Republican candidate, Donald Trump. These Republican victories created unified government in Washington for the first time since 2009, although the expectation that Republicans would be able to enact significant policy changes must be tempered by the reality of significant differences among Republican elected officials on many issues, disagreements between Republican members of Congress and their new president, and the fact that Democratic senators can still filibuster Republican initiatives.

Practice Quiz Questions

12. **What is the most accurate statement about the role of economic conditions in the 2016 election?**
    a. Looking across the entire nation, economic uncertainty shifted votes to Trump.
    b. The Trump campaign's mobilization efforts offset the loss of support from a weak economy.
    c. Hillary Clinton's campaign blamed President Obama for slow economic growth.
    d. Economic conditions did not matter because most Americans based their vote on other issues.
    e. The Clinton campaign convinced voters that Republican Senate leaders were to blame for the poor economy.

13. How did the electoral map favor Democratic Senate candidates in 2016?

a. Democratic efforts at redistricting gave them a sharp advantage in Senate contests.

b. Economic growth was uneven across the states, particularly in Senate seats controlled by the Democrats.

c. Republicans had to defend a disproportionate number of Senate seats, and many of these seats were in states where Democrats outnumbered Republicans.

d. Independent candidates drew votes away from Republican candidates.

e. Republican candidates were more likely to lose in states where a majority of voters supported Donald Trump.

14. Which of the following is the most important factor in explaining Donald Trump's victory over Hillary Clinton in the 2016 election?

a. The fact that more Americans are Republicans than Democrats

b. Perceptions of Trump as trustworthy and honest

c. Reduced turnout by minority groups that supported Democrats in 2008 and 2012

d. Widespread dislike of Barack Obama

e. Decisions by President Obama and Senator Bernie Sanders to not campaign for Clinton

Suggested Reading

Abramson, Paul, John Aldrich, and David Rohde. *Change and Continuity in the 2012 and 2014 Elections*. Washington, DC: CQ Press, 2015.

Bartels, Larry M., and Christopher H. Achen. *Democracy for Realists: Why Elections Do Not Produce Responsive Government*. Princeton, NJ: Princeton University Press, 2016.

Cramer, Richard Ben. *What It Takes: The Way to the White House*. New York: Vintage Books, 1993.

Fiorina, Morris P. *Retrospective Voting in American National Elections*. New Haven, CT: Yale University Press, 1981.

Grimmer, Justin, Sean J. Westwood, and Solomon Messing. *The Impression of Influence: Legislator Communications, Representation, and Democratic Accountability*. Princeton, NJ: Princeton University Press, 2015.

Halperin, Mark, and John Heilemann. *Double Down: Game Change 2012*. New York; Penguin Books, 2013.

Key, V. O. *The Responsible Electorate*. New York: Vintage Books, 1966.

Popkin, Samuel. *The Reasoning Voter*. Chicago: University of Chicago Press, 1991.

Sides, John, and Lynn Vavreck. *The Gamble: Choice and Chance in the 2012 Presidential Election*. Princeton, NJ: Princeton University Press, 2013.

10

Interest Groups

Do interest groups serve the needs of the many, or the privileged few?

There are nearly 20 million college students in America today. Many of these students (or their parents) take on large student loans to fund their education. Over the last 20 years, there have been several proposals to change how these loans are made. These policy suggestions range from a system whereby banks and other financial institutions provide the money to a plan that has the federal government making the loans directly to students and their parents. Either of these proposals would reduce borrowing costs and free up billions of dollars for Pell grants and other programs benefiting college students.

At first glance, reducing the cost of student loans would be an easy sell—who would oppose making college more affordable? The answer is the companies and institutions that make money originating and managing these loans—financial institutions such as Sallie Mae, Citibank, and others. If the country were to move to direct loans, these financial institutions would lose a lucrative source of income. To avert this kind of legislation, these institutions spent millions on lobbyists to make their case before the public and Congress, emphasizing that a move to direct loans would put thousands of their employees out of work (and reminding politicians that many of those who work for the financial institutions live and vote in political swing states like Florida).

For most Americans, this story looks all too common: organized, well-funded groups lobbying against changes that would benefit broader segments of the population. How can individuals have a voice in the policy process when they are fighting against organizations that have millions of dollars and extensive connections on their side? Even if individuals try to form new groups to advance their policy goals, their battle against well-entrenched and well-funded groups does not seem like a fair fight. Surprisingly, the case of student loans is one where David appears to have beaten Goliath. Despite intense, well-funded lobbying against direct loans, legislation implementing this change was enacted in 2010—meaning that you and your parents are now able to get lower-interest loans directly from the federal government. Placed

★

CHAPTER GOALS

Define *interest groups* and describe the characteristics of different types of groups.
pages 332–341

Explain how successful interest groups overcome collective action problems.
pages 341–343

Explore the ways interest groups try to influence government policies.
pages 343–353

Evaluate interest group influence.
pages 353–358

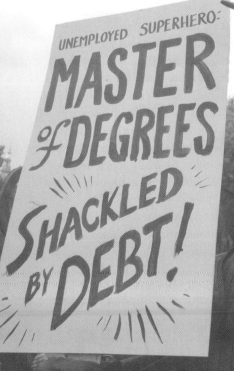

The debate over federal direct student loans pitted well-funded banks and other financial institutions against millions of college students and their parents. Did the banks' ability to lobby members of Congress and bureaucrats translate into a policy victory?

against concerns about interest group power, this example only deepens the mystery: if lobbying always works, how did the side with all the lobbyists lose the fight over direct loans?

This chapter surveys the wide range of interest groups in American politics—from large, powerful groups such as the National Rifle Association (NRA) to small organizations that lobby on issues that concern only a few Americans. Our aim is to get to the bottom of examples like student loan reform and the NRA's apparent control over gun control to understand what they really tell us about the power of interest groups in American politics. How do interest groups work? How often do they get what they want, and where does their influence come from? Do lobbying victories always go to the side with the most money?

interest group
An organization of people who share common political interests and aim to influence public policy by electioneering and lobbying.

lobbying
Efforts to influence public policy through contact with public officials on behalf of an interest group.

interest group state
A government in which most policy decisions are determined by the influence of interest groups.

What are interest groups?

Interest groups are organizations that seek to influence government policy by helping to elect candidates who support their policy goals and by lobbying elected officials and bureaucrats. In its most basic form, lobbying involves persuasion—using reports, protests, informal meetings, or other techniques to convince an elected official or bureaucrat to help enact a law, craft a regulation, or do something else that a group wants. The members of an interest group can be individual citizens, local governments, businesses, foundations or nonprofit organizations, churches, or virtually any other entity. An interest group's employees or members may lobby on the group's behalf, or a group may hire a lobbyist or lobbying firm to do the work for it. Groups may lobby on their own or work with other groups to enact compromise proposals. (See Nuts & Bolts 10.1 for some examples of the types of interest groups found in contemporary American politics.)

Sometimes interest groups are primarily political organizations. One such group is Public Citizen, which conducts research projects, lobbies legislators and bureaucrats, and tries to rally public opinion on a range of environmental, health, and energy issues. In some cases, lobbying is only one part of what an organization does. The NRA, for example, endorses candidates, contributes to campaigns, and lobbies elected officials. But it also runs gun safety classes, holds competitions, and sells gun accessories to its members. In other cases, interest group activity is almost hidden within an organization. For example, most drivers know that AAA (formerly the Automobile Association of America) provides emergency roadside service and maps, but many people are not aware that AAA is also an interest group that lobbies for policies such as limiting new drivers to daylight-only hours.

As these descriptions suggest, interest groups and lobbying are ubiquitous in American politics. Many organizations have lobbying operations or hire lobbyists to work on their behalf. You may think that you don't belong to a group that lobbies the federal government, but the odds are that you do.

In fact, one important view of American politics, *pluralism*, identifies interest groups as America's fundamental political actors.[1] Pluralists argue that most Americans participate in politics through their membership in interest groups like Public Citizen, the NRA, or even AAA. These groups lobby, try to elect candidates who share their views, and negotiate among themselves to encourage legislators to pursue policies that benefit their members. Others describe America as an interest group state, meaning that these groups are involved whenever policy is made.[2]

The business of lobbying

Interest group lobbying is heavily regulated.[3] Lobbying firms must file annual reports identifying their clients and specifying how much each client paid. Similarly, interest groups and corporations must file reports listing staff members who spent more than 20 percent of their time lobbying Congress, and detailing expenditures to lobbying firms. Also, most executive or legislative branch employees who take lobbying jobs are legally required to refrain from lobbying people in their former office or agency for one year; elected officials who become lobbyists must wait two years.

Today lobbying involves billions of dollars a year. Figure 10.1 presents annual lobbying expenditures for 2000 through 2015. As the figure shows, a total of $3.2 billion was spent on lobbying in 2015. The amount spent as well as the number of groups lobbying government has increased significantly over the last decade, although it has declined slightly in the last few years.

Why are there so many interest groups and registered lobbyists, and why are their numbers increasing? Figure 10.1 suggests that this proliferation is related to the large size and widespread influence of the federal government. Corporations lobby to get a government contract, or they want a new regulation to favor their business sector. Individuals lobby to limit what citizens can do or to get the government to relax restrictions on behavior—or to change corporate behavior. Simply put, the federal government does so many things and spends so much money that many individuals, organizations, and corporations have strong incentives for lobbying. Studies of Washington-based lobbying operations confirm this: interest groups are more likely to form around issues that have high levels of government involvement or when new programs or changes in government policy are likely.[4] Moreover, as groups form on one side of a policy question and start to lobby, people who oppose them may form their own interest groups and start lobbying as well, either separately or in concert.[5] The pressure of lobbying is especially strong when new policies are under consideration, such as in the proposed move to direct student loans. Firms such as Sallie Mae had always lobbied elected officials and bureaucrats, but the prospect of losing lucrative student loan operations gave these institutions a strong incentive to increase their efforts. In fact, the data show that over

Types of Interest Groups

Scholars often divide interest groups into categories based on who their members are or the number or kinds of things they lobby for.

- **Businesses** are for-profit enterprises that aim to influence policy in ways that will increase profits or satisfy other goals. Many corporations such as Google, Exxon, Boeing, Facebook, Citibank, and Sallie Mae have lobbying operations that petition government for contracts or favorable regulations of their firm or industry.
- **Trade or peak associations** are groups of businesses (often in the same industry) that band together to lobby for policies that benefit all of them.
- **Professional associations** represent individuals who have a common interest such as a profession.
- **Labor organizations** lobby for regulations that make it easy for workers to form labor unions, as well as for a range of other policies. The largest of these is the American Federation of Labor and Congress of Industrial Organizations (AFL-CIO).

- **Citizen groups** range from those with mass membership (such as the Sierra Club) to those that have no members but claim to speak for large segments of the population. One such group is the Family Research Council (FRC), which describes itself as "promoting the Judeo-Christian worldview as the basis for a just, free, and stable society." FRC Action (the lobbying arm of the organization) promotes a range of policies, from legislation that defines marriage as between a man and a woman to legislation that would eliminate estate taxes.
- **Institutional interest groups** are formed by nonprofits such as universities, think tanks, or museums. For example, the CIC (Committee on Institutional Cooperation) is a group of universities including the Big 10 in the Midwest that prepares research that helps individual universities make the case for continued federal support.

Growth in Spending on Lobbying and Total Federal Spending, 2000–2015

These data show that in recent years interest groups have spent several billion dollars lobbying the federal government. Does this amount seem surprisingly large or surprisingly small, given what lobbyists do and given the total federal outlays of money?

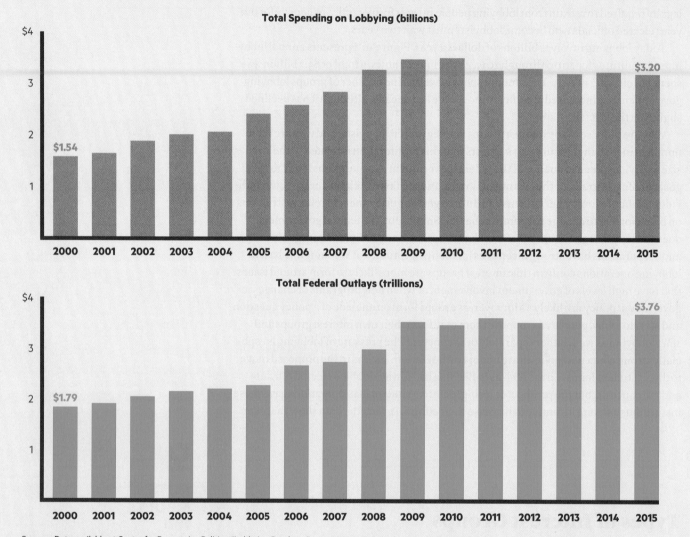

Total Spending on Lobbying (billions)

Total Federal Outlays (trillions)

Sources: Data available at Center for Responsive Politics, "Lobbying Database," www.opensecrets.org (accessed 2/7/16); Office of Management and Budget, Table 1.1, www.whitehouse.gov/omb/budget/historicals (accessed 2/1/16).

the last 15 years Sallie Mae spent over $40 million on direct lobbying, and even more was spent by associations and other groups that the firm was a member of.

The expenditures on lobbying, which are shown in Figure 10.1 (top), pay for many things. For example, at the same time that engineers at the Lockheed Martin Corporation worked to build the new F-35 fighter-attack plane for the military, Lockheed's lobbyists were working to ensure that the program retained its government funding and that Lockheed had government approval for exporting the plane to other countries. These meetings involved members of Congress, congressional staff, senior members of President Bush's (and later Obama's) staff, and the leaders of labor unions whose members worked for Lockheed.[6] Lockheed also ran ads in newspapers in Washington, D.C., promoting its new warplane. Thus, to support its goal of F-35 sales, Lockheed paid the salaries of its employees who planned and executed the lobbying effort, paid for outside lobbyists and their meetings on Capitol Hill, and spent money on broader publicity efforts.

Figure 10.2 shows lobbying expenditures for several different firms and associations during the 2015–2016 election cycle. Members of the first group—three associations and one company—were the highest spenders on lobbying during this time. For each one, it's not hard to imagine why they devote so much effort to lobbying: Realtors, for example, might be concerned about maintaining government policies that make it almost essential to hire a Realtor to help buy or sell a home. Even so, the fact that the National Association of Realtors spent only about $83 million on lobbying is something of a surprise. After all, over a million people work in real estate, generating billions of dollars in profits every year. The surprise is that real estate brokers are only willing to spend a tiny fraction of their profits to keep their near monopoly in place. The same is true for the large firms listed in Figure 10.2. Apple, for example, is one of the largest firms in the United States, but it only spends about $8 million per year on lobbying. And only one of the influential interest groups in Figure 10.2 (the AARP) spends more than $10 million per year on lobbying. Clearly, the big spenders on lobbying are exceptions to the rule, and most interest groups and firms spend relatively little on lobbying.[7] The group that

FIGURE 10.2

Variation in Lobbying Expenditures

Lobbying expenditures vary widely. Some influential groups (such as the U.S. Chamber of Commerce) spend hundreds of millions of dollars a year, but many other influential groups (such as the NARAL and the Family Research Council) spend relatively little. How can groups have influence over government policy despite spending almost nothing on lobbying?

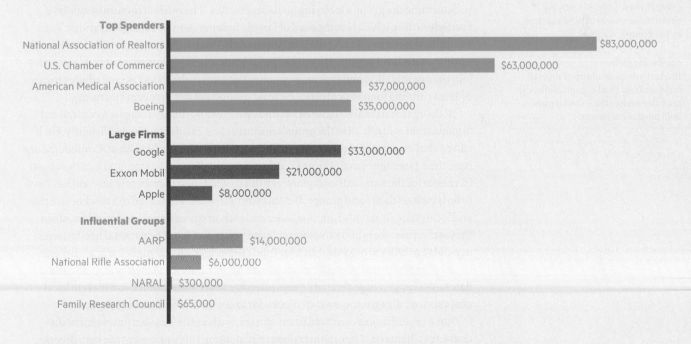

Top Spenders
- National Association of Realtors: $83,000,000
- U.S. Chamber of Commerce: $63,000,000
- American Medical Association: $37,000,000
- Boeing: $35,000,000

Large Firms
- Google: $33,000,000
- Exxon Mobil: $21,000,000
- Apple: $8,000,000

Influential Groups
- AARP: $14,000,000
- National Rifle Association: $6,000,000
- NARAL: $300,000
- Family Research Council: $65,000

Sources: Data available at Center for Responsive Politics, "Lobbying Database," www.opensecrets.org/lobby/index.php (accessed 11/6/16).

sends a turkey to the White House for a ceremonial pardon every year at Thanksgiving, the National Turkey Federation, spends less than a hundred thousand dollars every year to lobby the federal government on a relatively small range of issues. Many other groups spend even less, barely scraping together enough cash to send someone to plead their case in Washington. In fact, a few groups account for a substantial fraction of total lobbying expenditures.

Other companies lobby through their membership in trade associations. Consider the National Beer Wholesalers Association (NBWA), a nationwide group of local businesses that buy beer from brewers and resell it to stores and restaurants. NBWA's principal lobbying goal is to ensure that laws remain in place requiring intermediaries between beer producers and the stores, bars, and restaurants that sell beer to consumers. If the rules change to allow beer producers to deal with the end sellers directly, then NBWA's members would likely lose business.

Although the amount of money spent on lobbying by interest groups may seem like a lot (and often leads to calls for restrictions on lobbying, as discussed in the Take a Stand feature), it is small compared with how much is at stake.[8] The federal government now spends more than $3 trillion every year. In recent years, spending by interest groups and by the lobbying arms of organizations and corporations amounts to $3 billion every year. That's a lot of money, but it's still only about 1 percent of total federal spending. This difference raises a critical question: If interest groups could control policy choices by spending money on lobbying, why aren't they spending more?

Organizational structures

There are two main models of interest group structure. Most large, well-known organizations like the AARP and the NRA are centralized groups. These national organizations typically have headquarters in Washington, D.C., field offices in large state capitals, and members nationwide. Their defining feature is that the organization's leadership is concentrated in its headquarters. These leaders have the responsibility to determine the group's lobbying goals and tactics. The other structural model is a confederation, which is composed of largely independent, local organizations. For example, the National Independent Automobile Dealers Association (NIADA) is made up of 50 state-level organizations that provide membership benefits to car dealers who join the organization and that raise much of the money that NIADA contributes to candidates running for political office (several million dollars in recent elections).

Both organizational structures have advantages and disadvantages. A centralized organization controls all of the group's resources and can deploy them efficiently, but it can be challenging for these groups to find out what their members want. Confederations have the advantage of maintaining independent chapters at the state and local levels, so it is easier for the national headquarters to learn what their members want—all they have to do is contact their local groups. But this strength is closely related to a weakness. State and local chapters mostly function independently of the national headquarters, since they attract members and raise money largely on their own. The national headquarters depends on the local organizations for funds to pay its staff and make campaign contributions, and in return allow the locals to direct contributions to their preferred candidates. As a result, confederated groups often are beset with conflict, as different local chapters may disagree over what to lobby for and which candidates to support.

Some organizations are hard to categorize, such as the Tea Party movement discussed in Chapter 8. The organizations that make up this movement are very diverse. Some hold meetings or public protests, some endorse candidates, and some simply consist of a website run by one or two people. The issues that motivate each Tea Party

---

trade association
An interest group composed of companies in the same business or industry (the same "trade") that lobbies for policies that benefit members of the group.

"

If you can't eat their food, drink their booze, take their money and then vote against them, you've got no business being up here.

—**Jessie Unruh,** California state legislator

centralized groups
Interest groups that have a headquarters, usually in Washington, D.C., as well as members and field offices throughout the country. In general, these groups' lobbying decisions are made at headquarters by the group leaders.

confederations
Interest groups made up of several independent, local organizations that provide much of their funding and hold most of the power.

Restrictions on Interest Group Lobbying

Under current congressional rules, members of Congress and their staffs are severely limited in the size of gifts they can receive from lobbyists. Similar restrictions had existed for decades but were tightened in the mid-2000s after it was revealed that former congressional staffer-turned-lobbyist Jack Abramoff had used "golf junkets, free meals at the restaurant he owned, seats at sporting events, and, in some cases, old-fashioned cash" to lobby members of Congress.[a] The current restrictions limit members and their staffs to accepting gifts only if they are valued at less than $50—moreover, the total worth of the gifts that any lobbyist can give to a particular member of Congress or staffer is limited to $100 per year. Are these restrictions fair? Do they help or hurt the political process?

Keep the rules, and maybe tighten them.
Supporting this option seems like a no-brainer. These regulations are based on a sensible intuition that laws are needed to prevent well-funded, unscrupulous lobbyists from offering inducements to members of Congress and their staffs in return for policy change. Simply put, groups that can send people to Washington to wine and dine members of Congress, congressional staff, and bureaucrats, might gain a significant advantage over those who are unable to do so. Even if a fancy lunch doesn't buy a legislator's vote, it might help with access—that is, give the group a chance to make their arguments and perhaps change some minds. In this way, rules that allow even small gifts create an advantage for some interest groups (those that can open a Washington office or hire lobbyists) and a disadvantage for others. As a result, many reform proposals would go further, preventing lobbyists from giving anything to a member of Congress, legislative staffer, or bureaucrat—even a cup of coffee.

Relax the rules (a little).
Some argue that worries about interest group influence seem a little overstated. Suppose an interest group takes some congressional staff out to lunch or invites them to an evening reception. Nice treatment might increase the chances that the staffers would meet with the group's lobbyists or look at the group's proposals. But congressional staff and the legislators they work for are going to support a group's proposals only if they help the member's constituents or if they move policy in a way the member favors, not just because of an interest group's free lunch. Also, the targets of lobbying know

📷 When scandals surrounding Jack Abramoff came to light in 2005, many Americans considered him a typical lobbyist. Abramoff's actions were illegal, but the question remains: Are his tactics common in Washington, or was he a rare exception?

what's going on—they're not going to think a lobbyist is their new friend and ally just because of a small gift.

Finally, there are downsides to tight controls on these gifts and perks. The current rules on lobbyists' gifts create a lot of paperwork for members and their staffs, who have to file reports on just about anything they receive from a lobbyist, even if that individual is a former colleague, neighbor, or friend. The rules are also extremely complicated—for example, legislators are allowed to eat the hors d'oeuvres provided at a reception, but they cannot sit down to a full meal without violating the gift restrictions. The disclosure requirements are also a burden to smaller interest groups and firms, which have to document everything they do on complex forms. As a result, members of Congress, their staff, interest groups, and lobbying firms spend considerable time and effort on documenting small gifts that are unlikely to have any effect on policy outcomes.

take a stand

1. To what extent do you think current congressional rules limiting the size of gifts that members of Congress and their staffers can receive from lobbyists have curbed illegal behavior by interest groups?

2. Are these rules aimed at exceptional cases or average interest groups?

organization also vary widely, from opposition to President Obama to calls for radical changes in government. Virtually all lack formal dues-paying members, a headquarters, or a formal organizational structure, and few engage in the wide range of lobbying activities that we describe later in this chapter. Moreover, it is unclear whether many of these organizations will survive more than a few months or years. For all these reasons, very few of the organizations that identify themselves as part of the Tea Party are interest groups as we describe them here, although some may evolve into formal interest groups in the future.

Staff

Interest group staff fall into two categories: experts on the group's main policy areas and people with useful government connections and knowledge of procedures. The first group includes scientists, engineers, and others with advanced degrees; the second is dominated by people who have worked inside government as elected officials, bureaucrats, or legislative staff.[9] Sometimes these former members of government are also policy experts, but their unique contribution is their knowledge of how government works and their relationships with officeholders and other former coworkers.

The practice of moving from a government position to a job with an interest group or lobbying firm, or of transitioning from a lobbyist to an officeholder, is often called the **revolving door**.[10] For example, as of 2016, over half of the members of Congress who retired at the end of the 113th Congress had moved to lobbying jobs.[11] The percentages are similar for congressional staff and bureaucrats. The concern is that past government employees might capitalize on personal ties with their former colleagues—or that people working in government may favor a corporation that might hire them as a lobbyist in the future. These concerns have led to proposals to ban former elected officials, staff, and bureaucrats from working as lobbyists for some time period after they have left government service—and banning former lobbyists named to government positions from administering programs that they previously lobbied for.

Restrictions on the revolving door have costs as well as benefits. On the one hand, people who have worked in industry or as lobbyists know a particular field and the relevant laws, making them well qualified to work in this area of the executive branch. Similarly, former officeholders, congressional staff, and bureaucrats are attractive to lobbying firms, as they have firsthand knowledge of how policies are made and enjoy established relationships with people in government. Thus, a ban on hiring lobbyists may lead to a shortage of experienced candidates for government positions. On the other hand, the problem with the revolving door is that people in government may try to help particular firms and interest groups in return for a well-paid position after they leave government service. Or, when the influence works in the opposite direction, lobbyists-turned-lawmakers may favor the firms and organizations that once employed them. It is very hard to craft restrictions that avoid these problems.

Membership

Interest groups can also be distinguished by the size of their membership and the members' role in the group's activities. Some are **mass associations** with many dues-paying

---

President Barack Obama uses the headquarters of the U.S. Chamber of Commerce to propose making the corporate tax code simpler. By having Obama speak at their headquarters, the Chamber signals their strong support for the proposal, in effect lobbying every member of Congress without having to make a single visit to the Capital. @USChamber

DID YOU KNOW?

427

former members of Congress were registered lobbyists as of 2015.
Source: Opensecrets.org

revolving door
The movement of individuals from government positions to jobs with interest groups or lobbying firms, and vice versa.

mass associations
Interest groups that have a large number of dues-paying individuals as members.

members. One example is the Sierra Club, which has over 2 million members who each pay annual dues of about $30. Besides keeping its members informed about the implementation of environmental policy in Washington, D.C., the Sierra Club endorses judicial nominees and candidates for elected positions, files lawsuits to increase environmental protection on government projects, and works with members of Congress to develop legislative proposals. The group's members elect the organization's board of directors.

Yet not all mass associations give members a say in selecting their leaders or determining their mission. To join the AARP, which has more than 40 million members, you have to be at least 50 years old and pay dues of about $16 per year. Members get discounts on insurance, car rentals, and hotels, as well as driver safety courses and help doing their taxes. The AARP claims to lobby for policies its members favor, but members actually have no control over which legislative causes the group chooses. Moreover, the AARP does not poll members to determine its issue positions, nor do members pick AARP leadership.

Peak associations have a different type of membership,[12] exemplified by the Business-Industry Political Action Committee (BIPAC). This association of several hundred businesses and trade associations aims to elect "pro-business individuals" to Congress.[13] Individuals cannot join peak associations—they may work for member companies or organizations, but they cannot become dues-paying members on their own. The umbrella organization that led efforts to enact direct funding for student loans, the Student Aid Alliance, was another such peak association.

Resources

The resources that interest groups use to support their lobbying efforts are people, money, and expertise. We examine interest group strategies in a later section; here we emphasize that a group's resources influence its available lobbying strategies. Some large groups have sufficient funding and staff to pursue a wide range of strategies, whereas some smaller groups with fewer resources have only a few lobbying options.

People A crucial resource for most interest groups is the membership. Group members can write to or meet with elected officials, travel to Washington for demonstrations, and even offer expertise or advice to their leaders. When the "members" of a group are corporations, as is the case with trade associations, CEOs and other corporate staff can help with the group's lobbying efforts.

Many mass organizations try to get their members involved in the lobbying process. MoveOn.org, for example, has a Web page that helps people send letters to the editors of various national and local newspapers. MoveOn.org hopes to bring public attention to its political priorities by getting these Web-generated letters printed. Using the organization's site, you provide your address, choose from a list of papers to contact, and compose a message—using MoveOn.org's "talking points," which cover a wide range of issues—if you so choose. The page automatically imports your message into correctly addressed e-mails to your selected newspapers.[14] Other groups have similar pages that send e-mails to members of Congress or to the president.

Interest groups' ability to use people as a resource faces two major challenges. First, it requires having members, and recruiting new members can be difficult and expensive. The second challenge is motivating members to participate. As we discuss later, although some interest groups have managed to change government policy by persuading their members to write to and visit elected officials, the more common situation is that interest groups ask for members' help but receive little response.[15]

peak associations
Interest groups whose members are businesses or other organizations rather than individuals.

Many interest groups speak for large numbers of Americans, but some lobby for changes that would benefit only a few people or a single corporation. The Coalition for Luggage Security, for example, has only one member: a company that specializes in shipping travelers' baggage, which would gain considerable business if the coalition's lobbying efforts succeeded.

Money Virtually everything interest groups do, from meeting with elected officials to fighting for what they want in court, can be purchased as services. Money can also go toward campaign contributions or developing and running campaign ads. And, of course, money is necessary to fund interest groups' everyday operations.

Well-funded interest groups and firms have a considerable advantage in the lobbying process. If they need an expert, a lobbyist, or a lawyer, they can hire one or open a Washington office to increase contacts with legislators and bureaucrats. They can pay for campaign ads and make contributions to candidates and parties, whereas groups with less cash cannot use these strategies. Smaller firms might join a trade association to lobby for policies that help all of the association's members. The importance of money for interest group operations is evident in their funding appeals to members. For example, the donations page from the Sierra Club's website shows that supporters can give a membership as a gift, join as a life member, or pay dues monthly. They can make commemorative or memorial gifts, set up a planned giving scheme, or donate stock. The group even offers gift-giving plans for non-U.S. residents and a Spanish-language version of its donations page.

Interest groups use a variety of tactics to draw attention to their concerns, including events designed to generate media coverage. People for the Ethical Treatment of Animals (PETA), known for its bold media campaigns, stationed a life-size mechanical elephant outside the Ringling Bros. circus to protest the company's treatment of its elephants. @peta

Still, groups can be effective without spending much. They can rely on members to lobby for them, hire staff willing to work for low pay because they share the group's goals, or cite published research rather than funding their own studies to bolster their case for policy change. Moreover, the fact that a group has lots of money is no guarantee that its lobbying efforts will succeed. As we discussed earlier, even though Sallie Mae and the other firms that opposed student loan reform spent a considerable sum on lobbying, they were unable to prevent this policy change.

Expertise Expertise takes many forms. Some lobbying firms (especially those that employ former members of Congress or congressional staff) have inside information on the kinds of policies that might be enacted in the House or Senate. Interest groups with dues-paying members (such as the AARP) can poll their membership to find out what they would like government to do. Groups can also employ staff (or can hire experts) to conduct research or develop policy proposals. A firm's in-house lobbyists can provide information about how a change in government policy will affect the firm's profits and employment. All of this information can be deployed to persuade elected officials or bureaucrats about the merits of a group's or a firm's demands (as well as the political consequences of inaction) and offer ready-made solutions to the problems the group has identified.

Consider the AARP, whose website offers a vast array of research and analyses, including information about seniors' part-time employment, how people invest their 401(k) retirement accounts, and a comparison of long-term care policies in Europe and the United States.[16] The AARP's lobbyists use this research when arguing for policy changes in their public testimony and in private meetings with members of Congress and congressional staff. The AARP also routinely surveys their members to assess support for different policy options. And they hire former members of Congress and bureaucrats so they are well informed about the preferences of these groups.

Of course, only a few interest groups can match the AARP's wealth of expertise. Individual lobbyists also vary in what they can offer to a group or corporation. Former members of Congress might know a lot about policy options and the preferences of their former colleagues but be less informed about public opinion or the business challenges faced by a firm that hires them to lobby. In-house lobbyists might know a lot about the firm they work for but much less about congressional preferences. And an interest group's policy expert might know everything there is to know about current government policies in some area but nothing about how to sell new proposals to a skeptical member of Congress.

"Why Should I Care?"

When you think of a lobbyist, don't imagine a guy in an expensive suit carrying a briefcase of cash (or a campaign contribution). More often, people become lobbyists because they believe in the goals of the group they represent. And they generally don't wear expensive suits. Understanding who lobbyists really are, and what they really do, is key to evaluating whether or not they have too much influence in American politics.

Getting organized

★
EXPLAIN HOW SUCCESSFUL INTEREST GROUPS OVERCOME COLLECTIVE ACTION PROBLEMS

A new interest group's first priority is to get organized, which involves raising the money needed to hire staff, renting an office, setting up a website, and formulating policy goals and a lobbying strategy. In some cases, a lobbying firm is hired to perform these jobs. Once organized, the group must continue to attract funds for ongoing operations. These tasks are not easy. Even if a group of people (or corporations) shares the same goals, the challenge is to persuade them to donate time or money to the lobbying operation.

The logic of collective action

Research has found that a problem arises when a group of individuals (or corporations) has an opportunity to make itself better off through the provision of public goods. (For interest groups, the public good would be a change in government policy desired by group members.) Scholars refer to these situations as involving collective action. Even when all members of a group agree on the desirability of a public good and the costs of producing the good are negligible, cooperation is neither easy nor automatic (see Nuts & Bolts 10.2). Scholars refer to this situation as a **collective action problem**.

The logic of collective action provides insights into how interest groups are organized and how they make lobbying decisions. First, the logic of collective action tells us that group formation is not automatic. Even when a number of citizens want the same things from government, their common interest may not lead them to organize. Some groups remain latent and are not able to organize, which explains why certain debates in Washington feature well-organized groups on one side of the issue but few on the other. Unless people can easily see benefits from participating, which does not happen often, group leaders must worry about finding the right strategies to get people to join. Thus, given the logic of collective action, attracting members is just as important for a group's success as its lobbying strategy.

Society is full of groups of like-minded people (such as college students) who do not organize to lobby or who choose to engage in **free riding** and so enjoy the benefits of organizations without participating. Most organizations develop mechanisms to

collective action problem
A situation in which the members of a group would benefit by working together to produce some outcome, but each individual is better off refusing to cooperate and reaping benefits from those who do the work.

free riding
The result of relying on others to contribute to a collective effort while failing to participate on one's own behalf, yet still benefiting from the group's successes.

Collective Action Problems

NUTS & BOLTS

10.2

What is collective action?

"Collective action" refers to situations in which a group of individuals can work together to provide themselves with public goods. For example, changes in government policy (such as those lobbied for by interest groups) are public goods: if the government changes policy, such as increasing the size of college tuition grants, everyone who is eligible for the grants benefits from the increase.

What are the problems?

Situations like those described above make it hard to motivate people to contribute to collective efforts, because each would-be member can see that his or her contribution would be only a minuscule portion of what the group needs to succeed. Regardless of how many other people join, an individual is better off free riding—refusing to join but still being able to enjoy the benefits of any successes the group might have.

Why are collective action problems important?

Groups of like-minded citizens who seek changes in government policy may be unable to lobby effectively because they cannot solve their collective action problem. And organization matters. Groups that remain unorganized are less likely to get what they want from government.

How do interest groups solve collective action problems?

Interest groups solve collection action problems in three ways: (1) like some labor unions, they force people to join; (2) they are small enough where every member's voice matters and free rider problems are lessened; and (3) they encourage a larger, engaged membership by offering incentives for people to join and participate.

---

solidary benefits

Satisfaction derived from the experience of working with like-minded people, even if the group's efforts do not achieve the desired impact.

purposive benefits

Satisfaction derived from the experience of working toward a desired policy goal, even if the goal is not achieved.

coercion

A method of eliminating nonparticipation or free riding by potential group members by requiring participation, as in many labor unions.

promote cooperation in such situations. These solutions fall into three categories: benefits from participation, coercion, and selective incentives.

Studies of political parties and interest groups find that some individuals volunteer out of a sense of duty or because they enjoy working together toward a common goal. Scholars refer to these benefits of participation as either **solidary benefits**, which come from working with like-minded people, or **purposive benefits**, which come from working to achieve a desired policy goal.[17] If most people were spurred to political action because of participation benefits, the free rider problem wouldn't exist. However, when these benefits are not enough, groups try other measures in order to organize.

Another way to solve the free rider problem is through **coercion**, or requiring participation. Consider labor unions. They provide public goods to workers by negotiating with management on behalf of worker-members over pay and work requirements. Why don't union members free ride? Because in many cases they have to join the union: union shop laws require them to pay union dues as a condition of their employment. These laws are critical to unions; states with laws that make union membership optional typically have weak unions—if any.

AAA (formerly the Automobile Association of America) is a well-known provider of emergency road service, yet few people are aware of its role as an interest group that lobbies for a wide range of policy changes and builds awareness of key transportation issues. #AAA

DUU
IT COSTS MORE THAN YOU THINK!

ESTIMATED COSTS FOR A
FIRST DUI CONVICTION:

Fine (minimum)	$390
Penalties	$1,245
Vehicle Tow/Storage	$350
Alcohol Education Class	$575
Victim Restitution Fund	$140
DMV License Re-Issue	$125
Booking	$170
Insurance Increase	$10,154
Legal Fees	$2,500
TOTAL COST	**$15,649**

Finally, **selective incentives** are benefits given only to the members of an interest group. These incentives are not public goods; an individual can receive a selective incentive only by joining the group. Thus, interest groups offer selective incentives in the hope of providing a new reason to participate. One of the most interesting cases of selective incentives provided by an interest group involves AAA. Members with car trouble can call AAA at any time for emergency service. AAA also provides annotated maps and travel guides to its members, a travel agency, a car-buying service, discounts at hotels and restaurants, and other benefits. These services mask the interest group role of AAA. For example, its Foundation for Traffic Safety delivers research reports to legislators on topics ranging from lowering the blood alcohol level threshold that legally defines drunk driving to increasing the restrictions on driving by senior citizens.[18] It's unlikely that many AAA members—who join for the selective incentives— are aware of the organization's lobbying efforts. The inducements drive membership, which funds the organization's lobbying operation.

selective incentives
Benefits that can motivate participation in a group effort because they are available only to those who participate, such as member services offered by interest groups.

The logic of collective action says that organization is neither automatic nor easy. Rather than complaining about how many lobbyists there are or how much they spend, we should consider whether some groups in society are ignored because they are never able to organize themselves and lobby for their concerns.

"Why Should I Care?"

Interest group strategies

Once a group has organized and determined its goals, the next step is to decide how to lobby. There are two types of possible tactics: **inside strategies**, which are actions taken in Washington, D.C., and **outside strategies**, which involve actions taken outside Washington, D.C. (see How It Works: Lobbying the Federal Government).[19] In general, these strategies involve a single group that is working on its own, sometimes in opposition to another group or groups. However, as we discuss later, interest groups sometimes work together toward common legislative goals.

★

EXPLORE THE WAYS INTEREST GROUPS TRY TO INFLUENCE GOVERNMENT POLICIES

Inside strategies

Inside strategies involve some form of contact with elected officials or bureaucrats. Thus, inside strategies require a group to establish an office in Washington, D.C., or to hire a lobbying firm to act on its behalf.

Direct Lobbying When interest group staff meet with officeholders or bureaucrats, they plead their case through **direct lobbying**, asking government officials to change policy in line with the group's goals.[20] Such contacts are very common—on any given day, each congressional or administrative office gets phone calls, visits, or e-mails from dozens of lobbyists.

    Direct lobbying is generally aimed at officials and bureaucrats who are sympathetic to the group's goals.[21] In their efforts, interest groups and their representatives do not

inside strategies
The tactics employed within Washington, D.C., by interest groups seeking to achieve their policy goals.

outside strategies
The tactics employed outside Washington, D.C., by interest groups seeking to achieve their policy goals.

direct lobbying
Attempts by interest group staff to influence policy by speaking with elected officials or bureaucrats.

Lobbying the Federal Government: Inside and Outside Strategies

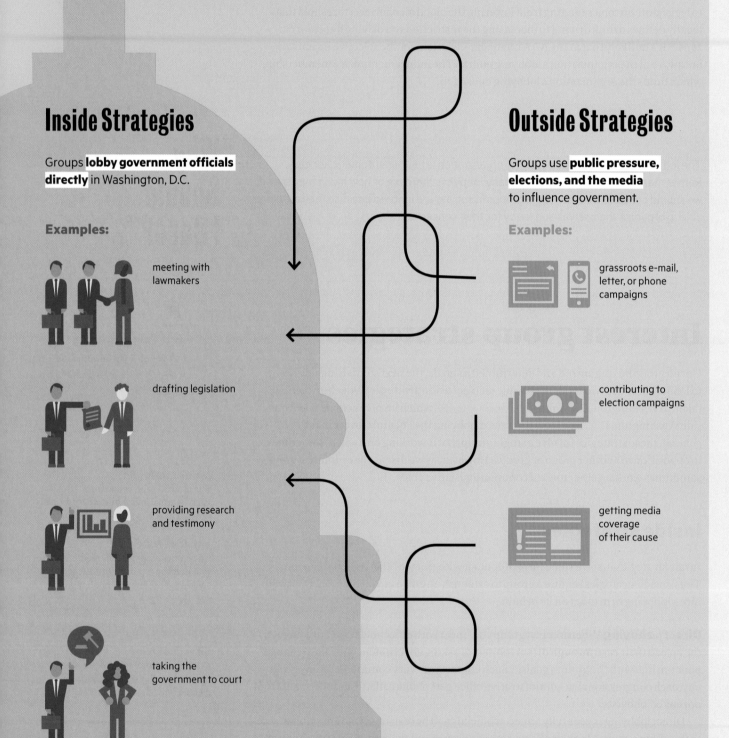

Inside Strategies

Groups **lobby government officials directly** in Washington, D.C.

Examples:

meeting with lawmakers

drafting legislation

providing research and testimony

taking the government to court

Outside Strategies

Groups use **public pressure, elections, and the media** to influence government.

Examples:

grassroots e-mail, letter, or phone campaigns

contributing to election campaigns

getting media coverage of their cause

AIPAC and the Iran Nuclear Deal

Throughout negotiations between Iran and the United States and its allies over limiting Iran's nuclear research program, and especially during congressional consideration of this agreement, the American Israel Public Affairs Committee (AIPAC)—an influential pro-Israel interest group—strongly opposed the deal. Using their connections throughout the country and in Washington, as well as their high level of funding, AIPAC engaged in a diverse set of lobbying activities with the goal of persuading members of Congress to disapprove the deal before a crucial deadline passed and the deal was enacted.

● Inside strategies

● Outside strategies

Do we have a deal?

July 14, 2015
The United States and its negotiation partners announce details of their **nuclear agreement with Iran.**

And they're off!

July 15, 2015
AIPAC announces its opposition to the Iran deal and **forms a new advocacy group to lobby** against the agreement.

Gathering forces.

July 2015
AIPAC organizes a series of **speeches** and **town hall meetings** in congressional districts and states of undecided legislators.

Making introductions.

July 28–29, 2015
AIPAC arranges a "Washington fly-in"—a series of **meetings between lawmakers and hundreds of constituents** who are opposed to the deal.

Running ads.

August 2015
AIPAC spends over **20 million dollars** running **television ads** opposing the deal in 23 states.

Funding trips.

August 2015
AIPAC organizes a **trip to Israel for 58 members of Congress** to meet with Israeli citizens and officials.

Going right to the source.

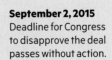

August 2015
AIPAC representatives **lobby undecided senators** to oppose the agreement.

We still have a deal!

September 2, 2015
Deadline for Congress to disapprove the deal passes without action.

While AIPAC's efforts were **ultimately unsuccessful**, they illustrate the many ways interest groups can work to influence the policy process.

Critical Thinking

1. **Despite its lobbying efforts, AIPAC's** side did not prevail in this situation. If you were advising them, what lobbying strategy would you suggest they spend more time on, if any? Why?

2. **Suppose you are the head of AIPAC.** How could you use the Iran agreement to illustrate AIPAC's power and influence in Washington, despite the fact that the group's position did not prevail?

try to convert opponents into supporters; rather, they help like-minded legislators secure policy changes that they both want. Their help can range from sharing information about proposed changes, to providing lists of legislators who might be persuadable, to drafting legislative proposals or regulations.

These efforts usually do not involve a trade in which the group expects legislative action in return for its help. Rather, the group's efforts are a way of helping legislators to enact policies that they prefer—and that the group prefers as well.[22] The legislator knows that a like-minded group has no reason to misrepresent its policy information. In fact, the legislator and his or her staff will be happy to meet with the group's representatives, as their information may be vital to the legislator's efforts to enact legislation, manage the bureaucracy, or keep the support of constituents back home in the district.[23] For example, corporations that stood to lose business if the government moved to direct student loans lobbied legislators whose districts included the companies' call centers and headquarters. For these legislators, helping these companies might be good public policy, but it was also a way of preserving their constituents' jobs.

Interest groups also contact legislators who disagree with their goals as well as fence-sitters (legislators who are not supporters or opponents), with the goal of converting them into supporters. These efforts are less extensive than the lobbying of supporters, however, because opponents are unlikely to change their minds unless a group can provide new information that causes them to rethink their position. But lobbying opponents may be useful if it forces opposing interest groups to use some of their limited resources in lobbying their own supporters to make sure that they do not change their position.[24]

As these descriptions indicate, interest groups place a high priority on maintaining access to their lobbying targets and being able to present their arguments, regardless of whether they expect to get what they want. Of course, interest groups want to achieve their policy goals, but access is the necessary first step that makes persuasion possible. Therefore, many interest groups try to keep their efforts low-key, providing information to friends and opponents alike, avoiding threats or harsh words, in the hope that they will leave a favorable impression and be able to gain access the next time they want to lobby these opponents. After all, people who are opposed to a group's current priorities one day may agree with them on some future issue.

Whom do these groups contact for direct lobbying? Analysis of lobbyists' annual disclosure forms shows that they contact people throughout the federal government: elected officials, members of the president's staff, and bureaucrats in the executive branch. They seek this wide range of contacts because different officials play distinct roles in the policy-making process and thus have various types of influence. Members of Congress shape legislation and budgets; members of the president's staff influence the formation of new policies and obtain presidential consent for new laws; and executive branch bureaucrats change the ways regulations are written and policies are implemented.

Drafting Legislation and Regulations Interest groups sometimes draft legislative proposals and regulations, which they deliver to legislators and bureaucrats as part of their lobbying efforts.[25] Surveys of interest groups found that more than three-quarters reported drafting proposals for members of Congress.[26] In the case of direct student loans, for example, the antireform forces developed a plan that would cut fees and lower interest rates for student loans but preserve the existing system.

Interest groups do not give proposals to just anyone. As with direct lobbying, they seek out legislators who already support their cause and who have significant influence within Congress. A lobbying effort aimed at cutting interest rates on student loans would target supporters of this change who are also members of the congressional committee with jurisdiction over student loan programs—preferably someone who chairs the committee or one of its subcommittees.[27] Interest groups also lobby bureaucrats to influence the details of new regulations.[28] If the types of regulations involved can go into effect without congressional approval, then lobbying can give groups what they want directly. But even if new regulations require approval by Congress or White House staff, interest groups can increase their chances of success by getting involved in the initial drafting.

Research Interest groups often prepare research reports on topics of interest to the group. For example, Public Citizen featured on its website a series of research reports on topics such as medical malpractice, the house-building industry, toy safety, and international trade.[29] Such reports serve multiple purposes. They may sway public opinion or help persuade elected officials or bureaucrats, and they are another way for lobbyists to directly influence an industry. They also help interest group staff claim expertise on some aspect of public policy. Members of Congress are more likely to accept a group's legislative proposal if they think that the group's staff has research to back up their claims. Journalists are also more likely to respond to an interest group's requests for publicity if they think that the group's staff has evidence supporting their claims.

The American Civil Liberties Union is an interest group that often uses litigation strategies in its efforts to change government policy. Here, members of the ACLU chapter in Washington State announce their filing of an abortion rights lawsuit against several local hospitals. #ACLU

Hearings Interest group staff often testify before congressional committees. In part, this activity is aimed at informing members of Congress about issues that matter to the interest group. For example, the NRA's website shows that its staff has testified in favor of "right-to-carry" laws as well as laws that would grant immunity to gun manufacturers for harm committed with weapons they produced.[30]

Litigation Another inside strategy involves taking the government to court. In bringing their case, interest groups can argue that the government's actions are not consistent with the Constitution or that the government has misinterpreted the existing law.[31] Interest groups can bring these actions via lawyers on their staff, a hired law firm, or lawyers who will work for no fees. Interest groups can also become involved in an existing case by filing amicus curiae ("friend of the court") briefs, documents that offer judges the group's rationale for how the case should be decided. The drawback of litigation is that it is costly and time-consuming—cases can take years to work through the federal court system. At a minimum, groups that use the litigation strategy generally combine it with direct lobbying or other strategies.

Working Together To increase their chances for success, interest groups can work together in their lobbying efforts, formulating a common strategy and future plans. In general, these collaborations are short-term efforts focused on achieving a specific outcome, like supporting or opposing the confirmation of judicial and cabinet nominees.[32] The fight against direct student loans, for example, involved corporations such as Citibank and Sallie Mae, along with the U.S. Chamber of Commerce. Support for change came from the Student Aid Alliance, a group comprised of colleges, think tanks, and associations of law schools and other professional schools. This group had formed in 1999 to lobby for increases in student aid, then stayed together to lobby on other issues.

Why do groups work together? The most obvious reason lies in the power of large numbers: legislators are more likely to respond, or at least provide access, when many groups with large or diverse memberships are all asking for the same thing.[33]

The problem with working together is that groups may agree on general goals but disagree on specifics, thereby requiring negotiation. If differences cannot be bridged, groups may undertake separate and possibly conflicting lobbying efforts or decide against lobbying entirely. For example, although there are many groups pressing for climate change legislation, they have not developed a unified lobbying effort. The problem? The groups disagree on which policies should be implemented, who should pay for them, and whether the government should aid companies that would be forced to purchase new antipollution equipment. Without an agreement, working alone seems a better strategy.[34]

Outside strategies

Outside strategies involve things that groups do across the country rather than in Washington. Again, these activities can be orchestrated by the group or be organized by a firm hired by the group.

Grassroots Lobbying Directly involving interest group members in lobbying efforts is called grassroots lobbying. Members may send letters, make telephone calls, participate in a protest, or express their demands in other ways. Many groups encourage grassroots lobbying. For example, the AARP's website has a page where members can find contact information for their representatives in Congress.[35] Other links allow members to e-mail or to fax their representatives letters that are prewritten by the AARP to express the group's positions on various proposals, such as pension protection legislation and proposals to curb identity theft. The AARP also organizes district meetings with elected officials and encourages its members to attend.

Mass protests are another form of grassroots lobbying. In addition to trying to capture the attention of government officials, mass protests also seek to draw media attention, with the idea of publicizing the group's goals and perhaps gaining new members or financial support. During the 2013 debate over gun control, groups such as Moms Demand Action for Gun Sense in America held many such rallies—although their efforts were overshadowed in some communities by counterprotests in which gun owners took advantage of open-carry laws to attend rallies while brandishing assault rifles and shotguns.[36]

Grassroots strategies are useful because elected officials are loath to act against a large group of citizens who care enough about an issue to express their position.[37] These officials may not agree with the group's goals, but they are likely to at least arrange a meeting with its staff, so that they appear willing to

grassroots lobbying
A lobbying strategy that relies on participation by group members, such as a protest or a letter-writing campaign.

Mass protests such as the 2014 People's Climate March in New York City are intended to attract media attention and demonstrate the depth of public support for a group's goals.

learn about their constituents' demands.[38] However, these member-based strategies work only for a small set of interest groups. To take advantage of these strategies, groups first need a large number of members. Legislators begin to pay attention to a letter-writing campaign only when they receive several thousand pieces of mail.

In addition, for grassroots lobbying to be effective, the letters or other efforts have to come from a Congress member's own constituents. The effectiveness of grassroots lobbying also depends on perceptions of how much a group has done to motivate participation. Suppose a representative gets 10,000 e-mails demanding an increase in student aid. However, virtually all the messages contain the same appeal because they were generated and sent from a group's website. Congressional staff refer to these efforts as **Astroturf lobbying**.[39] Given the similarity of the letters, the representative may discount the effort, believing that it says more about the group's ability to make campaign participation accessible than it does about the number of district residents who strongly support an increase in student aid. Even so, politicians are sometimes reluctant to completely dismiss Astroturf efforts—the fact that so many people participated, even with facilitation by an interest group, means that their demands must at least be considered.

Mobilizing Public Opinion One strategy related to grassroots lobbying involves trying to change what the public thinks about an issue. The goal is not to get citizens to do anything but to influence public opinion in the hope that elected officials will see this change and respond by enacting (or opposing) new laws or regulations to keep their constituents happy.

Virtually all groups try to influence opinion. Most maintain a Web page that presents their message, and they write press releases to get media coverage. Any contact with citizens, whether to encourage them to join the group, contribute money, or engage in grassroots lobbying, also involves elements of persuasion—trying to transform citizens into supporters and supporters into true believers and even activists. In the case of gun control, for example, the NRA has an aggressive campaign to make it easier for members to contact their elected officials and to express their opinions.

A focused mobilization effort involves contacting large numbers of potential supporters through e-mail, phone calls, direct mail, television advertising, print media, social media, and websites. In order to get legislators to respond, a group has to persuade large numbers of people to get involved. One example of mobilization occurs during congressional hearings on nominees to the Supreme Court or other federal judgeships. One study found that about one-third of the groups that lobbied for or against these nominees also deployed direct mail and leaflets and ran phone banks as a way to influence public opinion.[40]

Electioneering Interest groups get involved in elections by making contributions to candidates, mobilizing people (including their own staff) to help in a campaign, endorsing candidates, funding campaign ads, or mobilizing a candidate's or party's supporters. All these efforts seek to influence who gets elected, with the expectation that changing who gets elected will affect what government does.

Federal laws limit groups' electioneering and lobbying efforts. (See Nuts & Bolts 10.3.) For example, most private organizations and associations in America are organized as 501(c)(3) organizations, a designation based on their Internal Revenue Service classification, which means that donations to the group are tax deductible. However, 501(c)(3) organizations are not allowed to engage in any political activities or lobbying (other than certain voter-education programs or voter-registration drives that are conducted in a nonpartisan manner), although some groups are always looking for loopholes in these restrictions. Groups that want to engage in lobbying or electioneering without looking for exceptions can incorporate under other IRS designations

Astroturf lobbying
Any lobbying method initiated by an interest group that is designed to look like the spontaneous, independent participation of many individuals.

Interest Groups and Electioneering: Types of Organizations

An interest group's ability to engage in electioneering depends on how it is organized—specifically, what section of the IRS code applies to the organization. The following table gives details on four common organizations: 501(c) organizations, 527 organizations, PACs, and so-called Super PACs. Therefore, many choose to contribute money to nonprofits organized as 501(c)(4) groups, which can lobby and engage in electioneering as long as their "primary activity" (at least half of their overall activity) is not political.

Type of Organization	Advantages	Disadvantages
501(c)(3)	Contributions tax deductible	Cannot engage in political activities or lobbying, only voter education and mobilization
527	Can spend unlimited amounts on issue advocacy and voter mobilization	Cannot make contributions to candidates or coordinate efforts with candidates or parties
501(c)(4)	Can spend unlimited amounts on electioneering; do not have to disclose contributors	At least half of their activities must be nonpolitical; cannot coordinate efforts with candidates or parties
PACs	Can contribute directly to candidates and parties	Strict limits on direct contributions
Super PACs	Can spend unlimited amounts on electioneering; can support or oppose specific candidates	Cannot make contributions to candidates or coordinate efforts with candidates or parties

political action committee (PAC)

An interest group or a division of an interest group that can raise money to contribute to campaigns or to spend on ads in support of candidates. The amount a PAC can receive from each of its donors and the amount it can spend on federal campaigning are strictly limited.

527 organization

A tax-exempt group formed primarily to influence elections through voter mobilization efforts and issue ads that do not directly endorse or oppose a candidate. Unlike PACs, 527s are not subject to contribution limits and spending caps.

and operate as a **political action committee (PAC)**, a **527 organization**, or a 501(c)(4). Although contributions to these organizations are not tax deductible, such organizations have fewer restrictions on the size of the contributions they can make and on how their money is spent—for example, 527 organizations have no contribution or spending limits. Two new options for electioneering by interest groups emerged in recent elections: "Super PACs" and 501(c)(4) organizations. The former was a consequence of the *Citizens United* Supreme Court decision that authorized unlimited independent spending by corporations and labor unions in federal elections.[41] Many groups set up new PACs to take advantage of these latest rules—the "Super" label reflects the fact that these groups take in and spend much more money than the typical PAC. All of the major 2016 presidential candidates had an independent Super PAC running ad campaigns on their behalf.

In 2016, federally focused 527 organizations spent more than $400 million on electioneering and PACs and Super PACS spent over $2 billion on electioneering and contributions to candidates and parties.[42] However, these large numbers mask some important details, as illustrated by Figure 10.3. To begin with, look at the right-hand side of the figure—some of the largest firms in America (Google, Walmart, and Exxon Mobil) have PACs that spend only a million or so on contributions. Another large firm, Apple, has no PAC. The AMA's PAC is also small, and the other influential interest groups mentioned earlier (the AARP and Family Research Council) spend even less or don't have a PAC or a 527. These numbers suggest that money doesn't buy elections or policy outcomes—if it did, these organizations would probably spend a lot more on campaign donations and television ads.

The other groups in Figure 10.3 were some of the largest spenders in the 2016 election cycle. But even then, spending totals can be deceptive. The National Association of Realtors, for example, made over $10 million in contributions—but spread out over 500 candidates, with slightly more going to Republicans and Democrats. The PAC for

EMILY's List collects over $40 million in contributions but spends most of this on the direct mail operation that generates funds, leaving only a fraction left for contributions. The Gay and Lesbian Victory Fund focuses on recruiting and endorsing candidates and makes no contributions at all. Finally, the largest spender in 2016, NextGen Climate Action, was funded largely by a single wealthy donor. Moreover, most of the candidates the organization supported in 2014 and 2016 lost their elections.

Finally, while the over $2 billion for overall spending by all of these groups seems large, the average each group spent is much smaller. Most PACs contribute to only a few candidates. And while there were over a thousand Super PACs active in the 2016 election and they spent over a billion dollars in total, most are small, with the average spending just over $500,000. These data highlight a sharp difference in electioneering strategies between the very few large, well-funded interest groups and everyone else. A few 527s, Super PACs, 501(c)(4)s, and PACs have the money to deploy massive advertising and mobilizing efforts for a candidate or issue they like or against those they don't like. There are also some very large associations that can persuade large numbers of members to work for and vote for candidates whom the group supports or against candidates that the group wants to defeat. And just a few rich individuals can make outsized contributions to a candidate they favor. But these strategies are not available to the vast majority of interest groups, which simply don't have the resources. Most interest groups hope to give modest help to a few candidates who are sympathetic to the group's goals.

Contributions by PACs and 527s in 2016: A Closer Look

FIGURE 10.3

Although estimates of total campaign spending suggest that donors have tremendous influence over candidates, the reality is more complicated. Contributions don't buy victories; a substantial amount of campaign cash goes to administrative costs or is distributed across many candidates, and some organizations spend surprisingly little on campaign contributions. How could you use this data to argue against claims that interest groups are all-powerful players in American elections?

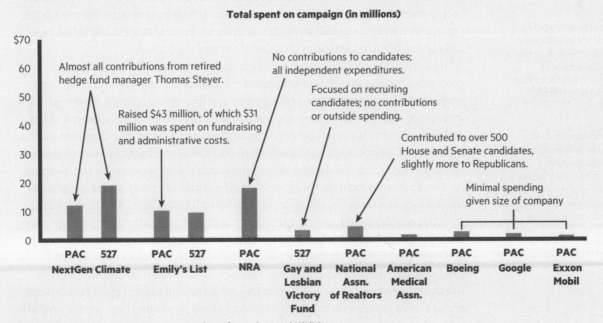

Sources: Data available at www.opensecrets.org and www.fec.gov (accessed 11/6/16).

Conservative Super PACs, such as the Conservative Political Action Committee (CPAC), hold conventions that give candidates a venue to present themselves to conservative activists and donors. @CPAC

These contributions are generally made in the hope that, once elected, the officeholder will remember their contribution when the group asks for a meeting. It is important to remember that electioneering is only one strategy available to interest groups. Some groups do not do any electioneering at all, possibly because they lack sufficient funds, because they want to avoid making enemies based on whom they support or don't support, or because other strategies are more promising given the resources that are available to them. Many groups opt for quiet lobbying efforts that use their expertise, or they undertake grassroots efforts to build public support for their policy goals. Massive electioneering operations by interest groups are relatively rare.

Cultivating Media Contacts Media coverage helps a group publicize its concerns without spending any money. Thus, most interest group leaders talk often with journalists to suggest news stories that pertain to the group's issues and to pursue favorable coverage. Such attention may mobilize public opinion indirectly, by getting people to join the group, contribute money, or demand that elected officials support the group's agenda. Favorable media coverage also helps a group's leaders assure members that they are actively working on members' concerns.

Journalists listen when interest groups call if they feel that the group's story will catch their readers' attention or address their concerns. Smart interest group leaders make it easy for journalists to cover their cause, holding events that produce intriguing news stories. These stories may not change anyone's mind, but the media coverage provides free publicity for the groups' policy agendas.

Bypassing Government: The Initiative Process A final outside strategy for interest groups bypasses government entirely: a group can work to get its proposed policy change voted on by the public in a general election through an initiative or a referendum. Referenda and initiatives allow citizens to vote on specific proposed changes in policy. The difference between these procedures lies in the source of the proposal. In a **referendum** the legislature or another government body proposes the question that is put to a vote, whereas an **initiative** allows citizens to put questions on the ballot, typically after gathering signatures of registered voters on a petition.

Initiatives can occur only in states and municipalities that have the appropriate procedures in place; there is no mechanism for a nationwide vote on an interest group's proposal. So if a group wants to use this process to effect national change, it has to get its measure on the ballot in one state at a time. Moreover, only some states allow initiatives and some permit this kind of vote only on a narrow range of issues. The champion state for initiatives is California, whose citizens often vote on dozens of initiatives in each general election, ranging from funding for stem-cell research to limits on taxation and spending.[43]

There are many examples of groups using the initiative process to change government policy. Most notably, advocates of term limits for state legislators have used the initiative process to establish such limits in 21 states, although the limits in some states have since been overturned by legislative action or subsequent initiatives.[44]

One of the principal concerns about the initiative process is that it favors well-funded groups that can advertise heavily in support of their proposals and can mobilize their supporters to vote on Election Day.[45] But spending a lot of money often is not enough: even groups with substantial resources have sometimes been unable to reform policy through the initiative process.[46]

referendum
A direct vote by citizens on a policy change proposed by a legislature or another government body. Referenda are common in state and local elections, but there is no mechanism for a national-level referendum.

initiative
A direct vote by citizens on a policy change proposed by fellow citizens or organized groups outside government. Getting a question on the ballot typically requires collecting a set number of signatures from registered voters in support of the proposal. There is no mechanism for a national-level initiative.

Choosing strategies

Most groups give testimony, do research, contact elected officials and bureaucrats, talk with journalists, and develop legislative and regulatory proposals.[47] A particular group's decisions about which strategies to use depend partly on its resources and partly on what approach the group believes will be most effective in promoting its particular issues. Some strategies that work well for one group's agenda might not be appropriate for another's. The Humane Society of the United States is an organization that lobbies to prevent the abuse and neglect of animals. It had a $190 million annual budget in 2015 but only a small Washington office. Its lobbying expenses for the 2016 election cycle are less than $300,000. Rather than lobbying members of Congress, the group's focus is on investigations and grassroots organizing, highlighting situations where corporations and countries are not behaving according to existing laws against animal cruelty.

Other interest groups advance their cause in ways that don't look like lobbying. For example, as NASA begins to formulate plans for sending humans to Mars in the 2030s, the Boeing Company has released a series of films and videos about these plans. At one level, Boeing's efforts are all about highlighting the many important discoveries that a voyage to Mars might generate—but they are also a way to increase the chances that NASA's plans will attract public support and be funded by Congress, which, if it happens, will likely generate a series of very lucrative contracts to Boeing to build and help operate exploration hardware.

"Why Should I Care?"

At first glance, lobbying victories should go to the groups that can spend a lot on contributions to candidates or on direct lobbying. But there are many other ways to succeed in the battle to shape public policy, from organizing American citizens to preparing new proposals or doing background research. Policy influence isn't as much about the size of a group's budget as it is about factors such as the size of the group's membership or the perception of its expertise. Even poorly funded groups can find ways to win. If there's an issue that you believe in, find a group that supports it and get involved.

How much power do interest groups have?

★

EVALUATE INTEREST GROUP INFLUENCE

One 2016 presidential candidate, Democrat Lawrence Lessig, built his entire campaign around a pledge to convince members of Congress to enact campaign-finance reform. This, he argued, is the only way to break the influence of special interests over policy making in Washington. Once reform was enacted, Lessig promised to resign from office. While Lessig's campaign went nowhere, his pledge illustrates a widely held belief about how Washington works, that interest groups have too much power and something drastic must be done to end their domination over policy making in Washington.

As we discuss in the What Do the Numbers Say? section, some studies of interest group influence support Lessig's claims—but others tell a very different story, one where a group's chances of getting what it wants depend on whether there is organized

While many observers credit lobbying by the pharmaceutical industry for policies such as the Medicare Prescription Drug Benefit (and its ban on importing medicines), favorable public opinion, the efforts of the AARP, and bureaucrats' independent judgments probably had greater influence on passing the Drug Benefit Act. @PHRMA @AARP

99

But this is the great danger America faces. That we will cease to be one nation and become instead a collection of interest groups: city against suburb, region against region, individual against individual. Each seeking to satisfy private wants.

—**Barbara Jordan,** civil rights leader and former member of Congress

opposition to their demand. In other words, as one analysis put it, "the solution to lobbying is more lobbying."[48]

Scholarly research also reveals just how hard it is to measure interest group influence. For one thing, we know that interest groups usually lobby their friends in government rather than their enemies and moderate their demands in the face of resistance. As a result, what looks like success may in fact be a signal of something else. For example, the NRA leadership would probably favor a new federal law that made it legal to carry a concealed handgun throughout the nation. Why doesn't the NRA demand enactment of this legislation? Because there is no sign that Congress would comply. A proposal that would force states to honor concealed carry permits issued by other states has been introduced in Congress several times but never brought up for debate or a vote.[49] Thus, the NRA's decision to forgo lobbying on this issue shows the limits of the organization's power.

Second, some complaints about the power of interest groups come from the losing side in the political process. Consider the Alliance for Retired Americans and its claims about the Medicare Prescription Drug Benefit. The Alliance lobbied against the Medicare legislation just as the drug companies lobbied for it. However, the Alliance was on the losing side and many of the provisions the group favored were not enacted, making it more prone to complain about the influence of "special interests."

Third, many interest groups claim responsibility for policies and election outcomes regardless of whether their lobbying made the difference. Consider former senator Kay Hagan (D-NC), who was defeated in her 2014 reelection bid. Many interest groups funded ads criticizing Hagan or contributed to her opponent's campaign. The ads may have helped defeat Hagan, but she was also hurt by having a well-funded, experienced opponent, Thom Tillis; President Obama's unpopularity; and the nearly even ratio of Democrats to Republicans in the state. Yet the leaders of interest groups have a considerable incentive to make strong claims about their group's influence and impact, as these claims help them attract members and keep their jobs.[50]

Fourth, arguments about the impact of interest groups on election outcomes, such as Hagan's defeat in 2014, ignore the fact that interest groups are almost always active on both sides of an election campaign. Although Hagan was the target of attack ads funded by interest groups and many groups gave contributions to her opponent, Hagan also received support from interest groups in the form of campaign contributions and independent ads. Thus, it doesn't make sense to attribute Hagan's defeat to actions taken by one set of groups without asking why similar efforts on Hagan's behalf had no effect. You can't conclude that interest groups are all-powerful without explaining why Hagan's supporters were unable to save her seat.

In sum, dire claims about the overwhelming influence of interest groups and lobbying on Washington policy making are probably wrong. Rather than making a blanket

Interest Group Power

Conventional wisdom says that business interest groups have too much power over policy outcomes in Washington. But what do the numbers say?

To address this question, a group of political scientists tracked a series of issues through years of lobbying, congressional debate, legislative action, and implementation by the bureaucracy. Their goal was to determine whether business groups were successful in getting what they want from Congress, particularly when their efforts were opposed by citizen groups or government officials. Here's what they found:

Which Interests Groups Win . . . and When?

After four years...

■ Business Groups Win   ■ Other Side Wins   ■ Both/Neither Win

Business groups v. citizen groups or unions

40%	40%	20%

Business groups v. citizen groups or unions

36%	36%	27%

Business groups unopposed

89%	11%

Think about it

- Many people believe that business groups always succeed in their lobbying efforts. Does this chart confirm or deny these suspicions?
- After looking at these data, do you think business groups have too much power? How do these data help us understand the winners and losers in the student loan reform debate discussed at the beginning of this chapter?

Source: Marie Hojnacki, Kathleen Marchetti, Frank Baumgartner, Jeffrey M. Berry, David C. Kimball, and Beth L. Leech, "Assessing Business Advantage in Washington Lobbying," Interest Groups and Advocacy 4 (2015): 206–24.

claim about interest group influence, a better response is to ask, "What are the conditions that enhance a group's influence over policy, and what are the conditions that reduce it?" That is, what determines when interest groups succeed?

What determines when interest groups succeed?

Three factors shape interest group influence. The first is what the group is trying to do—change a policy (including enacting a new policy) or prevent change. The second is salience: How many Americans care about what a group is trying to do? The third is conflict: To what extent do other groups or the public oppose the policy change?

Change versus Preventing Change In general, groups are going to have an easier time preventing a change than working to implement one. As we discuss in Chapter 2, enacting a new policy requires the approval of both houses of Congress, the president's signature (or a veto override), and implementation from the appropriate bureaucratic agency. Each of these steps provides an opportunity for interest groups to lobby in favor of doing nothing. And if groups are successful in the process, change will not occur. Studies show that groups are much more likely to be successful when their goals involve negative lobbying—blocking changes in policy.[51] Most of the NRA's legislative victories in recent years fit this description: they have successfully lobbied against a new ban on assault weapons, against reforms to the system of national background checks for hand-gun purchases, and against new limits on ownership of guns by mentally ill people.

While the success of the NRA's negative lobbying attracts considerable attention, its failures in lobbying for policy change do not. Consider the NRA's advocacy of concealed carry laws. As noted earlier, there is little doubt that the NRA's leaders and most of its members favor the passage of such laws nationwide, but efforts to lobby Congress in favor of such laws are unlikely to be successful given public opposition and well-funded interest groups who are against concealed carry. These groups could respond with negative lobbying against any effort the NRA might make. As a result, the NRA does not lobby for concealed carry—and the limits on its power over legislation are not evident.

salience
The level of familiarity with an interest group's goals among the general population

Salience Interest groups are more likely to succeed when their request has low **salience** or attracts little public attention.[52] When the average voter does not know or care about a group's request, legislators and bureaucrats do not have to worry about the political consequences of giving the group what it wants. The only question is whether the officials themselves favor the request or can be convinced that the group's desired change is worthwhile. In contrast, when salience is high legislators' response to lobbying will hinge on their judgment of constituent opinion: Do voters favor what the group wants? After all, the average legislator has a strong interest in reelection and is unlikely to act against his or her constituents' wishes. As a result, lobbying may count for nothing in the face of public opposition or be superfluous when the group's position already has public support.[53]

Low-salience issues are surprisingly common. The idea of interest group lobbying probably brings to mind titanic struggles on controversial issues, such as gun control, abortion rights, or judicial nominations, over which groups try to capture public attention as a way of pressuring people in government. And, in fact, many groups are active for or against these issues. However, the typical issue attracts much less activity. One analysis of lobbying disclosure forms found that 5 percent of issues attracted more than 50 percent of lobbying activity and 50 percent of issues attracted less than 3 percent.[54] Thus, the typical issue debated by members of Congress may involve relatively little interest group activity and a group's request may generate little or no opposition from other groups. Remember the National Turkey Federation—the people who give the president a turkey every Thanksgiving? In the winter of 2014, the federation successfully lobbied federal bureaucrats to increase propane supplies to Midwest states facing record cold temperatures, including areas where the federation's members use propane to heat their barns. The policy change resulting from the federation's lobbying efforts attracted no publicity, which is precisely the point. When few people know or care about a policy change, interest groups are able to dominate the policy-making process.

Conflict Interest group influence is much less apparent on conflictual issues—those over which public opinion is split and groups are typically active on both sides of the question. Consider a high-salience issue such as gun control. The ongoing debate over gun control attracts many well-funded interest groups and coalitions, which support different versions of gun control or want no change at all. There is no consensus among either members of Congress, interest groups, or the American public about which policy changes were needed. Under these conditions, access doesn't count for very much; legislators have a keen sense of the political costs of accommodating a group's demands. As a result, stalemate is the likely result, which is exactly what has happened over the last few years. If policy change occurs at all, it is likely to reflect a complex process of bargaining and compromise, with no groups getting exactly what they want. In such cases, it is hard to say whether a particular group won or lost or to attribute any aspect of the final bargain to a particular group's efforts.

The case of gun control illustrates that being large or well-funded often does not help an interest group convince government officials to comply with its requests. As mentioned earlier, many people worry that well-funded interest groups will use their financial resources to dominate the policy-making process, even if public opinion is against them, but these fears are largely unfounded. The conditions that are ripe for well-funded interest groups to become involved in a policy debate typically ensure that there will be well-funded groups on all sides of a question. Under these conditions, no group is likely to get everything it wants and no group's lobbying efforts are likely to be decisive. Some groups may not get anything.

However, gun control is not a typical case. Most cases of interest group influence look a lot like the Turkey Federation's request for more propane: a group asks for

If you have ever heard of the National Turkey Federation, it's probably because of its participation in the annual presidential "pardoning" of a turkey before Thanksgiving. The federation's relative anonymity has been beneficial: its effort to increase the amount of turkey served in federally funded school lunches was aided by most Americans' lack of awareness of the proposal. @TurkeyGal

While Congress has considered various forms of gun control legislation in recent years, the NRA has been successful at blocking such measures at the federal level and even liberalizing state-level gun laws. Members of the NRA and other gun rights supporters are gathered here in the Texas state capital to rally against stricter limits on firearms. @NRA

something, there is relatively little opposition, and Congress or the bureaucracy responds with appropriate policy changes. The situation might have been very different if another group had lobbied on the other side against the Turkey Federation. If so, satisfying one group would have required displeasing at least one other group. Faced with this no-win situation, bureaucrats or legislators would be less likely to give the group what it wanted. At a minimum, they would have had to measure the Turkey Federation's arguments against those made by the other groups.

"Why Should I Care?"

Suppose you want to change some federal government policy—you want more funding for a program or an end to some regulation. Does having enough money guarantee a win? Generally speaking, the answer is no. What matters more is the salience of the policy or regulation you're trying to change and whether there is organized opposition on the other side. If your group is the only one lobbying, chances are good that you'll win. But if the issue is highly salient and you have opposition, your prospects aren't good, regardless of the size of your bankroll.

Conclusion

Many Americans think that interest groups are powerful manipulators of the American policy process and that they are able to get what they want regardless of the impact on everyone else. Federal direct student loans are seemingly a perfect example: a small number of well-funded lobbyists worked to defeat a policy change that would lower the cost of attending college for most students.

As you have seen, the truth is much more complex. Interest groups represent many different Americans, many of whom are unaware that lobbying occurs on their behalf. Moreover, for many groups the challenge is to get organized in the first place or to scrape together enough resources to start lobbying. These efforts don't always succeed. Interest groups are more likely to get what they want when their demands attract little public attention and no opposition from other groups. When a group asks for a large or controversial policy change, it stands little chance of success, even if the group has many members, a large lobbying budget, or an influential leader directing its operation.

The debate over direct student loans exemplifies all of these findings. Although the corporations that stood to lose from the direct loan proposal had significant lobbying operations, the proposal had relatively high salience and was controversial. Consequently, legislators' voting decisions were less likely to be affected by lobbying or other interest group strategies such as electioneering. These lobbying efforts may have helped to inform members of Congress about the details of the proposal or the impact that the change would have on employment in their districts, but there is no evidence that support for these proposals was shaped by lobbying. And although these lobbying efforts delayed the move to direct loans, they did not prevent it.

In sum, while individual lobbying efforts often reflect the efforts of small groups to achieve favored policy outcomes at the expense of the majority, when we look across the entire range of interest group activities a different picture emerges: in the main, interest groups reflect the conflictual nature of American politics and the resulting drive of individuals, groups, and corporations to shape American public policy in line with their policy goals. The average citizen benefits as well as loses from lobbying activities.

STUDY GUIDE

What are interest groups?

Define *interest groups* and describe the characteristics of different types of groups. (Pages 332–341)

Summary

Interest groups are organizations that seek to influence government policy by helping elect candidates who support their policy goals and by lobbying elected officials and bureaucrats. Although they are generally viewed with disdain, interest groups are ubiquitous—most organizations have lobbyists working on their behalf—and, under the theory of pluralism, are regarded as fundamental actors in American politics.

Key terms

interest group (p. 332)
lobbying (p. 332)
interest group state (p. 332)
trade association (p. 336)
centralized groups (p. 336)

confederations (p. 336)
revolving door (p. 338)
mass associations (p. 338)
peak associations (p. 339)

Practice Quiz Questions

1. **In contrast to political parties, interest groups _____.**
   a. run candidates for office
   b. coordinate the activities of elected officials
   c. guarantee that certain candidates appear on electoral ballots
   d. directly influence government activity
   e. indirectly influence government activity

2. **Why is the number of lobbyists increasing?**
   a. The federal government is growing in size and influence.
   b. Lobbying is not closely regulated.
   c. Citizens are now more supportive of special interests.
   d. Politicians can concurrently serve their terms and work as lobbyists.
   e. Interest groups have more money to spend.

3. **In contrast to a confederation, a centralized interest group _____.**
   a. maintains lots of independent chapters
   b. often has local chapters competing over resources
   c. deploys the group's resources more efficiently
   d. is able to find out what its members want
   e. has no weaknesses

4. **The practice of moving from government positions to working for interest groups is called _____.**
   a. interest-group capture
   b. the revolving door
   c. an iron triangle
   d. escalator politics
   e. the spoils system

Getting organized

Explain how successful interest groups overcome collective action problems. (Pages 341–343)

Summary

A primary challenge in operating an interest group is getting members to coordinate with one another. Interest groups have a number of different ways of overcoming the problem of collective action, with varying degrees of success.

Key terms

collective action problem (p. 341)
free riding (p. 341)
solidary benefits (p. 342)

purposive benefits (p. 342)
coercion (p. 342)
selective incentives (p. 343)

Practice Quiz Questions

5. **The logic of collective action says that when people _____ on policy priorities and the costs are _____ cooperation is not easy.**
   a. agree; high
   b. agree; covered by one person
   c. agree; low
   d. disagree; high
   e. disagree; low

6. **Purposive benefits come from _____, while solidary benefits come from _____.**
   a. working with like-minded people; working to achieve a desired policy goal
   b. receiving material goods; working with like-minded people
   c. receiving material goods; working to achieve a desired policy goal
   d. working to achieve a desired policy goal; receiving material goods
   e. working to achieve a desired policy goal; working with like-minded people

7. **Labor unions are generally able to overcome the collective action problem through the use of _____.**
   a. solidary benefits
   b. purposive benefits
   c. coercion
   d. selective incentives
   e. recruitment

Interest group strategies

Explore the ways interest groups try to influence government policies. (Pages 343–353)

Summary

Interest groups have two types of tactics for lobbying elected officials. They can attempt to influence politics by taking action in Washington or they can take action elsewhere. The decision to pursue an inside or outside strategy comes down to the interest group's resources and which strategy members think will be most effective.

Key terms
inside strategies (p. 343)
outside strategies (p. 343)
direct lobbying (p. 343)
grassroots lobbying (p. 348)
Astroturf lobbying (p. 349)
political action committee (PAC) (p. 350)
527 organization (p. 350)
referendum (p. 352)
initiative (p. 352)

Practice Quiz Questions

8. **Asking government officials to change policy in line with the group's goals is _____.**
   a. revolving door lobbying
   b. Astroturf lobbying
   c. direct lobbying
   d. indirect lobbying
   e. outside lobbying

9. **Interest groups generally _____ draft legislation; they generally _____ provide testimony before committees.**
   a. do; do
   b. do not; do
   c. do; do not
   d. do not; do not

10. **Directly involving interest group members in lobbying efforts is called _____.**
    a. Astroturf lobbying
    b. grassroots lobbying
    c. democratic lobbying
    d. lobbying through referendum
    e. inside lobbying

11. **For grassroots lobbying to be effective, _____.**
    a. only a few pieces of mail are necessary
    b. mail must come from all over the country
    c. all messages have to have exactly the same appeal
    d. letters have to come from constituents
    e. letters have to come from prominent officials

12. **Interest groups that want to maximize the amount of access they receive in return for a campaign contribution will sometimes _____.**
    a. contribute to weak candidates who need the money
    b. contribute to candidates who oppose the group's goals
    c. wait until the general election to make a contribution
    d. help candidates who support them, even if they are electorally safe
    e. avoid electioneering efforts altogether

How much power do interest groups have?

Evaluate interest group influence. (Pages 353–358)

Summary

It is commonly argued that elected officials are letting interest groups define their agenda. However, the evidence on interest groups does not support these claims: there is no correlation between the amount of money spent on lobbying and a group's success, nor is there conclusive evidence that group lobbying influences policy. Groups are generally most influential when the issues attract little public attention and when an issue does not have organized opposition.

Key term
salience (p. 356)

Practice Quiz Questions

13. **Interest groups generally lobby _____ in government.**
    a. their opponents
    b. their friends
    c. the undecided
    d. the newly elected
    e. the less informed

14. **Interest groups are more likely to succeed when their request has _____ salience and when it has _____ conflict.**
    a. low; little
    b. high; little
    c. low; high
    d. high; high
    e. high; zero

Suggested Reading

Ainsworth, Scott. *Analyzing Interest Groups: Group Influence on People and Policies*. New York: W. W. Norton, 2002.

Baumgartner, Frank, Jeffrey M. Berry, Marie Hojnacki, David C. Kimball, and Beth L. Leech. *Lobbying and Policy Change: Who Wins, Who Loses, and Why*. Chicago: University of Chicago Press, 2009.

Carpenter, Daniel. *The Forging of Bureaucratic Autonomy: Reputations, Networks, and Policy Innovation in Executive Agencies, 1862-1928*. Princeton, NJ: Princeton University Press, 2002.

Gilens, Martin, and Benjamin Page. *Testing Theories of American Politics: Elites, Interest Groups, and Average Citizens*. Princeton, NJ: Princeton University Press, 2014.

Kollman, Kenneth. *Outside Lobbying: Public Opinion and Interest Group Strategies*. Princeton, NJ: Princeton University Press, 1998.

Olson, Mancur. *The Logic of Collective Action*, 2nd ed. Cambridge, MA: Harvard University Press, 1971.

Schattschneider, E. E. *The Semisovereign People*. New York: Harper and Row, 1959.

Schlozman, Kay Lehman, and John Tierney. *Organized Interests and American Democracy*. New York: HarperCollins, 1986.

Stigerwalt, Amy. *The Battle over the Bench: Senators, Interest Groups, and Lower Court Confirmations*. Charlottesville: University of Virginia Press, 2010.

Verba, Sidney, Kay Lehman Schlozman, and Henry Brady. *Voice and Equality: Civic Participation in America*. Cambridge, MA: Harvard University Press, 1995.

11

Congress

Who does Congress represent?

Early in March 2014, the casual observer reading the headline "Senate Approves McCaskill Sexual Assault Bill in 97–0 Vote" may have reasonably assumed that there was massive bipartisan agreement on this important issue.[1] However, digging past the headline would have revealed bruising partisan (and intraparty) conflict. Despite the unanimous support for the compromise bill in the Senate, the House declined to take up the bill, with then-Speaker John Boehner saying he wanted to see how previous reforms worked out: "I don't frankly see any reason at this point for any further action to be taken."[2]

A 2013 Pentagon report showed that 26,000 troops had "unwanted sexual contact" in 2012, comprising 6.1 percent of active-duty women and 1.2 percent of active-duty men. This was a 37 percent increase in incidents of unwanted sexual contact compared with such incidents in 2010 and more than eight times the 3,374 sexual assaults reported in 2010.[3] The report led to an outcry in Congress, with two senators, Claire McCaskill (D-MO) and Kirsten Gillibrand (D-NY), providing alternative plans. Both bills provided much stronger protections for victims of sexual assaults by removing the "good soldier" defense (a defense that takes an accused soldier's good military record into account, even if it is unrelated to the alleged crime) and strengthening prosecutors' role in advising commanders on whether to go to court martial. But Senator Gillibrand pushed for an even stronger overhaul that would have removed prosecutions for sexual assaults from the military chain of command, while Senator McCaskill did not. This difference led to a protracted battle that lasted nearly a year and isolated McCaskill as the only one of the 16 Democratic women senators to vote against Gillibrand's bill.[4] Nonetheless, as we noted earlier, McCaskill's version of the bill was the one that passed by a unanimous vote in the Senate. While supporters of the stronger reforms were disappointed, this case shows that even on a deeply conflictual issue such as how to address the problem of sexual assaults in the military, it is possible to find common ground and a compromise that can win the support of a majority in the Senate and, perhaps at some point, the House.

The essential nature of conflict and compromise in the legislative process is not very well understood by the general public. Americans often view the type

★
CHAPTER
GOALS

Explain how members of Congress represent their constituents and how elections hold members accountable.
pages 364–381

Examine how parties, the committee system, and staffers enable Congress to function.
pages 381–392

Trace the steps in the legislative process.
pages 392–400

Describe how Congress ensures that the bureaucracy implements policies correctly.
pages 400–401

Kirsten Gillibrand (D-NY) greets panel members testifying at a Senate hearing on sexual assault in the military. Senator Gillibrand is trying to change how the Pentagon handles the increase in sexual assaults. Here, Gillibrand shakes hands with air force lieutenant general Richard Harding before greeting army lieutenant general Dana Chipman, who is next to him.

of wheeling and dealing that is necessary to reach compromises as improper and wonder why there is so much conflict. A typical sentiment is, "Why does there have to be so much partisan bickering? Can't they just implement the best solutions to our problems?" Many don't even attempt to understand the legislative process and the nature of conflict and compromise because it seems hopelessly complex. Anyone who has watched congressional debates on C-SPAN knows that legislative maneuvers can make your head spin, and the discussions can seem mind-numbing.

In this chapter, we show that the basic characteristics of Congress are straightforward and that the motivations that guide members' behavior and the way that Congress works are transparent. This chapter argues that members' behavior is driven by their desire to respond to constituent interests (and the closely related goal of reelection) and constrained by the institutional structures within which they operate (such as the committee system, parties, and leadership). At the same time, members try to be responsible for broader national interests, which are often at odds with their constituents' interests and, subsequently, the goal of reelection.

This tension between being responsible and responsive is a source of conflict and requires members of Congress to make tough decisions, often involving political trade-offs and compromises. Should a House member vote for dairy price supports for her local farmers even if it means higher milk prices for families around the nation? Should a senator vote to subsidize the production of tobacco, the biggest cash crop in his state, despite the tremendous health costs it imposes on millions of Americans? Should a member vote to close a military base, as requested by the Pentagon, even if it means the loss of thousands of jobs back home? These are difficult questions. On a complex issue, such as how best to deal with sexual assaults in the military, there is no obvious "responsible" solution and fair-minded people can disagree. These disagreements take on a partisan edge, as most Republicans favor maintaining the chain of command while most Democrats do not, which obviously leads to conflict.

This chapter begins by examining the constitutional underpinnings of the representational tensions Congress must address. After exploring different ways of understanding representation, we describe Congress's image problem, the incumbency advantage, and Congress's central institutional features. We conclude by considering some potential reforms that might make Congress work better. How can members of Congress best serve the collective interests of the nation while also representing their local constituents? How do the institutions of Congress, such as committees and political parties, help members pursue their goals? What did the Founders envision as the proper role for Congress within our political system?

What Congress does

Congress and the Constitution

Congress was the "first branch" in the early decades of our nation's history. The Constitution specified for Congress a vast array of enumerated powers, including regulating commerce, coining money, raising and supporting armies, creating the courts, establishing post offices and roads, declaring war, and levying taxes (see Article I, Section 8, of the Constitution in the appendix). In contrast, the president was given few explicit powers and played a much less prominent role early in our history. Furthermore, many of Congress's extensive powers came from its implicit powers, which were rooted in the elastic clause of Article I of the Constitution, which gives Congress the power "to make all Laws which shall be necessary and proper for carrying into Execution the foregoing Powers."

As noted in Chapter 2, the compromises that gave rise to Congress's initial structure reflected an attempt to reconcile the competing interests of the day (large versus small states, northern versus southern interests, and proponents of strong national power versus state power). These compromises included establishing a system of **bicameralism**—that is, a bicameral (two-chambered) institution made up of a popularly elected House and a Senate chosen by state legislatures—allowing each slave to count as three-fifths of a person for purposes of apportionment for the House, and setting longer terms for senators (six years) than for House members (two years). But these compromises also laid the foundation for the split loyalties that members of Congress have between their local constituencies and the nation's interests. Although the Founders hoped that Congress would pass legislation that emphasized the national good over local interests, they also recognized the importance of local constituencies. Thus, the two-year House term was intended to tie legislators to public sentiment.

At the same time, the *Federalist Papers* made it clear that the new government was by no means a direct democracy that would put all policy questions to the public. In *Federalist 57*, Madison asserted that "the aim of every political constitution is, or ought to be, first to obtain for rulers men who possess most wisdom to discern, and most virtue to pursue, the common good of the society." This common good may often conflict with local concerns, such that members are expected to both "refine and enlarge the debate" to encompass the common good *and* represent their local constituents.

In general, the Founders viewed the Senate as the more likely institution to enlarge the debate and speak for the national interests; it was intended to check the more responsive and passionate House. Because senators were indirectly elected and served longer terms than House members, the Senate was more insulated from the people. A famous (although perhaps fictional) story that points out the differences between the House and Senate involves an argument between George Washington and Thomas Jefferson. Jefferson did not think the Senate was necessary, while Washington supported having two chambers. During the argument, Jefferson poured some coffee he was drinking into his saucer. Washington asked him why he had done so. "To cool it," replied Jefferson. "Even so," said Washington, "we pour legislation into the senatorial saucer to cool it."

This idea of a more responsible Senate survived well into the twentieth century, even after the Seventeenth Amendment in 1913 allowed the direct, popular election of senators. Today the Senate is still more insulated than the House. Because of the six-year terms of senators, only one-third of the 100 Senate seats are contested in each election, while all 435 House members are elected every two years. However, differences between the representational roles of the House and the Senate have become muted as senators seem to campaign for reelection 365 days a year, every year, just like House members.[5] This "permanent campaign" means that senators are less insulated from electoral forces than they were earlier.

The relationship between the president and Congress has also evolved significantly. Congress's roots in geographic constituencies made it well suited for the politics of the nineteenth century. Early in U.S. history, several great presidents left their mark on national politics (George Washington, Andrew Jackson, and Abraham Lincoln, among others), but Congress dominated much of the day-to-day politics, which revolved around issues such as the tariff (taxes on imported or exported goods), slavery, and internal improvements such as building roads and canals. Given the tendency to address these issues with patronage and the **pork barrel**—that is, jobs and policies

bicameralism
The system of having two chambers within one legislative body, like the House and Senate in the U.S. Congress.

The Founders viewed the House as more passionate than the Senate, or as the "hot coffee" that needed to be cooled in the "saucer" of the Senate. This perception probably did not include coming to blows over differences in policy as Congressmen Albert G. Brown and John A. Wilcox did in 1851 about whether Mississippi should secede from the Union.

A ROW IN CONGRESS.

pork barrel
Legislative appropriations that benefit specific constituents, created with the aim of helping local representatives win reelection.

descriptive representation
When a member of Congress shares the characteristics (such as gender, race, religion, or ethnicity) of his or her constituents.

DID YOU KNOW?

$1.1 million

was the average net worth of members of Congress in 2014. More than half of all members of Congress are millionaires (274 of 535).
Source: Center for Responsive Politics

targeted to benefit specific constituents—Congress was better suited for the task than the president was.

Beginning around the turn of the twentieth century and accelerating with the New Deal of the 1930s (which established modern social welfare and regulatory policies), the scope of national policy expanded and politics became more centered in Washington. With this nationalization of politics and the increasing importance of national security issues during World War II, the Cold War, the wars in Korea, Vietnam, and Iraq, and the War on Terror, the president has assumed a more central policy-making role. Nonetheless, the central tensions between representing local versus national interests remain essential in understanding the legislative process and the relationship between members of Congress and their constituents.

Congress represents the people (or tries to)

Americans have a love–hate relationship with Congress; that is, we love our own member of Congress, but we hate Congress as a whole. Well, "hate" is a strong word, but as we show later in this section, members of Congress routinely have approval ratings 30 to 40 points higher than the institution's. One poll found that members of Congress landed fifth from the bottom in a ranking of 26 professions in terms of perceived honesty and ethical standards.[6] A more whimsical poll by Public Policy Polling asked respondents questions such as, "What do you have a higher opinion of, Congress or root canals?" Root canals won handily, 56 to 32 percent. Congress was also less popular than head lice, traffic jams, cockroaches, and Donald Trump, but narrowly beat out Lindsay Lohan and had a comfortable margin over the Ebola virus, the Kardashians, and meth labs.[7] Why is Congress so unpopular? How do members of Congress try to represent their constituents? And how do elections influence this important dynamic?

Types of Representation Let's examine the two basic relationships between constituents and their member of Congress: descriptive representation and substantive representation. The former is rooted in the politician's side of the relationship. Does the member of Congress "look like" the constituents in demographic or socioeconomic terms—for example, AfricanAmerican, Latino, or white; male or female; Catholic, Protestant, or some other religion; middle-class or upper-class? Many people believe that such **descriptive representation** is a distinct value in itself. Having positive role models for various demographic groups helps create greater trust in the system. Moreover, there are benefits in being represented by someone who shares something as basic as skin color with constituents.

Descriptive representation is also related to the perceived responsiveness of a member of Congress. In general, constituents report higher levels of satisfaction with representatives who are of the same racial or ethnic background as the constituents themselves. Thus, descriptively represented constituents are more likely to assume that their interests are being represented than those who are not.[8] If you doubt that descriptive representation makes a difference, ask yourself whether it would be fair if all 435 House members and 100 senators were white male Protestants. Although the demographics of Congress are considerably more diverse than this, the legislature does not come close to "looking like us" on a nationwide scale (see the What Do the Numbers Say? feature). This is especially true in the Senate, where only ten African Americans and nine Latinos have served in the history of the institution (three African Americans and four Latinos currently are in the Senate as of 2017).[9]

Although descriptive representation is important, it goes only so far. More important than a member's race, gender, or religion, many argue, is the *substance* of what

Descriptive Representation in Congress

Compared with a generation ago, the number of women and racial and ethnic minorities in Congress has increased. But on these dimensions, how representative of the people is Congress? How close does Congress come to "looking like us"? What do the numbers say?

Sources: U.S. Census; Congressional Research Service

Gender in Congress

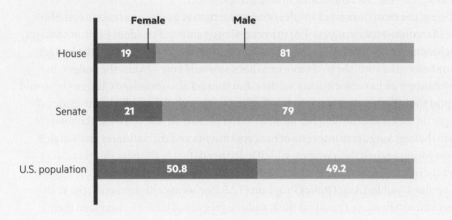

	Female	Male
House	19	81
Senate	21	79
U.S. population	50.8	49.2

Racial and Ethnic Composition of Congress

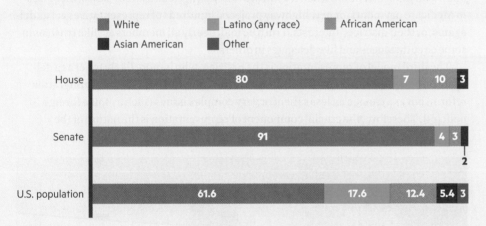

- White
- Latino (any race)
- African American
- Asian American
- Other

	White	Latino (any race)	African American	Asian American	Other
House	80	7	10	3	
Senate	91	4	3		2
U.S. population	61.6	17.6	12.4	5.4	3

Think about it

- Which comes closer to "looking like us," the House or the Senate?
- How could having more women or racial and ethnic minorities in Congress affect legislation and policy decisions?
- Latinos now make up the largest ethnic minority in the United States, yet they still lag behind African Americans in terms of representation in the House. Why do you think this is?

substantive representation
When a member of Congress represents constituents' interests and policy concerns.

trustee
A member of Congress who represents constituents' interests while also taking into account national, collective, and moral concerns that sometimes cause the member to vote against the preference of a majority of constituents.

delegate
A member of Congress who loyally represents constituents' direct interests.

politico
A member of Congress who acts as a delegate on issues that constituents care about (such as immigration reform) and as a trustee on more-complex or less-salient issues (such as some foreign policy or regulatory matters).

📷

Members of Congress spend a good deal of time in their districts, developing relationships with constituents. Here, Representative Jason Chaffetz (R-UT) meets constituents after a town hall meeting. @jasoninthehouse

that person does. Merely because a representative shares some characteristics with you does not necessarily mean that he or she will represent your interests. Substantive representation moves beyond appearances to specify how the member serves constituents' interests. Two long-standing models of representation are (1) the trustee, who represents the interests of constituents from a distance, weighing numerous national, collective, local, and moral concerns; and (2) the delegate, who carries out the direct desires of the voters. In a sense, trustees are more concerned with being responsible and delegates are more interested in being responsive.

One of the most famous examples of a representative acting as a trustee was Marjorie Margolies-Mezvinsky (D-PA) in a crucial 1993 vote on President Clinton's budget, which included controversial tax increases and spending cuts to balance the budget. Hours before the vote, she told reporters that she would vote against the budget, in accordance with her constituents' wishes. But she had also promised Clinton she would support the bill if her vote was needed. As she cast the critical vote in the 218–216 cliffhanger (in which she fulfilled her promise to the president), she did what she thought was in the best long-term interests of her constituents and the nation, even though it meant voting against their wishes, which led to her defeat in the next election. More recently, in 2008, bipartisan majorities in the House and Senate voted for the hugely unpopular Troubled Asset Relief Program (TARP or, as its critics called it, the Wall Street bailout) because President Bush and congressional leaders convinced them it was necessary to prevent a complete economic meltdown.

In contrast, a delegate does not have to worry about angering voters because he or she simply does what voters want. Examples are so numerous it is pointless to single out one member for attention: when it comes to tax cuts, agricultural subsidies, increases in Medicare payments, or new highway projects, hundreds of representatives act as delegates for their districts' interests. Truth be told, nearly all members act like trustees in some circumstances and like delegates in others.

The third model of representation is the politico, who is more likely to act as a delegate on issues that are highly salient to his or her constituency (such as immigration reform) but as a trustee on less salient or very complex issues (such as some foreign policies). Therefore, the crucial component of representation is the nature of the

constituency and how the member of Congress attempts to balance and represent constituents' conflicting needs and desires.

The Role of the Constituency Most voters do not monitor their representatives' behavior closely. Can representation work if voters are not paying attention?

Members of Congress behave as if voters were paying attention, even when constituents are inattentive. Incumbents know that at election time challengers may raise issues that become salient after the public thinks about them, so they try to deter challengers by anticipating what the constituents would want *if they were fully informed*.[10] For example, the public didn't know much about the FBI's inability to hack into locked phones, but it became an issue in the 2016 elections when the FBI tried to force Apple to allow them to access a phone used by a suspect in the San Bernardino shootings. Savvy incumbents would have tried to stake out a position consistent with what the voters would want *before* a strong challenger raised the issue in a campaign. Richard F. Fenno, one of the leading congressional scholars of the twentieth century, points out that some segments of the constituency are more attentive and more important for a member's reelection than others (see Figure 11.1).[11]

Another way to examine the representative–constituency relationship is to look at differences across districts. How do districts vary? First, they differ in size: Senate "districts" (that is, states) vary in terms of area and population. House districts all have about 745,000 people, but they vary tremendously in geographic size. Districts also differ in terms of who lives there and what they want from government. Some districts are located in poor city neighborhoods, where voters' concerns are economic development, crime control, antipoverty programs, and looser immigration regulations. Some are wealthy and urban, where citizens are more supportive of foreign aid and higher taxes. Some are suburban, where funding for education and transportation is critical. Some are conservative and rural, where agricultural policies, gun rights, and support for tax cuts dominate. Districts vary from the religious to the secular, from domination by one industry to a diversified corporate base to no industry at all. Some consider government a force for good, while others argue that government should get off people's backs. And some districts are a mixture of all these things.

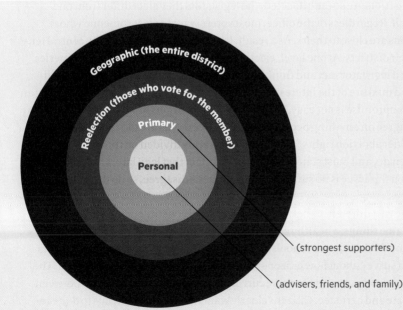

(strongest supporters)

(advisers, friends, and family)

FIGURE 11.1

Fenno's Concentric Circles

The concentric circles of a congressional constituency illustrate the various parts of a district that a member represents. Can you think of an issue on which House members would be more responsive to their reelection constituency than to their geographic constituency?

Source: Based on Richard F. Fenno, *Home Style: House Members in Their Districts* (Boston: Little, Brown, 1978).

What Do People Want from Congress?

Members of Congress are often criticized for being out of touch with their constituents. Based on a *USA Today* poll, Americans seem to want their congressional members to vote in line with their constituents' views, to work across party lines, and to spend more time in the district rather than Washington, D.C. But what happens if these goals conflict? What if the member represents a very partisan district where the majority does not want him or her to work with the other party? Also, is there no room for trustees who follow their conscience and stick to their principles?

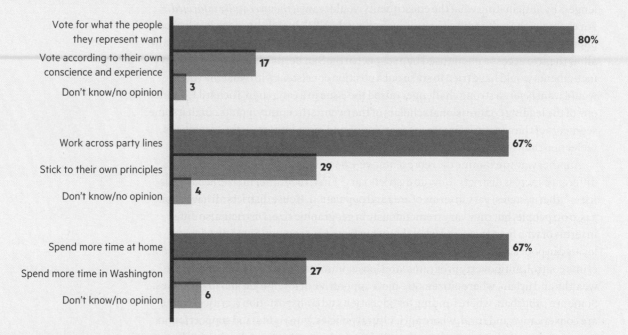

Source: "Divided We Still Stand—And Getting Used To It," *USA Today*, www.usatoday.com (accessed 4/11/14).

Because districts are so multifaceted, the legislators they elect differ from one another as well. Regardless of the office, most voters want to elect someone whose policy positions are close to theirs. As a result, legislators tend to reflect the central tendencies of their districts. At one level, electing a legislature that "thinks like America" sounds good: if legislators act and think like their districts, then the legislature will contain a good mixture of the interests representing the country or state. But finding an acceptable compromise is not easy. We elect legislators to get things done, but they may be unable to agree on anything because their disagreements are too fundamental to bridge. Consider abortion rights. The country is sharply divided on this issue, as are the House, the Senate, and most state legislatures. The fact that legislators have not come to a decision on this issue is no surprise: just as citizens disagree, so do their elected representatives.

Despite the vast differences between congressional constituencies, voters want many of the same things: a healthy economy, a safe country (in terms of national defense and local crime), good schools, and effective health care. Figure 11.2 reports responses to a survey about how citizens feel that legislators should do their jobs. The survey showed strong support for our recurring theme concerning tensions between being a delegate and a trustee. Citizens clearly want their elected officials to do **casework** for the district—that is, help their constituents to solve bureaucratic problems or

casework
Assistance provided by members of Congress to their constituents in solving problems with the federal bureaucracy or addressing other specific concerns.

address specific concerns related to government. But respondents showed little interest in having the representatives "spend more time in Washington" and would rather have them spend more time at home. Thus, responsibilities for national interests may be more difficult for members of Congress to explain to their constituents.

Members of Congress want to keep their jobs

Members' relationship to their constituents also must be understood within the context of their desire to be reelected. Political scientist David R. Mayhew argues in *Congress: The Electoral Connection* that reelection must come first.[12] Members certainly hold multiple goals, including making good policy, but if they cannot maintain their seats then they cannot attain other goals in office.

After assuming that reelection is central, Mayhew asks this question: "Members of Congress may be electorally motivated, but are they in a position to do anything about it?"[13] Although individual members of Congress cannot do much to alter national economic or political forces, they can control their own activities in the House or Senate. The importance of the electoral connection in explaining the behavior of members of Congress seems especially clear for marginal incumbents who are constantly trying to shore up their electoral base. But for those from safe districts, why should they worry?

Incumbents Work toward Reelection Objectively, it looks as though about 90 percent of House members (and a large proportion of senators) are absolutely safe, but incumbents realize that this security is not guaranteed. Even in elections with relatively low turnover, many incumbents are "running scared"; in every election, a few supposedly safe incumbents are unexpectedly defeated, and members tend to think that it could happen to them the next time around. Mayhew warns: "When we say 'Congressman Smith is unbeatable,' we do not mean that there is nothing he could do that would lose him his seat." As we noted in Chapter 9, this actually means: "Congressman Smith is unbeatable as long as he continues to do the things that he is doing."[14] Members recognize that becoming inattentive to their district, being on the wrong side of a key string of votes, or failing to bring home the district's share of pork could cost them their seats. A potential challenger is always waiting in the wings.

Mayhew outlines three ways that members promote their chances for reelection: advertising, credit claiming, and position taking. Each approach shapes the way members relate to their constituents. "Advertising" in this context refers to appeals or appearances without issue content that get the member's name in front of the public in a favorable way. Advertising includes activities associated with "working the district," such as attending town meetings; appearing in a parade; going to a local Rotary Club lunch; or sending letters of congratulation for graduations, birthdays, or anniversaries. Members of Congress also spend a fair amount of time meeting with their constituents in Washington, D.C., including seeing school groups, tourists, and interest groups from their districts.

With credit claiming, the member of Congress takes credit for something of value to the voter—most commonly, pork-barrel policies targeted to benefit specific constituents or the district as a whole. The goods must be specific and small enough in scale that the member of Congress may believably claim credit. In other words, it is far less credible to take credit for a national drop in violent crime or an increase in SAT scores than for the renovations at a local veterans' hospital or a highway improvement grant. The other main source of credit claiming is casework for individual constituents who request help with tasks such as tracking down a lost Social Security check or expediting

electoral connection
The idea that congressional behavior is centrally motivated by members' desire for reelection.

the processing of a passport. This activity, like advertising, has both district-based and Washington-based components.

"Position taking" refers to any public statement—such as a roll call vote, speech, editorial, or position paper—about a topic of interest to constituents or interest groups. This may be the toughest aspect of a member's job, because, on many issues, the member is likely to alienate a certain segment of the population no matter what position he or she takes. Members try to appeal to specific audiences within their district. For example, while speaking to the Veterans of Foreign Wars members might emphasize their support for a particular new weapons program, but in meetings with college students they might highlight their opposition to the National Security Agency's collection of millions of phone records.

The focus on reelection has some costs. We'll identify five common ones here: (1) There is a perception that Congress has granted itself too many special privileges aimed at securing reelection (such as funding for large staffs and sending mail at no cost). (2) Evidence suggests that some voters question the value of pork-barrel spending, even when it is targeted to their district.[15] (3) Members' desire to please means that Congress has a difficult time refusing any group's demands, which may lead to passage of contradictory policies. (4) Given that most members are experts at getting reelected, they achieve a certain level of independence from the party leadership—that is, they do not depend on party leaders for their reelection. This fact contributes to the fragmentation of Congress and creates difficulties for congressional leaders as they attempt to shepherd policies through the legislative maze. (5) Time spent actively campaigning takes time away from the responsibilities of enacting laws and overseeing their implementation.

The Incumbency Advantage The desire to be reelected influences House members' and senators' behavior both in their districts and in Congress. Consider the early career of Senator Tammy Baldwin (D-WI), who served as the representative of Wisconsin's 2nd congressional district from 1999 to 2013. Initially elected in 1998, she was Wisconsin's first female representative and the first openly gay person ever elected to a freshman term in Congress.[16] In her first two elections, she won with the overwhelming support of liberal voters in Madison, but she lost the surrounding rural areas and suburbs, narrowly winning districtwide. Baldwin recognized that she needed to shore up support outside Madison, and she spent time over the next several years meeting with constituents in the rural and suburban parts of her district. She also explored issues important to these voters, such as the dairy price support program and the problem of chronic wasting disease in Wisconsin deer. Having built up her electoral base (and having benefited from favorable redistricting in 2002), she cruised to victories in her next two elections, winning nearly two-thirds of the vote. After winning reelection to the House four more times, she became the first lesbian elected to the Senate in 2012.

Members' success at pleasing constituents produces large election rewards. As Figure 11.3 shows, very few members are defeated in their reelection races. One way that political scientists have documented the growth of **incumbency advantage** is to examine the electoral margins in House elections. If a member is elected with less than 55 percent of the vote, he or she is said to hold a marginal seat. Since the late 1960s, the number of marginal districts has been declining. Having fewer marginal districts does not necessarily translate into fewer incumbent defeats, but in the past two decades incumbent reelection rates have been near record high levels, with 95 to 98 percent of House incumbents winning in many years.[17]

In 2008, in an election that many called transformational, 95 percent of House incumbents were still reelected. Although the Democrats picked up some seats in the

incumbency advantage
The relative infrequency with which members of Congress are defeated in their attempts for reelection.

House and Senate Reelection Rates

FIGURE
11.3

The whole House is up for reelection every two years, so the line showing the reelection of House members in a given election year represents the percentage of the entire House. Since senators are up for reelection every six years, only one-third of the members are seeking reelection every two years. The line for the Senate represents the percentage of those who won who were up for reelection in that election year. Why do you think that House members have an easier time getting reelected than senators?

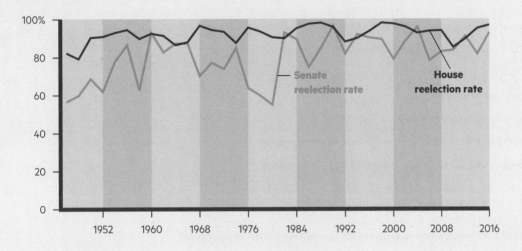

Sources: The 1946–2012 percentages were compiled from Norman J. Ornstein, Thomas E. Mann, Michael J. Malbin, and Andrew Rugg, "Vital Statistics on Congress," www.brookings.edu/vitalstats, pp. 49–50 (accessed 4/18/14); 2014 and 2016 percentages were calculated from election results.

Senate, reelection remained the norm there as well. Even in the "tsunami" election of 2010, in which Republicans made the largest gains in the House since 1948, picking up 63 seats, 86 percent of all incumbents were reelected. Why are incumbents so successful? Scholars have offered several reasons for this increase in incumbency advantage.

In the District: Home Style One explanation for increasing incumbency advantage is rooted in the diversity of congressional districts and states. Members typically respond to the diversity in their districts by developing an appropriate home style: a way of relating to the district.[18] A home style shapes the way members allocate resources, the way incumbents present themselves to their district, and the way they explain their policy positions.

Given the variation among districts, members' home styles vary as well. In some rural districts it is important for representatives to have local roots and voters expect extensive contact with members. Urban districts expect a different kind of style. They have a more mobile population, so it is not crucial to be homegrown. Voters expect less direct contact and place more emphasis on how members explain their policy positions. Incumbency advantage may be explained in part by the skill with which members have cultivated their individual home styles in the last two decades. Members are spending more time at home and less time in Washington than was true a generation ago. This familiarity with the voters has helped them remain in office.

Table 11.1 shows how one member, Senator Tammy Baldwin, spent her time in Washington and in her district as a House member. In general, a legislator's workday

Typical Workdays for a Congressional Representative

Members of Congress are generally busy from morning until late at night, both in Washington, D.C., and in their districts, attending meetings and events. This is the actual schedule from Tammy Baldwin when she represented Wisconsin's 2nd congressional district in the House.

In Washington, D.C. (votes scheduled throughout the day)	
9:15–9:45	Office time
9:45–10:00	Caucus, Democratic members, Subcommittee on Energy and Environment on markup legislation
10:00–12:00	Markup H.R. 3276, H.R. 3258, H.R. 2868, Subcommittee on Energy and Environment
11:30–11:45	Step outside markup to meet with constituents on specifics of health care reform legislation
12:00–12:15	Travel to Department of Justice
12:15–1:15	Lunch with Attorney General Eric Holder
1:30–1:45	Meet with health care CEO on specifics of health care reform legislation
2:00–3:00	Meet with members who support single-payer health care amendment
3:00–4:30	Markup H.R. 3792, Subcommittee on Health
4:30–5:30	Office time
5:30–6:00	Caucus, Democratic members, Energy and Commerce Committee on financial services bill
6:00–6:30	Meet with legislative staff
6:30–7:00	Meet with chief of staff
7:00–7:50	Office time
8:00–10:00	Dinner with chief of staff and political adviser
In the District	
7:00 ET–8:00 CT	Fly from Washington, D.C., to Madison, WI
8:15–10:30	Free time at home
10:30–10:40	Phone interview with area radio station on constituent survey, health care reform, and upcoming listening session
12:15–12:25	Travel to office
12:25–1:00	Office time, edit/sign correspondence
1:00–1:20	Travel to Madison West High School
1:30–1:55	Remarks at school plaza dedication ceremony
2:00–2:30	Travel to Stoughton, WI
2:45–5:00	Listening session (originally scheduled for one hour but continued until all present could speak)
5:00–5:40	Travel home
5:15–5:20	Phone interview with University of Wisconsin student radio station
6:15–6:45	Travel to Middleton, WI
7:00–8:00	Attend and give brief remarks at NAACP annual banquet
8:05–8:25	Travel home

Note: The authors would like to thank then-Representative Tammy Baldwin and her press secretary, Jerilyn Goodman, for sharing this information. Ms. Goodman emphasized that there really isn't a "typical day" for a member but said that these two days illustrate the workload. Baldwin was elected to the U.S. Senate in 2012.

in the Capitol is split between committee meetings, briefings, staff meetings, meetings with constituents, and various dinners and fund-raisers with interest groups and other organizations, punctuated by dashes to the floor of the House or Senate to vote. Days in the district are spent meeting with constituents to explain what is happening in Washington and to listen to voters' concerns.

Campaign Fund-Raising Raising money is also key to staying in office. Incumbents need money to pay for campaign staff, travel, and advertising. It takes at least $1 million to make a credible challenge to an incumbent in most districts, and in many areas with expensive media markets the minimum price tag is $2 million or more. Few challengers can raise that much money. The gap between incumbent and challenger spending has grown dramatically in the past decade, and incumbents now spend about three times as much, on average, as challengers. (For more on campaign finance, see Chapters 9 and 10.)

Money also functions as a deterrent to potential challengers. A sizable reelection fund signals that an incumbent knows how to raise money and will run a strong campaign. The aim is to convince would-be challengers that they have only a slim chance of beating the incumbent—and to convince contributors and party organizations that there's no point in trying to find or support a challenger.

This last point is crucial in explaining incumbency advantage, because it is nearly impossible to beat an incumbent with a weak challenger. Consider that only 10 to 15 percent of challengers in a typical election year have any previous elective experience; when such a high proportion of challengers are amateurs, it is not surprising that so many incumbents win.

Constituency Service Another thing incumbents do to get reelected is "work their districts," taking every opportunity to meet with constituents, listen to their concerns, and perform casework (helping constituents interact with government programs or agencies). Most legislators travel around their districts or states with several staffers whose job is to talk to people who meet the incumbent and to write down contact information and what the incumbent has promised to do. High levels of constituency service may help explain why some incumbents have become electorally secure.

House Speaker Paul Ryan (R-WI) with his constituents at a "listening session" in Kenosha, Wisconsin.
@SpeakerRyan

Members of Congress love doing constituency service because it is an easy way to make voters happy. If a member can help a constituent solve a problem, that person will be more likely to support the member in the future.[19] Many voters might give the incumbent some credit simply for being willing to listen. Therefore, most members devote a significant portion of their staff to constituency service, publish newsletters that tout their good deeds on behalf of constituents, and solicit citizens' requests for help through their newsletters and websites. Most House members have a "How can I help?" type of link on their home page that connects to information on government agencies, grants, internships, service academies, and visiting Washington, D.C.

Most House members work their districts to an extreme; they are said to be in the "Tuesday to Thursday Club," meaning they are in Washington only during the middle of the week, spending the rest of their time at home in their districts. These members go to diners and coffee shops on Saturday mornings to chat, spend the day at public events in their "Meet Your Representative" RV, then hit the bowling alleys at night to meet a few more people. One member has even joked that his wife has given up sending him out for groceries because he spends three hours talking with people while getting a loaf of bread.

This combination of factors gives incumbents substantial advantages over candidates who might run against them. By virtue of their position, they can help constituents who have problems with an agency or a program. They attract media attention because of their actions in office; small local newspapers will even reprint members' press releases verbatim because they do not have the resources to do their own reporting. Members can use the money and other resources associated with their position for casework and contact with voters (trips home to their district and the salaries of their staffers who do constituency service are taxpayer funded). And they use their official position as a platform for raising campaign cash. A contributor who donates as a way to gain access to the policy-making process will be inclined to give to someone already in office. Finally, most incumbents represent states or districts whose partisan balance (the number of likely supporters of their party versus the number likely to prefer the other party) is skewed in their favor—if it weren't, they probably wouldn't have won the seat in the first place.

Senator Mark Kirk (R-IL) is shown here campaigning for reelection. A Republican in a heavily Democratic state, Kirk lost to his Democratic challenger, Tammy Duckworth. @MarkKirk

National Forces in Congressional Elections There is also another consequence of the electoral connection. Because congressional politics tends to be local, voters generally are not strongly influenced by the president or the national parties. Because most incumbents can insulate themselves from national forces, it is more difficult to hold the government accountable. For example, in the 2016 elections 62 percent of the people believed the nation was "on the wrong track." Yet 97 percent of House incumbents won reelection.

Many House and Senate candidates distance themselves from the national party. For example, in the 2010 West Virginia Senate race Democratic candidate Joe Manchin made his opposition to the Democratic Party's energy policy very clear with an ad in which he shot a mock version of the bill with a rifle. However, there are nationalized "wave" elections in which national issues can overwhelm incumbents' attempts to insulate themselves. In 2006, many House Republicans tried to distance themselves from President Bush and the unpopular war in Iraq, but more than 20 Republicans were defeated and Democrats regained control of the House. In the 2010 midterms, the same thing happened to moderate Democrats who were ousted by voters who believed the government had gone too far in its response to the recession and health care. These national forces led the Democrats to lose 63 House seats (and 6 Senate seats), with the result that the Republicans regained control of the House.

National forces in congressional elections also may be evident in presidential years. In 2008, Republicans faced a backlash against Bush, whose approval ratings had hit record lows. Republican members of Congress avoided being seen with him, and Democrats highlighted their opponents' earlier support for the president. In 2012, the congressional elections ratified the status quo; despite Obama's solid win, the Republicans retained control of the House and the Democrats increased their majority in the Senate only slightly. The 2016 presidential election featured two nominees, Hillary Clinton and Donald Trump, who had the highest negative ratings of any pair of major-party candidates. Republican congressional candidates were especially likely to distance themselves from their party's nominee. Overall, the localized nature of congressional elections and the incumbency advantage promote congressional stability in the face of presidential change. This has profound implications for governance because they increase the likelihood that different parties will control the presidency and Congress. This kind of divided government complicates accountability because the president and Congress have become adept at blaming each other when things go wrong.

Redistricting Connects Representation and Elections The shape and makeup of congressional districts are critical to understanding representation in Congress and the electoral connection. District boundaries determine who is eligible to vote in any given congressional race, and these boundaries are re-drawn every 10 years, after each national census. **Redistricting** is the task of state legislatures. Its official purpose is to ensure that districts are roughly equal in population, which in turn ensures that every vote counts equally in determining the composition of the legislature.

District populations vary over time as people move from state to state or from one part of a state to another. At the national level, states gain or lose legislative seats after each census through **apportionment**, which is the process of dividing the fixed number of House seats (435) among the states based on increases and decreases in state populations. Thus, states growing the fastest gain seats and states that are not growing as fast or that are losing population lose seats (for example, after the 2010 census Texas gained four seats in Congress while Ohio lost two). The one legislature in America that is not redistricted is the U.S. Senate, which has two legislators elected per state, thus giving voters in small states proportionally more influence than those in large states when it comes to the Senate.

redistricting
Re-drawing the geographic boundaries of legislative districts. This happens every 10 years to ensure that districts remain roughly equal in population.

apportionment
The process of assigning the 435 seats in the House to the states based on increases or decreases in state population.

Types of Gerrymanders

We have learned that the redistricting process is a powerful tool politicians can use to help their party, or individual members, win and maintain seats in Congress. Let's look at two key types of gerrymandering.

Partisan gerrymanders

Elected officials from one party draw district lines that benefit candidates from their party and hurt candidates from other parties. This usually occurs when one party has majorities in both houses of the state legislature and occupies the governorship and can therefore enact redistricting legislation without input from the minority party.

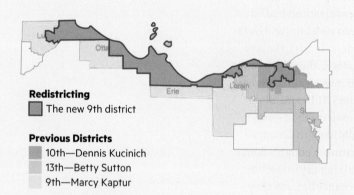

Redistricting
- The new 9th district

Previous Districts
- 10th—Dennis Kucinich
- 13th—Betty Sutton
- 9th—Marcy Kaptur

After the 2010 census, Ohio lost two seats in Congress (see our discussion of apportionment on page 377). Republicans controlled the redistricting process and wanted the loss of seats to come from the Democrats. So the Republicans drew a new 9th congressional district that cut across the districts of three existing Democratic members of Congress. Obviously only one could win the Democratic primary—that happened to be Marcy Kaptur. Democrats Kucinich and Sutton had to leave Congress.

Racial gerrymanders

Redistricting is used to help or hurt the chances of minority legislative candidates. The Voting Rights Act (VRA) of 1965 mandated that districting plans for many parts of the South be approved by the U.S. Department of Justice or a Washington, D.C., district court. Subsequent interpretations of the 1982 VRA amendments and Supreme Court decisions led to the creation of districts in which racial minorities are in the majority. The aim of these majority-minority districts was to raise the percentage of African-American and Latino elected officials.

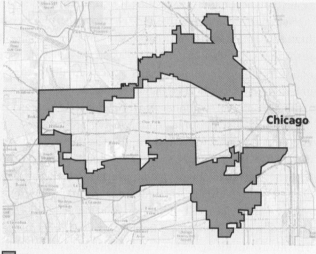

- The new 4th congressional district

Illinois's 4th congressional district is a clear example of racial gerrymandering. The district has a very odd shape, but it incorporates two heavily Latino areas. (The northern part has a high Puerto Rican population and the southern part is largely Mexican; both areas are heavily Democratic.) This district is a stronghold of Democrat Luis Gutierrez, who is of Puerto Rican descent, and is seen as a safe district for Democrats.

In theory, redistricting proceeds from a set of principles that define what districts should look like. One criterion is that districts should be roughly equal in population based on the principles of "one-person, one-vote" established by the Supreme Court in the 1960s.[20] They should also reflect "communities of interest," grouping like-minded voters into the same district. There are also technical criteria, including compactness (districts should not have extremely bizarre shapes) and contiguity (one part of a district cannot be completely separated from the rest of the district). Mapmakers also try to respect traditional natural boundaries, avoid splitting municipalities, preserve existing districts, and avoid diluting the voting power of racial minorities.

Partisan Redistricting Although the preceding principles are important, they are not the driving force in the redistricting process. Suppose a Democrat holds a state assembly seat from an urban district populated mainly by citizens with strong Democratic Party ties. After a census, the Republican-dominated state legislature develops a new plan that extends the representative's district into the suburbs, claiming that the change counteracts population declines within the city by adding suburban voters. However, these suburban voters will likely be Republicans, increasing the chance that the Democrat will face strong opposition in future elections and maybe lose his or her seat. Such changes have an important impact on voters as well. Voters who are "shifted" to a new district by a change in boundaries may be unable to vote for the incumbent they have supported for years and may instead get a representative who doesn't share their views.

In congressional redistricting, a reduction in the number of seats allocated to a state can lead to districting plans that put two incumbents in the same district, forcing them to run against each other. Incumbents from one party use these opportunities to defeat incumbents from the other party. Both parties use this technique and other tools of creative cartography to gain partisan advantage.

These attempts to use the redistricting process for political advantage are called gerrymandering. The term is named after Elbridge Gerry, a Massachusetts House member and governor, vice president under James Madison, and author of one of the original partisan redistricting plans (including a district with a thin, winding shape resembling a salamander). In addition to the partisan gerrymanders discussed here, see Nuts & Bolts 11.1 for examples of redistricting strategies.

gerrymandering
Attempting to use the process of re-drawing district boundaries to benefit a political party, protect incumbents, or change the proportion of minority voters in a district.

Racial Redistricting Redistricting may yield boundaries that look highly unusual. During the 1992 redistricting in North Carolina, the Justice Department told state legislators that they needed to create two districts with majority populations of minority voters (called majority-minority districts). Figure 11.4 shows the plan they enacted, in which the district boundaries look like a pattern of spiderwebs and ink blots. Moreover, one of the districts had parts that ended up being only as wide as I-85, following the highway off an exit ramp, over a bridge, and down the entrance ramp on the other side. This move prevented the I-85 district from bisecting the district it was traveling through, which would have violated the state law requiring contiguous districts.

The North Carolina example shows how convoluted redistricting plans can become. Part of the complexity is due to the availability of census databases that allow line drawers to divide voters as closely as they want, moving neighborhood by neighborhood, even house by house. Why bother with this level of detail? Because redistricting influences who gets elected; it is active politicking in its most fundamental form. The North Carolina plan was ultimately declared unconstitutional by the U.S. Supreme Court—a ruling that opened the door for dozens of lawsuits about racial redistricting (see discussion in Chapter 5 of the Voting Rights Act of 1965 and the more recent Supreme Court

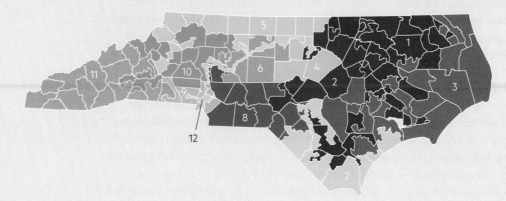

FIGURE 11.4

North Carolina Redistricting, 1992

This set of House districts was the subject of the landmark Supreme Court ruling *Shaw v. Reno* (1993), in which the Court said that "appearances matter" when drawing district lines. Do you agree? Should other factors such as race, party, and competitiveness play a greater role than district shape?

Source: North Carolina General Assembly, 1992 Congressional Base Plan No. 10, http://ncga.state.nc.us (accessed 10/26/12).

rulings on racial redistricting, especially the 2013 case in which the Court struck down the part of the law that had identified states that needed to have their redistricting plans preapproved by the Justice Department[21]). The current legal standard is that race cannot be the predominant factor in drawing congressional district lines, but it can be one of the factors. Nonetheless, there is still plenty of room to create districts that will be composed of voters who will vote in ways that will have profound political consequences. The obvious political implications of redistricting often lead to demands that district plans be prepared or approved by nonpartisan committees or by panels of judges who are theoretically immune from political pressure. Such a process, as in Iowa, often produces more competitive districts.

The Responsibility–Responsiveness Dilemma As mentioned earlier, polls show that despite generally approving of their own member of Congress, people hold Congress itself in very low esteem. This is rooted in the conflicts that arise from Congress's dual roles: responsibility for national policy making and responsiveness to local constituencies.[22] This duality may make members of Congress appear to be simultaneously small-minded seekers of meaningless symbolic legislation and great leaders who debate important issues. Indeed, the range of issues that Congress must address is vast, from taxes and health care reform to overseeing the classification of black-eyed peas, from authorizing the war with Afghanistan and expanding free trade to declaring a National Cholesterol Education Month. Part of the national frustration with Congress arises because we want our representatives to be responsible *and* responsive; we want them to be great national leaders *and* to take care of our local and, at times, personal concerns.

Difficult choices have to be made between being responsive and being responsible. Rather than understanding these issues as being inherent in the legislative process, we often accuse members of **gridlock** and partisan bickering when our conflicting demands are not met. For example, public-opinion polls routinely show that the public wants lower taxes; more spending on education, the environment, and health care; and balanced budgets. But those three things cannot happen simultaneously. We often expect the impossible from Congress and then are frustrated when it doesn't happen.

gridlock
An inability to enact legislation because of partisan conflict within Congress or between Congress and the president.

The responsibility–responsiveness dilemma brings us back to the puzzle we posed at the beginning of this section: Why is there a persistent 30 to 40 percent gap between approval ratings for individual members and for the institution? As Richard Fenno put it, "If Congress is the 'broken branch,' how come we love our congressman so much?"[23] The answer may simply be that members of Congress tend to respond more to their constituents' demands than to solving national problems. And when Congress becomes embroiled in debates about constituencies' conflicting demands, the institution may appear ineffectual. But as long as members keep the "folks back home" happy, their individual popularity will remain high. The next section describes how members structure the institutions of Congress to help them get reelected.

"Why Should I Care?"

How would you like your member of Congress to represent you? Should members just represent the interests of their district or the broader nation? Should they be responsive or responsible? Constituents have an interest in holding their members accountable, yet most congressional elections are not very competitive. So if you don't like how your member is representing you, what can you do about it? Understanding the nature of representation and the incumbency advantage can help answer these important questions.

The structure of Congress

★

EXAMINE HOW PARTIES, THE COMMITTEE SYSTEM, AND STAFFERS ENABLE CONGRESS TO FUNCTION

As we have seen, the goal of getting reelected greatly influences the behavior of members of Congress. The reelection goal also has a strong influence on the way that Congress is structured, both formally (staff, the committee system, parties, and the leadership) and informally (norms). Despite the importance of the electoral connection, the goal of being reelected cannot explain everything about members' behavior and the congressional structure. This section examines some other explanations for the way Congress is set up: the policy motivations of members, the partisan basis for congressional institutions, and the importance of the committee system.

Informal structures

Various norms provide an informal structure for the way Congress works. *Universalism* is a norm stating that when benefits are being divided up they should be awarded to as many districts and states as possible. Thus, when it comes to handing out federal highway dollars or expenditures for the Pentagon's weapons programs the benefits are broadly distributed across the entire country, which means that votes in support of these bills tend to be very lopsided. For example, the $305 billion 2015 transportation bill contained some spending in every part of the country and passed by an 83–16 vote in the Senate and a 359–65 margin in the House.[24]

Another norm, **logrolling**, reinforces universalism with the idea that "if you scratch my back, I'll scratch yours." This norm leads members of Congress to support bills that they otherwise might not vote for in exchange for other members' votes on bills that are very important to them. For example, House members from a dairy state might vote for tobacco price supports even if their state had no tobacco farmers and in return they would expect a member from the tobacco state to vote for the dairy price support bill. This norm can produce wasteful pork-barrel spending. For example, in the 2011 budget a $1.1 trillion omnibus appropriations bill contained more than 6,488 **earmarks** worth $8.3 billion, so nearly everyone gained something by passing it. The 2016 omnibus appropriations bill did not include any traditional earmarks, following the ban on formal earmarks in both the House and Senate in 2011, but there were still billions of dollars in targeted spending as members of Congress found ways to secure funding for their district or state. Senator John McCain (R-AZ), Senate Armed Services Committee chairman, called it a last-minute mess full of "wasteful, unnecessary, and inappropriate pork-barrel projects."[25] The Take a Stand feature describes some of the debates in Congress and among political commentators about the merits of this type of spending.[26]

The norm of *specialization* is also important, both for the efficient operation of Congress and for members' reelection. By specializing and becoming an expert on a given issue, members provide valuable information to the institution as a whole and also create a basis for credit claiming. This norm is stronger in the House, where members often develop a few areas of expertise, whereas senators tend to be policy generalists. For example, Representative John Lewis (D-GA) has dedicated much of his decades-long House career to the issue of civil rights, while Senator John McCain (R-AZ) has had his hand in a variety of issues, including campaign finance and lobbying reform, tax policy, telecommunications and aviation issues, national defense, foreign policy, and immigration policy.

The **seniority** norm also serves individual and institutional purposes. This norm holds that the member with the longest service on a committee will chair the committee. Although there have been numerous violations of the norm in the past 30 years, whereby the most senior member has been passed over for someone whom the party leaders favored instead, the norm benefits the institution by ensuring orderly succession in committee leadership.[27] The norm also benefits members by providing a tangible reason that voters should return them to Congress year after year. Many members of Congress make this point when campaigning, and the issue is more than just posturing. Committee chairs *are* better able to "bring home the bacon" than a junior member who is still learning the ropes.

---

logrolling
A form of reciprocity in which members of Congress support bills that they otherwise might not vote for in exchange for other members' votes on bills that are very important to them.

earmarks
Federally funded local projects attached to bills passed through Congress.

seniority
The informal congressional norm of choosing the member who has served the longest on a particular committee to be the committee chair.

The Politics of Pork

What is pork? Pork traditionally took the form of earmarked funding for a specific project that is not subject to standard, neutral spending formulas or a competitive process. However, since 2011 the House and Senate have banned formal earmarks, so members have created new ways to make sure that the benefits continue to flow to their constituents. Some broader definitions of pork include any benefit targeted to a particular political constituency (typically an important business in a member's district), even if the benefit is part of a stand-alone bill. Examples of this type of targeted federal largesse include the bill that provided federal support to the airlines after the September 11 attacks, which sailed through Congress without much debate, and the lucrative contracts to rebuild Iraq that were awarded to politically well-connected businesses.

Pork is simply wasteful spending.
Pork has plenty of critics. Citizens Against Government Waste, one of the most outspoken groups to tackle pork-barrel spending, compiles each year's federal pork-barrel projects into their annual *Congressional Pig Book* to draw attention to pork. The ban on earmarks has helped a great deal, but committee and informal earmarks are still pervasive. The arguments against pork are especially urgent during a time of massive budget deficits. According to this view, the national interest in a balanced budget should take priority over localized projects.

One common tactic previously used by legislators to win approval for pork was to insert earmarks into emergency spending bills that were expected to pass, such as disaster relief for flood and hurricane victims, spending for national security after the September 11 attacks, or funding for the wars in Iraq and Afghanistan. For example, the $636.3 billion defense appropriations bill in 2010 included $128.3 billion for the wars in Iraq and Afghanistan and was also stuffed with 1,719 earmarks worth $7.6 billion.[a] Even without specific earmarks, House members and senators were still claiming credit for plenty of pork in the 2016 omnibus spending bill: $120 million to upgrade the M1 Abrams tank, which is opposed by the Pentagon; $15 million for the Pacific Coastal Salmon Recovery Fund; and $4 million for an aquatic plant control program.[b] As one reporter explained, "[T]he truth is that earmarks haven't really vanished; they've merely changed shape.... Call it the era of vegan pork."[c] Members may simply be taking credit for something that was going to pass anyway or they may secure the project through "letter-marking"—writing a letter to the relevant agency to ask for the funding to be directed to their district. This type

President Obama signs the omnibus spending bill in Washington, D.C., in January 2014. This bill funded a broad range of military and discretionary programs.

of "asking nicely" for pork (sometimes referred to as "stealth pork") can be effective because agencies know that their funding depends on keeping members of Congress happy.

Pork has its good side.
Nonetheless, some argue that pork is the "glue of legislating," because these small side payments secure the passage of larger bills. If it takes a little pork for the home district or state in order to get important legislation through Congress, so be it. The motives of budget reform groups that call for greater fiscal discipline in Congress may also be questioned, since many of these groups oppose government spending in general—not just on pork. In some cases, policies they identify as pork have significant national implications: military readiness, road improvements to support economic infrastructure, or the development of new agricultural and food products. National interests can be served, in other words, by allowing local interests to take a dip into the pork barrel. Put another way, "pork is in the eye of the beholder," or one person's pork is another person's essential spending. Finally, defenders of pork point out that even according to the critics' own definition, pork spending constitutes about one-half of 1 percent of the total federal budget.

take a stand

1. If you were a member of Congress, would you work hard to deliver pork to your district or work to eliminate as much pork as you could from the budget?

2. Why is it so difficult to eliminate pork even in the face of massive budget deficits?

Formal structures

Formal structures also shape members' behavior in Congress. Political parties, party leadership, the committee system, and staff provide the context within which members of Congress make policy and represent their constituents (see Nuts & Bolts 11.2).

Parties and Party Leaders Political parties are important for allocating power in Congress. Party leaders are always elected on straight party-line votes, with the majority party determining committee leadership, the division of seats on committees, and the allocation of committee resources. Parties in Congress also become more important when opposing parties control the two chambers. This was the case between 1981 and 1986, when Republicans controlled the Senate and Democrats controlled the House, and in part of 2001 and 2002 and 2011–2014 when the opposite was true.

A leading theory of congressional organization points to the importance of parties in solving collective action problems in Congress. Without parties, the legislative process would be much more fractured and decentralized because members would be autonomous agents in battle with one another. Parties provide a team framework that allows members to work together for broadly beneficial goals. Just think how difficult it would be for a member of Congress to get a bill passed if he or she had to build a coalition from scratch every time. Instead, parties provide a solid base from which coalition building may begin. As discussed in Chapter 8, political parties provide brand name recognition for members.

The top party leader in the House—and the only House leader mentioned in the Constitution—is the Speaker of the House, who is the head of the majority party and influences the legislative agenda, committee assignments, scheduling, and overall party strategy. The Democratic Party made history in January 2007 when its representatives elected Nancy Pelosi as the first woman to serve as Speaker. John Boehner was elected Speaker in 2011 after Republicans regained control of the House in the 2010 midterm elections and was replaced by Paul Ryan in 2015. The Speaker is aided by the Majority Leader, the Majority Whip, and the caucus chair (in addition to many others in lower-level party positions). The Majority Leader is one of the national spokespersons for the party and also helps with the day-to-day operation of the legislative process. The Majority Whip oversees the extensive whip system, which has three functions: information gathering, information dissemination, and coalition building. The whips meet regularly to discuss legislative strategy and scheduling. The whips then pass along this information to colleagues in their respective parties and indicate the party's position on a given bill. Whips also take a head count of party members in the House on specific votes and communicate this information to the party leaders.

If a vote looks close, whips try to persuade members to support the party's position ("whip" comes from the fox-hunting term "whipper-in," meaning the person who keeps the hounds from wandering too far from the pack; similarly, party whips try to ensure that members do not stray too far from party positions). The conference chair for the Republicans (or caucus chair for the Democrats) runs the party meetings to elect floor leaders, to make committee assignments, and to set legislative agendas. The minority party in the House has a parallel structure: its leader is the Minority Leader, and the second in command is the Minority Whip.

The Senate leadership does not have as much power as the leadership of the House, mostly because individual senators have more power than individual House members due to the Senate's rule of unlimited debate. The Majority Leader and Minority Leader are the leaders of their respective parties, and second in command to them are the Assistant Majority and Minority Leaders. The Senate also has a whip system, but it is not as developed as the House system. Republicans have a separate position

Speaker of the House
The elected leader of the House of Representatives.

Majority Leader
The elected head of the party holding the majority of seats in the House or Senate.

whip system
An organization of House leaders who work to disseminate information and promote party unity in voting on legislation.

Minority Leader
The elected head of the party holding the minority of seats in the House or Senate.

Majority-Party Structure in the House of Representatives and the Senate

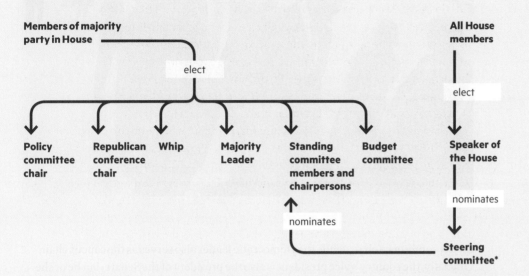

Members of majority party in House → **elect** →
- **Policy committee chair**
- **Republican conference chair**
- **Whip**
- **Majority Leader**
- **Standing committee members and chairpersons** ← nominates
- **Budget committee**

All House members → **elect** → **Speaker of the House** → **nominates** → **Steering committee***

*Steering committee includes the Speaker, majority leader, and whip, and some members who are appointed by the Speaker and some who are elected by the Conference.

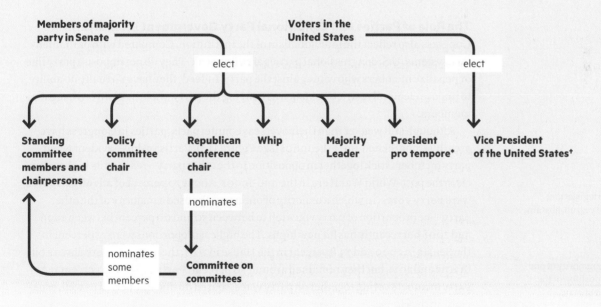

Members of majority party in Senate → **elect** →
- **Standing committee members and chairpersons** ← nominates some members
- **Policy committee chair**
- **Republican conference chair** → **nominates** → **Committee on committees**
- **Whip**
- **Majority Leader**
- **President pro tempore***

Voters in the United States → **elect** → **Vice President of the United States**†

*The president pro tempore is elected by the majority party members, but by custom is the most senior member of the majority party.
†The vice president of the United States is the president of the Senate, but rarely presides over the floor. The vice president's most important role is to break tie votes.

Party leadership is central in the legislative process. Senate Minority Leader Chuck Schumer (D-NY, left), Speaker of the House Paul Ryan (R-WI, right), and House Minority Leader Nancy Pelosi (D-CA, behind) must work together and with other members of Congress to pass legislation.

president pro tempore
A largely symbolic position usually held by the most senior member of the majority party in the Senate.

for the conference chair, while the Democratic leader also serves as the caucus chair. Officially, the country's vice president is also the president of the Senate, but he or she appears in the chamber only when needed to cast a tie-breaking vote. The Constitution also mentions the **president pro tempore** of the Senate, whose formal duties involve presiding over the Senate when the vice president is not there. This is typically the most senior member of the majority party, and the position does not have any real power. (In fact, the actual president pro tempore rarely presides over the Senate and the task is typically given to a more junior senator.)

The Role of Parties and Conditional Party Government Political parties in Congress also reflect the individualism of the institution. Compared with parliamentary systems, U.S. congressional parties are very weak. They do not impose a party line or penalize members who vote against the party. Indeed, they have virtually no ability to impose electoral restrictions (such as denying the party's nomination) on renegade members.

Although still weaker than their overseas counterparts, parties in Congress have greatly strengthened since the 1960s (see Figure 11.5). Partisanship—evident when party members stick together in opposition to the other party—reached its highest levels in the post–World War II era in the mid-1990s. About 70 percent of all **roll call votes** were **party votes**, in which a majority of one party opposed a majority of the other party. The proportion of party votes fell to between 50 and 60 percent between 1996 and 2008 but recently has hit new highs. The highest proportions were 72 percent in the Senate in 2009 and 75.8 percent in the House in 2011; the numbers were down a bit in 2012 and 2013, but they remained around 70 percent. **Party unity**, the percentage of party members voting together on party votes, soared during this period as well, especially in the House.

The Democratic Party has become much more cohesive as southern Democrats have started to vote more like their northern counterparts, partly because of the increasing importance of African-American voters who tend to vote for Democrats in the South. Moreover, increasing Republican strength in the South means that the remaining Democratic districts are more liberal, because Republicans defeat the more moderate Democrats. Similarly, there are fewer moderates within the Republican

roll call vote
A recorded vote on legislation; members may vote yes, no, abstain, or present.

party vote
A vote in which the majority of one party opposes the position of the majority of the other party.

party unity
The extent to which members of Congress in the same party vote together on party votes.

Party Votes and Unity in Congress, 1962–2015

(A) Party votes are said to occur when a majority of one party opposes a majority of the other party, and **(B)** party unity refers to the percentage of the party members who vote together on party votes. These two graphs make two important points. First, partisanship has increased in the last two decades, in terms of both the proportion of party votes and the level of party unity. Second, despite these increased levels of partisanship, only about two-thirds of all votes in the House and Senate divide the two parties. Given these potentially conflicting observations, how would you assess the argument that partisanship in Congress is far too intense?

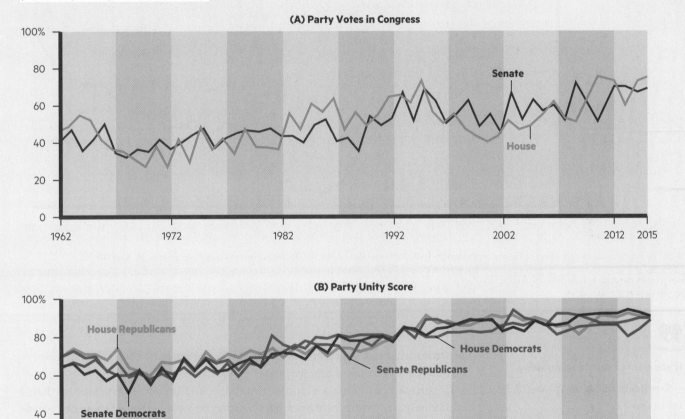

Source: CQ Roll Call http://cqrollcall.com/cq (accessed 7/28/16).

Party, as most regions of the country that used to elect moderate Republicans are now electing Democrats.[28]

Another way to examine changes in the composition of the parties is to examine the ideological distribution of members of Congress (see Figure 11.6). The parties in Congress are now more polarized than at any point in U.S. history. In the 1970s, there was considerable overlap between the Democratic and Republican parties. But in the most recent Congress, the two parties are almost completely separated—that is, only a few Democrats are more conservative than the most liberal Republican. At the same time,

FIGURE 11.6

Ideological Polarization in Congress, 1879-2015

Although party polarization in Congress has been high in the past, it lessened in the early twentieth century. Polarization has increased steadily in the last 70 years, and today's Congress is more polarized than ever. What do you think causes this extreme polarization?

Ideological distance between the parties in each chamber

House

Senate

Source: "More on Polarization through the 114th," Voteview blog, January 30, 2016, https://voteviewblog.wordpress.com (accessed 5/16/16).

> **If you want to get along, go along.**

—**Sam Rayburn,** former Speaker of the House

Speaker Paul Ryan (R-WI) discusses the policy battles Congress faced in November 2015, as they pushed to pass a $1.1 trillion spending bill and avoid a holiday season government shutdown. @SpeakerRyan

the parties are growing further apart, which makes it even harder for the Republicans and the Democrats to work together and compromise to pass legislation.

This greater cohesiveness within parties and separation across parties means that conditional party government (see Chapter 8) may be in play—that is, strong party leadership is possible in Congress, but it is conditional on the consent of party members.[29] That consent is more likely if there are strong differences between the parties but unity within parties. Leaders' chief responsibility is to get their party's legislative agenda through Congress, but they primarily have to rely on persuasion and control over the timing of when bills come up for a vote rather than telling members what to do. Leaders' success largely depends on personal skills, communicative abilities, and trust. Some of the most successful leaders, such as Lyndon Johnson (D-TX), Majority Leader of the Senate from 1955 to 1961, and Sam Rayburn (D-TX), Speaker of the House for more than 17 years, kept in touch with key members on a daily basis. Another important tool of the leadership is agenda control: both positive (getting bills to the floor that are favored by the party) and negative (preventing votes on bills that would divide the majority party).

Leaders also must have the ability to bargain and compromise. One observer noted, "To Senator Johnson, public policy evidently was an inexhaustibly bargainable product."[30] Such leaders find solutions where none appear possible. Leaders also do favors for members (such as making campaign appearances, helping with fund-raising, contributing to campaigns, helping them get desired committee assignments, or guiding pet projects through the legislative process) to engender a feeling of personal obligation to the leadership when it needs a key vote.

The party's most powerful positive incentives are in the area of campaign finance. In recent years the congressional campaign committees of both parties and the national party organizations have been supplying candidates with money and resources in an attempt to gain more influence in the electoral process. Party leaders may also help arrange a campaign stop or a fund-raiser for a candidate with party leaders or the president. For example, President Obama held dozens of fund-raisers for Democrats in 2014, earning him the label of "Fundraiser-in-Chief" from CNN.[31] Such events typically raise $500,000 to more than $1 million.

Despite these positive reinforcements, members' desire for reelection always comes before party concerns and leadership rarely tries to force a member to vote against his or her constituents' interests. For example, Democrats from rural areas, where most constituents support gun ownership and many are hunters, would not be expected to vote the party line favoring a gun control bill. But if a member of Congress did something much more extreme that crossed the party's leadership—for example, supporting the opposing party's candidate for Speaker or passing strategic information to the opposition—he or she could expect to be disciplined by the party's leaders.

Speaker Boehner disciplined four Tea Party House Republicans late in 2012 by removing them from their committees. Boehner had tired of the "brinkmanship" approach to budget politics favored by the Tea Party representatives, or Freedom Caucus as they are known now, and resented their willingness to go against the party leadership. Things deteriorated for Boehner over the next three years as Tea Partiers tried, unsuccessfully, to push the country off a "fiscal cliff" early in 2013 rather than agree to any tax increases (the "cliff" was the economic damage that would have been caused by automatic spending cuts and tax increases that were due to kick in). Boehner then was unable to prevent a government shutdown in the fall of 2013. The Freedom Caucus also pushed for repeated votes to repeal Obamacare, restrict President Obama's executive actions on immigration policy, and restrict funding for Planned Parenthood. Most significantly, they forced Boehner to resign as Speaker in September 2015 and then rejected the heir apparent, Majority Leader Kevin McCarthy, because he was too moderate. Finally, they agreed to accept Paul Ryan as Speaker, but nine Freedom Caucus members voted against him.[32]

The Committee System The committee system in the House and Senate is another crucial part of the legislative structure (see Table 11.2). There are four types of committees: standing, select, joint, and conference. **Standing committees**, which have ongoing membership and jurisdictions, are where most of Congress's work gets done. These committees draft legislation and oversee the implementation of the laws they pass. For example, the Agriculture Committee in the House and the one in the Senate have jurisdiction over farm programs such as commodity price supports, crop insurance, and soil conservation. But they also create and oversee policy for rural electrification and development; the food stamp and nutrition programs; and the inspection of livestock, poultry, seafood, and meat products. Many committees share jurisdiction on policy—for example, the House Natural Resources Committee oversees the National Forest Service and forests on federally owned lands, and the Agriculture Committee oversees policy for forests on privately owned lands.

Select committees typically address a specific topic for one or two terms, such as the Select Committee on Energy Independence and Global Warming that operated from 2007 to 2010. These committees do not have the same legislative authority as standing committees; rather, they mostly serve to collect information, provide policy options, and draw attention to a given issue.

Joint committees are made up of members of both the House and the Senate, and they rarely have legislative authority. The Joint Committee on Taxation, for example,

A sitting president can be a powerful ally in a campaign. In 2016, President Obama campaigned with Senate candidate Catherine Cortez Masto (D-NV), who ultimately won her race.

standing committees
Committees that are a permanent part of the House or Senate structure, holding more importance and authority than other committees.

select committees
Committees in the House or Senate created to address a specific issue for one or two terms.

joint committees
Committees that contain members of both the House and Senate but have limited authority.

does not have authority to send legislation concerning tax policy to the floor of the House or Senate. Instead, it gathers information and provides estimates of the consequences of proposed tax legislation. Joint committees may also be temporary, such as the "Supercommittee" (officially the Joint Select Committee on Deficit Reduction) that was formed in 2011.

conference committees
Temporary committees created to negotiate differences between the House and Senate versions of a piece of legislation that has passed through both chambers.

Conference committees are formed to resolve specific differences between House and Senate versions of legislation that are passed in each chamber. These committees mostly comprise standing committee members from each chamber who worked on the bill.

TABLE 11.2

Congressional Committees

There are equivalent committees in the House and Senate (and some joint committees) that work on similar problems and craft similar bills whose differences must be reconciled before a final bill becomes law. Equivalent or similar committees in both chambers are listed across from each other.

House Committees	Senate Committees	Joint Committees
Agriculture	Agriculture, Nutrition, and Forestry	Joint Economic Committee
Appropriations	Appropriations	Joint Committee on the Library
Armed Services	Armed Services	Joint Committee on Printing
Budget	Budget	Joint Committee on Taxation
Education and Workforce	Health, Education, Labor, and Pensions	
Energy and Commerce	Commerce, Science, and Transportation	
Ethics	Select Committee on Ethics	
Financial Services	Banking, Housing, and Urban Affairs	
Foreign Affairs	Foreign Relations	
Homeland Security	Homeland Security and Governmental Affairs	
House Administration	Rules and Administration	
Judiciary	Judiciary	
Natural Resources	Energy and Natural Resources	
Select Committee on Intelligence	Select Committee on Intelligence	
Small Business	Small Business and Entrepreneurship	
Transportation and Infrastructure	Environment and Public Works	
Veterans' Affairs	Veterans' Affairs	
Ways and Means	Finance	

Committees specific to the House	Committees specific to the Senate
Oversight and Government Reform	Special Committee on Aging
Rules	Indian Affairs
Science, Space, and Technology	

The committee system creates a division of labor that helps members get reelected by supporting their specialization and credit claiming. For example, a chair of the Agriculture Committee or of a key agricultural subcommittee may reasonably take credit for passing an important bill for the farmers back home, such as the Cottonseed Payment Program that provides assistance to cottonseed farmers who lost crops due to hurricanes.

The number of members who could make these credible claims expanded dramatically in the 1970s with the proliferation of subcommittees (there are 100 in the House and 67 in the Senate). Speaking about the House, one observer said, with some exaggeration, that if you ever forget a member's name you can simply refer to him or her as "Mr. or Ms. Chairman" and you will be right about half the time. This view of congressional committees is based on the **distributive theory**, which is rooted in the norm of reciprocity and the incentive to provide benefits for the district. The theory holds that members will seek committee assignments to best serve their district's interests, the leadership will accommodate those requests, and the floor will respect the views of the committees in a big institution-level logroll—that is, committee members will support one another's legislation. This means that members tend to have an interest in and to support the policies produced by the committees they serve on. For example, members from farm states would want to serve on the Agriculture Committee and members with a lot of military bases or defense contractors in their districts would want to be on the Armed Services Committee.

Nonetheless, the committee system does not exist simply to further members' electoral goals. According to **informational theory**, it also provides collective benefits to the rest of the members through committee members' expertise on policy, which helps reduce uncertainty about policy outcomes.[33] By deferring to expert committees, members are able to achieve beneficial outcomes while using their time more efficiently. This informational theory is also consistent with the argument made by Richard Fenno 40 years ago that members will serve on committees for reasons other than simply trying to achieve reelection (which is implied by the distributive theory). Fenno argued that members also were interested in achieving power within the institution and in making good policy.[34] Others argue that goals vary from bill to bill and all members pursue reelection advantage, institutional power, and effective policy in different circumstances.[35] Thus, the committee system does not exist only to further members' electoral goals, but it often serves that purpose.

Committees also serve the policy needs of the majority party, largely because it controls a majority of seats on every committee. The party ratios on each committee generally reflect the partisan distribution in the overall chamber, but the majority party gives itself somewhat larger majorities on the important committees such as Ways and Means (which controls tax policy), Appropriations, and Rules. This is especially true for the Rules Committee (in which the majority party controls 9 of the 13 seats). The Rules Committee is important to the majority party because it structures the nature of debate in the House by setting the length of debate and the type and number of amendments to a bill that will be allowed. These decisions are called *rules* and must be approved by a majority of the House members. The Rules Committee has become an arm of the majority-party leadership, and in many instances it provides rules that support the party's policy agenda or that protect its members from having to take controversial positions. For example, the Rules Committee prevented many amendments on the 2010 health care reform bill; if the amendments had come to a vote, they would have divided the Democratic Party. Majority members are expected to support their party on votes on rules, even if they end up voting against the related legislation.

distributive theory
The idea that members of Congress will join committees that best serve the interests of their district and that committee members will support one another's legislation.

informational theory
The idea that having committees in Congress made up of experts on specific policy areas helps to ensure well-informed policy decisions.

Congressional Staff The final component of the formal structure of Congress is congressional staff. The size of personal and committee staff exploded in the 1970s and 1980s and has since leveled off. The total number of congressional staff is more than four times as large as it was 50 years ago. Part of the motivation for this growth was to reduce the gap between the policy-making capability of Congress and the president, especially with regard to fiscal policy. The other primary motivation was electoral. By increasing the size of their personal staff, members were able to open multiple district offices and expand opportunities for helping constituents. When the Republicans took control of Congress in 1994, they vowed to cut the waste in the internal operation of the institution, in part by cutting committee staff. However, although they reduced committee staff by nearly a third, they made no cuts in personal staff.

"Why Should I Care?"

The Constitution says very little about the internal structure of Congress, so the institution is largely the one the members want. The norms of the institution and its formal structure facilitate members' electoral and policy goals, so if they don't like the way something works they can change it. This may sound very self-serving, but members of Congress also serve broader collective and policy goals or they would be booted out of office. Understanding this fundamental point provides great insight into why Congress is structured the way that it is.

★
TRACE THE STEPS IN THE LEGISLATIVE PROCESS

How a bill becomes a law

Every introductory textbook on American politics has an obligatory section including a neat little diagram that describes how a bill becomes a law (see How It Works: Passing Legislation). But we provide an important truth-in-advertising disclosure: many important laws do not follow this orderly path. In fact, Barbara Sinclair's book *Unorthodox Lawmaking* argues that "the legislative process for major legislation is now less likely to conform to the textbook model than to unorthodox lawmaking."[36] After presenting the standard view, we describe the most important deviations from that path.

The conventional process

The details of the legislative process can be incredibly complex, but its basic aspects are fairly simple. The most important thing to understand about the process is that before a piece of legislation can become a law it must be passed *in identical form* by both the House and the Senate and signed by the president. If the president vetoes the bill, it can still be passed with a two-thirds vote in each chamber. Here are the basic steps of the process (but see Nuts & Bolts 11.3 for a description of different types of legislation):

1. A member of Congress introduces the bill.
2. A subcommittee and committee craft the bill.
3. Floor action on the bill takes place in the first chamber (House or Senate).
4. Committee and floor action takes place in the second chamber.

Types of Legislation

- **Bill:** A legislative proposal that becomes law if it is passed by both the House and the Senate in identical form and approved by the president. Each is assigned a bill number, with "H.R." indicating bills that originated in the House and "S.R." denoting bills that originated in the Senate. Private bills are concerned with a specific individual or organization and often address immigration or naturalization issues. Public bills affect the general public if enacted into law.
- **Simple resolution:** Legislation used to express the sense of the House or Senate, designated by "H.Res." or "S.Res." Simple resolutions affect only the chamber passing the resolution, are not signed by the president and cannot become public law. Resolutions are often used for symbolic legislation, such as congratulating sports teams or naming a post office after a famous person (see Figure 11.7).
- **Concurrent resolution:** Legislation used to express the position of both chambers on a nonlegislative matter to set the annual budget or to fix adjournment dates, designated by "H.Con.Res" or "S.Con.Res." Concurrent resolutions are not signed by the president and therefore do not carry the weight of law.
- **Joint resolution:** Legislation that has few practical differences from a bill (passes both chambers in identical form, signed by the president) unless it proposes a constitutional amendment. In that case, a two-thirds majority of those present and voting in both the House and the Senate, and ratification by three-fourths of the states, are required for the amendment to be adopted and it does not require the president's signature.

5. The conference committee works out any differences between the House and Senate versions of the bill. (If the two chambers pass the same version, steps 5 and 6 are not necessary.)
6. The conference committee version is given final approval on the floor of each chamber.
7. The president either signs or vetoes the final version.
8. If the bill is vetoed, both chambers can attempt to override the veto with a two-thirds vote in both chambers.

The first part of the process, unchanged from the earliest Congresses, is the introduction of the bill. Only members of Congress can introduce the bill, either by dropping it into the "hopper," a wooden box at the front of the chamber in the House, or by presenting it to one of the clerks at the presiding officer's desk in the Senate. Even the president would need to have a House member or senator introduce his or her bill. Each bill has one or more sponsors and often many co-sponsors. Members may introduce bills on any topic they choose, but often the bills are related to a specific constituency interest. For example, Senator Cory Gardner (R-CO) introduced Senate Resolution 371 "Congratulating the Denver Broncos for winning Super Bowl 50" (see Figure 11.7). Obviously, most legislation is more substantive, but members of Congress are always attentive to issues their constituents care about.

The next step is to send the bill to the relevant committee. House and Senate rules specify committee jurisdictions (there are more than 200 categories), and the bill is matched with the committee that best fits its subject matter. In the House, major legislation may be sent to more than one committee in a practice known as multiple referral, but one of the committees is designated the primary committee and the bill is reviewed by the other committees sequentially or in parts. The practice is less common in the Senate, partly because senators have more opportunities to amend legislation on the floor. However, there were three committees in the House and two in the Senate that simultaneously worked on health care reform in 2009.

Once the bill goes to a committee, the chair refers it to the relevant subcommittee where much of the legislative work is done. One important point: 80 to 90 percent

How it works: in theory
Passing Legislation

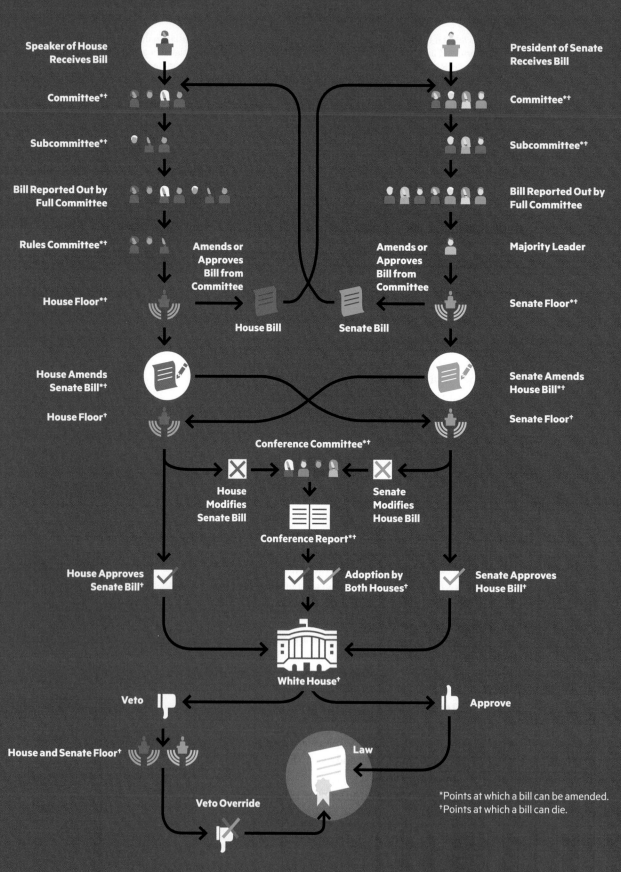

Speaker of House Receives Bill

President of Senate Receives Bill

Committee*†

Committee*†

Subcommittee*†

Subcommittee*†

Bill Reported Out by Full Committee

Bill Reported Out by Full Committee

Rules Committee*†

Amends or Approves Bill from Committee

Amends or Approves Bill from Committee

Majority Leader

House Floor*†

House Bill

Senate Bill

Senate Floor*†

House Amends Senate Bill*†

Senate Amends House Bill*†

House Floor†

Senate Floor†

Conference Committee*†

House Modifies Senate Bill

Senate Modifies House Bill

Conference Report*†

House Approves Senate Bill†

Adoption by Both Houses†

Senate Approves House Bill†

White House†

Veto

Approve

House and Senate Floor†

Law

Veto Override

*Points at which a bill can be amended.
†Points at which a bill can die.

How it works: in practice

Passing the Affordable Care Act

The 2010 Affordable Care Act (ACA) provides an example of how passing legislation often deviates from the conventional method.

In the House...

3 committees crafted the bill.

↓

She added things.

Speaker Nancy Pelosi assumed a critical role in shaping the final bill, **adding things that weren't in the committee version.**

↓

House passes its version.

Meanwhile...

President Obama was intensely involved. **The White House held daily meetings** with the committees.

In the Senate...

5 committees worked on the Senate version.

↓

He added things.

After a deadlock between two committees, Majority Leader Harry Reid pushed through a merged version of the bill, **adding things that weren't in the committee version.**

↓

Senate passes its version.

No conference committee. Instead, committee leaders, White House staff, and party leadership negotiated the details of the bills.

So then...

?!

The Senate version of the **bill was passed by the House.**

But...

!

The House added things.

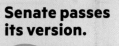

The House also passed a separate reconciliation bill that included many amendments to the Senate version.

Amended!

That reconciliation bill was then **amended by the Senate.**

Passed!

The amended reconciliation bill was then **passed by the House.**

Signed into law.

President Obama **signed the two acts into law,** both of which comprise the ACA.

❓ Critical Thinking

1. **What are the most significant ways in which** the process to pass the ACA deviated from the conventional method?
2. **Do you think the ACA could have been** passed without this unconventional process? Why or why not?

FIGURE 11.7

Taking Care of the Fans

The congratulatory resolution here is symbolic and commends the Denver Broncos for winning the Super Bowl in 2016. Why do you think members of Congress spend time passing seemingly trivial resolutions like this?

S. RES. 371

In the Senate of the United States
February 22, 2016

Congratulating the Denver Broncos for winning Super Bowl 50.

Whereas, on February 7, 2016, the Denver Broncos won Super Bowl 50, defeating the Carolina Panthers by a score of 24–10 at Levi's Stadium in Santa Clara, California;

Whereas the victory marks the third Super Bowl title for the Denver Broncos;

Whereas the Broncos' appearance in the Super Bowl was their National Football League record-tying eighth appearance;

Whereas quarterback Peyton Manning earned his 200th career win;

Whereas linebacker Von Miller earned the Most Valuable Player award while recording 2 ½ sacks and 2 forced fumbles;

Whereas running back C.J. Anderson rushed for 90 yards and 1 touchdown;

Whereas wide receiver Emmanuel Sanders caught 6 passes for 83 yards;

Whereas defensive tackle Malik Jackson recorded 5 tackles and a defensive touchdown;

Whereas wide receiver Jordan Norwood's 61-yard punt return was the longest in Super Bowl history; [...]

Whereas the Denver Broncos football team has proudly represented the City of Denver and the State of Colorado, and all of the loyal Broncos fans: Now, therefore, be it

Resolved, That the Senate—

(1) congratulates the Denver Broncos for winning Super Bowl 50;

(2) recognizes the achievements of all the players, coaches, and staff who contributed to the victory; [...]

Source: Congress.gov, www.congress.gov/bill/114th-congress/senate-resolution/371/text (accessed 3/19/16).

markup
One of the steps through which a bill becomes a law, in which the final wording of the bill is determined.

of bills die at this stage of the process; they never make it out of the subcommittee or committee. For bills that see some action, the subcommittee holds hearings, calls witnesses, and gathers the information necessary to rewrite, amend, and edit the bill. The final language of the bill is determined in a collaborative process known as the **markup**. During this meeting, members debate aspects of the issue and offer amendments to change the language or content of the bill. After all amendments have been considered, a final vote is taken on whether to send the bill to the full committee. If it is sent, the full committee then considers whether to pass it along to the floor. This committee also has the option of amending the bill, passing it as is, or tabling it (which kills the bill). Every bill sent to the floor by a committee is accompanied by a report and full documentation of all the hearings. These documents constitute the bill's legislative history, which the courts, executive departments, and the public use to determine the purpose and meaning of the law.

When the bill makes it to the floor, it is placed on one of the various legislative calendars. Bills are removed from the calendar to be considered by the floor under a broad range of possible rules. When the bill reaches the floor, the majority party and minority party each designate a bill manager who is responsible for guiding the debate on the floor. In the House, debate proceeds according to tight time limits and rules governing the nature of amendments. Senate debate is much more open and unlimited in most circumstances (unless all the senators agree to a limit). If you have ever watched C-SPAN, you know that often there are very few people on the floor during debates. Typically only the small number of people who are most interested in the bill (usually members of the committee that produced it) actively participate and offer amendments.

When debate is completed and all amendments have been considered, the presiding officer calls for a voice vote, with those in favor saying "aye" and those opposed "no." If it is unclear which side has won, any member may call for a "division vote," which requires members on each side to stand and be counted. At that point, any member may call for a recorded vote (there is no way of recording members' positions on voice votes and division votes). If at least 25 members agree that a recorded vote is desired, buzzers go off in the office buildings and committee rooms, calling members to the floor for the vote. Once they reach the floor, members vote by an electronic system in which they insert ATM-like cards into slots and each vote is recorded on a big board at the front of the House or Senate chamber.

If the bill passes the House and the Senate in different forms, the discrepancies have to be resolved. On many minor bills, one chamber may simply accept the other chamber's version to solve the problem. On other minor bills and some major bills, differences are resolved through a process known as amendments between the chambers. In this case, one chamber modifies a bill passed by the other chamber and sends it back. These modifications can go back and forth several times before both houses agree on an identical bill. A complicated version of this approach was used to pass health care reform in 2010.

The most common way to resolve differences on major legislation is through a conference committee made up of key players in the House and the Senate. A majority of major bills go to a conference committee, but minor bills rarely do.[37] Sometimes the conferees split the difference between the House and Senate versions, but at other times the House and Senate approaches are so different that one must be chosen—an especially tricky prospect when different parties control the two chambers. Sometimes the conference cannot resolve differences and the bill dies. If the conference committee can agree on changes, each chamber must pass the final version, the conference report, by a majority vote and neither chamber is allowed to amend it.

The bill is then sent to the president. If the president approves and signs the measure within 10 days (not counting Sundays), it becomes law. If he or she objects to the bill, the president may **veto** it within 10 days, sending it back to the chamber where it originated, along with a statement of objections. Unless both the House and the Senate vote to override the veto by a two-thirds majority, the bill dies. If the president does not act within 10 days and Congress is in session, the bill becomes law without the president's approval. If Congress is not in session, the measure dies through what is known as a **pocket veto**.

One final point on how a bill becomes a law is important: any bill that appropriates money must pass through the two-step process of authorization and appropriation. In the authorization process, members debate the merits of the bill, determine its language, and limit the amount that can be spent on the bill. The appropriations process involves the Budget Committees in both the House and the Senate, which set the overall guidelines for the national budget, and the Appropriations Committees in the two chambers, which determine the actual amounts of money that will be spent. In recent years, Congress has been unable to pass its appropriations bills in time for the start of the new fiscal year, so it ends up having to pass "continuing resolutions" that spend money at the last year's levels in order to keep the government open. Congress passed three continuing resolutions for the 2016 fiscal year. That may sound like a lot, but the record is 21 for the 2001 fiscal year.[38]

veto
The president's rejection of a bill that has been passed by Congress. A veto can be overridden by a two-thirds vote in both the House and Senate.

pocket veto
The automatic death of a bill passed by the House and Senate when the president fails to sign the bill in the last 10 days of a legislative session.

Deviations from the conventional process

There are many ways in which legislation may not follow the typical path. First, in some Congresses up to 20 percent of *major* bills bypass the committee system. This may be done by a discharge petition, in which a majority of the members force a bill out of its assigned committee, or by a special rule in the House. In some cases, a bill may go to the relevant committee, but then party leadership may impose its version of the bill later in the process. For example, in the wake of the terrorist attacks of September 11, the House Judiciary Committee after hard bipartisan work quickly approved a version of the Patriot Act to be considered by the full House to give the government stronger surveillance powers. But a few days later, according to committee member Representative Jerrold Nadler (D-NY), "Then the bill just disappeared. And we had a new several hundred page bill revealed from the Rules Committee" that had to be voted on the next day. Most members of Congress did not have a chance to read it.[39] The ACA also deviated from the standard path (see How It Works: In Practice, earlier in this chapter.)

Second, about one-third of major bills are adjusted post-committee and before the legislation reaches the floor by supporters of the bill to increase the chances of passage. Sometimes the bill goes back to the committee after these changes, and sometimes it does not. Thus, although most of the legislative work is accomplished in committees, a significant amount of legislation bypasses committee review.

Third, summit meetings between the president and congressional leaders may bypass or jump-start the normal legislative process. For example, rather than going through the Budget Committees to set budgetary targets, the president may meet with top leaders from both parties and hammer out a compromise that is presented to Congress as a done deal. This technique is especially important on delicate budget negotiations or when the president is threatening to use the veto. Often the congressional rank and file go along with the end product of the summit meeting, but occasionally they reject it—as happened in February 2014, when all but 28 House Republicans voted against their leadership on the extension of the debt ceiling that had been agreed to by President Obama and House and Senate leaders.

Fourth, omnibus legislation—massive bills that run hundreds of pages long and cover many different subjects and programs—often requires creative approaches by the leadership to guide the bill through the legislative maze. Leadership task forces may be used in place of committees, and alternatives to the conference committee may be devised to resolve differences between the two chambers. In addition, the massive legislation often carries riders—extraneous legislation attached to the "must pass" bill to secure approval for pet projects that would otherwise fail. This is a form of pork-barrel legislation and another mechanism used in the quest for reelection.

Differences in the House and Senate legislative processes

There are three central differences in the legislative processes of the House and the Senate: (1) the continuity of the membership and the impact this has on the rules, (2) the way in which bills get to the floor, and (3) the structure of the floor process, including debate and amendments. First, as discussed earlier, the Senate is a continuing body, with two-thirds of its members returning to the next session without facing reelection (because of the six-year term), whereas all House members are up for reelection every two years. This has an important impact on the rules of the two chambers: there has been much greater stability in the rules of the Senate than the House. Whereas the

omnibus legislation
Large bills that often cover several topics and may contain extraneous, or pork-barrel, projects.

House adopts its rules anew at the start of each new session (sometimes with major changes, sometimes with only minor modifications), the Senate has not had a general reaffirmation of its rules since 1789. However, the Senate rules can be changed at the beginning of a session to meet the needs of the new members.

The floor process is much simpler and less structured in the Senate than in the House. In part, this is due to the relative size of the two chambers: the House with its 435 members needs to have more rules than the Senate with its 100 members. Ironically, however, the floor process is actually much easier to navigate in the House because of its structure. Since the adoption of Reed's Rules in 1890, the House has been a very majoritarian body—that is, a majority of House members can almost always have their way. Named after Speaker Thomas Reed, the rules were an implementation of his view that "the best system is to have one party govern and the other party watch."[40] In contrast, the Senate has always been a much more individualistic body. Former Majority Leader Howard Baker compared leading the Senate to "herding cats," saying it was difficult "trying to make ninety-nine independent souls act in concert under rules that encourage polite anarchy and embolden people who find majority rule a dubious proposition at best."[41]

The Filibuster Part of the challenge in getting the Senate to act collectively is rooted in the Senate's unlimited debate and very open amendment process. Unless restricted by a unanimous consent agreement, senators can speak as long as they want and offer any amendment to a bill, even if it isn't directly related to the underlying bill. Debate may be cut off only if a supermajority of 60 senators agrees in a process known as invoking **cloture**. Therefore, one senator can stop any bill by threatening to talk the bill to death if 40 of his or her colleagues agree. This practice is known as a **filibuster**.

The filibuster strengthens the hand of the minority party in the Senate, giving it veto power over legislation unless the majority party has 60 senators who unanimously support a bill.

Before the 1960s, senators really did hold the floor for hours by reading from the phone book or reciting recipes. The late Strom Thurmond, the senator from South Carolina who was the longest-serving and oldest senator until his retirement in January 2003 (at 100 years old and after 48 years in the Senate), holds the record of 24 hours and 18 minutes of continuous talking. Today it is rare for a filibuster to tie up Senate business, since a senator's threat to filibuster a bill is often enough to take the bill off the legislative agenda. If the bill is actually filibustered, it goes on a separate legislative track so that it does not bring the rest of the business of the Senate to a halt. Alternatively, if supporters of the bill think they have enough votes they can invoke cloture to stop the filibuster and bring the bill to the floor for a vote. Frustrated over repeated Republican filibusters on President Obama's nominations to federal courts and agencies, in November 2013 Senate Democrats removed the filibuster for all presidential nominations, except those to the Supreme Court.[42]

Because of the practice of unlimited debate in the Senate, much of its business is conducted under unanimous consent agreements by which senators agree to adhere to time limits on debate and amendments. However, because these are literally *unanimous* agreements, a single senator can obstruct the business of the chamber by issuing a **hold** on the bill or presidential nomination. This practice is often a bargaining tool to extract concessions from the bill's supporters, but sometimes, especially late in a session when time gets tight, a hold can actually kill a bill by removing it from the active agenda.

House Rules In contrast to the Senate, the House is a more orderly, if complex, institution. The Rules Committee exerts great control over the legislative process,

cloture
A procedure through which the Senate can limit the amount of time spent debating a bill (cutting off a filibuster) if a supermajority of 60 senators agree.

filibuster
A tactic used by senators to block a bill by continuing to hold the floor and speak—under the Senate rule of unlimited debate—until the bill's supporters back down.

Senator Ted Cruz (R-TX) held forth on the Senate floor for more than 21 hours expressing his opposition to the ACA in September 2013. @TedCruz

hold
An objection to considering a measure on the Senate floor.

closed rules
Conditions placed on a legislative debate by the House Rules Committee prohibiting amendments to a bill.

open rules
Conditions placed on a legislative debate by the House Rules Committee allowing relevant amendments to a bill.

modified rules
Conditions placed on a legislative debate by the House Rules Committee allowing certain amendments to a bill while barring others.

especially on major legislation, through special rules that govern the nature of debate on a bill. There are three general types of rules: closed rules do not allow any amendments to the bill, open rules allow any germane amendments, and modified rules allow some specific amendments but not others. Once a special rule is adopted and the Committee of the Whole convenes, general debate is tightly controlled by the floor managers. All amendments are considered under a five-minute rule, but this rule is routinely bent as members offer phantom "pro forma" amendments to, for example, "strike the last word" or "strike the requisite number of words." This means that the member is not really offering an amendment but is simply going through the formal procedure of offering one in order to get an additional five minutes to talk about the amendment.

These descriptions of the two chambers show that although the Senate is formally committed to unlimited debate, senators often voluntarily place limits on themselves through unanimous consent, which makes them operate much more like the House. Similarly, although the House has very strict rules concerning debate and amendments, there are ways of bending those rules to make the House operate a bit more like the potentially freewheeling Senate.

"Why Should I Care?"

Otto von Bismarck, the Prussian statesman of the late nineteenth century, famously said, "Laws are like sausages; it is better not to see them being made." Indeed, the legislative process may be messy, but knowledge of how laws are made is important both for being an effective legislator and for being a good democratic citizen. Understanding how a bill becomes a law, seeing the various stages of the process, and recognizing the various veto points at which a bill may die all help put into context the simplistic complaints about gridlock and conflict. Now that you have a better understanding of the legislative process, you should have a stronger basis for evaluating what Congress is doing.

★

DESCRIBE HOW CONGRESS ENSURES THAT THE BUREAUCRACY IMPLEMENTS POLICIES CORRECTLY

Oversight

Once a bill becomes a law, Congress plays another crucial role by overseeing the implementation of the law to make sure the bureaucracy interprets it as Congress intended. Other motivations drive the oversight process as well, such as the desire to gain publicity that may help in the reelection quest or to embarrass the president if he or she is of the opposite party. For example, in 2015 Republicans used their oversight powers to call attention to Hillary Clinton's use of private servers for her work-related e-mail as secretary of state and the way that she handled the attack on the U.S. embassy in Benghazi. While these hearings were, at least in part, politically motivated (she was no longer secretary of state), the most important motivation for oversight is to ensure that laws are implemented properly.[43]

There are several mechanisms that Congress may use to accomplish this goal (see also Chapter 13). First, the bluntest instrument is the power of the purse. If members of Congress think an agency is not properly implementing their programs, they can simply cut off the funds to that agency. However, this approach to punishment is rarely used because it often eliminates good aspects of the agency along with the bad.

Second, Congress can hold hearings and investigations. By summoning administration officials and agency heads to a public hearing, Congress can use the media spotlight to focus attention on problems within the bureaucracy or on issues that have been overlooked. For example, House Republicans called former Health and Human Services secretary Kathleen Sebelius to testify several times in 2013 and 2014 about the rocky rollout of the healthcare.gov website for Obamacare. This type of oversight is known as "fire alarm oversight"—that is, members wait until there is a crisis before they spring to action.[44] This is in contrast to "police patrol" oversight, which involves constant vigilance in overseeing the bureaucracy. For example, the House Veterans' Affairs Committee recently investigated extremely long waits for medical appointments at VA hospitals and the falsification of records to cover up how long veterans had to wait to be seen by doctors, which eventually led to General Eric Shinseki's resignation as the secretary of Veterans' Affairs.[45] Of the two, fire alarm oversight is far more common because Congress does not have the resources to constantly monitor the entire bureaucracy.

Finally, the Senate exercises specific control over other executive functions through its constitutional responsibilities to provide "advice and consent" on presidential appointments and approval of treaties. The Senate typically defers to the president on these matters, but it may assert its power, especially when constituent interests are involved. One current example would be the Senate's increasing skepticism about free-trade agreements negotiated by the president's trade representatives and holds on presidential nominations.

The ultimate in congressional oversight is the process of removing the president, vice president, other civil officers, or federal judges through impeachment. The House and Senate share this power: the House issues articles of impeachment, which outline the charges against the official, and the Senate conducts the trial of the impeached officials. Two presidents have been impeached: Andrew Johnson in the controversy over Reconstruction after the Civil War, and Bill Clinton over the scandal involving White House intern Monica Lewinsky. However, neither president was convicted and removed by the Senate.

Former secretary of state and Democratic presidential candidate Hillary Clinton testifies before the House Select Committee on Benghazi in October 2015. Clinton faced tough questioning over her response to the attack on the U.S. diplomatic compound in Benghazi and her use of a private e-mail server while serving as secretary of state. #Benghazi @HillaryClinton

Conclusion

Although the details of the legislative process and the institutions of Congress can be complicated, the basic explanations for members' behavior are quite straightforward when viewed in terms of the trade-off between responsiveness and responsibility. Members of Congress want to be reelected, so they are generally quite responsive to constituents' interests. They spend considerable time on casework—meeting with people in their district and delivering benefits for their district. At the same time, members are motivated to be responsible—to rise above local interests and attend to the nation's best interests. The conflict between these two impulses can create contradictory policies that contribute to Congress's image problem. For example, we subsidize tobacco farming at the same time that we spend billions of dollars to treat the health problems that tobacco use creates. We have laws on water rights that encourage farmers to irrigate the desert at the same time that we pay farmers to leave parts of their land unplanted in areas of the country that are well suited for agriculture. These policies, and others, can be explained both by the desire to serve local interests and by the norms of reciprocity and universalism.

Considering members' motivations is crucial to understanding how Congress functions, but their behavior is also constrained by the institutions in which they operate. The committee system is an important source of expertise and information, and it provides a platform from which members can take positions and claim credit. Parties in Congress provide coherence to the legislative agenda and help structure voting patterns on bills. Rules and norms constrain the nature of debate and the legislative process. Although these institutions shape members' behavior, it is important to remember that members can also change those rules and institutions. Therefore, Congress has the ability to evolve with changing national conditions and demands from voters, groups, and the president.

In this context, much of what Congress does can be understood in terms of the conflicts inherent in politics. How can members act responsibly without sacrificing responsiveness? Can Congress be structured in a way that allows members to be responsive (and therefore have a better chance of getting reelected) without losing the ability to make unpopular decisions when needed, like cutting budget deficits? The example discussed in the chapter introduction concerning sexual assaults in the military demonstrates that, even on issues that nearly everyone would agree are problems (nobody is in favor of sexual assaults), there are important differences of opinion about what actions should be taken. The compromise position that passed with nearly universal support in the Senate was not ideal for those who wanted stronger reforms, but compromise means that many people will not be completely satisfied with the final version.

This chapter also sheds light on some of the ways that political process matters. With a clearer understanding of how Congress operates, you are better able to assess the outputs of government. For example, this chapter provided a closer look at party leaders and pork-barrel spending: party leaders in Congress help members solve their collective action problems rather than causing gridlock and policy failure, as is commonly assumed. Some pork may be wasteful, but in other cases it is important for the districts that receive the benefits and may serve broader collective interests as well. Congress does not always live up to the expectations of being the "first branch" of government, but it often does an admirable job of balancing the conflicting pressures it faces.

> "
>
> **I have seen in the Halls of Congress more idealism, more humanness, more compassion, more profiles of courage than in any other institution that I have ever known.**
>
> —**Hubert Humphrey,** former senator and vice president

📷

Members of Congress want to be reelected, and this goal explains much of their behavior. In 2016, House Majority Leader Kevin McCarthy (R-CA) won reelection. Given his leadership position within the party, McCarthy must be especially careful to balance local interests with the good of the nation as a whole.
@KevinOMcCarthy

What Congress does

Explain how members of Congress represent their constituents and how elections hold members accountable. (Pages 364–381)

Summary

The Constitution gave Congress vast enumerated powers, making it the "first branch" of government. While Congress has long dominated day-to-day politics, the president has become considerably more powerful over time. Despite the low approval ratings for Congress itself, most voters like their members of Congress. Members of Congress work hard to strike a balance between responding to what constituents want, and what is in the constituency's best interest. In the balance, however, they prioritize district interests over national policy.

Key terms

bicameralism (p. 365)
pork barrel (p. 365)
descriptive representation (p. 366)
substantive representation (p. 368)
trustee (p. 368)
delegate (p. 368)
politico (p. 368)

casework (p. 370)
electoral connection (p. 371)
incumbency advantage (p. 372)
redistricting (p. 377)
apportionment (p. 377)
gerrymandering (p. 379)
gridlock (p. 380)

Practice Quiz Questions

1. **What did the Seventeenth Amendment do?**
   a. repeal Prohibition
   b. grant women's suffrage
   c. give senators six-year terms
   d. allow for direct election of senators
   e. lower the voting age to 18

2. **Why do senators have longer terms than members of the House of Representatives?**
   a. to reduce the number of candidates in each election
   b. to make sure that senators were tied to public sentiment
   c. to provide more opportunities for pork-barrel legislation
   d. to make elections easier to administer
   e. to make sure that senators were somewhat insulated from the people

3. **What is the most common style of representation in Congress?**
   a. trustee
   b. politico
   c. delegate
   d. consulate
   e. adviser

4. **Most constituents are _____; most members of Congress act as if the constituency _____ paying attention.**
   a. inattentive; is not
   b. inattentive; is
   c. attentive; is not
   d. attentive; is
   e. selectively attentive; is not

5. **Members of Congress generally hold multiple goals. Which goal comes first?**
   a. getting reelected
   b. passing good policy
   c. serving their political party
   d. blocking the opposing party
   e. serving special interests

6. **What is apportionment?**
   a. determining presidential primary election winners
   b. determining whether the state legislature or courts will re-draw district lines
   c. determining which states gain/lose seats in the Senate
   d. determining which states gain/lose seats in the House
   e. determining how many seats a party has in Congress

7. **A home style shapes the way members of Congress _____.**
   a. work with party leaders
   b. vote in Congress
   c. write legislation in committees
   d. present themselves to their district
   e. spend campaign money

8. **On average, incumbents spend _____ times as much as challengers.**
   a. one and one-half
   b. three
   c. five
   d. ten
   e. twenty

The structure of Congress

Examine how parties, the committee system, and staffers enable Congress to function. (Pages 381–392)

Summary

Many aspects of Congress are set up to meet the needs of its members. The norms of universalism and reciprocity still dominate, meaning that members of Congress share resources more broadly than partisan politics would dictate.

Key terms

logrolling (p. 382)

earmarks (p. 382)

seniority (p. 382)

Speaker of the House (p. 384)

Majority Leader (p. 384)

whip system (p. 384)

Minority Leader (p. 384)

president pro tempore (p. 386)

roll call vote (p. 386)

party vote (p. 386)

party unity (p. 386)

standing committees (p. 389)

select committees (p. 389)

joint committees (p. 389)

conference committees (p. 390)

distributive theory (p. 391)

informational theory (p. 391)

Practice Quiz Questions

9. **The norm of ___ says that federal highway dollars are likely to be divided up so that many districts benefit.**

   a. reciprocity

   b. seniority

   c. party unity

   d. universalism

   e. specialization

10. **Committee leadership, division of seats on committee, and allocation of committee resources are determined by ___.**

    a. the majority party

    b. the size of the election margin

    c. unanimous consent

    d. seniority

    e. the president pro tempore

11. **The Senate leadership is ___ the House leadership.**

    a. more powerful than

    b. as powerful as

    c. less powerful than

    d. irrelevant to

12. **Party leaders have the power to ___.**

    a. force members of Congress to vote a particular way

    b. keep a member of Congress off the ballot in the next election

    c. force their members to share their campaign money

    d. exclude a member from a roll call vote

    e. help their members get favorable committee assignments

How a bill becomes a law

Trace the steps in the legislative process. (Pages 392–400)

Summary

Most bills become law in a conventional manner, but major pieces of legislation generally deviate considerably from this path. The legislative process differs for the House and Senate, sometimes making it difficult to reconcile differences between bills.

Key terms

markup (p. 396)

veto (p. 397)

pocket veto (p. 397)

omnibus legislation (p. 398)

cloture (p. 399)

filibuster (p. 399)

hold (p. 399)

closed rules (p. 400)

open rules (p. 400)

modified rules (p. 400)

Practice Quiz Question

13. **Compared with the Senate, the floor process in the House is very ___ and ___.**

    a. unstructured; majoritarian

    b. structured; majoritarian

    c. unstructured; individualistic

    d. structured; individualistic

    e. individualistic; majoritarian

14. **Which of the following is the most important characteristic of how a bill becomes a law?**

    a. The bill must be passed by a conference committee comprised of House and Senate members.

    b. The bill must be signed by the Speaker of the House.

    c. A majority of the majority party members of the House and Senate must support the bill.

    d. The bill must pass the House and Senate in identical form.

    e. The bill must be introduced by the president or one of his staff members.

Oversight

Describe how Congress ensures that the bureaucracy implements policies correctly. (Pages 400–401)

Summary

After passing bills into law, Congress oversees the bureaucracy in its implementation of the law, making sure it fits Congress's intentions. Although controlling funding is the most powerful mechanism for this, Congress has a number of other mechanisms for achieving bureaucratic fidelity. Generally, Congress does not actively patrol the bureaucracy, but waits until a crisis emerges to act.

Practice Quiz Questions

15. Waiting for a crisis to emerge before taking action is called _____.

  a. police patrol oversight
  b. fire alarm oversight
  c. emergency room oversight
  d. reactionary oversight
  e. bureaucratic oversight

16. The most important reason for congressional oversight is

  a. to try to embarrass political opponents.
  b. to help raise funds for a political campaign.
  c. to support the president's policymaking efforts.
  d. to make sure that laws are implemented properly.
  e. to amend previously passed legislation.

Suggested Reading

Adler, Scott E., and John D. Wilkerson. *Congress and the Politics of Problem Solving*. New York: Cambridge University Press, 2013.

Bianco, William T. *Trust: Representatives and Constituents*. Ann Arbor: University of Michigan Press, 1994.

Canon, David T. *Race, Redistricting and Representation: The Unintended Consequences of Black Majority Districts*. Chicago: University of Chicago Press, 1999.

Fenno, Richard F. *Congressmen in Committees*. Boston: Little, Brown, 1973.

Hall, Richard L. *Participation in Congress*. New Haven, CT: Yale University Press, 1996.

Jacobson, Gary C. *The Politics of Congressional Elections*, 8th ed. New York: Pearson, 2012.

Lapinski, John S. *The Substance of Representation: Congress, American Political Development, and Lawmaking*. Princeton, NJ: Princeton University Press, 2013.

Mayhew, David R. *Congress: The Electoral Connection*, 2nd ed. New Haven, CT: Yale University Press, 2004.

Theriault, Sean. *Party Polarization in Congress*. New York: Cambridge University Press, 2008.

12

The Presidency

Why can't the president get more done?

Presidential campaigns often make it sound like the winner is going to be the most powerful person in the world. Candidates routinely promise to revitalize the economy, end poverty and injustice, defeat America's enemies, and whip the government into shape. It certainly matters who wins the election. Presidents can order military and covert forces into action. They lead the federal bureaucracy's implementation of congressional mandates. They serve as America's head of state. America looks different today because Barack Obama defeated John McCain in 2008 and Mitt Romney in 2012. And four years from now, America will look different because Donald Trump won the 2016 election rather than his opponent, Hillary Clinton.

At the same time, descriptions of the president as some all-powerful force are clearly an exaggeration. Presidents have limited power to affect the economy. Their control over America's military is constrained by public opinion, congressional authority, and the reality that the use of force is often counterproductive. Bureaucrats have many ways to evade presidential directives. Members of Congress, even those from the president's party, are often in open revolt against presidential proposals. Given these problems, the question is not how Donald Trump will transform the government. Rather, the question is why he will be able to do anything at all.

This chapter examines the extent, and the limits, of presidential power. America's presidents possess considerable power over U.S. foreign and domestic policy, and they have used this power to do things that have a massive effect on the lives of ordinary Americans. Even so, presidents are often driven to compromise or are forced to abandon deeply held policy goals in the face of opposition from Congress, bureaucrats, judges, or the American public. Why are presidents all-powerful in some cases and seemingly powerless in others?

This chapter shows that while U.S. presidents can sometimes change policy unilaterally, most times they require cooperation or consent from others. As a result, presidential success is not automatic. Presidents may face obstacles in their efforts to achieve their own policy goals, yet at the same time they must

★

CHAPTER GOALS

Trace the evolution of presidential power.
pages 408–411

Describe the constitutional and statutory powers of the president today.
pages 411–424

Explain how the Executive Office of the President, the vice president, the first spouse, and the Cabinet help the president.
pages 424–427

Explain how modern presidents have become even more powerful.
pages 428–435

📷

The transfer of presidential power pushes us to ask fundamental questions about the tone and policy direction of the country. What will Trump do with the power of the presidency? Will he work with Congress, or act more unilaterally? What policies from the past will he keep? What will he abandon? Will President Trump be able to accomplish all he promised?

attempt to satisfy the demands of supporters and opponents—while trying to avoid alienating people who disagree with presidential decisions. To put it another way, although presidents are powerful, they are not kings or dictators. Presidents must also cultivate public opinion in order to get reelected or to help members of their party to be elected or reelected to office. Moreover, presidents and their staff must monitor the bureaucracy to make sure that presidential decisions are faithfully implemented. And sometimes presidents must decide whether to scale back on a proposal to make it more likely to pass Congress or to risk complete failure by holding firm to the original goal.

With these considerations in mind, we ask these fundamental questions in this chapter: What are the sources and limits of presidential power? When are presidents able to prevail in the face of conflict in the country, in Congress, or in the bureaucracy? Has presidential power grown over time? How does conflict affect the decisions that presidents make and the ways they try to implement their policy goals? How does the presidency really work?

★

TRACE THE EVOLUTION OF
PRESIDENTIAL POWER

The development of presidential power

As we consider the history of America's 44 presidents and look ahead to the forty-fifth, four facts stand out: (1) Presidents matter. Their actions have had profound consequences for the nation, in both domestic and foreign policy. (2) Presidents get their power from a variety of sources, from provisions of the Constitution to their management of and the actions taken by the executive branch of government. (3) Presidential power has increased over time, not because of changes in the Constitution but because of America's growth as a nation, its emergence as a dominant actor in international politics, the expansion of the federal government, and various acts of legislation that have given new authority to the president. (4) There are sharp limits to presidential power. Presidents are often forced to compromise or abandon their plans in the face of public, congressional, or foreign opposition.

Early years through World War I

Since the early years of the Republic, presidents' actions have had profound consequences for the nation. Presidents George Washington, John Adams, and Thomas Jefferson forged compromises on issues such as choosing a permanent location for the nation's capital, establishing the federal courts, and financing the government. Presidents Andrew Jackson and Martin Van Buren were instrumental in forming the Democratic Party and its local party organizations.[1]

Early presidents also made important foreign policy decisions. For example, the Monroe Doctrine issued by President James Monroe in 1823 stated that America would remain neutral in wars involving European nations and that these nations must cease attempts to colonize or occupy areas in North and South America.[2] Presidents John Tyler and James Polk oversaw the admission of the huge territory of Texas into the Union following the Mexican-American War, as well as the acquisition of land that later became Oregon, Washington, Idaho, and parts of Montana and Wyoming.[3]

Presidents also played key roles in the conflict over slavery in America. President Millard Fillmore's support helped to enact the Compromise of 1850, which limited slavery in California, and Franklin Pierce supported the Kansas-Nebraska Act, which regulated slavery in those territories. And, of course, Abraham Lincoln, who helped form the Republican Party in the 1850s, played a transformative role in setting policy as president during the Civil War. His orders raised the huge Union army, and as commander in chief he directed the conduct of the bloody war that ultimately brought the southern states back into the Union. Moreover, he issued the Emancipation Proclamation, which freed the slaves in the South.[4]

During the late 1800s and early 1900s, presidents were instrumental in federal responses to the nation's rapid expansion and industrialization.[5] The country's growing size and economy generated conflict over which services the federal government should provide to citizens and the extent to which the government should regulate individual and corporate behavior.[6] Various acts of legislation created new federal agencies and, in doing so, also created new presidential powers and responsibilities. For example, Republican president Theodore Roosevelt used the Sherman Antitrust Act to break up the Northern Securities Company, a mammoth nationwide railroad trust. Roosevelt also increased the power of the Interstate Commerce Commission to regulate businesses and expanded federal conservation programs. Democratic president Woodrow Wilson further increased the government's role in managing the economy through his support of the Clayton Antitrust Act, the Federal Reserve Act, the first federal income tax, and legislation banning child labor.[7]

As these examples illustrate, presidential power has grown over time with the expansion of the federal government, as the president and members of the executive branch have obtained new regulatory powers over corporations and individual Americans and as presidents have responded to shifts in public opinion by proposing new policies. Moreover, the power of the presidency grew during this era due to the actions of presidents, particularly Roosevelt and Wilson, who firmly believed that the presidency was the most important federal office.

Yet Wilson's foreign policy initiatives illustrate the limits of presidential power. Although he campaigned in the 1916 election on a promise to keep America out of World War I, Wilson ultimately ordered American troops to fight on the side of the Allies. After the war, Wilson offered a peace plan that proposed reshaping the borders of European countries in order to mitigate future conflicts; creating an international organization, the League of Nations, to prevent future conflicts; and taking other measures to encourage free trade and democracy.[8] However, America's allies rejected most of Wilson's proposals and the Senate refused to allow American participation in the League of Nations.

The Great Depression through the present

Presidential actions defined the government's response to the Great Depression—the worldwide economic collapse in the late 1920s and 1930s marked by high unemployment, huge stock market declines, and many bank failures. After winning the 1932 election, Democrat Franklin Roosevelt and his staff began reshaping American government. Roosevelt's New Deal reforms created many federal agencies that helped individual Americans and imposed many new corporate regulations.[9] This expansion continued under Roosevelt's successors. Even Republican Dwight Eisenhower, whose party had initially opposed many New Deal reforms, presided over the creation of new agencies and the building of the interstate highway system.[10]

George Washington remains, for many Americans, the presidential ideal—a leader whose crucial domestic and foreign policy decisions shaped the growth of America's democracy.

President Franklin Delano Roosevelt called on the public to support his New Deal programs and other policies. Here, he delivers one of his "fireside chat" radio broadcasts, designed to communicate his arguments to the American people and to win their support.

The president plays a predominant role in American foreign policy. In the 1980s, President Ronald Reagan negotiated numerous arms agreements with the Soviet Union. Here, Reagan and Soviet leader Mikhail Gorbachev sign a treaty eliminating certain types of nuclear missiles.

Presidents were instrumental in the civil rights reforms and expansion of the federal government in the 1960s. With congressional approval, President Lyndon Johnson's administration created a wide range of domestic programs, such as the Department of Housing and Urban Development, Medicare, Medicaid, and federal funding for schools. The job of enacting voting rights and civil rights legislation also took place during LBJ's presidency.

Both Johnson and his successor, Richard Nixon, directed America's involvement in the Vietnam War, with the goal of forcing the North Vietnamese to abandon their plans to unify North and South Vietnam. But presidential efforts in Vietnam did not meet with success. Despite enormous deployments of American forces and more than 58,000 American soldiers killed, Nixon eventually signed an agreement that allowed American troops to leave but did not end the conflict, which concluded only after a North Vietnamese victory in 1975.

The two presidents immediately after Nixon, Republican Gerald Ford and Democrat Jimmy Carter, faced the worst economic conditions since the Great Depression, largely due to increased energy prices. Both presidents offered plans to reduce unemployment and inflation, restore economic growth, and enhance domestic energy sources. But their efforts were largely unsuccessful, which became a critical factor in their failed reelection bids.

In the last generation, the political and policy importance of presidential actions has continued to increase. This trend continued during the presidency of Republican Ronald Reagan despite his platform of tax cuts, fewer regulations, and smaller government. Reagan and his staff also negotiated important arms control agreements with the Soviet Union. Reagan's successor, Republican George H. W. Bush, led American and international participation in the Persian Gulf War during 1990 and 1991, which succeeded in removing Iraqi forces from Kuwait with minimal American casualties.

Democrat Bill Clinton's presidency was marked by passage of the North American Free Trade Agreement, welfare reform, arms control agreements, and successful peacekeeping efforts by U.S. troops in Haiti and the Balkans. His presidency also was distinguished by having one of the longest periods of economic growth in U.S. history and the first balanced budgets since the 1960s. President George W. Bush won congressional approval of his tax cuts and education reforms, but he is remembered for managing America's response to the September 11 attacks, including the wars in Iraq and Afghanistan.

President Obama secured several notable changes in domestic and foreign policy, including the enactment of health care reform, economic stimulus legislation, new financial regulations, and the appointment of two Supreme Court justices. However, he had to compromise in enacting many of the new policies, and in areas such as immigration reform and gun control he has been largely unsuccessful in achieving his policy goals.

"Why Should I Care?"

Presidents' performance is often evaluated as though their powers and foresight were unlimited. However, the history of presidential successes and failures highlights how presidents are often constrained by circumstances. Many of the problems they faced were totally unanticipated or had no good solutions. Other times, attempts to address national needs failed because of congressional or bureaucratic intransigence. Thus, before we make judgments about presidential performance we need to understand their job and the resources they have to accomplish it.

The president's job description

★

DESCRIBE THE CONSTITUTIONAL AND STATUTORY POWERS OF THE PRESIDENT TODAY

This section describes the president's constitutional authority (powers derived from the provisions of the Constitution), statutory authority (powers that come from laws), and the additional capabilities that presidents derive from their position as the head of the executive branch of government. Constitutional and statutory powers are summarized in Nuts & Bolts 12.1. As the box indicates, some presidential powers arise from one source, such as the Constitution, and others derive from a combination of constitutional and statutory authority. Our aim is to show how these provisions operate in modern-day American politics: what kinds of opportunities and constraints they create for the current president and future holders of the office.

constitutional authority (presidential)
Powers derived from the provisions of the Constitution that outline the president's role in government.

statutory authority (presidential)
Powers derived from laws enacted by Congress that add to the powers given to the president in the Constitution.

vesting clause
Article II, Section 1, of the Constitution, which states: "The executive Power shall be vested in a President of the United States of America," making the president both the head of government and the head of state.

Head of the executive branch

A president's responsibilities and the source of presidential power begin with the constitutional responsibilities of the office. The Constitution's vesting clause—"The executive Power shall be vested in a President of the United States of America"—makes

Presidential Powers

Power	Source of Power
Head of Government, Head of State (Vesting Clause)	Constitutional authority
Implementation of Laws ("Faithful Execution")	Constitutional and statutory authority
Executive Orders and Similar Directives (Rare)	Constitutional and statutory authority
Administration of Executive Branch	Constitutional authority
Nominations and Appointments to Executive Branch and Judiciary	Constitutional and statutory authority
Commander in Chief of Armed Forces	Constitutional authority
Negotiation of Treaties and Executive Agreements	Constitutional and statutory authority
Veto of Congressional Actions	Constitutional authority
Presidential Pardons	Constitutional authority
Other Ceremonial Powers	Constitutional authority
Executive Privilege	Other
Recommendation of Spending Levels and Other Legislative Initiatives	Other

head of government
One role of the president, through which he or she has authority over the executive branch.

head of state
One role of the president, through which he or she represents the country symbolically and politically.

the president the **head of government**, granting authority over the executive branch, as well as **head of state**, or the symbolic and political representative of the country. The precise meaning of the vesting clause has been debated for more than 200 years. Presidents and their supporters argue for an expansive meaning; their opponents counter that the clause is so vague as to be meaningless. These debates are an important clue that a president's power is only partially due to the specific constitutional grants of power—some of it comes from how each president interprets less concrete statements such as the vesting clause.

The Constitution also places the president in charge of the implementation of laws, saying "he shall take Care that the Laws be faithfully executed." Sometimes the implementation of a law is nearly automatic, as was the case with a 2014 law that raised the cost of federal flood insurance for homeowners who lived in flood-prone areas. In that case, all the president needed to do to implement the law was to ensure that bureaucrats in FEMA collected the higher premiums from policyholders.

More commonly, the president's authority to implement the law requires using judgment to translate legislative goals into programs, budgets, and regulations. For example, the Affordable Care Act (ACA) of 2010 gave the president and the Department of Health and Human Services the authority to modify provisions of the new program, including the deadlines for people to purchase health insurance through the new federal and state exchanges. Although critics charged that congressional consent was required, the ACA was typical of major legislation in that it gave the administration significant leeway as it implemented the policy changes mandated by the law's passage.[11]

Finally, the president's control of the executive branch allows him or her to issue orders to government agencies that make significant policy changes. For example, in 2015 President Obama granted quasi-legal status and work permits to nearly a million illegal immigrants who entered the country as children. While many Republicans and some Democrats criticized the president's action, they were unable to take the steps

needed to overturn it—write legislation, shepherd it through the House and Senate, and override a veto. Ultimately, Obama's order was struck down by a federal appeals court with this decision upheld by a tied Supreme Court. And of course, the order could have been removed by President Trump on his first day in office.

Appointments The president appoints ambassadors, senior bureaucrats, and members of the federal judiciary, including Supreme Court justices.[12] As the head of the executive branch, the president controls about 8,000 positions, ranging from high-profile jobs such as secretary of state to mundane administrative and secretarial positions. About 1,200 of these appointments—generally high-level positions such as cabinet secretaries—require Senate confirmation. Because federal judgeships are lifetime appointments, they enable the president to put people into positions of power who will remain after he or she leaves office. For example, President Obama's two Supreme Court appointments, Sonia Sotomayor and Elena Kagan, emerged as influential voices on such issues as health care and the rights of criminal defendants. The full effects of these and other judicial appointments by Obama will not be completely apparent for years to come.

The need for Senate confirmation of the president's appointments is one of the fundamental limits on presidential power. Historically, the Senate has approved virtually all nominees without much debate or controversy, although in recent years senators (particularly Republicans during Obama's presidency) have blocked votes on many judicial and agency nominees. For example, Republican senators refused to hold hearings or a vote on Merrick Garland, Obama's 2016 Supreme Court nominee, which left the seat vacant for an entire year. If the Senate is in recess (adjourned for more than three days), the president can make a **recess appointment**, whereby an appointee is temporarily given a position without a Senate vote and holds the office until the beginning of the next congressional session. All presidents make recess appointments, but typically for relatively minor offices and for noncontroversial nominees—it would have been highly unusual (and highly controversial) for President Obama to appoint Garland to the Supreme Court via a recess appointment, and the constitutionality of this act is questionable. In any case, the Senate can eliminate the possibility of recess appointments by holding brief working sessions as often as needed to ensure that no recess lasts more than three days.

Executive Orders Presidents have the power to issue **executive orders**—that is, proclamations that unilaterally change government policy without subsequent congressional consent[13]—as well as other kinds of orders that change policy, such

recess appointment
Selection by the president of a person to be an ambassador or the head of a department while the Senate is not in session, thereby bypassing Senate approval. Unless approved by a subsequent Senate vote, recess appointees serve only to the end of the congressional term.

executive orders
Proclamations made by the president that change government policy without congressional approval.

as National Security Presidential Directives and Presidential Findings (see the How It Works feature in this chapter). Responding to the December 2012 mass shooting of schoolchildren at Sandy Hook Elementary School in Newtown, Connecticut, President Obama signed 23 executive orders relating to gun control in January 2013.[14] Many of these orders were relatively modest, such as releasing an analysis of how many lost or stolen guns are used in subsequent crimes. Other orders had more significant effects, such as ordering the Consumer Product Safety Commission (CPSC) to develop new requirements for gun locks. More significant policy changes proposed by Obama, such as banning the possession of armor-piercing bullets, limiting the size of hand-gun ammunition magazines, and increasing federal funding for local police officers, were part of a gun control package sent to Congress at the same time that the executive orders were signed. None of these proposals were enacted. As the What Do the Numbers Say? feature shows, all presidents issue many numbers of executive orders. Most are not consequential, like the annual order that gives federal employees an early dismissal on the last working day before Christmas. But some executive orders implement large changes in federal policy. Lincoln's Emancipation Proclamation was issued as an executive order.

Executive orders may appear to give the president authority to do whatever he or she wants, even in the face of strong opposition from Congress. However, as the gun control example illustrates, a president's power to issue executive orders generally involves purely administrative matters (such as releasing the study of lost and stolen guns). Or the president may be able to issue an executive order on a specific question because Congress passed a law giving him or her specific authority in this case (such as the ability to direct the CPSC to develop new gun lock regulations). Moreover, regardless of the authority used to issue an order, if members of Congress had objected to the policy changes or new regulations they could have passed a law overturning the orders. In light of congressional opposition to Obama's gun control legislation, if the president had tried to implement these changes through executive orders he would surely have faced either legislative or judicial action to overturn the orders.

Commander in Chief The Constitution makes the president the commander in chief of America's military forces but gives Congress the power to declare war. These provisions are potentially contradictory, and the Constitution leaves open the broader question of who controls the military.[15] In practice, however, the president controls day-to-day military operations through the Department of Defense and has the power to order troops into action without explicit congressional approval. For example, in the summer of 2014 the Obama administration joined over a dozen other nations to aid rebel forces in the Syrian civil war. This included conducting air strikes against Syrian government forces and the ISIL terrorist organization. Members of Congress did not approve this action: an authorization resolution was proposed but never voted on in the Senate, and the House took no action at all. Similarly, the 2011 attack on Osama bin Laden's compound was carried out without prior congressional approval, although some congressional leaders were notified in advance. In fact, even though the United States has been involved in hundreds of military conflicts, there have been only five declarations of war: the War of 1812, the Mexican-American War (1846), the Spanish-American War (1898), World War I (1917), and World War II (1941).

As a way of restraining presidential war-making power, Congress enacted the War Powers Resolution of 1973 (see Nuts & Bolts 12.2). However, a 2004 report by the Congressional Research Service found that between 1975 and 2003, despite dozens of U.S. military actions—ranging from embassy evacuations to large-scale operations, including the 1991 Persian Gulf War and the invasions of Iraq and Afghanistan—the War Powers Resolution has been invoked only once.[16] Moreover, despite being in effect

President Obama's Executive Orders

Many critics argued that President Obama issued an unprecedented number of executive orders. They said this was his strategy to bypass a Republican Congress that was unsympathetic to his policy proposals. What do the numbers say?

Executive Orders Issued by Recent Presidents

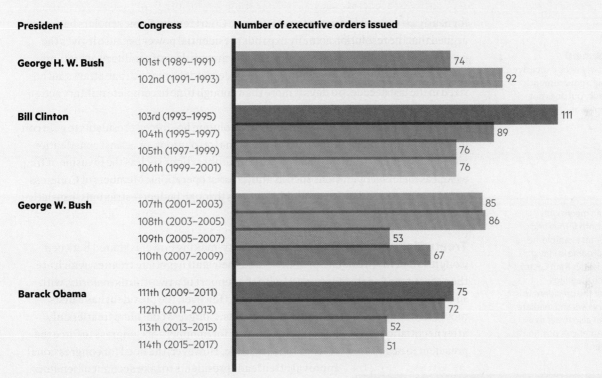

■ Divided government (president from one party and at least one branch of Congress from the other)

■ Unified government (president and both branches of Congress from the same party)

President	Congress	Number of executive orders issued
George H. W. Bush	101st (1989–1991)	74
	102nd (1991–1993)	92
Bill Clinton	103rd (1993–1995)	111
	104th (1995–1997)	89
	105th (1997–1999)	76
	106th (1999–2001)	76
George W. Bush	107th (2001–2003)	85
	108th (2003–2005)	86
	109th (2005–2007)	53
	110th (2007–2009)	67
Barack Obama	111th (2009–2011)	75
	112th (2011–2013)	72
	113th (2013–2015)	52
	114th (2015–2017)	51

Think about it

- Is there any evidence that Obama issued more executive orders than his predecessors?
- In light of past patterns, how many executive orders would you expect from incoming president Donald Trump?

Source: "Executive Orders Disposition Tables Index," *Federal Register*, www.archives.gov (accessed 11/6/16).

The War Powers Resolution of 1973

1. The president is required to report to Congress any introduction of U.S. forces into hostilities or imminent hostilities.
2. The use of force must be terminated within 60 days unless Congress approves of the deployment. The time limit can be extended to 90 days if the president certifies that additional time is needed to safely withdraw American forces.
3. The president is required whenever possible to consult with Congress before introducing American forces into hostilities or imminent hostilities.
4. Any congressional resolution authorizing the continued deployment of American forces will be considered under expedited procedures.

Source: Richard F. Grimmett, "The War Powers Resolution: After Thirty Years," Congressional Research Service Report RL32267, March 11, 2004.

executive agreement
An agreement between the executive branch and a foreign government, which acts as a treaty but does not require Senate approval.

The president often meets with foreign leaders in both formal and informal settings—for example, he watched a baseball game in Havana, Cuba, with Cuban leader Raul Castro in March 2016. Such meetings provide a venue for the president to present American views and mediate disagreements, but also to act as a visible symbol of America's position as a world superpower.

for nearly 40 years, it has never faced Supreme Court review. Some scholars have even argued that the resolution actually expands presidential power because it gives the president essentially unlimited control for the first 90 days of a military operation—and in some cases, such as the killing of bin Laden and the many drone attacks authorized in the last decade, 90 days is more than enough time to complete military action without getting Congress involved.[17]

Despite its limitations, the War Powers Resolution has forced presidents to gain congressional approval, in the form of congressional resolutions, or at least consultation with congressional leaders, for large-scale military actions such as the invasion of Iraq, as well as for lesser operations such as antiterrorist operations. Members of Congress can also curb a president's war-making powers through budget restrictions, legislative prohibitions, and, ultimately, impeachment.[18]

Treaty Making and Foreign Policy Treaty-making power is shared between Congress and the president: presidents and their staff negotiate treaties, which are then sent to the Senate for approval with the support of a two-thirds majority, with some treaties only needing a simple majority. However, the president has a first-mover advantage in the treaty-making process. Congress considers treaties only after negotiations have ended; there is no way for members of Congress to force the president to negotiate a treaty or limit its scope. However, the need for congressional approval often leads presidents to take account of senators' preferences when negotiating treaties, leading again to significant compromise between the two branches.

Presidents have two strategies for avoiding a congressional treaty vote. One is to announce that the United States will voluntarily abide by a treaty without ratifying it. In the case of the 2015 Paris Climate Accord, one of the reasons why the United States supported voluntary targets for reductions in greenhouse gases was that such an agreement did not require Senate approval. It is also possible to structure a deal as an **executive agreement** between the executive branch and a foreign government, which does not require Senate approval. Relative to a ratified treaty, which remains in force after the president who negotiated it leaves office, both voluntary compliance and executive agreements have the disadvantage that a subsequent president can simply undo the action.

The president also serves as the principal representative of the United States in foreign affairs other than treaty negotiations. Presidential duties include communicating with foreign leaders, nongovernmental organizations, and even ordinary citizens to persuade them to act in ways that the president believes are in the best interest of the United States. For example, in March 2016 President Barack Obama traveled to Cuba, where he toured Cuba's capital, Havana, watched a baseball game between American and Cuban teams, met with Cuban dissidents, and gave a speech on Cuban television that criticized the regime for human rights violations. While speeches and baseball games have no direct effect on policy, they can raise public awareness of their government's shortcomings and perhaps increase pressures for change.

The amount of time the administration devotes to foreign policy is subject to domestic and world events and therefore not entirely under presidential control. Barack Obama campaigned on a pledge to reduce American military operations abroad and, six years into his time in office, America no longer had combat operations in Iraq and Afghanistan. But Obama expanded drone and Special Forces attacks on members of terrorist organizations, promoted American participation in Libya and Syria, and sent American forces to eastern Europe in response to Russia's annexation of Crimea. Obama and his aides also spent considerable time coordinating the global response to the financial crisis of 2008–2009, as well as natural disasters such as the 2010 earthquake in Haiti.

Legislative Power The Constitution establishes lawmaking as a shared power between the president and Congress, and compromise between the two branches is fundamental to passing laws that satisfy both the president and Congress.[19] The president can recommend policies to Congress, notably in the annual State of the Union address. The president and staff also work with members of Congress to develop legislative proposals, and although the president cannot formally introduce legislation, it is typically easy to find a member of Congress willing to sponsor a presidential proposal.[20] Presidents and their legislative staff also spend considerable time lobbying members of Congress to support their proposals and negotiating with legislative leaders over policy details.

The president's legislative power also stems from the ability to veto legislation (see Nuts & Bolts 12.3). Once both chambers of Congress have passed a bill by simple majority, the president must decide within two weeks of congressional action whether to sign it or issue a veto. Signed bills become law, but vetoed bills return to the House and Senate for a vote to override the veto. If both chambers enact the bill again with at least two-thirds majorities, the bill becomes law; otherwise, it is defeated. If Congress adjourns before the president has made a decision, the president can pocket veto the proposal by not responding to it. Pocket vetoes cannot be overridden, but as has happened in recent years, congressional leaders can avoid them by keeping Congress in session for two weeks after a bill is enacted.

Figure 12.1 shows the number of vetoes issued by recent presidents—and the number overridden by Congress. In general, vetoes are most likely to occur under divided government, when a president from one party faces a House and Senate controlled by the other party (in the case of Obama, the relatively small number of vetoes reflects a sharp reduction in the number of laws enacted by Congress).[21] Vetoes are much less likely under unified government, when one party controls both Congress and the presidency, because the chances are much higher that the president and legislators from his or her party hold similar policy priorities.

A president's threats to veto legislation provide an additional source of power: they allow the president to specify what kinds of proposals he or she is willing or unwilling

State of the Union
An annual speech in which the president addresses Congress to report on the condition of the country and to recommend policies.

pocket veto
A president's ability to veto a piece of legislation by taking no action on it (possible only when Congress is not in session).

to accept from Congress. Legislators then know that they need to write a proposal that attracts two-thirds support in both houses or accede to a president's demands. For example, during the 2012–2013 debate over raising the federal debt limit President Obama said he would veto any legislation that included a repeal of his health care

The Veto Process

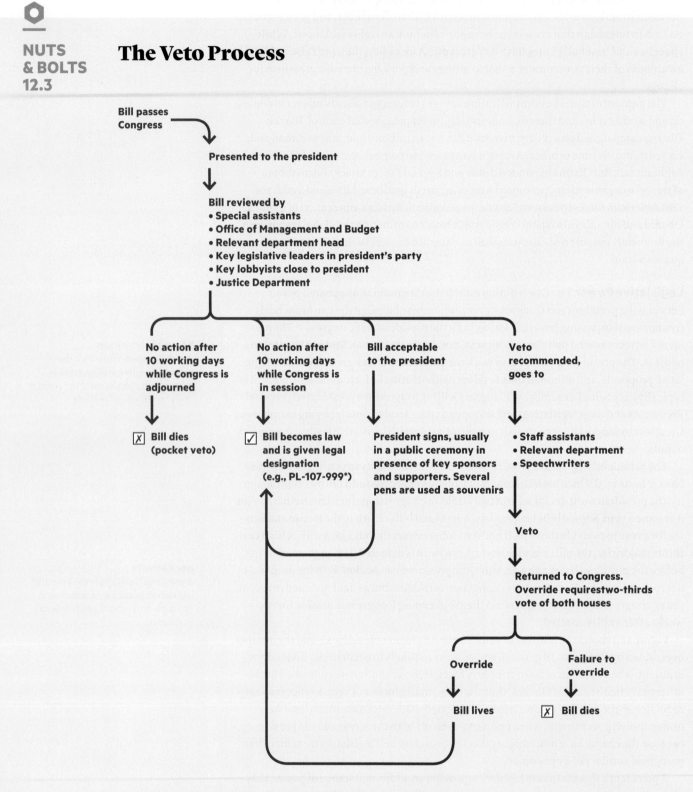

Bill passes
Congress

→ Presented to the president

↓

Bill reviewed by
- Special assistants
- Office of Management and Budget
- Relevant department head
- Key legislative leaders in president's party
- Key lobbyists close to president
- Justice Department

No action after 10 working days while Congress is adjourned

↓

☒ Bill dies (pocket veto)

No action after 10 working days while Congress is in session

↓

☑ Bill becomes law and is given legal designation (e.g., PL-107-999*)

Bill acceptable to the president

↓

President signs, usually in a public ceremony in presence of key sponsors and supporters. Several pens are used as souvenirs

Veto recommended, goes to

↓

- Staff assistants
- Relevant department
- Speechwriters

↓

Veto

↓

Returned to Congress. Override requires two-thirds vote of both houses

Override

↓

Bill lives

Failure to override

↓

☒ Bill dies

*PL = public law; 107 = number of Congress (107th was 2001–2003); 999 = number of the law.

legislation, even if a veto led to a government shutdown. Whether Obama was willing to follow through with his threat is unclear, but the threat worked. In this sense, the veto power can facilitate compromise between presidents and members of Congress—compromises that favor the president's point of view.

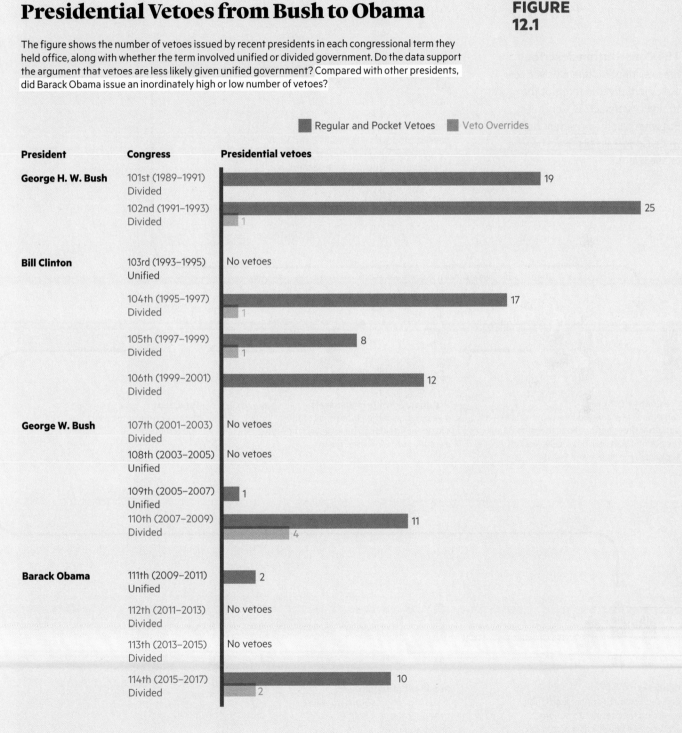

FIGURE 12.1

Presidential Vetoes from Bush to Obama

The figure shows the number of vetoes issued by recent presidents in each congressional term they held office, along with whether the term involved unified or divided government. Do the data support the argument that vetoes are less likely given unified government? Compared with other presidents, did Barack Obama issue an inordinately high or low number of vetoes?

■ Regular and Pocket Vetoes ■ Veto Overrides

President	Congress	Presidential vetoes
George H. W. Bush	101st (1989–1991) Divided	19
	102nd (1991–1993) Divided	25 / 1
Bill Clinton	103rd (1993–1995) Unified	No vetoes
	104th (1995–1997) Divided	17 / 1
	105th (1997–1999) Divided	8 / 1
	106th (1999–2001) Divided	12
George W. Bush	107th (2001–2003) Divided	No vetoes
	108th (2003–2005) Unified	No vetoes
	109th (2005–2007) Unified	1
	110th (2007–2009) Divided	11 / 4
Barack Obama	111th (2009–2011) Unified	2
	112th (2011–2013) Divided	No vetoes
	113th (2013–2015) Divided	No vetoes
	114th (2015–2017) Divided	10 / 2

Source: Data aggregated by the author.

How Presidents Make Policy outside the Legislative Process

The Constitution describes the president's influence over new policy initiatives in terms of the power to sign or veto acts of Congress. But what can the president do when Congress fails to act how he or she wants?

President + White House staff develop proposals—they talk to the public, members of Congress, interest groups, union and corporation heads, party leaders, and others. Some of these groups initiate contact and submit their own ideas or even fully drafted plans.

President + Congress sometimes find compromise proposals—but other times negotiations reveal that the president's plans will not receive majority support in the House and Senate.

President + White House staff investigate whether some or all of the president's goals can be achieved through executive order or other means.

President issues appropriate orders and directives.

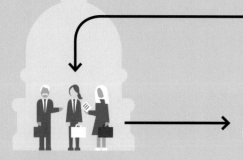

Congress decides whether to enact legislation reversing the president's actions. They need a two-thirds majority in both houses to override an expected presidential veto.

Presidential appointees, assuming congressional attempts to reverse the new policies are unsuccessful, administer implementation of the new policies.

Obama Reestablishes Relations with Cuba

The reopening of diplomatic ties with Cuba illustrates how the president can bypass Congress and initiate meaningful policy change. Obama announced a series of policy changes in December 2014 after a long series of negotiations with the Cuban government, including an agreement to swap spies held by each government.

President + staff:

We're open to it.

2008: During the 2008 presidential campaign, Obama **said he was willing to meet with Cuban leaders.**

Here's a start.

After the election, Obama **eased restrictions** on Cuban Americans sending money to relatives in Cuba.

President + staff + Congress

Let's talk.

2014: Secret negotiations began with the Cuban regime.

...but just us.

Obama and his staff **decided against consulting members of Congress.**

Because...

They believed that Republicans and others who opposed a deal with Cuba would respond **by doing everything they could to end the talks.**

Welcome!

December 2014: Obama announces the **restoration of diplomatic relations with Cuba.**

Let's rebuild.

Florida

Cuba

Easing of restrictions on travel to Cuba, removal of Cuba from the list of state sponsors of terrorism, and other moves to rebuild ties between the two nations.

Welcome home!

The spy exchange takes place soon thereafter. Some Republicans in Congress criticized the spy swap.

President + presidential appointees + Congress

One more (big) thing.

Post-April 2015: Obama and his appointees lobbied Congress to **lift the trade embargo with Cuba.**

Just one catch.

Since the embargo was created by an act of legislation, **Congress must enact a new law to reverse it.** Moreover, all of the Obama administration's changes can be revoked by President Trump.

❓ Critical Thinking

1. **In addition to concerns about congressional opposition,** why else would the Obama administration decide to keep initial negotiations with Cuba a secret?

2. **Based on what you've read in this chapter,** what would Congress need to do to reverse Obama's actions?

DID YOU KNOW?

Through November 8, 2016, President Obama pardoned or commuted the sentences of

844

individuals convicted of federal crimes.

Source: U.S. Department of Justice

executive privilege
The right of the president to keep executive branch conversations and correspondence confidential from the legislative and judicial branches.

Other Duties and Powers The Constitution gives the president several additional powers, including the authority to pardon people convicted of federal crimes or to commute (reduce) their sentences. The only limit on this power is that a president cannot pardon anyone who has been impeached and convicted by Congress. (Thus, if a president is removed from office via impeachment he or she can neither pardon him- or herself nor be pardoned when the vice president assumes the presidency.)

Although most presidential pardons attract little attention, some have been extremely controversial. Presidents have pardoned their own appointees for crimes committed while serving in their administrations, and also have pardoned campaign contributors and personal friends. For example, in July 2007 President Bush commuted a 30-month jail term given to Lewis "Scooter" Libby, Vice President Dick Cheney's former aide. Libby had been convicted of lying to a grand jury about his role in leaking the name of Valerie Plame, a covert CIA agent, to several journalists. Yet, in the main, most pardons attract little attention.

Executive Privilege Finally, although this power is not formally set out in the Constitution or a statute, all presidents have claimed to hold the power of **executive privilege**. This refers to the ability to shield themselves and their subordinates from revealing White House discussions, decisions, or documents (including e-mails) to members of the legislative or judicial branches of government.[22]

Although claims of executive privilege have been made since the ratification of the Constitution in 1789, it is still not clear exactly what falls under the privilege and what does not. In the 1974 case *United States v. Nixon*, a special prosecutor appointed by the Justice Department to investigate the Watergate scandal challenged President Nixon's claims of executive privilege to force him to hand over tapes of potentially incriminating Oval Office conversations involving Nixon and his senior aides. The Supreme Court ruled unanimously that executive privilege does exist, but that the privilege is not absolute. The Court's decision required Nixon to release the tapes, which proved his involvement with attempts to cover up the scandal—but the ruling did not clearly

Congressional investigations of the Justice Department's failed attempt to prevent illegal arms shipments into the United States (the operation was code-named Fast and Furious) were stymied by President Obama's use of executive privilege to limit testimony by his appointees.

The Limits of Executive Privilege

Deciding what information a president can be compelled to release to the public or to other branches of government and what information can be kept confidential requires confronting fundamentally political questions. There are no right answers, and the limits of executive privilege remain unclear. On the one hand, members of Congress need facts, predictions, and estimates from the executive branch to make good public policy. On the other hand, the president and his or her staff have a right to keep their deliberations confidential, as well as a practical need to keep some things secret.

Consider the controversy over the Obama administration's policy of targeting terrorists using attacks by uncrewed drone aircraft. Compared with deployments of other military forces, on the one hand drone attacks have the advantages of surprise (drones are small and fly high enough to be invisible), low cost (drones are cheaper than fighters or bombers), and lower risk (the drones can be controlled from anywhere, so there is no risk of American casualties in an attack). On the other hand, drone attacks carry the risk of collateral damage—an attack may also hurt or kill innocent civilians. Moreover, because drone attacks are conducted in secret, there is little to no congressional oversight of who gets targeted by drone strikes or the potential for collateral damage. Should drone attacks fall under executive privilege?

Keep the attacks secret.

Clearly, revealing the targets of drone strikes in advance of the actual attacks would destroy the secrecy that makes these strikes so effective—terrorists could stop using cell phones, stay indoors as much as possible, travel only at night, and take other actions to make themselves hard to spot from the air. But there would be danger even in forcing an administration to release information after an attack, as such documents would reveal the criteria used to decide which terrorists to target, the limits of the drone technology, and what factors made it easier to carry out a successful attack. All of this information would help terror targets to evade future drone attacks and perhaps require a return to using Special Forces to attack terror targets, which would place American lives at risk.

Reveal the information.

The problem with imposing a high level of secrecy on drone attacks is that it is an exception to the rule of keeping Congress informed about the use of military force. In the end, a

📷 The president's role as commander in chief of America's armed forces gives him or her a tremendous amount of power—power that often can be exercised secretly. What should be the limits on presidential secrecy?

drone is simply a different way of attacking terrorists or their organization. While the need for secrecy in advance of an attack makes sense, it is not obvious why it should continue after an attack has been carried out. In general, presidents are required to give Congress (in the case of secret operations, the chairs and ranking members of the Intelligence Committees) "prompt notification" of all secret operations. This rule was intended to govern reporting of all covert operations. Should drone attacks be given a higher level of secrecy, or should presidents be forced to keep members of Congress informed? Take a stand.

take a stand

1. One argument for using drones to attack terrorist targets highlights their greater effectiveness and lower costs than other options. But drone attacks also involve lower political risks to the president. Explain why this is so.

2. Under current law, the president only has to inform a few members of Congress about covert operations, and can wait until an operation is in progress before releasing information. Why would members of Congress want to expand notification requirements, such as informing more members or requiring disclosure during the planning of an operation?

state the conditions under which a future president could withhold such information.[23] President Obama invoked executive privilege several times, in cases ranging from demands by congressional Republicans for documents related to Operation Fast and Furious (a failed Justice Department sting operation involving the sale of illegal firearms at the U.S.-Mexico border) to requests by both Republicans and Democrats for information on drone strikes against terrorist groups (see the Take a Stand feature). In the former case, federal courts rejected Obama's claim, forcing release of the documents; in the latter, members of Congress did not pursue their claims in the courts.

Claims of executive privilege present a dilemma. On the one hand, members of Congress need to know what is happening in the executive branch. In the case of President Nixon and the Watergate scandal, claims of executive privilege allowed the Watergate cover-up to continue for more than a year and would have kept this information secret permanently if the Supreme Court had ruled in Nixon's favor.[24] Exercising executive privilege can also weaken accountability to the public, as restricting information may leave the average voter unaware of what an administration is doing. On the other hand, the president and his or her staff need to be able to communicate freely, discussing alternative strategies and hypothetical situations or national security secrets without fearing that they will be forced to reveal conversations that could become politically embarrassing or costly.

"Why Should I Care?"

Criticisms of a president often center on cases of inaction or failure, where a president does nothing to address a national problem or where he or she tries to change policy but is unsuccessful. The underlying expectation is that presidents are powerful and can do anything. The reality is that presidents are more powerful in some areas than others—for example, when they negotiate with foreign leaders versus when they propose changes in spending, which requires congressional approval. Thus, when we judge presidents' performance we must consider what they were trying to do and whether they required the assistance of others to make their proposals a reality.

★

EXPLAIN HOW THE EXECUTIVE OFFICE OF THE PRESIDENT, THE VICE PRESIDENT, THE FIRST SPOUSE, AND THE CABINET HELP THE PRESIDENT

The presidency as an institution

As head of the executive branch, the president runs a huge, complex organization with hundreds of thousands of employees. This section describes the organizations and staff who help the president exercise his or her vast responsibilities, from managing disaster-response efforts to implementing policy changes.[25] Among these employees are appointees who hold senior positions in the government. These individuals serve as the president's eyes and ears in the bureaucracy, making sure that bureaucrats are following presidential directives.

The Executive Office of the President

Executive Office of the President (EOP)
The group of policy-related offices that serve as support staff to the president.

The executive branch's organizational chart begins with the Executive Office of the President (EOP), which has employed about 1,800 people in recent administrations. About one-third of these employees are concentrated in two offices: the Office of Management and Budget, which develops the president's budget proposals and monitors

The Executive Office of the President

NUTS & BOLTS 12.4

Council of Economic Advisers	Office of National Drug Control Policy
Council on Environmental Quality	Office of Science and Technology Policy
Domestic Policy Council	Office of the First Lady
Homeland Security Council	Office of the United States Trade Representative
National Economic Council	President's Foreign Intelligence Advisory Board
National Security Council	Privacy and Civil Liberties Oversight Board
Office of Administration	USA Freedom Corps
Office of Faith-Based and Community Initiatives	White House Fellows Office
Office of Management and Budget	White House Military Office
Office of National AIDS Policy	White House Office

spending by government agencies, and the Office of the United States Trade Representative, which negotiates trade agreements with other nations. Nuts & Bolts 12.4 lists the organizations that make up the EOP.

One of the most important duties of EOP staff is helping presidents achieve their policy goals and get reelected. For example, two of President Obama's key political operatives, David Plouffe and David Axelrod, served in the EOP as senior advisers during Obama's first term. Their job was to link the administration and the reelection campaign—as one article put it, "making sure that the actions of one did not threaten the success of the other."[26] Similarly, Donald Trump named two key campaign advisers, Reince Priebus and Steve Bannon, as chief of staff and senior counselor, respectively. The most influential EOP staff occupy the offices in the West Wing of the White House. The West Wing contains the president's office, known as the Oval Office, and space for the president's chief aide and personal secretary, as well as senior aides such as the vice president, the president's press secretary, and the chief of staff, who manages all aspects of White House operations—including, as former Reagan chief of staff James Baker put it, who gets to play tennis on the White House courts. Many recent chiefs of staff have been central in the development of policy proposals and negotiations with members of Congress. However, the chief of staff serves as the agent of the president—what matters is what the president wants, not a chief of staff's policy preferences.

Most EOP staff members are presidential appointees who retain their positions only as long as the president who appointed them remains in office. These individuals are often drawn to government service out of loyalty to the president or because they share the president's policy goals. However, most leave their positions after two or three years to escape the pressures of the job, the long hours, and the relatively low government salaries.[27] Some EOP offices—such as the Office of Management and Budget, the Office of the United States Trade Representative, and the National Security Council (NSC)—also have a significant number of permanent staff analysts and experts.[28] The emphasis on loyalty in presidential appointments has obvious drawbacks: appointees may not know much about the jobs they are given, and they may not be very effective at managing the agencies they are supposed to control. For example, Ron Klain, Obama's choice to lead the government's efforts to stem the spread of the Ebola virus, was criticized for his lack of experience in medicine and public health.

> You don't need to know who's playing on the White House tennis court to be a good president.
>
> —James Baker, former White House Chief of Staff

The president's closest advisers are chosen for their loyalty to the president and his or her policy goals. President Trump named Reince Priebus (Chairman of the Republican National Committee, left) as his chief of staff and Steve Bannon (head of Breitbart News and campaign CEO, right) as chief strategist and senior counselor.

While many people perceive the vice president's position to be ceremonial and relatively powerless, recently the vice president's role has expanded significantly. President Obama's vice president Joe Biden served as a trusted policy adviser and directed several initiatives such as the Cancer Moonshot 2020. @JoeBiden #CancerMoonshot

The vice president

As set out in the Constitution, the vice president's job is to preside over Senate proceedings. This largely ceremonial job is usually delegated to the president pro tempore of the Senate, who in turn typically gives the duty to a more junior member. The vice president also has the power to cast tie-breaking votes in the Senate. As mentioned earlier, the vice president's other formal responsibility is to become president if the current president dies, becomes incapacitated, resigns, or is impeached. Of the 45 people who have become president, 9 were vice presidents who became president in midterm.

These rather limited official duties of the vice president pale in comparison with the influential role played by recent vice presidents. Vice President Dick Cheney, who served with President George W. Bush, exerted a significant influence over many policy decisions, including the rights of terror suspects, tax and spending policy, environmental decisions, and the writing of new government regulations.[29] Although Cheney's level of influence was unique, other recent vice presidents have also had real power. For example, Vice President Al Gore was an important adviser to President Bill Clinton. And Barack Obama's vice president, Joe Biden, played an important role, attending all significant meetings and serving as the last person the president talked to before making a decision. Donald Trump's vice president, Mike Pence, will likely play a similar role in his administration.

The first spouse

Presidential spouses have also played a key but largely informal role in presidential administrations, typically as one of a president's most important advisers. There are examples where they have been an informal conduit for expressing the president's opinions to political appointees, members of Congress, or the media. They also represent America at a wide range of international events, from funerals to conferences. And of course, presidential spouses are a highly visible symbol of the nation, performing a role similar to the president's role as head of state.

Attempts by first spouses to have an official policy-making role in a president's administration are generally limited. For one thing, a first spouse's staff is not set up to assess policy problems or solutions. The commitments of first spouses often keep them out of Washington for substantial periods. Finally, insofar as the first spouse's work is controversial at all, opponents can always argue that the first spouse should not be involved in policy making, as he or she was not elected to do so. Thus, during Bill Clinton's presidency then-first spouse Hillary Clinton was criticized for her leadership role in health care reform efforts.

In light of these constraints, most first spouses pick a largely noncontroversial policy area to focus their official efforts. For example, George W. Bush's spouse, Laura Bush, made numerous public appearances to support education and literacy programs as well as international HIV/AIDS treatment and prevention efforts. Michelle Obama worked to support exercise and healthy eating programs (including changes to federal student lunch guidelines). Similarly, after the failure of health care reform in the Clinton presidency Hillary Clinton changed her focus to less visible, less controversial initiatives, such as efforts to expand human rights and women's rights throughout the world. Donald Trump's spouse, Melania Trump, has suggested that she will focus her efforts on steps to deter cyberbullying.

The president's Cabinet

The president's **Cabinet** is composed of the heads of the 15 executive departments in the federal government, along with other appointees given cabinet rank by the president. Nuts & Bolts 12.5 lists the Cabinet and cabinet-level positions. The cabinet members' principal job is to be the frontline implementers of the president's agenda in their executive departments. As we discuss in Chapter 13, these appointees monitor the actions of the lower-level bureaucrats who retain their jobs regardless of who is president and are not necessarily sympathetic to the president's priorities.

Like other presidential appointees, cabinet members are chosen for a combination of loyalty to the president and expertise. Although he served under a Democratic president, President Obama's first secretary of defense Chuck Hagel was a former Republican senator and a Vietnam veteran. And Obama's secretary of Energy Ernest Moniz was a nuclear physicist who served on Obama's Science and Technology Advisory Council prior to his appointment.

Cabinet
The group of 15 executive department heads who implement the president's agenda in their respective positions.

Cabinet and Cabinet-Level Positions

NUTS & BOLTS 12.5

The president's Cabinet is composed of the heads of the 15 executive departments along with other appointees given cabinet rank by the president.

Secretary of Agriculture	Secretary of Transportation
Secretary of Commerce	Secretary of the Treasury
Secretary of Defense	Secretary of Veterans Affairs
Secretary of Education	Vice president
Secretary of Energy	White House chief of staff
Secretary of Health and Human Services	Attorney general
Secretary of Homeland Security	Head of the Environmental Protection Agency
Secretary of Housing and Urban Development	Head of the Office of Management and Budget
Secretary of the Interior	Head of the Office of National Drug Control Policy
Secretary of Labor	United States Trade Representative
Secretary of State	

Having read the job description for America's president, you might reasonably ask, how does any one person handle all of these responsibilities? The answer is that presidents have help, trusted advisers and people chosen for policy knowledge, political skills, and loyalty. Put another way, if you want to know whether someone will make a good president don't look at his or her experience or campaign promises—look at the people he or she picks to help run the government.

"Why Should I Care?"

Presidential power today

Throughout American history, presidents have accomplished major achievements. They have expanded the territorial boundaries of the United States, fought wars, and enacted large government programs. Yet the Constitution grants the president only limited powers. Presidents have also gained powers from new statutory authority (laws passed by Congress). Even so, assessing presidential power requires expanding our notions of where this power comes from. Saying that the presidents became more powerful because of the expansion of the United States or the increased size of the federal budget or bureaucracy tells only part of the story. What about these circumstances made presidents more powerful?

One important clue about where presidential power comes from is that after more than two centuries many of the limits to these powers—including which executive actions require congressional approval and which ones can be reversed by Congress—are not well defined. In addition to these ambiguities, presidents also gain real power from other, more informal aspects of their office. Recall our discussion of the president's ability to influence the legislative process. In the Constitution, the president's powers are limited to advising Congress on the state of the union and to vetoing legislation, subject to congressional override. But presidents often have very real influence at all points in the legislative process. Presidents can offer a variety of small inducements, such as visits to the Oval Office and campaign assistance, and they can draw on the natural respect that most people (including members of Congress) feel for the presidency regardless of who holds the office, thereby securing compromises that achieve the president's policy goals.[30]

The very ambiguity of the Constitution also creates opportunities for the exercise of presidential power. As we have seen, the Constitution makes the president military commander in chief but gives Congress the power to declare war and to raise and support armies, without specifying which branch of government is in charge of the military. Thus, at least part of presidential authority must be derived or assumed from what the Constitution and statutes *do not say*—ways in which they fail to define or delineate presidential power—and how presidents use this ambiguity to pursue their goals.

The Constitution makes the president commander in chief but limits that power by giving Congress the power to raise and support armies. Thus, while President Obama could order American forces to conduct air strikes on the ISIL terrorist organization in Syria, members of Congress had several legislative options to limit or even stop these operations.

Presidents and unilateral action

Political scientists Terry M. Moe and William G. Howell argue that constitutional and statutory ambiguities in some cases enable presidents to take unilateral action, changing policy on their own without consulting Congress or anyone else.[31] Although Congress can, in theory, undo unilateral actions through legislation, court proceedings, or impeachment, Moe and Howell maintain that the costs of doing so, in terms of time, effort, and public perceptions, are often prohibitive. The result is that presidents can take unilateral action despite congressional opposition, knowing that their actions stand little chance of being reversed.

The 2011 debate over U.S. military action in Syria provides a good example of how constitutional ambiguities create opportunities for unilateral action. The Obama administration argued that because the operation only involved air strikes and very limited deployment of advisers, it did not trigger the "hostilities or imminent hostilities" provisions of the War Powers Act. While some in Congress disagreed and wanted to vote on whether to authorize the operation, no such vote was ever taken. This example is far from the first time that a president has argued that military operations were not subject to congressional review. During the Iraq War, some Democrats in Congress wanted to cut off war funding to force the withdrawal of American forces, but supporters of the Bush administration responded with what they called the unitary executive theory. They argued that the Constitution's vesting clause allows the president to issue orders and policy directives that members of Congress cannot undo unless the Constitution explicitly gives them this power. In the case of funding the Iraq War, they maintained that the Constitution's description of the president as commander in chief of America's armed forces meant that, even if Congress refused to appropriate funds for the war, the president could order American forces to stay in Iraq and order the Department of the Treasury to spend any funds necessary to continue operations.

In both cases, the position of the Obama and Bush administrations left members of Congress with a single unattractive option: they could invoke the War Powers Resolution to force the end of combat operations. This option would take time, as it would require building majority support in the House and the Senate for the resolution. It would also trigger Supreme Court review of the War Powers Resolution, which is a significant risk—if the Court were to rule in favor of the president and to hold that the resolution was unconstitutional, it would sharply reduce Congress's control over future military operations.

Presidents act unilaterally to make domestic policy as well. For example, during his second term in office President Obama ordered federal contractors to increase the minimum wage they paid their employees.[32] Obama also gave several directives to the Justice Department that limited deportations of undocumented immigrants. And the Obama administration made several important policy changes to smooth the implementation of the ACA. While all of these actions can be undone by an act of legislation or by an order issued by a future president, they remain in place until one of those moves occur.

It is important to understand that all presidents take unilateral actions. President Bush, for example, authorized wiretaps of Americans' international phone conversations without obtaining warrants from the Foreign Intelligence Surveillance Court, a special federal court created to approve such requests.[33] Throughout the nation's history there have been many other examples of unilateral presidential actions, such as the annexation of Texas, the freeing of slaves in the Emancipation Proclamation, the desegregation of the U.S. military, the initiation of affirmative action programs, and the creation of agencies such as the Peace Corps.[34]

unilateral action (presidential)
Any policy decision made and acted upon by the president and presidential staff without the explicit approval or consent of Congress.

unitary executive theory
The idea that the vesting clause of the Constitution gives the president the authority to issue orders and policy directives that cannot be undone by Congress.

Control over the interpretation and implementation of laws

Most presidents have tried to control the implementation of laws by issuing a **signing statement** when signing a bill into law. These documents, which explain the president's interpretation of the new law, are issued most often when the president disagrees with the interpretation of members of Congress who supported the legislation but still wishes to approve the bill. Presidents issue signing statements so that if the courts have to resolve uncertainties about the bill's intent judges can take into account not only the views expressed during congressional debates about the bill but also the president's interpretation of it.[35] The president can also influence the implementation of a law through a signing statement, essentially telling the bureaucracy to follow his or her interpretation of the law rather than Congress's.

Congress has the power to block most types of presidential action, if it chooses. For example, in 2009 President Obama ordered the closure of the detention center for terror suspects at Guantánamo Bay, Cuba, but Congress passed legislation preventing the closure until the Obama administration developed detailed plans for relocating the prisoners.

In some cases, presidents have found loopholes in laws that were initially designed to restrict their power. An analysis of legislation designed to curb presidential power found that subsequent presidents actually used these laws to justify unilateral actions—the opposite of what was intended.[36] For example, current law requires the president to give congressional leaders "timely notification" of secret intelligence operations. During the Reagan administration, senior officials did not reveal the existence of ongoing operations for several months. When these operations were eventually discovered, officials claimed they were within the letter of the law because it did not specify a time limit for notification.[37]

Congressional responses to unilateral action

In theory, members of Congress can undo a president's unilateral action by enacting a law to overturn it, but this is harder than it may sound.[38] Some members of Congress

Federal courts can undo unilateral presidential actions. A series of Supreme Court rulings forced the George W. Bush administration to allow terror suspects, such as Salim Hamdan, an Al Qaeda member captured in Afghanistan, to challenge their imprisonment. This courtroom sketch from the U.S. naval base in Guantánamo, Cuba, shows Hamdan (far left) and his legal team.

may approve of what the president has done or be indifferent to it, or they may give a higher priority to other policies. Still, reversals do happen: after President Obama announced plans to close the Guantánamo Bay detention center for terrorist suspects, the House and Senate added an amendment to a spending bill stating that the prison could not be closed until the administration released plans explaining where the prisoners would be sent. The facility remains open to this day.

Members of Congress can also write laws in a way that limits the president's authority over their implementation.[39] The problem with this approach is that members of Congress delegate authority to the president or the executive branch bureaucracy for good reasons—either because it is difficult for legislators to predict how a policy should be implemented or because they cannot agree among themselves on an implementation plan.[40] Members of Congress from the president's party may also want to grant presidential authority because they hold policy goals similar to the president's and would therefore benefit from the exercise of unilateral power.

Even if members of Congress tried to use these strategies to limit the president's authority, it could still be argued—along the lines of the unitary executive theory—that Congress could not overturn the president's actions because the Constitution did not explicitly give the legislature this power. The only option for members of Congress would be to take the president to court (probably all the way to the Supreme Court) to demonstrate that he or she had overstepped his authority. In February 2014, Senator Rand Paul (R-KY) filed a lawsuit challenging the Obama administration's decision to allow the NSA to collect Americans' telephone call metadata (the caller, receiver, time and length of call—but not the content of the conversation) without a warrant.[41] While the Obama administration voluntarily ended this data collection soon after Paul filed his lawsuit, in general lawsuits are not a very practical or expedient option. Aside from the fact that the Court might not side with Congress, these legal proceedings could take years.

Congress also has the power to remove the president or vice president from office through the impeachment process. However, removing a president is much more difficult than passing a law to undo a unilateral action. First, House members must impeach (indict) the president by majority vote, which accuses him or her of a crime or breach of his or her sworn duties. Then senators hold a trial, followed by a vote—in which a two-thirds majority is required to remove the president from office. Only two presidents have faced an impeachment vote: Andrew Johnson in 1866 and Bill Clinton in 1999 (a third president, Richard Nixon, resigned from office to prevent an impeachment vote). Johnson was involved in a political dispute over administration of the southern states after the Civil War; Clinton was alleged to have lied under oath in a sexual harassment lawsuit. Although both of these presidents were impeached by the House, they were not convicted by the Senate, so they stayed in office. One reason impeachment is difficult is that members of Congress who are upset about certain presidential actions might nevertheless oppose removing the president from office. They might approve of the president's other initiatives, want to prevent the vice president from becoming president, or have concerns about the political backlash that impeachment could generate against them or their party.

In sum, ambiguities in the Constitution create opportunities for unilateral presidential action. These actions are subject to reversal through legislation, court decisions, and impeachment, but members of Congress face significant costs if they undertake any of these options. As long as presidents are careful to limit their exercise of unilateral power to actions that do not generate intense opposition in Congress, they can implement a wide range of policy goals without official congressional consent—provided that bureaucrats go along with the president's wishes, a question we take up in the next chapter.

President as politician

As we have discussed, statutory and constitutional authority give the president considerable influence over policy. However, the reality of presidential power is closer to President Harry Truman's description of what incoming president (and former army general) Dwight Eisenhower would find when he entered the White House: much of what presidents do (or want to do) requires support from others, including legislators, bureaucrats, and citizens. As a result, the presidency is an inherently political office—something that all presidents learn is true, regardless of their expectations when they took office.[42] Presidents have to take into account the political consequences of their decisions: their effect on their political support, reelection prospects, and their party. A president must also contend with the reality that achieving his or her personal policy goals often requires bargaining and compromising with others, both inside and outside government.

In part, presidents must keep their eyes on the political implications of their actions in office because they want to be reelected to a second term. One important indicator of presidential performance is the **presidential approval rating**, the percentage of the public who think the president is doing a good job in office. Figure 12.2, which shows the presidential approval ratings for the last six presidents who ran for reelection, reveals that first-term presidents with less than 50 percent approval are in real trouble. No recent president has been reelected with less than a 50 percent approval rating.

Of course, it would be wrong to say that presidents are single-mindedly focused on keeping their approval rating as high as possible. For one thing, presidential approval is shaped by factors that they have only limited control over, such as the state of the economy. And every president has taken actions that were politically costly because they believed that the policies were worthwhile—for example, President Obama ordered U.S. armed forces to intervene in the Syrian civil war despite polls showing that a majority of Americans opposed this strategy. Even so, presidents and their advisers are

presidential approval rating
The percentage of Americans who think that the president is doing a good job in office.

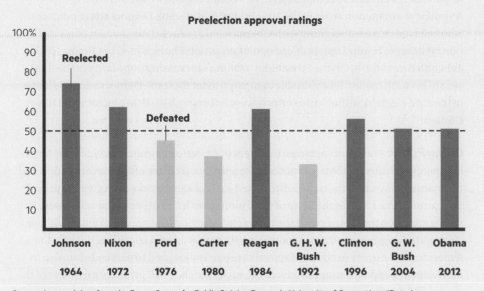

FIGURE 12.2

Presidential Popularity and Reelection

This figure shows the preelection year average approval ratings for recent presidents who ran for reelection. It shows that a president's chances of winning reelection are related to his popularity. At what level of approval would you say that an incumbent president is likely to be reelected?

Preelection approval ratings

Reelected

Defeated

| Johnson | Nixon | Ford | Carter | Reagan | G. H. W. Bush | Clinton | G. W. Bush | Obama |
| 1964 | 1972 | 1976 | 1980 | 1984 | 1992 | 1996 | 2004 | 2012 |

Source: Approval data from the Roper Center for Public Opinion Research, University of Connecticut, "Data Access: Presidential Approval," http://webapps.ropercenter.uconn.edu/CFIDE/roper/presidential/webroot/presidential_rating.cfm (accessed 10/26/12).

keenly aware of the political consequences of their actions and there is no doubt that these consequences shape both their decisions and how they explain these actions to American citizens.

The President as Party Leader The president is the unofficial head of his or her political party and generally picks the party's day-to-day leadership or at least has considerable influence over the selection. This process begins when a presidential candidate captures the party's nomination. For example, in 2008, soon after Barack Obama became the presumptive Democratic Party nominee, some of his senior aides and advisers took on leadership positions in the Democratic Party organization.[43] During the 2012 campaign, some of these individuals returned to help Obama get reelected, such as Deputy Campaign Manager Jennifer O'Malley Dillon, who had served as the executive director of the Democratic National Committee.

The president's connection to the party reflects intertwining interests. The president needs support from members of his or her party in Congress to enact legislation, and the party and its candidates need the president to compile a record of policy achievements that reflect well on the organization and to help raise the funds needed for the next election. Therefore, party leaders generally defer to a presidential candidate's (or a president's) staffing requests and most presidents and presidential candidates take time to meet with national party leaders and the congressional leadership from their party to plan legislative strategies, make joint campaign appearances, and raise funds for the party's candidates.

The president's value to the party also depends on his or her popularity. When presidential approval ratings drop to low levels, most members of Congress see no political advantage to campaigning with the president or supporting White House proposals and they may become increasingly reluctant to comply with the president's requests. In the 2002 and 2004 elections, Republican legislators stressed their connection to President Bush and gladly accepted offers of joint campaign appearances. In 2006 and 2008, however, as Bush's approval ratings declined because of the war in Iraq, many

Republican candidates deemphasized their connection to Bush as much as possible.[44] A similar phenomenon arose in the 2014 midterms for some Democratic candidates who believed that campaigning with Obama would reduce their chances of reelection, as it would remind voters of unpopular proposals championed by Obama, such as health care reform. On the other hand, Obama's increasing popularity in the final year of his term made him a valuable campaign asset for some Democratic candidates in the 2016 election, although his efforts were not enough to secure victory for Hillary Clinton.

Going Public Presidents are in an excellent position to communicate with the American people because of their prominent role and the extensive media coverage devoted to anything they say to the nation. Broadcast and cable networks even give the president prime-time slots for the State of the Union speech and other major addresses. The media attention that comes with the presidency provides the president with a unique strategy for shaping government policy: **going public**, that is appealing directly to American citizens.[45] Presidential appeals are partly designed to persuade but also to motivate the president's supporters, in the hope that they will pressure members of the House and Senate to support the president's requests.

Going public sometimes works—but more often it is ineffectual or often counterproductive. A president's appeals may energize supporters; they may also have a similar effect on opponents.[46] Thus, rather than facilitating compromise (or a wholesale presidential victory), publicizing an issue may deepen existing conflicts. More generally, studies suggest that most Americans ignore or reject a president's attempts to go public. As presidency scholar George C. Edwards III notes, people who disapprove of a president's time in office are not going to change their minds just because of a presidential speech.[47] Thus, unless a president is extraordinarily popular going public is not going to help enact the president's agenda. This pattern is part of the explanation of why President Obama had little success in enacting major legislative proposals in his second term. Consider Figure 12.3, which shows data on presidential approval for Obama's eight years in office. As you can see, after initially high ratings President Obama's approval rating hovered in the 45 to 50 percent range for most of his presidency. This reflected on the one

going public
A president's use of speeches and other public communications to appeal directly to citizens about issues the president would like the House and Senate to act on.

DID YOU KNOW?

President Obama made

18

major speeches (often televised) calling for new regulations on handgun purchases and ownership.

The president is the unofficial head of his party and works with fellow party members in government. Here, President Obama meets with Vice President Joe Biden and Democratic House leaders, clockwise from the bottom left, Steve Israel (D-NY), Chris Van Hollen (D-MD), Steny Hoyer (D-MD), House Minority Leader Nancy Pelosi (D-CA), James Clyburn (D-SC), Xavier Becerra (D-CA), and Joseph Crowley (D-NY).

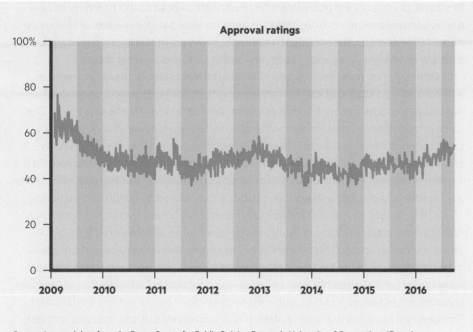

Approval ratings

Source: Approval data from the Roper Center for Public Opinion Research, University of Connecticut, "Data Access: Presidential Approval," https://presidential.roper.center (accessed 11/15/16).

FIGURE 12.3

Presidential Approval Ratings for Barack Obama

Barack Obama's approval ratings were remarkably stable during his presidency, reflecting slow but steady economic growth and high levels of partisan polarization. During the last two years of Obama's term in office, many Republicans said that Obama should be blamed for not dealing with ISIL and the threat of terrorist attacks in the United States. Does the data on Obama's approval ratings suggest these attacks were successful or unsuccessful?

hand the relatively weak state of the American economy until 2016 and on the other the lack of significant scandals or international crises during his presidency, and high levels of partisan polarization among American citizens, which makes people more likely to approve of a president who shares their party ID. Given these middling popularity ratings, it is no surprise that Obama had little success in building public support for proposals such as increased controls on gun ownership or immigration reform.

The difficulty presidents have in shaping public opinion is another reason why some presidents seem to accomplish more than others. Political scientist Stephen Skowronek argues that presidents are constrained by the era in which they govern.[48] Some presidents (such as Ronald Reagan in 1981) take office when public opinion is strongly behind their policy agenda, making it easier for them to persuade Congress and bureaucrats to comply with their requests. Other presidents have the misfortune to hold office when public opinion is not supportive of new programs and increased regulations (such as exists now), which strongly limits what the president can do, even with all of his or her powers and capability for unilateral action. On the other side of the coin, President Donald Trump holds office with unified Republican control of the House and Senate. At a minimum, he will make significant policy changes through the exercise of executive authority, similar to how we have described Barack Obama's presidency. Legislative successes are possible, but will require Trump to forge compromises with members of Congress to secure enactment of these proposals.

Conclusion

President Donald Trump occupies an office whose power is derived from constitutional authority, statutory authority, and ambiguities that enable unilateral action. Even so, presidential power is limited. The president shares many powers with Congress.

Moreover, presidents are politicians who need public support, both to win reelection and to persuade members of Congress to approve their policy initiatives. Public evaluation is based on how the president handles those issues that are considered a priority by many Americans, such as the economy, health care, and national security.

Taken together, these factors help to explain why presidents appear powerful in some situations but not others. Military actions, such as drone attacks on terrorist organizations, do not require congressional assent, at least not in the short term. The same is true of many other foreign policy actions. However, major changes in policy (particularly domestic policy) or spending are unlikely unless the president's party controls both houses of Congress. A president can also change policy by controlling the implementation of existing legislation or by acting unilaterally, but this process requires a compliant bureaucracy and is subject to being overturned by congressional action.

All this considered, Donald Trump's presidency may be less transformational than his supporters believe. Some of Trump's proposals can be implemented through unilateral executive action. Others will require the cooperation of members of Congress, bureaucrats, or even the leaders of other nations. Given these constraints, it is almost surely true that Trump will fall short of achieving a fundamental renovation of American government. However, this outcome—if it occurs—does not reflect any limitations that Trump might have as a politician. Rather, it is a consequence of how the rules and institutions of American politics both empower and constrain presidential actions.

STUDY GUIDE

responsibilities. The president has many duties, but the primary responsibilities of the office are to oversee the executive branch and implement laws passed by Congress. Although some presidents might prefer to focus on either domestic or foreign policy, most find that their priorities are determined by domestic and world events.

Key terms

constitutional authority (p. 411)
statutory authority
(presidential) (p. 411)
vesting clause (p. 411)
head of government (p. 412)
head of state (p. 412)

recess appointment (p. 413)
executive orders (p. 413)
executive agreement (p. 416)
State of the Union (p. 417)
pocket veto (p. 417)
executive privilege (p. 422)

The development of presidential power

Trace the evolution of presidential power. (Pages 408–411)

Summary

Presidents get their powers from a variety of sources: some powers are from the Constitution; others have more informal origins. Although the president's constitutional powers have not changed, presidential power has grown substantially over time. Nonetheless, even presidents' power is still limited in a number of contexts.

Practice Quiz Questions

1. **Presidential power has increased over time for all of the reasons below except:**
   a. changes in the Constitution
   b. America's growth as a nation
   c. America's emergence as a dominant actor in international politics
   d. the expansion of the federal government
   e. acts of legislation passed by Congress

2. **Which of the following events during Barack Obama's presidency best illustrates the limits of presidential power?**
   a. congressional consideration of new gun control laws
   b. the failure of Obama's Social Security reforms
   c. the deployment of U.S. forces in Libya in 2011
   d. the enactment of health care reform legislation
   e. Obama's defeat of Mitt Romney in 2012

The president's job description

Describe the constitutional and statutory powers of the president today. (Pages 411–424)

Summary

The president's formal powers arise from a combination of constitutional provisions and additional laws that give him or her increased

Practice Quiz Questions

3. **Presidents use recess appointments when they are trying to _____.**
   a. fill a judicial vacancy outside the scheduled period
   b. fill a vacant seat in Congress
   c. temporarily dodge the need for Senate approval
   d. temporarily dodge the need for House approval
   e. fill vacancies with a permanent replacement

4. **A presidential proclamation that unilaterally changes government policy without congressional consent is called _____.**
   a. an executive privilege
   b. a fast-track authority
   c. an executive agreement
   d. an executive order
   e. statutory authority

5. **Some scholars argue that the War Powers Resolution has effectively expanded the power of _____.**
   a. the president
   b. Congress
   c. the Supreme Court
   d. the Department of Defense
   e. the State Department

6. **The first-mover advantage refers to the president's negotiating advantage over _____.**
   a. foreign leaders
   b. governors
   c. the bureaucracy
   d. Congress
   e. international organizations

The presidency as an institution

Explain how the Executive Office of the President, the vice president, the first spouse, and the Cabinet help the president. (Pages 424–427)

Summary

The executive branch is a huge, complex organization that helps the president exercise vast responsibilities. Appointees to the branch serve as the president's eyes and ears on the bureaucracy. Almost all appointees are replaced when a new administration begins.

Key terms

Executive Office of the President (EOP) (p. 424)

Cabinet (p. 427)

Practice Quiz Questions

7. In most appointments to EOP positions, presidents generally emphasize _____.
   a. experience
   b. expertise
   c. effectiveness
   d. public opinion
   e. loyalty

8. Recent vice presidents have had _____ official duties and/but _____ been influential in their role.
   a. no; have not
   b. limited; have
   c. limited; have not
   d. extensive; have
   e. extensive; have not

9. The primary job of most of the people who work in the Executive Office of the President is _____.
   a. to help the president manage the federal bureaucracy
   b. to lobby members of Congress to enact the president's program
   c. to manage the president's reelection campaign
   d. to find ways to build public support for the president
   e. to oversee the organization of the president's party

Presidential power today

Explain how modern presidents have become even more powerful. (Pages 428–435)

Summary

While presidents have gained power over time, the Constitution grants the president rather limited powers. The growth of presidential power is closely related to the fact that most limits on it are not well-defined and presidents have succeeded in taking advantage of these ambiguities.

Key terms

unilateral action (presidential) (p. 429)

unitary executive theory (p. 429)

signing statement (p. 430)

presidential approval rating (p. 432)

going public (p. 434)

Practice Quiz Questions

10. The _____ was used by the George W. Bush administration to argue in favor of the power to station American forces in Iraq.
    a. principal-agent theory
    b. unitary executive theory
    c. unilateral agreement theory
    d. dual presidency theory
    e. signing statement power

11. Most presidents use the _____ to control the interpretation and implementation of laws.
    a. line-item veto
    b. recess appointment
    c. executive order
    d. signing statement
    e. pocket veto

12. Congressional challenges to presidential unilateral action are _____ used and are generally _____ at constraining presidential power.
    a. rarely; successful
    b. rarely; unsuccessful
    c. commonly; successful
    d. commonly; unsuccessful

13. Presidential approval is generally based on _____.
    a. economic conditions
    b. policy positions
    c. presidential actions
    d. presidential appointments
    e. an absence of scandals

14. What is the best explanation for the ability of presidents to act unilaterally in the face of congressional opposition?
    a. Americans' dislike of Congress
    b. The perception that presidents only act in the interests of the entire nation
    c. The doctrine of executive privilege
    d. The difficulty of enacting a law to reverse a president's actions
    e. The theory of the unitary executive

15. For most presidents, the problem with going public is that _____.

   a. the public is more focused on Congress

   b. the president's speeches are not very persuasive

   c. they energize their opponents

   d. they generally address unimportant issues

   e. they do not reach their target audience

Suggested Reading

Alter, Jonathan. *The Promise: President Obama, Year One.* New York: Simon and Schuster, 2010.

Canes-Wrone, Brandice. *Who Leads Whom? Presidents, Policy, and the Public.* Chicago: University of Chicago Press, 2006.

Edwards, George C., III. *Predicting the Presidency: The Potential of Persuasive Leadership.* Princeton, NJ: Princeton University Press, 2015.

Hallett, Brian. *Declaring War: Congress, the President, and What the Constitution Does Not Say.* New York: Cambridge University Press, 2012.

Howell, William G. *Power without Persuasion: The Politics of Direct Presidential Action.* Princeton, NJ: Princeton University Press, 2003.

Katznelson, Ira. *Fear Itself: The New Deal and the Origins of Our Time.* New York: W. W. Norton, 2013.

Lewis, David E. *Presidents and the Politics of Agency Design: Political Insulation in the United States Government Bureaucracy, 1946–1997.* Palo Alto, CA: Stanford University Press, 2003.

Mayer, Kenneth. *With the Stroke of a Pen: Executive Orders and Presidential Power.* Princeton, NJ: Princeton University Press, 2001.

Neustadt, Richard E. *Presidential Power and the Modern Presidents: The Politics of Leadership from Roosevelt to Reagan.* New York: Free Press, 1990.

Rudalevige, Andrew. *Managing the President's Program: Presidential Leadership and Legislative Policy Formation.* Princeton, NJ: Princeton University Press, 2002.

Skowronek, Stephen. *Presidential Leadership in Political Time: Reprise and Reappraisal,* 2nd ed. Lawrence: University of Kansas Press, 2011.

The Bureaucracy

What's with all this red tape?

Millions of Americans work in the federal bureaucracy, doing everything from processing paperwork to driving scientific rovers on Mars. In some cases, these individuals find themselves as poster children for epic government failures. Consider the case of Flint, Michigan, where residents discovered in 2016 that their drinking water was contaminated by dangerously high levels of lead. Most of the blame falls on state officials, who allowed the local water authority to stop using chemicals to prevent lead pipes from contaminating the water supply. However, while scientists in the U.S. Environmental Protection Agency (EPA) were aware of the risks created by this decision, agency officials spent months debating whether it had the authority to order the state to change its policy even as many Flint children began to show symptoms of lead poisoning. In the end, the EPA did a poor job of safeguarding the health of the people of Flint even though this task is a fundamental part of its mission statement.

In other cases, though, civil servants produce near miracles. NASA's *Opportunity* rover, for example, was built to last only 90 days on Mars—but NASA's scientists have managed to keep it operating for more than 12 years after it landed. *Opportunity* and its sister rover, *Spirit* (which lasted nine years before getting trapped in a Martian sand dune), have made many important discoveries about Martian geology, including clues about the presence of water on the surface of Mars and prospects for life on the planet.

These two examples illustrate only a tiny part of the federal bureaucracy. Americans encounter the bureaucracy every day: when they sort through mail delivered by the Postal Service, drive on highways funded by the Department of Transportation, or purchase food inspected by the Food and Drug Administration (FDA). The prices Americans pay to surf the Web, watch television, or use a cell phone are influenced by regulations issued by the FCC. When people go on vacation, their bags are inspected by the Transportation Security Administration (TSA), the aircraft and pilots are scrutinized by the Federal Aviation Administration (FAA), and many beaches are maintained by the Army Corps of Engineers.

Although many federal bureaucrats work diligently to serve the American public, the comparison of the EPA's inaction on Flint's water supply to the long-lasting Mars rovers illustrates a fundamental fact: the same federal

📷

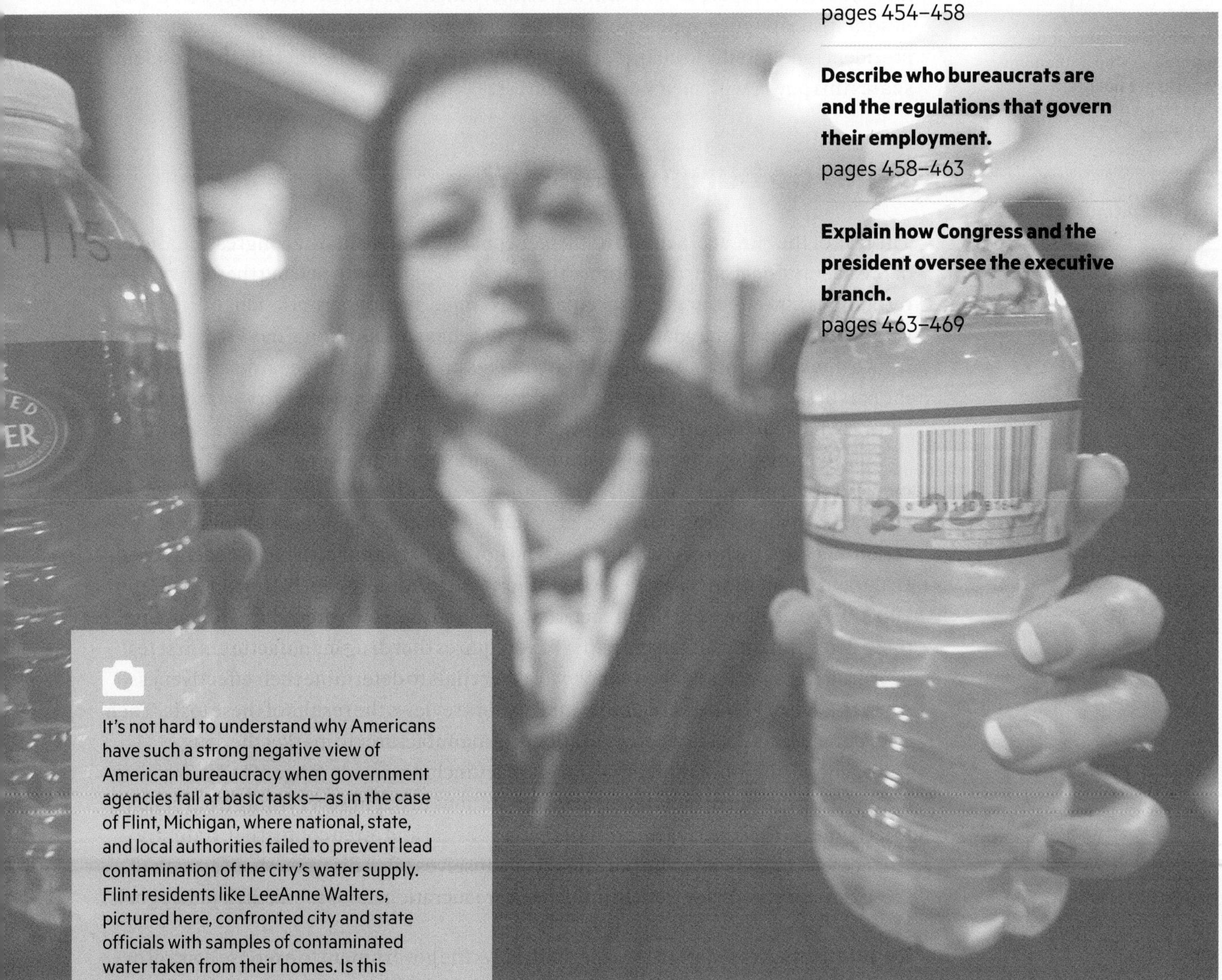

It's not hard to understand why Americans
have such a strong negative view of
American bureaucracy when government
agencies fail at basic tasks—as in the case
of Flint, Michigan, where national, state,
and local authorities failed to prevent lead
contamination of the city's water supply.
Flint residents like LeeAnne Walters,
pictured here, confronted city and state
officials with samples of contaminated
water taken from their homes. Is this
negative view accurate? How can we trust
government to act in our interests given
such failures?

bureaucracy that accomplishes so many big tasks also does things that are inefficient, wasteful, and downright dumb. Do these shortcomings result from inevitable accidents—or are they the consequence of deliberate actions? And if so, why were agencies designed to fail or to do things that look a lot like failure? How does conflict over what government should do translate into bureaucratic successes and failures?

bureaucracy
The system of civil servants and political appointees who implement congressional or presidential decisions; also known as the *administrative state*.

civil servants
Employees of bureaucratic agencies within the government.

political appointees
People selected by an elected leader, such as the president, to hold a government position.

regulation
A rule that allows the government to exercise control over individuals and corporations by restricting certain behaviors.

What is the federal bureaucracy?

The federal bureaucracy that makes up the government's executive branch is composed of millions of civil servants, who work for the government in permanent positions, and thousands of political appointees, who hold short-term, usually senior positions and are appointed by an elected leader, such as the president. Another name for the bureaucracy is the *administrative state*, which refers to the role bureaucrats play in administering government policies.[1] Most constitutional scholars agree that the president is nominally in charge of the bureaucracy—although generally the president shares this power with members of Congress.

What do bureaucrats do?

The task of the bureaucracy is to implement policies established by congressional acts or presidential decisions. Sometimes the tasks associated with putting these laws and resolutions into effect are very specific. For example, in the appropriations bill for fiscal year 2016 Congress mandated that the navy purchase an additional five F-35 attack jets from defense contractor Lockheed Martin. This provision required no discretion on the part of the bureaucrats tasked to implement it—all they needed to do was sign the contract and make sure that the jets were delivered and Lockheed Martin was paid.

More commonly, however, legislation determines only the general guidelines for meeting governmental goals, allowing bureaucrats to develop specific policies and programs. In these cases, bureaucrats' actions determine the essence of government action, deciding "who gets what, when, and how."[2] For example, the 1938 Federal Food, Drug, and Cosmetic Act gave the FDA the job of determining which drugs are safe and effective, but it allowed FDA bureaucrats to develop their own procedures for making these determinations.[3] Currently, the FDA requires that drug manufacturers first test new drugs for safety, and then conduct further trials to determine their effectiveness. An FDA advisory board of scientists and doctors reviews the results of these tests. Then FDA bureaucrats decide whether to allow the manufacturer to market the drug.

In general, the job of the federal bureaucracy includes a wide range of tasks, from regulating the behavior of individuals and corporations to buying everything from pencils to jet fighters. These activities are inherently political and often conflictual: ordinary citizens, elected officials, and bureaucrats themselves often disagree about aspects of these activities, and they work to influence bureaucratic actions to suit their policy goals.

Regulations A regulation is a rule that allows the government to exercise control over individuals and corporations by restricting their behaviors. It does so by either allowing or prohibiting behavior, setting out the conditions under which certain behaviors can occur, or assessing costs or granting benefits based on behavior. Bureaucrats gain

Although the term "bureaucracy" may suggest workers sitting behind desks in offices, the agencies of the federal bureaucracy perform a wide range of tasks. Following the explosion of BP's *Deepwater Horizon* oil rig in 2010, the Coast Guard—a government agency—responded to try to put out the fire. #DeepwaterHorizon #BPoilspill #USCG

the authority to write regulations by the statute that sets up their agency or by a subsequent act of Congress. Consider the EPA's Clean Power Plan, which imposes limits on the amount of carbon dioxide that can be emitted from electrical power plants. These new regulations, as well as limits on other power plant emissions, follow from authority given to the EPA by the Clean Air Act, legislation that was enacted in the 1970s (for more details, see How it Works: Bureaucracy and Legislation).

Regulations are developed according to the **notice-and-comment procedure**.[4] Before a new regulation can take effect, it must be published in the *Federal Register*, an official publication that includes rules, proposed rules, and other types of government documents. Individuals and companies that the regulation will affect can then respond to the agency that proposed it, either supporting or opposing it, and offering different versions for consideration. Those potentially affected can also appeal to members of Congress or to the president's staff for help in getting the proposed rule revised. The agency then issues a final regulation, incorporating changes based on the comments. This final regulation is also published in the *Federal Register* and then put into effect. The process is time-consuming. The FAA's release in 2015 of regulations on the use of drone aircraft—including a provision requiring all but the smallest drones to be registered with the agency—began with a congressional mandate issued in 2012. Many regulations can take even longer to craft from beginning to end.

The process of devising or modifying regulations is often political. Members of Congress and the president usually have strong opinions about how new regulations should look—and even when they don't, they may still get involved on behalf of a constituent or an interest group. Bureaucrats take account of these pressures from elected officials for two reasons: (1) The bureaucrats' policy-making power may derive from a statute that members of Congress could overturn; and (2) bureaucrats need congressional support to get larger budgets and to expand their agency's mission. Thus, despite bureaucrats' power to implement policies, their agencies' budgets, appointed leaders, and overall missions are subject to elected officials' oversight.

Many regulations are issued each year. Lately, the *Federal Register* has contained more than 22,000 pages and about 4,000 new regulations a year.[5] Although nearly all government agencies issue regulations, most come from a few agencies, including the Federal Trade Commission, which regulates commerce; the FCC, which regulates media companies that create content as well as telecommunications companies that transmit information; and the FDA, which regulates drugs, medical products, food, and cosmetics.

notice-and-comment procedure
A step in the rule-making process in which proposed rules are published in the *Federal Register* and made available for debate by the general public.

Bureaucracy and Legislation

After Congress passes legislation and the president signs it, the transition from legislation to regulation begins. Input from local government officials, interest groups, and others helps to refine the regulations as they are developed, and has a strong influence on how regulations will affect people "on the ground."

Congress passes legislation.

↓

The president signs the bill into law.

↓

Bureaucrats interpret the law and design appropriate regulations.

↓

Courts respond to challenges to the law, and they can provide guidelines for implementation.

Other bureaucrats disseminate regulations to state and local governments, corporations, and individuals, and they monitor compliance.

Citizens and interest groups provide information and proposals to bureaucrats, and they lobby for their preferred implementation of the legislation.

↓

Regulations can be revised in light of changing circumstances, different political climates, or unanticipated consequences.

Regulating Greenhouse Gas Emissions

In August 2015, the Environmental Protection Agency (EPA) announced its Clean Power Plan, which imposes new state-by-state limits on emissions of CO_2 (carbon dioxide) from fossil fuel power plants. This regulatory change was the product of a decade-long process of judicial decisions and actions by EPA bureaucrats.

New Acts!

Congressional Action: Congress enacts two Clean Air Acts in 1963 and 1970, with amendments in 1977 and 1990, authorizing the government to monitor and limit emissions of harmful chemicals into the atmosphere.

Although... maybe not?

Bureaucratic Action (2003): The EPA announces that the **Clean Air Act does not give it the authority to regulate CO_2** and other greenhouse gases.

Actually...yes.

Judicial Action (2007): In response to a case brought by 12 states, the Supreme Court rules that **greenhouse gases are covered by the Clean Air Act.**

Second try.

March 2012: The EPA **issues a draft of a new regulation** that would limit CO_2 emissions from new power plants.

Obama weighs in.

Presidential Directive, June 2013: President Obama **directs the EPA to develop additional regulations** for limiting CO_2 emission from new and existing power plants.

Results?

September 2013: The EPA modifies its draft regulations to place **CO_2 standards** on new power plants and issues a revised proposal.

June 2014: The EPA proposes an additional rule that aims to **cut CO_2 emissions from existing power plants.**

Critical Thinking

1. **Critics of the regulatory process complain that unelected** bureaucrats make most of the decisions while elected officials sit on the sidelines. Is this complaint supported by the case of the Clean Power Plan?

2. **The Clean Power Plan illustrates how acts of legislation are often** reinterpreted years after their passage. Why don't members of Congress write legislation in ways that prevent this from happening?

Feedback.

September 2013– March 2014: Supporters and opponents of the new rules submit over **6 million comments.**

Third try!

New Regulations Finalized (August 2015): The EPA **announces its Clean Power Plan,** which will regulate CO_2 emissions from both new and existing power plants.

Please stand by.

February 2016: The Supreme Court puts implementation of the Clean Power Plan for existing plants on hold, pending litigation. Moreover, these regulations are subject to change by the Trump administration.

Federal regulations influence many aspects of everyday life that would not seem likely to be affected by government action. The increase in the number of women's intercollegiate athletic teams is partly due to regulations that require equal funding for men's and women's teams. Pictured here is the University of Connecticut's 2016 NCAA women's basketball championship team. @UConnWBB #TitleIX

The nine most terrifying words in the English language are: I'm from the government, and I'm here to help.
—President Ronald Reagan

DID YOU KNOW?

In 2015, the federal government completed work on

2,353

new regulations or rules, 81 of which were "major" (with annual costs exceeding $100 million).

Federal regulations affect most aspects of everyday life. They influence the gas mileage of cars sold in the United States, the materials used to build roads, and the price of gasoline. They determine the amounts that doctors can charge senior citizens for medical procedures; the hours that medical residents can work; the criteria used to determine who gets a heart, lung, or kidney transplant—and the allowable emissions from power plants. Regulations set the eligibility criteria for student loans, limit how the military can recruit on college campuses, determine who can get a home mortgage and what their interest rate will be, and describe what constitutes equal funding for men's and women's college sports teams. Regulations also shape contribution limits and spending decisions in political campaigns.

Regulations are often controversial because they involve trade-offs between incompatible goals, as well as decisions made under uncertain circumstances. For example, the FDA drug-approval process prioritizes the goal of preventing harmful drugs from coming to market.[6] As a result, patients sometimes cannot get access to experimental treatments because FDA approval has not been granted, even when those treatments are the patients' only remaining option.[7] Advocates for patients have argued that people with dire prognoses should be allowed to use an experimental treatment as a potentially lifesaving last resort.[8] However, current FDA regulations prevent them from doing so except under very special circumstances, arguing that unapproved treatments may do more harm than good and that allowing wider access to these drugs may tempt manufacturers to market new drugs without adequate testing.

Research, Development, and New Policies Government scientists work in areas from medicine to astronomy to agriculture. Sometimes they do basic research, such as working for the National Institutes of Health (NIH) to discover mechanisms that govern cell reproduction and death. Government scientists also do applied research, from developing new cancer drugs to improving crop-management techniques. Federal funds support university and corporate research that examines similar issues.

Bureaucrats are also an important source of changes in government policies. For example, Congress and the president give civilian and military personnel in the Department of Defense the job of revising military doctrines—broad directives on how our armed forces should go about accomplishing specific tasks such as fighting the ISIL terrorist organization in Syria, building civil society in Afghanistan, or running military training operations in Africa. While military doctrines reflect input from members of Congress, the State Department and the president's appointees, and groups outside government (including lobbyists, think tanks, and defense contractors), they also reflect the preferences of the bureaucrats assigned to the task. Thus, as in the case of regulations, bureaucrats are not just implementers; they have a significant influence on what government does and does not do.

Bureaucratic expertise and its consequences

Bureaucrats are experts. Even compared with most members of Congress or presidential appointees, the average bureaucrat is a specialist in a certain policy area (often holding an advanced degree), with a better grasp of his or her agency's mission. For example, people who hold scientific or management positions in the FDA usually know more about the benefits and risks of new drugs than people outside the agency do. Their decision to deny unapproved drugs to seriously ill patients may seem cruel, but it may also reflect a thoughtful balancing of two incompatible goals: preventing harmful drugs from reaching the market and allowing people who have exhausted all other treatments access to risky, experimental products. A bureaucracy of experts is an important part of what political scientists call **state capacity**—the knowledge, personnel, and institutions needed to effectively implement policies.[9]

Red Tape and Standard Operating Procedures Despite bureaucrats' policy expertise, their decisions often appear to take too much time, rely on arbitrary judgments of what is important, and have unintended consequences—to the point that actions designed to solve one problem may create worse ones. Many critics cite the abundance of **red tape**, which refers to excessive or unnecessarily complex regulations, or **standard operating procedures**, which are the rules that lower-level bureaucrats must follow when implementing policies regardless of whether they are applicable.

Cases of bureaucratic ineptitude and failed reform efforts raise a critical question: How can an organization full of experts develop such dysfunctional ways of doing business? Bureaucrats are neither clueless nor malevolent. What, then, explains red tape and counterproductive standard operating procedures? The answer is the very strength of the American bureaucracy: its expertise.

Because bureaucrats know things that elected officials do not and because bureaucrats have their own policy goals, it is hard for elected officials to evaluate what bureaucrats are doing. For example, building the *Opportunity* and *Spirit* Mars rovers cost considerably more than planned. But did NASA bureaucrats mislead Congress about the difficulty of building the rovers, or was the overrun an honest mistake, resulting from factors that could not be anticipated? Of course, given that *Spirit* and *Opportunity* have far outlasted their expected lifetimes, the program is seen as a success and a bargain. But if things had turned out differently (if one or both of the rovers had crash-landed on Mars or had stopped working shortly after landing) members of Congress might easily have thought that NASA had presented the best-case scenario in order to secure funding.

Of course, sometimes bureaucrats simply make mistakes. For example, the FDA has delayed helpful drugs

state capacity
The knowledge, personnel, and institutions that the government requires to effectively implement policies.

red tape
Excessive or unnecessarily complex regulations imposed by the bureaucracy.

standard operating procedures
Rules that lower-level bureaucrats must follow when implementing policies.

📷

After news of an $800,000 General Services Administration (GSA) conference at a Las Vegas resort came to light in 2012, Congress held hearings on the agency's practices. Here, former Representative John Mica (R-FL) criticizes the apparent misuse of taxpayer money.

Despite their policy expertise, bureaucrats still make mistakes. When the Medicare program implemented the Prescription Drug Benefit in 2006, information about the coverage was available on an easy-to-read website, but the agency soon learned that many seniors who needed the information did not know how to use a Web browser.

from reaching the market and has approved drugs that were later found to have harmful side effects. However, these decisions may have been justified based on the information available to bureaucrats at the time. Here, again, it is hard to say that bureaucrats are at fault for such decisions.

The Problem of Control Political scientists refer to the difficulty that elected officials and their staff face when they try to interpret or influence bureaucratic actions as the **problem of control**.[10] A classic example is the **principal–agent game**. The principal–agent game describes an interaction where an individual or a group (an "agent") acts on behalf of another (the "principal"). In the federal government, for example, the president and Congress are principals and bureaucrats are agents. An agent may not want to work or may prefer outcomes that the principal does not like. Moreover, because the agent is an expert at the task he or she has been given, he or she has additional knowledge and experience that is inaccessible to the principal. The conundrum for the principal, then, is this: giving the agent very specific orders prevents the agent from acting based on expertise, but if the principal gives the agent the freedom to make decisions based on expertise the principal has less control over the agent's actions.

For example, suppose Congress and the president directed the FDA to shorten its drug-approval process. FDA officials might have mandated a lengthy process based on their expert assessment of the best way to screen out harmful drugs. By giving orders that superseded the FDA officials' screening process, elected officials would be sacrificing the valuable bureaucratic expertise behind the policy and risking the hasty approval of unsafe drugs. On the other hand, if Congress and the president allowed FDA bureaucrats to devise their own procedures and regulations there would be a chance that the FDA could use this freedom to pursue goals that have nothing to do with drug safety. For example, critics of the FDA's procedures have asserted that a drawn-out approval process is designed to favor large companies that already have drugs on the market over smaller companies trying to get approval for drugs that would compete with existing products. The principal–agent game can also be framed in terms of citizens. Figure 13.1 shows that a majority of survey respondents agreed that

problem of control
A difficulty faced by elected officials in ensuring that when bureaucrats implement policies they follow these officials' intentions but still have enough discretion to use their expertise.

principal–agent game
The interaction between a principal (such as the president or Congress), who needs something done, and an agent (such as a bureaucrat), who is responsible for carrying out the principal's orders.

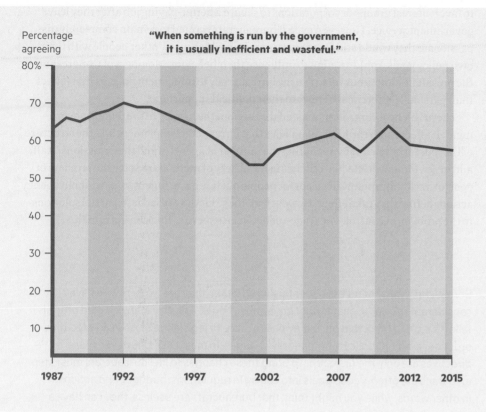

Percentage agreeing

"When something is run by the government, it is usually inefficient and wasteful."

FIGURE 13.1

How Americans View the Federal Bureaucracy

Many Americans believe the bureaucracy is wasteful and inefficient. Note, however, that the magnitude of negative feelings varies over time. Consider the time frame represented on the graph. What happened during these years that might explain the changes in citizens' opinions about the government?

Source: Pew Research Center, "Beyond Distrust: How Americans View Their Government," November 23, 2015, www.people-press.org (accessed 5/6/16).

the federal government is typically inefficient and wasteful—although the percentage agreeing with this assessment declined from its peak in 1992 until more recent years, when it again increased. Such opinions give citizens a strong motivation to demand that elected officials control the bureaucracy—to reduce the waste and inefficiency or, as the earlier quote from Ronald Reagan suggests, to prevent bureaucrats from overly intruding into American society.

Members of Congress and citizens are sometimes right to question the motives of members of the bureaucracy. Sometimes bureaucratic actions are the result of **regulatory capture**, which occurs when bureaucrats cater to a small group of individuals or corporations, regardless of the impact of these actions on public welfare. For example, until very recently the FCC allowed telecommunications companies to charge very high rates for phone calls made by individuals in federal prisons to their families, friends, or legal counsel. The companies have long argued to the FCC that these rates were justified by the cost of special hardware needed to monitor prison calls—but no one was lobbying the FCC in favor of federal prisoners, who have no alternative but to pay what the companies charge.[11]

You might think that the problem of control isn't too difficult to solve as long as bureaucrats act as impartial experts and set aside their own policy goals. Many studies of bureaucracies, beginning with the work of the early political theorist Max Weber, argue that bureaucrats should provide information and expertise and avoid taking sides on policy questions or being swayed by elected officials, people outside government, or their own policy goals.[12] However, bureaucrats' behavior doesn't always fit Weber's vision. Many enter the bureaucracy with their own ideas about what government should do, and they make decisions in line with those goals. For example, in the case of Flint's water supply, some EPA scientists felt strongly that the federal government should have demanded quick action by state and local authorities, bypassing the investigative procedure that their superiors wanted. Bureaucrats may also be tempted

regulatory capture
A situation in which bureaucrats favor the interests of the groups or corporations they are supposed to regulate at the expense of the general public.

to favor interest groups or corporations to secure a better-paying job after they leave government service. However, even if bureaucrats wanted to remain completely dispassionate they would still face a government in which many other people with their own policy goals would attempt to influence their behavior. Members of Congress or the president sometimes try to use the bureaucracy to implement policies that reflect their personal preferences or reward their political supporters.[13]

The problem of control has existed throughout the history of the federal government. It affects both the kinds of policies that bureaucrats implement and the structure of the federal bureaucracy, including the number of agencies and their missions, staff, and tasks. Moreover, elected officials use a variety of methods to solve the problem of control, including making it easier for people outside government to learn about agency actions before they take effect. However, all these tactics are, at best, partial solutions to the problem of control. The trade-off between expertise and control remains.

"Why Should I Care?"

Bureaucrats aren't mindless paper pushers. Rather, they are experts who have considerable power to shape what government does. The way many elected officials talk, it's easy to think that once they pass a piece of legislation or issue an executive order government policy automatically changes. In most cases, however, these directives are only the first step. To bring these changes to life, bureaucrats must step in to translate often-vague goals into concrete regulations, budgets, and actions. In other words, while you might think that bureaucrats are useless, they can have a profound effect on your daily life.

★

TRACE THE EXPANSION OF THE FEDERAL BUREAUCRACY OVER TIME

How has the American bureaucracy grown?

The evolution of America's federal bureaucracy was not steady or smooth. Most of its important developments occurred during three short periods: the late 1890s and early 1900s, the 1930s, and the 1960s.[14] In all three periods, the driving force was a combination of demands from citizens for enhanced government services and the desire of people in government to either respond to these demands or increase the size and scope of the federal government to be more in line with their own policy goals.

The beginning of America's bureaucracy

From the Founding of the United States until the election of Andrew Jackson in 1828, the staff of the entire federal bureaucracy numbered at most in the low thousands. There were only three executive departments (State, Treasury, and War), along with a postmaster general.[15] The early federal government also performed a narrow range of tasks. It collected taxes on imports and exports and delivered the mail. The national army consisted of a small Corps of Engineers and a few frontier patrols. The attorney general was a private attorney who had the federal government as one of his clients. Members of Congress outnumbered civil servants in Washington, and the president had very little staff at all.[16]

The small size of the federal government during those years reflected Americans' deep suspicion of government, especially unelected officials. In the Declaration of Independence, one of the charges against George III was that he had "erected a multitude of new offices and sent hither swarms of officers to harass our people and eat out their substance."[17] Executive branch offices were formed only when absolutely necessary. Nonetheless, conflicts soon arose around control of the bureaucracy. The legislation that established the departments of State, Treasury, and War allowed the president to nominate the people in charge of these departments but made these appointments subject to Senate approval. (The same is true today for the heads of all executive departments and many other presidential appointments.)

The election of Andrew Jackson in 1828 brought the first large-scale use of the spoils system, in which people who had worked in Jackson's campaign were rewarded with new positions in the federal government (usually working as local postmasters).[18] The spoils system was extremely useful to party organizations, as it gave them a powerful incentive with which to convince people to work for the party—a particularly important tool for Jackson, as his campaign organization was at that time the largest ever organized.

The challenge facing the spoils system was ensuring that these government employees, who often lacked experience in their new fields, could actually carry out their jobs. The solution was to develop procedures for these employees, so that they knew exactly what to do even if they had little or no experience or training.[19] These instructions became one of the earliest uses of standard operating procedures. They ensured that the government could function even if large numbers of employees had been hired in reward for political work rather than because of their qualifications.[20]

As America expanded in size, so did the federal government, which saw an almost eightfold increase in the bureaucracy between 1816 and the beginning of the Civil War in 1861. This growth did not reflect a fundamental change in what the government did; in fact, much of the increase came in areas such as the Post Office, which needed to serve a geographically larger nation—and, of course, to provide "spoils" for party workers in the form of government jobs.[21] Even by the end of the Civil War, the federal government still had very little involvement in the lives of ordinary Americans. State and local governments provided services such as education, public works, and welfare benefits, if they were provided at all. The federal government's role in daily life was limited to mail delivery, collecting import and export taxes, and a few other areas.

Building a new American state: the Progressive Era

Changes in the second half of the nineteenth century transformed America's bureaucracy.[22] This transformation began after the Civil War, but the most significant changes occurred during the Progressive Era, 1890–1920. Many laws and executive actions increased the government's regulatory power during this period, including the Sherman Antitrust Act of 1890, the Pure Food and Drug Act of 1906, the Federal Meat Inspection Act of 1906, expansion of the Interstate Commerce Commission, and various conservation measures.[23] Now the federal government was no longer simply a deliverer of mail and a defender of borders; rather, it had an indirect impact on several aspects of everyday life. When Americans bought food or other products, went to work, or traveled on vacation, the choices available to them were shaped by the actions of federal bureaucrats in Washington and elsewhere.

These developments were matched by a fundamental change in the federal bureaucracy following passage of the 1883 Pendleton Civil Service Act. This measure created the **federal civil service**, in which the merit system (qualifications, not political

This cartoon of a monument to President Andrew Jackson riding a pig decries his involvement in the spoils system, which allowed politicians to dole out government service jobs in return for political support.

federal civil service
A system created by the 1883 Pendleton Civil Service Act in which bureaucrats are hired on the basis of merit rather than political connections.

connections) would be the basis for hiring and promoting bureaucrats.[24] In other words, when new presidents took office they could not replace government workers with their own campaign workers. Initially, only about 13,000 federal jobs acquired civil service protections, but over the next two decades many additional positions were incorporated into the civil service, to the point that in the modern era virtually all full-time, permanent government employees have civil service protection. In some cases, presidents gave civil service protections to people who had been hired under the spoils system to prevent the next president from replacing these bureaucrats with his or her own loyalists. Over time, these reforms created a bureaucracy in which people were hired for their expertise and allowed to build a career in government without having to fear being fired when a new president or Congress took office.[25]

The New Deal, the Great Society, and the Reagan Revolution

Dramatic expansion of the federal bureaucracy occurred during the New Deal period in the 1930s and during the mid-1960s Great Society era. In both cases, the changes were driven by a combination of citizen demands and the preferences of elected officials who favored an increased role of government in society. This expansion was only marginally curtailed during the Reagan Revolution of the 1980s.

The New Deal "The New Deal" refers to the government programs implemented during Franklin Roosevelt's first term as president in the 1930s. At one level, these programs were a response to the Great Depression and the inability of local governments and private charities to provide adequate support to Americans during this economic crisis. Many advocates of the New Deal also favored an expanded role for government in American society, regardless of the immediate need for intervention.[26] Roosevelt's programs included reforms to the financial industry as well as efforts to help people directly, including stimulating employment, economic growth, and the formation of labor unions. The Social Security Act, the first federally funded pension program for all Americans, was also passed as part of the New Deal.[27]

These reforms represented a vast increase in the size, responsibilities, and capacity of the bureaucracy, as well as a large transfer of power to bureaucrats and to the president.[28] While the Progressive Era reforms created an independent bureaucracy and increased its state capacity, the New Deal reforms broadened the range of policy areas in which this capacity could be applied. Before the New Deal, the federal government influenced citizens' choices through activities such as regulating industries and workplace conditions. After the New Deal, the federal government took on the role of directly delivering to individuals a wide range of benefits and services—ranging from jobs to electricity. It also increased the regulation of many industries, including those in the banking and financial sectors.

The expansion of the federal government and the subsequent delegation of power to bureaucrats and to the president were controversial changes, both when they were enacted and as they were implemented in subsequent years.[29] Many Republicans opposed New Deal reforms because they believed that the federal government could not deliver services efficiently and that an expanded federal bureaucracy would create a modern spoils system. Many southerners worried that the federal government's increased involvement in everyday life would endanger the system of racial segregation in southern states.[30] Even so, Democratic supporters of the New Deal, aided by public support, carried the day.

Franklin Roosevelt's New Deal programs greatly expanded the power of the federal government and the bureaucracy. As this cartoon shows, these changes were controversial, with some seeing them as moving too much power from Congress to the president and bureaucracy.

The Great Society The Great Society was a further expansion in the size, capacity, and activities of the bureaucracy that occurred during Lyndon Johnson's presidency (1963–1969). During these years, Johnson proposed and Congress enacted programs that funded bilingual education, loans and grants for college students, special education, preschools, construction of elementary and secondary schools, mass-transit programs in many cities, health care for seniors and poor people, job training and urban renewal, enhanced voting rights and civil rights for minorities, environmental protection, funding for the arts and cultural activities, and space exploration.[31]

The Great Society programs had mixed success. Voting rights and civil rights reforms ended the "separate but equal" system of social order in southern states and dramatically increased political participation by African Americans.[32] But many antipoverty programs were dismal failures. Poverty rates among most groups remained relatively constant, and other indicators, such as the rate of teen pregnancy, actually increased.[33] In retrospect, the people who designed and implemented these programs did not realize the complexities of the problems they were trying to address.[34] For example, many antipoverty programs were built on the assumption that most people receiving welfare needed job training programs in order to transition from welfare to permanent, paid employment. However, additional data that were available a decade later showed that most people receiving welfare do so for short periods because of medical or family crises—problems that the Great Society programs did not touch.[35] Despite these shortcomings, the expansion of the federal government during the New Deal and Great Society has remained in place well into the twenty-first century.

The Reagan Revolution and Afterward The election of Ronald Reagan to the presidency in 1980, along with a Republican takeover of the Senate and Republican gains in the House of Representatives, created an opportunity for conservatives to roll back the size and scope of the federal government. However, 30 years after Reagan's presidency, despite the election of two subsequent Republican presidents and many years with unified Republican control of Congress, the growth of the federal government has not slowed. Members of Congress and presidents from both parties have fought for large expansions in government policy. For example, while Democrat Barack Obama's administration issued many new environmental regulations and profoundly changed the American health care system, these changes are not too different in magnitude from the reforms championed by Republican George W. Bush, including education policies that increased federal control over local school districts, new drug financing benefits for seniors, and changes to financial regulations that increased financial reporting requirements for corporations. Over the next four years, the Trump administration will have a similar impact on the bureaucracy and its policies.

Under President George W. Bush the federal bureaucracy continued to expand. Programs like No Child Left Behind increased the role of government in society. #NCLB

"Why Should I Care?"

Though sometimes their rhetoric seems otherwise, the difference between Republicans and Democrats is not over the size of the federal government but over what government should do. While Republicans often argue for making government smaller and Democrats respond by highlighting the consequences of even a small cut in services, the fact is that most people on both sides accept the fact that a large federal government is here to stay. Knowing how the federal bureaucracy has grown, and evaluating whether this growth has caused problems or created benefits, is central to building your own ideas about what government should do.

The modern federal bureaucracy

The size and scope of the modern federal bureaucracy reflect the expansion of the federal government over the last half century and its increased role in the lives of everyday Americans. The structure of the bureaucracy also reflects ongoing attempts by presidents, members of Congress, and others to control bureaucratic actions in line with their policy goals.

The structure of the federal government

Nuts & Bolts 13.1 shows the structure of the executive branch of the federal government. As discussed in Chapter 12, the Executive Office of the President (EOP) contains organizations that support the president and implement presidential policy initiatives—individuals working in these organizations are part of the administrative presidency that works to ensure that bureaucrats implement the president's policy priorities, bringing the actions of bureaucrats (agents) in line with the president's (principal's) preferences.[36] Among its many offices, the EOP contains the Office of Management and Budget, which prepares the president's annual budget proposal to Congress and monitors government spending and the development of new regulations. Below the EOP are the 15 executive departments, from the Department of Agriculture to the Department of Veterans Affairs, which constitute the major divisions within the executive branch. The heads of these 15 organizations make up the president's Cabinet.

Each executive department contains many smaller organizations. Nuts & Bolts 13.2 shows the organizational chart for the Department of Agriculture. As you can see, the Department of Agriculture includes offices that help farmers produce and sell their crops, as well as offices that ensure food safety, but it also houses the Forest Service and offices that manage issues related to housing and utilities in rural areas. The Department of Agriculture also administers the food stamps program, even though the program has no direct connection to farming or food safety.

Below the executive departments, but not subordinate to them, are a set of agencies, commissions, and government corporations that are called independent agencies, or independent establishments, to highlight that they are not part of an executive department. Most of these carry out specialized functions, such as the Federal Reserve System (which manages the money supply, banking system, and interest rates) and the Federal Deposit Insurance Corporation (which regulates the banking industry). The figure includes only some noteworthy or well-known agencies; there are many more.

There are two important lessons to draw from these charts. First, the federal government handles an enormous range of functions. Second, the division of activities among executive departments and independent agencies does not always have an obvious logic. Why, for example, does the Department of Agriculture administer rural utilities programs and food stamps? Similarly, it is not always clear why certain tasks are handled by an independent agency whereas others fall within the scope of an executive department.[37] Why is the Federal Reserve an independent agency rather than part of the Department of the Treasury?

Organizational decisions like these often reflect elected officials' attempts to shape agency behavior—and the extent to which political process matters. Part of the difference between independent agencies and the organizations contained within executive departments has to do with the president's ability to control these organizations'

Office of Management and Budget
An office within the EOP that is responsible for creating the president's annual budget proposal to Congress, reviewing proposed rules, and performing other budget-related tasks.

independent agencies
Government offices or organizations that provide government services and are not part of an executive department.

The Executive Branch of the Federal Government

The executive branch includes the 15 cabinet offices, as well as several independent agencies, commissions, and government corporations.

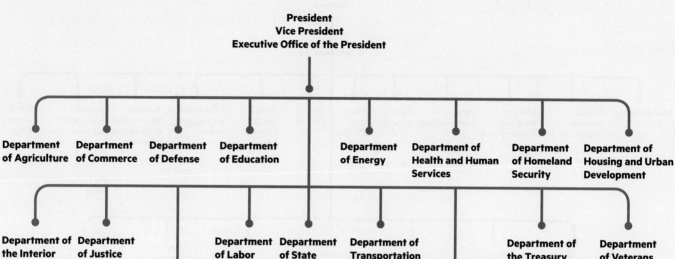

President
Vice President
Executive Office of the President

| Department of Agriculture | Department of Commerce | Department of Defense | Department of Education | Department of Energy | Department of Health and Human Services | Department of Homeland Security | Department of Housing and Urban Development |

| Department of the Interior | Department of Justice | Department of Labor | Department of State | Department of Transportation | Department of the Treasury | Department of Veterans Affairs |

Selected Independent Establishments and Government Corporations

Central Intelligence Agency
Consumer Product Safety Commission
Environmental Protection Agency
Equal Employment Opportunity Commission
Federal Communications Commission
Federal Deposit Insurance Corporation
Federal Election Commission
Federal Reserve System

Federal Trade Commission
General Services Administration
National Aeronautics and Space Administration
National Foundation on the Arts and the Humanities
National Labor Relations Board
National Railroad Passenger Corporation (Amtrak)
National Science Foundation
Occupational Safety and Health Review Commission

Peace Corps
Securities and Exchange Commission
Selective Service System
Small Business Administration
Social Security Administration
U.S. Agency for International Development
U.S. Postal Service

Source: Based on *GPO Access: Guide to the U.S. Government,* http://bensguide.gpo.gov/files/gov_chart.pdf (accessed 9/22/12).

activities. Organizations that fall within an executive department, such as the FAA or the Federal Highway Administration (FHA) (both within the Department of Transportation), can be controlled by the president (to some extent) through his or her appointees.[38] In contrast, independent agencies have more freedom from oversight and control by the president and Congress. For example, the president nominates governors of the Federal Reserve, who (if the Senate confirms them) can serve for 14 years. Outside the nomination and confirmation process, the president and Congress have very little control over the Federal Reserve's policies; the organization is self-financing, and its governors can be removed from office only if Congress takes the extreme step of impeaching them.

These details about the hiring and firing of bureaucrats and the location of agencies in the structure of the federal government matter because they determine the amount of political control that other parts of the government can exercise over an agency, as well as who gets to exercise this power. As political scientist Terry M. Moe puts it, "The bureaucracy rises out of politics, and its design reflects the interests, strategies, and compromises of those who exercise political power."[39]

The Structure of the Department of Agriculture

The Department of Agriculture is headed by the secretary of Agriculture and the deputy secretary of Agriculture and includes various assistant secretaries and undersecretaries for specific areas such as natural resources and the environment, farm services, rural development, and food safety.

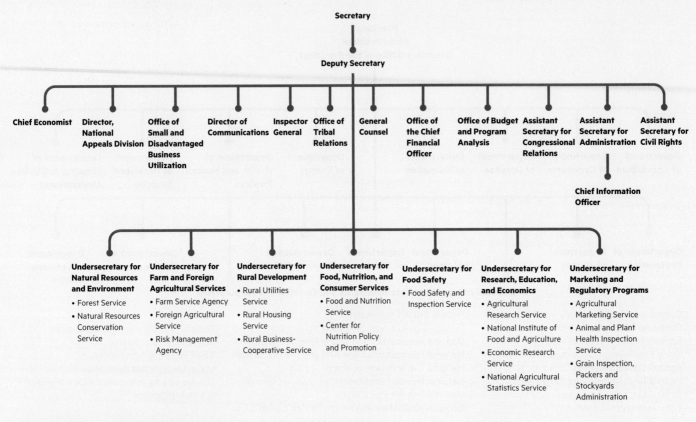

Secretary

Deputy Secretary

Chief Economist

Director, National Appeals Division

Office of Small and Disadvantaged Business Utilization

Director of Communications

Inspector General

Office of Tribal Relations

General Counsel

Office of the Chief Financial Officer

Office of Budget and Program Analysis

Assistant Secretary for Congressional Relations

Assistant Secretary for Administration

Assistant Secretary for Civil Rights

Chief Information Officer

Undersecretary for Natural Resources and Environment
- Forest Service
- Natural Resources Conservation Service

Undersecretary for Farm and Foreign Agricultural Services
- Farm Service Agency
- Foreign Agricultural Service
- Risk Management Agency

Undersecretary for Rural Development
- Rural Utilities Service
- Rural Housing Service
- Rural Business-Cooperative Service

Undersecretary for Food, Nutrition, and Consumer Services
- Food and Nutrition Service
- Center for Nutrition Policy and Promotion

Undersecretary for Food Safety
- Food Safety and Inspection Service

Undersecretary for Research, Education, and Economics
- Agricultural Research Service
- National Institute of Food and Agriculture
- Economic Research Service
- National Agricultural Statistics Service

Undersecretary for Marketing and Regulatory Programs
- Agricultural Marketing Service
- Animal and Plant Health Inspection Service
- Grain Inspection, Packers and Stockyards Administration

Source: U.S. Department of Agriculture, "USDA Organization Chart," www.usda.gov/documents/AgencyWorkflow.pdf (accessed 4/23/10).

The size of the federal government

The federal government employs millions of people. Table 13.1 shows the number of employees in each executive department. The Department of Defense is the largest cabinet department, with more than 700,000 civilian personnel. The Department of Education is the smallest, with only 4,500 employees. Many departments are on the small side: four cabinet departments have fewer than 20,000 employees. The same is true for many independent agencies. The General Services Administration (GSA) of the EOP, for example, has only about 12,000 employees. Millions of additional people work for the government as members of the armed forces, as employees of the Postal Service, for civilian companies that contract with the government, or as recipients of federal grant money.

The What Do the Numbers Say? feature in this chapter shows the size of the federal budget from 2012 to 2016. Clearly, the budget has steadily increased, to the point that annual spending in recent years is nearly $4 trillion per year. The best explanation for the size of the federal government is the size of America itself—more than 320 million

TABLE
13.1

Employment in Selected Cabinet Departments

Organization	Total Employees
Defense (civilian only)	732,000
Veterans Affairs	366,500
Homeland Security	188,100
Justice	119,800
Treasury	103,000
Agriculture	90,500
Health and Human Services	74,400
Interior	66,700
Transportation	56,200
Commerce	45,600
State	34,500
Labor	17,700
Energy	16,100
Housing and Urban Development	8,400
Education	4,500

Source: "Budget of the United States Government Fiscal Year 2017: Analytical Perspectives, Chapter 11—Improving the Federal Workforce," www.whitehouse.gov/sites/default/files/omb/budget/fy2017/assets/ap_8_strengthening.pdf (accessed 5/6/16).

people spread out over an area more than twice the size of the EU—coupled with America's position as the most powerful nation in the world with the largest military. However, some observers argue that the real explanation has to do with bureaucrats themselves—that bureaucrats are **budget maximizers** who never pass up a chance to increase their own funding, regardless of whether the new spending is worthwhile.[40]

This argument misses some important points. First, the increase in total federal spending masks the fact that many agencies see their budgets shrink.[41] Particularly in recent administrations, one of the principal missions of presidential appointees, both in agencies and in the EOP, has been to scrutinize budget requests with an eye to cutting spending as much as possible.[42] And every year, some government agencies are eliminated (in fact, most of the executive department head counts in Table 13.1 have grown smaller in recent editions of this text).[43]

Moreover, public-opinion data provide an explanation for the overall growth in government: the American public's demand for services.[44] Despite complaints about the federal bureaucracy, polls find little evidence of demands for less government. When the Pew Research Center asked people in 2013 to decide which two programs should have their spending cut as a way of reducing the budget deficit, a majority favored cutting relatively small programs: 34 percent picked the State Department and 48 percent picked foreign economic aid (see Table 13.2). Far fewer people favored cuts in the programs that account for the overwhelming majority of federal spending: defense, health care spending, and Social Security. In other words, while in the abstract Americans might want a smaller government that is less involved in everyday life, they do not support the large-scale budget cuts that would be necessary to achieve this goal. The public's desire for more government services is often encouraged by elected officials, who create new government programs (and expand existing ones in response to constituent demands) as a way of building support and improving their chances of reelection.

budget maximizers
Bureaucrats who seek to increase funding for their agency whether or not that additional spending is worthwhile.

DID YOU KNOW?

Since 1992, the federal civilian workforce has shrunk by

18%

Source: Office of Management and Budget

TABLE
13.2

Public Opinion on Spending Cuts

Many Americans complain about the size of the federal government. However, their complaints do not translate into support for reductions in policy areas or cuts in specific programs that could significantly reduce spending. Based on these data, are there any kinds of proposals for significantly reducing the size of the federal government that might attract widespread support?

Source: Pew Research Center, "As Sequester Deadline Looms, Little Support for Cutting Most Programs," February 22, 2013, www. people-press.org (accessed 3/31/14).

Policy area	Percent favoring reduction
Aid to world's needy	48%
State Department	34
Unemployment aid	32
Military defense	24
Aid to needy in United States	24
Health care	22
Environmental protection	22
Energy	21
Scientific research	20
Agriculture	20
Antiterrorism defenses	19
Roads and infrastructure	17
Medicare	15
Combating crime	14
Food and drug inspection	14
Natural disaster relief	12
Education	10
Social Security	10
Veterans' benefits	6

"Why Should I Care?"

You might think that the government spends too much and that the bureaucracy is too large. The questions you have to ask yourself are: What am I willing to sacrifice to make government smaller? Am I OK with a smaller military, fewer regulations on banks and credit card companies, less oversight of food and drug safety? And how much would these changes save? We have a large, costly federal government because in the end, most people want it that way.

★

DESCRIBE WHO BUREAUCRATS ARE AND THE REGULATIONS THAT GOVERN THEIR EMPLOYMENT

The human face of the bureaucracy

The term "bureaucrat" applies to a wide range of people with different qualifications and job descriptions. Figure 13.2 shows data on the range of jobs that federal workers do. The federal government includes so many different kinds of jobs because of the vast array of services it provides. This section describes who these people are and the terms of their government employment.

Types of Federal Workers

FIGURE 13.2

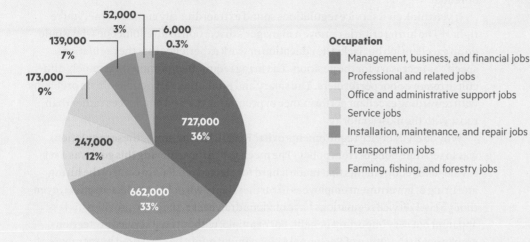

Occupation
- Management, business, and financial jobs
- Professional and related jobs
- Office and administrative support jobs
- Service jobs
- Installation, maintenance, and repair jobs
- Transportation jobs
- Farming, fishing, and forestry jobs

Source: Based on the U.S. Bureau of Labor Statistics, "Occupational Employment Statistics NAICS 999100–Federal Executive Branch," www.bls.gov (accessed 5/6/16).

Although complaints are often heard about the efficiency or motivations of federal bureaucrats, surveys show that many employees in these positions have a strong interest in public service or implementing good public policy. In fact, these motivations are often strong enough that scholars such as James L. Perry have argued against attempts to motivate federal workers with monetary incentives—bureaucrats who work hard because they feel it is the right thing to do may resent incentive schemes that presume they are lazy or only interested in money.[45]

Civil service regulations

A key characteristic of most jobs in the federal bureaucracy is that they are subject to the civil service regulations mentioned earlier.[46] The current civil service system sets out a job description and pay ranges for all federal jobs.[47] The civil service system also establishes tests that determine who is hired for low-level clerical and secretarial positions; people with less than a college degree are generally eligible for clerical and low-level technical jobs. As in the private sector, a college degree or an advanced degree and work experience qualify an individual for higher-level positions. Federal salaries are supposed to be comparable to what people earn in similar, private-sector positions, and salaries are increased somewhat for federal employees who work in areas with a high cost of living.

Civil service regulations provide job security. After three years of satisfactory performance, employees cannot be fired except "for cause," meaning that the firing agency must cite a reason. Civil service regulations set out a multistep procedure for firing someone, beginning with low performance evaluations, then warning letters given to the employee, followed by a lengthy appeals process before a firing takes place. One study found that only about 11,000 civil servants are fired in a given year—a

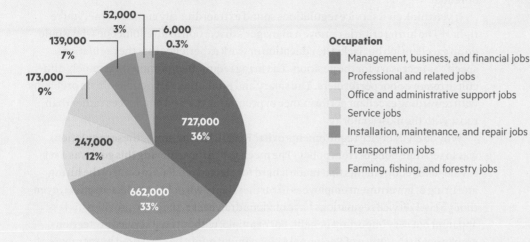

very small percentage of the total civilian federal workforce of about 2 million people.[48] A subpar performer may be assigned other duties, transferred to another office, or even given nothing to do in the hope that the person will leave voluntarily out of boredom.

If you think civil service regulations sound extraordinarily cumbersome, you're right.[49] The hiring criteria remove a manager's discretion to hire someone who would do an excellent job but lacks the education or work experience that the regulations specify as necessary for the position. The firing requirements make it extremely difficult to remove poor performers. The salary and promotion restrictions create problems with rewarding excellent performance or promoting the best employees rather than those with the most seniority.

Why do civil service requirements exist? Recall that the aim of these regulations was to separate politics from policy. The mechanism for achieving this goal was a set of rules and requirements that made it hard for elected officials to control the hiring and firing of government employees to further their own political goals. In effect, even though civil service regulations have obvious drawbacks, they also provide this less apparent but very important benefit. For example, without civil service protections, employees in the Office of Personnel Management might be pressured by members of Congress who wanted to increase pensions for retiring federal workers who were their constituents.

Although loyalty to the president is a widely accepted criterion for hiring agency heads and other presidential appointees, professionals with permanent civil service positions are supposed to be hired on the basis of their qualifications, not their political beliefs. In fact, it is illegal to bring politics into these hiring decisions. However, there is no doubt that all presidential administrations worry about the political loyalties of midlevel bureaucrats—after all, these individuals are most likely to be experts and therefore the biggest example of the problem of control. For example, during the presidency of George W. Bush, Justice Department officials admitted to screening job applicants based on their ideological leanings. Membership in a liberal organization such as Greenpeace listed on a candidate's résumé reduced the likelihood of the person's being hired, while membership in a conservative organization such as the Federalist Society boosted an applicant's chances.[50]

Limits on political activity

Federal employees are limited in their political activities. The Hatch Act, enacted in 1939 and amended in 1940, prohibited federal employees from engaging in organized political activities.[51] Under the act, employees could vote and contribute to candidates but could not work for candidates or for political parties. These restrictions were modified in the 1993 Federal Employees Political Activities Act, allowing federal employees to undertake a wider range of political activities, including fund-raising and serving as an officer of a political party. Senior members of the president's White House staff and political appointees are exempt from most of these restrictions, although they cannot use government resources for political activities.

While the Hatch Act is often invoked when government employees express controversial views, the key restriction is on activities that directly help a particular political candidate, such as a public endorsement at a mass rally. For example, during James Hansen's tenure as a NASA scientist (he retired in 2013) he wrote and testified about the dangers of global warming, taking positions that contradicted the then-official statements of NASA leadership.[52] However, because Hansen did not speak for or against a

Is the Federal Bureaucracy Too Big?

One of the most intense conflicts in American political life is over the size of the federal government. Generally, Republicans say that the size of federal bureaucracy should be reduced, while Democrats tend to favor increasing the size of government programs. However, the size of government has increased steadily over time. Has the size of the bureaucracy gotten out of control? What do the numbers say?

■ Democratic administrations ■ Republican administrations

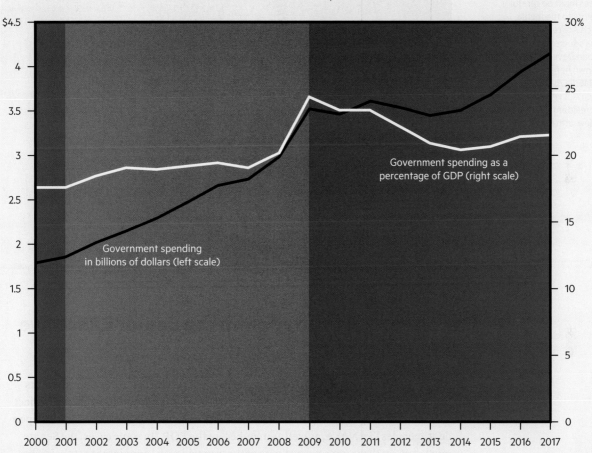

Think about it

- **Some people worry that the level of government spending is growing too fast. Does this graph support or refute this argument?**
- **The debate between Republicans and Democrats is often framed as an argument over increased government spending (Democrats favor increases; Republicans don't). Does this graph support or refute this argument?**

Source: Office of Management and Budget, "The President's Budget for Fiscal Year 2017," www.whitehouse.gov/omb/budget (accessed 5/6/16).

candidate, his actions did not fall under the Hatch Act. Even so, the Hatch Act makes life especially difficult for presidential appointees whose job duties often mix government service with politics, such as helping the president they work for get reelected. In order to comply with Hatch Act restrictions, these officials need to carry separate cell phones to make calls related to their political activities and maintain separate e-mail accounts—usually provided by the party or campaign committee—for their political communications.

Federal employees must be careful that their comments to the media comply with Hatch Act restrictions. President Obama's secretary of Housing and Urban Development, Julian Castro, shown here at the Common Sense Media Awards in 2016, violated the Hatch Act when he spoke about the 2016 presidential campaign during an interview with journalist Katie Couric.

Political appointees and the Senior Executive Service

Not every federal employee is a member of the civil service. The president appoints over 7,000 individuals to senior positions in the executive branch that are not subject to civil service regulations, such as the leaders of executive departments and independent agencies like NASA, as well as members of the EOP. (In some cases, the Senate must confirm these nominees.) Some of these presidential appointees get their jobs as a reward for working on the campaign staff, contributing substantial funds, or raising money from other donors. These individuals may not be given positions with real decision-making power. Some government agencies have the reputation of being **turkey farms**, places where campaign stalwarts can be appointed without the risk that their lack of experience will lead to bad policy.[53]

turkey farms
Agencies to which campaign workers and donors can be appointed in reward for their service because it is unlikely that their lack of qualifications will lead to bad policy.

The majority of a president's appointees act as the president's eyes, ears, and hands throughout the executive branch. They hold positions of power within government agencies, serving as secretaries of executive departments, agency heads, or senior deputies. Their jobs involve finding out what the president wants from their agency and ordering, persuading, or cajoling their subordinates to implement presidential directives.

In many agencies, people in the top positions are members of the Senior Executive Service (SES), who are also exempt from civil service restrictions.[54] As of 2014, there were a few thousand SES members, most of whom were career government employees who held relatively high-level agency positions before moving to the SES. This change of employment status costs them their civil service protections but allows them to apply for senior leadership positions in the bureaucracy. Some political appointees are also given SES positions, although most do not have the experience or expertise held by career bureaucrats who typically move to the SES.

The president's ability to appoint bureaucrats in many different agencies helps him or her control the bureaucracy. By selecting people who are loyal or like-minded, a president can attempt to control the actions of lower-level bureaucrats and implement his or her policy agenda. The SES also provides civil servants an incentive to do their jobs well, as good performance in an agency position can help build a career that might allow them to transfer to the SES.

The problem of control shapes the kinds of people who are hired as bureaucrats as well as their job protections. Political appointees and members of the SES are supposed to ride herd on the rest of the bureaucracy. Civil service protections exist to ensure that bureaucrats' decisions reflect expertise rather than political considerations.

Controlling the bureaucracy

★

EXPLAIN HOW CONGRESS AND THE PRESIDENT OVERSEE THE EXECUTIVE BRANCH

As the expert implementers of legislation and presidential directives, bureaucrats hold significant power to influence government policy. This situation creates the problem of political control illustrated by the principal–agent game: elected officials must figure out how to reap the benefits of bureaucratic expertise without simply giving bureaucrats free rein to do whatever they want.

One strategy is to take away discretion entirely and give bureaucrats simple, direct orders. For example, from 1996 to 2015 a law passed by Congress forbade the U.S. Centers for Disease Control from conducting research that would "advocate or promote gun control"—which was interpreted by the CDC as limiting all gun-related research by agency scientists or by outside researchers who received agency funds.[55] (The ban was repealed after a series of mass shootings in 2013, although to this day the CDC conducts very little gun-related research.) The problem with eliminating bureaucrats' discretion in this way is that it limits the positive influence of their expertise. Particularly when new policies are being developed, taking away bureaucratic discretion is costly for legislators or presidential appointees, as it forces them to work out the policy details themselves—and may still produce less effective policies than those constructed by bureaucrats with specialized knowledge.[56] Moreover, preventing bureaucrats from using their judgment makes it impossible for them to craft policies that take into account new developments or unforeseen circumstances.[57]

bureaucratic drift
Bureaucrats' tendency to implement policies in a way that favors their own political objectives rather than following the original intentions of the legislation.

For all these reasons, elected officials must find other ways to reduce or eliminate **bureaucratic drift**—that is, bureaucrats pursuing their own goals rather than their assignments from officeholders or appointees—while still reaping the benefits of bureaucratic expertise. This section describes two common strategies: changing the way agencies are organized and staffed and using standardized procedures for monitoring agency actions. In both cases, the aim is to set up the agency so that bureaucrats can use their expertise, while making sure their actions are consistent with elected officials' wishes.[58] These measures mitigate—but do not eliminate—the problem of control discussed earlier (see the Take a Stand feature).

The Senate's power over the confirmation of senior agency officials is often used as a tool to shape agency policy and operations. Richard Cordray, the first head of the Consumer Financial Protection Agency, was nominated after some senators objected to President Obama's first nominee, Elizabeth Warren, who was a Harvard Law professor at the time.

Agency organization

Over the last 20 years, political scientists have shown how agencies can be organized to minimize bureaucratic drift.[59] Specifically, when an agency is set up or given new responsibilities, the officials who initiate the change don't simply tell the agency what to do. To make sure that they get the policies they want, they also determine where the agency is located within the federal government structure and who runs it. These efforts may occur solely within Congress, involve both Congress and the president, or be arranged by presidential actions.[60]

For example, one of the Obama administration's responses to the 2008–2009 financial crisis was to form a new agency, the Consumer Financial Protection Bureau, which would help to enforce new bank regulations and investigate consumer complaints about financial firms. In 2011, it was expected that Elizabeth Warren, a Harvard law professor who had helped to set up the agency, would become the first head of the agency. However, many Republican and some Democratic senators and financial-industry lobbyists opposed Warren's appointment, believing she would encourage her subordinates to be excessively pro-consumer in their investigations. As a result, Obama appointed the former attorney general of Ohio, Richard Cordray, who was more acceptable to more senators, while Warren was elected as a U.S. senator from Massachusetts in 2012.

Monitoring

One of the most important ways elected officials prevent bureaucratic drift is to know what bureaucrats are doing or planning to do. Information gathering by members of Congress about bureaucratic actions is termed **oversight**. Congressional committees often hold hearings to question agency heads, secretaries of executive departments, or senior agency staff. Similarly, one of the primary responsibilities of presidential appointees is to monitor how bureaucrats are responding to presidential directives. The problem is that presidential appointees may be unable to fulfill this role. Because they are chosen for their loyalty to the president, they may lack the experience needed to fully understand what bureaucrats in their agency are doing. Moreover, given that appointees typically hold their position for only a year or two, they have little time to learn the details of agency operations.

Advance Warning Members of Congress, the president, and his or her staff gain advance knowledge of bureaucratic actions through the notice-and-comment

oversight
Congressional efforts to make sure that laws are implemented correctly by the bureaucracy after they have been passed.

TAKE A STAND

Is Political Control of the Bureaucracy Beneficial?

When working with bureaucrats, elected officials (the president or members of Congress) face the problem of political control: Should they allow bureaucrats to exercise judgment when implementing policies or give them specific, narrow directives? Compounding this problem is the fact that most bureaucrats are civil service employees, meaning they cannot be fired except under very extreme circumstances. As a result, even when elected officials give very specific directives to an agency they may find that bureaucrats essentially ignore the directives and that very little can be done to force compliance (after all, regardless of what bureaucrats do or don't do, they will still have a job). Civil service protections also mean that members of Congress or a new presidential administration cannot clean house in an agency, replacing untrustworthy bureaucrats with individuals who will do what they are told. Should civil service protections be abolished?

Get rid of civil service protections.

The civil service system began in an era when few government jobs required specialized knowledge, expertise, or an advanced degree. Under these conditions, a new administration might be tempted to implement mass firings, rewarding political supporters with jobs in the federal bureaucracy, as the new workers would be just as effective as the people they replaced. At the same time, there would be little cost to getting rid of a bureaucrat who refused an order, as most positions could be filled by anyone.

The modern federal bureaucracy is exactly the opposite: most jobs, particularly those that involve real policy-making power, require expertise to be done effectively. Under these conditions, civil service protections are to some extent unnecessary, as bureaucrats have considerable job security because of their expertise and experience. Getting rid of recalcitrant bureaucrats involves significant costs: by removing their knowledge of the policies being decided and the procedures by which decisions are made, it may become impossible for an agency to function at all. Moreover, a bureaucrat's reluctance to behave as ordered may be a sign that something is wrong—that the directive makes no sense or that there are easier ways of accomplishing the task.

Civil service protections are still needed.

The fact that firing bureaucrats costs the government the benefit of their experience and expertise does not mean that elected officials will never threaten to do so, or even carry out their threats. A new president might simply decide that he or

The State Department's backlog of passport applications is a good example of how bureaucrats' actions (or inactions) can affect the lives and plans of ordinary Americans.

she wants a loyal bureaucracy, even if this outcome requires getting rid of everyone who has any experience with agency operations. A congressional majority might want a new policy enough to enact a bill that freezes the salaries of any bureaucrats who do not behave as ordered. In both cases, removing civil service protections—making bureaucrats vulnerable to threats about their future employment—could easily lead to bad policy outcomes.

The deeper problem with removing civil service protections is that it would likely change the kinds of people who undertake careers in government service. Civil service protections enable policy experts to work for the government without fearing that they will be fired for simply voicing their concerns or because a new administration places a high value on loyalty. Without the protections afforded by civil service regulations, these individuals might choose a different career, depriving the federal government (and the American people) of the benefits of their knowledge and training.

take a stand

1. In general, contemporary Democratic politicians tend to favor civil service protections, while Republicans want to weaken them. Does this preference make sense in light of what we know about the differences between the parties in their beliefs about the size and scope of government?

2. Not all jobs in the federal bureaucracy require specialized knowledge and expertise. Would it make sense to abandon civil service protections for low-level jobs such as clerical positions? Would such a change help elected officials manage the problem of control? Why or why not?

procedure described earlier in the chapter, which requires bureaucrats to disclose proposed changes before they take effect.[61] This delay gives opponents the opportunity to register complaints with their congressional representatives, and it allows these legislators time either to pressure the agency to revise the regulation or even to enact another law undoing or modifying the agency action. Members of Congress also pressure bureaucrats to release memos, working drafts, and other documents as a way of keeping track of what bureaucrats are doing—for example, in 2015 Republicans on the House Science and Technology Committee demanded the release of e-mails sent by scientists analyzing climate change for the National Oceanographic and Atmospheric Administration.[62] (Some of the scientists later testified before the committee, but the e-mail request was rejected.)

Investigations: Police Patrols and Fire Alarms Investigations involve Congress, legislative staff, or presidential appointees selecting some government program or office and scrutinizing the organization, its expenditures, and its activities. There are two types of oversight: police patrols and fire alarms. Ideally, every agency would be investigated as often as possible, with agencies that had large budgets or carried out important functions being investigated more frequently. These investigations may involve fact-finding trips to local offices, interviews with senior personnel, audits of agency accounts, and calls to the agency to see how it responds to citizens' requests. This method of investigation is called police patrol oversight.[63] Think of a police officer walking his or her beat, rattling doors to see if they are locked, checking out broken windows, and looking down alleys for suspicious behavior.

The disadvantage of police patrol oversight is that it is costly in terms of money and staff time. Moreover, these investigations often find that agencies are doing what they should. Because of these problems, Congress and the president also look outside government for information on what bureaucrats are doing. Rather than undertaking a series of investigations, they wait until they receive a complaint about bureaucratic actions, then focus investigative efforts on those cases, a practice labeled fire alarm oversight.[64] The so-called fire alarm can take many different forms. Representatives and their staff meet frequently with constituents, who may let them know of a problem with the bureaucracy. Similarly, the president and his or her staff are often contacted by lobbyists, corporate executives, and ordinary citizens with complaints about bureaucratic actions. Newspaper reporters and Internet bloggers also provide information on what bureaucrats are doing. Some agencies have advisory committees that not only help make agency decisions but also serve to keep Congress and the president informed about them.[65]

The case of NASA climate change scientist James Hansen described earlier provides a clear example of fire alarm oversight. At one point, NASA managers required that Hansen submit all his public statements and work for review before publication. But this order soon became known when the *New York Times* and other newspapers reported it. The resulting firestorm of protest from members of Congress forced NASA head Michael Griffin to rescind the order. These fire alarms provide exactly the sort of information that Congress and the president often lack about how bureaucrats are implementing laws and directives, including cases when bureaucrats are doing (or planning to do) something that contradicts their mandate. Such communications tell Congress and the president where to focus their efforts to monitor the bureaucracy, drawing their attention to agencies or programs in which problems have been reported, rather than driving them to try to oversee the entire government at once.

police patrol oversight A method of oversight in which members of Congress constantly monitor the bureaucracy to make sure that laws are implemented correctly.

fire alarm oversight A method of oversight in which members of Congress respond to complaints about the bureaucracy or problems of implementation only as they arise rather than exercising constant vigilance.

Correcting violations

When members of Congress or the president find a case of bureaucratic drift, they can take steps to influence the bureaucrats' actions. Many tactics can be used to bring a wayward agency into line. Legislation or an executive order can send a clear directive to an agency or remove its discretion, tasks and programs can be moved to an agency that is more closely aligned with elected officials' goals, political appointees at an agency can be replaced, and agencies can be reorganized. For example, after the water crisis in Flint became public the EPA swung into action by establishing a task force to provide expert advice to state and local authorities. It also made all of this advice public so that people in Flint could assess the efficacy of solutions proposed by local agencies.

One of the most significant difficulties in dealing with bureaucratic drift is disagreement between members of Congress and the president about whether an agency is doing the right thing—regardless of whether the agency is following its original orders. Most of the tactics discussed earlier require joint action by the president and congressional majorities. Without presidential support, members of Congress need a two-thirds majority to impose corrections. Without congressional support, the president can only threaten to cut an agency's proposed budget, change its home within the federal bureaucracy, or set up a new agency to do what the errant agency refuses to do. Actually carrying out these threats requires congressional approval. As a result, disagreements between the president and Congress can give an agency significant freedom, as long as it retains the support of at least one branch of government.

An agency may also be able to fend off elected officials' attempts to take political control if it has a reputation for expertise. For example, one reason that attempts to pass legislation forcing the FDA to alter its drug-approval process have had little success is that the FDA's process is thought to have worked mostly as intended, approving new drugs that are safe and effective and keeping ineffective or unsafe drugs off the market. At the same time, the FDA has responded to pressure from Congress and the president to revise some rules on its own.[66]

Finally, agencies can sometimes combat attempts to control their behavior by appealing to groups who benefit from agency actions.[67] For example, since the 1980s, the Occupational Safety and Health Administration (OSHA) has resisted attempts by Republican presidents and Republican members of Congress to eliminate the agency or limit its operations.[68] One element of its strategy has been to build strong ties to labor unions. As a result, OSHA is much more likely to receive complaints about workplace safety from companies with strong unions. The second prong of the strategy has involved building cooperative arrangements with large companies to prevent workplace accidents, an approach that not only protects workers but can save companies a lot of money over the long term. Moreover, when OSHA levies fines against companies that violate safety regulations the fines are generally much less than would be allowed by law. As a result, when proposals to limit or eliminate OSHA are debated in Congress members hear from unions as well as many large corporations in support of keeping the agency in place. Over time, this strategy has generated support for the agency from Democrats and Republicans in the House and Senate.

The consequences of control

This discussion of attempts to control what bureaucrats do while at the same time tapping their expertise explains many of the seemingly dysfunctional aspects of the bureaucracy. Part of the problem is the nature of the tasks given to bureaucrats. Even when members of Congress and the president agree on which problems deserve attention, bureaucrats often face the much harder task of translating these officials' lofty problem-solving goals into concrete policies. Given the magnitude of this job, it is no surprise that even the best efforts of government agencies do not always succeed.

Many government regulations work as intended. An increase in regulatory attention to environmental protection and cleanup of polluted sites has dramatically improved water quality nationwide, including that of the Hudson River in New York, shown here.

Most important, the use of standard operating procedures is rooted partly in the complexity of bureaucrats' tasks—but also in the desire of agency heads and elected officials to control the actions of lower-level staff. Some of the EPA's delays in responding to the crisis in Flint were the product of preset plans and procedures that did not anticipate the need for fast action to protect a community from an unsafe water supply. Moreover, giving laptops to government employees so they can work while out of the office sounds like a good idea, but it also puts sensitive data at risk because laptops are easily lost or stolen. And while the FDA's drug-approval process succeeds for the most part at preventing harmful drugs from coming to market, the delays imposed by the process do prevent some patients from receiving lifesaving treatments. However, in all these cases the decisions do not reflect incompetence or malice. Rules and procedures are needed in any organization to ensure that decisions are made fairly and that they reflect the goals of the organization. But it is impossible to find procedures that will work well in all cases, particularly for the kinds of policy decisions made by bureaucrats.

"Why Should I Care?"

Cases of bureaucratic failure (poorly conceived policies or regulations, inaction, red tape) are often cited to "prove" that bureaucrats are incompetent, lazy, or dumb. The real story is that bureaucrats are often given nearly impossible tasks or political mandates that limit their authority. In this sense, complaints about bureaucrats have more to do with what we want them to do rather than their unwillingness or inability to execute these missions.

Conclusion

Bureaucrats implement government policy—often in situations in which the problems as well as potential solutions are vast and poorly understood and in the face of sharp disagreements about what government should do. On the government's behalf, bureaucrats spend money on everything from pencils to Mars rovers. They formulate regulations that determine what can be created, produced, transported, bought, sold, consumed, and disposed of in America. Elected officials want to control what bureaucrats do while also tapping into their expertise on policy matters. In this way, conflict over public policy often translates into conflicting ideas about what bureaucrats should do, resulting in complex, often-contradictory mandates and directions imposed on bureaucrats. For example, EPA inaction on the Flint water crisis was driven by disagreements within the agency on whether they had the authority to force state and local officials to address the problem.

 These characteristics of the bureaucracy and the fundamentally political nature of bureaucrats' jobs explain many cases of ineptitude and red tape. Sometimes bureaucrats simply make mistakes, choosing the wrong policy because they—and, in some cases, everyone else—lack full information about the tasks they were given. Bureaucrats may drag their feet when they oppose their tasks on policy grounds. Policies may reflect direct or implicit orders given by elected officials or political appointees. For example, the EPA's reluctance to act in the case of Flint may reflect a lack of easy solutions or the desire not to get involved in a purely local problem. Attempts at political control also shape the structure of the bureaucracy, from influencing which agencies function independently and which ones fall within executive departments to determining the qualifications for commissioners and agency heads and the rules they must follow when making decisions.

STUDY GUIDE

What is the federal bureaucracy?

Define *bureaucracy* and explain its major functions.
(Pages 442–450)

Summary

The bureaucracy is composed of both civil servants and political appointees and is in charge of interpreting and implementing a wide range of government policies. While bureaucrats are policy experts, most members of Congress are not. Nonetheless, Congress tries to control how the bureaucracy operates, which can result in inefficiencies.

Key terms

bureaucracy (p. 442)

civil servants (p. 442)

political appointees (p. 442)

regulation (p. 442)

notice-and-comment procedure (p. 443)

state capacity (p. 447)

red tape (p. 447)

standard operating procedures (p. 447)

problem of control (p. 448)

principal–agent game (p. 448)

regulatory capture (p. 449)

Practice Quiz Questions

1. **A government rule that affects the choices that individuals or corporations make is called _____.**

   a. an initiative

   b. a referendum

   c. a regulation

   d. a procurement

   e. an appropriation

2. **One of the reasons bureaucrats respond to pressure from elected officials is because _____.**

   a. they need congressional support to get larger budgets

   b. elected officials are experts

   c. they are all appointed by members of Congress

   d. their offices are housed in the Congress

   e. they are required by law to do so

3. **In the problem of control, the _____ is the principal and the _____ is the agent.**

   a. bureaucracy; president

   b. bureaucracy; Congress

   c. president; Congress

   d. president; bureaucracy

   e. Congress; president

4. **_____ occurs when bureaucrats cater to a small group of individuals regardless of the impact of these actions on the public welfare.**

   a. Bureaucratic drift

   b. Regulatory capture

   c. The revolving door

   d. An iron triangle

   e. Neutral competence

How has the American bureaucracy grown?

Trace the expansion of the federal bureaucracy over time.
(Pages 450–453)

Summary

The bureaucracy has grown substantially since the turn of the twentieth century, largely in response to citizen demands that the government do more for the people. The federal government had a very limited role in daily life for much of the nineteenth century, but it expanded during the Progressive Era, when regulatory activity increased and the spoils system was replaced by the federal civil service. The bureaucracy expanded again with the New Deal and Great Society programs, which increased the number of services the government provided.

Key term

federal civil service (p. 451)

Practice Quiz Questions

5. **How did the bureaucracy change during the Progressive Era?**

   a. It expanded the delivery of government services directly to individuals.

   b. The spoils system was first established.

   c. It created a number of antipoverty and educational programs.

   d. It reduced the government's regulatory activity.

   e. It increased the government's regulatory activity.

6. The civil service reforms of the Progressive Era _____ the spoils system and _____ the power of party organizations.

   a. ended; increased
   b. ended; decreased
   c. instituted; increased
   d. instituted; decreased
   e. expanded; increased

7. What effect did the Reagan Revolution have on bureaucracy?

   a. The government stopped passing regulatory policies.
   b. The size of the federal government shrank.
   c. The size of the federal government increased.
   d. The civil service reforms were weakened.
   e. The civil service reforms were strengthened.

The modern federal bureaucracy

Describe the size and structure of the executive branch today. (Pages 454–458)

Summary

The modern bureaucracy serves a wide range of functions, but the division of labor within the bureaucracy does not always have an obvious logic. Overlapping or confusing jurisdictions can be the result of elected officials attempting to shape the agency behavior by assigning a task to an executive department rather than an independent agency. The overall size of the bureaucracy reflects the demands of constituents but also fits the needs of elected officials to improve their chances of reelection.

Key terms

Office of Management and Budget (p. 454)

independent agencies (p. 454)

budget maximizers (p. 457)

Practice Quiz Questions

8. What is the job of the Office of Management and Budget?

   a. to prepare the president's annual budget proposal for the Congress
   b. to prepare a response to the budget passed by Congress
   c. to prepare annual budget proposals for the states
   d. to monitor government spending for the Supreme Court
   e. to monitor government spending for Congress

9. Independent agencies have _____ freedom from oversight than executive departments do and _____ be controlled by the president through his appointees.

   a. more; cannot
   b. more; can

   c. less; cannot
   d. less; can

10. The federal budget is growing in size because _____.

   a. bureaucrats are budget maximizers
   b. politicians do not scrutinize budget requests
   c. government agencies are never eliminated
   d. the public does not support large-scale budget cuts
   e. a growing percentage of Americans are going into civil service

The human face of the bureaucracy

Describe who bureaucrats are and the regulations that govern their employment. (Pages 458–463)

Summary

The regulations within the civil service system were established to separate politics from policy. Rather than getting and retaining a job for political reasons, individuals are hired based on merit and are quite difficult to fire. However, the president makes senior-level appointments that are not protected by civil service regulations and are more political in nature. These appointments are instrumental in helping the president control the bureaucracy.

Key term

turkey farms (p. 462)

Practice Quiz Questions

11. Compared with employees in private business, government employees are motivated _____ by salary and benefits than/as by the chance to make a difference.

    a. more
    b. just as much
    c. less

12. The civil service regulations _____ the flexibility that managers have in their hiring decisions and _____ the influence of elected officials.

    a. decrease; decrease
    b. increase; increase
    c. increase; decrease
    d. decrease; increase
    e. increase; have no effect on

Controlling the bureaucracy

Explain how Congress and the president oversee the executive branch. (Pages 463–469)

Summary

With their expertise, bureaucrats have the power to significantly influence government policy. This creates a dilemma for elected officials, who want to enjoy the benefits of the expertise while retaining control of the bureaucracy. Lawmakers can generally organize agencies and monitor their behavior to reduce, but not eliminate, bureaucratic drift.

Key terms

bureaucratic drift (p. 464)   police patrol oversight (p. 466)
oversight (p. 464)   fire alarm oversight (p. 466)

Practice Quiz Questions

13. When bureaucrats pursue their own goals rather than their assignments from officeholders, this is called _____.

a. an iron triangle

b. regulatory capture

c. problem of control

d. turkey farming

e. bureaucratic drift

14. Giving direct orders to bureaucrats _____ the influence of their policy expertise and _____ the potential to respond to unforeseen circumstances.

a. limits; reduces

b. increases; reduces

c. limits; increases

d. increases; increases

e. limits; has no effect on

15. While police patrol oversight has the advantage of being _____, it has the drawback of being _____.

a. affordable; unresponsive

b. responsive; costly

c. affordable; generally unnecessary

d. responsive; unpopular

e. affordable; ineffective

Suggested Reading

Brehm, John, and Scott Gates. *Teaching, Managing Tasks, and Brokering Trust: Functions of the Public Executive*. New York: Russell Sage Foundation, 2008.

Carpenter, Daniel P. *The Forging of Bureaucratic Autonomy: Reputations, Networks, and Policy Innovation in Executive Agencies, 1862–1928*. Princeton, NJ: Princeton University Press, 2001.

Huber, John D., and Charles R. Shipan. *Deliberate Discretion? The Institutional Foundations of Bureaucratic Autonomy*. New York: Cambridge University Press, 2002.

Lewis, David E. *The Politics of Presidential Appointments: Political Control and Bureaucratic Performance*. Princeton, NJ: Princeton University Press, 2010.

Light, Paul. *A Government Well-Executed: Public Service and Public Performance*. Washington, DC: Brookings Institution Press, 2003.

McCubbins, Mathew D., Roger G. Noll, and Barry R. Weingast. "Structure and Process as Solutions to the Politician's Principal-Agency Problem," *Virginia Law Review* 74 (1989): 431–82.

Miller, Gary. *Managerial Dilemmas: The Political Economy of Hierarchy*. New York: Cambridge University Press, 1987.

Moe, Terry M. "Political Control and the Power of the Agent." *Journal of Law, Economics, and Organization* 22 (2006): 1–21.

Nelson, Michael. "A Short, Ironic History of American National Bureaucracy." *Journal of Politics* 44 (1982): 747–78.

Skowronek, Stephen. *Building a New American State: The Expansion of National Administrative Capacities, 1877–1920*. New York: Cambridge University Press, 1982.

Workman, Samuel. *The Dynamics of Bureaucracy in the U.S. Government*. New York: Cambridge University Press, 2015.

14

The Courts

What is the role of courts in our political system?

On February 13, 2016, Justice Antonin Scalia died in his sleep while visiting a West Texas ranch. Scalia was an intellectual force on the Court known for his sharp wit, tough (and frequent) questions during oral arguments, and scathing dissents. His death had momentous political implications: with the Court now divided 4–4 between liberals and conservatives, President Obama could tip the balance in favor of the liberals for the first time in a generation. However, within an hour of the confirmation of Scalia's death Senate Majority Leader Mitch McConnell announced that there would be no hearing and no vote on any nomination by President Obama. The next president would get to decide the future balance of the Court.[1]

About a month later, President Obama nominated Merrick Garland to fill the vacancy. A respected judicial moderate, Garland served for nearly two decades on the Washington, D.C., appeals court, the second most important court in the nation. Despite a nomination that was intended to appeal to moderate Republican senators, Senate leadership held firm to their vow to let the vacancy be filled by the next president.

The immediate implication of the deadlock was that five cases were split 4–4, meaning that no new precedents were established and the lower courts' decisions would stand. Several of these cases, including a California case on public sector unions and a Texas case concerning immigration policy, were significant cases that will likely be addressed by a future Court.[2] Some cases appeared to be unanimous, but masked a 4–4 split. For example, the Court punted on the question of whether a religious organization could be required to provide coverage of contraceptives in a parallel insurance plan (they cannot be forced to provide coverage directly). Rather than deciding whether this was an infringement of the group's religious freedom, the Court sent the case back to lower court in a unanimous 8–0 decision, which meant the case would

Explain how the power of judicial review was established.

Outline the structure of the court system.

Describe how cases reach the Supreme Court.

Describe the Supreme Court's procedures for hearing a case.

Analyze the factors that influence Supreme Court decisions.

Assess the Supreme Court's power in the political system.

People outside the Supreme Court in April 2016 urge the Senate to "do [their] job" and hold hearings on the nomination of Merrick Garland. The vacancy in 2016 was one of the longest for the Court in U.S. history. #DoYourJob

ultimately be decided by a future court. The Court also responded by deciding to hear far fewer cases in their fall term (8 compared to 13 at this same time the previous year). Supreme Court politics also spilled over to the 2016 elections. Democrats urged Republican senators to "do [their] job," pointing out that every Supreme Court nominee since 1875 had received a hearing or vote and since 1900 six justices were confirmed during a presidential election year.[3] It became a central issue in the presidential campaign, with exit polls showing that 21 percent of voters said the Supreme Court vacancy was the most important factor in determining their vote. Another 48 percent said it was "an important factor." Of those saying it was "most important," 56 percent voted for Trump and 41 percent for Clinton (while those saying it was important split evenly).

Why all the fuss? If justices are simply interpreting the Constitution and neutrally applying it to law, why should it matter so much which president gets to fill a vacancy? The simple answer is that justices are more than baseball umpires calling the balls and strikes, as Chief Justice John G. Roberts Jr. famously said. As they interpret the Constitution, they also play one of two roles in our political system: either asserting their own policy-making authority or deferring to the decisions of others (Congress, the president, or the people). The Court's decision about which path to take in a given case is often political, involving conflict, trade-offs, and compromise, much like decision making in Congress.

That the Supreme Court is a policy-making and political institution may seem inappropriate. After all, the guiding principles of the "rule of law" in the American political system—embodied in the words carved above the entrance to the Supreme Court ("equal justice under the law") and the statue of Justice represented as a blindfolded women holding a set of scales—seem to contradict the view of a political Supreme Court. We normally think of the courts as objectively applying the law and interpreting the Constitution for each case. Indeed, there is often consensus among the justices on how to rule in a given case. In the 2015–2016 term, nearly half of the decisions were unanimous (38 of 82) and 12 more only had one dissenting vote. But, the recent immigration case illustrates that politics is an inherent part of the judiciary and a single set of objective standards is not always available for a given case. The 4–4 split upheld the lower court's injunction blocking Obama's deferred deportation program for illegal immigrants. The one-sentence decision offered no clues about the Court's reasoning, but the oral arguments made it clear that four justices saw Obama's actions as executive overreach and four viewed them as proper bureaucratic discretion.[4] On the other hand, the Court also issued a 4–3 decision upholding the University of Texas's affirmative action policy. This type of deference to state policy is an example of judicial restraint.[5]

For those who resist the view that the courts are a policy-making institution, the theme "political process matters" may not seem to apply in this chapter. However, the courts often *do* make policy, and the way they make decisions has an impact on outcomes. To see how political process matters for the courts, it is important to answer the following questions: What are the different roles of the courts? What is the structure of the judicial system? How do court decisions shape policy? In a nutshell, what is the nature of judicial decision making? This chapter also examines the questions suggested by the immigration and affirmative action cases: What is the proper place of the courts within our political system? How do the courts work? How much power should unelected judges have? Are the courts a necessary check on the other branches of government or a source of unaccountable power that contradicts core principles of democracy? Before addressing these questions, we discuss how the Founders viewed the judicial system.

The development of an independent and powerful federal judiciary

The Constitution did not definitively establish the role of the courts in American politics and the Supreme Court's authority as the ultimate interpreter of the Constitution. The powers of the Supreme Court evolved over time, and debates about its proper role continue to this day.

The Founders' views of the courts: the weakest branch?

The Federalists and Antifederalists did not see eye to eye on much, and the judiciary was no exception. Alexander Hamilton, writing in *Federalist 78*, said that the Supreme Court would be "beyond comparison the weakest of the three departments of power." In contrast, one of the authors of the *Antifederalist Papers* wrote: "The supreme court under this constitution would be exalted above all other power in the government and subject to no control."[6] Hmmm, which is it, weakest or strongest? Although the framers could not agree on the likely relative power of the Court, there was surprisingly little debate at the Constitutional Convention about the judiciary. Article III of the Constitution, which concerns the judicial branch of government (see Nuts & Bolts 14.1), created one Supreme Court and gave the courts independence by providing federal judges with lifetime terms (assuming "good behavior").

NUTS & BOLTS 14.1

Jurisdiction of the Federal Courts as Defined in Article III of the Constitution

Source: Lee Epstein and Thomas G. Walker, *Constitutional Law for a Changing America: Institutional Powers and Constraints*, 5th ed. (Washington, DC: CQ Press, 2004), p. 65.

Jurisdiction of Lower Federal Courts

- Cases involving the U.S. Constitution, federal laws, and treaties.
- Controversies between two or more states. (Congress passed a law giving the Supreme Court exclusive jurisdiction over these cases.)
- Controversies between citizens of different states.
- Controversies between a state and citizens of another state. (The Eleventh Amendment removed federal jurisdiction in these cases.)
- Controversies between a state or its citizens and any foreign states, citizens, or subjects.
- Cases affecting ambassadors, public ministers, and consuls.
- Cases of admiralty and maritime jurisdictions.
- Controversies between citizens of the same state claiming lands under grants of different states.

Jurisdiction of the Supreme Court
Original Jurisdiction*

- Cases involving ambassadors, public ministers, and consuls.
- Cases to which a state is a party.

Appellate Jurisdiction

- Cases falling under the jurisdiction of the lower federal courts, "with such exceptions, and under such Regulations as the Congress shall make."

---

* This does not imply exclusive jurisdiction. For example, the Supreme Court may refer to a district court for a case involving an ambassador (the more likely outcome).

The main disagreements about the judiciary had to do with how independent the courts should be *vis-à-vis* the other branches of government and how much power to give to the courts. Some of the framers feared a tyrannical Congress and wanted to create judicial and executive branches that could check this power. Others argued for making the executive and judicial branches more closely related so they would be better able to balance Congress. A central debate was whether to give the judiciary some "revisionary power" over Congress, similar to the president's veto power. This idea of judicial review would have given the Supreme Court the power to strike down laws passed by Congress that violated the Constitution. The framers could not agree on judicial review, so the Constitution remained silent on the matter. As the power of judicial review has evolved, it has become a central part of the system of checks and balances (see Chapter 2).

Many details about the Supreme Court were left up to Congress, including its size, the time and place it would meet, and its internal organization. These details, and the system of lower federal courts, were outlined in the Judiciary Act of 1789. This law set the number of justices at six (one chief justice and five associates). The number of justices gradually increased to ten by the end of the Civil War and was then restricted to seven under Reconstruction policies. The number was set at nine in 1869, where it has remained ever since.[7] The 1789 act also created a system of federal courts, which included 13 district courts and 3 circuit courts—the intermediate-level courts with appellate jurisdiction (cases heard on appeal from lower courts). The district courts each had one judge, while the circuit courts had two Supreme Court justices and one district judge. This odd arrangement for staffing the circuit courts remained in place for more than 100 years, over the objections of the justices who resented having to "ride circuit" in difficult traveling conditions.[8] Today separate judges are appointed to fill the circuit courts (what we call appeals courts). The Supreme Court had a rough start. Indeed, it seemed determined to prove Alexander Hamilton right, that it was the weakest branch. Of the six original justices appointed by George Washington, one declined to serve and another never showed up for a formal session. The Court's first sessions lasted only a few days because it did not have much business. In fact, the Court did not decide a single case in 1791 or 1792. When Justice Rutledge resigned in 1791 to take a state court position, two potential appointees turned down the job in order to keep their positions in their state legislatures! Such career decisions would be unimaginable today, when serving on the Supreme Court is considered the pinnacle of a legal career.[9]

Judicial review and *Marbury v. Madison*

The Court started to gain more power when John Marshall was appointed chief justice in 1801. Marshall single-handedly transformed the Court into an equal partner in the system of checks and balances. The most important step was the decision *Marbury v. Madison* (1803), which gave the Supreme Court the power of judicial review. As noted earlier, the framers were split on the wisdom of giving the Court the power to strike down laws passed by Congress, and the Constitution does not explicitly address the issue. However, historians have established that a majority of the framers, including the most influential ones, favored judicial review. Given that the Constitution did not address the issue of judicial review, Marshall simply asserted that the Supreme Court had the power to determine when a law was unconstitutional.

The facts and legal reasoning behind *Marbury* are worth explaining because this is one of the most important court cases in American history. The Federalists had just lost the election of 1800 to Thomas Jefferson and the Democratic-Republicans. In a

Judiciary Act of 1789
The law in which Congress laid out the organization of the federal judiciary. The law refined and clarified federal court jurisdiction and set the original number of justices at six. It also created the Office of the Attorney General and established the lower federal courts.

district courts
Lower-level trial courts of the federal judicial system that handle most U.S. federal cases.

appellate jurisdiction
The authority of a court to hear appeals from lower courts and change or uphold the decision.

judicial review
The Supreme Court's power to strike down a law or an executive branch action that it finds unconstitutional.

last-minute power grab, the Federalist-controlled lame-duck Congress gave outgoing President Adams an opportunity to appoint 42 new justices of the peace for the District of Columbia and Alexandria, Virginia. Adams made the appointments, and the Senate confirmed them, but not before time ran out and the new administration took over. The secretary of state, John Marshall (the same Marshall who had just been confirmed as chief justice before President Adams left office), failed to ensure that all the commissions for the new judges were delivered by midnight. When President Jefferson assumed office, he ordered his new secretary of state, James Madison, not to deliver the remaining commissions that had been issued by the outgoing Federalist administration. William Marbury was one of the people who did not receive his commission, and he asked the Supreme Court to issue an order giving him the position.

As leading figures in opposing parties, Chief Justice Marshall and President Jefferson did not like each other. This put Marshall in a difficult position. He was concerned that if he issued the order that Marbury wanted (giving Marbury his job) Jefferson probably would ignore it (technically, Secretary of State Madison was the other party in the lawsuit, but Jefferson was calling the shots). Given the weakness of the Court, having such an order disregarded by the president could have been a final blow to its position in the national government. However, if the Court did not issue the order it would be giving in to Jefferson despite the merits of Marbury's case—he really had been cheated out of his job. It appeared that the Court would lose whether it issued the order or not.

To get out of the predicament, Marshall applied the idea of judicial review. Although the idea was not original to Marshall (as noted, the framers debated the issue and Hamilton endorsed it in some detail in *Federalist 78*), the Court had never exercised its authority to rule on the constitutionality of a federal law. Marshall's reasoning was quite clever: the Court's opinion said that Marbury was due his commission, but the Court did not have the power to give him his job because the part of the Judiciary Act of 1789 that gave it that power was unconstitutional! The core issue was Section 13 of the Act, which gave the Court the power to issue orders (writs of mandamus) to anyone holding federal office. This section expanded the original jurisdiction of the Supreme Court, and that was where Congress overstepped its bounds, according to Marshall. The original jurisdiction of the Court is clearly specified in the Constitution, so any attempt by Congress to change that jurisdiction through legislation would be unconstitutional; the only way to change original jurisdiction would be through a constitutional amendment.[10] Marshall writes: "It is emphatically the province and duty of the judicial department to say what the law is.... If two laws conflict with each other, the courts must decide on the operation of each. So if a law be in opposition to the Constitution ... the court must determine which of these conflicting rules governs the case. This is of the very essence of judicial duty."[11]

Judicial review in practice

Chief Justice Marshall lost the battle—poor Mr. Marbury never did get his job, and Jefferson appointed the people he wanted to be justices of the peace—but the Supreme Court won the war. By asserting its power to review the constitutionality of laws passed by Congress, the Court became an equal partner in the institutional balance of power. Although it would be more than 50 years until the Court would use judicial review again to strike down a law passed by Congress (in the unfortunate 1857 *Dred Scott* case, which concerned slavery and effectively led to the Civil War), the reasoning behind *Marbury* has never been challenged by subsequent presidents or Congresses.[12]

original jurisdiction
The authority of a court to handle a case first, as in the Supreme Court's authority to initially hear disputes between two states. However, original jurisdiction for the Supreme Court is not exclusive; it may assign such a case to a lower court.

Chief Justice John Marshall favored the idea of judicial review and claimed this power for the Court in the *Marbury v. Madison* decision.

Interpreting federal laws may seem like a logical responsibility for the Supreme Court, but what about state laws? Should the Supreme Court have final say over them as well? The Constitution does not answer this question. But the supremacy clause requires that the Constitution and national laws take precedence over state constitutions and state laws when they conflict. The Judiciary Act of 1789 made it clear that the Supreme Court would rule on these matters.

It didn't take long for the Court to assert its power in this area. In 1796, the Court heard a case concerning a British creditor who was trying to collect a debt from the state of Virginia. The state had passed a law canceling all debts owed by Virginians (or the state) to British subjects. However, the Treaty of Paris, which ended the Revolutionary War and recognized American independence, ensured the collection of such debts. This conflict was resolved when the Court struck down the state law and upheld Americans' commitments under the treaty.[13] Advocates of states' rights were not happy with this ruling, but it was crucial for the national government that the Constitution be applied uniformly rather than be subject to different interpretations by every state.

The contours of the relationship between the national government and the states were largely defined by how active the Supreme Court was in asserting judicial review and how willing it was to intervene in matters of state law. For much of the nineteenth century, the Court embraced dual federalism, in which the national government and the states operated on two separate levels (see Chapter 3). Later the Court involved itself more in state law as it moved toward a more active role for the national government in regulating interstate commerce and using the Fourteenth Amendment to selectively incorporate the amendments that constitute the Bill of Rights (see Chapter 4).

All in all, the Court has struck down more than 180 acts of Congress (and about 1,400 state laws). This sounds like a lot, but Congress passed more than 60,000 laws in its first 225 years. Over time, the Court has ruled on state laws in many important areas, including civil liberties, desegregation and civil rights, abortion, privacy, redistricting, labor laws, employment and discrimination, and business and environmental regulation.

When the Supreme Court strikes down a congressional or state law, it engages in constitutional interpretation—that is, it determines that the law is unconstitutional. But the Supreme Court also engages in statutory interpretation—that is, it applies national and state laws to particular cases (statutes are laws that are passed by legislatures). Often the language of a statute may be unclear and the Court must interpret how to apply the law. For example, should the protection of endangered species prevent economic development that may destroy the species' habitat? How does one determine if an employer is responsible for sexual harassment in the workplace? How should the voting rights of minorities be protected? In each case, the Court must interpret the relevant statutes to determine what Congress really meant. In addition, in the third main area of the law—administrative law—the Court is sometimes required to assess the appropriateness of statutory interpretation by federal agencies that are responsible for implementing the laws. Often this involves the controversial practice of consulting legislative histories—floor debates, congressional hearings, and so on—to determine legislative intent. But the late Justice Antonin Scalia argued that such searches are inherently subjective and that justices should only interpret the actual statutory text.

Although politicians and other political actors accept judicial review as a central part of the political system, critics are concerned about its antidemocratic nature. Why, for example, do we give nine unelected justices such extraordinary power over our elected representatives? Debates about the proper role for the Court will continue as long as it is involved in controversial decisions. We will take up this question later in the chapter when we address the concepts of judicial activism and judicial restraint.

constitutional interpretation
The process of determining whether a piece of legislation or governmental action is supported by the Constitution.

statutory interpretation
The various methods and tests used by the courts for determining the meaning of a law and applying it to specific situations. Congress may overturn the courts' interpretation by writing a new law; thus, it also engages in statutory interpretation.

Judicial review may seem like "inside baseball" that doesn't really matter for most Americans. However, the power to strike down laws and government actions means that the Court may act against political majorities to strike down unconstitutional actions such as segregating schools by race and discriminating against same-sex marriage. Judicial review may also be used, however, to frustrate popular majorities during times of political change, such as during the New Deal of the 1930s. In either case, this is an awesome political power that puts the Supreme Court on an equal institutional footing with Congress and the president.

★

OUTLINE THE STRUCTURE OF THE COURT SYSTEM

The American legal and judicial system

Two sets of considerations are necessary to understand the overall nature of our judicial system: the fundamentals of the legal system that apply to all courts in the United States, and the structure of the court system within our system of federalism.

Court fundamentals

The general characteristics of the court system begin with the people who are in the courtroom. The **plaintiff** brings the case, and the **defendant** is the person or party who is being sued or charged with a crime. If the case is appealed, the petitioner is the person bringing the appeal and the respondent is on the other side of the case. In a civil case, the plaintiff sues to determine who is right or wrong and to gain something of value, such as monetary damages, the right to vote, or admission to a university. For example, imagine that your neighbor accidentally backs his car into the fence that divides your property, destroying a large section of it. The neighbor does not have adequate insurance to cover the damages and refuses to pay for the repairs. You do not want to pay the $1,000 deductible on your insurance policy, so you (the plaintiff) sue your neighbor (the defendant) to see whether your neighbor has to pay for the repairs. In a criminal case, the plaintiff is the government and the prosecutor attempts to prove the guilt of the defendant (the person accused of the crime).

Many, but not all, civil and criminal cases are heard before a jury that decides the outcome in the case, which is called the verdict. Often cases get settled before they go to trial (or even in the middle of the trial) in a process known as **plea bargaining**. In a civil case, this would mean that the plaintiff and the defendant agree on a monetary settlement and admission of guilt (or not; in some cases the defendant may agree to pay a fine or damages but not to admit guilt). In a criminal case, the defendant may agree to plead guilty in exchange for receiving a shorter sentence or being charged with a lesser crime. Plea bargaining is an excellent example of how legal conflict between two parties can be resolved through compromise.

Differences between Civil and Criminal Cases

There are important differences between civil and criminal cases. One is the standard of proof that serves to determine the outcome of the case. In civil cases, the jury has to determine whether the "preponderance of evidence"—that is, a majority of the evidence—proves that the plaintiff wins.

plaintiff
The person or party who brings a case to court.

defendant
The person or party against whom a case is brought.

plea bargaining
Negotiating an agreement between a plaintiff and a defendant to settle a case before it goes to trial or the verdict is decided. In a civil case, this usually involves an admission of guilt and an agreement on monetary damages; in a criminal case, this often involves an admission of guilt in return for a reduced charge or sentence.

O. J. Simpson dons a pair of gloves during testimony in his double-murder trial in Los Angeles in June 1995. The jury was not convinced of his guilt "beyond a reasonable doubt" and thus acquitted Simpson in this criminal trial. However, a subsequent civil trial found that a "preponderance of evidence" was against him.

class-action lawsuit
A case brought by a group of individuals on behalf of themselves and others in the general public who are in similar circumstances.

common law
Law based on the precedent of previous court rulings rather than on legislation. It is used in all federal courts and 49 of the 50 state courts.

precedent
A legal norm established in court cases that is then applied to future cases dealing with the same legal questions.

In criminal cases, a much stiffer burden must be met—the defendant must be found guilty "beyond a reasonable doubt."

Another difference is where the burden of proof lies. In criminal cases, there is a presumption of "innocent until proven guilty"—that is, the state must prove the guilt of the defendant. However, in civil cases the burden of proof may be on the plaintiff or the defendant, depending on the law that governs the case. Even more complicated, in civil cases the plaintiff may have to prove certain points and the defendant other points. For example, in certain race-based voting rights cases the plaintiff would have to prove that race was the predominant motivation for creating a black-majority congressional district. If that point is demonstrated, then the burden of proof shifts to the defendant to show that there was some "compelling state interest" to justify the use of race as a predominant factor.

One type of civil suit is the **class-action lawsuit**, a case brought by a group of individuals on behalf of themselves and others in similar circumstances. The target may be a corporation that produced hazardous or defective products or that engaged in illegal behavior that harmed a particular group. For example, 1.5 million current and former female Walmart employees sued the retailing giant for sex discrimination in 2011, claiming that the store had paid women less than men for the same work and had promoted fewer women than men.[14] Suits are often filed on behalf of shareholders of companies that have lost value because of fraud committed by corporate leaders. Cases like these are an important mechanism for providing accountability and justice in our economic system. Federal regulators do not have the ability to ensure the complete safety of food, drugs, and consumer products or to continually monitor all potential business fraud. Therefore, consumers rely on the legal system and class-action lawsuits to ensure that businesses act fairly and produce safe products.

Common Elements of the Judicial System Several characteristics of the judicial system apply to all cases. First, ours is an adversarial system in which lawyers on both sides have an opportunity to present their case, challenge the testimony of the opposing side, and try to convince the court that their version of the events is true. The process of "discovery," in which both sides share the information that will be presented in court, ensures a fair process and few last-minute surprises. Second, 49 of the 50 states and the federal courts operate under a system of **common law**, which means that legal decisions build from precedent established in previous cases and apply commonly throughout the jurisdiction of the court. The alternative, which is practiced only in Louisiana, is the civil law tradition, which is based on a detailed codification of the law that is applied to each specific case.

The notion of **precedent** (or stare decisis—"let the decision stand") deserves special attention. Precedent is a previously decided case or set of decisions that serves as a guide for future cases on the same topic. Lower courts are bound by Supreme Court decisions when there is a clear precedent that is relevant for a given case. In many cases, following precedent is not clear-cut because several precedents may seem relevant. The lower courts have considerable discretion in sorting out which precedents are the most important. The Supreme Court tries to follow its own precedents, but in the past 50 years justices have been willing to deviate from earlier decisions when they think that the precedent is flawed. The Court has overruled more than twice as many decisions since 1953 than in the previous 164 years. Part of this can be explained by the relatively small number of precedents that *could* have been overturned in the first few decades of our nation's history. But even when accounting for the natural accumulation of more precedents to potentially overturn, recent Courts have been much more willing to deviate from precedent than previous Courts. For example, in a recent campaign finance case the Court overturned part of a 38-year-old precedent that had upheld aggregate limits on contributions.[15] As this record indicates, precedent is not a rule the Court must follow but a norm that constrains its behavior.

Two more points must be considered before a case is filed. First, the person bringing the case must have **standing** to sue in a civil case, which means that the person has a legitimate basis for bringing the case. This usually means that the individual has suffered some direct and personal harm from the action addressed in the court case. Standing is easy to establish for private parties—as in the previous example, if your neighbor destroys your fence, you have been harmed. However, it gets more interesting when the government is a party. For example, when an environmental group challenged the Interior Department's interpretation of the Endangered Species Act the Supreme Court ruled that the group did not have standing because it did not demonstrate that the government's policy would cause "imminent" injury to the group.[16] Similarly, federal courts ruled that 10 members of Congress did not have standing to challenge American bombing in Libya and that taxpayers do not have standing to sue the government if they disagree with a specific policy.[17] Depending on your politics, you may not want your hard-earned cash going to buy school lunches for poor children or to fund various wars. However, your status as a taxpayer does not give you enough of a personal stake in these policies to challenge them in court, and so you do not have standing. Later, in the section discussing how cases get to the Supreme Court, we will see that justices have some leeway in defining standing.

The final general characteristic of the legal system is the **jurisdiction** of the court—when bringing a case before the court, you must choose a court that actually has the power to hear your case. For example, if you wanted to contest a speeding ticket you would not file your case in the state supreme court or in the federal district court; you would file it in your local traffic court. What if you believed you were the victim of discrimination in the workplace? Would you sue in state or federal court? You probably could do either, but the decision would be based on which set of laws would provide you with more protection from discrimination. This varies by state, so the proper jurisdiction for a given case is often a judgment call based on specific legal questions (this practice of seeking the best court for your case is called *venue shopping*).

Structure of the court system and federalism

The structure of the court system is like the rest of the political system: it is divided within and across levels of government. Across the levels of government, the court system operates on two parallel tracks within (1) the state and local courts and (2) the federal courts. Within each level of government, both tracks include courts of original jurisdiction, appeals courts, and courts of special jurisdiction. As shown in the How It Works graphic, the state courts are entirely separate from the federal courts, with the exception of the small proportion of cases that are appealed from a state supreme court to the U.S. Supreme Court. There is much variation in the structure of state courts in terms of their names and the number of levels of courts. However, they all follow the same general pattern of trial courts with limited and general original jurisdiction and appeals courts (either one or two levels, depending on the state).

District Courts Workhorses of the federal system, the district courts handle more than a quarter of a million filings a year. There are 89 districts in the 50 states, with at least one district court for each state. There are also district courts in Puerto Rico, the Virgin Islands, the District of Columbia, Guam, and the Northern Mariana Islands to bring the total to 94 districts with 677 judges.[18] There are two limited-jurisdiction district courts: the Court of International Trade, which addresses cases involving international trade and customs issues, and the U.S. Court of Federal Claims, which handles most claims for money damages against the United States, disputes over federal

standing
Legitimate justification for bringing a civil case to court.

jurisdiction
The sphere of a court's legal authority to hear and decide cases.

The Court System

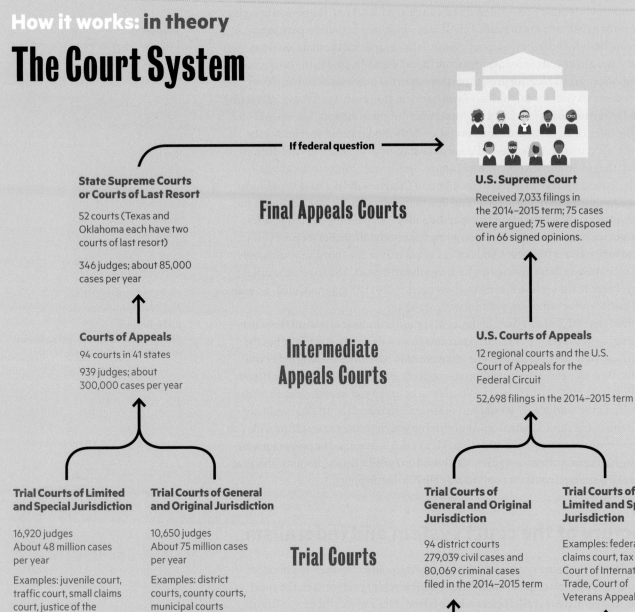

If federal question →

Final Appeals Courts

State Supreme Courts or Courts of Last Resort

52 courts (Texas and Oklahoma each have two courts of last resort)

346 judges; about 85,000 cases per year

U.S. Supreme Court

Received 7,033 filings in the 2014–2015 term; 75 cases were argued; 75 were disposed of in 66 signed opinions.

Intermediate Appeals Courts

Courts of Appeals

94 courts in 41 states

939 judges; about 300,000 cases per year

U.S. Courts of Appeals

12 regional courts and the U.S. Court of Appeals for the Federal Circuit

52,698 filings in the 2014–2015 term

Trial Courts

Trial Courts of Limited and Special Jurisdiction

16,920 judges
About 48 million cases per year

Examples: juvenile court, traffic court, small claims court, justice of the peace, family court

Trial Courts of General and Original Jurisdiction

10,650 judges
About 75 million cases per year

Examples: district courts, county courts, municipal courts

Trial Courts of General and Original Jurisdiction

94 district courts
279,039 civil cases and 80,069 criminal cases filed in the 2014–2015 term

Trial Courts of Limited and Special Jurisdiction

Examples: federal claims court, tax court, Court of International Trade, Court of Veterans Appeals

State and Local Courts

Federal Courts

Sources: Data on federal courts are from the U.S. Supreme Court, "2015 Year-End Report on the Federal Judiciary," www.supremecourt.gov/publicinfo/year-end/2015year-endreport.pdf (accessed 3/11/16). Data on state courts are from National Center for State Courts, www.ncsc.org (accessed 10/26/16); Ballotpedia.org, "Intermediate Appellate Courts," https://ballotpedia.org/Intermediate_appellate_courts (accessed 3/18/16) and Ron Malega and Thomas H. Cohen, "State Court Organization, 2011," U.S. Department of Justice, Bureau of Justice Statistics, www.bjs.gov/content/pub/pdf/sco11.pdf (accessed 3/18/16).

Same-Sex Marriage through the Court System

Same-sex marriage has been addressed in dozens of state and federal court cases in the past decade. A landmark case decided in June 2015 illustrates how cases make their way through the court system and how the Supreme Court resolves conflicts between the lower courts.

Okay, let's resolve this.

Supreme Court: The Supreme Court resolved this conflict in a landmark 5–4 decision, *Obergefell v. Hodges* (2015), holding that the fundamental **right to marry is guaranteed to same-sex couples** by both the due process clause and the equal protection clause of the Fourteenth Amendment to the U.S. Constitution.

The conflict between the circuit courts meant that same-sex marriage was legal in some states, but not in others. At the end of June 2015, same-sex couples could marry in 29 states and the District of Columbia, but not in 21 states.

It's constitutional.

Federal Court of Appeals: Appeals court rulings from the Fourth, Seventh, Ninth, and Tenth Circuits, representing 23 states, **struck down state-level bans on same-sex marriage** as unconstitutional.

It's unconstitutional.

Federal Court of Appeals: Six federal district court cases from Michigan, Ohio, Kentucky, and Tennessee were appealed to the Sixth Circuit Court, which **upheld the bans on same-sex marriage in these four states.**

Yeah, but...

Eleven federal district court decisions were appealed by states attempting to uphold their bans.

Rights awarded!

State and Federal Trial Courts: Following the Supreme Court's landmark ruling in 2013 striking down the Defense of Marriage Act, more than **two dozen state courts and federal district courts struck down bans on same-sex marriage.**

?

Critical Thinking

1. **What are the advantages and disadvantages** of having such a complex court system?

2. **When does a case that goes through the state courts** end up in the U.S. Supreme Court? Can you think of an issue other than same-sex marriage where this is likely to occur?

appeals courts
The intermediate level of federal courts that hear appeals from district courts. More generally, an appeals court is any court with appellate jurisdiction.

contracts, unlawful "takings" of private property by the federal government, and other claims against the United States.

Appeals Courts The appeals courts (called circuit courts until 1948)[19] are the intermediate courts of appeals, but in practice they are the final court for most federal cases that are appealed from the lower courts. The losing side in a federal case can appeal to the Supreme Court, but given that the highest court in the land hears so few cases, the appeals courts usually get the final word. Appeals courts did not always have this much power; in fact, through much of the nineteenth century they had very limited appellate jurisdiction and did not hear many significant cases.

The number of appeals courts in the nation slowly expanded as the workload of these courts grew, to the current 12 regional courts and the court of appeals for the Federal Circuit, which handles specialized cases from all over the country. The smallest of the regional appeals courts is the First Circuit, which has 6 judges, and the largest is the Ninth Circuit, which has 29 judges.[20] In 2015, there were 179 appeals court judges and 84 "senior judges" (these numbers include the appeals court for the federal circuit).[21] Senior judges are semiretired judges who hear certain cases to help out with the overall federal court system workload; they typically handle about 15 percent of the workload for the federal court system.

The Supreme Court The Supreme Court sits at the top of the federal court system. The Supreme Court is the "court of last resort" for cases coming from both the state and the federal courts. One important function of the Court is to ensure that the application and interpretation of the Constitution are consistent nationwide by resolving conflicts between lower courts, or between a state law and a federal law, or between laws in different states. A district court or appeals court ruling is applicable only for the specific region of that court, whereas Supreme Court rulings apply to the entire country.

Although the Supreme Court is the most important interpreter of the Constitution, the president and Congress also interpret the Constitution on a regular basis. This means that the Supreme Court does not always have the final say. For example, if the Court strikes down a federal law for being overly vague Congress can rewrite the law to clarify the offending passage. When this happens, Congress may have the final word. For example, Congress overturned *Ledbetter v. Goodyear Tire & Rubber Co.* (2007) when it passed the Lilly Ledbetter Fair Pay Act in 2009. The law said that the Supreme Court had misinterpreted the 1964 Civil Rights Act when it ruled that Ledbetter would have had to file her pay discrimination suit within 180 days of being hired.[22]

Even on matters of constitutional interpretation rather than statutory interpretation, Congress can fight back by passing a constitutional amendment. However, this is a difficult and time-consuming process (see Chapter 2). Nevertheless, that option is available as a way of overturning an unpopular Court decision. Perhaps the best example of this is the very first major case ever decided by the Supreme Court—*Chisholm v. Georgia* (1793). This case upheld the right of a citizen of one state to sue another state in federal court. The states were shocked by this challenge to their sovereignty, and a constitutional amendment to overturn the decision quickly made its way through Congress. By 1795, the Eleventh Amendment had been ratified and citizens could no longer sue a state (in federal court) in which they did not live.[23]

How judges are selected

There are many mechanisms for placing judges in courts. At the national level, the president makes the appointments with the advice and consent of the Senate. This process may be extremely contentious, as discussed in the chapter opener about filling Justice Scalia's vacancy. At the state level, various methods are in use.

State-Level Judges At the state level, there are 147 trial courts (some states have multiple levels), 94 appeals courts, and 52 supreme courts. At the state level, judges can be selected for trial courts in five different ways: appointment by the governor (6 courts), appointment by the state legislature (5 courts), partisan elections (39 courts), nonpartisan elections (34 courts), and the system called the Missouri Plan in which the governor makes appointments from a list compiled by a nonpartisan screening committee (46 courts). Seventeen courts use some combination of these methods.[24] With this last method, the appointed judge usually has to run in a retention election within several years of the appointment, making this system a hybrid of the political nomination and popular election routes to the court.

There is some controversy over the wisdom of electing judges, as doing so may undermine the courts' role as the protector of unpopular minority rights. Even in states where judicial elections are officially nonpartisan, it is clear who the liberal and conservative candidates are, so judicial elections can be very partisan. Interest groups often get involved by making endorsements or running their own advertisements for or against the judicial candidates. Electing judges also raises the potential for conflicts of interest if campaign contributors have cases before the court.[25] However, elected judges will be more responsive to public opinion, especially on salient issues such as the death penalty[26] and abortion.[27] Furthermore, the alternative to elections—appointing judges—has been criticized as elitist. These critics also say that there's not much evidence that the process of appointing judges is more "merit based" than judicial elections.[28]

Federal Judges The Constitution does not specify requirements for serving on the federal courts, unlike the detailed stipulations for Congress and the president. Federal judges don't even have to have a law degree! (This is probably due to the limited number of law schools at the time of the Founding; when the Constitution was written, someone who wanted to be a lawyer generally would serve as an apprentice in a law office to learn the trade.) The president appoints federal judges with the "advice and consent" of the Senate (the Senate must approve the nominees with a majority vote).

Nomination battles for federal judges can be intense, because the stakes are high. As the discussion of judicial review made clear, the Supreme Court plays a central role in the policy process, and because a justice has life tenure a justice's impact can outlive the president and Senate who put him or her on the Court. The justices often serve for decades, much longer than the people who appoint them.

The Role of the President Given the Constitution's silence on the qualification of federal judges, presidents have broad discretion over whom to nominate. Presidents have always tried to influence the direction of the federal courts and especially the Supreme Court by picking people who share their views. Because the Senate often has different ideas about the proper direction for the Court, nomination disputes end up being a combination of debates over the merit of a nominee and partisan battles about the ideological composition of the Court.

Although presidents would *like* to influence the direction of the Court, it is not always possible to predict how judges will behave once they are on the Court. Earl Warren is a good example. He was appointed by Republican president Dwight Eisenhower and had been the Republican governor of California, yet he turned out to be one of the most liberal chief justices of the last century. Eisenhower called Warren's nomination the biggest mistake he ever made.[29] Former justices William Joseph Brennan Jr., David Souter, and John Paul Stevens also were nominated by Republican presidents but regularly voted with the liberal bloc on the Court.

Nonetheless, the president can make a good guess about how a justice is likely to vote based on the nominee's party affiliation and the nature of his or her legal writings and decisions (if the nominee has prior judicial experience). Not surprisingly, 102 of 112 justices who have served on the Court have shared the nominating president's party (91 percent). Overall, more than 90 percent of the lower-court judges appointed by presidents in the twentieth century have also belonged to the same party as the president.

Presidents can influence the direction of the federal courts by selecting judges who share their views. President Obama is shown with Judge Merrick B. Garland, whom he nominated to the U.S. Supreme Court to fill the vacancy created by the death of Justice Antonin Scalia.

The most partisan move to influence the Court was President Franklin Delano Roosevelt's infamous plan to pack the Court. FDR was frustrated because the Court had struck down several pieces of important New Deal legislation, so to get a more sympathetic Court he proposed nominating a new justice for every justice who was over 70 years old. Six justices were over 70, so this would have increased the size of the Court to 15 justices. This effort to disguise the partisan power play as a humanitarian gesture (to help the old-timers with their workload) didn't fool anyone. The plan to pack the Court ran into opposition, but in the so-called switch in time that saved nine the Court started ruling in favor of the New Deal legislation, so the plan was dropped.

In addition to the ideological considerations about whom to nominate, the president also considers the individual's reputation as a legal scholar and his or her personal relationship to the candidate. Further considerations are the candidate's ethical standards, gender, and race (see Figure 14.1 for data on the latter two points). Donald Trump thrust judges' demographic backgrounds into the limelight when he said that federal district judge Gonzalo P. Curie could not be objective in the lawsuit concerning Trump University because Curie was a Mexican (the judge was born in Indiana and his parents are from Mexico).

The Role of the Senate The Senate is the other half of the equation that determines the composition of the federal courts. The Senate has shifted from a very active role in providing "advice and consent" on court appointments to a passive role and then back

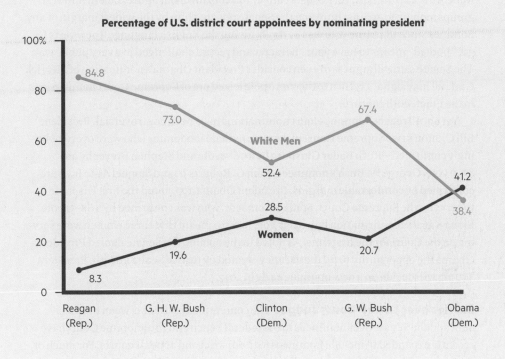

Percentage of U.S. district court appointees by nominating president

- 84.8 — White Men
- 73.0
- 52.4
- 67.4
- 41.2
- 38.4

- 8.3 — Women
- 19.6
- 28.5
- 20.7

Reagan (Rep.)	G. H. W. Bush (Rep.)	Clinton (Dem.)	G. W. Bush (Rep.)	Obama (Dem.)

FIGURE 14.1

Race and Gender on Federal District Courts

Since the 1980s, the proportion of women on the federal bench has gone up fivefold while the percentage of white men has plummeted by more than half. Do you think that descriptive representation in the judicial branch is important?

Source: Max Ehrenfreund, "The Number of White Dudes Becoming Judges Has Plummeted under Obama," *Washington Post*, February 18, 2016, www.washingtonpost.com (accessed 6/8/16).

to an active role. One constant is that the Senate rarely rejects nominees because of their qualifications; rather, it tends to reject them for political reasons. Of 28 Supreme Court nominees rejected by the Senate in the history of the United States, only 2 were turned down because they were seen as unqualified: George Williams in 1873 and G. Harrold Carswell in 1970. Serious questions were also raised about a third justice, Clarence Thomas, who had served for only 18 months as a federal judge before being nominated to the Court. Thomas also was accused of sexual harassment by former colleague Anita Hill. Nonetheless, Thomas ultimately won confirmation by a 52–48 vote, the second-narrowest successful margin in history. The other 26 nominees were rejected for political reasons. Most commonly, when a president makes a nomination close to an election and the Senate is controlled by the opposing party the Senate will kill the nomination, hoping that its party will win the presidency and nominate a justice more to its liking.

Throughout the nineteenth century, the Senate was very willing to turn down Court nominations for political reasons. In fact, between 1793 and 1894 the Senate did not confirm 21 nominees to the Court, which was about a third of the total number nominated. In contrast, between 1894 and 1968 the Senate did not even require nominees to testify and during that period only 4 nominees were rejected.

A rethinking of this passive role occurred in the late 1960s. President Nixon vowed to pull the Court back from the "liberal excesses" of the Warren Court, but the Senate stiffened its spine and rejected two nominees in a row: Clement Haynsworth (in 1969) and G. Harrold Carswell (in 1970). With Haynsworth, there were ethical problems involving his participation in cases in which he had a financial interest. Carswell had a mediocre judicial record, and civil rights groups raised questions about his commitment to enforcing antidiscrimination laws. Nixon must have thought that the Senate wouldn't reject his choice twice in a row! The most recent Senate rejection was of Judge

Robert Bork, a brilliant, very conservative, and controversial figure. Liberal interest groups mobilized against him, and the Senate rejected him by the widest margin of any nominee since 1846 (the vote was 42 to 58), giving the English language a new verb: to get "borked" means to have your character and record challenged in a very public way. The Senate's unwillingness to even consider President Obama's nomination of Merrick Garland may signal a return to the more politicized era of Supreme Court nominations in the nineteenth century.

Yet not all recent Supreme Court nominations have been controversial. President Bill Clinton's two Supreme Court picks were judicial moderates who were overwhelmingly confirmed—Ruth Bader Ginsburg by a 96–3 vote and Stephen Breyer by an 87–9 vote. George W. Bush's nominees, John G. Roberts Jr. and Samuel Alito Jr., were confirmed by comfortable margins. President Obama appointed the first Hispanic to serve on the Supreme Court, Sonia Sotomayor, who was confirmed by a 68–31 vote. Elena Kagan's confirmation by a 63–37 vote in 2010 meant that three women were serving on the Court for the first time. As noted in the opener, the Senate denied President Obama the opportunity to fill the vacancy created by Justice Scalia's death. President Trump will decide on a new nominee early in 2017.

Battles over Lower-Court Judges The contentious battles between the president and the Senate over nominees to the federal bench and the Supreme Court have recently expanded to include nominees to the district and appeals courts. For much of the nation's history, the president did not play a very active role in the nomination process for district courts, instead deferring to the home-state senators of the president's party to suggest candidates—a norm called senatorial courtesy. If neither senator from the state was from the president's party, he would consult House members from his party and other high-ranking party members from the state for district court nominees. The president typically has shown more interest in appeals court nominations. The Justice Department plays a key role in screening candidates, but the local senators of the president's party remain active as well through the "blue slip" process: home-state senators record their support or opposition to nominees on blue slips of paper. Some committee chairs have allowed a single home-state senator to use the blue slip to veto a nominee, but others have not followed the process so strictly.

Recently the process has become much more contentious. While the confirmation rate for federal judges has been relatively stable in the past 35 years (between 80 and 90 percent), the average time to confirm nominees has increased dramatically. The average length of delay from nomination to confirmation has increased from a little over 50 days in the 1980s to over 200 days in recent years (see Figure 14.2 for data on noncontroversial nominations; when all nominations are included, the waits are even longer, especially for George W. Bush's nominees), and the situation has intensified. Democrats blocked 39 of President Bush's nominees between 2001 and 2009,[30] and Republicans have been returning the favor since then, blocking dozens of President Obama's nominees, which included employing a record number of filibusters of lower-court nominees. After the Senate blocked three nominees to the D.C. Court of Appeals, the second-most important court in the nation, Democrats responded in November 2013 by eliminating the filibuster on lower-court and executive branch nominations but not Supreme Court nominations (see the Take a Stand feature).[31] In mid-2016 there were 19 district court nominations that were supported by the Judiciary Committee with voice votes (so they were not controversial), and they had been waiting on the Senate floor for an average of 307 days (a median of 299 days).[32] The confirmation process has slowed to a trickle, with only 17 judges confirmed in the previous 16 months, compared with 45 for President George W. Bush in the comparable period, 40 for Clinton,

senatorial courtesy
A norm in the nomination of district court judges in which the president consults with his or her party's senators from the relevant state in choosing the nominee.

Senate hearings on Supreme Court nominations have been more conflictual since the 1960s. Although President Obama's nomination of Sonia Sotomayor was confirmed by a 68–31 vote in 2009, Senate Republicans challenged her to explain and defend her views on several issues.

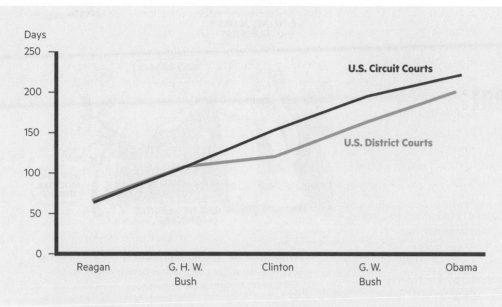

Source: Barry J. McMillion, "Length of Time from Nomination to Confirmation for 'Uncontroversial' U.S. Circuit and District Court Nominees: Detailed Analysis," Congressional Research Service, September 18, 2012, http://fas.org (accessed 6/25/14). "Uncontroversial" nominees are those who were reported from the Judiciary Committee by a voice vote or a unanimous vote and were confirmed by the Senate with a voice vote or no more than five votes in opposition.

FIGURE 14.2

Average Confirmation Delay for Uncontroversial Federal Court Nominations, 1981–2012

Since the 1980s, the length of time needed to confirm federal court nominations has increased dramatically. Why do you think this happened? Why does it matter?

and 82 for George H. W. Bush.[33] The partisan battle over nominations means that more than 10 percent of all federal judgeships remain vacant, which increases the workload for current judges and creates a growing backlog of cases.

Although there is no definitive answer as to how active the Senate should be in giving "advice and consent"—especially how much power a minority of 41 senators (the number of senators who, until recently, could block a nomination through agreeing to a filibuster; see Chapter 11) should have—it is clear that the Founders intended the Senate to play an active role. The first draft of the Constitution gave the Senate the sole power to appoint Supreme Court justices. However, the final version made appointment a shared power with the president. It was not expected that the Senate would compete with the president over whom to nominate, but it *was* assumed that the Senate would exercise independent judgment as to the suitability of the president's nominees.

"Why Should I Care?"

It is safe to assume that most Americans do not follow the details of battles over court nominations. However, these battles are every bit as important as the elections that *do* capture much attention. Unelected judges often serve for 20 or 30 years, much longer than the average member of Congress, and then have the power to strike down laws that Congress passes. These confirmation battles also support our argument that politics is conflictual and that we should expect it to be that way. The Founders certainly did not expect that the process would be free of politics or that the Senate would be an essentially passive and subordinate player in a nominally joint enterprise. Even George Washington had two of his nominations turned down by the Senate for political reasons. Therefore, politics will continue to play an important role in deciding who serves on the federal bench.

Advice and Consent: Detonating the Nuclear Option

When they have been the minority party in the Senate, both Democrats and Republicans have been willing to use the filibuster to block judicial nominees.

The use of the filibuster to stop presidential nominations to the federal courts has been the source of intense partisan battles in the past 20 years (until recently, 41 senators could stop action on any nomination through a filibuster). However, the positions in those battles are determined by which party controls the Senate and the presidency. Democrats who railed against Republican obstruction when Clinton was president used the same tactics when they were the minority party and George W. Bush was president. The tables were turned again as Republicans filibustered many of Obama's court nominees.

For nearly 10 years, there have been serious discussions about limiting the use of the filibuster for court nominations. When the Democrats blocked many of President George W. Bush's lower-court nominees, the Republican leadership in the Senate considered implementing the "nuclear option," which would have prevented filibusters on judicial nominations. (This plan gets its name because Democrats threatened to essentially shut down the Senate if they lost the use of the filibuster.) This crisis was defused when the "Gang of 14"—seven moderate Republicans and seven moderate Democrats—agreed to a compromise that preserved the Democrats' right to filibuster a nominee, but only in the most extreme cases. The compromise was honored for a while, but then Republicans obstructed many of President Obama's nominees. Between 1967 and 2013, there were 77 attempts to invoke cloture (to stop a filibuster) on a court nomination. More than half of those (41) came during Obama's presidency.[a]

The compromise dissolved in 2013 when Republicans refused to act on *any* nominee to the D.C. Court of Appeals, the second-most important court in the nation, in an effort to preserve the even partisan balance on that court. When Democrats were unable to stop filibusters on three nominees to that court, they detonated the nuclear option, so a simple majority of the Senate could stop a filibuster for lower-court nominations (but the filibuster was preserved for Supreme Court nominations). Republicans responded by forcing Democrats to invoke cloture on every judicial nomination and generally slowing down the process.

Abolish the filibuster for Supreme Court nominations.

For purposes of this exercise, we are going to do a thought experiment to try to strip partisanship from this issue and figure out if you support the principle of filibustering judicial nominations for the Supreme Court. President Donald Trump has nominated a strong conservative for the open seat on the Court, but Senate Democrats are filibustering the nomination in hopes of getting a more moderate nominee. There are 52 votes in favor of the nomination, but not the 60 needed to cut off the filibuster. Supporters of the nomination are urging Senate leadership to abolish the filibuster for Supreme Court nominations, arguing that the voters have spoken by electing President Trump and that he should be able to nominate who he wants to serve on the Supreme Court. The filibuster is overturning the will of the people.

Preserve the filibuster.

Supporters of the filibuster argue that the Constitution gives the Senate the power to "advise and consent" on presidential nominations and that senators should be able to have significant influence on who serves on the Supreme Court. Most senators who are opposing President Trump's nominee say that they would support a more moderate nominee (a conservative version of Merrick Garland). They argue that this is consistent with the Gang of 14 compromise.

Would you support the filibuster? Take a stand.

take a stand

1. What would you do in the situation just described? Why?

2. Now to complete the thought experiment, assume that Hillary Clinton had been elected and she has nominated a judicial liberal to fill the vacancy on the Court and Republicans are filibustering the nomination. Is your position still the same?

Access to the Supreme Court

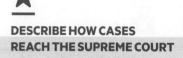

It is extremely difficult to have a case heard by the Supreme Court. Currently the Court hears about 1 percent of the cases submitted (76 of 7,509 cases in the most recent completed term). This section explains how the Court decides which cases to hear. When a case is submitted, the clerk of the Court assigns it a number and places it on the docket, which is the schedule of cases.

The Court's workload

Statistics on the Supreme Court's workload initially suggest that the size of the docket has increased dramatically since the 1970s (see Figure 14.3). However, a majority of cases are frivolous and are dismissed after limited review. The Court has become increasingly impatient with these frivolous petitions and has moved to prevent "frequent filers" from harassing the Court. One often-cited case involved Michael Sindram, who asked the Court to order the Maryland courts to remove a $35 traffic ticket from his record. Our favorite example concerned a wealthy drug dealer, Frederick W. Bauer, who was convicted on 10 counts of dealing drugs and petitioned the Court 12 times on various issues. The justices finally had enough and directed "the Clerk not to accept any further petitions for certiorari or petitions for extraordinary writs from Bauer in non-criminal matters" unless he paid his docketing fees. They concluded that the order will allow this Court to focus on "petitioners who have not abused our processes."[34]

Although the increase in workload is not as significant as it appears due to the high number of frivolous cases, another change is more important: the number of opinions issued by the Court has fallen by more than half in the past 20 years. The Court heard roughly 150 cases a year through the 1980s, but this number has fallen to only 75 to 85 cases in recent years (see Figure 14.3).[35] The change is even more dramatic when one considers that the Court has reduced the number of "summary decisions" it issues (cases that do not receive a full hearing but on which the Court rules on the merits of the case) from 150 a year in the 1970s to a handful today. The number of summary judgments declined when Congress gave the Court more control over its docket and dramatically reduced the number of cases that it was *required* to hear on appeal. However, there is no good explanation for why the Court issues half as many opinions as it used to, other than that the chief justices have decided that the Court shouldn't issue so many opinions. The 2016–2017 term is almost certain to show an additional drop in the number of cases heard because of the vacancy created by Justice Scalia's death. Because of the potential 4–4 deadlock, justices were unwilling to take on some cases until they were back to full strength.[36]

Rules of access

With the smaller number of cases being heard, it is even more important to understand how the Court decides which cases to consider. There are four paths that a case may take to get to the Supreme Court. First, Article III of the Constitution specifies that the Court has original jurisdiction in cases involving a foreign ambassador or foreign countries or cases in which a state is a party. As a practical matter, the Court shares jurisdiction with the lower courts on these issues.

In recent years, the Court has invoked original jurisdiction only in cases involving disputes between two or more states over territorial or natural resource issues. For example, New Jersey and New York had a disagreement about which state should

On rare occasions the Supreme Court serves as a court of original jurisdiction. One of those unusual times is when there is a dispute between two states, such as when the Court had to settle a disagreement between New York and New Jersey over Ellis Island.

control 24 acres of filled land that the federal government had added around Ellis Island. Another case involved a dispute between Kansas and Colorado over which state should have access to water from the Arkansas River (recent disputes often concern water rights).[37] If original jurisdiction is granted and there are factual issues to be resolved, the Court will appoint a "special master" (usually a retired federal judge) to hold a hearing, gather evidence, and make a recommendation to the Court. This process is necessary because the Supreme Court is not a trial court. In the history of our nation, only about 175 cases have made it to the Court through this path, an average of less than 1 per year, and typically these cases do not have any broader significance beyond the parties involved.[38]

The other three routes to the Court are all on appeal: as a matter of right (usually called on appeal), through certification (a process that has been used only five times since 1982), or through a writ of *certiorari*. Cases on appeal are those that Congress has determined to be so important that the Supreme Court must hear them. Before 1988, these cases constituted a larger share of the Court's docket and they included (1) cases in which a lower court declared a state or federal law unconstitutional and (2) cases in which a state court upheld a state law that had been challenged as unconstitutional under the U.S. Constitution. The Court currently has much more discretion on these cases, however; the only ones that the Court is still compelled to take on appeal are some voting rights and redistricting cases.

The third path is the most common: at least 95 percent of the cases in most sessions arrive through a **writ of *certiorari*** (from the Latin "to be informed"). In these cases, a litigant who lost in lower court can file a petition to the Supreme Court explaining why the Court should hear the case. If four justices agree, the case will get a full hearing (this is called, reasonably enough, the Rule of Four). This process may sound simple, but sifting through the 7,500 or so cases that the Court receives every year and deciding which 75 of them will be heard is daunting. Former justice William O. Douglas said that this winnowing process is "in many respects the most important and interesting of all our functions."[39]

The Court's criteria

How does the Court decide which cases to hear? Several factors come into play, including the specific characteristics of the case and the broader politics surrounding it.

writ of *certiorari*
The most common way for a case to reach the Supreme Court, in which at least four of the nine justices agree to hear a case that has reached them via an appeal from the losing party in a lower court's ruling.

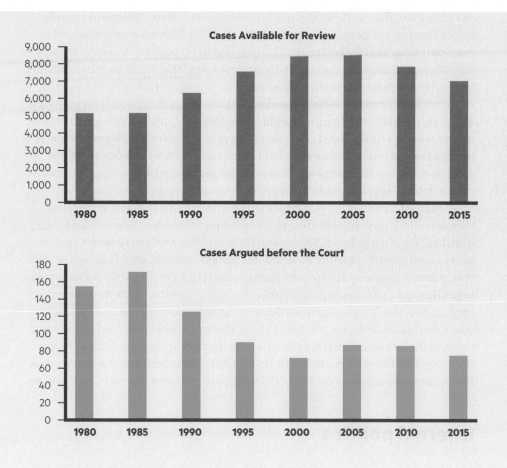

Cases Available for Review

Cases Argued before the Court

FIGURE 14.3

The Court Sees More Opportunities ... but Hears Fewer Cases

The Supreme Court's workload appears to be headed in two directions: the Court is receiving more cases but hearing fewer of them. What are the implications of having the Supreme Court hear fewer cases? Should something be done to try to get the Court to hear more cases?

Source: Data compiled from "Chief Justice's Year-End Reports on the Federal Judiciary," www.supremecourt.gov (accessed 5/24/16).

Although several criteria generally must be met before the Court will hear the case, justices still have leeway in defining the boundaries of these conditions.

Collusion, Standing, and Mootness First, there are the constitutional guidelines, which are sparse. The Constitution limits the Court to hearing actual "cases and controversies," which has been interpreted to mean that the Court cannot offer advisory opinions about hypothetical situations but must deal with actual cases. The term "actual controversy" also includes several other concepts that limit whether a case will be heard: collusion, standing, and mootness. Collusion simply means that the litigants in the case cannot want the same outcome and cannot be testing the law without an actual dispute between the two parties.[40]

Standing is the most general criterion; as we noted earlier, it means that the party bringing the case must have a personal stake in the outcome. The Court has discretion in defining standing: it may hear cases that it thinks are important even when the plaintiff may not have standing, as traditionally understood, or it may avoid hearing cases that may be politically sensitive on the grounds that there is no standing. For example, on the one hand, the Court decided several important racial redistricting cases even when the white plaintiffs had not suffered any personal harm by being in the black-majority districts.[41] On the other hand, in a politically sensitive case involving the Pledge of Allegiance and the First Amendment the Court decided not to hear the case, saying that the father of the student who brought the case did not have standing because he did not have sufficient custody over his daughter (he was divorced and the mother had primary custody).[42] Clearly, the Court was more eager to voice its views

mootness
The irrelevance of a case by the time it is received by a federal court, causing the Court to decline to hear the case.

on redistricting than on the Pledge of Allegiance, because it could have just as easily avoided hearing the former case by saying the plaintiffs did not have standing and ruled on the merits of the latter case. This is an important point to consider: the Court may often avoid hearing a controversial case based on a "threshold" issue like standing and not have to decide the merits of the case.

A controversy must still be relevant when the Court hears the case; mootness is when a case is irrelevant by the time it is brought before a federal court. Nonetheless, there have to be exceptions to this principle, because some types of cases would always be moot by the time they got to the Supreme Court. For example, exceptions have been made for abortion cases because a pregnancy lasts only nine months and for a case to get from district court to the appeals court to the Supreme Court always takes longer than that.

Thousands of cases every year meet the basic criteria. One very simple guideline eliminates the largest number of cases: if a case does not involve a "substantial federal question," it will not be heard. This essentially means that the Court does not have to hear a case if the justices do not think the case is important enough. Of course, the "federal" part of this standard is also important: if a case is governed by state law rather than federal law, the Court would decline to hear the case unless there are constitutional implications. The "political question doctrine," discussed later, is another basis upon which the Court may decide not to hear a case. This still leaves about 20 to 30 percent of the cases that are winnowed to the final list with the more specific guidance of Rule 10 in the Supreme Court rules (see Nuts & Bolts 14.2). Of the criteria listed in Rule 10, conflict between appeals court decisions is most likely to produce a Supreme Court hearing.

Internal politics

Not much is known about the actual discussions that determine which cases will be heard by the Court. The justices meet in conference with no staff or clerks. Leaks are rare, but a few insider accounts and the papers of retired justices provide some insights to the process. First, since the late 1970s most justices have used a cert pool, whereby their law clerks take a first cut at the cases (law clerks to the justices are top graduates of elite law schools who help justices with background research at several stages of the process). Clerks write joint memos about groups of cases, providing their recommendations about which cases should be heard. The ultimate decisions are up to the justices, but clerks have significant power to help shape the agenda.

cert pool
A system initiated in the Supreme Court in the 1970s in which law clerks screen cases that come to the Supreme Court and recommend to the justices which cases should be heard.

NUTS & BOLTS 14.2

Deciding to Hear a Case in the Supreme Court

Rule 10 of the *Rules of the U.S. Supreme Court* says that a case is more likely to be heard when

- there is conflict between appeals court opinions or between a state supreme court opinion and another state supreme court on an important federal question,
- there is conflict between a federal appeals court and a state supreme court on an important federal question,
- a lower-court decision has "departed from the accepted and usual course of judicial proceedings,"
- a state supreme court or appeals court has ruled on a substantial federal question that has not yet been addressed by the Court, or
- a state supreme court or appeals court ruling conflicts with Supreme Court precedent.

Rule 10 also states that *certiorari* is unlikely to be granted when "the asserted error consists of erroneous factual findings or the misapplication of a properly stated rule of law."

Source: U.S. Supreme Court, *Rules of the U.S. Supreme Court*, adopted April 19, 2013, effective July 1, 2013 (accessed 5/27/16).

Second, the chief justice has an important agenda-setting power: he or she decides the "discuss list" for a given day. Any justice can add a case to the list, but there is no systematic evidence on how often this happens. Only 20 to 30 percent of the cases are discussed in conference, which means that about three-quarters of the cases that are submitted to the Supreme Court are never even discussed by the Court. In most cases, this is justified because of the high proportion of frivolous suits submitted to the Court.[43]

Many factors outside the legal requirements or internal processes of the Court influence access to the Court and which cases will be heard. Cases that have generated a lot of activity from interest groups or other governmental parties, such as the solicitor general, are more likely to be heard. The **solicitor general** is a presidential appointee who works in the Justice Department and supervises the litigation of the executive branch. In cases in which the federal government is a party, the solicitor general or someone else from that office will represent the government in court. The Court accepts about 70 to 80 percent of cases in which the U.S. government is a party compared with about 1 percent overall.[44]

Even with these influences, the Court has a great deal of discretion as to which cases it hears. Well-established practices such as standing and mootness may be ignored (or modified) if the Court wants to hear a specific case. However, one final point is important: although the justices may pick and choose their cases, they cannot set their own agenda. They can select only from the cases that come to them.

solicitor general
A presidential appointee in the Justice Department who conducts all litigation on behalf of the federal government before the Supreme Court and supervises litigation in the federal appellate courts.

Hearing cases before the Supreme Court

★

DESCRIBE THE SUPREME COURT'S PROCEDURES FOR HEARING A CASE

A surprisingly small proportion of the Court's time is actually spent hearing cases—only about 37 days per term. The Court is in session from the first Monday in October through the end of June. It hears cases on Mondays through Wednesdays in alternating two-week cycles in which it is in session from 10 A.M. to 3 P.M., with a one-hour break for lunch. In the other two weeks of the cycle when it is not in session, justices review briefs, write opinions, and sift through the next batch of petitions. On most Fridays when the Court is in session, the justices meet in conference to discuss cases that have been argued and decide which cases they will hear. Opinions are released throughout the term, but the bulk of them come in May and June.[45]

The Court is in recess from July through September. Justices may take some vacation, but they mostly use the time for study, reading, writing, and preparing for the next term. During the summer, the Court also considers emergency petitions (such as stays of execution) and occasionally hears important cases. For example, on September 9, 2009 (nearly a month before the fall session started), the Court heard a challenge to the Bipartisan Campaign Reform Act, more commonly known as the McCain-Feingold Act after its two principal sponsors. Congress urged the Court to give the law a speedy review, given its importance for the upcoming 2010 elections. In the blockbuster case *Citizens United v. Federal Election Commission*, the Supreme Court decided that independent spending in campaigns by corporations and labor unions is protected by the First Amendment.

Briefs

During the regular sessions, the Court follows rigidly set routines. The justices prepare for a case by reading the briefs that both parties submit. Because the Supreme

Court hears only appeals, it does not call witnesses or gather new evidence. Instead, in structured briefs of no more than 50 pages the parties present their arguments about why they either support the lower-court decision or believe the case was improperly decided. Interest groups often submit **amicus curiae** ("friend of the court") briefs that convey their opinions to the Court; in fact, 85 percent of cases before the Supreme Court have at least one amicus brief.[46] The federal government also files amicus briefs on important issues such as school busing, school prayer, abortion, reapportionment of legislative districts, job discrimination against women and minorities, and affirmative action in higher education.

It is difficult to determine the impact of amicus briefs on the outcome of a case, but those that are filed early in the process increase the chances that the case will be heard.[47] Given the limited information that justices have about any given case, interest group involvement can be a strong signal about the importance of a case.

Oral argument

Once the briefs are filed and have been reviewed by the justices, cases are scheduled for **oral arguments**. Except in unusual circumstances, each case gets one hour, which is divided evenly between the two parties. In especially important cases, extra time may be granted (for example, the Obamacare case had six hours of oral argument, which was the most since a VRA case in 1966).[48] Usually there is only one lawyer for each side who presents the case, but parties who have filed amicus briefs may participate if their arguments "would provide assistance to the Court not otherwise available." Given the tight time pressures, the Court is usually unwilling to extend the allotted time to allow "friends of the court" to testify.[49]

The Court is strict about its time limits and uses a system of three lights to show the lawyers how much of their allotted 30 minutes is left. A green light goes on when the speaker's time begins, a white light provides a five-minute warning, and a red light means to stop. Most textbooks cite well-known examples of justices cutting people off in midsentence or walking out of the courtroom as the lawyer drones on. One source implies that these anecdotes are generally revealing of Court procedure, saying:

Cameras are not allowed in the Supreme Court, so artists' sketches are the only images of oral arguments. Depicted here is the oral argument in the 2016 case concerning the affirmative action policy at the University of Texas, Austin.

"Anecdotes probably tell as much about the proceeding of the Court during oral argument as does any careful study of the rules and procedures."[50]

However, having a preference for "careful study" over anecdotes, we were curious about how common it was for justices to strictly impose the time limits. Initially, we examined 42 cases from the 2004–2005 term, using the online transcripts on the Court's website.[51] We found that most lawyers did not use all their allotted time, with 62 percent of the cases coming in under 60 minutes, 17 percent at exactly an hour, and 21 percent at over an hour. One-sixth of the lawyers still had at least five minutes left on the clock. We found only two instances in which a justice cut someone off in midsentence after the person had gone over the half-hour limit. We updated the analysis for the Roberts Court, examining all 74 cases argued in the 2009 calendar year. Roberts was not much of a stickler for adhering to the time limits: nearly 60 percent of oral arguments went past their allotted time (most by only a minute or two), 13.5 percent were exactly one hour, and 27 percent were under an hour. Again, only 2 of the 74 oral arguments ended with an attorney being cut off in midsentence by the chief justice. Thus, while the Court tries to encourage attorneys to stay within the time limits, it is not as draconian as some anecdotes imply.

Some lawyers may not use all of their time because their train of thought is interrupted by aggressive questioning. Transcripts reveal that justices jump in with questions almost immediately and some attorneys never regain their footing. The frequency and pointedness of the questions vary by justice, with Justices Breyer, Roberts, and Sotomayor being the most aggressive on the current Court, while Justice Thomas went more than 10 years without asking a single question. Justice Thomas broke his streak in 2016, perhaps feeling the need to fill the void created by the death of Justice Scalia.[52] Cameras are not allowed in the courtroom, so most Americans have never seen the Court in action—although a small live audience is admitted every morning the Court is in session. If you are curious about oral arguments, audio recordings of every case since 1995 are available at www.oyez.org.

Conference

After oral arguments, the justices meet in conference to discuss and then vote on the cases. As with the initial conferences, these meetings are conducted in secret. We know, based on notes in the personal papers of retired justices, that the conferences are orderly and structured but can become quite heated. The justices take turns discussing the cases and outlining the reasons for their positions. Justice Thurgood Marshall described the decision-making process in conference and the need for secrecy as

> a continuing conversation among nine distinct individuals on dozens of issues simultaneously. The exchanges are serious, sometimes scholarly, occasionally brash and personalized, but generally well-reasoned and most often cast in understated, genteel language. . . . In other cases, a majority of justices start down one path, only to reverse direction. . . . This is the kind of internal debate that the justices have argued should remain confidential, taking the position that only their final opinions have legal authority. They have expressed concern that premature disclosure of their private debates and doubts may undermine the Court's credibility and inhibit their exchange of ideas.[53]

Opinion writing

After the justices indicate how they are likely to vote on a case, if the chief justice is in the majority (which is most of the time) the chief justice decides who will write the majority opinion. For example, Warren Burger assigned 1,891 of the 2,201 opinions (about 86 percent) when he was chief justice in the 1970s and 1980s.[54] Otherwise, the most senior justice in the majority assigns the opinion. Many considerations determine how a case will be assigned. First, the chief justice will try to ensure the smooth operation of the Court. Along these lines, in 1989 Chief Justice Rehnquist announced a change in how he assigned opinions. In his first three terms he tried to give each justice the same number of cases, but he recognized that "this policy does not take into consideration the difficulty of the opinion assigned or the amount of work that the 'assignee' may currently have backed up in his chambers. . . . It only makes sense in the assignment of additional work to give some preference to those who are 'current' with respect to past work."[55] A second factor is the justices' individual areas of expertise. For example, Justice Harry Blackmun had developed expertise in medical law when he was in private practice. This experience played a role in Chief Justice Burger's decision to assign Blackmun the majority opinion in the landmark abortion decision *Roe v. Wade* (1973). Likewise, Justice Sandra Day O'Connor developed expertise in racial redistricting cases and authored most of those decisions in the 1990s.

Strategy on the Court Another factor in how opinions are assigned is more strategic: it includes the Court's external relations, internal relations, and the personal policy goals of the opinion assigner. The Court must be sensitive to how others might respond to its decisions because it must rely on the other branches of government to enforce its decisions. One famous example of this consideration in an opinion assignment came in a case from the 1940s that struck down a practice that had prevented African Americans from voting in Democratic primaries.[56] Originally, the opinion was assigned to Justice Felix Frankfurter, but Justice Robert Jackson wrote a memo suggesting that it might be unwise to have a liberal, politically independent Jew from the Northeast write an opinion that was sure to be controversial in the South. Chief Justice Harlan Fiske Stone agreed and reassigned the opinion to Justice Stanley Reed, a Protestant and Democrat from Kentucky.[57] It may not seem that the Court is sensitive to public opinion,

If he or she is in the majority, the chief justice decides who will write the majority opinion. Otherwise, the most senior justice in the majority makes the assignment. Since being named chief justice in 2005, John Roberts has spread opinion-writing duties fairly evenly among the justices.

but these kinds of considerations happen fairly frequently in important cases. Internal considerations occasionally cause justices to vote strategically—differently from the justice's sincere preference—in order to be in the majority so that the justice can assign the opinion (often to himself or herself) as the most senior justice in the majority.

Justices may also assign opinions to help achieve their personal policy goals. The most obvious strategy is for the chief justice to assign opinions to justices who are closest to his position. Obviously, this practice is constrained by the first point—ensuring the smooth operation of the Court. If the chief justice assigned all the opinions to the justices who are closest to him ideologically, then justices with other ideological leanings would get a chance to write opinions only in the 15 to 20 percent of cases in which the chief is in the minority. That wouldn't work. Charles Hughes, chief justice from 1930 to 1941, sometimes assigned opinions on liberal decisions to conservative justices and cases with conservative outcomes to liberal justices in order to downplay the importance of ideology on the Court.[58]

After the opinions are assigned, the justices work on writing a draft opinion. Law clerks typically help with this process. Some justices insist on writing all of their opinions, whereas others allow a clerk to write the first draft. The drafts are circulated to the other justices for comment and reactions. Some bargaining may occur, in which a justice says he or she will withdraw support unless a provision is changed. Justices may join the majority opinion, may write a separate concurring opinion, or may dissent (see Nuts & Bolts 14.3 for details on the types of opinions).

Dissents Two final points about the process of writing and issuing opinions are important. First, until 1940, there was a premium placed on unanimous decisions. John Marshall, who was chief justice from 1800 to 1835, started this practice. Through the 1930s, about 80 to 90 percent of decisions were unanimous. This changed dramatically in the 1940s, when most cases had at least one dissent. In recent decades, about two-thirds of cases have had a dissent.[59] However, in the 2013–2014 term two-thirds of the cases were unanimous, the highest proportion since at least 1946. That proportion fell to 46 percent in the 2015–2016 term.[60] Second, dissents serve an important purpose. Not only do they allow the minority view to be expressed, but they also often

> "
> So that's the dissenter's hope: that they are writing not for today but for tomorrow.
> —Justice Ruth Bader Ginsburg

Types of Supreme Court Decisions

- **Majority opinion:** The core decision of the Court that must be agreed upon by at least five justices. The majority opinion presents the legal reasoning for the Court's decision.

- **Concurring opinion:** Written by a justice who agrees with the outcome of the case but not with part of the legal reasoning. Concurring opinions may be joined by other justices. A justice may sign on to the majority opinion and write a separate concurring opinion.

- **Plurality opinion:** Occurs when a majority cannot agree on the legal reasoning in a case. The plurality opinion is the one that has the most agreement (usually three or four justices). Because of the fractured nature of these opinions, they typically are not viewed as having as much clout as majority opinions.

- **Dissent:** Submitted by a justice who disagrees with the outcome of the case. Other justices can sign on to a dissent or write their own, so there can be as many as four dissents. Justices can also sign on to part of a dissent but not the entire opinion.

- **Per curiam (Latin for "by the court") opinion:** An unsigned opinion of the Court or a decision written by the entire Court. However, this is not the same as a unanimous decision that is signed by the entire Court. Per curiam opinions are usually very short opinions on noncontroversial issues, but not always. For example, *Bush v. Gore*, which decided the outcome of the 2000 presidential election, was a per curiam opinion. Per curiam decisions may also have dissents.

provide the basis for reversing a poorly reasoned case. When justices strongly oppose the majority opinion, they may take the unusual step of reading a portion of the dissent from the bench.

The process of hearing cases before the Court, including the written briefs, oral arguments, discussions in conference, and opinion assignment, is a very political one. As discussed in the chapter opener, it may be disturbing to think of the Court as a political institution that bargains and considers external forces like public opinion. Despite not having to answer to voters, justices are still sensitive to a broad range of considerations in hearing cases.

★

ANALYZE THE FACTORS THAT INFLUENCE SUPREME COURT DECISIONS

Supreme Court decision making

Judicial decision making is influenced by many different factors, but the two main categories are *legal* and *political*. Legal factors include the precedents of earlier cases and norms that justices must follow the language of the Constitution. Political influences include the justices' preferences or ideologies, their stances on whether the Court should take a restrained or activist role with respect to the elected branches, and external factors such as public opinion and interest group involvement. Some scholars argue that all Court behavior is political and that the use of legal factors is just a smoke screen for hiding personal preferences.

Legal factors

Those who put forward the legal view usually present their position in normative terms—that is, justices *should* follow precedent and the words of the Constitution. Advocates of this view recognize that justices often stray from these legal norms, but these critics see the interjection of personal preferences as a harmful politicization of the courts. While legal factors may be used as justification for political positions on the Court, they also independently influence judicial decision making on a broad range of cases.

Precedent The most basic legal factor is precedent, discussed earlier. Precedent does not determine the outcome of any given case, because every case has a range of precedents that can serve to justify a justice's decision. The "easy" cases, in which settled law makes the outcome obvious, are less likely to be heard by the Court because of the justices' desire to focus on the more controversial areas of unsettled law or when there is conflict between lower courts' decisions. However, there are areas of the law—such as free speech, the death penalty, and search and seizure—in which precedent is an important explanation for how the justices decide a case.

The Language of the Constitution The various perspectives that emphasize the language of the Constitution all fall under the heading of **strict construction**. The most basic of these is the literalist view of the Constitution. Sometimes this view is called a textualist position because it sees the text of the document as determining the outcome

strict construction
A way of interpreting the Constitution based on its language alone.

of any given case. Literalists argue that justices need to look no further than the actual words of the Constitution.

Justice Hugo Black was one of the most famous advocates of the literalist position. When the First Amendment says that "Congress shall make no law ... abridging the freedom of speech," that literally means *no* law. Justice Black said, "My view is, without deviation, without exception, without any ifs, buts, or whereases, that freedom of speech means that government shall not do anything to people ... either for the views they have or the views they express or the words they speak or write."[61] While that may be clear enough with regard to political speech, how about pornography, Internet speech, or symbolic speech, such as burning an American flag or wearing an armband to protest the Vietnam War? A literal interpretation of the Constitution does not necessarily help determine whether these forms of speech should be restricted. (Indeed, Black was one of the two dissenters in a case that upheld students' right to wear armbands as a form of symbolic speech. Black believed that school officials should be allowed to decide whether a symbolic protest would be too disruptive in the classroom and argued that only spoken and written speech should be afforded the strongest protection of the First Amendment. So much for "without deviation, without exception" concerning restricting expression of the "views ... [people] have"!)

Critics of strict construction also point out that the Constitution is silent on many important points (such as a right to privacy) and could not have anticipated the many legal implications of changes in technology in the twentieth and twenty-first centuries, such as eavesdropping devices, cloning, and the Internet. Also, although the language

Mary Beth Tinker and two other students in the Des Moines, Iowa, public schools were suspended for wearing armbands to protest the Vietnam War. The Supreme Court ruled that the First Amendment protected symbolic political speech, even in public schools. Mary Beth is shown here with her mother at the trial.

original intent
The theory that justices should surmise the intentions of the Founders when the language of the Constitution is unclear.

of the First Amendment is relatively clear when it comes to political speech, other equally important words of the Constitution such as "necessary and proper," "executive power," "equal protection," and "due process" are open-ended and vague. Some strict constructionists respond by arguing that, if the words of the Constitution are not clear, the justices should be guided by what the Founders *intended*, a perspective called the original intent or originalist perspective. Clarence Thomas is the current justice who is most influenced by this view, especially on issues of federalism.

Justice Antonin Scalia had a similar view, arguing that the text of the Constitution should be closely followed and, if the text is ambiguous, justices should figure out what the words generally meant to people at the time they were written. This view led Scalia to some unpopular positions, such as his view that the Sixth Amendment provision that "in all criminal prosecutions the accused shall enjoy the right ... to be confronted with the witnesses against him" applies even in the case of an accused child molester. The majority of the Court disagreed and held that it was acceptable to have the child testify in front of the prosecutor and defense attorney, with the judge, the jury, and the accused viewing from another room over closed-circuit television because of the potential trauma the child would experience by having to confront the defendant face-to-face.[62]

living Constitution
A way of interpreting the Constitution that takes into account evolving national attitudes and circumstances rather than the text alone.

Critics of the strict constructionist view are often described as supporting a living Constitution perspective on the document (see Chapter 2). They argue that originalism or other versions of strict construction can "make a nation the prisoner of its past, and reject any constitutional development save constitutional amendment."[63] If the justices are bound to follow the literal words of the Constitution, *with the meaning they had when the document was written*, we certainly could be legally frozen in time. The option of amending the Constitution is a long and difficult process, so that is not always a viable way for the Constitution to reflect changing norms and values. Justice William Brennan, a critic of originalism, also argued it was "arrogance cloaked in humility" to presume to know what the framers intended. According to this view, interpreting the Constitution is always somewhat subjective and it is misleading to claim otherwise.[64]

> "
>
> **The words of the Constitution ... are so unrestricted by their intrinsic meaning or by their history or by tradition or by prior decisions that they leave the individual Justice free, if indeed they do not compel him, to gather meaning not from reading the Constitution but from reading life.**
>
> —Justice Felix Frankfurter

Political factors

The living Constitution perspective points to the second set of influences on Supreme Court decision making: political factors. Indeed, many people are uncomfortable thinking about the Court in political terms and prefer to think of the image of "blind justice," in which constitutional principles are fairly applied. However, political influences are clearly evident in the Court—maybe less than in Congress or the presidency, but they are certainly present. This means that the courts respond to and shape politics in ways that often involve compromise, both within the courts themselves and in the broader political system.

attitudinalist approach
A way of understanding decisions of the Supreme Court based on the political ideologies of the justices.

Political Ideology and Attitudes The most important political factor is the justices' ideology or attitudes about various issues (this is often called the attitudinalist approach to understanding Supreme Court decision making). Liberal judges are strong defenders of individual civil liberties (including defendants' rights), tend to be pro-choice on abortion, support regulatory policy to protect the environment and workers, support national intervention in the states, and favor race-conscious policies such as affirmative action. Conservative judges favor state regulation of private conduct (especially on moral issues), support prosecutors over defendants, tend to be pro-life on abortion, and support the free market and property rights over the environment and workers, states' rights over national intervention, and a color-blind policy on race. See the What Do the Numbers Say? feature for more on how the balance between liberal and conservative judges has shifted.

The Shifting Ideological Balance of the Court

After Justice Antonin Scalia died in early 2016, the open seat on the Supreme Court became a major issue in the presidential election. Why? As this figure shows, when justices are replaced the ideological shifts can be quite large (as when Clarence Thomas replaced Thurgood Marshall) or nonexistent (as when Sonia Sotomayor replaced David Souter). Many people said that replacing Scalia would drastically alter the ideological makeup of the Court, given the 4–4 split on the Court between liberal and conservative justices. What do the numbers say?

Arrows represent a shift in ideology when a vacancy is filled on the Court, either to a more conservative or more liberal justice.

Each dot represents the ideology of the incoming and outgoing justice.

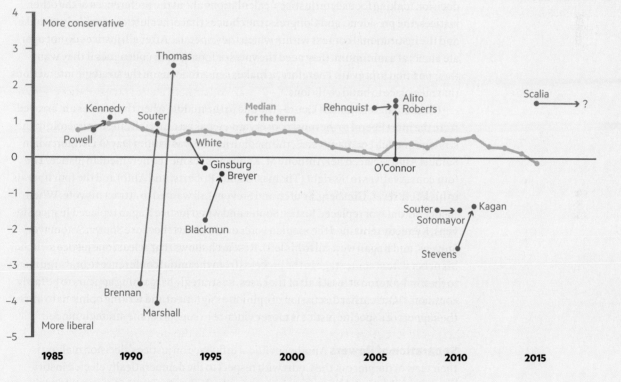

Think about it

- Look at where Scalia is on the ideological scale. If Hillary Clinton had been elected, where would Scalia's dot have likely moved?
- President Trump is expected to nominate a conservative, similar to Scalia. What will happen to the median justice in that case?
- Will the ideological shift of the Court's median be large, small or stay the same? Why?

Source: The Upshot, "A Supreme Court with Merrick Garland Would Be the Most Liberal in Decades," www.nytimes.com (accessed 8/26/16).

These are, of course, just general tendencies. However, they do provide a strong basis for explaining patterns of decisions, especially on some types of cases. For example, there were dramatic differences in the chief justices' rulings on civil liberties cases from 1953 to 2001: Earl Warren took the liberal position on 79 percent of the 771 cases he participated in, Warren Burger took the liberal position on 30 percent of 1,429 cases, and William Rehnquist took the liberal position on only 22 percent of his 2,127 cases.[65] If justices were neutrally applying the law, there would not be such dramatic differences.

Proponents of the attitudinalist view also argue that justices who *claim* to be strict constructionists or originalists are really driven by ideology because they selectively use the text of the Constitution. For example, Justice Thomas voted against the University of Michigan's affirmative action program without considering whether the authors of the Fourteenth Amendment supported the practice (the historical record shows that they supported similar policies for the newly freed slaves). Therefore, if Justice Thomas had been true to his originalist perspective he would have supported affirmative action, but his ideology led him to oppose the policy. The example of Hugo Black's contradictory position on free speech rights cited earlier demonstrates that a liberal textualist view may also be inconsistently applied.

The Strategic Model A strategic approach to understanding Supreme Court decision making focuses on justices' calculations about the preferences of the other justices, the president, and Congress; the choices that other justices are likely to make; and the institutional context within which they operate. After all, justices do not operate alone: at a minimum, they need the votes of four of their colleagues if they want their position to prevail. Therefore, it makes sense to focus on the strategic interactions that take place to build coalitions.

The median voter on the Court—the one in the middle when the justices are arrayed from the most liberal to the most conservative—has an especially influential role in the strategic model. For many years, the median justice was Sandra Day O'Connor; when Samuel Alito replaced her Anthony M. Kennedy became the new median justice. The four conservatives to his right (Thomas, Scalia, Roberts, and Alito) and the four liberals to his left (Breyer, Ginsberg, Souter, and Stevens) all wanted to attract his vote. When Justice Sotomayor replaced Justice Souter and when Justice Kagan replaced Justice Stevens, Kennedy remained the median voter on the Court (because Souter, Sotomayor, Stevens, and Kagan were all to his left). Research shows that at least one justice switches his or her vote at some stage in the process (from the initial conference to oral arguments to the final vote) on at least half of the cases, so strategic bargaining appears to be fairly common.[66] Our earlier discussion of opinion assignment and writing opinions to attract the support of a specific justice is more evidence in support of the strategic model.

Separation of Powers Another political influence on justices' decision making is their view of the place of the Court with respect to the democratically elected institutions (Congress and the president). Specifically, do they favor an activist or a restrained role for the Court? Advocates of **judicial restraint** argue that judges should defer to the elected branches and not strike down their laws or other actions. In contrast, advocates of **judicial activism** argue that the Court must play an active role in interpreting the Constitution to protect minority rights even if it means overturning the actions of the elected branches. Yet another approach says that these normative arguments about how restraint or activism ought to work don't really matter because the Court usually follows public opinion and rarely plays a lead role in promoting policy change. One scholar found that three-fifths to two-thirds of Supreme Court decisions are consistent with public opinion when the public has a clear preference on an issue.[67] Nonetheless, there are plenty of examples of when the Court has stood up for unpopular views, such as banning prayer in schools, allowing flag burning, and protecting criminal defendants' rights.

judicial restraint
The idea that the Supreme Court should defer to the democratically elected executive and legislative branches of government rather than contradicting existing laws.

judicial activism
The idea that the Supreme Court should assert its interpretation of the law even if it overrules the elected executive and legislative branches of government.

Judicial Activism Often assessments of the Court's role vary with the views of a specific line of cases. A political conservative may favor activist decisions striking down environmental laws or workplace regulations but oppose activist decisions that defend flag burning or defendants' rights. Political liberals may do the opposite—calling for judicial restraint on the first set of cases but for judicial activism to protect civil liberties. The term "activist judges" often appears in the media. Sometimes the media mistakenly assert that liberal justices are more activist than conservative justices. In fact, though, that is not always the case. The current Court is quite conservative, but it is also activist.[68] Two conservative justices, Kennedy and Thomas, have voted to overturn laws passed by Congress 93 percent and 81 percent of the time, respectively, whereas two of the most liberal justices, Breyer and Ginsburg, have taken the activist position in only 42 percent and 48 percent of the cases.[69] The 1930s Court that struck down much of the New Deal legislation was also conservative and activist, but the Warren Court of the late 1950s and early 1960s was liberal and activist.

In a survey taken about the judicial branch, most respondents were unable to name any Supreme Court justices. Just so you are not in danger of falling into that category, as of the fall of 2016 the justices were (front row, left to right) Clarence Thomas, a blank space representing the justice who will replace Antonin Scalia, John G. Roberts Jr. (chief justice), Anthony M. Kennedy, Ruth Bader Ginsburg, (standing, left to right) Sonia Sotomayor, Stephen Breyer, Samuel Alito Jr., and Elena Kagan.

A prominent legal journalist observed that the way the popular media describe activism and restraint typically boils down to ideology: if you like a decision, it is restrained; if you do not like a decision, it is activist. For example, *Bush v. Gore*, the decision that decided the outcome of the 2000 presidential election, shows that "most conservatives tie themselves in knots to defend judicial activism when they like the results and to denounce it when they do not. As the reactions to *Lawrence* [the gay sex case discussed in Chapter 4] and, earlier, *Roe* [the landmark abortion case] have shown, liberals have been no less selective in their outrage at judicial adventurousness."[70] However, there are instances in which restraint reflects more than ideology and preferences. Justice O'Connor, for example, took restrained positions on abortion and affirmative action, despite her personal views against these policies. And in a more recent example of judicial restraint, shown in the health care reform decision, Chief Justice Roberts said that some decisions "are entrusted to our nation's elected leaders, who can be thrown out of office if the people disagree with them." However, despite providing the pivotal vote to uphold central provisions of the law, he made his personal views against the law clear. "It is not our job," he said, "to protect the people from the consequences of their political choices."[71]

It is important to define activism and restraint in terms of the Court's role in our nation's system of separated powers: Does it check the elected branches by overturning their decisions through judicial review? If so, the Court has taken an activist position.

Outside Influences: Interest Groups and Public Opinion Finally, there are external influences on the Court, such as public opinion and interest groups. We have already talked about the role of interest groups in filing amicus briefs. This is the only avenue of influence open to interest groups; other tactics such as lobbying and fund-raising are either inappropriate or irrelevant (because justices are not elected). The role of public opinion is more complex. Obviously, justices do not consult public opinion polls the way elected officials do. However, the Court expresses the public's preferences in several indirect ways.

The first was most colorfully expressed by Mr. Dooley, a fictional Irish-American bartender whom newspaper satirist Finley Peter Dunne created in 1898. Mr. Dooley offered keen insights on politics and general social criticism, including this gem on the relationship between the Supreme Court and the public: "th' supreme coort always follows th' iliction returns."[72] That is, the public elects the president and the Senate, who nominate and confirm the justices. Therefore, sooner or later, the Court should reflect the views of the public. Subsequent work by political scientists has confirmed this to be largely the case,[73] especially in recent years when Supreme Court nominations have become more political and more important to the public.[74]

The second mechanism through which public opinion may influence the Court is more direct: when the public has a clear position on an issue that is before the Court, the Court tends to agree with the public. One study found that the "public mood" and Court opinions correlated very highly between 1956 and 1981, but their association was weaker through the rest of the 1980s.[75] More recent work demonstrates that the Court is constrained by public opinion, in part because they may fear resistance to implementing an unpopular decision.[76]

Several high-profile examples support the idea that the Court is sensitive to public opinion: the Court's switch during the New Deal in the 1930s to support Roosevelt's policy agenda after standing in the way for four years, giving in to wartime opinion to support the internment of Japanese Americans during World War II, limiting an accused child molester's right to confront his accuser in a courtroom, and declaring that laws limiting sex between consenting gay adults were unconstitutional. In each of these cases, the justices reflected the current public opinion of the nation rather than a strict reading of the Constitution or the Founders' intent.

Sometimes the Court may shift its views to reflect *international* opinion. The most recent example struck down the death penalty for minors in 12 states. Ruling by a 5–4 vote that the execution of 16- or 17-year-olds violated the Eighth Amendment's prohibition against "cruel and unusual punishments," the majority opinion overturned a 1989 case and said that the new decision was necessary to reflect the "evolving standards of decency" concerning the definition of "cruel and unusual punishments." Justice Kennedy, who had voted on the other side of this issue 16 years earlier, wrote: "It is fair to say that the United States now stands alone in a world that has turned its face against the juvenile death penalty." Justice Kennedy said that although the Court was not obligated to follow foreign developments, "it is proper that we acknowledge the overwhelming weight of international opinion" for its "respected and significant confirmation for our own conclusions."[77] This explicit recognition of the role of public opinion firmly placed a majority of the Court on the side of the "living Constitution" perspective on this issue, while rejecting the strict constructionist view of the dissenters.

Another way that the Court may consider the public mood is to shift the timing of a decision. The best example here is the landmark school desegregation case,

> The Supreme Court, of course, has the responsibility of ensuring that our government never oversteps its proper bounds or violates the rights of individuals. But the Court must also recognize the limits on itself and respect the choices made by the American people.
> —Justice Elena Kagan

Brown v. Board of Education (1954), that the Court sat on for more than two years—until after the 1952 presidential election—because it didn't think the public was ready for its bombshell ruling.[78] Others have argued that the Court rarely *changes* its views to reflect public opinion,[79] but at a minimum the evidence supports the notion that the Court is usually in step with the public.

Shouldn't the Court be neutrally applying the words of the Constitution to the cases it hears? While a normatively appealing view, this textualist view ignores many of the realities of how the Court actually operates. Justices often let their own political views shape their decisions, but more neutral forces such as precedent and deferring to the elected branches also play important roles. Having a realistic understanding of the various factors that go into a justice's decision explains why the Court strikes down some laws and upholds others.

"Why Should I Care?"

★

ASSESS THE SUPREME COURT'S POWER IN THE POLITICAL SYSTEM

The role of the Court in our political system

We conclude with the topic addressed early in the chapter—the place of the Court within the political system. Is the Court the "weakest branch"? As Alexander Hamilton pointed out, the Court has "neither the power of the purse nor the sword." Therefore, it is not clear how it can enforce decisions. In some instances the Court can force its views on the other branches; in other cases it needs their support to enforce its decisions.

Compliance and implementation

To gain compliance with its decisions, the Court can rely only on its reputation and on the actions of Congress and the president to back them up. If the other branches don't support the Court, there isn't much it can do. The Court's lack of enforcement power is especially evident when a ruling applies broadly to millions of people who care deeply about the issue. Consider school prayer, which still exists in hundreds of public schools nationwide despite having been ruled unconstitutional more than 50 years ago. It is impossible to enforce the ban unless someone in a school complains and is willing to bring a lawsuit.

In most cases that involve a broad policy, the Court depends on the president for enforcement. After *Brown v. Board of Education* (1954), the landmark school desegregation case, presidents Eisenhower and Kennedy had to send in federal troops to desegregate public schools and universities. However, presidential foot-dragging can have a big impact on how the law is enforced. President Nixon attempted to lessen the impact of a school busing decision in 1971 that forced the integration of public schools by interpreting it very narrowly. Republican presidents who oppose abortion have limited the scope of *Roe v. Wade*, which legalized abortion in 1973, by denying federal support for abortions for Medicaid recipients, banning abortions on military bases, and preventing doctors from mentioning abortion as an option during pregnancy counseling. The Court must rely on its reputation and prestige to compel the president and Congress not to stray too far from its decisions.

High school students in Maize, Kansas, join hands around a flagpole at the annual nationwide event calling Christian youth to pre-class schoolyard prayer at the start of the new school year. Enforcing the prohibition of school prayer and drawing the line between permissible and impermissible prayer have both been difficult for the Court.

Relations with the other branches

Relations with the other branches of government may become strained when the Court rules on fundamental questions about institutional power. In some cases, the other branches may fight back; in others, the Court may exercise self-restraint and not get involved.

Resistance from the Other Branches The president and Congress often fight back when they think the Court is exerting too much influence, which can limit the Court's power as a policy-making institution. For the president, this can escalate to open conflict. One example was FDR's court-packing scheme, which was his response to the obstructionist New Deal Court. Another example is more recent: President Obama's criticism of the Supreme Court in his 2010 State of the Union message for the Court's ruling in *Citizens United v. Federal Election Commission* (2010). When Obama stated in his speech that the decision had opened the floodgates for corporate spending—including foreign corporations—in elections, Justice Alito was caught on camera mouthing the words "not true." Washington was abuzz for days about whether the president's comment or Alito's response was out of line. Chief Justice Roberts added fuel to the fire a few weeks later when he said that he found the president's comment and the partisan atmosphere of the speech "very troubling" and indicated that justices might not attend State of the Union addresses in the future.

The president can counter the Court's influence in a more restrained way by failing to enforce a decision vigorously. Congress can try to control the Court by blocking appointments it disagrees with (however, this often involves a disagreement with the president more than the Court), limiting the jurisdiction of the federal courts, changing the size of the Court, or even impeaching a judge. The latter three options are rarely used, but Congress often threatens to take these drastic steps. The most common way for Congress to respond to a Court decision that it disagrees with is simply to pass legislation that overturns the decision (if the case concerns the interpretation of a law).

Self-Imposed Restraint In general, the Court avoids stepping on the toes of the other branches unless it is absolutely necessary. The Court often exercises self-imposed restraint and refuses to act on "political questions"—issues that are outside the judicial domain and should be decided by elected officials. The practice dates back to an 1804 dispute over whether a piece of land next to the Mississippi River belonged to Spain or the United States. The Court observed: "A question like this, respecting the boundaries of nations, is . . . more a political than a legal question, and in its discussion, the courts of every country must respect the pronounced will of the legislature."[80]

A more recent application of the doctrine came when the Washington, D.C., district court dismissed a lawsuit from Rep. Charles Rangel (D-NY) against former Speaker John A. Boehner (R-OH) concerning the House of Representatives' censure of Rangel for tax evasion and other unethical behavior. The district court dismissed the suit, in part on the grounds that this was a political question that should be decided by Congress, not the Court: "The House has wide discretion to discipline its Members under the Discipline Clause, and this Court may not lightly intrude upon that discretion."[81] The Court is generally reluctant to get involved in internal congressional disputes.

Although this self-imposed limitation on judicial power is important, one must also recognize that the Court reserves the right to decide what a political question is. Therefore, one could argue that this is not much of a limit on judicial power after all. For example, for many decades the Court avoided the topic of legislative redistricting,

saying that it did not want to enter that "political thicket." However, it changed its position in the 1960s in a series of cases that imposed the idea of "one person, one vote" on the redistricting process, and it has been intimately involved in redistricting ever since. The Court's ability to define the boundaries of political questions is an important source of its policy-making power.

The Court's Multifaceted Role This "big picture" question about the relationship of the Court to the other branches boils down to this: Does the judiciary constrain the other branches, or does it defer to their wishes? Given the responsiveness of the elected branches to the will of the people, this question can alternatively be stated: Does the Court operate against the political majority to protect minority interests, or does it defer to the popular will? The evidence on this is mixed.

The judicial branch as a whole contains a basic paradox: it may be simultaneously seen as the least democratic and most democratic branch.[82] The least democratic part is obvious: federal judges and many state and local judges are unelected and are not accountable to the voters (except indirectly through the elected leaders who appoint them). But the judiciary can also be seen as the most democratic branch. Cases that are brought to the courts come from the people and, as long as the legal criteria for bringing a case are met, the courts must hear those cases. Although people have the right to petition "the government for a redress of grievances," there is no guarantee that Congress or the executive branch will listen to them. Of course, only a small fraction of the cases brought to the Supreme Court are heard, so the antidemocratic charge carries more weight at the top. However, the court system as a whole may be seen as providing an important outlet for participation in our political system.

Whether the Supreme Court goes against our elected leaders—that is, is the Court a countermajoritarian force in our political system?—is also a complicated question to sort out. The Court is activist on many issues, exercising judicial review, but on many other issues it defers to the elected institutions. Sometimes an activist Court defends minority interests on issues such as criminal defendants' rights, school prayer, gay rights, and flag burning, but that is not always the case. Is the Court acting undemocratically when it exercises its power of judicial review (or, as critics would say, "legislates from the bench")? Or is it playing its vital role in our constitutional system as a check on the other branches, as with some of its recent cases concerning the legal rights of enemy combatants in the War on Terror? The immigration case mentioned in the chapter opener, *United States v. Texas*, would be seen as the former by supporters of President Obama's immigration policy and the latter by those who viewed his policy on deportation deferrals as executive overreach.

The answers depend somewhat on one's political views. Conservatives would generally applaud the activism of the Rehnquist and Roberts Courts, while liberals would see it as an unwarranted check on the elected branches. Moreover, the Court's role has varied throughout history: in some instances, it defended unpopular views and strongly protected minority rights; in other cases, it followed majority opinion and declined to play that important role. But clearly, the Court has the *potential* to play an important policy-making role in our system of checks and balances; whether it actually plays that role depends on the political, personal, and legal factors outlined in this chapter.

Conclusion

The courts demonstrate that politics is conflictual. And many conflicts demonstrate that the courts are political. Although plenty of unanimous Supreme Court decisions do not involve much conflict among the justices, many landmark cases deeply divide the Court on constitutional interpretation and how to balance those competing interpretations against other values and interests. These conflicts in the Court often reveal deeper fault lines in the broader political system.

It shouldn't be surprising that political process matters in the courts. The rules of courtroom procedures, including discovery and how evidence is presented, can have an important impact on outcomes. Political process is also important for selecting judges and determining which cases the Supreme Court hears.

Politics is indeed everywhere, even in the courts, where you would least expect to see it. Despite the idealized image of Justice as a blindfolded woman holding a set of scales, politics affects everything from the selection of judges to the decisions they make. Some characteristics of the federal courts (the most important of which is judges' lifetime tenure) insulate the system from politics. However, courts are subject to influence by judges' ideologies, interest groups, and the president and Senate, who try to shape the courts' composition through the nomination process.

The chapter-opening example demonstrates the important role that the courts play in the political system. Recall that the Supreme Court deferred to the elected branches of Texas in upholding their affirmative action policy for college admissions. But that same week, the Court struck down President Obama's deportation deferral program, throwing 4.3 million immigrants into legal limbo. Thus, the federal courts can serve as a referee between the other branches of government, and between the national and state governments, by defining the boundaries of permissible conduct.

STUDY GUIDE

The development of an independent and powerful federal judiciary

Explain how the power of judicial review was established. (Pages 477–481)

Summary

In contrast to other branches of government, the Constitution offers few specifics on the organization of the judiciary. In fact, most of the details on the arrangement of the judiciary do not come from the Constitution at all, but from congressional action. In addition, the Supreme Court's strongest power—judicial review—is not even mentioned in the Constitution but was established in the *Marbury v. Madison* decision.

Key terms

Judiciary Act of 1789 (p. 478)
district courts (p. 478)
appellate jurisdiction (p. 478)
judicial review (p. 478)

original jurisdiction (p. 479)
constitutional interpretation (p. 480)
statutory interpretation (p. 480)

Practice Quiz Questions

1. **Most of the details about the Supreme Court were established in _____.**
    a. the Judiciary Act of 1789
    b. Article I of the Constitution
    c. Article II of the Constitution
    d. the *Federalist Papers*
    e. *Marbury v. Madison*

2. **_Marbury v. Madison_ is significant because it _____.**
    a. established the Supreme Court
    b. introduced the process of selective incorporation
    c. changed the manner of judicial selection
    d. established judicial review
    e. gave Supreme Court justices lifetime appointments

3. **Judicial review enables the Supreme Court to _____.**
    a. submit legislation to Congress
    b. strike down laws passed by Congress
    c. revise laws passed by Congress
    d. oversee presidential appointments to the bureaucracy
    e. approve judicial appointments to lower courts

4. **The Court's application of national and state laws to particular cases is called _____.**
    a. constitutional interpretation
    b. judicial restraint
    c. judicial activism
    d. original jurisdiction
    e. statutory interpretation

The American legal and judicial system

Outline the structure of the court system. (Pages 481–492)

Summary

All courts within the United States have a similar set of fundamental attributes, such as the distinction between civil and criminal cases and the reliance on legal precedent. The judicial system is divided between state and federal courts, and within each level of government there are courts of original jurisdiction and appeals courts.

Key terms

plaintiff (p. 481)
defendant (p. 481)
plea bargaining (p. 481)
class-action lawsuit (p. 482)
common law (p. 482)

precedent (p. 482)
standing (p. 483)
jurisdiction (p. 483)
appeals courts (p. 486)
senatorial courtesy (p. 490)

Practice Quiz Questions

5. **A system of _____ relies on legal decisions that are built from precedent established in previous cases.**
    a. common law
    b. civil law
    c. statutory law
    d. stare decisis
    e. plea bargaining

6. **When one has suffered direct and personal harm from the action addressed in a case, it is called _____.**
    a. precedent
    b. appellant
    c. plea bargaining
    d. jurisdiction
    e. standing

7. The president appoints federal judges with the "advice and consent" of the _____.
   a. House of Representatives
   b. Senate
   c. Supreme Court
   d. attorney general
   e. vice president

Access to the Supreme Court

Describe how cases reach the Supreme Court. (Pages 493–497)

Summary

The Supreme Court hears only about 1 percent of the cases that are brought to it. To help decide which cases to hear, the Court generally uses three factors: collusion, standing, and mootness. Ultimately, the justices have a great deal of discretion in deciding to hear a case, but they can only hear cases that come to them.

Key terms

writ of *certiorari* (p. 494)   cert pool (p. 496)

mootness (p. 496)   solicitor general (p. 497)

Practice Quiz Questions

8. When a litigant who lost in a lower court files a petition, the case reaches the Supreme Court _____.
   a. as a matter of right
   b. through a writ of certification
   c. through a writ of *certiorari*
   d. as a matter of original jurisdiction
   e. through senatorial courtesy

9. _____ means that the controversy is not relevant when the Court hears the case.
   a. Mootness
   b. Amicus
   c. Collusion
   d. Standing
   e. Precedent

10. Most justices _____ in initially deciding which cases should be heard.
    a. personally review all cases
    b. personally review a random sample of cases
    c. follow the recommendations of the chief justice
    d. use a random selection process
    e. use a cert pool

Hearing cases before the Supreme Court

Describe the Supreme Court's procedures for hearing a case. (Pages 497–502)

Summary

When hearing a case, the justices prepare by reading briefs before they hear the oral arguments. After oral arguments, the justices meet in conference to discuss and vote on the cases. The majority opinion explains the rationale for how a decision is reached, although justices can also write dissenting and concurring opinions.

Key terms

amicus curiae (p. 498)   oral arguments (p. 498)

Practice Quiz Questions

11. The most important impact of a case having a large number of amicus curiae briefs is _____.
    a. the decision is more likely to be unanimous
    b. the case is more likely to be heard
    c. the decision is more likely to go against the government
    d. the case is less likely to be heard
    e. the decision is more likely to have a liberal outcome

12. Oral arguments generally last _____, and justices _____ wait until the end of the arguments to ask questions.
    a. one hour; will
    b. one hour; do not
    c. one day; will
    d. one week; will
    e. one week; do not

13. Generally, the chief justice or the _____ justice decides who writes the majority opinion; justices' individual areas of expertise _____ a factor in making this assignment.
    a. most junior; are not
    b. most junior; are
    c. most senior; are not
    d. most senior; are
    e. dissenting; does not

Supreme Court decision making

Analyze the factors that influence Supreme Court decisions. (Pages 502–509)

Summary

The Court makes decisions based on legal factors such as precedent and informal norms, and political factors such as the justices' own ideologies and positions on the role that the Court plays in government. Although the Court does not consider public opinion the way elected officials do, most decisions generally stay in step with the public.

Key terms

strict construction (p. 502)   attitudinalist approach (p. 504)
original intent (p. 504)   judicial restraint (p. 506)
living Constitution (p. 504)   judicial activism (p. 506)

Practice Quiz Questions

14. **The perspective that when the Constitution is not clear the justices should be guided by what the Founders wanted is called _____.**

    a. judicial activism

    b. strict construction

    c. original intent

    d. the attitudinalist approach

    e. interpretive statute

15. **Advocates of _____ argue that the Court must defer to the elected branches and not strike down their laws.**

    a. judicial restraint

    b. judicial activism

    c. judicial limitation

    d. legal maximization

    e. the strategic model

The role of the Court in our political system

Assess the Supreme Court's power in the political system. (Pages 502–512)

Summary

Given the constitutional weakness of the Court, it is unclear how it is able to enforce its decisions. Depending on context, the Court is occasionally able to force its views on the elected branches, although more often it requires their support.

Practice Quiz Question

16. **In general, the Court _____ challenges with the elected branches and often _____ to act on "political questions."**

    a. avoids; agrees

    b. avoids; refuses

    c. pursues; agrees

    d. pursues; refuses

Suggested Reading

Baum, Lawrence. *Judges and Their Audiences: A Perspective on Judicial Behavior.* Princeton, NJ: Princeton University Press, 2006.

Black, Ryan C., and Ryan J. Owens, *The Solicitor General and the United States Supreme Court: Executive Influence and Judicial Decisions.* New York: Cambridge University Press, 2012.

Cornell University Law School, Supreme Court Collection, www.law.cornell.edu/supremecourt/text/home.

Eisgruber, Christopher L. *Constitutional Self-Government.* Cambridge, MA: Harvard University Press, 2001.

Hansford, Thomas G., and James F. Spriggs II. *The Politics of Precedent on the U.S. Supreme Court.* Princeton, NJ: Princeton University Press, 2006.

Northwestern University, Oyez: Supreme Court Multimedia, www.oyez.org.

O'Brien, David M. *Storm Center: The Supreme Court in American Politics,* 10th ed. New York: W. W. Norton, 2014.

Rosen, Jeffrey. *The Most Democratic Branch: How the Courts Serve America.* New York: Oxford University Press, 2006.

Sunstein, Cass R., David Schkade, Lisa M. Ellman, and Andres Sawicki. *Are Judges Political? An Empirical Analysis of the Federal Judiciary.* Washington, DC: Brookings Institution Press, 2006.

Tushnet, Mark. *A Court Divided: The Rehnquist Court and the Future of Constitutional Law.* New York: W. W. Norton, 2006.

U.S. Supreme Court website, www.supremecourt.gov.

APPENDIX

The Declaration of Independence

In Congress, July 4, 1776

The unanimous Declaration of the thirteen united States of America,

When in the Course of human events, it becomes necessary for one people to dissolve the political bands which have connected them with another, and to assume among the powers of the earth, the separate and equal station to which the Laws of Nature and of Nature's God entitle them, a decent respect to the opinions of mankind requires that they should declare the causes which impel them to the separation.

We hold these truths to be self-evident, that all men are created equal, that they are endowed by their Creator with certain unalienable Rights, that among these are Life, Liberty and the pursuit of Happiness.—That to secure these rights, Governments are instituted among Men, deriving their just powers from the consent of the governed. —That whenever any Form of Government becomes destructive of these ends, it is the Right of the People to alter or to abolish it, and to institute new Government, laying its foundation on such principles and organizing its powers in such form, as to them shall seem most likely to effect their Safety and Happiness. Prudence, indeed, will dictate that Governments long established should not be changed for light and transient causes; and accordingly all experience hath shewn, that mankind are more disposed to suffer, while evils are sufferable, than to right themselves by abolishing the forms to which they are accustomed. But when a long train of abuses and usurpations, pursuing invariably the same Object evinces a design to reduce them under absolute Despotism, it is their right, it is their duty, to throw off such Government, and to provide new Guards for their future security.—Such has been the patient sufferance of these Colonies; and such is now the necessity which constrains them to alter their former Systems of Government. The history of the present King of Great Britain is a history of repeated injuries and usurpations, all having in direct object the establishment of an absolute Tyranny over these States. To prove this, let Facts be submitted to a candid world.

He has refused his Assent to Laws, the most wholesome and necessary for the public good.

He has forbidden his Governors to pass Laws of immediate and pressing importance, unless suspended in their operation till his Assent should be obtained; and when so suspended, he has utterly neglected to attend to them.

He has refused to pass other Laws for the accommodation of large districts of people, unless those people would relinquish the right of Representation in the Legislature, a right inestimable to them and formidable to tyrants only.

He has called together legislative bodies at places unusual, uncomfortable, and distant from the depository of their public Records, for the sole purpose of fatiguing them into compliance with his measures.

He has dissolved Representative Houses repeatedly, for opposing with manly firmness his invasions on the rights of the people.

He has refused for a long time, after such dissolutions, to cause others to be elected; whereby the Legislative powers, incapable of Annihilation, have returned to the People at large for their exercise; the State remaining in the mean time exposed to all the dangers of invasion from without, and convulsions within.

He has endeavoured to prevent the population of these States; for that purpose obstructing the Laws for Naturalization of Foreigners; refusing to pass others to encourage their migrations hither, and raising the conditions of new Appropriations of Lands.

He has obstructed the Administration of Justice, by refusing his Assent to Laws for establishing Judiciary powers.

He has made Judges dependent on his Will alone, for the tenure of their offices, and the amount and payment of their salaries.

He has erected a multitude of New Offices, and sent hither swarms of Officers to harrass our people, and eat out their substance.

He has kept among us, in times of peace, Standing Armies without the Consent of our legislatures.

He has affected to render the Military independent of and superior to the Civil power.

He has combined with others to subject us to a jurisdiction foreign to our constitution, and unacknowledged by our laws; giving his Assent to their Acts of pretended Legislation:

For Quartering large bodies of armed troops among us:

For protecting them, by a mock Trial, from punishment for any Murders which they should commit on the Inhabitants of these States:

For cutting off our Trade with all parts of the world:

For imposing Taxes on us without our Consent:

For depriving us in many cases, of the benefits of Trial by Jury:

For transporting us beyond Seas to be tried for pretended offences:

For abolishing the free System of English Laws in a neighboring Province, establishing therein an Arbitrary government, and enlarging its Boundaries so as to render it at once an example and fit instrument for introducing the same absolute rule into these Colonies:

For taking away our Charters, abolishing our most valuable Laws, and altering fundamentally the Forms of our Governments:

For suspending our own Legislatures, and declaring themselves invested with power to legislate for us in all cases whatsoever.

He has abdicated Government here, by declaring us out of his Protection and waging War against us.

He has plundered our seas, ravaged our Coasts, burnt our towns, and destroyed the lives of our people.

He is at this time transporting large Armies of foreign Mercenaries to compleat the works of death, desolation and tyranny, already begun with circumstances of Cruelty & perfidy scarcely paralleled in the most barbarous ages, and totally unworthy the Head of a civilized nation.

He has constrained our fellow Citizens taken Captive on the high Seas to bear Arms against their Country, to become the executioners of their friends and Brethren, or to fall themselves by their Hands.

He has excited domestic insurrections amongst us, and has endeavoured to bring on the inhabitants of our frontiers, the merciless Indian Savages, whose known rule of warfare, is an undistinguished destruction of all ages, sexes and conditions.

In every stage of these Oppressions We have Petitioned for Redress in the most humble terms: Our repeated Petitions have been answered only by repeated injury. A Prince whose character is thus marked by every act which may define a Tyrant, is unfit to be the ruler of a free people.

Nor have We been wanting in attentions to our Brittish brethren. We have warned them from time to time of attempts by their legislature to extend an unwarrantable jurisdiction over us. We have reminded them of the circumstances of our emigration and settlement here. We have appealed to their native justice and magnanimity, and we have conjured them by the ties of our common kindred to disavow these usurpations, which, would inevitably interrupt our connections and correspondence. They too have been deaf to the voice of justice and of consanguinity. We must, therefore, acquiesce in the necessity, which denounces our Separation, and hold them, as we hold the rest of mankind, Enemies in War, in Peace Friends.

We, Therefore, the Representatives of the United States of America, in General Congress, Assembled, appealing to the Supreme Judge of the world for the rectitude of our intentions, do, in the Name, and by Authority of the good People of these Colonies, solemnly publish and declare, That these United Colonies are, and of Right ought to be Free and Independent States; that they are Absolved from all Allegiance to the British Crown, and that all political connection between them and the State of Great Britain, is and ought to be totally dissolved; and that as Free and Independent States, they have full Power to levy War, conclude Peace, contract Alliances, establish Commerce, and to do all other Acts and Things which Independent States may of right do. And for the support of this Declaration, with a firm reliance on the protection of divine Providence, we mutually pledge to each other our Lives, our Fortunes and our sacred Honor.

The foregoing Declaration was, by order of Congress, engrossed, and signed by the following members:

John Hancock

New Hampshire
Josiah Bartlett
William Whipple
Matthew Thornton

Massachusetts Bay
Samuel Adams
John Adams
Robert Treat Paine
Elbridge Gerry

Rhode Island
Stephen Hopkins
William Ellery

Connecticut
Roger Sherman
Samuel Huntington
William Williams
Oliver Wolcott

New York
William Floyd
Philip Livingston
Francis Lewis
Lewis Morris

New Jersey
Richard Stockton
John Witherspoon
Francis Hopkinson
John Hart
Abraham Clark

Pennsylvania
Robert Morris
Benjamin Rush
Benjamin Franklin
John Morton
George Clymer
James Smith
George Taylor
James Wilson
George Ross

Delaware
Caesar Rodney
George Read
Thomas M'Kean

Maryland
Samuel Chase
William Paca
Thomas Stone
Charles Carroll, of Carrollton

Virginia
George Wythe
Richard Henry Lee
Thomas Jefferson
Benjamin Harrison
Thomas Nelson, Jr.
Francis Lightfoot Lee
Carter Braxton

North Carolina
William Hooper
Joseph Hewes
John Penn

South Carolina
Edward Rutledge
Thomas Heyward, Jr.
Thomas Lynch, Jr.
Arthur Middleton

Georgia
Button Gwinnett
Lyman Hall
George Walton

Resolved, That copies of the Declaration be sent to the several assemblies, conventions, and committees, or councils of safety, and to the several commanding officers of the continental troops; that it be proclaimed in each of the United States, at the head of the army.

The Articles of Confederation

Agreed to by Congress November 15, 1777;
ratified and in force March 1, 1781

To all whom these Presents shall come, we the undersigned Delegates of the States affixed to our Names, send greeting. Whereas the Delegates of the United States of America, in Congress assembled, did, on the fifteenth day of November, in the Year of Our Lord One thousand Seven Hundred and Seventy seven, and in the Second Year of the Independence of America, agree to certain articles of Confederation and perpetual Union between the States of Newhampshire, Massachusetts-bay, Rhodeisland and Providence Plantations, Connecticut, New-York, New-Jersey, Pennsylvania, Delaware, Maryland, Virginia, North-Carolina, South-Carolina and Georgia in the words following, viz. "Articles of Confederation and perpetual Union between the states of Newhampshire, Massachusettsbay, Rhodeisland and Providence Plantations, Connecticut, New-York, New-Jersey, Pennsylvania, Delaware, Maryland, Virginia, North-Carolina, South-Carolina and Georgia.

Art. I. The Stile of this confederacy shall be "The United States of America."

Art. II. Each state retains its sovereignty, freedom and independence, and every Power, Jurisdiction and right, which is not by this confederation expressly delegated to the United States, in Congress assembled.

Art. III. The said states hereby severally enter into a firm league of friendship with each other, for their common defence, the security of their Liberties, and their mutual and general welfare, binding themselves to assist each other, against all force offered to, or attacks made upon them, or any of them, on account of religion, sovereignty, trade, or any other pretence whatever.

Art. IV. The better to secure and perpetuate mutual friendship and intercourse among the people of the different states in this union, the free inhabitants of each of these states, paupers, vagabonds and fugitives from Justice excepted, shall be entitled to all privileges and immunities of free citizens in the several states; and the people of each state shall have free ingress and regress to and from any other state, and shall enjoy therein all the privileges of trade and commerce, subject to the same duties, impositions and restrictions as the inhabitants thereof respectively, provided that such restriction shall not extend so far as to prevent the removal of property imported into any state, to any other state, of which the Owner is an inhabitant; provided also that no imposition, duties or restriction shall be laid by any state, on the property of the united states, or either of them.

If any Person guilty of, or charged with treason, felony, or other high misdemeanor in any state, shall flee from Justice, and be found in any of the united states, he shall, upon demand of the Governor or executive power, of the state from which he fled, be delivered up and removed to the state having jurisdiction of his offence.

Full faith and credit shall be given in each of these states to the records, acts and judicial proceedings of the courts and magistrates of every other state.

Art. V. For the more convenient management of the general interests of the united states, delegates shall be annually appointed in such manner as the legislature of each state shall direct, to meet in Congress on the first Monday in November, in every year, with a power reserved to each state, to recall its delegates, or any of them, at any time within the year, and to send others in their stead, for the remainder of the Year.

No state shall be represented in Congress by less than two, nor by more than seven Members; and no person shall be capable of being a delegate for more than three years in any term of six years; nor shall any person, being a delegate, be capable of holding any office under the united states, for which he, or another for his benefit receives any salary, fees or emolument of any kind.

Each state shall maintain its own delegates in a meeting of the states, and while they act as members of the committee of the states.

In determining questions in the united states, in Congress assembled, each state shall have one vote.

Freedom of speech and debate in Congress shall not be impeached or questioned in any Court, or place out of Congress, and the members of congress shall be protected in their persons from arrests and imprisonments, during the time of their going to and from, and attendance on congress, except for treason, felony, or breach of the peace.

Art. VI. No state without the Consent of the united states in congress assembled, shall send any embassy to, or receive any embassy from, or enter into any conference, agreement, or alliance or treaty with any King, prince or state; nor shall any person holding any office or profit or trust under the united states, or any of them, accept of any present, emolument, office or title of any kind whatever from any king, prince or foreign state; nor shall the united states in congress assembled, or any of them, grant any title of nobility.

No two or more states shall enter into any treaty, confederation or alliance whatever between them, without the consent of the united states in congress assembled, specifying accurately the purposes for which the same is to be entered into, and how long it shall continue.

No state shall lay any imposts or duties, which may interfere with any stipulations in treaties, entered into by the united states in congress assembled, with any king, prince or state, in pursuance of any treaties already proposed by congress, to the courts of France and Spain.

No vessels of war shall be kept up in time of peace by any state, except such number only, as shall be deemed necessary by the united states in congress assembled, for the defence of such state, or its trade; nor shall any body of forces be kept up by any state, in time of peace, except such number only, as in the judgment of the united states, in congress assembled, shall be deemed requisite to garrison the forts necessary for the defence of such state; but every state shall always keep up a well regulated and disciplined militia, sufficiently armed and accoutred, and shall provide and constantly have ready for use, in public stores, a due number of field pieces and tents, and a proper quantity of arms, ammunition and camp equipage.

No state shall engage in any war without the consent of the united states in congress assembled, unless such state be actually invaded by enemies, or shall have received certain advice of a resolution being formed by some nation of Indians to invade such state, and the danger is so imminent as not to admit of a delay, till the united states in congress asssembled can be consulted; nor shall any state grant commissions to any ships or vessels of war, nor letters of marque or reprisal, except it be after a declaration of war by the united states in congress assembled, and then only against the kingdom or state and the subjects thereof, against which war has been so declared, and under such regulations as shall be established by the united states in congress assembled, unless such state be infested by pirates; in which case vessels of war may be fitted out for that occasion, and kept so long as the danger shall continue, or until the united states in congress assembled shall determine otherwise.

Art. VII. When land-forces are raised by any state for the common defence, all officers of or under the rank of colonel, shall be appointed by the legislature of each state respectively, by whom such forces shall be raised, or in such manner as such state shall direct, and all vacancies shall be filled up by the state which first made the appointment.

Art. VIII. All charges of war, and all other expences that shall be incurred for the common defence or general welfare, and allowed by the united states in congress assembled, shall be defrayed out of a common treasury, which shall be supplied by the several states in proportion to the value of all land within each state, granted to or surveyed for any Person, as such land and the buildings and improvements thereon shall be estimated according to such mode as the united states in congress assembled, shall from time to time direct and appoint.

The taxes for paying that proportion shall be laid and levied by the authority and direction of the legislatures of the several states within the time agreed upon by the united states in congress assembled.

Art. IX. The united states in congress assembled, shall have the sole and exclusive right and power of determining on peace and war, except in the cases mentioned in the sixth article—of sending and receiving ambassadors—entering into treaties and alliances, provided that no treaty of commerce shall be made whereby the legislative power of the respective states shall be restrained from imposing such imposts and duties on foreigners, as their own people are subjected to, or from prohibiting the exportation of any species of goods or commodities whatsoever—of establishing rules for deciding in all cases, what captures on land or water shall be legal, and in what manner prizes taken by land or naval forces in the service of the united states shall be divided or appropriated—of granting letters of marque and reprisal in times of peace—appointing courts for the trial of piracies and felonies committed on the high seas and establishing courts for receiving and determining finally appeals in all cases of captures, provided that no member of congress shall be appointed a judge of any of the said courts.

The united states in congress assembled shall also be the last resort on appeal in all disputes and differences now subsisting or that hereafter may arise between two or more states concerning boundary, jurisdiction or any other cause whatever; which authority shall always be exercised in the manner following. Whenever the legislative or executive authority or lawful agent of any state in controversy with another shall present a petition to congress stating the matter in question and praying for a hearing, notice thereof shall be given by order of congress to the legislative or executive authority of the other state in controversy, and a day assigned for the appearance of the parties by their lawful agents, who shall then be directed to appoint by joint consent, commissioners or judges to constitute a court for hearing and determining the matter in question: but if they cannot agree, congress shall name three persons out of each of the united states, and from the list of such persons each party shall alternately strike out one, the petitioners beginning, until the number shall be reduced to thirteen; and from that number not less than seven, nor more than nine names as congress shall direct, shall in the presence of congress be drawn out by lot, and the persons whose names shall be so drawn or any five of them, shall be commissioners or judges, to hear and finally determine the controversy, so always as a major part of the judges who shall hear the cause shall agree in the determination: and if either party shall neglect to attend at the day appointed, without shewing reasons, which congress shall judge sufficient, or being present shall refuse to strike, the congress shall proceed to nominate three persons out of each state, and the secretary of congress shall strike in behalf of

such party absent or refusing; and the judgment and sentence of the court to be appointed, in the manner before prescribed, shall be final and conclusive; and if any of the parties shall refuse to submit to the authority of such court, or to appear to defend their claim or cause, the court shall nevertheless proceed to pronounce sentence, or judgment, which shall in like manner be final and decisive, the judgment or sentence and other proceedings being in either case transmitted to congress, and lodged among the acts of congress for the security of the parties concerned: provided that every commissioner, before he sits in judgment, shall take an oath to be administered by one of the judges of the supreme or superior court of the state, where the cause shall be tried, "well and truly to hear and determine the matter in question, according to the best of his judgment, without favour, affection or hope of reward:" provided also, that no state shall be deprived of territory for the benefit of the united states.

All controversies concerning the private right of soil claimed under different grants of two or more states, whose jurisdictions as they may respect such lands, and the states which passed such grants are adjusted, the said grants or either of them being at the same time claimed to have originated antecedent to such settlement of jurisdiction, shall on the petition of either party to the congress of the united states, be finally determined as near as may be in the same manner as is before prescribed for deciding disputes respecting territorial jurisdiction between different states.

The united states in congress assembled shall also have the sole and exclusive right and power of regulating the alloy and value of coin struck by their own authority, or by that of the respective states—fixing the standard of weights and measures throughout the united states—regulating the trade and managing all affairs with the Indians, not members of any of the states, provided that the legislative right of any state within its own limits be not infringed or violated—establishing and regulating post-offices from one state to another, throughout all the united states, and exacting such postage on the papers passing thro' the same as may be requisite to defray the expences of the said office—appointing all officers of the land forces, in the service of the united states, excepting regimental officers—appointing all the officers of the naval forces, and commissioning all officers whatever in the service of the united states—making rules for the government and regulation of the said land and naval forces, and directing their operations.

The united states in congress assembled shall have authority to appoint a committee, to sit in the recess of congress, to be denominated "A Committee of the States," and to consist of one delegate from each state; and to appoint such other committees and civil officers as may be necessary for managing the general affairs of the united states under their direction—to appoint one of their number to preside, provided that no person be allowed to serve in the office of president more than one year in any term of three years; to ascertain the necessary sums of Money to be raised for the service of the united states, and to appropriate and apply the same for defraying the public expenses—to borrow money, or emit bills on the credit of the united states, transmitting every half year to the respective states an account of the sums of money so borrowed or emitted,—to build and equip a navy—to agree upon the number of land forces, and to make requisitions from each state for its quota, in proportion to the number of white inhabitants in such state; which requisition shall be binding, and thereupon the legislature of each state shall appoint the regimental officers, raise the men and cloath, arm and equip them in a soldier like manner, at the expense of the united states; and the officers and men so cloathed, armed and equipped shall march to the place appointed, and within the time agreed on by the united states in congress assembled: But if the united states in congress assembled shall, on consideration of circumstances judge proper that any state should not raise men, or should raise a smaller number than its quota, and that any other state should raise a greater number of men than the quota thereof, such extra number shall be raised, officered, cloathed, armed and equipped in the same manner as the quota of such state, unless the legislature of such state shall judge that such extra number cannot be safely spared out of the same, in which case they shall raise officer, cloath, arm and equip as many of such extra number as they judge can be safely spared. And the officers and men so cloathed, armed and equipped, shall march to the place appointed, and within the time agreed on by the united states in congress assembled.

The united states in congress assembled shall never engage in a war, nor grant letters of marque and reprisal in time of peace, nor enter into any treaties or alliances, nor coin money, nor regulate the value thereof, nor ascertain the sums and expenses necessary for the defence and welfare of the united states, or any of them, nor emit bills, nor borrow money on the credit of the united states, nor appropriate money, nor agree upon the number of vessels of war, to be built or purchased, or the number of land or sea forces to be raised, nor appoint a commander in chief of the army or navy, unless nine states assent to the same: nor shall a question on any other point, except for adjourning from day to day be determined, unless by the votes of a majority of the united states in congress assembled.

The congress of the united states shall have power to adjourn to any time within the year, and to any place within the united states, so that no period of adjournment be for a longer duration than the space of six Months, and shall publish the Journal of their proceedings monthly, except such parts thereof relating to treaties, alliances or military operations, as in their judgment require secrecy; and the yeas and nays of the delegates of each state on any question shall be entered on the Journal, when it is desired by any delegate; and the delegates of a state, or any of them, at his or their request shall be furnished with a transcript of the said Journal, except such parts as are above excepted, to lay before the legislatures of the several states.

Art. X. The committee of the states, or any nine of them, shall be authorised to execute, in the recess of congress, such of the powers of congress as the united states in congress assembled, by the consent of nine states, shall from time to time think expedient to vest them with; provided that no power be delegated to the said committee, for the exercise of which, by the articles of confederation, the voice of nine states in the congress of the united states assembled is requisite.

Art. XI. Canada acceding to this confederation, and joining in the measures of the united states, shall be admitted into, and entitled to all the advantages of this union: but no other colony shall be admitted into the same, unless such admission be agreed to by nine states.

Art. XII. All bills of credit emitted, monies borrowed and debts contracted by, or under the authority of congress, before the assembling of the united states, in pursuance of the present confederation, shall be deemed and considered as a charge against the united states, for payment and satisfaction whereof the said united states and the public faith are hereby solemnly pledged.

Art. XIII. Every state shall abide by the determinations of the united states in congress assembled, on all questions which by this confederation are submitted to them. And the Articles of this confederation shall be inviolably observed by every state, and the union shall be perpetual; nor shall any alteration at any time hereafter be made in any of them; unless such alteration be agreed to in a congress of the united states, and be afterwards confirmed by the legislatures of every state.

And Whereas it hath pleased the Great Governor of the World to incline the hearts of the legislatures we respectively represent in congress, to approve of, and to authorize us to ratify the said articles of confederation and perpetual union. Know Ye that we the undersigned delegates, by virtue of the power and authority to us given for that purpose, do by these presents, in the name and in behalf of our respective constituents, fully and entirely ratify and confirm each and every of the said articles of confederation and perpetual union, and all and singular the matters and things therein contained: And we do further solemnly plight and engage the faith of our respective constituents, that they shall abide by the determinations of the united states in congress assembled, on all questions, which by the said confederation are submitted to them. And that the articles thereof shall be inviolably observed by the states we respectively represent, and that the union shall be perpetual. In Witness whereof we have hereunto set our hands in Congress. Done at Philadelphia in the state of Pennsylvania the ninth day of July, in the Year of our Lord one Thousand seven Hundred and Seventy-eight, and in the third year of the independence of America.

The Constitution of the United States of America

[handwritten: Intro to Constitution Gives purpose of Document]

[PREAMBLE]

We the People of the United States, in Order to form a more perfect Union, establish Justice, insure domestic Tranquility, provide for the common defence, promote the general Welfare, and secure the Blessings of Liberty to ourselves and our Posterity, do ordain and establish this Constitution for the United States of America.

[handwritten: Good measure to how good Constitution is is how well it acheives three things]

Article I

[handwritten: About Congress, Legislative Branch]

SECTION 1
[LEGISLATIVE POWERS]

All legislative Powers herein granted shall be vested in a Congress of the United States, which shall consist of a Senate and House of Representatives.

SECTION 2
[HOUSE OF REPRESENTATIVES, HOW CONSTITUTED, POWER OF IMPEACHMENT] *[handwritten: (every 2 years)]*

The House of Representatives shall be composed of Members chosen every second Year by the People of the several States, and the Electors in each State shall have the Qualifications requisite for Electors of the most numerous Branch of the State Legislature.

No Person shall be a Representative who shall not have attained to the Age of twenty five Years, and been seven Years a Citizen of the United States, and who shall not, when elected, be an Inhabitant of that State in which he shall be chosen. *[handwritten: Requirements]*

[handwritten: House of Representatives]

Representatives and *direct Taxes*[1] shall be apportioned among the several States which may be included within this Union, according to their respective Numbers, *which shall be determined by adding to the whole Number of free Persons, including those bound to Service for a Term of Years, and excluding Indians not taxed, three fifths of all other Persons.*[2] The actual Enumeration shall be made within three Years after the first Meeting of the Congress of the United States, and within every subsequent Term of ten Years, in such Manner as they shall by Law direct. The Number of Representatives shall not exceed one for every thirty Thousand, but each State shall have at Least one Representative; *and until such enumeration shall be made, the State of New Hampshire shall be entitled to chuse three, Massachusetts eight, Rhode-Island and Providence Plantations one, Connecticut five, New-York six, New Jersey four, Pennsylvania eight, Delaware one, Maryland six, Virginia ten, North Carolina five, South Carolina five, and Georgia three.*[3]

When vacancies happen in the Representation from any State, the Executive Authority thereof shall issue Writs of Election to fill such Vacancies.

The House of Representatives shall chuse their Speaker and other Officers; and shall have the sole Power of Impeachment.

SECTION 3
[THE SENATE, HOW CONSTITUTED, IMPEACHMENT TRIALS] *[handwritten: Senate]*

The Senate of the United States shall be composed of two Senators from each State, *chosen by the Legislature thereof,*[4] for six Years; and each Senator shall have one Vote.

[handwritten: originally no popular elections for Senators Changed in Early 20th century]

[handwritten: Italicized = No longer part]

Immediately after they shall be assembled in Consequence of the first Election, they shall be divided as equally as may be into three Classes. The Seats of the Senators of the first Class shall be vacated at the Expiration of the second Year, of the second Class at the Expiration of the fourth Year, and of the third Class at the Expiration of the sixth Year, so that one third may be chosen every second Year; *and if Vacancies happen by Resignation, or otherwise, during the Recess of the Legislature of any State, the Executive thereof may make temporary Appointments until the next Meeting of the Legislature, which shall then fill such Vacancies.*[5]

[handwritten: slightly higher requirements]

No Person shall be a Senator who shall not have attained to the Age of thirty Years, and been nine Years a Citizen of the United States, and who shall not, when elected, be an Inhabitant of that State for which he shall be chosen.

[handwritten: Pres. & VP Senate is VP]

The Vice President of the United States shall be President of the Senate, but shall have no Vote, unless they be equally divided.

[handwritten: only significant is tiebreaking vote]

The Senate shall chuse their other Officers, and also a President pro tempore, in the Absence of the Vice President, or when he shall exercise the Office of President of the United States.

The Senate shall have the sole Power to try all Impeachments. When sitting for that Purpose, they shall be on Oath or Affirmation. When the President of the United States is tried, the Chief Justice shall preside: And no Person shall be convicted without the Concurrence of two thirds of the Members present.

Judgment in Cases of Impeachment shall not extend further than to removal from Office, and disqualification to hold and enjoy any Office of honor, Trust or Profit under the United States: but the Party convicted shall nevertheless be liable and subject to Indictment, Trial, Judgment and Punishment, according to Law.

SECTION 4
[ELECTION OF SENATORS AND REPRESENTATIVES]

The Times, Places and Manner of holding Elections for Senators and Representatives, shall be prescribed in each State by the Legislature thereof; but the Congress may at any time by Law make or alter such Regulations, except as to the Places of chusing Senators.

The Congress shall assemble at least once in every Year, and such Meeting shall be on the first Monday in December, unless they shall by Law appoint a different Day.[6]

SECTION 5
[QUORUM, JOURNALS, MEETINGS, ADJOURNMENTS]

Each House shall be the Judge of the Elections, Returns and Qualifications of its own Members, and a Majority of each shall constitute a Quorum to do Business; but a smaller Number may adjourn from day to day, and may be authorized to compel the

---

[1] Modified by Sixteenth Amendment.
[2] Modified by Fourteenth Amendment.
[3] Temporary provision.
[4] Modified by Seventeenth Amendment.
[5] Modified by Seventeenth Amendment.
[6] Modified by Twentieth Amendment.

Attendance of absent Members, in such Manner, and under such Penalties as each House may provide.

Each House may determine the Rules of its Proceedings, punish its Members for disorderly Behaviour, and, with the Concurrence of two thirds, expel a Member.

Each House shall keep a Journal of its Proceedings, and from time to time publish the same, excepting such Parts as may in their Judgment require Secrecy; and the Yeas and Nays of the Members of either House on any questions shall, at the Desire of one fifth of those Present, be entered on the Journal.

Neither House, during the Session of Congress, shall, without the Consent of the other, adjourn for more than three days, nor to any other Place than that in which the two Houses shall be sitting.

SECTION 6
[COMPENSATION, PRIVILEGES, DISABILITIES]

The Senators and Representatives shall receive a Compensation for their Services, to be ascertained by Law, and paid out of the Treasury of the United States. They shall in all Cases, except Treason, Felony and Breach of the Peace, be privileged from Arrest during their Attendance at the Session of their respective Houses, and in going to and returning from the same; and for any Speech or Debate in either House, they shall not be questioned in any other Place.

No Senator or Representative shall, during the Time for which he was elected, be appointed to any civil Office under the Authority of the United States, which shall have been created, or the Emoluments whereof shall have been encreased during such time; and no Person holding any Office under the United States, shall be a Member of either House during his Continuance in Office.

SECTION 7
[PROCEDURE IN PASSING BILLS AND RESOLUTIONS]

All Bills for raising Revenue shall originate in the House of Representatives; but the Senate may propose or concur with Amendments as on other Bills.

Every Bill which shall have passed the House of Representatives and the Senate, shall, before it become a Law, be presented to the President of the United States: If he approve he shall sign it, but if not he shall return it, with his Objections to that House in which it shall have originated, who shall enter the Objections at large on their Journal, and proceed to reconsider it. If after such Reconsideration two thirds of that House shall agree to pass the Bill, it shall be sent, together with the Objections, to the other House, by which it shall likewise be reconsidered, and if approved by two thirds of that House, it shall become a Law. But in all such Cases the Votes of both Houses shall be determined by yeas and Nays, and the Names of the Persons voting for and against the Bill shall be entered on the Journal of each House respectively. If any Bill shall not be returned by the President within ten Days (Sundays excepted) after it shall have been presented to him, the Same shall be a Law, in like Manner as if he had signed it, unless the Congress by their Adjournment prevent its Return, in which Case it shall not be a Law.

Every Order, Resolution, or Vote to which the Concurrence of the Senate and House of Representatives may be necessary (except on a question of Adjournment) shall be presented to the President of the United States; and before the Same shall take Effect, shall be approved by him, or being disapproved by him, shall be repassed by two thirds of the Senate and House of Representatives, according to the Rules and Limitations prescribed in the Case of a Bill.

SECTION 8
[POWERS OF CONGRESS]

The Congress shall have Power

To lay and collect Taxes, Duties, Imposts and Excises, to pay the Debts and provide for the common Defence and general Welfare of the United States; but all Duties, Imposts and Excises shall be uniform throughout the United States;

To borrow Money on the credit of the United States;

To regulate Commerce with foreign Nations, and among the several States, and with the Indian Tribes;

To establish an uniform Rule of Naturalization, and uniform Laws on the subject of Bankruptcies throughout the United States;

To coin Money, regulate the Value thereof, and of foreign Coin, and fix the Standard of Weights and Measures;

To provide for the Punishment of counterfeiting the Securities and current Coin of the United States;

To establish Post Offices and post Roads;

To promote the Progress of Science and useful Arts, by securing for limited Times to Authors and Inventors the exclusive Right to their respective Writings and Discoveries;

To constitute Tribunals inferior to the supreme Court;

To define and punish Piracies and Felonies committed on the high Seas, and Offences against the Law of Nations;

To declare War, grant Letters of Marque and Reprisal, and make Rules concerning Captures on Land and Water;

To raise and support Armies, but no Appropriation of Money to that Use shall be for a longer Term than two Years;

To provide and maintain a Navy;

To make Rules for the Government and Regulation of the land and naval Forces;

To provide for calling forth the Militia to execute the Laws of the Union, suppress Insurrections and repel Invasions;

To provide for organizing, arming, and disciplining, the Militia, and for governing such Part of them as may be employed in the Service of the United States, reserving to the States respectively, the Appointment of the Officers, and the Authority of training the Militia according to the discipline prescribed by Congress;

To exercise exclusive Legislation in all Cases whatsoever, over such District (not exceeding ten Miles square) as may, by Cession of particular States, and the Acceptance of Congress, become the Seat of the Government of the United States, and to exercise like Authority over all Places purchased by the Consent of the Legislature of the State in which the Same shall be, for the Erection of Forts, Magazines, Arsenals, dock-Yards, and other needful Buildings;—And

To make all Laws which shall be necessary and proper for carrying into Execution the foregoing Powers, and all other Powers vested by this Constitution in the Government of the United States, or in any Department or Officer thereof.

SECTION 9
[SOME RESTRICTIONS ON FEDERAL POWER]

The Migration or Importation of such Persons as any of the States now existing shall think proper to admit, shall not be prohibited by the Congress prior to the Year one thousand eight hundred and eight, but a Tax or duty may be imposed on such Importation, not exceeding ten dollars for each Person.[7]

---

[7] Temporary provision.

The Privilege of the Writ of Habeas Corpus shall not be suspended, unless when in Cases of Rebellion or Invasion the public Safety may require it.

No Bill of Attainder or ex post facto Law shall be passed.

No Capitation, or other direct, Tax shall be laid, unless in Proportion to the Census or Enumeration herein before directed to be taken.[8]

No Tax or Duty shall be laid on Articles exported from any State.

No Preference shall be given by any Regulation of Commerce or Revenue to the Ports of one State over those of another; nor shall Vessels bound to, or from, one State, be obliged to enter, clear, or pay Duties in another.

No Money shall be drawn from the Treasury, but in Consequence of Appropriations made by Law; and a regular Statement and Account of the Receipts and Expenditures of all public Money shall be published from time to time.

No Title of Nobility shall be granted by the United States: And no Person holding any Office of Profit or Trust under them, shall, without the Consent of the Congress, accept of any present, Emolument, Office, or Title, of any kind whatever, from any King, Prince, or foreign State.

SECTION 10
[RESTRICTIONS UPON POWERS OF STATES]

No State shall enter into any Treaty, Alliance, or Confederation; grant Letters of Marque and Reprisal; coin Money; emit Bills of Credit; make any Thing but gold and silver Coin a Tender in Payment of Debts; pass any Bill of Attainder, ex post facto Law, or Law impairing the Obligation of Contracts, or grant any Title of Nobility.

No State shall, without the Consent of the Congress, lay any Imposts or Duties on Imports or Exports, except what may be absolutely necessary for executing its inspection Laws: and the net Produce of all Duties and Imposts, laid by any State on Imports or Exports, shall be for the Use of the Treasury of the United States; and all such Laws shall be subject to the Revision and Control of the Congress.

No State shall, without the Consent of Congress, lay any Duty of Tonnage, keep Troops, or Ships of War in time of Peace, enter into any Agreement or Compact with another State, or with a foreign Power, or engage in War, unless actually invaded, or in such imminent Danger as will not admit of delay.

Article II

SECTION 1
[EXECUTIVE POWER, ELECTION, QUALIFICATIONS OF THE PRESIDENT]

The executive Power shall be vested in a President of the United States of America. *He shall hold his Office during the Term of four Years, and, together with the Vice President, chosen for the same Term, be elected, as follows*[9]

Each State shall appoint, in such Manner as the Legislature thereof may direct, a Number of Electors, equal to the whole Number of Senators and Representatives to which the State may be entitled in the Congress: but no Senator or Representative, or Person holding an Office of Trust or Profit under the United States, shall be appointed an Elector.

The electors shall meet in their respective States, and vote by ballot for two Persons, of whom one at least shall not be an Inhabitant of the same State with themselves. And they shall make a List of all the Persons voted for, and of the Number of Votes for each; which List they shall sign and certify, and transmit sealed to the Seat of the Government of the United States, directed to the President of the Senate. The President of the Senate shall, in the Presence of the Senate and House of Representatives, open all the Certificates, and the Votes shall then be counted. The Person having the greatest Number of Votes shall be the President, if such Number be a Majority of the whole Number of Electors appointed; and if there be more than one who have such Majority, and have an equal Number of Votes, then the House of Representatives shall immediately chuse by Ballot one of them for President; and if no Person have a Majority, then from the five highest on the List the said House shall in like Manner chuse the President. But in chusing the President, the Votes shall be taken by States, the Representation from each State having one Vote; A quorum for this Purpose shall consist of a Member or Members from two thirds of the States, and a Majority of all the States shall be necessary to a Choice. In every Case, after the Choice of the President, the person having the greatest Number of Votes of the Electors shall be the Vice President. But if there should remain two or more who have equal Votes, the Senate shall chuse from them by Ballot the Vice President.[10]

The Congress may determine the Time of chusing the Electors, and the Day on which they shall give their Votes; which Day shall be the same throughout the United States.

No Person except a natural born Citizen, or a Citizen of the United States, at the time of the Adoption of this Constitution, shall be eligible to the Office of President; neither shall any Person be eligible to that Office who shall not have attained to the Age of thirty five Years, and been fourteen Years a Resident within the United States.

In Case of the Removal of the President from Office, or his Death, Resignation, or Inability to discharge the Powers and Duties of the said Office, the Same shall devolve on the Vice President, and the Congress may by Law provide for the Case of Removal, Death, Resignation or Inability, both of the President and Vice President, declaring what Officer shall then act as President, and such Officer shall act accordingly, until the Disability be removed, or a President shall be elected.

The President shall, at stated Times, receive for his Services, a Compensation, which shall neither be increased nor diminished during the Period for which he shall have been elected, and he shall not receive within that Period any other Emolument from the United States, or any of them.

Before he enter on the Execution of his Office, he shall take the following Oath or Affirmation:—"I do solemnly swear (or affirm) that I will faithfully execute the Office of President of the United States, and will to the best of my Ability, preserve, protect and defend the Constitution of the United States."

SECTION 2
[POWERS OF THE PRESIDENT]

The President shall be Commander in Chief of the Army and Navy of the United States, and of the Militia of the several States, when called into the actual Service of the United States; he may require the Opinion, in writing, of the principal Officer in each of the executive Departments, upon any Subject relating to the Duties of their respective Offices, and he shall have Power to grant Reprieves and Pardons for Offences against the United States, except in Cases of Impeachment.

He shall have Power, by and with the Advice and Consent of the Senate, to make Treaties, provided two thirds of the Senators present concur; and he shall nominate, and by and with the Advice

---

[8] Modified by Sixteenth Amendment.
[9] Number of terms limited to two by Twenty-second Amendment.
[10] Modified by the Twelfth and Twentieth Amendments.

and Consent of the Senate, shall appoint Ambassadors, other public Ministers and Consuls, Judges of the supreme Court, and all other Officers of the United States, whose Appointments are not herein otherwise provided for, and which shall be established by Law: but the Congress may by Law vest the Appointment of such inferior Officers, as they think proper, in the President alone, in the Courts of Law, or in the Heads of Departments.

The President shall have Power to fill up all Vacancies that may happen during the Recess of the Senate, by granting Commissions which shall expire at the End of their next Session.

SECTION 3
[POWERS AND DUTIES OF THE PRESIDENT]

He shall from time to time give to the Congress Information of the State of the Union, and recommend to their Consideration such Measures as he shall judge necessary and expedient; he may, on extraordinary Occasions, convene both Houses, or either of them, and in Case of Disagreement between them, with Respect to the Time of Adjournment, he may adjourn them to such Time as he shall think proper; he shall receive Ambassadors and other public Ministers; he shall take Care that the Laws be faithfully executed, and shall Commission all the Officers of the United States.

SECTION 4
[IMPEACHMENT]

The President, Vice President and all civil Officers of the United States, shall be removed from Office on Impeachment for, and Conviction of, Treason, Bribery, or other high Crimes and Misdemeanors.

Article III

SECTION 1
[JUDICIAL POWER, TENURE OF OFFICE]

The judicial Power of the United States, shall be vested in one supreme Court, and in such inferior Courts as the Congress may from time to time ordain and establish. The Judges, both of the supreme and inferior Courts, shall hold their Offices during good Behaviour, and shall, at stated Times, receive for their Services, a Compensation, which shall not be diminished during their Continuance in Office.

SECTION 2
[JURISDICTION]

The judicial Power shall extend to all Cases, in Law and Equity, arising under this Constitution, the Laws of the United States, and Treaties made, or which shall be made, under their Authority;—to all Cases affecting Ambassadors, other public Ministers and Consuls;—to all Cases of admiralty and maritime Jurisdiction;—to Controversies to which the United States shall be a Party;—to Controversies between two or more States;—*between a State and Citizens of another State;*—between Citizens of different States,—between Citizens of the same State claiming Lands under Grants of different States, *and between a State,* or the Citizens thereof, *and foreign States, Citizens or Subjects.*[11]

In all Cases affecting Ambassadors, other public Ministers and Consuls, and those in which a State shall be Party, the supreme Court shall have original Jurisdiction. In all the other Cases before

mentioned, the supreme Court shall have appellate Jurisdiction, both as to Law and Fact, with such Exceptions, and under such Regulations as the Congress shall make.

The Trial of all Crimes, except in Cases of Impeachment, shall be by Jury; and such Trial shall be held in the State where the said Crimes shall have been committed; but when not committed within any State, the Trial shall be at such Place or Places as the Congress may by Law have directed.

SECTION 3
[TREASON, PROOF, AND PUNISHMENT]

Treason against the United States, shall consist only in levying War against them, or in adhering to their Enemies, giving them Aid and Comfort. No Person shall be convicted of Treason unless on the Testimony of two Witnesses to the same overt Act, or on Confession in open Court.

The Congress shall have Power to declare the Punishment of Treason, but no Attainder of Treason shall work Corruption of Blood, or Forfeiture except during the Life of the Person attainted.

Article IV

SECTION 1
[FAITH AND CREDIT AMONG STATES]

Full Faith and Credit shall be given in each State to the public Acts, Records, and judicial Proceedings of every other State. And the Congress may by general Laws prescribe the Manner in which such Acts, Records and Proceedings shall be proved, and the Effect thereof.

SECTION 2
[PRIVILEGES AND IMMUNITIES, FUGITIVES]

The Citizens of each State shall be entitled to all Privileges and Immunities of Citizens in the several States.

A Person charged in any State with Treason, Felony or other Crime, who shall flee from Justice, and be found in another State, shall on Demand of the executive Authority of the State from which he fled, be delivered up, to be removed to the State having Jurisdiction of the Crime.

No person held to Service or Labour in one State, under the Laws thereof, escaping into another, shall, in Consequence of any Law or Regulation therein, be discharged from such Service or Labour, but shall be delivered up on Claim of the Party to whom such Service or Labour may be due.[12]

SECTION 3
[ADMISSION OF NEW STATES]

New States may be admitted by the Congress into this Union; but no new State shall be formed or erected within the Jurisdiction of any other State; nor any State be formed by the Junction of two or more States, or Parts of States, without the Consent of the Legislatures of the States concerned as well as of the Congress.

The Congress shall have Power to dispose of and make all needful Rules and Regulations respecting the Territory or other Property belonging to the United States; and nothing in this Constitution shall be so construed as to Prejudice any Claims of the United States, or of any particular State.

---

[11] Modified by the Eleventh Amendment.

[12] Repealed by the Thirteenth Amendment.

SECTION 4
[GUARANTEE OF REPUBLICAN GOVERNMENT]

The United States shall guarantee to every State in this Union a Republican Form of Government, and shall protect each of them against Invasion; and on Application of the Legislature, or of the Executive (when the Legislature cannot be convened), against domestic Violence.

Article V
[AMENDMENT OF THE CONSTITUTION]

The Congress, whenever two thirds of both Houses shall deem it necessary, shall propose Amendments to this Constitution, or, on the Application of the Legislatures of two thirds of the several States, shall call a Convention for proposing Amendments, which, in either Case, shall be valid to all Intents and Purposes, as Part of this Constitution, when ratified by the Legislatures of three fourths of the several States, or by Conventions in three fourths thereof, as the one or the other Mode of Ratification may be proposed by the Congress; *Provided that no Amendment which may be made prior to the Year One thousand eight hundred and eight shall in any Manner affect the first and fourth Clauses in the Ninth Section of the first Article;* and that no State, without its Consent, shall be deprived of its equal Suffrage in the Senate.

Article VI
[DEBTS, SUPREMACY, OATH]

All Debts contracted and Engagements entered into, before the Adoption of this Constitution, shall be as valid against the United States under this Constitution, as under the Confederation.

This Constitution, and the Laws of the United States which shall be made in Pursuance thereof; and all Treaties made, or which shall be made, under the Authority of the United States, shall be the supreme Law of the Land; and the Judges in every State shall be bound thereby, any Thing in the Constitution or Laws of any State to the Contrary notwithstanding.

The Senators and Representatives before mentioned, and the Members of the several State Legislatures, and all executive and judicial Officers, both of the United States and of the several States, shall be bound by Oath or Affirmation, to support this Constitution; but no religious Test shall be required as a Qualification to any Office or public Trust under the United States.

Article VII
[RATIFICATION AND ESTABLISHMENT]

The Ratification of the Conventions of nine States, shall be sufficient for the Establishment of this Constitution between the States so ratifying the Same.

Done in Convention by the Unanimous Consent of the States present the Seventeenth Day of September in the Year of our Lord one thousand seven hundred and Eighty seven and of the Independence of the United States of America the Twelfth. *In Witness* whereof We have hereunto subscribed our Names,

G:º WASHINGTON—
Presidt. and deputy from Virginia

New Hampshire
John Langdon
Nicholas Gilman

Massachusetts
Nathaniel Gorham
Rufus King

Connecticut
Wm. Saml. Johnson
Roger Sherman

New York
Alexander Hamilton

New Jersey
Wil: Livingston
David Brearley
Wm. Paterson
Jona: Dayton

Pennsylvania
B Franklin
Thomas Mifflin
Robt. Morris
Geo. Clymer
Thos. FitzSimons
Jared Ingersoll
James Wilson
Gouv Morris

Delaware
Geo: Read
Gunning Bedford jun
John Dickinson
Richard Bassett
Jaco: Broom

Maryland
James McHenry
Dan of St Thos. Jenifer
Danl. Carroll

Virginia
John Blair—
James Madison Jr.

North Carolina
Wm. Blount
Richd. Dobbs Spaight
Hu Williamson

South Carolina
J. Rutledge
Charles Cotesworth Pinckney
Charles Pinckney
Pierce Butler

Georgia
William Few
Abr Baldwin

Amendments to the Constitution

Proposed by Congress and Ratified by the Legislatures of the Several States, Pursuant to Article V of the Original Constitution.

Amendments I–X, known as the Bill of Rights, were proposed by Congress on September 25, 1789, and ratified on December 15, 1791.

Amendment I
[FREEDOM OF RELIGION, OF SPEECH, AND OF THE PRESS]

Congress shall make no law respecting an establishment of religion, or prohibiting the free exercise thereof; or abridging the freedom of speech, or of the press; or the right of the people peaceably to assemble, and to petition the Government for a redress of grievances.

Amendment II
[RIGHT TO KEEP AND BEAR ARMS]

A well regulated Militia, being necessary to the security of a free State, the right of the people to keep and bear Arms, shall not be infringed.

Amendment III
[QUARTERING OF SOLDIERS]

No Soldier shall, in time of peace be quartered in any house, without the consent of the Owner, nor in time of war, but in a manner to be prescribed by law.

Amendment IV
[SECURITY FROM UNWARRANTABLE SEARCH AND SEIZURE]

The right of the people to be secure in their persons, houses, papers, and effects, against unreasonable searches and seizures, shall not be violated, and no Warrants shall issue, but upon probable cause, supported by Oath or affirmation, and particularly describing the place to be searched, and the persons or things to be seized.

Amendment V
[RIGHTS OF ACCUSED PERSONS IN CRIMINAL PROCEEDINGS]

No person shall be held to answer for a capital, or otherwise infamous crime, unless on a presentment or indictment of a Grand Jury, except in cases arising in the land or naval forces, or in the Militia, when in actual service in time of War or in public danger; nor shall any person be subject for the same offence to be twice put in jeopardy of life or limb; nor shall be compelled in any criminal case to be a witness against himself, nor be deprived of life, liberty, or property, without due process of law; nor shall private property be taken for public use, without just compensation.

Amendment VI
[RIGHT TO SPEEDY TRIAL, WITNESSES, ETC.]

In all criminal prosecutions, the accused shall enjoy the right to a speedy and public trial, by an impartial jury of the State and district wherein the crime shall have been committed, which district shall have been previously ascertained by law, and to be informed of the nature and cause of the accusation; to be confronted with the witnesses against him; to have compulsory process for obtaining witnesses in his favor, and to have the Assistance of Counsel for his defence.

Amendment VII
[TRIAL BY JURY IN CIVIL CASES]

In suits at common law, where the value in controversy shall exceed twenty dollars, the right of trial by jury shall be preserved, and no fact tried by a jury, shall be otherwise reexamined in any Court of the United States, than according to the rules of the common law.

Amendment VIII
[BAILS, FINES, PUNISHMENTS]

Excessive bail shall not be required, nor excessive fines imposed, nor cruel and unusual punishments inflicted.

Amendment IX
[RESERVATION OF RIGHTS OF PEOPLE]

The enumeration in the Constitution, of certain rights, shall not be construed to deny or disparage others retained by the people.

Amendment X
[POWERS RESERVED TO STATES OR PEOPLE]

The powers not delegated to the United States by the Constitution, nor prohibited by it to the States, are reserved to the States respectively, or to the people.

Amendment XI
[*Proposed by Congress on March 4, 1794; declared ratified on January 8, 1798.*]
[RESTRICTION OF JUDICIAL POWER]

The Judicial power of the United States shall not be construed to extend to any suit in law or equity, commenced or prosecuted against one of the United States by Citizens of another State, or by Citizens or Subjects of any Foreign State.

Amendment XII
[*Proposed by Congress on December 9, 1803; declared ratified on September 25, 1804.*]
[ELECTION OF PRESIDENT AND VICE PRESIDENT]

The Electors shall meet in their respective states and vote by ballot for President and Vice-President, one of whom, at least, shall not be an inhabitant of the same state with themselves; they shall name in their ballots the person voted for as President, and in distinct ballots the person voted for as Vice-President, and they shall make distinct lists of all persons voted for as President, and of all persons voted for as Vice-President, and of the number of votes for each, which lists they shall sign and certify, and transmit sealed to the seat of the government of the United States, directed to the President of the Senate;—the President of the Senate shall, in presence of the Senate and House of Representatives, open all the certificates and the votes shall then be counted;—The person having the greatest number of votes for President, shall be the President, if such number be a majority of the whole number of Electors appointed; and if no person have such majority, then from the persons having the highest numbers not exceeding three on the list of those voted for as President, the House of Representatives shall choose immediately, by ballot, the President. But in choosing the President, the votes shall be taken by states, the representation from each state having one vote; a quorum for this purpose shall consist of a member or members from two-thirds of the states, and a majority of all the states shall be necessary to a choice. And if the House of Representatives shall not choose a President whenever the right of choice shall devolve upon them, before the fourth day of March next following, then the Vice-President shall act as President, as in the case of the death or other constitutional disability of the President.—The person having the greatest number of votes as Vice-President, shall be the Vice-President, if such number be a majority of the whole number of Electors appointed, and if no person have a majority, then from the two highest numbers on the list, the Senate shall choose the Vice-President; a quorum for the purpose shall consist of two-thirds of the whole number of Senators, and a majority of the whole number shall be necessary to a choice. But no person constitutionally ineligible to the office of President shall be eligible to that of Vice-President of the United States.

Amendment XIII

[*Proposed by Congress on January 31, 1865; declared ratified on December 18, 1865.*]

SECTION 1
[ABOLITION OF SLAVERY]

Neither slavery nor involuntary servitude, except as a punishment for crime whereof the party shall have been duly convicted, shall exist within the United States, or any place subject to their jurisdiction.

SECTION 2
[POWER TO ENFORCE THIS ARTICLE]

Congress shall have power to enforce this article by appropriate legislation.

Amendment XIV

[*Proposed by Congress on June 13, 1866; declared ratified on July 28, 1868.*]

SECTION 1
[CITIZENSHIP RIGHTS NOT TO BE ABRIDGED BY STATES]

All persons born or naturalized in the United States, and subject to the jurisdiction thereof, are citizens of the United States and of the State wherein they reside. No State shall make or enforce any law which shall abridge the privileges or immunities of citizens of the United States; nor shall any State deprive any person of life, liberty, or property, without due process of law; nor deny to any person within its jurisdiction the equal protection of the laws.

SECTION 2
[APPORTIONMENT OF REPRESENTATIVES IN CONGRESS]

Representatives shall be apportioned among the several States according to their respective numbers, counting the whole number of persons in each State, excluding Indians not taxed. But when the right to vote at any election for the choice of electors for President and Vice-President of the United States, Representatives in Congress, the Executive and Judicial officers of a State, or the members of the Legislature thereof, is denied to any of the male inhabitants of such State, being twenty-one years of age, and citizens of the United States, or in any way abridged, except for participation in rebellion, or other crime, the basis of representation therein shall be reduced in the proportion which the number of such male citizens shall bear to the whole number of male citizens twenty-one years of age in such State.

SECTION 3
[PERSONS DISQUALIFIED FROM HOLDING OFFICE]

No person shall be a Senator or Representative in Congress, or elector of President and Vice-President, or hold any office, civil or military, under the United States, or under any State, who, having previously taken an oath, as a member of Congress, or as an officer of the United States, or as a member of any State legislature, or as an executive or judicial officer of any State, to support the Constitution of the United States, shall have engaged in insurrection or rebellion against the same, or given aid or comfort to the enemies thereof. But Congress may by a vote of two-thirds of each House, remove such disability.

SECTION 4
[WHAT PUBLIC DEBTS ARE VALID]

The validity of the public debt of the United States, authorized by law, including debts incurred for payment of pensions and bounties for services in suppressing insurrection or rebellion, shall not be questioned. But neither the United States nor any State shall assume or pay any debt or obligation incurred in aid of insurrection or rebellion against the United States, or any claim for the loss or emancipation of any slave; but all such debts, obligations and claims shall be held illegal and void.

SECTION 5
[POWER TO ENFORCE THIS ARTICLE]

The Congress shall have power to enforce, by appropriate legislation, the provisions of this article.

Amendment XV

[*Proposed by Congress on February 26, 1869; declared ratified on March 30, 1870.*]

SECTION 1
[NEGRO SUFFRAGE]

The right of citizens of the United States to vote shall not be denied or abridged by the United States or by any State on account of race, color, or previous condition of servitude.

SECTION 2
[POWER TO ENFORCE THIS ARTICLE]

The Congress shall have power to enforce this article by appropriate legislation.

Amendment XVI

[*Proposed by Congress on July 2, 1909; declared ratified on February 25, 1913.*]

[AUTHORIZING INCOME TAXES]

The Congress shall have power to lay and collect taxes on incomes, from whatever source derived, without apportionment among the several States, and without regard to any census or enumeration.

Amendment XVII

[*Proposed by Congress on May 13, 1912; declared ratified on May 31, 1913.*]

[POPULAR ELECTION OF SENATORS]

The Senate of the United States shall be composed of two Senators from each State, elected by the people thereof, for six years; and each Senator shall have one vote. The electors in each State shall have the qualifications requisite for electors of the most numerous branch of the State legislatures.

When vacancies happen in the representation of any State in the Senate, the executive authority of such State shall issue writs of election to fill such vacancies: *Provided,* That the legislature of any State may empower the executive thereof to make temporary appointments until the people fill the vacancies by election as the legislature may direct.

This amendment shall not be so construed as to affect the election or term of any Senator chosen before it becomes valid as part of the Constitution.

Amendment XVIII

[*Proposed by Congress December 18, 1917; declared ratified on January 29, 1919.*]

SECTION 1
[NATIONAL LIQUOR PROHIBITION]

After one year from the ratification of this article the manufacture, sale, or transportation of intoxicating liquors within, the importation thereof into, or the exportation thereof from the United States and all territory subject to the jurisdiction thereof for beverage purposes is hereby prohibited.

SECTION 2
[POWER TO ENFORCE THIS ARTICLE]

The Congress and the several States shall have concurrent power to enforce this article by appropriate legislation.

SECTION 3
[RATIFICATION WITHIN SEVEN YEARS]

This article shall be inoperative unless it shall have been ratified as an amendment to the Constitution by the legislatures of the several States, as provided in the Constitution, within seven years from the date of the submission hereof to the States by the Congress.[1]

Amendment XIX

[*Proposed by Congress on June 4, 1919; declared ratified on August 26, 1920.*]

---

[1] Repealed by the Twenty-first Amendment.

[WOMAN SUFFRAGE]

The right of citizens of the United States to vote shall not be denied or abridged by the United States or by any State on account of sex.

Congress shall have power to enforce this article by appropriate legislation.

Amendment XX

[*Proposed by Congress on March 2, 1932; declared ratified on February 6, 1933.*]

SECTION 1
[TERMS OF OFFICE]

The terms of the President and Vice President shall end at noon on the 20th day of January, and the terms of Senators and Representatives at noon on the 3d day of January, of the years in which such terms would have ended if this article had not been ratified; and the terms of their successors shall then begin.

SECTION 2
[TIME OF CONVENING CONGRESS]

The Congress shall assemble at least once in every year, and such meeting shall begin at noon on the 3d day of January, unless they shall by law appoint a different day.

SECTION 3
[DEATH OF PRESIDENT-ELECT]

If, at the time fixed for the beginning of the term of the President, the President elect shall have died, the Vice President elect shall become President. If a President shall not have been chosen before the time fixed for the beginning of his term, or if the President elect shall have failed to qualify, then the Vice President elect shall act as President until a President shall have qualified; and the Congress may by law provide for the case wherein neither a President elect nor a Vice President elect shall have qualified, declaring who shall then act as President, or the manner in which one who is to act shall be selected, and such person shall act accordingly until a President or Vice President shall have qualified.

SECTION 4
[ELECTION OF THE PRESIDENT]

The Congress may by law provide for the case of the death of any of the persons from whom the House of Representatives may choose a President whenever the right of choice shall have devolved upon them, and for the case of the death of any of the persons from whom the Senate may choose a Vice President whenever the right of choice shall have devolved upon them.

SECTION 5
[AMENDMENT TAKES EFFECT]

Sections 1 and 2 shall take effect on the 15th day of October following the ratification of this article.

SECTION 6
[RATIFICATION WITHIN SEVEN YEARS]

This article shall be inoperative unless it shall have been ratified as an amendment to the Constitution by the legislatures of three-fourths of the several States within seven years from the date of its submission.

Amendment XXI

[*Proposed by Congress on February 20, 1933; declared ratified on December 5, 1933.*]

SECTION 1
[NATIONAL LIQUOR PROHIBITION REPEALED]

The eighteenth article of amendment to the Constitution of the United States is hereby repealed.

SECTION 2
[TRANSPORTATION OF LIQUOR INTO "DRY" STATES]

The transportation or importation into any State, Territory, or Possession of the United States for delivery or use therein of intoxicating liquors, in violation of the laws thereof, is hereby prohibited.

SECTION 3
[RATIFICATION WITHIN SEVEN YEARS]

This article shall be inoperative unless it shall have been ratified as an amendment to the Constitution by conventions in the several States, as provided in the Constitution, within seven years from the date of the submission hereof to the States by the Congress.

Amendment XXII

[*Proposed by Congress on March 21, 1947; declared ratified on February 27, 1951.*]

SECTION 1
[TENURE OF PRESIDENT LIMITED]

No person shall be elected to the office of President more than twice, and no person who has held the office of President or acted as President, for more than two years of a term to which some other person was elected President shall be elected to the office of the President more than once. But this Article shall not apply to any person holding the office of President when this Article was proposed by the Congress, and shall not prevent any person who may be holding the office of President, or acting as President, during the term within which this Article becomes operative from holding the office of President or acting as President during the remainder of such term.

SECTION 2
[RATIFICATION WITHIN SEVEN YEARS]

This article shall be inoperative unless it shall have been ratified as an amendment to the Constitution by the legislatures of three-fourths of the several States within seven years from the date of its submission to the States by the Congress.

Amendment XXIII

[*Proposed by Congress on June 16, 1960; declared ratified on March 29, 1961.*]

SECTION 1
[ELECTORAL COLLEGE VOTES FOR THE DISTRICT OF COLUMBIA]

The District constituting the seat of Government of the United States shall appoint in such manner as the Congress may direct:

A number of electors of President and Vice President equal to the whole number of Senators and Representatives in Congress to which the District would be entitled if it were a State, but in no event more than the least populous State; they shall be in addition to those appointed by the States, but they shall be considered, for the purposes of the election of President and Vice President, to be electors appointed by a State; and they shall meet in the District and perform such duties as provided by the twelfth article of amendment.

SECTION 2
[POWER TO ENFORCE THIS ARTICLE]

The Congress shall have power to enforce this article by appropriate legislation.

Amendment XXIV

[*Proposed by Congress on August 27, 1962; declared ratified on January 23, 1964.*]

SECTION 1
[ANTI-POLL TAX]

The right of citizens of the United States to vote in any primary or other election for President or Vice President, for electors for President or Vice President, or for Senator or Representative of Congress, shall not be denied or abridged by the United States or any State by reason of failure to pay any poll tax or other tax.

SECTION 2
[POWER TO ENFORCE THIS ARTICLE]

The Congress shall have power to enforce this article by appropriate legislation.

Amendment XXV

[*Proposed by Congress on July 6, 1965; declared ratified on February 10, 1967.*]

SECTION 1
[VICE PRESIDENT TO BECOME PRESIDENT]

In case of the removal of the President from office or his death or resignation, the Vice President shall become President.

SECTION 2
[CHOICE OF A NEW VICE PRESIDENT]

Whenever there is a vacancy in the office of the Vice President, the President shall nominate a Vice President who shall take the office upon confirmation by a majority vote of both houses of Congress.

SECTION 3
[PRESIDENT MAY DECLARE OWN DISABILITY]

Whenever the President transmits to the President pro tempore of the Senate and the Speaker of the House of Representatives his written declaration that he is unable to discharge the powers and duties of his office, and until he transmits to them a written declaration to the contrary, such powers and duties shall be discharged by the Vice President as Acting President.

SECTION 4
[ALTERNATE PROCEDURES TO DECLARE AND TO END PRESIDENTIAL DISABILITY]

Whenever the Vice President and a majority of either the principal officers of the executive departments, or of such other body as Congress may by law provide, transmit to the President pro tempore of the Senate and the Speaker of the House of Representatives their written declaration that the President is unable to discharge the powers and duties of his office, the Vice President shall immediately assume the powers and duties of the office as Acting President.

Thereafter, when the President transmits to the President pro tempore of the Senate and the Speaker of the House of Representatives his written declaration that no inability exists, he shall resume the powers and duties of his office unless the Vice President and a majority of either the principal officers of the executive department, or of such other body as Congress may by law provide, transmit within four days to the President pro tempore of the Senate and the Speaker of the House of Representatives their written declaration that the President is unable to discharge the powers and duties of his office. Thereupon Congress shall decide the issue, assembling within forty eight hours for that purpose if not in session. If the Congress, within twenty one days after receipt of the latter written declaration, or, if Congress is not in session, within twenty one days after Congress is required to assemble, determines by two-thirds vote of both Houses that the President is unable to discharge the powers and duties of his office, the Vice President shall continue to discharge the same as Acting President; otherwise, the President shall resume the powers and duties of his office.

Amendment XXVI

[*Proposed by Congress on March 23, 1971; declared ratified on July 1, 1971.*]

SECTION 1
[EIGHTEEN-YEAR-OLD VOTE]

The right of citizens of the United States, who are eighteen years of age or older, to vote shall not be denied or abridged by the United States or by any State on account of age.

SECTION 2
[POWER TO ENFORCE THIS ARTICLE]

The Congress shall have power to enforce this article by appropriate legislation.

Amendment XXVII

[*Proposed by Congress on September 25, 1789; declared ratified on May 8, 1992.*]
[CONGRESS CANNOT RAISE ITS OWN PAY]

No law varying the compensation for the services of the Senators and Representatives, shall take effect, until an election of representatives shall have intervened.

The Federalist Papers

No. 10: Madison

Among the numerous advantages promised by a well constructed Union, none deserves to be more accurately developed than its tendency to break and control the violence of faction. The friend of popular governments never finds himself so much alarmed for their character and fate, as when he contemplates their propensity to this dangerous vice. He will not fail therefore to set a due value on any plan which, without violating the principles to which he is attached, provides a proper cure for it. The instability, injustice, and confusion introduced into the public councils have, in truth, been the mortal diseases under which popular governments have everywhere perished, as they continue to be the favorite and fruitful topics from which the adversaries to liberty derive their most specious declamations. The valuable improvements made by the American constitutions on the popular models, both ancient and modern, cannot certainly be too much admired; but it would be an unwarrantable partiality to contend that they have as effectually obviated the danger on this side, as was wished and expected. Complaints are everywhere heard from our most considerate and virtuous citizens, equally the friends of public and private faith and of public and personal liberty, that our governments are too unstable, that the public good is disregarded in the conflicts of rival parties, and that measures are too often decided, not according to the rules of justice and the rights of the minor party, but by the superior force of an interested and overbearing majority. However anxiously we may wish that these complaints had no foundation, the evidence of known facts will not permit us to deny that they are in some degree true. It will be found, indeed, on a candid review of our situation, that some of the distresses under which we labor have been erroneously charged on the operation of our governments; but it will be found, at the same time, that other causes will not alone account for many of our heaviest misfortunes; and, particularly, for that prevailing and increasing distrust of public engagements and alarm for private rights which are echoed from one end of the continent to the other. These must be chiefly, if not wholly, effects of the unsteadiness and injustice with which a factious spirit has tainted our public administration.

By a faction I understand a number of citizens, whether amounting to a majority or minority of the whole, who are united and actuated by some common impulse of passion, or of interest, adverse to the rights of other citizens, or to the permanent and aggregate interests of the community.

There are two methods of curing the mischiefs of faction: the one, by removing its causes; the other, by controlling its effects.

There are again two methods of removing the causes of faction: the one, by destroying the liberty which is essential to its existence; the other, by giving to every citizen the same opinions, the same passions, and the same interests.

It could never be more truly said than of the first remedy, that it is worse than the disease. Liberty is to faction what air is to fire, an aliment without which it instantly expires. But it could not be a less folly to abolish liberty, which is essential to political life, because it nourishes faction, than it would be to wish the annihilation of air, which is essential to animal life, because it imparts to fire its destructive agency.

The second expedient is as impracticable, as the first would be unwise. As long as the reason of man continues fallible, and he is at liberty to exercise it, different opinions will be formed. As long as the connection subsists between his reason and his self-love, his opinions and his passions will have a reciprocal influence on each other; and the former will be objects to which the latter will attach themselves. The diversity in the faculties of men, from which the rights of property originate, is not less an insuperable obstacle to a uniformity of interests. The protection of these faculties is the first object of Government. From the protection of different and unequal faculties of acquiring property, the possession of different degrees and kinds of property immediately results; and from the influence of these on the sentiments and views of the respective proprietors, ensues a division of the society into different interests and parties.

The latent causes of faction are thus sown in the nature of man; and we see them everywhere brought into different degrees of activity, according to the different circumstances of civil society. A zeal for different opinions concerning religion, concerning Government, and many other points, as well of speculation as of practice; an attachment to different leaders ambitiously contending for pre-eminence and power; or to persons of other descriptions whose fortunes have been interesting to the human passions, have in turn divided mankind into parties, inflamed them with mutual animosity, and rendered them much more disposed to vex and oppress each other, than to co-operate for their common good. So strong is this propensity of mankind to fall into mutual animosities, that where no substantial occasion presents itself, the most frivolous and fanciful distinctions have been sufficient to kindle their unfriendly passions, and excite their most violent conflicts. But the most common and durable source of factions has been the various and unequal distribution of property. Those who hold and those who are without property have ever formed distinct interests in society. Those who are creditors, and those who are debtors, fall under a like discrimination. A landed interest, a manufacturing interest, a mercantile interest, a moneyed interest, with many lesser interests, grow up of necessity in civilized nations, and divide them into different classes, actuated by different sentiments and views. The regulation of these various and interfering interests forms the principal task of modern Legislation, and involves the spirit of party and faction in the necessary and ordinary operations of Government.

No man is allowed to be judge in his own cause, because his interest would certainly bias his judgment and, not improbably, corrupt his integrity. With equal, nay with greater reason, a body of men are unfit to be both judges and parties at the same time; yet what are many of the most important acts of legislation but so many judicial determinations, not indeed concerning the rights of single persons, but concerning the rights of large bodies of citizens; and what are the different classes of legislators but advocates and parties to the causes which they determine? Is a law proposed concerning private debts? It is a question to which the creditors are parties on one side and the debtors on the other. Justice ought to hold the balance between them. Yet the parties are, and must be, themselves the judges; and the most numerous party, or in other words, the most powerful faction must be expected to prevail. Shall domestic manufacturers be encouraged, and in what degree, by restrictions on foreign manufacturers? are questions which would be differently decided by the landed and the manufacturing classes, and probably by neither with a sole regard to justice and the public good. The apportionment of taxes on the various descriptions of property is an act which seems to require the most exact impartiality; yet there is, perhaps, no legislative act in which greater opportunity and temptation are given to a predominant party to trample on the rules of justice. Every shilling with which they overburden the inferior number is a shilling saved to their own pockets.

It is in vain to say that enlightened statesmen will be able to adjust these clashing interests and render them all subservient to the public good. Enlightened statesmen will not always be at the helm. Nor, in many cases, can such an adjustment be made at all without taking into view indirect and remote considerations, which will rarely prevail over the immediate interest which one party may find in disregarding the rights of another or the good of the whole.

The inference to which we are brought is that the *causes* of faction cannot be removed and that relief is only to be sought in the means of controlling its *effects*.

If a faction consists of less than a majority, relief is supplied by the republican principle, which enables the majority to defeat its sinister views by regular vote. It may clog the administration, it may convulse the society; but it will be unable to execute and mask its violence under the forms of the Constitution. When a majority is included in a faction, the form of popular government, on the other hand, enables it to sacrifice to its ruling passion or interest both the public good and the rights of other citizens. To secure the public good and private rights against the danger of such a faction, and at the same time to preserve the spirit and the form of popular government, is then the great object to which our enquiries are directed. Let me add that it is the great desideratum by which alone this form of government can be rescued from the opprobrium under which it has so long labored and be recommended to the esteem and adoption of mankind.

By what means is this object attainable? Evidently by one of two only. Either the existence of the same passion or interest in a majority at the same time must be prevented, or the majority, having such co-existent passion or interest, must be rendered, by their number and local situation, unable to concert and carry into effect schemes of oppression. If the impulse and the opportunity be suffered to coincide, we well know that neither moral nor religious motives can be relied on as an adequate control. They are not found to be such on the injustice and violence of individuals, and lose their efficacy in proportion to the number combined together, that is, in proportion as their efficacy becomes needful.

From this view of the subject it may be concluded that a pure Democracy, by which I mean a Society consisting of a small number of citizens, who assemble and administer the Government in person, can admit of no cure for the mischiefs of faction. A common passion or interest will, in almost every case, be felt by a majority of the whole; a communication and concert results from the form of Government itself; and there is nothing to check the inducements to sacrifice the weaker party or an obnoxious individual. Hence it is that such Democracies have ever been spectacles of turbulence and contention; have ever been found incompatible with personal security or the rights of property; and have in general been as short in their lives as they have been violent in their deaths. Theoretic politicians, who have patronized this species of Government, have erroneously supposed that by reducing mankind to a perfect equality in their political rights, they would at the same time be perfectly equalized and assimilated in their possessions, their opinions, and their passions.

A Republic, by which I mean a Government in which the scheme of representation takes place, opens a different prospect and promises the cure for which we are seeking. Let us examine the points in which it varies from pure Democracy, and we shall comprehend both the nature of the cure and the efficacy which it must derive from the Union.

The two great points of difference between a Democracy and a Republic are: first, the delegation of the Government, in the latter, to a small number of citizens elected by the rest; secondly, the greater number of citizens and greater sphere of country over which the latter may be extended.

The effect of the first difference is, on the one hand, to refine and enlarge the public views by passing them through the medium of a chosen body of citizens, whose wisdom may best discern the true interest of their country and whose patriotism and love of justice will be least likely to sacrifice it to temporary or partial considerations. Under such a regulation it may well happen that the public voice, pronounced by the representatives of the people, will be more consonant to the public good than if pronounced by the people themselves, convened for the purpose. On the other hand, the effect may be inverted. Men of factious tempers, of local prejudices, or of sinister designs, may, by intrigue, by corruption, or by other means, first obtain the suffrages, and then betray the interests of the people. The question resulting is, whether small or extensive Republics are most favorable to the election of proper guardians of the public weal; and it is clearly decided in favor of the latter by two obvious considerations.

In the first place it is to be remarked that however small the Republic may be, the Representatives must be raised to a certain number in order to guard against the cabals of a few; and that however large it may be they must be limited to a certain number in order to guard against the confusion of a multitude. Hence, the number of Representatives in the two cases not being in proportion to that of the Constituents, and being proportionally greatest in the small Republic, it follows that if the proportion of fit characters be not less in the large than in the small Republic, the former will present a greater option, and consequently a greater probability of a fit choice.

In the next place, as each Representative will be chosen by a greater number of citizens in the large than in the small Republic, it will be more difficult for unworthy candidates to practise with success the vicious arts by which elections are too often carried; and the suffrages of the people being more free, will be more likely to centre on men who possess the most attractive merit and the most diffusive and established characters.

It must be confessed that in this, as in most other cases, there is a mean, on both sides of which inconveniencies will be found to lie. By enlarging too much the number of electors, you render the representative too little acquainted with all their local circumstances and lesser interests; as by reducing it too much, you render him unduly attached to these, and too little fit to comprehend and pursue great and national objects. The Federal Constitution forms a happy combination in this respect; the great and aggregate interests being referred to the national, the local and particular to the State legislatures.

The other point of difference is the greater number of citizens and extent of territory which may be brought within the compass of Republican than of Democratic Government; and it is this circumstance principally which renders factious combinations less to be dreaded in the former than in the latter. The smaller the society, the fewer probably will be the distinct parties and interests composing it; the fewer the distinct parties and interests, the more frequently will a majority be found of the same party; and the smaller the number of individuals composing a majority, and the smaller the compass within which they are placed, the more easily will they concert and execute their plans of oppression. Extend the sphere and you take in a greater variety of parties and interests; you make it less probable that a majority of the whole will have a common motive to invade the rights of other citizens; or if such a common motive exists, it will be more difficult for all who feel it to discover their own strength and to act in unison with each other. Besides other impediments, it may be remarked, that where there is a consciousness of unjust or dishonorable purposes, communication is always checked by distrust in proportion to the number whose concurrence is necessary.

Hence, it clearly appears that the same advantage which a Republic has over a Democracy in controlling the effects of faction is enjoyed by a large over a small republic—is enjoyed by the Union over the States composing it. Does this advantage consist in the substitution of representatives whose enlightened views and virtuous sentiments render them superior to local prejudices and to schemes of injustice? It will not be denied that the representation of the Union will be most likely to possess these requisite endowments. Does it consist in the greater security afforded by a greater variety of parties, against the event of any one party being able to outnumber and oppress the rest? In an equal degree does the increased variety of parties comprised within the Union increase this security? Does it, in fine, consist in the greater obstacles opposed to the concert and accomplishment of the secret wishes of an unjust and interested majority? Here again the extent of the Union gives it the most palpable advantage.

The influence of factious leaders may kindle a flame within their particular States but will be unable to spread a general conflagration through the other States: a religious sect may degenerate into a political faction in a part of the Confederacy; but the variety of sects dispersed over the entire face of it must secure the national Councils against any danger from that source: a rage for paper money, for an abolition of debts, for an equal division of property, or for any other improper or wicked project, will be less apt to pervade the whole body of the Union than a particular member of it; in the same proportion as such a malady is more likely to taint a particular county or district than an entire State.

In the extent and proper structure of the Union, therefore, we behold a republican remedy for the diseases most incident to Republican Government. And according to the degree of pleasure and pride we feel in being republicans ought to be our zeal in cherishing the spirit and supporting the character of federalist.

PUBLIUS

No. 51: Madison

To what expedient, then, shall we finally resort, for maintaining in practice the necessary partition of power among the several departments as laid down in the constitution? The only answer that can be given is that as all these exterior provisions are found to be inadequate the defect must be supplied, by so contriving the interior structure of the government as that its several constituent parts may, by their mutual relations, be the means of keeping each other in their proper places. Without presuming to undertake a full development of this important idea I will hazard a few general observations which may perhaps place it in a clearer light, and enable us to form a more correct judgment of the principles and structure of the government planned by the convention.

In order to lay a due foundation for that separate and distinct exercise of the different powers of government, which to a certain extent is admitted on all hands to be essential to the preservation of liberty, it is evident that each department should have a will of its own; and consequently should be so constituted that the members of each should have as little agency as possible in the appointment of the members of the others. Were this principle rigorously adhered to, it would require that all the appointments for the supreme executive, legislative, and judiciary magistracies should be drawn from the same fountain of authority, the people, through channels having no communication whatever with one another. Perhaps such a plan of constructing the several departments would be less difficult in practice than it may in contemplation appear. Some difficulties, however, and some additional expense would attend the execution of it. Some deviations, therefore, from the principle must be admitted. In the constitution of the judiciary department in particular, it might be inexpedient to insist rigorously on the principle: first, because peculiar qualifications being essential in the members, the primary consideration ought to be to select that mode of choice which best secures these qualifications; second, because the permanent tenure by which the appointments are held in that department must soon destroy all sense of dependence on the authority conferring them.

It is equally evident that the members of each department should be as little dependent as possible on those of the others for the emoluments annexed to their offices. Were the executive magistrate, or the judges, not independent of the legislature in this particular, their independence in every other would be merely nominal.

But the great security against a gradual concentration of the several powers in the same department consists in giving to those who administer each department the necessary constitutional means and personal motives to resist encroachments of the others. The provision for defence must in this, as in all other cases, be made commensurate to the danger of attack. Ambition must be made to counteract ambition. The interest of the man must be connected with the constitutional rights of the place. It may be a reflection on human nature that such devices should be necessary to control the abuses of government. But what is government itself but the greatest of all reflections on human nature? If men were angels, no government would be necessary. If angels were to govern men, neither external nor internal controls on government would be necessary. In framing a government which is to be administered by men over men, the great difficulty lies in this: You must first enable the government to control the governed; and in the next place oblige it to control itself. A dependence on the people is, no doubt, the primary control on the government; but experience has taught mankind the necessity of auxiliary precautions.

This policy of supplying, by opposite and rival interests, the defect of better motives, might be traced through the whole system of human affairs, private as well as public. We see it particularly displayed in all the subordinate distributions of power, where the constant aim is to divide and arrange the several offices in such a manner as that each may be a check on the other; that the private interest of every individual may be a sentinel over the public rights. These inventions of prudence cannot be less requisite in the distribution of the supreme powers of the State.

But it is not possible to give to each department an equal power of self-defense. In republican government, the legislative authority necessarily predominates. The remedy for this inconveniency is to divide the legislature into different branches; and to render them, by different modes of election and different principles of action, as little connected with each other as the nature of their common functions and their common dependence on the society will admit. It may even be necessary to guard against dangerous encroachments by still further precautions. As the weight of the legislative authority requires that it should be thus divided, the weakness of the executive may require, on the other hand, that it should be fortified. An absolute negative on the legislature appears, at first view, to be the natural defense with which the executive magistrate should be armed. But perhaps it would be neither altogether safe nor alone sufficient. On ordinary occasions it might not be exerted with the requisite firmness, and on extraordinary occasions it might be perfidiously abused. May not this defect of an absolute negative be supplied by some qualified connection between this weaker branch of the stronger department, by which the latter may be led to support the constitutional rights of the former, without being too much detached from the rights of its own department?

If the principles on which these observations are founded be just, as I persuade myself they are, and they be applied as a criterion to the several State constitutions, and to the federal Constitution, it will be found that if the latter does not perfectly correspond with them, the former are infinitely less able to bear such a test.

There are, moreover, two considerations particularly applicable to the federal system of America, which place that system in a very interesting point of view.

First. In a single republic, all the power surrendered by the people is submitted to the administration of a single government; and usurpations are guarded against by a division of the government into distinct and separate departments. In the compound republic of America, the power surrendered by the people is first divided between two distinct governments, and then the portion allotted to each subdivided among distinct and separate departments. Hence a double security arises to the rights of the people. The different governments will control each other, at the same time that each will be controlled by itself.

Second. It is of great importance in a republic not only to guard the society against the oppression of its rulers, but to guard one part of the society against the injustice of the other part. Different interests necessarily exist in different classes of citizens. If a majority be united by a common interest, the rights of the minority will be insecure. There are but two methods of providing against this evil: The one by creating a will in the community independent of the majority—that is, of the society itself; the other, by comprehending in the society so many separate descriptions of citizens as will render an unjust combination of a majority of the whole very improbable, if not impracticable. The first method prevails in all governments possessing an hereditary or self-appointed authority. This, at best, is but a precarious security; because a power independent of the society may as well espouse the unjust views of the major as the rightful interests of the minor party, and may possibly be turned against both parties. The second method will be exemplified in the federal republic of the United States. Whilst all authority in it will be derived from and dependent on the society, the society itself will be broken into so many parts, interests and classes of citizens, that the rights of individuals, or of the minority, will be in little danger from interested combinations of the majority. In a free government the security for civil rights must be the same as that for religious rights. It consists in the one case in the multiplicity of interests, and in the other in the multiplicity of sects. The degree of security in both cases will depend on the number of interests and sects; and this may be presumed to depend on the extent of country and number of people comprehended under the same government. This view of the subject must particularly recommend a proper federal system to all the sincere and considerate friends of republican government: Since it shows that in exact proportion as the territory of the Union may be formed into more circumscribed Confederacies, or States, oppressive combinations of a majority will be facilitated; the best security, under the republican form, for the rights of every class of citizens, will be diminished; and consequently the stability and independence of some member of the government, the only other security, must be proportionally increased. Justice is the end of government. It is the end of civil society. It ever has been and ever will be pursued until it be obtained, or until liberty be lost in the pursuit. In a society under the forms of which the stronger faction can readily unite and oppress the weaker, anarchy may as truly be said to reign as in a state of nature, where the weaker individual is not secured against the violence of the stronger: And as, in the latter state, even the stronger individuals are prompted, by the uncertainty of their condition, to submit to a government which may protect the weak as well as themselves: So, in the former state, will the more powerful factions or parties be gradually induced, by a like motive, to wish for a government which will protect all parties, the weaker as well as the more powerful. It can be little doubted that if the State of Rhode Island was separated from the Confederacy and left to itself, the insecurity of rights under the popular form of government within such narrow limits would be displayed by such reiterated oppressions of factious majorities that some power altogether independent of the people would soon be called for by the voice of the very factions whose misrule had proved the necessity of it. In the extended republic of the United States, and among the great variety of interests, parties, and sects which it embraces, a coalition of a majority of the whole society could seldom take place on any other principles than those of justice and the general good; and there being thus less danger to a minor from the will of the major party, there must be less pretext, also, to provide for the security of the former, by introducing into the government a will not dependent on the latter, or, in other words, a will independent of the society itself. It is no less certain than it is important, notwithstanding the contrary opinions which have been entertained, that the larger the society, provided it lie within a practicable sphere, the more duly capable it will be of self-government. And happily for the *republican cause,* practicable sphere may be carried to a very great extent by a judicious modification and mixture of the *federal principle.*

PUBLIUS

No. 78: Hamilton

To the People of the State of New York:

we proceed now to an examination of the judiciary department of the proposed government.

In unfolding the defects of the existing Confederation, the utility and necessity of a federal judicature have been clearly pointed out. It is the less necessary to recapitulate the considerations there urged, as the propriety of the institution in the abstract is not disputed; the only questions which have been raised being relative to the manner of constituting it, and to its extent. To these points, therefore, our observations shall be confined.

The manner of constituting it seems to embrace these several objects: 1st. The mode of appointing the judges. 2d. The tenure by which they are to hold their places. 3d. The partition of the judiciary authority between different courts, and their relations to each other.

First. As to the mode of appointing the judges; this is the same with that of appointing the officers of the Union in general, and has been so fully discussed in the two last numbers, that nothing can be said here which would not be useless repetition.

Second. As to the tenure by which the judges are to hold their places; this chiefly concerns their duration in office; the provisions for their support; the precautions for their responsibility.

According to the plan of the convention, all judges who may be appointed by the United States are to hold their offices DURING GOOD BEHAVIOR; which is conformable to the most approved of the State constitutions and among the rest, to that of this State. Its propriety having been drawn into question by the adversaries of that plan, is no light symptom of the rage for objection, which disorders their imaginations and judgments. The standard of good behavior for the continuance in office of the judicial magistracy, is certainly one of the most valuable of the modern improvements in the practice of government. In a monarchy it is an excellent barrier to the despotism of the prince; in a republic it is a no less excellent barrier to the encroachments and oppressions of the representative body. And it is the best expedient which can be devised in any government, to secure a steady, upright, and impartial administration of the laws.

Whoever attentively considers the different departments of power must perceive, that, in a government in which they are separated from each other, the judiciary, from the nature of its functions, will always be the least dangerous to the political rights of the Constitution; because it will be least in a capacity to annoy or injure them. The Executive not only dispenses the honors, but holds the sword of the community. The legislature not only commands the purse, but prescribes the rules by which the duties and rights of every citizen are to be regulated. The judiciary, on the contrary, has no influence over either the sword or the purse; no direction either of the strength or of the wealth of the society; and can take no active resolution whatever. It may truly be said to have neither FORCE nor WILL, but merely judgment; and must ultimately depend upon the aid of the executive arm even for the efficacy of its judgments.

This simple view of the matter suggests several important consequences. It proves incontestably, that the judiciary is beyond comparison the weakest of the three departments of power; that it can never attack with success either of the other two; and that all possible care is requisite to enable it to defend itself against their attacks. It equally proves, that though individual oppression may now and then proceed from the courts of justice, the general liberty of the people can never be endangered from that quarter; I mean so long as the judiciary remains truly distinct from both the legislature and the Executive. For I agree, that "there is no liberty, if the power of judging be not separated from the legislative and executive powers." And it proves, in the last place, that as liberty can have nothing to fear from the judiciary alone, but would have every thing to fear from its union with either of the other departments; that as all the effects of such a union must ensue from a dependence of the former on the latter, notwithstanding a nominal and apparent separation; that as, from the natural feebleness of the judiciary, it is in continual jeopardy of being overpowered, awed, or influenced by its co-ordinate branches; and that as nothing can contribute so much to its firmness and independence as permanency in office, this quality may therefore be justly regarded as an indispensable ingredient in its constitution, and, in a great measure, as the citadel of the public justice and the public security.

The complete independence of the courts of justice is peculiarly essential in a limited Constitution. By a limited Constitution, I understand one which contains certain specified exceptions to the legislative authority; such, for instance, as that it shall pass no bills of attainder, no ex-post-facto laws, and the like. Limitations of this kind can be preserved in practice no other way than through the medium of courts of justice, whose duty it must be to declare all acts contrary to the manifest tenor of the Constitution void. Without this, all the reservations of particular rights or privileges would amount to nothing.

Some perplexity respecting the rights of the courts to pronounce legislative acts void, because contrary to the Constitution, has arisen from an imagination that the doctrine would imply a superiority of the judiciary to the legislative power. It is urged that the authority which can declare the acts of another void, must necessarily be superior to the one whose acts may be declared void. As this doctrine is of great importance in all the American constitutions, a brief discussion of the ground on which it rests cannot be unacceptable.

There is no position which depends on clearer principles, than that every act of a delegated authority, contrary to the tenor of the commission under which it is exercised, is void. No legislative act, therefore, contrary to the Constitution, can be valid. To deny this, would be to affirm, that the deputy is greater than his principal; that the servant is above his master; that the representatives of the people are superior to the people themselves; that men acting by virtue of powers, may do not only what their powers do not authorize, but what they forbid.

If it be said that the legislative body are themselves the constitutional judges of their own powers, and that the construction they put upon them is conclusive upon the other departments, it may be answered, that this cannot be the natural presumption, where it is not to be collected from any particular provisions in the Constitution. It is not otherwise to be supposed, that the Constitution could intend to enable the representatives of the people to substitute their will to that of their constituents. It is far more rational to suppose, that the courts were designed to be an intermediate body between the people and the legislature, in order, among other things, to keep the latter within the limits assigned to their authority. The interpretation of the laws is the proper and peculiar province of the courts. A constitution is, in fact, and must be regarded by the judges, as a fundamental law. It therefore belongs to them to ascertain its meaning, as well as the meaning of any particular act proceeding from the legislative body. If there should happen to be an irreconcilable variance between the two, that which has the superior obligation and validity ought, of course, to be preferred; or, in other words, the Constitution ought to be preferred to the statute, the intention of the people to the intention of their agents.

Nor does this conclusion by any means suppose a superiority of the judicial to the legislative power. It only supposes that the power of the people is superior to both; and that where the will of the legislature, declared in its statutes, stands in opposition to that of the people, declared in the Constitution, the judges ought to be governed by the latter rather than the former. They ought to regulate their decisions by the fundamental laws, rather than by those which are not fundamental.

This exercise of judicial discretion, in determining between two contradictory laws, is exemplified in a familiar instance. It not uncommonly happens, that there are two statutes existing at one time, clashing in whole or in part with each other, and neither of them containing any repealing clause or expression. In such a case, it is the province of the courts to liquidate and fix their meaning and operation. So far as they can, by any fair construction, be reconciled to each other, reason and law conspire to dictate that this should be done; where this is impracticable, it becomes a matter of necessity to give effect to one, in exclusion of the other. The rule which has obtained in the courts for determining their relative validity is, that the last in order of time shall be preferred to the first. But this is a mere rule of construction, not derived from any positive law, but from the nature and reason of the thing. It is a rule not enjoined upon the courts by legislative provision, but adopted by themselves, as consonant to truth and propriety, for the direction of their conduct as interpreters of the law. They thought it reasonable, that between the interfering acts of an equal authority, that which was the last indication of its will should have the preference.

But in regard to the interfering acts of a superior and subordinate authority, of an original and derivative power, the nature and reason of the thing indicate the converse of that rule as proper to be followed. They teach us that the prior act of a superior ought to be preferred to the subsequent act of an inferior and subordinate authority; and that accordingly, whenever a particular statute contravenes the Constitution, it will be the duty of the judicial tribunals to adhere to the latter and disregard the former.

It can be of no weight to say that the courts, on the pretense of a repugnancy, may substitute their own pleasure to the constitutional intentions of the legislature. This might as well happen in the case of two contradictory statutes; or it might as well happen in every adjudication upon any single statute. The courts must declare the sense of the law; and if they should be disposed to exercise WILL instead of judgment, the consequence would equally be the substitution of their pleasure to that of the legislative body. The observation, if it prove any thing, would prove that there ought to be no judges distinct from that body.

If, then, the courts of justice are to be considered as the bulwarks of a limited Constitution against legislative encroachments, this consideration will afford a strong argument for the permanent tenure of judicial offices, since nothing will contribute so much as this to that independent spirit in the judges which must be essential to the faithful performance of so arduous a duty.

This independence of the judges is equally requisite to guard the Constitution and the rights of individuals from the effects of those ill humors, which the arts of designing men, or the influence of particular conjunctures, sometimes disseminate among the people themselves, and which, though they speedily give place to better information, and more deliberate reflection, have a tendency, in the meantime, to occasion dangerous innovations in the government, and serious oppressions of the minor party in the community. Though I trust the friends of the proposed Constitution will never concur with its enemies, in questioning that fundamental principle of republican government, which admits the right of the people to alter or abolish the established Constitution, whenever they find it inconsistent with their happiness, yet it is not to be inferred from this principle, that the representatives of the people, whenever a momentary inclination happens to lay hold of a majority of their constituents, incompatible with the provisions in the existing Constitution, would, on that account, be justifiable in a violation of those provisions; or that the courts would be under a greater obligation to connive at infractions in this shape, than when they had proceeded wholly from the cabals of the representative body. Until the people have, by some solemn and authoritative act, annulled or changed the established form, it is binding upon themselves collectively, as well as individually; and no presumption, or even knowledge, of their sentiments, can warrant their representatives in a departure from it, prior to such an act. But it is easy to see, that it would require an uncommon portion of fortitude in the judges to do their duty as faithful guardians of the Constitution, where legislative invasions of it had been instigated by the major voice of the community.

But it is not with a view to infractions of the Constitution only, that the independence of the judges may be an essential safeguard against the effects of occasional ill humors in the society. These sometimes extend no farther than to the injury of the private rights of particular classes of citizens, by unjust and partial laws. Here also the firmness of the judicial magistracy is of vast importance in mitigating the severity and confining the operation of such laws. It not only serves to moderate the immediate mischiefs of those which may have been passed, but it operates as a check upon the legislative body in passing them; who, perceiving that obstacles to the success of iniquitous intention are to be expected from the scruples of the courts, are in a manner compelled, by the very motives of the injustice they meditate, to qualify their attempts. This is a circumstance calculated to have more influence upon the character of our governments, than but few may be aware of. The benefits of the integrity and moderation of the judiciary have already been felt in more States than one; and though they may have displeased those whose sinister expectations they may have disappointed, they must have commanded the esteem and applause of all the virtuous and disinterested. Considerate men, of every description, ought to prize whatever will tend to beget or fortify that temper in the courts: as no man can be sure that he may not be to-morrow the victim of a spirit of injustice, by which he may be a gainer to-day. And every man must now feel, that the inevitable tendency of such a spirit is to sap the foundations of public and private confidence, and to introduce in its stead universal distrust and distress.

That inflexible and uniform adherence to the rights of the Constitution, and of individuals, which we perceive to be indispensable in the courts of justice, can certainly not be expected from judges who hold their offices by a temporary commission. Periodical appointments, however regulated, or by whomsoever made, would, in some way or other, be fatal to their necessary independence. If the power of making them was committed either to the Executive or legislature, there would be danger of an improper complaisance to the branch which possessed it; if to both, there would be an unwillingness to hazard the displeasure of either; if to the people, or to persons chosen by them for the special purpose, there would be too great a disposition to consult popularity, to justify a reliance that nothing would be consulted but the Constitution and the laws.

There is yet a further and a weightier reason for the permanency of the judicial offices, which is deducible from the nature of the qualifications they require. It has been frequently remarked, with great propriety, that a voluminous code of laws is one of the inconveniences necessarily connected with the advantages of a free government. To avoid an arbitrary discretion in the courts, it is indispensable that they should be bound down by strict rules and precedents, which serve to define and point out their duty in every particular case that comes before them; and it will readily be conceived from the variety of controversies which grow out of the folly and wickedness of mankind, that the records of those precedents must unavoidably swell to a very considerable bulk, and must demand long and laborious study to acquire a competent knowledge of them. Hence it is, that there can be but few men in the society who will have sufficient skill in the laws to qualify them for the stations of judges. And making the proper deductions for the ordinary depravity of human nature, the number must be still smaller of those who unite the requisite integrity with the requisite knowledge. These considerations apprise us, that the government can have no great option between fit character; and that a temporary duration in office, which would naturally discourage such characters from quitting a lucrative line of practice to accept a seat on the bench, would have a tendency to throw the administration of justice into hands less able, and less well qualified, to conduct it with utility and dignity. In the present circumstances of this country, and in those in which it is likely to be for a long time to come, the disadvantages on this score would be greater than they may at first sight appear; but it must be confessed, that they are far inferior to those which present themselves under the other aspects of the subject.

Upon the whole, there can be no room to doubt that the convention acted wisely in copying from the models of those constitutions which have established good behavior as the tenure of their judicial offices, in point of duration; and that so far from being blamable on this account, their plan would have been inexcusably defective, if it had wanted this important feature of good government. The experience of Great Britain affords an illustrious comment on the excellence of the institution.

PUBLIUS

Endnotes

Chapter 1

1. Thomas Hobbes, *Leviathan* (1651; repr., Indianapolis, IN: Bobbs, Merrill, 1958).

2. Alexander Hamilton, James Madison, and John Jay, *The Federalist Papers*, ed. Roy P. Fairfield, 2nd ed. (1788; repr., Baltimore, MD: Johns Hopkins University Press, 1981), p. 160.

3. Hamilton, Madison, and Jay, *The Federalist Papers*, p. 18.

4. Examples include E. E. Schattschneider, *The Semisovereign People: A Realist's View of Democracy in America* (New York: Holt, Rinehart, and Winston, 1960); Larry Bartels, *Unequal Democracy: The Politics of the New Gilded Age* (Princeton, NJ: Princeton University Press, 2008); and Jeffrey A. Segal and Howard Spaeth, *The Supreme Court and the Attitudinal Model Revisited* (New York: Cambridge University Press, 2002).

5. Morris Rosenberg, "Some Determinants of Political Apathy," *Public Opinion Quarterly* 18 (Winter 1954–55): 349–66; Jane Mansbridge, *Beyond Adversary Democracy* (New York: Basic Books, 1980); Nina Eliasoph, *Avoiding Politics: How Americans Produce Apathy in Everyday Life* (New York: Cambridge University Press, 1998); Melanie C. Green, Penny S. Visser, and Philip E. Tetlock, "Coping with Accountability Cross-Pressures: Low-Effort Evasive Tactics and High-Effort Quests for Complex Compromises," *Personality and Social Psychology Bulletin* 26:11 (2000): 1380–91.

6. John R. Hibbing and Elizabeth Theiss-Morse, *Stealth Democracy: Americans' Beliefs about How Government Should Work* (New York: Cambridge University Press, 2002), p. 147. See Diana E. Hess, *Controversy in the Classroom: The Democratic Power of Discussion* (New York: Routledge, 2009), for evidence that diverse viewpoints in the classroom have important effects on discussion.

7. Donald Green, Bradley Palmquist, and Eric Schickler, *Partisan Hearts and Minds* (New Haven, CT: Yale University Press, 2004); Christopher Achen, "Political Socialization and Rational Party Identification," *Political Behavior* 24:2 (2002): 151–70.

8. Robert S. Erikson, Michael B. MacKuen, and James A. Stimson, *The Macro Polity* (New York: Cambridge University Press, 2002).

9. Congressional Budget Office, "Current Budget Projections," www.cbo.gov/ftpdocs/108xx/doc10871/budgetprojections. pdf; The President's Budget for Fiscal Year 2016, "Historical Federal Workplace Tables," Office of Policy and Management, https://www.opm.gov/policy-data-oversight/data-analysis-documentation/federal-employment-reports/historical-tables/total-government-employment-since-1962; *Federal Register*, www.gpoaccess.gov/fr (all accessed 2/15/16).

10. For details, see Paul R. Abramson, John H. Aldrich, and David W. Rohde, *Change and Continuity in the 2012 and 2014 Elections* (Washington, DC: Congressional Quarterly Press, 2015).

11. Charles Taylor, *Multiculturalism: Examining the Politics of Recognition*, ed. Amy Gutmann, with commentary by K. Anthony Appiah, Jürgen Habermas, Steven C. Rockefeller, Michael Walzer, and Susan Wolf (Princeton, NJ: Princeton University Press, 1994); Will Kymlicka, *Multicultural Citizenship: A Liberal Theory of Minority Rights* (New York: Oxford University Press, 1995).

12. Morris P. Fiorina, with Samuel J. Abrams and Jeremy C. Pope, *Culture War: The Myth of a Polarized America*, 3rd ed. (New York: Pearson, Longman, 2010), pp. 46–7.

13. For more on political culture, see Herbert McClosky and John Zaller, *The American Ethos* (Cambridge, MA: Harvard University Press, 1984), and Pippa Norris, *Democratic Deficit: Critical Citizens Revisited* (New York: Cambridge University Press, 2011).

14. Frank M. Bryan, *Real Democracy: The New England Town Meeting and How It Works* (Chicago: University of Chicago Press, 2004).

Chapter 2

1. Jim DeMint, "Constitution of No," *National Review Online*, June 8, 2010, www.nationalreview.com/articles/229909/constitution-no/jim-demint?pg=2 (accessed 10/16/11).

2. Jennifer Steinhauer, "Constitution Has Its Day (More or Less) in House," *New York Times*, January 6, 2011, www.nytimes.com/2011/01/07/us/politics/07constitution.html (accessed 10/14/11).

3. Mark Trumbull, "On Constitution Day, Tea Party and Foes Duel over Our Founding Document," *Christian Science Monitor*, September 17, 2011, www.csmonitor.com/USA/Politics/2011/0917/On-Constitution-Day-tea-party-and-foes-duel-over-our-founding-document (accessed 10/16/11).

4. For a good overview of the political thought of the American Revolution, see Gordon S. Wood, *The Radicalism of the American Revolution* (New York: Vintage Books, 1993). For an excellent summary of the history, see Wood's *The American Revolution: A History* (New York: Modern Library, 2003).

5. David McCullough, *John Adams* (New York: Simon and Schuster, 2001), p. 90.

6. A classic text on the Founding period is Gordon S. Wood, *The Creation of the American Republic* (New York: W. W. Norton, 1969).

7. J. W. Peltason, *Corwin and Peltason's Understanding the Constitution*, 7th ed. (Hinsdale, IL: Dryden Press, 1976), p. 12.

8. The pamphlet sold 120,000 copies within a few months of publication, a figure that would leave the Harry Potter books in the dust in terms of the proportion of the literate public that purchased the book.

9. Thomas Hobbes, *Leviathan* (1651; repr., Indianapolis, IN: Bobbs, Merrill, 1958); John Locke, *Second Treatise of Government* (1690; repr., Indianapolis, IN: Bobbs, Merrill, 1952).

10. Robert A. Dahl, *How Democratic Is the American Constitution?* (New Haven, CT: Yale University Press, 2001), p. 12.

11. Alexander Hamilton, John Jay, and James Madison, *The Federalist Papers*, ed. Roy P. Fairfield, 2nd ed. (1788; repr., Baltimore, MD: Johns Hopkins University Press, 1981), p. 22.

12. Many delegates probably assumed that the electors would reflect the wishes of the voters in their states, but there is no clear indication of this in Madison's notes. (Hamilton makes this argument in the *Federalist Papers*.) Until the 1820s, many electors were directly chosen by state legislatures rather than by the people. In the first presidential election, George Washington won the unanimous support of the electors, but in only five states were the electors chosen by the people.

13. The actual language of the section avoids the term "slavery." Instead, it says: "The Migration or Importation of such Persons as any of the States now existing shall think proper to admit, shall not be prohibited by Congress prior to the Year one thousand eight hundred and eight." The ban on the importation of slaves was implemented on the earliest possible date, January 1, 1808.

14. Patrick Henry, "Shall Liberty or Empire Be Sought?," in *America, 1761–1837*, vol. 8 of *The World's Famous Orations*, ed. William Jennings Bryan (New York: Funk and Wagnalls, 1906), pp. 73, 76.

15. Thomas Jefferson to John Adams, 1787, in *The Writings of Thomas Jefferson*, Memorial Edition, ed. Andrew A. Lipscomb and Albert Ellery Bergh (Washington, DC: Thomas Jefferson Memorial Association of the United States, 1903), vol. 6, p. 370.

16. Charlie Savage, "Obama's War on Terror May Resemble Bush's in Some Areas," *New York Times*, February 17, 2009, p. A1.

17. Peter M. Shane, *Madison's Nightmare: How Executive Power Threatens American Democracy* (Chicago: University of Chicago Press, 2009).

18. "Is There a Constitutional Right to Own a Home or a Pet?," Annenberg Public Policy Center, September 16, 2015, http://www.annenbergpublicpolicycenter.org/is-there-a-constitutional-right-to-own-a-home-or-a-pet (accessed 9/30/15).

19. "Characters from 'The Simpsons' More Well Known to Americans than Their First Amendment Freedoms," McCormick Tribune Freedom Museum survey, March 1, 2006, http://documents.mccormickfoundation.org/news/2006/pr030106.aspx (accessed 10/30/15).

20. Thomas Jefferson to James Madison, in *Thomas Jefferson on Democracy*, ed. Saul Padover (New York: Mentor Books, 1953), p. 153.

21. Cass R. Sunstein, "Making Amends," *New Republic*, March 3, 1997, p. 42.

22. *Furman v. Georgia*, 408 U.S. 238 (1972).

23. Walter F. Murphy, "The Nature of the American Constitution," The Edmund Janes James lecture, December 6, 1987 (Department of Political Science, University of Illinois at Urbana-Champaign, 1989), p. 8, http://babel.hathitrust.org/cgi/pt?id=mdp.39015078286518;view=1up;seq=12.

Take a Stand

a. Jocelyn Kiley, "Americans Divided on How the Supreme Court Should Interpret the Constitution," Pew Research Center, July 31, 2014, www.pewresearch.org/fact-tank/2014/07/31/americans-divided-on-how-the-supreme-court-should-interpret-the-constitution (accessed 10/30/15).

b. Clarence Thomas, "How to Read the Constitution," *Wall Street Journal*, October 20, 2008.

c. *State of Missouri v. Holland*, 252 U.S. 416 (1920), 252.

d. William Rehnquist, "The Notion of a Living Constitution," *Harvard Journal of Law and Public Policy* 29 (2006): 402.

e. Rehnquist, "The Notion," p. 405.

f. Thurgood Marshall at the Annual Seminar of the San Francisco Patent and Trademark Law Association, Maui, Hawaii, May 6, 1987, www.thurgoodmarshall.com/speeches/constitutional_speech.htm (accessed 12/20/13).

Chapter 3

1. The full title of the law is the Patient Protection and Affordable Care Act (PPACA).

2. Ashby Jones, "Conservative Duo Tests Health Law," *Wall Street Journal*, September 13, 2010, http://online.wsj.com/article/SB10001424052748703897204575487963449135280.html#U301253590305VF (accessed 11/12/11).

3. Tenth Amendment Center, "Ohio Votes to Nullify Insurance Mandates," November 8, 2011, www.tenthamendmentcenter.com/2011/11/08/ohio-votes-to-nullify-insurance-mandates/ (accessed 11/12/11).

4. *National Federation of Independent Business v. Sebelius*, 132 S. Ct. 2566 (2012).

5. Obamacare Medicaid expansion, http://obamacarefacts.com/obamacares-medicaid-expansion (accessed 10/14/16).

6. Robert Pear, "Missouri Citizens Face Obstacles to Coverage," *New York Times*. August 2, 2013, www.nytimes.com/2013/08/03/us/missouri-citizens-face-obstacles-to-coverage.html?_r=1& (accessed 10/22/14).

7. See www.cisstat.com/eng/cis.htm for more information on the CIS.

8. *United States v. Windsor*, 570 U.S. (2013).

9. *Obergefell v. Hodges*, 576 U.S. (2015).

10. "The Supreme Court: Excerpts from Court's Welfare Ruling and Rehnquist's Dissent," *New York Times*, May 18, 1999, p. A20.

11. John W. Wright, ed., *New York Times 2000 Almanac* (New York: Penguin Reference, 1999), p. 165. Estimates from various online sources are quite a bit higher, averaging about 620,000 deaths.

12. Slaughterhouse Cases, 83 U.S. 36 (1873). See Ronald M. Labbe and Jonathan Lurie, *The Slaughterhouse Cases: Regulation, Reconstruction, and the Fourteenth Amendment* (Lawrence: University Press of Kansas, 2003).

13. Civil Rights Cases, 109 U.S. 3 (1883).

14. *United States v. E. C. Knight Co.*, 156 U.S. 1 (1895).

15. *Hammer v. Dagenhart*, 247 U.S. 251 (1918).

16. *Lochner v. New York*, 198 U.S. 45 (1905).

17. Wendy J. Schiller and Charles Stewart, *Electing the Senate: Indirect Democracy before the Seventeenth Amendment* (Princeton, NJ: Princeton University Press, 2014).

18. *Schechter Poultry Corporation v. United States*, 295 U.S. 495 (1935).

19. Four key cases are *West Coast Hotel Company v. Parrish* (1937), *Wright v. Vinton Branch* (1937), *Virginia Railway Company v. System Federation* (1937), and *National Labor Relations Board v. Jones and Laughlin Steel Corporation* (1937).

20. Martin Grodzins, *The American System* (New York: Rand McNally, 1966).

21. John Shannon, "Middle Class Votes Bring a New Balance to Federalism," February 1, 1997, policy paper 10 from the Urban

Institute series "The Future of the Public Sector," www.urban.org/url.cfm?ID=307051 (accessed 6/30/16).

22. This number varies depending on which grants are counted. Tim Conlan finds 15 block grants in this period. See his *From New Federalism to Devolution* (Washington, DC: Brookings Institution, 1998).

23. *Brown v. Board of Education*, 347 U.S. 483 (1954); *Swann v. Charlotte-Mecklenburg Board of Education*, 402 U.S. 1 (1971).

24. *Baker v. Carr*, 369 U.S. 186 (1962); *Reynolds v. Sims*, 377 U.S. 533 (1964); *Wesberry v. Sanders*, 376 U.S. 1 (1964); Martha Derthick, *Keeping the Compound Republic: Essays in American Federalism* (Washington, DC: Brookings Institution, 2001).

25. *Miranda v. Arizona*, 384 U.S. 436 (1966); *Mapp v. Ohio*, 367 U.S. 643 (1961).

26. *Shelby County v. Holder*, 570 U.S. (2013).

27. "Impact of Unfunded Mandates and Cost Shifts on U.S. Cities," U.S Conference of Mayors, June 2005, www.usmayors.org (accessed 11/13/11).

28. John Kincaid, "Governing the American States," in *Developments in American Politics*, ed. Gillian Peele, Christopher J. Bailey, Bruce Cain, and Guy Peters (Chatham, NJ: Chatham House, 1995), pp. 208–16.

29. Paul Posner, "The Politics of Coercive Federalism in the Bush Era," *Publius* 37:3 (May 2007): 390–412.

30. Gallup, "Trust in Government," September 9–13, 2015, www.gallup.com/poll/5392/trust-government.aspx (accessed 12/10/15).

31. Barry Rabe, "Environmental Policy and the Bush Era: The Collision between the Administrative Presidency and State Experimentation," *Publius* 37:3 (May 2007): 413–31.

32. Lois Beckett, "Nullification: How States Are Making It a Felony to Enforce Federal Gun Laws," *ProPublica*, May 2, 2013, www.propublica.org/article/nullification-how-states-are-making-it-a-felony-to-enforce-federal-gun-laws (accessed 11/15/13).

33. From a review of Michael S. Greve, *Real Federalism: Why It Matters, How It Could Happen* (Washington, DC: American Enterprise Institute Press, 1999), www.federalismproject.org/publications/books (accessed 10/10/07).

34. Cass Sunstein, *Designing Democracy: What Constitutions Do* (New York: Oxford University Press, 2001), p. 107.

35. J. W. Peltason, *Corwin and Peltason's Understanding the Constitution*, 7th ed. (Hinsdale, IL: Dryden Press, 1976), p. 177.

36. *Garcia v. San Antonio Metropolitan Transit Authority*, 469 U.S. 528 (1985).

37. *Gregory v. Ashcroft*, 501 U.S. 452 (1991).

38. *City of Boerne v. Flores*, 521 U.S. 507 (1997), 520.

39. *Kimel et al. v. Florida Board of Regents*, 528 U.S. 62 (2000).

40. *Alabama v. Garrett*, 531 U.S. 356 (2001).

41. *Shelby County v. Holder*, 570 U.S. (2013).

42. *United States v. Lopez*, 514 U.S. 549 (1995).

43. *United States v. Morrison*, 529 U.S. 598 (2000); Nia-Malika Henderson, "Obama Signs a Strengthened Violence Against Women Act," *Washington Post*, March 7, 2013, www.washingtonpost.com/politics/obama-signs-a-strengthened-violence-against-women-act/2013/03/07/e50d585e-8740-11e2-98a3-b3db6b9ac586_story.html (accessed 3/21/14).

44. *Romer v. Evans*, 517 U.S. 620 (1996).

45. *Atkins v. Virginia*, 536 U.S. 304 (2002); *Roper v. Simmons*, 543 U.S. 551 (2005).

46. *Gonzales v. Raich*, 545 U.S. 1 (2005); *Gonzales v. Oregon*, 546 U.S. 243 (2006).

47. *National Federation of Independent Business v. Sebelius*, 132 S. Ct. 2566 (2012).

48. *National Federation of Independent Business v. Sebelius*, 132 S. Ct. 2566 (2012), p. 51.

49. Jonathan Turley, "It's Not the Cannabis, It's the Constitution," *Los Angeles Times*, August 5, 2002, Metro section, part 2, p. 11.

50. Robert S. Erikson, Gerald C. Wright, and John P. McIver, *Statehouse Democracy: Public Opinion and Policy in the American States* (Cambridge: Cambridge University Press, 1993). For the policy specific evidence see Jeffrey R. Lax and Justin H. Phillips, "The Democratic Deficit in the States," *American Journal of Political Science* 56:1 (January 2012): 148–66. While Lax and Phillips show that states are responsive to opinion in eight specific policy areas, they also show that there is a "democratic deficit" in that majority opinion is often ignored in state policy.

51. American Society of Civil Engineers, "Report Card for America's Infrastructure: 2009," www.infrastructurereportcard.org (accessed 11/14/11).

52. Martha Derthick, *Keeping the Compound Republic: Essays in American Federalism* (Washington, DC: Brookings Institution, 2001), pp. 9–32.

Take a Stand

a. Steven Nelson, "Spending Deal Protects Medical Pot, Blocks Legalization in D.C.," *U.S. News and World Reports*, December 9, 2014, www.usnews.com/news/articles/2014/12/09/spending-deal-protects-medical-pot-blocks-legalization-in-dc (accessed 12/11/15).

Chapter 4

1. Alan Blinder, "Kentucky Clerk in Gay Marriage Dispute, Kim Davis, Joining G.O.P.," *New York Times*, September 25, 2015, www.nytimes.com/2015/09/26/us/kentucky-clerk-in-gay-marriage-dispute-kim-davis-joining-gop.html?_r=0 (accessed 1/6/16).

2. Elizabeth Daley, "Gov. Matt Bevin Just Removed All Clerks' Names from Kentucky Marriage Licenses," *Advocate*, December 22, 2015, www.advocate.com/marriage-equality/2015/12/22/gov-matt-bevin-grant-kim-davis-christmas-wish-no-clerks-marriage (accessed 1/6/16).

3. Ariane De Vogue, "Hobby Lobby Wins Contraceptive Ruling in Supreme Court," ABC News, June 30, 2014, http://abcnews.go.com/Politics/hobby-lobby-wins-contraceptive-ruling-supreme-court/story?id=24364311 (accessed 1/6/16).

4. Maggie Fox, "Supreme Court on Birth Control: What Hobby Lobby Ruling Means," NBC News, June 30, 2014, www.nbcnews.com/health/health-care/supreme-court-birth-control-what-hobby-lobby-ruling-means-n144526 (accessed 1/6/16).

5. *Arar v. Ashcroft et al.*, WL 346439 (E.D. N.Y. 2006). The case was also dismissed because Arar, a Canadian citizen, did not have standing to sue the U.S. government. Supporters of this decision (and the practice more generally) say that it is an essential part of the War on Terror and that the enemy combatants who are arrested have no legal rights. Opponents say that the practice violates international law and our own standards of decency; furthermore, torture almost never produces useful information because people will say anything to get the torture to stop.

6. *State v. Massey et al.*, 51 S.E.2d 179 (N.C. 1949). The case was appealed to the Supreme Court, but the Court declined to hear the case, which means that the state decision stands (*Bunn v. North Carolina*, 336 U.S. 942 [1949]).

7. Alan Blinder, "Tennessee Pastor Disputes a Wildlife Possession Charge by State," *New York Times*, November 15, 2013, www.nytimes.com/2013/11/16/us/tennessee-pastor-disputes-wildlife-possession-charge-by-state.html?_r=0 (accessed 1/24/14).

8. *Pennsylvania v. Miller*, Court of Common Pleas, WL 31426193 (Penn. 2002). However, supreme courts in Minnesota, Wisconsin, and several other states have decided that requiring the Amish to use orange SMV triangles violates their free exercise of religion.

9. *Wisconsin v. Yoder*, 403 U.S. 205 (1972).

10. Jeffrey Rosen, "Lemon Law," *New Republic*, March 29, 1993, p. 17.

11. Max Farrand, ed., *The Records of the Federal Convention of 1787*, rev. ed. (New Haven, CT: Yale University Press, 1937), pp. 587–88, 617–18.

12. *The Papers of Thomas Jefferson*, ed. J. Boyd (Princeton, NJ: Princeton University Press, 1958), pp. 557–83, cited in Lester S. Jayson, ed., *The Constitution of the United States of America: Analysis and Interpretation* (Washington, DC: U.S. Government Printing Office, 1973), p. 900.

13. Ralph Ketcham, *The Anti-Federalist Papers and the Constitutional Convention Debates* (New York: Signet Classic, Penguin Putnam, 2003), p. 247.

14. The two that were not ratified by the states were a complicated amendment on congressional apportionment and the pay raise amendment.

15. *Annals of Congress* 755 (August 17, 1789), cited in Lester S. Jayson, ed., *The Constitution of the United States of America* (Washington, DC: U.S. Government Printing Office, 1973), p. 898.

16. There is an intense scholarly debate on whether the authors of the Fourteenth Amendment intended for it to apply the Bill of Rights to the states. The strongest argument against this position is Raoul Berger's *The Fourteenth Amendment and the Bill of Rights* (1989), and a good book in support is Amar's *The Bill of Rights* (1998).

17. *Barron v. Baltimore* 32 U.S. 243 (1833), 250. The 1873 case was *Slaughter-House Cases*, 83 U.S. 36 (1873). The Supreme Court also declined to apply the Bill of Rights to the states in the *Civil Rights Cases*, 109 U.S. 3 (1883), in which the Court ruled that the Fourteenth Amendment did not give Congress the power to regulate the conduct of private business (thus the Civil Rights Act of 1875 was unconstitutional and private businesses could discriminate on the basis of race).

18. *Chicago, Burlington, and Quincy Railroad v. Chicago*, 166 U.S. 226 (1897).

19. *Twining v. New Jersey*, 211 U.S. 78, 98 (1908).

20. *Gitlow v. New York*, 268 U.S. 652 (1925).

21. James Hutson, "'A Wall of Separation,'" *Library of Congress Information Bulletin* 57:6 (June 1998), www.loc.gov/loc/lcib/9806/danbury.html (accessed 3/3/08).

22. Henry J. Abraham and Barbara A. Perry, *Freedom and the Court: Civil Rights and Civil Liberties in the United States*, 8th ed. (Lawrence: University Press of Kansas, 2003), p. 300.

23. *Engel v. Vitale*, 370 U.S. 421 (1962).

24. *Wallace v. Jaffree*, 482 U.S. 38 (1985).

25. *Lee v. Weisman*, 505 U.S. 577 (1992); *Santa Fe Independent School District v. Doe*, 530 U.S. 290 (2000).

26. *Marsh v. Chambers*, 463 U.S. 783 (1983); *Jones v. Clear Creek Independent School*, 61 LW 3819 (1993); *Town of Greece, N.Y. v. Galloway*, 572 U.S. ___ (2014).

27. *Lemon v. Kurtzman*, 403 U.S. 602 (1971).

28. *Lynch v. Donnelly*, 465 U.S. 668 (1984), 672–73.

29. Jeffrey Rosen, "Big Ten," *New Republic*, March 14, 2004, p. 11.

30. *Zelman v. Simmons-Harris*, 536 U.S. 639 (2002).

31. *Arizona Christian School Tuition Organization v. Winn*, U.S. Supreme Court slip. op. 09-987 and 09-991 (2011).

32. *Mitchell v. Helms*, 530 U.S. 793 (2000).

33. *Zobrest v. Catalina School District*, 509 U.S. 1 (1993). A similar decision in 1997 allowed a public school teacher to teach in a special program in a parochial school, *Agostini v. Felton*, 521 U.S. 203 (1997).

34. *Minersville School District v. Gobitis*, 310 U.S. 586 (1940).

35. *West Virginia Board of Education v. Barnette*, 319 U.S. 624 (1943), 642.

36. We will not cite all the cases here. See Abraham and Perry, *Freedom and the Court*, Chapter 6, for a summary of cases on this topic, especially Tables 6.1 and 6.2.

37. *Employment Division, Department of Human Resources of Oregon v. Smith*, 494 U.S. 872 (1990), 878–80. This case is often erroneously reported as having banned the religious use of peyote. In fact, the Court said: "Although it is constitutionally permissible to exempt sacramental peyote use from the operation of drug laws, it is not constitutionally required."

38. *City of Boerne v. Flores*, 521 U.S. 527 (1997); *Cutter v. Wilkinson*, No. 03-9877 (2005); *Gonzales v. O Centro Espirita Beneficente Uniao do Vegetal (UDV) et al.*, 546 U.S. 418 (2006). The Sherbert test comes from *Sherbert v. Verner*, 374 U.S. 398 (1963).

39. *Burwell v. Hobby Lobby*, 573 U.S. ___ (2014).

40. *Police Department of Chicago v. Mosley*, 408 U.S. 92 (1972).

41. *United States v. O'Brien*, 391 U.S. 367 (1968); *Ladue v. Gilleo*, 512 U.S. 43 (1994).

42. *Schenck v. United States*, 249 U.S. 47 (1919), 52.

43. Alan Dershowitz, *Shouting Fire: Civil Liberties in a Turbulent Age* (New York: Little, Brown, 2002).

44. *Abrams v. United States*, 250 U.S. 616 (1919), 630–31.

45. *Dennis v. United States*, 341 U.S. 494 (1951).

46. *Brandenburg v. Ohio*, 395 U.S. 444 (1969).

47. *Snyder v. Phelps*, 131 S.Ct. 1207 (2011).

48. *Smith v. Goguen*, 415 U.S. 566 (1974).

49. *Tinker v. Des Moines School District*, 393 U.S. 503 (1969).

50. *Spence v. Washington*, 418 U.S. 405 (1974).

51. *Spence v. Washington*, 418 U.S. 409–10 (1974).

52. *Texas v. Johnson*, 491 U.S. 397 (1989).

53. *United States v. Eichman*, 496 U.S. 310 (1990).

54. *United States v. O'Brien*, 391 U.S. 367, 376 (1968).

55. *Walker v. Texas Division, Sons of Confederate Veterans*, 576 U.S. ___ (2015).

56. *Buckley v. Valeo*, 424 U.S. 1 (1976).

57. *Davis v. Federal Election Commission*, 554 U.S. 724 (2008).

58. *Citizens United v. Federal Election Commission*, 558 U.S. 310 (2010); *McCutcheon v. Federal Election Commission*, 572 U.S. ___ (2014).

59. *McConnell v. Federal Election Commission*, 540 U.S. 93 (2003).

60. *Board of Regents of the University of Wisconsin System et al., Petitioners v. Scott Harold Southworth et al.*, 529 U.S. 217 (2000).

61. Kermit L. Hall, "Free Speech on Public College Campuses: Overview," www.firstamendmentcenter.org/speech/pubcollege/overview.aspx (accessed 2/10/08).

62. Carolyn J. Palmer, Sophie W. Penney, Donald D. Gehring, and Jan A. Neiger, "Hate Speech and Hate Crimes: Campus Conduct Codes and Supreme Court Rulings," *National Association of Student Personnel Administrators Journal* 34:2 (1997), http://publications.naspa.org/naspajournal/vol34/iss2/art4 (accessed 12/18/07).

63. Liam Stacknov, "Yale's Halloween Advice Stokes a Racially Charged Debate," *New York Times,* November 8, 2015, www.nytimes.com/2015/11/09/nyregion/yale-culturally-insensitive-halloween-costumes-free-speech.html?_r=0 (accessed 12/30/15).

64. Michael D. Regan, "Yale Lecturer Resigns over Halloween Costume Email Controversy," *Christian Science Monitor,* December 8, 2015, www.csmonitor.com/USA/Education/2015/1208/Yale-lecturer-resigns-over-Halloween-costume-email-controversy (accessed 12/30/15).

65. Yanan Wang, "Obama to Campus Protesters: Don't 'Shut Up' Opposing Viewpoints," *Washington Post,* December 22, 2015, www.washingtonpost.com/news/morning-mix/wp/2015/12/22/obama-to-campus-protesters-dont-shut-up-opposing-viewpoints (accessed 12/30/15).

66. *City of St. Paul v. RAV*, 505 U.S. 377 (1992).

67. *Virginia v. Black*, 538 U.S. 343 (2003).

68. The Editorial Board, "Hate Speech on Facebook," *New York Times,* May 30, 2013, www.nytimes.com/2013/05/31/opinion/misogynist-speech-on-facebook.html (accessed 1/28/14).

69. Facebook "community standards" on hate speech, www.facebook.com/communitystandards (accessed 1/28/14).

70. Jeffrey Rosen, "Who Decides? Civility v. Hate Speech on the Internet," *Insights on Law and Society* 13:2 (Winter 2013), www.americanbar.org/publications/insights_on_law_and_society/13/winter_2013/who_decides_civilityvhatespeechontheinternet.html (accessed 1/29/14).

71. Pete Kasperowicz, "13 House Democrats Offer Bill Demanding Government Study on Internet Hate Speech," *The Hill,* January 16, 2014, www.thehill.com/blogs/floor-action/technology/195647-dems-demand-government-study-on-internet-hate-speech (accessed 1/29/14).

72. *De Jonge v. State of Oregon*, 299 U.S. 353 (1937); *Edwards v. South Carolina*, 372 U.S. 229 (1963).

73. The Supreme Court declined to review the case in *Smith v. Collin*, 439 U.S. 916 (1978), which meant that the lower-court rulings stood (447 F. Supp. 676 [1978], 578 F.2d 1197 [1978]). See Donald A. Downs, *Nazis in Skokie: Freedom, Community and the First Amendment* (Notre Dame, IN: University of Notre Dame Press, 1985), for an excellent analysis of this important case.

74. *Forsyth County v. Nationalist Movement*, 505 U.S. 123 (1992).

75. *Frisby et al. v. Schultz et al.*, 487 U.S. 474 (1988).

76. *New York Times Co. v. United States*, 403 U.S. 713 (1971).

77. *New York Times v. United States*, 403 U.S. 713 (1971).

78. *Chaplinsky v. State of New Hampshire*, 315 U.S. 568 (1942).

79. *Chaplinsky v. State of New Hampshire.*

80. *New York Times v. Sullivan*, 376 U.S. 254 (1964), cited in Henry J. Abraham and Barbara A. Perry, *Freedom and the Court: Civil Rights and Civil Liberties in the United States,* 8th ed. (Lawrence: University Press of Kansas, 2003), p. 193.

81. *Hustler v. Falwell*, 485 U.S. 46 (1988).

82. *Valentine v. Chrestensen*, 316 U.S. 52 (1942).

83. *Virginia State Board of Pharmacy v. Virginia Citizens Consumer Council, Inc.*, 425 U.S. 748 (1976); *City of Cincinnati v. Discovery Network, Inc. et al.*, 507 U.S. 410 (1993).

84. *Lorillard Tobacco v. Reilly*, 533 U.S. 525 (2001).

85. In 1996, Congress passed the Child Pornography Prevention Act. This law makes the possession, production, or distribution of child pornography a criminal offense punishable with up to 15 years in jail and a fine. However, two parts of the law were struck down by the Court for being "overbroad and unconstitutional." *Ashcroft v. Free Speech Coalition*, 353 U.S. 234 (2002).

86. *Jacobellis v. Ohio*, 378 U.S. 184, 197 (1964).

87. *Roth v. United States*, 354 U.S. 476 (1957).

88. *Miller v. California*, 413 U.S. 15 (1973).

89. *Reno et al. v. American Civil Liberties Union et al.*, 521 U.S. 844 (1997).

90. *Ashcroft v. American Civil Liberties Union*, 535 U.S. 564 (2004).

91. *Federal Communications Commission v. Pacifica Foundation*, 438 U.S. 726 (1978).

92. *Federal Communications Commission et al. v. Fox Television Stations*, 556 U.S. 502 (2009).

93. *Federal Communications Commission and United States v. CBS Corporation*, 556 U.S. 1218 (2009).

94. *Federal Communications Commission v. Fox Television Stations*, 567 U.S. ____ (2012); *Federal Communications Commission v. CBS Corporation*, no. 11-1240 (2012), writ of certiorari denied.

95. *United States v. Stevens*, 559 U.S. 460 (2010).

96. *Brown v. Entertainment Merchants Association*, 564 U.S. (2011).

97. Edward Walsh, "U.S. Argues for Wider Gun Rights; Supreme Court Filing Reverses Past Policy," *Washington Post,* May 8, 2002, p. A1. For a lengthy memo from the attorney general that explores the individual rights argument, see www.justice.gov/olc/secondamendment2.pdf (accessed 3/22/12).

98. Law Center to Prevent Gun Violence, New Gun Legislation: Summary of Enacted Laws since Newtown, January 22, 2015, http://smartgunlaws.org/category/gun-laws-policies/new-gun-legislation (accessed 1/5/16).

99. *District of Columbia v. Heller*, 554 U.S. 290 (2008).

100. *McDonald v. Chicago*, 08-1521 (2010).

101. Robert J. Spitzer, *The Politics of Gun Control* (Chatham, NJ: Chatham House, 1995). Also see www.bradycenter.org/cases for a complete list of the cases (accessed 8/21/12). The two cases recognizing the individual right to bear arms were *United States v. Timothy Joe Emerson*, 46 F. Supp. 2d 598 (1999), and the D.C. Circuit Court case that was appealed in the landmark ruling *Parker v. District of Columbia*, 478 F.3d 370 (D.C. Cir. 2007).

102. Juliet Eilperin and David Nakamura, "Obama Moves to Further Regulate Gun Sales with Executive Actions that Circumvent Congress," *Washington Post,* January 5, 2016, www.washingtonpost.com/politics/obama-moves-on-guns-with-executive-actions-that-circumvent-congress/2016/01/05/97f23336-b3bc-11e5-a76a-0b5145e8679a_story.html?hpid=hp_hp-top-table-main_obamaguns-1215pm%3Ahomepage%2Fstory (accessed 1/5/16).

103. Legal Community against Violence, "Post *Heller* Litigation Summary," November 8, 2011, www.lcav.org/content/post-heller_summary.pdf (accessed 12/5/11).

104. *New Jersey v. T. L. O.*, 469 U.S. 325 (1985); *Safford United School District No. 1 et al. v. Redding*, 557 U.S. 364 (2009).

105. See Abraham and Perry, *Freedom and the Court*, Chapter 4, for a discussion of these cases. The most recent case is *Kentucky v. King*, 563 U.S. ___ (2011).

106. *Florence v. County of Burlington*, U.S. 10–945 (2012).

107. *Maryland v. King*, 133 S.Ct. 1958 (June 3, 2013).

108. *Riley v. California*, 513 U.S. ___ (2014).

109. *United States v. Jones*, 565 U.S. ___ (2012).

110. *Mapp v. Ohio*, 367 U.S. 643 (1961).

111. *Herring v. United States*, 555 U.S. 135 (2009).

112. *Utah v. Strieff*, 579 U.S. ___ (2016).

113. *Vernonia School District v. Acton*, 515 U.S. 646 (1995); *Board of Education of Pottawatomie County v. Earls*, 536 U.S. 832 (2002).

114. *Chandler v. Miller*, 520 U.S. 305 (1997).

115. Leslie Cauley, "NSA Has Massive Database of Americans' Phone Calls," *USA Today*, May 11, 2006, p. 1.

116. Lorraine Woellert and Dawn Kopecki, "The Snooping Goes beyond Phone Calls," *Business Week*, May 29, 2006, p. 38; "Data Mining: Federal Efforts Cover a Wide Range of Uses," GAO Report 04-548, May 2004, www.gao.gov/assets/250/242241.pdf (accessed 5/13/14).

117. Eric Lichtblau and James Risen, "Officials Say U.S. Wiretaps Exceeded Law," *New York Times*, April 16, 2009.

118. *Miranda v. Arizona*, 384 U.S. 436 (1966).

119. *New York v. Quarles*, 467 U.S. 649 (1984).

120. *Dickerson v. United States*, 530 U.S. 428 (2000).

121. *Benton v. Maryland*, 395 U.S. 784 (1969).

122. *Lucas v. South Carolina Coastal Council*, 505 U.S. 1003 (1992).

123. *Kelo v. City of New London*, 545 U.S. 469 (2005).

124. National Conference of State Legislatures, "Eminent Domain Overview," January 1, 2012, www.ncsl.org/research/environment-and-natural-resources/eminent-domain-overview.aspx (accessed 1/31/14).

125. *Powell v. Alabama*, 287 U.S. 45 (1932).

126. *Gideon v. Wainwright*, 372 U.S. 335 (1963).

127. *Evitts v. Lucy*, 469 U.S. 387 (1985); *Wiggins v. Smith*, 539 U.S. 510 (2003). See Elizabeth Gable and Tyler Green, "*Wiggins v. Smith*: The Ineffective Assistance of Counsel Standard Applied Twenty Years after *Strickland*," *Georgetown Journal of Legal Ethics* (Summer 2004): 755–71, for a discussion of many of these issues.

128. *Klopfer v. North Carolina*, 386 U.S. 213 (1967).

129. The law is 18 U.S.C. § 3161(c)(1) and the ruling is *Zedner v. United States*, 05-5992 (2006).

130. The case concerning African Americans is *Batson v. Kentucky*, 106 S.Ct. 1712 (1986); the case about Latinos is *Hernandez v. New York*, 500 U.S. 352 (1991); and the gender case is *J. E. B. v. Alabama ex rel. T. B.*, 511 U.S. 127 (1994). Two more-recent cases affirming that peremptory challenges could not be used in a racially discriminatory fashion were *Miller-El v. Dretke*, 545 U.S. 231 (2005), and *Snyder v. Louisiana*, 552 U.S. 472 (2008).

131. Death Penalty Information Center, "Number of Executions since 1976," www.deathpenaltyinfo.org/executions-year (accessed 3/5/16); *Hall v. Florida*, 572 U.S. ___ (2014).

132. Erik Eckholm, "One Execution Botched, Oklahoma Delays the Next," *New York Times*, April 29, 2014, www.nytimes.com/2014/04/30/us/oklahoma-executions.html (accessed 5/13/14).

133. *Furman v. Georgia*, 408 U.S. 238 (1972); *Gregg v. Georgia*, 428 U.S. 513 (1976).

134. See Abraham and Perry, *Freedom and the Court*, pp. 72–73, for a discussion of the earlier cases, and Charles Lane, "5–4 Supreme Court Abolishes Juvenile Executions," *Washington Post*, March 2, 2005, p. A1, for a discussion of the 2002 and 2005 cases. The cases were *Atkins v. Virginia*, 536 U.S. 304 (2002); *Roper v. Simmons*, 543 U.S. 551 (2005); and *Kennedy v. Louisiana*, 554 U.S. 407 (2008).

135. *Griswold v. Connecticut*, 381 U.S. 479 (1965), 482–86.

136. *Griswold v. Connecticut*, 511–12.

137. *Roe v. Wade*, 410 U.S. 113 (1973), 129.

138. *Planned Parenthood of Southeastern Pennsylvania v. Casey*, 505 U.S. 833 (1992).

139. Katharine Q. Seeyle, "Mississippi Voters Reject Anti-Abortion Measure," *New York Times*, November 8, 2011, www.nytimes.com/2011/11/09/us/politics/votes-across-the-nation-could-serve-as-a-political-barometer.html (accessed 12/5/11).

140. Erik Eckholm, "Access to Abortion Falling as States Pass Restrictions," *New York Times*, January 3, 2014, www.nytimes.com/2014/01/04/us/women-losing-access-to-abortion-as-opponents-gain-ground-in-state-legislatures.html (accessed 1/31/14).

141. *Whole Woman's Health v. Hellerstedt*, 579 U.S. ___ (2016).

142. *Bowers v. Hardwick*, 478 U.S. 186 (1986).

143. *Lawrence v. Texas*, 539 U.S. 558 (2003).

Take a Stand

a. *Florida v. Jardines*, 569 U.S. ___ (2013), 6–7.

b. Oral arguments in *U.S. v. Jones* (2012), November 8, 2011, www.supremecourt.gov/oral_arguments/argument_transcripts/10-1259.pdf, p. 44 (accessed 8/20/12).

Chapter 5

1. Complaint in *United States v. Maricopa County, Arizona, and Joseph M. Arpaio*, Federal District Court of Arizona, May 10, 2012, www.justice.gov/iso/opa/resources/512012510134311376158.pdf (accessed 4/6/14).

2. Mark Lacey, "U.S. Finds Pervasive Bias against Latinos by Arizona Sheriff," *New York Times*, December 16, 2011, www.nytimes.com/2011/12/16/us/arizona-sheriffs-office-unfairly-targeted-latinos-justice-department-says.html?ref=josephmarpaio (accessed 1/31/12).

3. "The Persistence of Racial and Ethnic Profiling in the United States," American Civil Liberties Union and the Rights Working Group, New York, August 2009, p. 42, www.aclu.org/files/pdfs/humanrights/cerd_finalreport.pdf (accessed 1/31/12).

4. Supplemental Permanent Injunction, *Manuel de Jesus Ortega Melendres v. Joseph M. Arpaio*, Federal District Court of Arizona, October 2, 2013, www.aclu.org/sites/default/files/assets/2013.10.02.606_supplemental_permanent_injunction_judgment_order.pdf (accessed 4/6/14).

5. Fernanda Santos, "Angry Judge Says Sheriff Defied Order on Latinos," *New York Times*, March 24, 2014, www.nytimes.com/2014/03/25/us/judge-says-arpaio-defied-order-on-profiling-latinos.html (accessed 4/6/14).

6. Jacques Billeaud, "Arizona Sheriff's Bid for Leniency Met with Skepticism," *Arizona Daily Sun*, July 22, 2016, http://azdailysun.com/news/state-and-regional/arizona-sheriff-s-bid-for-leniency-met-with-skepticism/

article_aa3322a5-48f7-5be7-8629-d86198f01c4d.html (accessed 8/11/16).

7. Julia Preston and John H. Cushman Jr., "Obama to Permit Young Migrants to Remain in U.S.," *New York Times*, June 15, 2012, www.nytimes.com/2012/06/16/us/us-to-stop-deporting-some-illegal-immigrants.html?pagewanted=all (accessed 4/6/14).

8. There are eight commissioners on the U.S. Commission on Civil Rights, four appointed by the president and four by Congress. The commissioners serve six-year terms and do not require Senate confirmation, and no more than four members may be of the same political party.

9. Howard Dodson, "How Slavery Helped Build a World Economy," in Schomburg Center for Research in Black Culture of the New York Public Library, *Jubilee: The Emergence of African-American Culture* (Washington, DC: National Geographic Press, 2003).

10. John W. Wright, ed., *New York Times 2000 Almanac* (New York: Penguin Reference, 1999), p. 165. Estimates from various online sources are quite a bit higher, averaging about 620,000 deaths.

11. V. O. Key Jr., *Southern Politics in State and Nation* (New York: Knopf, 1949), p. 538. For example, the Louisiana grandfather clause read: "No male person who was on January 1, 1867, or at any date prior thereto, entitled to vote under the Constitution of the United States, wherein he then resided, and no son or grandson of any such person not less than twenty-one years of age at the date of the adoption of this Constitution . . . shall be denied the right to register and vote in this State by reason of his failure to possess the educational or property qualifications." Grandfather clauses as they applied to voting were ruled unconstitutional in 1915.

12. Chandler Davidson, "The Voting Rights Act: A Brief History," in *Controversies in Minority Voting: The Voting Rights Act in Perspective*, ed. Bernard Grofman and Chandler Davidson (Washington, DC: Brookings Institution, 1992), p. 21.

13. "Indian Removal: 1814–1848," Public Broadcasting System, www.pbs.org/wgbh/aia/part4/4p2959.html (accessed 1/26/12).

14. *Cherokee Nation v. Georgia*, 30 U.S. 1 (1831).

15. *United States v. Wong Kim Ark*, 169 U.S. 649 (1898).

16. Bilal Qureshi, "From Wrong to Right: A U.S. Apology for Japanese Internment," August 9, 2013, National Public Radio, www.npr.org/sections/codeswitch/2013/08/09/210138278/japanese-internment-redress (accessed 1/29/16).

17. Institute for Advanced Technology in the Humanities, University of Virginia, Abigail Adams to John Adams, March 31, 1776, www.iath.virginia.edu/seminar/unit1/text/adams.htm (accessed 7/30/08).

18. *Bradwell v. Illinois*, 83 U.S. 130 (1873).

19. *Hoyt v. Florida*, 368 U.S. 57 (1961).

20. Lucian K. Truscott IV, "The Real Mob at Stonewall," *New York Times*, June 25, 2009, p. A19.

21. "Law and Civil Rights," Pollingreport.com, various surveys, www.pollingreport.com/civil.htm (accessed 1/29/16).

22. *Obergefell v. Hodges*, 576 U.S. ____ (2015).

23. "Charge Statistics, FY 1997 Through FY 2014," U.S. Equal Employment Opportunity Commission, www.eeoc.gov/eeoc/statistics/enforcement/charges.cfm (accessed 1/29/16).

24. "Where You Live Matters: 2015 Fair Housing Trends Report," National Fair Housing Alliance, www.nationalfairhousing.org/Portals/33/2015-04-30%20NFHA%20Trends%20Report%202015.pdf, p.17 (accessed 1/29/16).

25. "Recent Accomplishments of the Housing and Civil Enforcement Section," U.S. Department of Justice, January 6, 2016, www.justice.gov/crt/recent-accomplishments-housing-and-civil-enforcement-section (accessed 1/29/16).

26. Davidson, "The Voting Rights Act," p. 22; also see U.S. Department of Justice, Civil Rights Division, "About Section 5 of the Voting Rights Act," www.usdoj.gov/crt/voting/sec_5/obj_activ.htm, for a complete list of cases in which the Justice Department has denied "preclearance" of a change in an electoral practice under Section 5 of the Voting Rights Act. Note that in racially homogeneous single-member districts minority candidates usually win. But in at-large elections, in which representatives are elected citywide or countywide (and which thus may contain a mix of minority and white voters from the districts making up the city or county), the majority-white voters can outvote the minority voters and elect an all-white city council or school board.

27. "The Long Shadow of Jim Crow: Voter Suppression in America," Special Report, People for the American Way Foundation and NAACP, http://67.192.238.60/sites/default/files/thelongshadowofjimcrow.pdf (accessed 1/23/12); Wendy Weiser and Margaret Chen, "Voter Suppression Incidents, 2008 Analysis," November 3, 2008, www.brennancenter.org/content/resource/voter_suppression_incidents (accessed 1/19/10).

28. "New Voting Restrictions in Place for 2016 Presidential Election," Brennan Center for Justice, http://www.brennancenter.org/voting-restrictions-first-time-2016 (accessed 10/16/16).

29. Bernadette D. Proctor, Jessica L. Semega, and Melissa A. Kollar, "Income and Poverty in the United States: 2015," United States Census, Current Population Reports, September 2016, poverty rates from Table 3, p. 13, income from Table 1, p. 6, https://www.census.gov/content/dam/Census/library/publications/2016/demo/p60-256.pdf (accessed 10/17/16).

30. Jesse Bricker et al., "Changes in U.S. Family Finances from 2010 to 2013: Evidence from the Survey of Consumer Finances," *Federal Reserve Bulletin* 100:4 (September 2014), Table 2, p. 12, www.federalreserve.gov/pubs/bulletin/2014/pdf/scf14.pdf (accessed 9/30/14).

31. Employment Situation Summary, Bureau of Labor Statistics, Tables A2 and A3, October 7, 2016, www.bls.gov/news.release/empsit.t02.htm (accessed 10/16/16).

32. "America's Families and Living Arrangements: 2015," U.S. Census, Table C3, www.census.gov/hhes/families/data/cps2015C.html (accessed 10/17/16).

33. Federal Bureau of Investigation, "Crime in the United States, 2014, Expanded Homicide Data Tables, Table 2," https://ucr.fbi.gov/crime-in-the-u.s/2014/crime-in-the-u.s.-2014/tables/expanded-homicide-data/expanded_homicide_data_table_2_murder_victims_by_age_sex_and_race_2014.xls (accessed 10/17/16).

34. Life expectancy data are from Elizabeth Arias, "United States Life Tables, 2009," *National Vital Statistics Reports*, Centers for Disease Control and Prevention, January 6, 2014, www.cdc.gov/nchs/data/nvsr/nvsr62/nvsr62_07.pdf. Infant mortality numbers are from Marian F. MacDorman, PhD, and T. J. Mathews, "Understanding Racial and Ethnic Disparities in U.S. Infant Mortality Rates," NCHS Data Brief, Centers for Disease Control and Prevention, September 2011, www.cdc.gov/nchs/data/databriefs/db74.pdf. Maternal mortality rates are from "Pregnancy Mortality Surveillance System," March 3, 2014, Centers for Disease Control and Prevention, www.cdc.gov/reproductivehealth/maternalinfanthealth/pmss.html. (All sources accessed 4/7/14.)

35. See the National Resource Defense Council's research on the Environmental Justice Movement, www.nrdc.org/ej/history/hej.asp, and the Environmental Justice and Health Alliance for Chemical Policy reform's report "Who's in Danger? Race, Poverty, and Chemical Disasters," May 2014, www.comingcleaninc.org/assets/media/images/Reports/Who's%20in%20Danger%20Report%20and%20Table%20FINAL.pdf (accessed 1/30/16).

36. Greg Botelho, Sarah Jorgensen, and Joseph Netto, "Water Crisis in Flint, Michigan, Draws Federal Investigation," CNN.com, January 9, 2016, www.cnn.com/2016/01/05/health/flint-michigan-water-investigation (accessed 1/30/16).

37. Evelyn Diaz, "Nick Cannon Accuses L.A. Cops of Racial Profiling," BET News, www.bet.com/news/celebrities/2011/11/18/nick-cannon-accuses-la-cops-of-racial-profiling.html (accessed 1/29/12).

38. Benjamin Weiser and Joseph Goldstein, "Mayor Says New York City Will Settle Suits on Stop-and-Frisk Tactics," *New York Times*, January 30, 2014, www.nytimes.com/2014/01/31/nyregion/de-blasio-stop-and-frisk.html (accessed 4/6/14).

39. Hundreds of studies have examined these patterns, and, not surprisingly, there are divergent findings. However, most have found differences in sentencing based on race. A meta-analysis of 85 studies by Ojmarrh Mitchell and Doris L. MacKenzie funded by the U.S. Department of Justice found "after taking into account defendant criminal history and current offense seriousness, African-Americans and Latinos were generally sentenced more harshly than whites." See Mitchell and MacKenzie, "The Relationship between Race, Ethnicity, and Sentencing Outcomes: A Meta-Analysis of Sentencing Research," December 2004, www.ncjrs.gov/pdffiles1/nij/grants/208129.pdf. For government studies of racial profiling, see the Justice Department's "A Resource Guide on Racial Profiling Data Collection Systems," November 2000, www.ncjrs.gov/pdffiles1/bja/184768.pdf. For President Bush's statement on racial profiling, see Department of Justice, "Fact Sheet: Racial Profiling," June 17, 2003, www.usdoj.gov/opa/pr/2003/June/racial_profiling_fact_sheet.pdf. For a Government Accountability Office study, see "Racial Profiling: Limited Data on Motorist Stops," March 2000, www.gao.gov/new.items/gg00041.pdf. Government statistics on crime may be found on the FBI site at www.fbi.gov. (All documents accessed 3/21/08.)

40. The Counted, *The Guardian*, www.theguardian.com/us-news/ng-interactive/2015/jun/01/the-counted-police-killings-us-database# (accessed 1/30/16).

41. "Trayvon Martin, George Zimmerman Case," *Orlando Sentinel*, www.orlandosentinel.com/news/local/trayvon-martin (accessed 4/6/14).

42. "2014 Hate Crime Statistics," U.S. Department of Justice, www.fbi.gov/about-us/cjis/ucr/hate-crime/2014/tables/table-1 (accessed 1/30/16).

43. Rosa Parks with James Haskins, *Rosa Parks: My Story* (New York: Dial Books, 1992), p. 116.

44. Clayborne Carson, David J. Garrow, Gerald Gill, Vincent Harding, and Darlene Clark Hine, eds., *The Eyes on the Prize Civil Rights Reader* (New York: Penguin Books, 1997).

45. *Boynton v. Virginia*, 363 U.S. 454 (1960).

46. David Halberstam, *The Children* (New York: Ballantine Books, 1999).

47. Nate Silver, "Tea Party Nonpartisan Attendance Estimates: Now 300,000," April 16, 2009, www.fivethirtyeight.com/2009/04/tea-party-nonpartisan-attendance.html (accessed 1/19/10).

48. *Pearson v. Murray*, 169 Md. 478 (1936).

49. *Brown v. Board of Education*, 347 U.S. 483 (1954).

50. *Brown v. Board of Education II*, 349 U.S. 294 (1955).

51. Paul Brest and Sanford Levinson, *Process of Constitutional Decision Making: Cases and Material* (Boston: Little, Brown, 1982), pp. 471–80.

52. *Swann v. Charlotte-Mecklenberg Board of Education*, 402 U.S. 1 (1971).

53. *Milliken v. Bradley*, 418 U.S. 717 (1974).

54. *Parents Involved in Community Schools Inc. v. Seattle School District*, 05-98 (2007); *Meredith v. Jefferson County (Ky.) Board of Education*, 551 U.S. 701 (2007).

55. *Heart of Atlanta Motel, Inc. v. United States*, 379 U.S. 241 (1964).

56. *Katzenbach v. McClung*, 379 U.S. 294 (1964).

57. *Griggs v. Duke Power*, 401 U.S. 424 (1971).

58. *Easley v. Cromartie*, 532 U.S. 234 (2001), rehearing denied, 532 U.S. 1076 (2001).

59. *Easley v. Cromartie*, 532 U.S. 1076 (2001).

60. *Shelby County v. Holder*, 570 U.S. (2013).

61. *Reed v. Reed*, 404 U.S. 71 (1971).

62. *Frontiero v. Richardson*, 411 U.S. 677 (1973).

63. *Korematsu v. United States*, 323 U.S. 214 (1944).

64. *Craig v. Boren*, 429 U.S. 190 (1976).

65. *Orr v. Orr*, 440 U.S. 268 (1979).

66. *United States v. Virginia*, 518 U.S. 515 (1996).

67. *Johnson v. Transportation Agency of Santa Clara*, 480 U.S. 616 (1987).

68. *Harris v. Forklift Systems*, 510 U.S. 17 618 (1993).

69. *Ledbetter v. Goodyear Tire & Rubber Co.*, 550 U.S. 618 (2007).

70. Julie Hirschfeld Davis, "Obama Moves to Expand Rules Aimed at Closing Gender Pay Gap," *New York Times*, January 29, 2016, www.nytimes.com/2016/01/29/us/politics/obama-moves-to-expand-rules-aimed-at-closing-gender-pay-gap.html (accessed 1/30/16).

71. "Women Present Widespread Discrimination at Wal-Mart," press release, April 28, 2003, www.walmartclass.com/staticdata/press_releases/wmcc.html (accessed 10/4/12).

72. David Savage, "Supreme Court Blocks Huge Class-Action Suit against Wal-Mart," *Los Angeles Times*, June 21, 2011. The case is *Dukes v. Wal-Mart Stores, Inc.* (2011).

73. *Bowers v. Hardwick*, 478 U.S. 186 (1986), rehearing denied, 478 U.S. 1039 (1986).

74. *Romer v. Evans*, 517 U.S. 620 (1996).

75. *Lawrence v. Texas*, 539 U.S. 558 (2003). Because the basis for the decision was the due process clause of the Fourteenth Amendment and not the equal protection clause, this ruling upheld a civil liberty rather than a civil right. As such, it applied to all laws regarding sodomy, not just those that applied to gays. However, the decision has been widely regarded as a landmark civil rights case because it provided equal rights for gays.

76. The three cases are *Hollingsworth v. Perry*, 570 U.S. (2013), *United States v. Windsor*, 570 U.S. ____ (2013), and *Obergefell v. Hodges*, 576 U.S. ____ (2015).

77. Quoted in Voting Rights Act Extension: Report of the Subcommittee of the Constitution of the Committee on the Judiciary, U.S. Senate, 97th Congress, 2nd session, May 25, 1982, S. Rept. 97-417, 4.

78. Drew S. Days III, "Section 5 Enforcement and the Justice Department," in *Controversies in Minority Voting: The Voting Rights Act in Perspective*, ed. Bernard Grofman and Chandler Davidson (Washington, DC: Brookings Institution Press,

1992), p. 52; Frank R. Parker, *Black Votes Count* (Chapel Hill: University of North Carolina Press, 1990), p. 1.

79. Davidson, "The Voting Rights Act," p. 21.

80. "Fair Housing: It's Your Right." U.S. Department of Housing and Urban Development, http://portal.hud.gov/hudportal/HUD?src=/program_offices/fair_housing_equal_opp/FHLaws/yourrights (accessed 2/2/12).

81. *United States v. Morrison*, 529 U.S. 598 (2000).

82. *Board of Trustees of the University of Alabama v. Garrett*, 531 U.S. 356 (2001). However, in *State of Tennessee v. George Lane and Beverly Jones*, 541 U.S. 509 (2004), the Court ruled that the disabled must have access to courthouses.

83. The White House, "Remarks by the Reception Commemorating the Enactment of the Matthew Shepard and James Byrd Jr. Hate Crimes Prevention Act," October 28, 2009, www.whitehouse.gov/the-press-office/remarks-president-reception-commemorating-enactment-matthew-shepard-and-James-Byrd (accessed 1/21/10).

84. Tim Mak, "Post 'Don't Ask,' Gay Navy Lt. Marries," *Politico*, September 20, 2011, www.politico.com/news/stories/0911/63909.html (accessed 1/24/12).

85. *Public Papers of the Presidents of the United States: Lyndon B. Johnson, 1965*, vol. 2, entry 301 (Washington, DC: Government Printing Office, 1966), pp. 635–40.

86. *New York Times*/CBS poll, December 6–9, 1997. Fifty-nine percent of whites and 82 percent of blacks favored education programs to assist minority students in competing for college admissions, while 57 percent of whites but only 23 percent of blacks opposed preferences in hiring and promotion "to make up for past discrimination."

87. State of California, article 1, section 31.

88. The training program case was *United Steel Workers of America v. Weber*, 443 U.S. 193 (1979); the labor union case was *Sheet Metal Workers v. EEOC*, 478 U.S. 421 (1986); and the Alabama state police case was *U.S. v. Paradise*, 480 U.S. 149 (1987).

89. *Ricci v. DeStefano*, 557 U.S. (2009).

90. *Regents of the University of California v. Bakke*, 438 U.S. 265 (1978).

91. *Smith v. University of Washington*, 233 F3d 1188 (9th Cir. 2000).

92. *Grutter v. Bollinger*, 539 U.S. 306 (2003), was the law school case and *Gratz v. Bollinger*, 539 U.S. 244 (2003), was the undergraduate admissions case.

93. In *Bakke*, Justice Lewis Powell was the only member of the Court who held this position, even if it became the basis for all affirmative action programs over the next 25 years. Four justices in the *Bakke* decision wanted to get rid of race as a factor in admissions, and another four thought that the "strict scrutiny" standard should not even be applied in this instance.

94. *Schuette v. Coalition to Defend Affirmative Action*, 572 U.S. ____ (2014).

95. *Fisher v. University of Texas, Austin*, 579 U.S. ____ (2016).

96. James Vicini, "Supreme Court to Decide Arizona Immigration Law," Reuters, December 12, 2011, www.reuters.com/article/2011/12/12/us-usa-immigration-arizona-idUSTRE7BB0XJ20111212 (accessed 2/2/12).

97. *Arizona v. United States*, 567 U.S. ____ (2012).

98. Fernanda Santos, "Arizona Immigration Law Survives Ruling," *New York Times*, September 6, 2012, www.nytimes.com/2012/09/07/us/key-element-of-arizona-immigration-law-survives-ruling.html?r=0 (accessed 10/5/12).

99. Immigration, various polls, www.pollingreport.com/immigration.htm (accessed 1/30/16).

100. "An Act Providing for the Collection of Data Relative to Traffic Stops," Massachusetts state law, Chapter 228 of the Acts of 2000, www.mass.gov/legis/laws/seslaw00/sl000228.htm (accessed 7/22/08).

Chapter 6

1. Christopher Ingram, "Voldemort Is Polling Better than Many Republican Presidential Candidates," June 9, 2015, www.washingtonpost.com/news/wonk/wp/2015/06/09/the-shark-from-jaws-is-polling-better-than-all-of-the-2016-candidates (accessed 8/30/16).

2. The Harris Poll, "Wingnuts and President Obama," March 6, 2015, http://media.theharrispoll.com/documents/Harris-Interactive-Poll-Research-Politics-Wingnuts-2010-03.pdf (accessed 11/3/15).

3. For a review, see Arthur Lupia and Mathew D. McCubbins, *The Democratic Dilemma* (New York: Cambridge University Press, 1998).

4. Larry Bartels, "Partisanship and Voting Behavior, 1952–1996," *American Journal of Political Science* 44 (2000): 35–50.

5. Robert S. Erikson, Michael B. MacKuen, and James A. Stimson, *The Macro Polity* (New York: Cambridge University Press, 2002).

6. John Zaller, "Coming to Grips with V. O. Key's Concept of Latent Opinion" (unpublished paper, University of California, Los Angeles, 1998).

7. Morris Fiorina, *Retrospective Voting in American National Elections* (Cambridge, MA: Harvard University Press, 1981).

8. John Zaller, *The Nature and Origins of Mass Opinion* (New York: Cambridge University Press, 1992).

9. R. Michael Alvarez and John Brehm, *Hard Choices, Easy Answers* (Princeton, NJ: Princeton University Press, 2002).

10. John Zaller and Stanley Feldman, "A Theory of the Survey Response: Revealing Preferences versus Answering Questions," *American Journal of Political Science* 36 (1992): 579–616.

11. Janet M. Box-Steffensmeier and Susan DeBoef, "Macropartisanship and Macroideology in the Sophisticated Electorate," *Journal of Politics* 63:1 (2001): 232–48.

12. Jack Citrin, Donald P. Green, Christopher Muste, and Cara Wong, "Public Opinion toward Immigration Reform: The Role of Economic Motivations," *American Journal of Political Science* 59:3 (1997): 858–82.

13. William G. Jacoby, "Issue Framing and Public Opinion on Government Spending," *American Journal of Political Science* 44:4 (2000): 750–67; L. M. Bartels, "Beyond the Running Tally: Partisan Bias in Political Perceptions," *Political Behavior* 24:2 (2002): 117–50.

14. Donald R. Kinder, "Exploring the Racial Divide: Blacks, Whites, and Opinion on National Policy," *American Journal of Political Science* 45:2 (2001): 439–49; Paul M. Sniderman and Thomas Piazza, *The Scar of Race* (Cambridge, MA: Harvard University Press, 1993).

15. Robert Huckfeldt, Jeffery Levine, William Morgan, and John Sprague, "Accessibility and the Political Utility of Partisan and Ideological Orientations," *American Journal of Political Science* 43:3 (July 1999): 888–911.

16. George E. Marcus, John L. Sullivan, Elizabeth Theiss-Morse, and Sandra L. Wood, *With Malice toward Some: How People Make Civil Liberties Judgments* (New York: Cambridge University Press, 1995).

17. Stanley Feldman and Marco R. Steenbergen, "The Humanitarian Foundation of Public Support for Social

Welfare," *American Journal of Political Science* 45:3 (2001): 658–77.

18. R. Michael Alvarez and John Brehm, "American Ambivalence towards Abortion Policy: Development of a Heteroskedastic Probit Model of Competing Values," *American Journal of Political Science* 39:4 (1995): 1055–82.

19. R. Michael Alvarez and John Brehm, "Are Americans Ambivalent towards Racial Policies?," *American Journal of Political Science* 41 (1997): 345–74.

20. Jamie Druckman, with Toby Bolsen and Fay Lomax Cook, "The Influence of Partisan Motivated Reasoning on Public Opinion," *Political Behavior* 36 (2014): 235–52.

21. Virginia Sapiro, "Not Your Parents' Political Socialization: Introduction for a New Generation," *Annual Review of Political Science* 7 (2004): 1–23.

22. Christopher Achen, "Parental Socialization and Rational Party Identification," *Political Behavior* 24 (2002): 151–70.

23. Alan S. Gerber, Gregory A. Huber, David Doherty, Conor M. Dowling, and Shang E. Ha, "Personality and Political Attitudes: Relationships across Issue Domains and Political Contexts," *American Political Science Review* 104 (February 2010): 111–33.

24. M. Kent Jennings and Richard G. Niemi, *Generations and Politics: A Panel Study of Young Adults and Their Parents* (Princeton, NJ: Princeton University Press, 1981).

25. Robert Putnam, *Bowling Alone: The Collapse and Revival of American Community* (New York: Simon and Schuster, 2000).

26. Richard G. Niemi and Mary Hepburn, "The Rebirth of Political Socialization," *Perspectives on Politics* 24 (1995): 7–16.

27. David Campbell, *Why We Vote: How Schools and Communities Shape Our Civic Life* (Princeton, NJ: Princeton University Press, 2006).

28. Sidney Verba, Kay Schlozman, and Henry Brady, *Voice and Equality: Civic Volunteerism in American Politics* (Cambridge, MA: Harvard University Press, 1995).

29. Paul Allen Beck and M. Kent Jennings, "Pathways to Participation," *American Political Science Review* 76 (1982): 94–108.

30. Fiorina, *Retrospective Voting in American National Elections*.

31. Pew Research Center, "In Gay Marriage Debate, Both Supporters and Opponents See Legal Recognition as 'Inevitable,'" June 6, 2013, www.people-press. org/2013/06/06/in-gay-marriage-debate-both-supporters-and-opponents-see-legal-recognition-as-inevitable (accessed 10/30/15).

32. Pew Research Center, "United in Remembrance, Divided over Policies: Ten Years after 9/11," September 1, 2011, www.people-press.org/2011/09/01/united-in-remembrance-divided-over-policies/1 (accessed 9/5/12).

33. Pew Research Center, "Terrorism Worries Little Changed; Most Give Government Good Marks for Reducing Threat," January 15, 2015, www.people-press.org/2015/01/12/terrorism-worries-little-changed-most-give-government-good-marks-for-reducing-threat (accessed 10/28/15).

34. John Zaller, *The Nature and Origins of Mass Opinion* (New York: Cambridge University Press, 1992).

35. Richard Nadwau et al., "Class, Party, and South–Nonsouth Differences," *American Politics Research* 32 (2004): 52–67.

36. James H. Kuklinski et al., "Racial Prejudice and Attitudes toward Affirmative Action," *American Journal of Political Science* 41 (1997): 402–19.

37. Donald P. Green, Bradley Palmquist, and Eric Schickler, *Partisan Hearts and Minds* (New Haven, CT: Yale University Press, 2002).

38. Pew Research Center, "Young Voters Supported Obama Less, but May Have Mattered More," November 26, 2012, www. people-press.org/2012/11/26/young-voters-supported-obama-less-but-may-have-mattered-more (accessed 3/17/14).

39. Jack Citrin and David O. Sears, *American Identity and the Politics of Multiculturalism* (New York: Cambridge University Press, 2014).

40. For elaboration on this point, see William T. Bianco, Richard G. Niemi, and Harold W. Stanley, "Partisanship and Group Support over Time: A Multivariate Analysis," *American Political Science Review* 80 (September, 1986): 969–76.

41. Arthur Lupia and Mathew D. McCubbins, *The Democratic Dilemma* (New York: Cambridge University Press, 1998).

42. Lawrence R. Jacobs and Robert Y. Shapiro, *Politicians Don't Pander: Political Manipulation and the Loss of Democratic Responsiveness* (Chicago: University of Chicago Press, 2000).

43. Kaiser Family Foundation, Kaiser Health Tracking Poll: The Public's Views on the ACA, 2016, http://kff.org/interactive/kaiser-health-tracking-poll-the-publics-views-on-the-aca/#?response=Favorable--Unfavorable&aRange=twoYear (accessed 11/1/15).

44. Christopher Wlezien and Robert S. Erikson, "The Horse Race: What Polls Reveal as the Election Campaign Unfolds," *International Journal of Public Opinion Research* 19:1 (2007): 74–88.

45. Pollster.com, "IVR and Internet: How Reliable?" September 28, 2006, www.pollster.com/mystery_pollster/ivr_internet_how_reliable.php (accessed 2/21/08).

46. For data on reported and actual turnout, see Chapter 9.

47. Anton J. Nederhof, "Methods of Coping with Social Desirability Bias: A Review," *European Journal of Social Psychology* 15:3 (2006): 263–80.

48. The Harris Poll, "Wingnuts and President Obama," March 6, 2015, http://media.theharrispoll.com/documents/Harris-Interactive-Poll-Research-Politics-Wingnuts-2010-03.pdf (accessed 11/3/15).

49. James H. Kuklinski et al., "Misinformation and the Currency of Democratic Citizenship," *Journal of Politics* 62:3 (2000): 790–816.

50. Sarah Kliff, "Obamacare Is 5 Years Old, and Americans Are Still Worried about Death Panels," Vox.com, May 23, 2015, www. vox.com/2015/3/23/8273007/obamacare-poll-death-panels (accessed 11/2/15).

51. George H. Bishop, *The Illusion of Public Opinion: Fact and Artifact in Public Opinion Polls* (Washington, DC: Rowman & Littlefield, 2004).

52. Michael X. Delli Carpini and Scott Keeter, *What Americans Know about Politics and Why It Matters* (New Haven, CT: Yale University Press, 1997).

53. Dan Diamond, "The Unemployment Rate Doubled under Bush. It's Fallen by More than One-Third under Obama," Vox. com, November 7, 2015, www.vox.com/2015/11/7/9684780/unemployment-rate-obama (accessed 11/7/15).

54. Delli Carpini and Keeter, *What Americans Know about Politics and Why It Matters*.

55. Nate Silver, "How FiveThirtyEight Calculates Pollster Ratings," September 25, 2014, http://fivethirtyeight.com/features/how-fivethirtyeight-calculates-pollster-ratings (accessed 11/6/15).

56. For a review of the literature on trust in government, see Karen Cook, Russell Hardin, and Margaret Levi, *Cooperation without Trust* (New York: Russell Sage Foundation, 2005), as well as Marc J. Hetherington, *Why Trust Matters: Declining Political*

Trust and the Demise of American Liberalism (Princeton, NJ: Princeton University Press, 2004).

57. William T. Bianco, *Trust: Representatives and Constituents* (Ann Arbor: University of Michigan Press, 1994).

58. Sean M. Theriault, *The Power of the People: Congressional Competition, Public Attention, and Voter Retribution* (Columbus: Ohio State University Press, 2005).

59. Thomas Rudolph and Jillian Evans, "Political Trust, Ideology, and Public Support for Government Spending," *American Journal of Political Science* 49 (2005): 660–71.

60. Patricia Moy and Michael Pfau, *With Malice toward All? The Media and Public Confidence in Democratic Institutions* (Boulder, CO: Praeger, 2000).

61. Robert S. Erikson, Michael B. MacKuen, and James A. Stimson, *The Macro Polity* (New York: Cambridge University Press, 2002).

62. James A. Stimson, *Public Opinion in America: Moods, Swings, and Cycles* (Boulder, CO: Westview Press, 1999).

63. Robert S. Erikson, Michael B. MacKuen, and James A. Stimson, "American Politics: The Model" (unpublished paper, Columbia University, 2000).

64. Larry Bartels, "Constituency Opinion and Congressional Policy Making: The Reagan Defense Buildup," *American Political Science Review* 85 (June 1991): 457–74; Jonathan Kastellec, Jeffrey R. Lax, and Justin H. Phillips, "Public Opinion and Senate Confirmation of Supreme Court Nominees," *Journal of Politics* 72 (2010): 767–84.

65. Lawrence R. Jacobs and Robert Y. Shapiro, *Politicians Don't Pander: Political Manipulation and the Loss of Democratic Responsiveness* (Chicago: University of Chicago Press, 2000).

Chapter 7

1. Jason Barabas, and Jennifer Jerit, "Estimating the Causal Effects of Media Coverage on Policy-Specific Knowledge," *American Journal of Political Science* 53 (2008): 73–89.

2. Thomas E. Patterson, *Out of Order* (New York: Alfred A. Knopf, 1993); Robert D. Putnam, *Bowling Alone* (New York: Basic Books, 2000).

3. Thomas Patterson, "Bad News, Period," *Political Science and Politics* 29 (1996): 17–20.

4. William H. Riker, *The Strategy of Rhetoric: Campaigning for the American Constitution* (New Haven, CT: Yale University Press, 1996).

5. Garry Wills, *Explaining America: The Federalist* (New York: Penguin Press, 2001).

6. Geoffrey R. Stone, *Perilous Times: Free Speech in Wartime from the Sedition Act of 1798 to the War on Terrorism* (New York: W. W. Norton, 2004).

7. John D. Stevens, *Sensationalism and the New York Press* (New York: Columbia University Press, 1991).

8. Robert C. Williams, *Horace Greeley: Champion of American Freedom* (New York: New York University Press, 2006).

9. Gay Talese, *The Kingdom and the Power* (New York: Calder and Boyars, 1983).

10. For a detailed history, see United States Early Radio History, www.earlyradiohistory.us (accessed 9/17/12).

11. This discussion draws on the summary "Merging Media: How Relaxing FCC Ownership Rules Has Affected the Media Business," www.pbs.org/newshour/media/conglomeration/fcc2.html (accessed 2/26/08).

12. The Project for Excellence in Journalism, "The State of the News Media, 2007: Ownership," 2007, www.stateofthenewsmedia.org/2007/narrative_overview_ownership.asp?cat=5&media=1 (accessed 2/26/08).

13. The *Columbia Journalism Review* maintains a list of holdings for major media companies at Who Owns What, www.cjr.org/tools/owners (accessed 9/17/12).

14. SCOTUSblog, www.scotusblog.com (accessed 9/17/12).

15. See www.themonkeycage.org (accessed 9/17/12).

16. The Center for Responsive Politics, www.opensecrets.org (accessed 9/17/12).

17. Pollster, www.pollster.com (accessed 9/17/12).

18. See, for example, James J. Cramer, "Newspapers Still Stumble Online," RealMoney.com, May 2, 2005, www.thestreet.com/p/_rms/rmoney/jamesjcramer/10221101.html (accessed 2/26/08).

19. Matthew Baum, "Sex, Lies and War: How Soft News Brings Foreign Policy to the Inattentive Public," *American Political Science Review* 96 (2002): 91–109.

20. Lance Bennett, *News: The Politics of Illusion* (New York: Pearson, 2012).

21. Danny Hayes and Matthew Guardino, *Influence from Abroad: Foreign Voices, the Media, and U.S. Public Opinion* (New York: Cambridge University Press, 2013).

22. Matthew Baum, "Talking the Vote: Why Presidential Candidates Hit the Talk Show Circuit?," *American Journal of Political Science* 49 (2005): 213–34.

23. Trip Gabriel, "Ben Carson Is Struggling to Grasp Foreign Policy, Advisors Say," *New York Times*, November 17, 2015, p. A1.

24. James Hohmann, "First-Time Candidate Carson Doesn't Understand What Running for President Entails," *Washington Post*, November 9, 2015.

25. Barton Gellman, "Code Name 'Verax': Snowden, in Exchanges with *Post* Reporter, Made Clear He Knew Risks," *Washington Post*, June 13, 2012, p. A1.

26. Sharon LaFraniere, "Math behind Leak Crackdown: 153 Cases, 4 Years, 0 Indictments," *New York Times*, July 20, 2013, p. A1.

27. Michael Kelly, "Bing Maps Appear to Show the 'Secret' U.S. Drone Base in Saudi Arabia," February 8, 2013, www.businessinsider.com/wired-finds-americas-drone-base-in-saudi-arabia-2013-2 (accessed 8/30/16).

28. For a discussion of these concepts, see Paul M. Sniderman and Sean M. Theriault, "The Structure of Political Argument and the Logic of Issue Framing," in *Studies in Public Opinion*, ed. William E. Saris and Paul M. Sniderman (Princeton, NJ: Princeton University Press, 2004); and Shanto Iyengar and Donald Kinder, *News That Matters* (Chicago: University of Chicago Press, 1987). See also Maxwell McCombs and Donald L. Shaw, "The Agenda-Setting Functions of Mass Media," *Public Opinion Quarterly* 36 (1972): 176–87; and Amos Tversky and Daniel Kahnemann, "The Framing of Decisions and the Psychology of Choice," *Science* 211 (1981): 453–58.

29. Markus Prior, "Media and Political Polarization," *Annual Review of Political Science* 16 (2013): 101–27.

30. Kevin Arceneaux et al., "The Influence of News Media on Political Elites: Investigating Strategic Responsiveness in Congress," *American Journal of Political Science*, 60:1 (2016): 5–29.

31. Matthew S. Levendusky, "Why Do Partisan Media Polarize Viewers?" *American Journal of Political Science* 57:3 (2013): 611–23.

32. Kevin Arceneaux, Martin Johnson, and Chad Murphy, "Polarized Political Communication, Oppositional Media Hostility, and Selective Exposure," *Journal of Politics* 74:01 (2012): 174–86.

33. See Eric Alterman, *What Liberal Media?* (New York: Basic Books, 2003), and Bernard Goldberg, *Bias* (New York: Regnery, 2001).

34. Eric Wemple, "*Fox & Friends* Fails on Obama–Muslim Museum Connection: No Surprise Here," *Washington Post*, October 7, 2013, www.washingtonpost.com/blogs/erik-wemple/wp/2013/10/07/fox-friends-fails-on-obama-muslim-museum-connection-no-surprise-here (accessed 12/26/13).

35. This description runs on the editorial masthead of every issue of the *Nation*.

36. Tal Kopan, "Carson Slams Reporters over Questions about His Past," November 6, 2015, www.cnn.com/2015/11/06/politics/ben-carson-responds-violent-past-new-day (accessed 11/20/15).

37. Stefano DellaVigna and Ethan Kaplan, "The Fox News Effect: Media Bias and Voting," *Quarterly Journal of Economics* 122 (2007): 1187–1234.

38. Project Censored, "Top 25 of 2014–2015," www.projectcensored.org/category/top-25-of-2014-2015 (accessed 11/20/15).

39. Carl Bialik, "Scare Headlines Exaggerated the US Crime Wave," September 11, 2015, http://fivethirtyeight.com/features/scare-headlines-exaggerated-the-u-s-crime-wave (accessed 11/20/15).

40. Pew Research Center, "Press Widely Criticized, but Trusted More than Other Information Sources," September 22, 2011, www.people-press.org/2011/09/22/press-widely-criticized-but-trusted-more-than-other-institutions (accessed 9/17/12).

41. Markus Prior, *Post-Broadcast Democracy: How Media Choice Increases Inequality in Political Involvement and Polarizes Elections* (New York: Cambridge University Press, 2007).

42. Pablo Boczkowski, *Imitation in an Age of Information Abundance* (Chicago: University of Chicago Press, 2010).

43. Jonathan Ladd, "Four Approaches to Providing Political News Given That So Many People Don't Want It," August 20, 2015, www.mischiefsoffaction.com/2015/08/four-approaches-to-providing-political.html?m=1 (accessed 11/5/15).

44. Patterson, "Bad News, Period."

45. Shanto Iyengar, Helmut Norpoth, and Kyu Hahn, "Consumer Demand for Election News: The Horserace Sells," *Journal of Politics* 66 (2004): 157–75.

46. Thomas Patterson, "Doing Well and Doing Good: How Soft News and Critical Journalism Are Shrinking the News Audience and Weakening Democracy—and What News Outlets Can Do about It" (Cambridge, MA: Joan Shorenstein Center on the Press, Politics, and Public Policy, Harvard University, 2000), www.ksg.harvard.edu/presspol/research_publications/reports/softnews.pdf (accessed 2/29/08).

47. Justin Peters, "Does Paris Matter More than Beirut?" November 18, 2015, www.slate.com/articles/news_and_politics/culturebox/2015/11/the_media_covered_the_paris_attacks_more_than_the_beirut_bombing_the_problem.html (accessed 11/21/15).

48. T. E. Patterson, *The Vanishing Voter* (New York: Knopf, 2002); J. N. Cappella and K. H. Jamieson, *Spiral of Cynicism: The Press and the Public Good* (New York: Oxford University Press, 1997).

49. Robert McChesney, *The Problem of the Media: U.S. Communication Politics in the 21st Century* (New York: Monthly Review Press, 2004).

Chapter 8

1. Marty Cohen et al., *The Party Decides: Presidential Nominations before and after Reform* (Chicago: University of Chicago Press, 2008).

2. Joseph Schlesinger, *Political Parties and the Winning of Office* (Ann Arbor: University of Michigan Press, 1994).

3. William Nesbit Chambers and Walter Dean Burnham, *The American Party Systems: Stages of Political Development* (Oxford, UK: Oxford University Press, 1966).

4. Donald H. Hickey, "Federalist Party Unity and the War of 1812," *Journal of American Studies* 12 (April 1978): 23–39; William T. Bianco, David B. Spence, and John D. Wilkerson, "The Electoral Connection in the Early Congress: The Case of the Compensation Act of 1816," *American Journal of Political Science* 40 (February 1996): 145–71.

5. John Aldrich, *Why Parties?* (Chicago: University of Chicago Press, 2005).

6. James MacPherson, *Battle Cry of Freedom: The Civil War Era* (New York: Oxford University Press, 1988).

7. Michael F. Holt, *The Rise and Fall of the Whig Party: Jacksonian Politics and the Onset of the Civil War* (New York: Oxford University Press, 1999).

8. Harold W. Stanley, William T. Bianco, and Richard G. Niemi, "Partisanship and Group Support over Time: A Multivariate Analysis," *American Political Science Review* 80 (1986): 969–76.

9. Eric Schickler, *Racial Realignment: The Transformation of American Liberalism, 1932—1965* (Princeton, NJ: Princeton University Press, 2016).

10. Hans Noel, *Political Ideologies and Political Parties in America* (New York: Cambridge University Press, 2014).

11. Aldrich, *Why Parties?*

12. James L. Sundquist, *Dynamics of the Party System*, rev. ed. (Washington, DC: Brookings Institution, 1983).

13. John H. Aldrich and Richard G. Niemi, "The Sixth American Party System: Electoral Change, 1952–1992," in *Broken Contract: Changing Relationships between Americans and Their Governments*, ed. Steven Craig (Boulder, CO: Westview Press, 1993).

14. Charles S. Bullock III, Donna R. Hoffman, and Ronald Keith Gaddie, "Regional Variations in the Realignment of American Politics, 1944–2004," *Social Science Quarterly* 87:3 (2006): 494–518.

15. The full list of Democratic constituency groups is available at www.democrats.org/people. A list of Republican coalition groups is available at www.gop.com/coalition-support (accessed 10/18/12).

16. Jon F. Hale, "The Making of the New Democrats," *Political Science Quarterly* 110:2 (1995): 207–32.

17. Christopher S. Parker and Matt A. Barreto, *Change They Can't Believe In: The Tea Party and Reactionary Politics in America* (Princeton, NJ: Princeton University Press, 2015).

18. James Monroe, *The Political Party Matrix* (Albany: SUNY Press, 2001).

19. Gary Cox and Mathew McCubbins, *Legislative Leviathan* (Berkeley: University of California Press, 1993); James M. Snyder and Michael M. Ting, "An Informational Rationale for Political Parties," *American Journal of Political Science* 46 (2002): 90–110.

20. Jason Roberts and Steven Smith, "Procedural Contexts, Party Strategy, and Conditional Party Government," *American Journal of Political Science* 47:2 (2003): 305–17.

21. David Rohde, *Parties and Leaders in the Post-reform House* (Chicago: University of Chicago Press, 1991); Keith Poole, "An Update on Polarization through the 113th Congress," *Voteview*, September 8, 2013, http://voteview.com/blog/?p=887 (accessed 4/24/14).

22. Catherine Rampell, "Tax Pledge May Scuttle a Deal on Deficit," *New York Times*, November 18, 2011, p. B1.

23. Donald Green, Bradley Palmquist, and Eric Schickler, *Partisan Hearts and Minds* (New Haven, CT: Yale University Press, 2004); Christopher Achen, "Political Socialization and Rational Party Identification," *Political Behavior* 24:2 (2002): 151-70.

24. Morris Fiorina, *Retrospective Voting in American National Elections* (New Haven, CT: Yale University Press, 1981).

25. Michael Meffert, Helmut Norpoth, and Anirudh V. S. Ruhil, "Realignment and Macropartisanship," *American Political Science Review* 95:4 (2001): 953-62.

26. Walter Dean Burnham, "The Reagan Heritage," in *The Election of 1988: Reports and Interpretations*, ed. Gerald M. Pomper et al. (Chatham, NJ: Chatham House, 1989).

27. Martin P. Wattenberg, *The Decline of American Political Parties: 1952-1994* (Cambridge, MA: Harvard University Press, 1996).

28. David S. Broder, *The Party's Over: The Failure of Partisan Politics in America* (New York: Harper and Row, 1971).

29. Donald P. Green and Bradley Palmquist, "Of Artifacts and Partisan Instability," *American Journal of Political Science* 34:3 (August 1990): 872-902.

30. Samara Kiar and Yanna Krupnikov, "*Independent Politics: How American Disdain for Parties Leads to Political Inaction* (New York: Cambridge University Press, 2016).

31. Larry M. Bartels, "Partisanship and Voting Behavior, 1952–1996," *American Journal of Political Science* 44:1 (2000): 35-50.

32. Daniel Schlotzman, *When Movements Anchor Parties: Electoral Alignments in American History* (Princeton, NJ: Princeton University Press, 2015).

33. Patrick Egan, *Partisan Priorities: How Issue Ownership Drives and Distorts American Politics* (New York: Cambridge University Press, 2013).

34. Jill Lawrence, "Party Recruiters Lead Charge for '06 Vote; Choice of Candidates to Run in Fall May Decide Who Controls the House," *USA Today*, May 25, 2006, p. A5.

35. Marty Cohen, David Karol, Hans Noel, and John Zaller, *The Party Decides: Presidential Nominations before and after Reform* (Chicago: University of Chicago Press, 2008).

36. Jonathan Bernstein, "Clinton Knows Who's Boss: Her Party," November 18, 2015, www.bloombergview.com/articles/2015-11-18/democratic-party-is-more-important-than-hillary-clinton (accessed 11/20/15).

37. S.A. Miller, "Recruits for 2010 Put Glee in GOP," *Washington Times*, January 6, 2010, p. A1.

38. Compiled from information available at www.ballot-access.org (accessed 12/17/09).

39. Kyle Mattes and David Redlawsk, *The Positive Case for Negative Campaigning* (Chicago: University of Chicago Press, 2014).

40. Patricia Zapor, "Pro-life Democrats Describe Lonely Role, but See Improvements," Catholic News Service, July 28, 2004, www.catholicnews.com/data/stories/cns/0404122.htm (accessed 3/27/08).

41. John Geering, *Party Ideologies in America, 1828-1996* (New York: Cambridge University Press, 2001).

42. See www.lp.org/our-history (accessed 9/17/12).

43. Steven J. Rosenstone, Roy L. Behr, and Edward Lazarus, *Third Parties in America: Citizen Response to Major Party Failure* (Princeton, NJ: Princeton University Press, 1984).

44. Janet Hook and Peter Wallsten, "GOP Feels Sting of Candidates' Rejection," *Los Angeles Times*, October 10, 2005, p. A1.

45. Gary Cox, *Making Votes Count: Strategic Coordination in the World's Electoral Systems* (Cambridge, UK: Cambridge University Press, 1997).

46. Peter Hanson, *Too Weak to Govern: Majority Party Power and Appropriations in the U.S. Senate* (New York: Cambridge University Press, 2015).

47. Thomas B. Edsall, "GOP Gains Advantage on Key Issues, Polls Say," *Washington Post*, January 27, 2002, p. A4.

48. John D. McKinnon, "Backing Away from Bush; Some Republican Candidates Avoid Ties with Unpopular President," *Wall Street Journal*, May 23, 2006, p. A4.

Take a Stand

a. Nelson Polsby, *Consequences of Party Reform* (New York: Oxford University Press, 1983).

b. Daniel A. Smith and Caroline J. Tolbert, *Educated by Initiative: The Effects of Direct Democracy on Citizens and Political Organizations in the American States* (Ann Arbor: University of Michigan Press, 2004).

Chapter 9

1. Morris P. Fiorina, *Retrospective Voting in American National Elections* (New Haven, CT: Yale University Press, 1981); V. O. Key, *The Responsible Electorate* (New York: Vintage Books, 1966).

2. David Mayhew, *Congress: The Electoral Connection* (New Haven, CT: Yale University Press, 1973).

3. For details on early voting, see the Early Voting Information Center site at http://earlyvoting.net (accessed 10/19/12).

4. Barry C. Burden, David T. Canon, Kenneth R. Meyer, and Donald P. Moynihan, "Election Laws, Mobilization, and Turnout: The Unexpected Consequences of Early Voting," *American Journal of Political Science* 58 (2014): 95-109.

5. Jonathan N. Wand, Kenneth W. Shotts, Jasjeet S. Sekhon, Walter R. Mebane, Michael C. Herron, and Henry E. Brady, "The Butterfly Ballot Did It: The Aberrant Vote for Buchanan in Palm Beach County, Florida," *American Political Science Review* 95 (2001): 793-809.

6. Michael Alvarez, Lonna Rae Atkeson, and Thad E. Hall, *Evaluating Elections: A Handbook of Standards and Methods* (New York: Cambridge University Press, 2013).

7. United States Government Accountability Office, "Issues Related to State Voter Identification Laws," 2014, www.gao.gov/assets/670/665966.pdf (accessed 3/4/16).

8. Minor-party candidates are typically selected during party conventions.

9. Barbara Norrander, "Presidential Nomination Politics in the Post-reform Era," *Political Research Quarterly* 49 (1996): 875-90.

10. Larry Bartels, *Presidential Primaries and the Dynamics of Public Choice* (Princeton, NJ: Princeton University Press, 1988).

11. William G. Mayer, "Forecasting Presidential Nominations or, My Model Worked Just Fine, Thank You," *Political Science and Politics* 36 (2003): 153-59.

12. Marty Cohen, David Karol, Hans Noel, and John Zaller, "Beating Reform: The Resurgence of Parties in Presidential Nominations, 1980 to 2000" (paper presented at the 2001 American Political Science Association Annual Meeting, San Francisco, CA).

13. Richard Herrera, "Are 'Superdelegates' Super?," *Political Behavior* 16 (1994): 79-93.

14. FairVote, "Maine and Nebraska," www.fairvote.org/e_college/me_ne.htm (accessed 10/19/12).

15. Robert Bennett, "The Problem of the Faithless Elector," *Northwestern University Law Review* 100 (2004): 121–30.

16. James Q. Wilson, "Is the Electoral College Worth Saving?," *Slate*, November 3, 2000, www.slate.com/id/92663 (accessed 10/19/12).

17. Robert Erikson and Christopher Wlezien, *The Timeline of Presidential Elections* (Chicago: University of Chicago Press, 2013).

18. Larry M. Bartels and Christopher H. Achen, *Democracy for Realists: Why Elections Do Not Produce Responsive Government* (Princeton, NJ: Princeton University Press, 2016).

19. Linda Fowler and Robert McClure, *Political Ambition: Who Decides to Run for Congress* (Ann Arbor: University of Michigan Press, 1989).

20. Robin Kolodny, *Pursuing Majorities: Congressional Campaign Committees in American Politics* (Norman: University of Oklahoma Press, 1999).

21. Steven Ansolabehere and Alan Gerber, "Incumbency Advantage and the Persistence of Legislative Majorities," *Legislative Studies Quarterly* 22 (1997): 161–80.

22. For a discussion of Johnson's decision, see Robert A. Caro, *The Path to Power* (New York: Knopf, 1983).

23. Thomas Mann and Norman Ornstein, *The Permanent Campaign and Its Future* (Washington, DC: American Enterprise Institute, 2000).

24. David Mayhew, *Congress: The Electoral Connection* (New Haven, CT: Yale University Press, 1973).

25. Henry Chappell and William Keech, "A New Model of Political Accountability for Economic Performance," *American Political Science Review* 79 (1985): 10–19.

26. Jonathan Krasno and Donald P. Green, "The Dynamics of Campaign Fundraising in House Elections," *Journal of Politics* 56 (1991): 459–74.

27. Michael J. Goff, *The Money Primary: The New Politics of the Early Presidential Nomination Process* (New York: Rowman & Littlefield, 2007).

28. Chris Cillizza, "Consulting Firms Face Conflict in 2008," *Roll Call*, June 20, 2005, p. 1.

29. For details, see Committee on Standards of Official Conduct, "Laws, Rules, and Standards of Conduct Governing Campaign Activity," memorandum, April 25, 2008, http://ethics.house.gov/sites/ethics.house.gov/files/m_campaign_activity_2008_0.pdf (accessed 11/6/12).

30. Cherie Maestas, Walter Stone, and L. Sandy Maisel, "Quality Counts: Extending the Strategic Politician Model of Incumbent Deterrence," *American Journal of Political Science* 48 (2004): 479–90.

31. Matt Bai, "Turnout Wins Elections," *New York Times Magazine*, December 14, 2003, p. 100.

32. Christopher Drew, "New Telemarketing Ploy Steers Voters on Republican Path," *New York Times*, November 6, 2006.

33. John Dickerson, "Weak Poll," *Slate*, October 30, 2006, www.slate.com/id/2152529 (accessed 10/19/12).

34. Michael Babaro, "Candidates Stick to Script, If Not the Truth, in the 2016 Race," *New York Times*, November 7, 2015, p. A1.

35. For a history of presidential debates, see the Commission on Presidential Debates site at www.debates.org (accessed 10/19/12).

36. For a video library of presidential campaign ads, see Museum of the Moving Image, "The Living Room Candidate: Presidential Campaign Commercials 1952–2012," http://livingroomcandidate.org (accessed 10/19/12).

37. Museum of the Moving Image, "The Living Room Candidate: 1964: Johnson vs. Goldwater," http://livingroomcandidate.org/commercials/1964/dowager (accessed 10/19/12).

38. Museum of the Moving Image, "The Living Room Candidate: 1964: Johnson vs. Goldwater."

39. For examples of this argument, see Thomas Patterson, *The Vanishing Voter* (New York: Knopf, 2002), and Jules Witcover, *No Way to Pick a President: How Money and Hired Guns Have Debased American Politics* (London: Routledge, 2001).

40. For examples of these and other campaign ads, see "Most Intriguing Campaign Ads of 2010," ABC News, http://abcnews.go.com/politics/slideshow/intriguing-political-ads-2010-10887147 (accessed 10/19/12).

41. Paul Freeman, Michael Franz, and Kenneth Goldstein, "Campaign Advertising and Democratic Citizenship," *American Journal of Political Science* 48 (2004): 723–41.

42. Constantine J. Spilotes and Lynn Vavreck, "Campaign Advertising: Partisan Convergence or Divergence?," *Journal of Politics* 64 (2002): 249–61.

43. Kathleen Hall Jameson, *Packaging the Presidency: A History and Criticism of Presidential Campaign Advertising* (New York: Oxford University Press, 1996).

44. Steven Ansolabehere and Shanto Iyengar, *Going Negative: How Political Advertisements Shrink and Polarize the Electorate* (New York: Free Press, 1997); Richard Lau, Lee Sigelman, Caroline Heldman, and Paul Babbitt, "The Effects of Negative Political Advertisements: A Meta-analytic Analysis," *American Political Science Review* 93 (1999): 851–70.

45. Jonathan Krasno and Frank J. Sorauf, "For the Defense," *Political Science and Politics* 37 (2004): 777–80.

46. Contribution and spending data are available from the Center for Responsive Politics at www.opensecrets.org.

47. Brian Stelter, "The Price of 30 Seconds," *New York Times*, October 1, 2007, http://mediadecoder.blogs.nytimes.com/2007/10/01/the-price-of-30-seconds (accessed 10/19/12).

48. For a review of this literature, see Michael Malbin, *The Election after Reform: Money, Politics, and the Bipartisan Campaign Reform Act* (Washington, DC: Rowman & Littlefield, 2006).

49. Lynda Powell, *The Influence of Campaign Contributions in State Legislatures* (Ann Arbor: University of Michigan Press, 2012).

50. David Karol, "If You Think Super PACS Have Changed Everything about Presidential Primaries, Think Again," 2015, www.washingtonpost.com/blogs/monkey-cage/wp/2015/09/21/if-you-think-super-pacs-have-changed-everything-about-the-presidential-primary-think-again (accessed 9/21/15).

51. For a discussion, see Patterson, *The Vanishing Voter*, especially Chapter 1, "The Incredible Shrinking Electorate," pp. 3–22.

52. William H. Riker and Peter Ordeshook, "A Theory of the Calculus of Voting," *American Political Science Review* 62 (1968): 25–39.

53. Michael McDonald, The United States Elections Project, http://elections.gmu.edu (accessed 10/19/12).

54. Pew Research Center, "Regular Voters, Intermittent Voters, and Those Who Don't," October 18, 2006, available at www.people-press.org/files/legacy-pdf/292.pdf (accessed 7/29/16).

55. For a review of the literature on issue voters, see Jon K. Dalager, "Voters, Issues, and Elections: Are Candidates' Messages Getting Through?," *Journal of Politics* 58 (1996): 486–515.

56. Richard P. Lau and David P. Redlawsk, *How Voters Decide: Information Processing during Electoral Campaigns* (New York: Cambridge University Press, 2006).

57. Samuel Popkin, *The Reasoning Voter* (Chicago: University of Chicago Press, 1991).

58. Richard R. Lau and David P. Redlawsk, "Advantages and Disadvantages of Cognitive Heuristics in Political Decision Making," *American Journal of Political Science* 45 (2001): 951-71.

59. For 2006 exit poll data, see Pew Research Center, "Public Cheers Democratic Victory," November 16, 2006, www.people-press.org/reports/display.php3?ReportID=296 (accessed 10/19/12).

Chapter 10

1. Robert A. Dahl, *A Preface to Democratic Theory* (Chicago: University of Chicago Press, 1951); David Truman, *The Governmental Process* (New York: Harper and Row, 1951).

2. Theodore Lowi, *The End of Liberalism: The Second Republic of the United States* (New York: W. W. Norton, 1979).

3. Lobbying regulations are often changed; the discussion here is just a general guide. Regular reports on past, current, and proposed lobbying regulations can be found on the website of the Congressional Research Service at www.opencrs.com (accessed 9/19/12).

4. Frank Baumgartner and Beth Leech, *Basic Interests: The Importance of Interest Groups in Politics and in Political Science* (Princeton, NJ: Princeton University Press, 1999), p. 109.

5. Beth L. Leech, Frank R. Baumgartner, Timothy M. La Pira, and Nicholas A. Semanko, "Drawing Lobbyists to Washington: Government Activity and the Demand for Advocacy," *Political Research Quarterly* 58: 1 (March 2005): 19-30.

6. Roxana Tiron, "Lockheed Martin Leads Expanded Lobbying by US Defense Industry," *Washington Post*, January 26, 2012, www.washingtonpost.com/business/economy/lockheed-martin-leads-expanded-lobbying-by-us-defense-industry/2012/01/26/gIQAlgQtaQ_story.html (accessed 2/4/14).

7. Tim LaPira, Lee Drutman, and Matthew Glassman, "The Interest Group Top Tier: More Groups, Concentrated Clout," paper presented at the 2014 American Political Science Association Annual Meeting.

8. For more on this argument, see Tim Harford, "There's Not Enough Money in Politics," *Slate*, April 1, 2006, www.slate.com/id/2138874 (accessed 7/29/16); and Stephen Ansolabehere, John M. de Figueiredo, and James M. Snyder, "Why Is There So Little Money in American Politics?" *Journal of Economic Perspectives* 17 (2003): 105-30.

9. Scott Ainsworth, *Analyzing Interest Groups: Group Influence on People and Policies* (New York: W. W. Norton, 2002).

10. Timothy LaPira and Hershel F. Thomas III, "Revolving Door Lobbyists and Interest Representation," *Interest Groups and Advocacy* 3 (2013): 4-29.

11. Data available at www.opensecrets.org/revolving/departing.php?cong=113 (accessed 7/29/16).

12. Robert H. Salisbury, John P. Heinz, Edward O. Laumann, and Robert L. Nelson, "Who Works with Whom? Interest Group Alliances and Opposition," *American Political Science Review* 81 (1987): 1217-34.

13. Business-Industry Political Action Committee, "About BIPAC," www.bipac.org/about/about.asp (accessed 4/8/08).

14. One example campaign is MoveOn.org Political Action Committee, "Letter to the Editor: Tell the Media: We Want to End the War. The President Wants Endless War," http://pol.moveon.org/lte/?lte_campaign_id=72 (accessed 4/8/08).

15. Thomas Holyoke, "Choosing Battlegrounds: Interest Group Lobbying across Multiple Venues," *Political Science Quarterly* 56 (2003): 325-36.

16. AARP, "Policy and Research for Professionals in Aging," www.aarp.org/research/ppi (accessed 4/8/08).

17. James Q. Wilson, *Political Organizations* (New York: Basic Books, 1974).

18. American Automobile Association, Foundation for Traffic Safety, www.aaafoundation.org/home (accessed 7/29/16).

19. Kenneth Kollman, *Outside Lobbying: Public Opinion and Interest Group Strategies* (Princeton, NJ: Princeton University Press, 1998).

20. Jack Walker, *Mobilizing Interest Groups in America* (Ann Arbor: University of Michigan Press, 1991).

21. John P. Heinz, Edward O. Laumann, and Robert Salisbury, *The Hollow Core: Private Interests in National Policymaking* (Cambridge, MA: Harvard University Press, 1993).

22. Richard L. Hall and Alan V. Deardorff, "Lobbying as Legislative Subsidy," *American Political Science Review* 100 (2006): 69-84.

23. Hall and Deardorff, "Lobbying as Legislative Subsidy."

24. David Austen-Smith and John R. Wright, "Counteractive Lobbying," *American Journal of Political Science* 38:1 (1994): 25-44.

25. Key Lehman Schlozman and John T. Tierney, *Organized Interests and American Democracy* (New York: HarperCollins, 1986).

26. Baumgartner and Leech, *Basic Interests*, p. 152.

27. Christine A. DeGregorio, *Networks of Champions: Leadership, Access, and Advocacy in the U.S. House of Representatives* (Ann Arbor: University of Michigan Press, 1992).

28. Daniel Carpenter, *The Forging of Bureaucratic Autonomy: Reputations, Networks, and Policy Innovation in Executive Agencies, 1862-1928* (Princeton, NJ: Princeton University Press, 2002).

29. Public Citizen Publications, www.citizen.org/publications (accessed 7/29/16).

30. Derived from a search of the NRA Institute for Legislative Action site, www.nraila.org (accessed 9/19/12).

31. Kim Scheppele and Jack L. Walker, "The Litigation Strategies of Interest Groups," in *Mobilizing Interest Groups in America*, ed. Jack Walker (Ann Arbor: University of Michigan Press, 1991).

32. Lauren Cohen Bell, *Warring Factions: Interest Groups, Money, and the New Politics of Senate Confirmation* (Columbus: Ohio State University Press, 2002).

33. Kevin W. Hula, *Lobbying Together: Interest Group Coalitions in Legislative Politics* (Washington, DC: Georgetown University Press, 1999).

34. Jeanne Cummings, "Word Games Could Threaten Climate Bill," June 9, 2009, www.politico.com/news/stories/0609/24059.html (accessed 9/19/12).

35. AARP, "Elected Officials," http://capwiz.com/aarp/dbq/officials (accessed 7/29/16).

36. Manny Fernandez, "Gun Sentiments and Guns on Display at Alamo Rally," *New York Times*, October 29, 2013, p. A23.

37. Richard Fenno, *Home Style: U.S. House Members in Their Districts* (Boston: Little, Brown, 1978). See also Brandice Caines-Wrone, David W. Brady, and John F. Cogan, "Out of Step, out of Office: Electoral Accountability and House Members' Voting," *American Political Science Review* 96 (2002): 127-40.

38. Emily Yoffe, "Am I the Next Jack Abramoff?," *Slate*, April 1, 2006, www.slate.com/id/2137886 (accessed 8/28/09).

39. Kollman, *Outside Lobbying*.

40. Gregory Calderia, Marie Hojnacki, and John R. Wright, "The Lobbying Activities of Organized Interests in Federal Judicial Nominations," *Journal of Politics* 62 (2000): 51–69.

41. *Citizens United v. Federal Election Commission*, 558 U.S. 310 (2010).

42. Data from www.opensecrets.org and www.fec.gov (accessed 11/1/16).

43. John G. Matsusaka, "Direct Democracy and Fiscal Gridlock: Have Voter Initiatives Paralyzed the California Budget?," *State Politics and Policy* 5 (2005): 346–62.

44. Thad Kousser, *Term Limits and the Dismantling of State Legislative Professionalism* (New York: Cambridge University Press, 2004).

45. John G. Matsusaka, *For the Many or the Few: The Initiative, Public Policy, and American Democracy* (Chicago: University of Chicago Press, 2004).

46. Elizabeth R. Gerber, *The Populist Paradox: Interest Group Influence and the Promise of Direct Legislation* (Princeton, NJ: Princeton University Press, 1999).

47. Baumgartner and Leech, *Basic Interests*, Chapter 8, pp. 147–67.

48. Lee Drutman, "The Solution to Lobbying Is More Lobbying," *Washington Post*, April 29, 2015, www.washingtonpost.com/blogs/monkey-cage/wp/2015/04/29/the-solution-to-lobbying-is-more-lobbying (accessed 2/16/16).

49. National Rifle Association Institute for Legislative Action, "Fact Sheet: Right-to-Carry: The Stearns/Boucher Right-to-Carry Reciprocity Bill," www.nraila.org/Issues/FactSheets/Read.aspx?id=189&issue=003 (accessed 4/9/08).

50. David Lowery, "Why Do Organized Interests Lobby? A Multi-Goal, Multi-Context Theory of Lobbying," *Polity* 39 (2007): 29–54.

51. Amy McKay, "Negative Lobbying and Policy Outcomes," *American Politics Review* 40 (2011): 116–46.

52. Jeffrey M. Berry, *The Interest Group Society* (New York: HarperCollins, 1997); Raymond A. Bauer, Ithiel de Sola Pool, and Lewis Dexter, *American Business and Public Policy* (New York: Atherton Press, 1963).

53. Ken Kollman, *Outside Lobbying* (Princeton, NJ: Princeton University Press, 1998).

54. Frank Baumgartner and Beth Leech, "Interest Niches and Policy Bandwagons: Patterns of Interest Group Involvement in National Politics," *Journal of Politics* 63 (2001): 1191–1213.

Take a Stand

a. Jacob Weisberg, "Three Cities, Three Scandals: What Jack Abramoff, Anthony Pellicano, and Jared Paul Stern Have in Common," *Slate*, April 9, 2006, www.slate.com/id/2140238 (accessed 10/25/12).

Chapter 11

1. Ramsey Cox and Jeremy Herb, "Senate Approves McCaskill Sexual Assault Bill in 97–0 Vote," *The Hill*, March 10, 2014, http://thehill.com/blogs/floor-action/senate/200393-senate-votes-97-0-for-military-sexual-assault-bill#ixzz2yaauKflt (accessed 4/9/14).

2. Lisa Mascaro, "Senate Rejects Gillibrand Bill on Sexual Assaults in Military," *Los Angeles Times*, March 6, 2014, http://articles.latimes.com/2014/mar/06/news/la-pn-military-sexual-assault-20140306 (accessed 6/6/14).

3. *Department of Defense Annual Report on Sexual Assault in the Military, Fiscal Year 2012*," vol. 1, May 3, 2013, www.sapr.mil/public/docs/reports/FY12_DoD_SAPRO_Annual_Report_on_Sexual_Assault-VOLUME_ONE.pdf (accessed 4/9/14).

4. Ed O'Keefe, "How Kirsten Gillibrand Won by Losing," *Washington Post*, March 6, 2014, www.washingtonpost.com/blogs/the-fix/wp/2014/03/06/how-kirsten-gillibrand-won-by-losing (accessed 4/9/14).

5. See Paul Gronke, *The Electorate, the Campaign, and the Office: A Unified Approach to Senate and House Elections* (Ann Arbor: University of Michigan Press, 2000), for research showing that the House and Senate elections share many similar characteristics. See Richard F. Fenno, *Senators on the Campaign Trail: The Politics of Representation* (Norman: University of Oklahoma Press, 1996), for a good general discussion of Senate elections.

6. All poll data except the poll comparing Congress with other occupations is from PollingReport.com (www.pollingreport.com). The occupations poll was cited in Karlyn Bowman and Everett Carll Ladd, "Public Opinion toward Congress: A Historical Look," in *Congress, the Press, and the Public*, ed. Thomas E. Mann and Norman J. Ornstein (Washington, DC: Brookings Institution Press, 1994), p. 50.

7. "Congress Less Popular than Cockroaches, Traffic Jams," Public Policy Polling, January 8, 2013, www.publicpolicypolling.com/pdf/2011/PPP_Release_Natl_010813_.pdf (accessed 4/11/14).

8. Claudine Gay, "Spirals of Trust? The Effect of Descriptive Representation on the Relationship between Citizens and Their Government," *American Journal of Political Science* 46:4 (October 2002): 717–32; Katherine Tate, *Black Faces in the Mirror: African Americans and Their Representatives in Congress* (Princeton, NJ: Princeton University Press, 2003), Chap. 7. However, Tate shows that African Americans who are represented by African Americans in Congress are not any more likely to vote, be involved in politics, or have higher overall approval rates of Congress than African Americans who are not descriptively represented.

9. In addition to those mentioned in the text, there were two other African Americans who were elected by state legislatures to serve in the Senate during the Reconstruction period. And in more recent times, there was an African American, Roland Burris (D-IL), who was appointed to serve the remainder of Senator Barack Obama's term.

10. R. Douglas Arnold, *The Logic of Congressional Action* (New Haven, CT: Yale University Press, 1990), pp. 60–71.

11. Richard F. Fenno, *Home Style: House Members in Their Districts* (Boston: Little, Brown, 1978).

12. David R. Mayhew, *Congress: The Electoral Connection* (New Haven, CT: Yale University Press, 1974).

13. Mayhew, *Congress*, p. 17.

14. Mayhew, *Congress*, p. 37.

15. Patrick J. Sellers, "Fiscal Consistency and Federal District Spending in Congressional Elections," *American Journal of Political Science* 41:3 (July 1997): 1024–41.

16. David T. Canon, "History in the Making: The 2nd District in Wisconsin," in *The Battle for Congress: Candidates, Consultants, and Voters*, ed. James A. Thurber (Washington, DC: Brookings Institution Press, 2001), pp. 199–238.

17. Gary C. Jacobson, *The Politics of Congressional Elections*, 5th ed. (New York: Longman, 2001), pp. 24–30.

18. Fenno, *Home Style*.

19. Morris Fiorina, *Congress: Keystone of the Washington Establishment*, rev. ed. (New Haven, CT: Yale University Press, 1989).

20. The language used by the Court in 1960 was "one-man, one-vote." The Court ruled in *Baker v. Carr*, 369 U.S. 186 (1962), that state legislative districts that were unequal in population violated the equal protection clause of the Fourteenth Amendment. *Wesberry v. Sanders*, 376 U.S. 1 (1964), applied the same principle to U.S. House districts.

21. *Shelby County v. Holder*, 570 U.S. (2013).

22. See Kenneth R. Mayer and David T. Canon, *The Dysfunctional Congress: The Individual Roots of an Institutional Dilemma*, 2nd ed. (New York: Columbia University Press, 2011), for an extended discussion of this argument.

23. Richard F. Fenno, "If as Ralph Nader Says, Congress Is the 'Broken Branch,' How Come We Love Our Congressmen So Much?," in *Congress in Change: Evolution and Reform*, ed. Norman J. Ornstein (New York: Praeger, 1975), pp. 277–87.

24. Russell Berman, "A Major Infrastructure Bill Clears Congress," *The Atlantic*, December 4, 2015, www.theatlantic.com/politics/archive/2015/12/a-major-infrastructure-bill-clears-congress/418827 (accessed 3/19/16).

25. Leo Shane III, "2016 Defense Budget Deal Finally Nailed Down by Congress," *Military Times*, December 18, 2015, www.militarytimes.com/story/military/capitol-hill/2015/12/18/omnibus-passage-partisan-success/77569538 (accessed 3/19/16).

26. Jonathan Weisman and Jim VandeHei, "Road Bill Reflects the Power of Pork; White House Drops Effort to Rein In Hill," *Washington Post*, August 11, 2005, p. A1.

27. An important qualification to the norm was imposed by Republicans in 1995 when they set a six-year term limit for committee and subcommittee chairs.

28. David W. Rohde, *Parties and Leaders in the Post-reform House* (Chicago: University of Chicago Press, 1991).

29. David Rohde and John Aldrich, "The Transition to Republican Rule in the House: Implications for Theories of Congressional Politics," *Political Science Quarterly* 112:4 (Winter 1997–1998): 541–67.

30. Nelson W. Polsby, *Congress and the Presidency*, 4th ed. (Englewood Cliffs, NJ: Prentice Hall, 1986), p. 111.

31. Paul Steinhauser, "Obama 2014 Campaign Role: Fundraiser-in-Chief," CNN Politics, March 20, 2014, http://politicalticker.blogs.cnn.com/2014/03/20/obama-2014-campaign-role-fundraiser-in-chief (accessed 4/16/14).

32. Christina Marcos, "The Republicans Who Didn't Vote for Ryan," *The Hill*, October 28–29, 2015, http://thehill.com/blogs/floor-action/house/258542-the-republicans-who-didnt-vote-for-ryan (accessed 3/19/16).

33. Keith Krehbiel, *Information and Legislative Organization* (Ann Arbor: University of Michigan Press, 1992).

34. Richard F. Fenno, *Congressmen in Committees* (Boston: Little, Brown, 1973).

35. Richard L. Hall, *Participation in Congress* (New Haven, CT: Yale University Press, 1996).

36. Barbara Sinclair, *Unorthodox Lawmaking* (Washington, DC: CQ Press, 2000), p. xiv.

37. Edward Epstein, "Dusting Off Deliberation," *CQ Weekly*, June 14, 2010, pp. 1434–42.

38. Kenneth Chamberlain, "Government Shutdown Scares through the Years," *National Journal*, December 14, 2011, www.nationaljournal.com/congress/government-shutdown-scares-through-the-years-20111214 (accessed 12/19/11); for 2016 see www.congress.gov/resources/display/content/Appropriations+for+Fiscal+Year+2016#AppropriationsforFiscalYear2016-continuingappropriations (accessed 3/19/16.)

39. Daphne Eviatar, "Patriot Act Renewal Kicks Off over Party Lines," *Washington Independent*, September 23, 2009, http://washingtonindependent.com/60575/debate-over-patriot-act-renewal-kicks-off-over-party-lines (accessed 12/19/11).

40. Congressional Record, 46th Congress, 2nd session, April 22, 1880, p. 2661.

41. Howard H. Baker, Jr., "Leaders Lecture Series Address to the Senate," July 14, 1998, www.senate.gov/artandhistory/history/common/generic/Leaders_Lecture_Series_Baker.htm (accessed 5/7/08).

42. Paul Kane, "Reid, Democrats Trigger 'Nuclear' Option; Eliminate Most Filibusters on Nominees," *Washington Post*, November 21, 2013, www.washingtonpost.com/politics/senate-poised-to-limit-filibusters-in-party-line-vote-that-would-alter-centuries-of-precedent/2013/11/21/d065cfe8-52b6-11e3-9fe0-fd2ca728e67c_story.html (accessed 6/6/14).

43. Philip Rucker and Robert Costa, "McCarthy's Comments on Benghazi Probe May Be a Political Gift to Clinton," *Washington Post*, October 1, 2015, www.washingtonpost.com/politics/mccarthys-comments-on-benghazi-probe-may-be-a-political-gift-to-clinton/2015/10/01/6ceb6e88-6857-11e5-9233-70cb36460919_story.html (accessed 3/20/16). House Majority Leader Kevin McCarthy told Fox News host Sean Hannity, "Everybody thought Hillary Clinton was unbeatable, right? But we put together a Benghazi special committee, a select committee. What are her numbers today? Her numbers are dropping. Why? Because she's un-trustable. But no one would have known any of that had happened had we not fought."

44. Mathew McCubbins and Thomas Schwartz, "Congressional Oversight Overlooked: Police Patrol versus Fire Alarm," *American Journal of Political Science* 28:1 (February 1984): 165–77.

45. Richard Simon, Christi Parsons, and Michael A. Memoli, "VA Chief and White House Spokesman Resign, Fueling Unease," *Los Angeles Times*, May 30, 2014, www.latimes.com/nation/la-na-shinseki-20140531-story.html#page=1 (accessed 6/6/14).

Take a Stand

a. This figure comes from a report by the Citizens Against Government Waste, "Pork Alert: Defense Conference Report Loaded with Earmarks," www.cagw.org/newroom/releases/2009/pork-alert-defense.html (accessed 1/6/10). A lower figure of $4 billion in earmarks was reported in John D. McKinnon and Brody Mullins, "Defense Bill Earmarks Total $4 Billion," *Wall Street Journal*, December 23, 2009, p. A1.

b. Sean Kennedy and Curtis Kalin, *2015 Congressional Pig Book*, Citizens Against Government Waste, http://cagw.org/reporting/pig-book (accessed 3/19/16).

c. Alex Altman, "Congress Feasts on Vegan Pork despite Earmark Ban," *Time*, January 16, 2014, http://swampland.time.com/2014/01/16/congress-feasts-on-vegan-pork-despite-earmark-ban (accessed 4/16/14).

Chapter 12

1. John Aldrich, *Why Parties?* (Chicago: University of Chicago Press, 1995).

2. Ernest R. May, *The Making of the Monroe Doctrine* (Cambridge, MA: Harvard University Press, 1975).

3. Arthur M. Schlesinger, Jr., *The Age of Jackson* (Boston: Little, Brown, 1945).

4. David Greenberg, "Lincoln's Crackdown," *Slate*, November 30, 2001, www.slate.com/id/2059132 (accessed 8/8/16).

5. Stephen Skowronek, *Building a New American State: The Expansion of National Administrative Capacities* (New York: Cambridge University Press, 1982).

6. Theda Skocpol, *Protecting Soldiers and Mothers: The Political Origins of Social Policy in the United States* (Cambridge, MA: Harvard University Press, 1995).

7. Kendrick Clements, *The Presidency of Woodrow Wilson* (Lawrence: University Press of Kansas, 1992).

8. Thomas J. Knock, *To End All Wars: Woodrow Wilson and the Quest for a New World Order* (New York: Oxford University Press, 1992).

9. William E. Leuchtenburg, *FDR Years: On Roosevelt and His Legacy* (New York: Columbia University Press, 1995).

10. Chester Pach and Elmo Richardson, *The Presidency of Dwight D. Eisenhower* (Lawrence: University Press of Kansas, 1991).

11. Sarah Kliff, "The White House Keeps Changing Obamacare. Is That Legal?," *Washington Post*, August 7, 2013, www.washingtonpost.com/blogs/wonkblog/wp/2013/08/07/the-white-house-keeps-changing-obamacare-is-that-legal (accessed 4/28/14).

12. Thomas J. Weko, *The Politicizing Presidency: The White House Personnel Office, 1948-1994* (Lawrence: University Press of Kansas, 1995).

13. Kenneth Mayer, *With the Stroke of a Pen: Executive Orders and Presidential Power* (Princeton, NJ: Princeton University Press, 2001).

14. What's in Obama's Gun Control Proposal?," *New York Times*, January 16, 2013, www.nytimes.com/interactive/2013/01/16/us/obama-gun-control-proposal.html (accessed 4/26/14).

15. Brian Hallett, *Declaring War: Congress, the President, and What the Constitution Does Not Say* (New York: Cambridge University Press, 2012).

16. Richard F. Grimmett, "The War Powers Resolution: After Thirty Years," Congressional Research Service Report RL32267, March 11, 2004, www.fas.org/man/crs/RL32267.html#_1_1 (accessed 6/2/14).

17. Lewis Fisher and David G. Adler, "The War Powers Resolution: Time to Say Goodbye," *Political Science Quarterly* 113:1 (1998): 1-20.

18. William G. Howell and Jon C. Pevehouse, *While Dangers Gather: Congressional Checks on Presidential War Powers* (Princeton, NJ: Princeton University Press, 2007).

19. Mark A. Peterson, *Legislating Together: The White House and Capitol Hill from Eisenhower to Reagan* (Cambridge, MA: Harvard University Press, 1990).

20. Andrew Rudalevige, *Managing the President's Program: Presidential Leadership and Legislative Policy Formation* (Princeton, NJ: Princeton University Press, 2002).

21. Charles Cameron and Nolan M. McCarty, "Models of Vetoes and Veto Bargaining," *Annual Review of Political Science* 7 (2004): 409-35.

22. Mark J. Rozell, "The Law: Executive Privilege: Definition and Standards of Application," *Presidential Studies Quarterly* 29:4 (1999): 918-30.

23. See Oyez, *United States v. Nixon*, 418 U.S. 683 (1974), www.oyez.org/cases/1970-1979/1974/1974_73_1766, for a summary of the case (accessed 11/1/12).

24. Mark J. Rozell, *Executive Privilege: The Dilemma of Secrecy and Democratic Accountability* (Baltimore, MD: Johns Hopkins University Press, 1994).

25. John Hart, *The Presidential Branch: From Washington to Clinton* (Chatham, NY: Chatham House, 1987).

26. Jackie Calmes, "As Plouffe Departs, a West Wing Job Is Redefined," *New York Times*, January 26, 2013, p. A17, www.nytimes.com/2013/01/27/us/politics/david-plouffe-senior-adviser-leaves-white-house.html?_r=0 (accessed 6/3/14).

27. Kelly Chang, David Lewis, and Nolan McCarthy, "The Tenure of Political Appointees" (paper presented at the 2003 Midwest Political Science Association Annual Meeting, Chicago, April 4, 2003).

28. David E. Lewis, "Staffing Alone: Unilateral Action and the Politicization of the Executive Office of the President, 1988-2004," *Presidential Studies Quarterly* 35 (2005): 496-514.

29. For a series of articles detailing Cheney's role, see "Angler: The Cheney Vice Presidency," *Washington Post*, June 24-27, 2007, www.washingtonpost.com/cheney (accessed 4/29/08).

30. Richard E. Neustart, *Presidential Power and the Modern Presidents* (New York: Simon and Schuster, 1991).

31. Terry M. Moe and William G. Howell, "The Presidential Power of Unilateral Action," *Journal of Law, Economics, and Organization* 15 (1999): 132-46.

32. Eugene Kontorovich, "Obama's Minimum Wage Proposal Has More Statutory Authority than Prior 'Unilateral' Actions," *Washington Post*, January 29, 2014, www.washingtonpost.com/news/volokh-conspiracy/wp/2014/01/29/obamas-minimum-wage-plan-has-more-statutory-authority-than-prior-unilateral-actions/?tid=pm_national_pop (accessed 5/1/14).

33. James Risen and Eric Lichtblau, "Spying Program Snared U.S. Calls," *New York Times*, December 21, 2005, p. A1; David E. Sanger, "After ABM Treaty: New Freedom for U.S. in Different Kind of Arms Control," *New York Times*, December 15, 2001, p. A8.

34. These examples appear throughout Moe and Howell, "The Presidential Power of Unilateral Action"; see also William G. Howell, "Unilateral Powers: A Brief Overview," *Presidential Studies Quarterly* 35:3 (2005): 417-39.

35. Louis Fisher, *Presidential War Power*, 2nd ed. (Lawrence: University Press of Kansas, 2004); James M. Lindsay, "Deference and Defiance: The Shifting Rhythms of Executive-Legislative Relations in Foreign Policy," *Presidential Studies Quarterly* 33:3 (2003): 530-46; Lawrence Margolis, *Executive Agreements and Presidential Power in Foreign Policy* (New York: Praeger, 1985), 209-32.

36. Phillip Cooper, "George W. Bush, Edgar Allan Poe, and the Use and Abuse of Presidential Signing Statements," *Presidential Studies Quarterly* 35:3 (2005): 515-32.

37. Andrew Rudalevige, *The New Imperial Presidency: Renewing Presidential Power after Watergate* (Ann Arbor: University of Michigan Press, 2005).

38. Christopher Deering and Forrest Maltzman, "The Politics of Executive Orders: Legislative Constraints on Presidential Power," *Political Research Quarterly* 52:4 (1999): 767-83.

39. David E. Lewis, *Presidents and the Politics of Agency Design: Political Insulation in the United States Government Bureaucracy, 1946-1997* (Palo Alto, CA: Stanford University Press, 2003).

40. David Epstein and Sharyn O'Halloran, *Delegating Powers* (Cambridge, UK: Cambridge University Press, 1999).

41. Jamie Fuller, "Rand Paul Files Suit against Obama, NSA Wednesday," *Washington Post*, February 12, 2014, www.washingtonpost.com/blogs/post-politics/wp/2014/02/12/rand-paul-files-suit-against-obama-nsa-today (accessed 5/1/14).

42. William G. Howell, *Thinking about the Presidency: The Primacy of Power* (Princeton, NJ: Princeton University Press, 2015).

43. Ben Smith and David Paul Kuhn, "Obama Moves Quickly to Reshape DNC," *Politico*, June 13, 2008, www.politico.com/news/stories/0608/11045.html (accessed 8/8/16).

44. John D. McKinnon, "Backing Away from Bush; Some Republican Candidates Avoid Ties with Unpopular President," *Wall Street Journal*, May 23, 2006, p. A4; Carrie Budoff, "Is Bush's Support Worse Than No Support?," *Politico*, July 16, 2007, www.politico.com/news/stories/0707/4960.html (accessed 8/8/16).

45. George C. Edwards III, *The Public Presidency* (New York: St. Martin's Press, 1983); George C. Edwards III, *On Deaf Ears: The Limits of the Bully Pulpit* (New Haven, CT: Yale University Press, 2003).

46. For evidence, see Edwards, *On Deaf Ears*.

47. George C. Edwards III, *Predicting the Presidency: The Potential of Persuasive Leadership* (Princeton, NJ: Princeton University Press, 2015).

48. Stephen Skowronek, *Presidential Leadership in Political Time: Reprise and Reappraisal*, 2nd ed., revised and expanded (Lawrence: University of Kansas Press, 2011).

Chapter 13

1. Dwight Waldo, *The Administrative State: A Study of the Political Theory of American Public Administration* (1948; repr. Piscataway, NJ: Transaction, 2006).

2. The original quote is from Robert Dahl and was used in this context in David E. Lewis, *Presidents and the Politics of Agency Design: Political Insulation in the United States Government* (Palo Alto, CA: Stanford University Press, 2003).

3. For a history of the FDA, see John P. Swann, FDA History Office, "History of the FDA," www.fda.gov/oc/history/historyoffda/section2.html (accessed 7/15/08).

4. For details, see Cornelius Kerwin, *Rulemaking: How Government Agencies Write Law and Make Policy* (Washington, DC: CQ Press, 1999).

5. Enterprise Risk Management Initiative, "Costs Associated with Regulatory Risks," www.mgt.ncsu.edu/erm/index.php/articles/entry/regulatory-risk-cost/ (accessed 2/3/10).

6. Andrew Pollack, "New Sense of Caution at FDA," *New York Times*, September 29, 2006, www.nytimes.com/2006/09/29/business/29caution.html?_r=0 (accessed 8/29/16).

7. There are two exceptions. A patient can enroll in a clinical trial for a new drug during the approval process, but there is a good chance that the patient will get a placebo or a previously approved treatment rather than the drug being tested. The FDA does allow companies to provide some experimental drugs to patients who cannot participate in a trial, but only those drugs that have passed early screening trials.

8. Susan Okie, "Access before Approval—a Right to Take Experimental Drugs?," *New England Journal of Medicine* 355 (2004): 437-40.

9. Stephen Skowronek, *Building a New American State: The Expansion of National Administrative Capacities, 1877-1920* (New York: Cambridge University Press, 1982).

10. Terry Moe, "An Assessment of the Positive Theory of Congressional Dominance," *Legislative Studies Quarterly* 4 (1987): 475-98.

11. Leon Neyfakh, 2015, "The FCC Just Voted to Reduce the Exorbitant Cost of Prison Phone Calls," www.slate.com/blogs/the_slatest/2015/10/22/prison_phone_calls_the_fcc_is_finally_making_them_cheaper.html (accessed 5/6/16).

12. Frances E. Rourke, "Responsiveness and Neutral Competence in American Bureaucracy," *Public Administration Review* 52 (1992): 539-46; Max Weber, *Essays on Sociology* (New York: Oxford University Press, 1958).

13. Samuel Workman, *The Dynamics of Bureaucracy in the U.S. Government* (New York: Cambridge University Press, 2015).

14. Karen Orren and Steven Skowronek, "Regimes and Regime Building in American Government: A Review of the Literature on the 1940s," *Political Science Quarterly* 113 (1998): 689-702.

15. Michael Nelson, "A Short, Ironic History of American National Bureaucracy," *Journal of Politics* 44 (1982): 747-78.

16. Nelson, "A Short, Ironic History of American National Bureaucracy."

17. Nelson, "A Short, Ironic History of American National Bureaucracy."

18. John Aldrich, *Why Parties?* (Chicago: University of Chicago Press, 1995).

19. Nelson, "A Short, Ironic History of American National Bureaucracy."

20. Matthew A. Crenson, *The Federal Machine: Beginnings of Bureaucracy in Jacksonian America* (Baltimore, MD: Johns Hopkins University Press, 1975).

21. James Q. Wilson, "The Rise of the Bureaucratic State," in *The American Commonwealth*, ed. Nathan Glazer and Irving Kristol (New York: Basic Books, 1976).

22. Skowronek, *Building a New American State*.

23. Robert Harrison, *Congress, Progressive Reform, and the New American State* (New York: Cambridge University Press, 2004).

24. The U.S. State Department has an excellent summary of the Pendleton Act at http://usinfo.state.gov/usa/infousa/facts/democrac/28.htm.

25. Lawrence C. Dodd and Richard L. Schott, *Congress and the Administrative State* (New York: Wiley, 1979).

26. Ira Katznelson and Bruce Pietrykowski, "Rebuilding the American State: Evidence from the 1940s," *Studies in American Political Development* 5:2 (1991): 301-39.

27. David Plotke, *Building a Democratic Political Order: Reshaping American Liberalism in the 1930s and 1940s* (New York: Cambridge University Press, 1996).

28. Theda Skocpol and Kenneth Finegold, "State Capacity and Economic Intervention in the Early New Deal," *Political Science Quarterly* 97 (1999): 255-70.

29. Michael Brown, "State Capacity and Political Choice: Interpreting the Failure of the Third New Deal," *Studies in American Political Development* 9 (1995): 187-212.

30. Ira Katznelson, Kim Geiger, and Daniel Kryder, "Limiting Liberalism: The Southern Veto in Congress, 1933-1950," *Political Science Quarterly* 108 (1993): 283-306.

31. Joseph Califano, "What Was Really Great about the Great Society," *Washington Monthly*, October 1999, www.washingtonmonthly.com/features/1999/9910.califano.html (accessed 7/16/08).

32. David T. Canon, *Race, Redistricting, and Representation: The Unintended Consequences of Black Majority Districts* (Chicago: University of Chicago Press, 1999).

33. Charles Murray, *Losing Ground: American Social Policy, 1950-1980* (New York: Basic Books, 1984).

34. Henry J. Aaron, *Politics and the Professors: The Great Society in Perspective* (Washington, DC: Brookings Institution Press, 1978).

35. Michael B. Katz, *In the Shadow of the Poorhouse: A Social History of Welfare in America* (New York: Basic Books, 1996).

36. Richard P. Nathan, *The Administrative Presidency* (New York: Wiley, 1983).

37. Andrew Rudalevige, "The Structure of Leadership: Presidents, Hierarchies, and Information Flow," *Presidential Studies Quarterly* 35 (2005): 333–60.

38. David E. Lewis, *Presidents and the Policy of Agency Design* (Palo Alto, CA: Stanford University Press, 2003).

39. Terry M. Moe, "An Assessment of the Positive Theory of Congressional Dominance," *Legislative Studies Quarterly* 4 (1987): 475–98.

40. William A. Niskanen, *Bureaucracy and Public Economics* (Washington, DC: Edward Elgar, 1976); Robert Whaples and Jac C. Heckelman, "Public Choice Economics: Where Is There Consensus?," *American Economist* 49 (2005): 66–78.

41. Alan Schick and Felix LoStracco, *The Federal Budget: Politics, Process, Policy* (Washington, DC: Brookings Institution Press, 2000).

42. Joel D. Aberbach, "The Political Significance of the George W. Bush Administration," *Social Policy and Administration* 39:2 (2005): 130–49.

43. David E. Lewis, "The Politics of Agency Termination: Confronting the Myth of Agency Immortality," *Journal of Politics* 64 (2002): 89–107.

44. Ronald A. Wirtz, "Put It on My . . . Er, His Tab: Opinion Polls Show a Big Gap between the Public's Desire for Services and Its Willingness to Pay for These Services," *Fedgazette*, January 2004, www.minneapolisfed.org/pubs/fedgaz/04-01/tab.cfm (accessed 7/16/08).

45. James L. Perry and Annie Hondeghem, *Motivation in Public Management: The Call of Public Service* (Oxford, UK: Oxford University Press, 2008).

46. Paul Light, *A Government Well-Executed: Public Service and Public Performance* (Washington, DC: Brookings Institution Press, 2003).

47. This discussion of the details of the civil service system is based on Bureau of Labor Statistics, "Career Guide to Industries," March 12, 2008, www.bls.gov/oco/cg/cgs041.htm (accessed 7/16/08).

48. Dennis Cauchon, "Some Federal Workers More Likely to Die Than Lose Jobs," *USA Today*, July 19, 2011, p. A1.

49. Ronald N. Johnson and Gary D. Liebcap, *The Federal Civil Service System and the Problem of Bureaucracy* (Chicago: University of Chicago Press, 1993).

50. Eric Lichtblau, "Report Sees Illegal Hiring Practices at Justice Department," *New York Times*, June 25, 2008, www.nytimes.com/2008/06/25/washington/24cnd-justice.html# (accessed 6/16/14).

51. For the details of the Hatch Act, see Daniel Engber, "Can Karl Rove Plot Campaign Strategy on the Government's Dime?," *Slate*, April 21, 2006, www.slate.com/id/2140418 (accessed 8/29/16).

52. Justin Gillis, "Climate Maverick to Retire from NASA." *New York Times*, April 1, 2013, p. D1.

53. Timothy Noah, "Low Morale at Homeland Security," *Slate*, September 14, 2005, www.slate.com/id/2126313 (accessed 8/29/16).

54. For details on the SES, see www.opm.gov/policy-data-oversight/senior-executive-service/ (accessed 4/7/14).

55. Todd Frankel, "Why the CDC Still Isn't Researching Gun Violence, Despite the Ban Being Lifted Two Years Ago," *Washington Post*. January 14, 2015, p. A01.

56. John D. Huber and Charles R. Shipan, *Deliberate Discretion? The Institutional Foundations of Bureaucratic Autonomy* (New York: Cambridge University Press, 2002).

57. David Epstein and Sharyn O'Halloran, *Delegating Powers: A Transaction Cost Politics Approach to Policy Making under Separate Powers* (New York: Cambridge University Press, 1999).

58. Mathew D. McCubbins, Roger G. Noll, and Barry R. Weingast, "Structure and Process as Solutions to the Politician's Principal–Agency Problem," *Virginia Law Review* 74 (1989): 431–82.

59. Barry R. Weingast, "Caught in the Middle: The President, Congress, and the Political–Bureaucratic System," in *Institutions of American Democracy: The Executive Branch*, ed. Joel D. Aberbach and Mark A. Peterson (New York: Oxford University Press, 2006).

60. Keith Whittington and Daniel P. Carpenter, "Executive Power in American Institutional Development," *Perspectives on Politics* 1 (2003): 495–513.

61. Roger Noll, Mathew McCubbins, and Barry Weingast, "Administrative Procedures as Instruments of Political Control," *Journal of Law, Economics and Organization* 3 (1987): 243–77.

62. Lisa Rein, "Climate Scientists to Be Grilled by Congressional Investigators, but Their E-Mails Are Still Off-Limits," *Washington Post*, November 16, 2015.

63. Mathew McCubbins and Thomas Schwartz, "Congressional Oversight Overlooked: Fire Alarms vs. Police Patrols," *American Journal of Political Science* 28 (1984): 165–79.

64. McCubbins and Schwartz, "Congressional Oversight Overlooked."

65. Steven J. Balla and John R. Wright, "Interest Groups, Advisory Committees, and Congressional Control of the Bureaucracy," *American Journal of Political Science* 45 (2001): 799–812.

66. Daniel P. Carpenter, "The Gatekeeper: Organizational Reputation and Pharmaceutical Regulation at the FDA" (unpublished paper, Harvard University, 2006).

67. Terry M. Moe, "Political Control and the Power of the Agent," *Journal of Law, Economics, and Organization* 22 (2006): 1–29.

68. See David Weil, "OSHA: Beyond the Politics," *Frontline*, January 9, 2003, www.pbs.org/wgbh/pages/frontline/shows/workplace/osha/weil.html (accessed 8/29/16).

Chapter 14

1. Burgess Everett and Glenn Thrush, "McConnell Throws Down the Gauntlet: No Scalia Replacement under Obama," Politico.com, February 13, 2016, www.politico.com/story/2016/02/mitch-mcconnell-antonin-scalia-supreme-court-nomination-219248#ixzz49VnIxZGz (accessed 5/23/16).

2. The union case was *Friedrichs v. California Teachers Association* and the immigration case was *United States v. Texas*.

3. www.whitehouse.gov/scotus (accessed 5/23/16).

4. *United States v. Texas*, 579 U.S. ____ (2016).

5. *Fisher v. University of Texas*, 579 U.S. ____ (2016).

6. Ralph Ketcham, *The Anti-Federalist Papers and the Constitutional Convention Debates* (New York: Penguin Putnam, 2003), p. 304.

7. Lester S. Jayson, ed., *The Constitution of the United States of America: Analysis and Interpretation* (Washington, DC: U.S. Government Printing Office, 1973), p. 585.

8. David G. Savage, *Guide to the U.S. Supreme Court*, 4th ed. (Washington, DC: CQ Press, 2004), p. 7.

9. Savage, *Guide to the U.S. Supreme Court*, pp. 5–7.

10. Winfield H. Rose, "*Marbury v. Madison*: How John Marshall Changed History by Misquoting the Constitution," *Political Science and Politics* 36:2 (April 2003): 209–14. Rose argues that in a key quotation in the case Marshall intentionally left out a clause of the Constitution that suggests that Congress *did* have the power to expand the original jurisdiction of the Court. Other constitutional scholars reject this argument.

11. *Marbury v. Madison*, 5 U.S. 1 Cranch 137 (1803).

12. Revisionist historians, legal scholars, and political scientists have challenged the landmark status of *Marbury v. Madison*. For example, Michael Stokes Paulsen's *Michigan Law Review* article points out that *Marbury* was not cited in subsequent Supreme Court cases as a precedent for judicial review until the late nineteenth century. Legal scholars in the early twentieth century were the first to promote the idea that *Marbury* was a landmark decision. Paulsen also notes that when the opinion was delivered in 1803 it was not controversial. Even the Jeffersonian Democrats, who were at odds with Marshall's Federalists, thought that it was a reasonable decision and not the institutional power grab that is described in modern accounts. Finally, Marshall made a very narrow case for judicial review, arguing that the Supreme Court could declare legislation that was contrary to the Court's interpretation of the Constitution null and void only if it concerned judicial powers. Revisionists argue that what appear to be broad claims of judicial power in *Marbury* (e.g., the Court has the power "to say what the law is") are taken out of the context of a much more narrow claim of power. Michael Stokes Paulsen, "Judging Judicial Review: *Marbury* in the Modern Era: The Irrepressible Myth of *Marbury*," *Michigan Law Review* 101 (August, 2003): 2706–43.

13. *Ware v. Hylton*, 3 U.S. 199 (1796).

14. *Wal-Mart v. Dukes*, 564 U.S. (2011). However, in 2011 the Court struck down any class-action claim unless there was "convincing proof of a companywide discriminatory pay and promotion policy"—statistical evidence of pay disparities would not suffice. David Savage, "Supreme Court Blocks Huge Class-Action Suit against Wal-Mart," *Los Angeles Times*, June 21, 2011, http://articles.latimes.com/2011/jun/21/nation/la-na-court-walmart-20110621 (accessed 7/13/16).

15. *Buckley v. Valeo*, 424 U.S. 1 (1976), upheld aggregate limits, saying that Congress had an interest in preventing the "appearance of corruption." *McCutcheon v. FEC*, 572 U.S. ___ (2014) limited Congress's interest in corruption to a more narrow "quid pro quo" corruption that is basically bribery (and already prohibited by other laws).

16. *Lujan v. Defenders of Wildlife*, 504 U.S. 555 (1992).

17. The case concerning the bombing in Libya was *Kucinich v. Obama*, 821 F.Supp. 2d 110 (Dist. of Columbia 2011). The cases limiting taxpayers' standing to challenge laws they disagree with are *Flast v. Cohen*, 392 U.S. 83 (1968), and *Arizona Christian School Tuition Org. v. Winn*, 131 S.Ct. 1436 (2011).

18. United States Courts, Judges & Judgeships, Federal Judgeships, www.uscourts.gov/judges-judgeships/authorized-judgeships (accessed 7/1/16).

19. The official name for each appeals court is the "United States Court of Appeals for the ___ Circuit."

20. United States Courts, Judges & Judgeships, Federal Judgeships, www.uscourts.gov/judges-judgeships/authorized-judgeships (accessed 7/1/16).

21. Ibid.

22. *Ledbetter v. Goodyear Tire & Rubber Co.*, 550 U.S. 618 (2007).

23. The Eleventh Amendment does not mention lawsuits against a state brought in federal court by citizens of that same state.

However, in *Alden v. Maine* (527 U.S. 706 [1999]) the Court extended the logic of sovereign immunity to apply to these cases as well.

24. "Judicial Selection in the States," Ballotpedia.org, https://ballotpedia.org/Judicial_selection_in_the_states (accessed 5/24/16).

25. See, for example, a case involving the West Virginia state supreme court and $3 million in campaign spending by a coal company that had a case pending before the court, *Caperton v. A. T. Massey Coal Co.*, 556 U.S. 868 (2009); the Court ruled that the losing party's due process rights under the Fourteenth Amendment had been violated when the justice who benefited from the campaign spending did not recuse himself from the case. Given the disproportionate and significant spending by Massey and the timing of the spending, the majority ruled: "On these extreme facts the probability of actual bias rises to an unconstitutional level."

26. Paul Brace and Brent D. Boyea, "State Public Opinion, the Death Penalty, and the Practice of Electing Judges," *American Journal of Political Science* 52:2 (April 2008): 360–72.

27. Richard P. Caldarone, Brandice Canes-Wrone, and Tom S. Clark, "Partisan Labels and Democratic Accountability: An Analysis of State Supreme Court Abortion Decisions," *Journal of Politics* 71 (2009): 560–73.

28. Stephen Ware, "The Missouri Plan in National Perspective," *Missouri Law Review* 74 (2009): 751–75.

29. Savage, *Guide to the U.S. Supreme Court*, p. 1003.

30. "President Bush Discusses Judicial Accomplishments and Philosophy," Cincinnati, Ohio, October 6, 2008, georgewbush-whitehouse.archives.gov/news/releases/2008/10/20081006-5.html (accessed 12/14/11).

31. Paul Kane, "Reid, Democrats Trigger 'Nuclear' Option; Eliminate Most Filibusters on Nominees," *Washington Post*, November 21, 2013, www.washingtonpost.com/politics/senate-poised-to-limit-filibusters-in-party-line-vote-that-would-alter-centuries-of-precedent/2013/11/21/d065cfe8-52b6-11e3-9fe0-fd2ca728e67c_story.html (accessed 5/2/14).

32. "Pending Judicial Nominations," Alliance for Justice, www.afj.org/wp-content/uploads/2014/11/ReportPendingNominees.pdf (accessed 5/24/16).

33. Mike DeBonis, "Mitch McConnell's Senate Is Confirming Very, Very Few Presidential Nominees," *Washington Post*, May 5, 2016, www.washingtonpost.com/news/powerpost/wp/2016/05/05/mitch-mcconnells-senate-is-confirming-very-very-few-presidential-nominees/ (accessed 5/24/16).

34. Supreme Court of the United States *In Re Frederick W. Bauer*, On Motion for Leave to Proceed in forma pauperis, No. 99-5440, Decided October 18, 1999, per curiam, http://supreme.lp.findlaw.com/supreme_court/decisions/99-5440.html (accessed 9/26/16).

35. John Roberts, U.S. Supreme Court, "2007 Year-End Report on the Federal Judiciary," January 1, 2008, www.supremecourt.gov/publicinfo/year-end/2007year-endreport.pdf (accessed 9/26/16).

36. For a critical account of the Supreme Court's reduced caseload, which dates back to the Rehnquist Court, see Philip Allen Lacovara, "The Incredible Shrinking Court," *American Lawyer*, December 1, 2003, pp. 53–58.

37. *New Jersey v. New York*, No. 120 Orig., 118 S.Ct. 1726 (1998), and *Kansas v. Colorado*, No. 105 Orig., 125 S.Ct. 526 (2004).

38. Henry J. Abraham, *The Judiciary: The Supreme Court in the Governmental Process*, 7th ed. (Boston: Allyn and Bacon, 1987), p. 25, says that original jurisdiction has been invoked "about 150 times." A Lexis search revealed an additional 27

original-jurisdiction cases between 1987 and December 2004. See U.S. Department of Justice, Help/Glossary, www.usdoj.gov/osg/briefs/help.html, for a basic discussion of the Supreme Court's original jurisdiction.

39. Savage, *Guide to the U.S. Supreme Court*, p. 848.

40. See Thomas G. Walker and Lee Epstein, *The Supreme Court of the United States: An Introduction* (New York: St. Martin's Press, 1993), pp. 80–85, for a more detailed discussion of these concepts and citations to the relevant court cases.

41. *Shaw v. Reno*, 509 U.S. 630 (1993).

42. *Elk Grove Unified School District v. Newdow*, 542 U.S. 1 (2004).

43. Gregory A. Caldeira and John R. Wright, "The Discuss List: Agenda Building in the Supreme Court," *Law and Society Review* 24 (1990): 813.

44. Walker and Epstein, *Supreme Court*, p. 89; Ryan C. Black and Ryan J. Owens, *The Solicitor General and the United States Supreme Court: Executive Branch Influence and Judicial Decisions* (New York: Cambridge University Press, 2012).

45. U.S. Supreme Court, "The Court and Its Procedures," www.supremecourtus.gov/about/procedures.pdf (accessed 5/27/16).

46. Lee Epstein, Jeffrey A. Segal, Harold J. Spaeth, and Thomas G. Walker, *The Supreme Court Compendium: Data, Decisions, and Developments*, 3rd ed. (Washington, DC: CQ Press, 2003), Table 7-25.

47. Gregory A. Caldeira and John R. Wright, "*Amicus Curiae* before the Supreme Court: Who Participates, When, and How Much?," *Journal of Politics* 52 (August 1990): 803.

48. Andrew Christy, "'Obamacare' Will Rank among the Longest Supreme Court Arguments Ever," National Public Radio, November 15, 2011, www.npr.org/blogs/itsallpolitics/2011/11/15/142363047/obamacare-will-rank-among-the-longest-supreme-court-arguments-ever (accessed 5/2/14).

49. U.S. Supreme Court, *Rules of the U.S. Supreme Court*, adopted April 19, 2013, effective July 1, 2013, Rule 28.7, www.supremecourt.gov/ctrules/2013RulesoftheCourt.pdf (accessed 5/27/16).

50. Savage, *Guide to the U.S. Supreme Court*, p. 852.

51. U.S. Supreme Court, Argument Transcripts, www.supremecourt.gov/oral_arguments/argument_transcripts (accessed 9/26/16).

52. Garrett Epps, "Clarence Thomas Breaks His Silence," *The Atlantic*, February 29, 2016, www.theatlantic.com/politics/archive/2016/02/clarence-thomas-supreme-court/471582/ (accessed 5/27/16).

53. Quoted in Savage, *Guide to the U.S. Supreme Court*, p. 854.

54. Forrest Maltzman, James F. Spriggs II, and Paul J. Wahlbeck, *Crafting Law on the Supreme Court: The Collegial Game* (New York: Cambridge University Press, 2000), p. 33.

55. William H. Rehnquist, "Memorandum to the Conference: Policy regarding Assignments," November 24, 1989, papers of Justice Thurgood Marshall, Library of Congress Manuscript Division, Washington, D.C., quoted in Maltzman, Spriggs, and Wahlbeck, *Crafting Law*, pp. 30–31.

56. *Smith v. Allwright*, 321 U.S. 649 (1944).

57. Walker and Epstein, *Supreme Court*, p. 110.

58. Savage, *Guide to the U.S. Supreme Court*, p. 854.

59. Lee Epstein, William M. Landes, and Richard A. Posner, "Are Even Unanimous Decisions in the United States Supreme Court Ideological?," *Northwestern University Law Review* 106:2 (2012), 702.

60. Adam Liptak, "Compromise at the Court Veils Its Rifts: Roberts Handiwork, Unanimous Rulings," *New York Times*, July 2, 2014, pp. A1, A17. For the recent term see Kedar Bhatia, "Final October Term 2015 Stat Pack," June 29th, 2016, www.scotusblog.com/wp-content/uploads/2016/06/SB_unanimity_OT15.pdf, accessed 7/1/16.

61. Quoted in Lee Epstein and Thomas G. Walker, *Constitutional Law for a Changing America: Institutional Powers and Constraints*, 5th ed. (Washington, DC: CQ Press, 2004), p. 29.

62. *Maryland v. Craig*, 497 U.S. 836 (1990).

63. Epstein and Walker, *Constitutional Law for a Changing America*, p. 31.

64. Seth Stern and Stephen Wermiel, *Justice Brennan: Liberal Champion* (Boston: Houghton Mifflin Harcourt, 2010).

65. Epstein, Segal, Spaeth, and Walker, *Supreme Court Compendium*, Table 6-2.

66. Forrest Maltzman and Paul J. Wahlbeck, "Strategic Policy Considerations and Vote Fluidity on the Burger Court," *American Journal of Political Science* 90 (1996): 581–92; Maltzman, Spriggs, and Wahlbeck, *Crafting Law on the Supreme Court*.

67. Thomas R. Marshall, *Public Opinion and the Supreme Court* (Boston: Unwin Hyman, 1989), p. 12; as cited in Epstein and Walker, *Constitutional Law for a Changing America*, p. 92.

68. Thomas M. Keck, *The Most Activist Supreme Court in History: The Road to Modern Judicial Conservatism* (Chicago: University of Chicago Press, 2004).

69. Marshall, *Public Opinion*, Table 6-8.

70. Jeffrey Rosen, "Has the Supreme Court Gone Too Far?," *Commentary* 116:3 (October 2003), pp. 41–2.

71. *National Federation of Independent Business v. Sebelius*, 567 U.S. (2012).

72. Finley Peter Dunne, Paul Green, and Jacques Barzun, *Mr. Dooley in Peace and in War* (1898; repr., Champaign-Urbana: University of Illinois Press, 2001).

73. Robert Dahl, "Decision-Making in a Democracy: The Supreme Court as a National Policy-Maker," *Journal of Public Law* 6 (1957): 279–95, is the classic work on this topic. More recent work challenged Dahl's methods but largely supports the idea that the Court follows the will of the majority.

74. Jeffrey A. Segal, Richard J. Timpone, and Robert M. Howard, "Buyer Beware? Presidential Success through Supreme Court Appointments," *Political Research Quarterly* 53:3 (September 2000): 557–73; Gregory A. Caldeira and Charles E. Smith Jr., "Campaigning for the Supreme Court: The Dynamics of Public Opinion on the Thomas Nomination," *Political Research Quarterly* 58:3 (August 1996): 655–81.

75. William Mishler and Reginald S. Sheehan, "The Supreme Court as a Countermajoritarian Institution? The Impact of Public Opinion on Supreme Court Decisions," *American Political Science Review* 87:1 (March 1993): 87–101.

76. Matthew E. K. Hall, "The Semiconstrained Court: Public Opinion, the Separation of Powers, and the U.S. Supreme Court's Fear of Nonimplementation," *American Journal of Political Science* 58:2 (April 2014): 352–66; Matthew E. K. Hall, *The Nature of Supreme Court Power* (New York: Cambridge University Press, 2011).

77. *Stanford v. Kentucky*, 492 U.S. 361 (1989); *Roper v. Simmons*, 543 U.S. 551 (2005).

78. David O'Brien, *Storm Center: The Supreme Court in American Politics*, 4th ed. (New York: W. W. Norton, 1996), p. 276.

79. Helmut Norpoth and Jeffrey A. Segal, "Popular Influence in Supreme Court Decisions," *American Political Science Review* 88 (1994): 711–16.

80. *Foster v. Neilson*, 27 U.S. 253 (1829).

81. *Charles B. Rangel v. John A. Boehner,* United States District Court for the District of Columbia, Civil Action No. 13-540, December 11, 2013, p. 48, https://ecf.dcd.uscourts.gov/cgi-bin/show_public_doc?2013cv0540-24 (accessed 5/2/14).

82. We thank Dan Smith for raising this point.

Take a Stand

a. Richard S. Beth, "Cloture Attempts on Nominations: Data and Historical Development," Congressional Research Service Report 7-5700, June 23, 2013, www.senate.gov/CRSReports/crs-publish.cfm?pid=%270E%2C*P%2C%3B%3C%20P%20%20%0A (accessed 5/2/2014); "President Obama's Judicial Nominations," 113th Congress, American Bar Association, www.americanbar.org/content/dam/aba/uncategorized/GAO/2014apr16_obamanomchart.authcheckdam.pdf (accessed 5/2/13).

Study Guide Answer Key

Chapter 1	Chapter 2	Chapter 3	Chapter 4	Chapterr 5
1. C	1. B	1. C	1. D	1. A
2. B	2. E	2. B	2. B	2. C
3. C	3. A	3. B	3. A	3. B
4. D	4. C	4. C	4. D	4. E
5. D	5. C	5. C	5. B	5. C
6. C	6. B	6. B	6. C	6. E
7. A	7. D	7. B	7. A	7. B
8. E	8. B	8. B	8. D	8. D
9. A	9. D	9. A	9. A	9. E
10. E	10. B	10. D	10. C	10. A
11. C	11. D	11. B	11. B	11. B
	12. B	12. A	12. C	12. C
	13. A	13. D	13. C	13. C
	14. B	14. A	14. B	14. A
	15. B	15. D	15. C	15. D

Chapter 6	Chapter 7	Chapter 8	Chapter 9	Chapter 10
1. D	1. E	1. C	1. A	1. E
2. B	2. B	2. A	2. B	2. A
3. A	3. D	3. E	3. D	3. C
4. D	4. B	4. B	4. B	4. B
5. C	5. D	5. E	5. B	5. C
6. E	6. C	6. A	6. B	6. E
7. A	7. A	7. E	7. C	7. C
8. D	8. C	8. A	8. E	8. C
9. D	9. A	9. E	9. A	9. A
10. C	10. D	10. B	10. C	10. B
11. B	11. B	11. C	11. B	11. D
12. D	12. E	12. C	12. A	12. D
13. A	13. A	13. E	13. C	13. B
14. C	14. C	14. C	14. C	14. A
15. B				

Chapter 11	Chapter 12	Chapter 13	Chapter 14
1. D	1. A	1. C	1. A
2. E	2. A	2. A	2. D
3. B	3. C	3. D	3. B
4. B	4. D	4. B	4. E
5. A	5. A	5. E	5. A
6. D	6. D	6. B	6. E
7. D	7. E	7. C	7. B
8. B	8. B	8. A	8. C
9. D	9. A	9. B	9. A
10. A	10. B	10. D	10. E
11. C	11. D	11. C	11. B
12. E	12. B	12. A	12. B
13. B	13. A	13. E	13. D
14. D	14. D	14. A	14. C
	15. C	15. B	15. A
			16. B

Credits

Line Art

Photographs

Chapter 13

Chapter 14

Glossary/Index

"consent of the governed," 33 The idea that government gains its legitimacy through regular elections in which the people living under that government participate to elect their leaders.

conservative, 193, *193*, 211–13, 261–62, 262 One side of the ideological spectrum defined by support for lower taxes, a free market, and a more-limited government; generally associated with Republicans.

constitutional authority, 411, 412 Powers derived from the provisions of the Constitution that outline the president's role in government.

constitutional interpretation, 480 The process of determining whether a piece of legislation or governmental action is supported by the Constitution.

cooperative federalism, 76–77, *77*, 78, 80, 86, 93 A form of federalism in which national and state governments work together to provide services efficiently. This form emerged in the late 1930s, representing a profound shift toward less concrete boundaries of responsibility in national-state relations.

culture wars, 15 Political conflict in the United States between "red-state" Americans, who tend to have strong religious beliefs, and "blue-state" Americans, who tend to be more secular.

equal time provision, 227–28, 228 An FCC regulation requiring broadcast media to provide equal air time on any non-news programming to all candidates running for an office.

Era of Good Feeling, 256

establishment clause, 103, 110, 111 Part of the First Amendment that states "Congress shall make no law respecting an establishment of religion," which has been interpreted to mean that Congress cannot sponsor or favor any religion.

ethnicity, 17
European Union (EU), 68
Everson v. Board of Education of Ewing Township, 109
Every Student Succeeds Act in, *11*

exclusionary rule, 128, 128–29 The principle that illegally or unconstitutionally acquired evidence cannot be used in a criminal trial.

executive agreement, 416–17 An agreement between the executive branch and a foreign government, which acts as a treaty but does not require Senate approval.

executive branch, 424–27, *426,* 478
   allocation of power to, 6, 47, 50, 55
   checks and balances on, 38, 40
   structure of, 454–55, *455, 456*
   see also president, U.S.; vice president, U.S.

Executive Office of the President (EOP), 424–25, 438, 457 The group of policy-related offices that serve as support staff to the president.

executive orders, 55, 412–14, 413, 415, 420 Proclamations made by the president that change government policy without congressional approval.

executive powers clause, 55 Part of Article II, Section 1, of the Constitution that states: "The executive Power shall be vested in a President of the United States of America." This broad statement has been used to justify many assertions of presidential power.

executive privilege, 422, 422–24 The right of the president to keep executive branch conversations and correspondence confidential from the legislative and judicial branches.

Facebook, 118, 229, 230, 232, 232

factions, 6, 33–34, 36–37 Groups of like-minded people who try to influence the

government. American government is set up to avoid domination by any one of these groups.
   see also interest groups

Fair Housing Act, 174
Falwell, Jerry, 121
families, 197, *198*
Family Leave Act, *88*
Farrakhan, Louis, 179
FBI (Federal Bureau of Investigation), 5
FCC (Federal Communications Commission), 123, 227–28, 228
FDA, *see* Food and Drug Administration (FDA)
Federal Aviation Administration (FAA), 13
federal bureaucracy, *see* bureaucracy
Federal Bureau of Investigation (FBI), 5
Federal Civil Rights Act, *160*

federal civil service, 451–52 A system created by the 1883 Pendleton Civil Service Act in which bureaucrats are hired on the basis of merit rather than political connections.

Federal Communications Commission (FCC), 123, 227–28, 228 A government agency created in 1934 to regulate American radio stations and later expanded to regulate television, wireless communications technologies, and other broadcast media.

Federal Election Commission, 117, 310 The government agency that enforces and regulates election laws; made up of six presidential appointees, of whom no more than three can be members of the same party.

Federal Election Commission, Citizens United v., 310, 350, 497, 510
Federal Election Commission, McCutcheon v., 310
Federal Emergency Management Agency (FEMA), 66
Federal Employees Political Activities Act, 460
federal government, *see* government, federal

federalism, 6, 64–97 The division of power across the local, state, and national levels of government.
   assessing, 91, *93,* 93–94, 97
   balance of power under, 41, 68–71, 91
   civil rights and, 94
   coercive, 64, *78,* 80, 83–85
   competitive, 86
   constitutional framework for, 68–71
   cooperative, 76–77, *77, 78,* 80, 86, 93
   court structure and, 483, *484, 485, 486*
   definition of, 66
   dual, 73–76, *74, 76, 77,* 80, 83, 86, 400
   early, 72–73, *73*
   environmental policy and, *79*
   fiscal, *80,* 80–81

ideological complexities of, 91
"layer cake" model of, 76–77, *78*
levels of government and autonomy in, 67–68
"marble cake" model of, 76–77, *78*
modern, 77, 80–81, 83–90, 96
New Federalism, *80,* 81
picket fence, 77, *78,* 80
see also government, federal

Federalist 78, 50, 477
Federalist Papers, 31, 33, 45–46, 365

Federalists, 61, 255, 255–56, 478 Those at the Constitutional Convention who favored a strong national government and a system of separated powers.
   Constitutional Convention role of, 35, 37
   government control by, 72
   separation of powers and, 45, 52, 70

Federalist Society, 45
federal judges, 487–90, *488, 490, 491,* 492
Federal Meat Inspection Act, 451

federal preemptions, 84–85 Impositions of national priorities on the states through national legislation that is based on the Constitution's supremacy clause.

Federal Reserve, 26
Federal Reserve Act, 409
Federal Speedy Trial Act, 133
FEMA (Federal Emergency Management Agency), 66
feminism, 18
Fenno, Richard, 381, 391
Ferguson, Missouri, 156
Ferguson, Plessy v., 147, 164
Fifteenth Amendment, 56, 75, 107, 147
Fifth Amendment, 74, *106, 109, 131,* 131–33, *134,* 173
fifth party system, *255,* 256, 257

fighting words, 121 Forms of expression that "by their very utterance" can incite violence. These can be regulated by the government but are often difficult to define.

filibuster, 399, 399, 490, 492, 492 A tactic used by senators to block a bill by continuing to hold the floor and speak—under the Senate rule of unlimited debate—until the bill's supporters back down.

Fillmore, Millard, 409

filtering, 238, 239, 241 The influence on public opinion that results from journalists' and editors' decisions about which of many potential news stories to report.

financial crisis of 2008–2009, 417

fire alarm oversight, 401, 466 A method of oversight in which members of Congress respond to complaints about the bureaucracy or problems of implementation only as they arise rather than exercising constant vigilance.

First Amendment, 59, 75, 98, *102*, 103, 104, *106*, *109*, 110–24, 135
  freedom of assembly and, 21, *102*, *109*, *119*, 119–20
  freedom of religion and, 21, 98, *99*, *102*, 103, 108, *109*, *110*, 110–13, *112*, 138, 139
  freedom of speech and, 21, 59, 75, *102*, 104, *109*, 113–24, *115*, *116*, 119, 122, 140
  freedom of the press and, 21, 75, *102*, *109*, *120*, 120–21
  symbolic speech protected by, *503*, 503–4
First Continental Congress, *30*
first party system, 255, *255*
first spouses (presidential spouses), 426, *426*
FISA (Foreign Intelligence Surveillance Act), 130–31
FISA Amendments Act of 2008, 131

fiscal federalism, *80*, 80–81 A form of federalism in which federal funds are allocated to the lower levels of government through transfer payments or grants.

Fisher v. Univ. of Texas, 171
FiveThirtyEight.com, 229, 230

527 organization, 258–59, 350 A tax-exempt group formed primarily to influence elections through voter mobilization efforts and to issue ads that do not directly endorse or oppose a candidate. Unlike PACs, 527 organizations are not subject to contribution limits and spending caps.

flag desecration, 116–17, *1116*
Flag Protection Act, 116
Flint, Mich., 154, 440, *441*, 442, *467*, 469–70
Flores, City of Boerne v., 88
Florida, 134
  2000 election and, 277–78, 291, *291*, 295
  jury duty in, 150
  Orlando shooting in June 2016, 190
  as a swing state, 330
Florida, Seminole Tribe v., 88
Food and Drug Administration (FDA), 440, 442, 448, 467, 469
Ford, Gerald, 302, 410
Foreign Intelligence Surveillance Act (FISA), 130–31
Foreign Intelligence Surveillance Court, 429
Foreign Miners Tax, 149
foreign policy, *410*, 416, 416–17
Founders of the United States, 5–6, 21, *28*, 28–29, 32–34, 59, 70, 95
Fourteenth Amendment, 56, 73, 75, 87–88, 90, 100, 107–8, 110, 134, 149
  due process clause of, 135, 172
  equal protection clause of, 100, 145, 147, 167–69, 173

Fourth Amendment, 104, 105, *106*, *109*, 126–31, *127*, *128*, *130*, 135, 164
fourth party system, *255*, 256
Fox & Friends, 240
Fox News Channel, 240

framing, *238*, *239*, 241 The influence on public opinion caused by the way a story is presented or covered, including the details, explanations, and context offered in the report.

France, 68, 195, *195*, 230
Frankfurter, Felix, 500
Franklin, Benjamin, 35, 43–44, 45
Freedmen's Bureau, 147
freedom, civil liberties and, 98, *99*, 100, 145
Freedom Caucus, 389
freedom of assembly, 21, *102*, *109*, *119*, 119–20
freedom of religion, 21, 98, *99*, *102*, 103, 108, *109*, *110*, 110–13, *112*, 138, 139
  see also religion
freedom of speech, 21, 59, 75, *102*, 104, *109*, 113–24, *115*, *116*, 119, 122, 140, 503
freedom of the press, 21, 75, *102*, *109*, *120*, 120–21
Freedom Riders, *160*, 161–62

free exercise clause, 97, 111–13, *112* Part of the First Amendment that states that Congress cannot prohibit or interfere with the practice of religion.

free market, 15, 25 An economic system based on competition among businesses without government interference.

free rider problem, 6–7, 14, 341–42 The incentive to benefit from others' work without making a contribution, which leads individuals in a collective action situation to refuse to work together.

free riding, 341 The result of relying on others to contribute to a collective effort while failing to participate on one's own behalf, yet still benefiting from the group's successes.

French and Indian War (1754–1763), 29
French Revolution, 114
Fugitive Slave Act, 146

full faith and credit clause, 70–71 Part of Article IV of the Constitution requiring that each state's laws be honored by the other states. For example, a legal marriage in one state must be recognized across state lines.

Gardner, Cory, 393
Garland, Merrick, *50*, 413, 474, *475*, 488, 490
Garner, Tyron, 137, *137*, 172
Garrett, Alabama v., 88

gay men and lesbians
  civil rights of, 90, 137, *137*, 150–51, *151*, 159, 163, 172–73, 175–76, *306*
  Constitution and, 54
  discrimination against, 94
  marriage and, *see* same-sex marriage
  military and, 177, *177*, 185
GDP (gross domestic product), 81, *82*
Geering, John, 275
gender
  federal district judges and, *489*
  juries and, 134
  laws concerning, *88*, 89
  political conflict and, 17, 18
  relationship of voting patterns to, 18
  see also women and women's rights
gender discrimination, *158*, *159*, 168–69, *169*, 170, 172, *172*, 176, 482
"gender gap," 17

general election, 289 The election in which voters cast ballots for House members, senators, and (every four years) a president and vice president.

general-election campaigns, 289–90, 303–7, *304*, *305*, *306*
General Services Administration (GSA), *447*, 456
General Social Survey, 200, *200*
George III, 451
Georgia, 172
Georgia, Chisholm v., 70, 74, 486
Gephardt, Richard, 293
Gerry, Elbridge, 44, 104, 106, 379

gerrymandering, *378*, 379 Attempting to use the process of re-drawing district boundaries to benefit a political party, protect incumbents, or change the proportion of minority voters in a district.

"get out the vote" (GOTV), 304
Gibbons v. Ogden, 72, 74
Gideon, Clarence, 133
Gideon v. Wainwright, *109*, 133
Gillibrand, Kirsten, 362, *363*
Ginsburg, Ruth Bader, 490, 506, 507, *507*
Gitlow, Benjamin, 108
Gitlow v. New York, 108, *109*

going public, 434 A president's use of speeches and other public communications to appeal directly to citizens about issues the president would like the House and Senate to act on.

Gonzales v. Raich, 92
Goodyear Tire and Rubber, Ledbetter v., 486
Goodyear Tire and Rubber Company, 168
Gorbachev, Mikhail, *410*
Gore, Al, 294
  in 2000 election, 277–78, 291, *291*, 298, 298–99
  expanded vice presidential role of, 426
Gore, Bush v., 507

Agriculture Committee of, *389, 390*
apportionment of seats in, 377
Appropriations Committee of,
    390, 391
bills in, 398–400, *399*
Budget Committee of, *390*
Committee on Foreign Affairs of, *390*
constitutional requirements of candi-
    dates for, *292*
Democratic control of, 384
election to, 365, 372–73, *373*
gerrymandering of districts of,
    378, *379*
gun control and, 190
incumbents in, *318,* 318–19, 372–73, *373,*
    375, 377
Intelligence Committee of, *390*
Judiciary Committee of, *390,* 398
Majority Leader in, 384, *385*
Minority Leader in, 384, *385*
Natural Resources Committee of,
    389, 390
redistricting and, 166–67, 379–80,
    380
Republican control of, 275, 320
rules and procedures in, 13, 399–400
Rules Committee in, 391, 399–400
Senate *vs.,* 365
Speaker of, 384, *385*
Transportation Committee of, *390*
typical workdays for, *373, 374,* 375
Veterans' Affairs Committee of, *390,* 401
Ways and Means Committee of, *390,* 391
whip system of, 384, *385*
see also Congress
Housing and Urban Development, Depart-
    ment of, 410
housing discrimination, 152
Howell, William, 429
Hoyer, Steny, *255, 434*
Hudson River, *468*
Hughes, Charles, 501
Humane Society, 353
human nature, Founders' views on, 33–34
Humphrey, Hubert, 402
Hustler, 121

Idaho, 408

**ideological polarization, 211–13, 387–88,
388** The effect on public opinion when
many citizens move away from moderate
positions and toward either end of the political spectrum, identifying themselves as
either liberals or conservatives.

ideology, 19 A cohesive set of ideas and
beliefs used to organize and evaluate the
political world.
    conservative, 193, *193,* 211–13
    definition of, 19
    federalism and, 91
    liberal, 193, 211–13
    political conflict and, 19
    public opinion and, 11, 193, *193,* 211–13

IGOs (intergovernmental organizations),
    68
"I Have a Dream" (King), *161, 162,* 163
Illinois, 150, 378
IMF (International Monetary Fund),
    68, 163
immigration and immigrants, 18, *18,* 144,
    148–49, 184–85, *413*
    in Arizona, 142, *143,* 184
    Clinton and, *306*
    illegal, 144, 184–85, *185,* 325, 412–13
    public opinion on, 185, 218
    Trump and, 144, 184, 201, *306*
immigration policy, 4, *4*

impeachment, 6, 51, 401 A negative or
checking power over the other branches that
allows Congress to remove the president,
the vice president, or other "officers of the
United States" (including federal judges) for
abuses of power.
    of A. Johnson, 432
    of Clinton, 432

implied powers, 57–59 Powers supported
by the Constitution that are not expressly
stated in it.

income inequality, 15, *17,* 18, *158*
income tax, 56, 409

**incumbency advantage, 372–73, 373,
376** The relative infrequency with which
members of Congress are defeated in their
attempts for reelection.

incumbent A politician running for reelection to the office he or she currently holds.
    definition of, 288
    high reelection rates of, *318,* 318–19
    retrospective evaluations of, 289
    work toward reelection, 371–72

independent agencies, 454 Government
offices or organizations that provide government services and are not part of an executive department.

independent voters, *265,* 265–66
Indian Removal Act, 148
individualism, economic, 15
industrialization, 77, 409

informational theory, 391 The idea that
having committees in Congress made up
of experts on specific policy areas helps to
ensure well-informed policy decisions.

initiative, 352 A direct vote by citizens on
a policy change proposed by fellow citizens
or organized groups outside government.
Getting a question on the ballot typically
requires collecting a set number of signatures from registered voters in support of
the proposal. There is no mechanism for a
national-level initiative.

In re Oliver 333 U.S. 257, 109

inside strategies, 343–48, 347 The tactics
employed within Washington, D.C., by
interest groups seeking to achieve their
policy goals.

institutional interest groups, *333*
intercontinental railroad, 149

interest group, 10, 13, 15, 330–60 An
organization of people who share common
political interests and aim to influence
public policy by electioneering and
lobbying.
    campaign contributions by, *312*
    definition of, 332, 359
    electioneering and, 349–52, *351, 352*
    financial expenditures of, 333–36, *334, 335*
    inside strategies of, 343–48, *347*
    membership size and role in, 338–39, *339*
    organizational structures of, 336, 338
    outside lobbying strategies of, 343, 344,
        345, 348, 348–53, *350, 351, 352*
    political influence and power of, 353–58,
        354, 357, 360
    public opinion and, 13
    regulation of, 333, 337
    resources used by, 339–41, *340*
    staff and revolving door of, 338
    Supreme Court and, 508–9
    types of, *333,* 359
    see also lobbying and lobbyists

interest group state, 332 A government in
which most policy decisions are determined
by the influence of interest groups.

**intergovernmental organizations (IGOs),
68** Organizations that seek to coordinate
policy across member nations.

intermediate scrutiny, 114 The middle
level of scrutiny the courts can use when
determining whether a law is constitutional. To meet this standard, the law or
policy must further an important government interest in a way that is "substantially
related" to that interest and must use means
that are a close fit to the government's goal
and not substantially broader than is necessary to accomplish that goal, and the policy
must be "content neutral."

intermediate scrutiny test, 114, 168, *170, 171*
Internal Revenue Service (IRS), 7
International Monetary Fund (IMF), 68, 163
Internet, 356, 582–83
    cyberbullying, 118
    fabricated photos on, 231, *231*
    information gathering and availability
        as transformed by, 228–31, *230, 231*
    pornography and, 122–23
interracial marriage, 147
Interstate Commerce Commission, 409,
    451

deviations from, *395, 398*
differences in House and Senate, 398–400, *399*

Lemon test, 111 The Supreme Court uses this test, established in *Lemon v. Kurtzman*, to determine whether a practice violates the First Amendment's establishment clause.

Lemon v. Kurtzman, 111
Leno, Jay, 60
lesbians, *see* gay men and lesbians
"Letter from the Birmingham Jail" (King), *161*, 162
Lewinsky, Monica, 401
Lewis, John, 382
LGBTQ community, 150–51, *151, 306*
  see also gay men and lesbians
Libby, I. Lewis "Scooter," 422

libel, 121–22 Written false statements that damage a person's reputation. They can be regulated by the government but are often difficult to distinguish from permissible speech.

liberal, 19, 91, 193, 211–13, 261–62, 262 One side of the ideological spectrum defined by support for stronger government programs and more market regulation; generally associated with Democrats.

liberal or conservative ideology, 193 A way of describing political beliefs in terms of a position on the spectrum running from liberal to moderate to conservative.

Libertarians, 19, 20, 278 Those who prefer very limited government and therefore tend to be conservative on issues such as welfare policy, environmental policy, and public support for education but liberal on issues of personal liberty such as free speech, abortion, and the legalization of drugs.

liberty, 21–23, 25, 33 Political freedom, such as the freedom of speech, press, assembly, and religion. These and other legal and due process rights protecting individuals from government control are outlined in the Bill of Rights of the U.S. Constitution.

Lilly Ledbetter Fair Pay Act, *159*, 169
Limbaugh, Rush, 231, 240

limited government, 29, 59 A political system in which the powers of the government are restricted to prevent tyranny by protecting property and individual rights.

Lincoln, Abraham, 73, 146
  Civil War and, 409
  on public opinion, 192
literacy tests, 147
litigation as lobbying strategy, 347, *347*
Little Rock, Ark., school desegregation in, *160*, 177

living Constitution, 54, 59, 504 A way of interpreting the Constitution that takes into account evolving national attitudes and circumstances rather than the text alone.

lobbying, 330, *331, 332* Efforts to influence public policy through contact with public officials on behalf of an interest group.
  astroturf, 349
  conflict in, *357*, 357–58
  definition of, 332
  direct, 343, 346
  drafting legislation and regulations in, 346–47
  financial spending on, 333–36, *334, 335*
  grassroots, *348*, 348–49
  media used in, 352
  mobilizing public opinion, 349
  regulation of, 333, 337
  see also interest groups

Locke, John, 33, *33*, 40
Lockett, Clayton, 134
Lockheed Martin Corporation, 334–35

logrolling, 42–44, 382 A form of reciprocity in which members of Congress support bills that they otherwise might not vote for in exchange for other members' votes on bills that are very important to them.

Lopez, Alfonso, 89
Lopez, United States v., 88, 89
López-Cantera, Carlos, 269
Los Angeles, Calif., 132
Louisiana, *164*
Louisiana, Duncan v., 109

Madison, James, 21, 31, 33–34, 35, *36*, 36–37, 56, 110, 227, 379, 479
  Constitutional Convention and, 40
  on judicial review, 52
  views on government of, 6, 56, 72
Madison, Marbury v., 52, 478–79, *479*

Majority Leader, 242, 384, *385* The elected head of the party holding the majority of seats in the House or Senate.

majority opinions, 501
majority rule, 36–38

majority voting, 290 A voting system in which a candidate must win more than 50 percent of votes to win the election. If no candidate wins enough votes to take office, a runoff election is held between the top two vote-getters.

Malcolm X, *161*
Malloy v. Hogan, 109
Manchin, Joe
Manning, Bradley, *120*, 120–21
Mapp, Dollree, 128, *128*
Mapp v. Ohio, 128

"marble cake" model of federalism, 76–77, *78*
Marbury v. Madison, 52, 478–79, *479*
March on Washington, *161, 162*, 162–63
margin of error, 202
Margolies-Mezvinsky, Marjorie, 368
marijuana
  drug-sniffing dogs in searches for, 105, *105*
  medical use of, 91, 92, *92*
marketplace of ideas, 124

markup, 396 One of the steps through which a bill becomes a law, in which the final wording of the bill is determined.

marriage
  interracial, 147
  same-sex, *see* same-sex marriage
Marshall, John, 53, 479
  judicial review established by, 478–79
  Marbury v. Madison and, 52, 478–79
  McCulloch v. Maryland and, 54
  unanimous decisions practice of, 501
Marshall, Thurgood, 54, 163, 505
Mars rovers, 440, 447
Martin, Trayvon, 156
Maryland, 163–64
Maryland, Benton v., 109
Maryland, McCulloch v., 54, 57–58, 72, 74, *74*
Mason, George, 44, 104, 106
Massachusetts, 44, 46, 91, 119

mass associations, 339–39 Interest groups that have a large number of dues-paying individuals as members.

mass media, 226, 244–45 Sources that provide information to the average citizen, such as newspapers, television networks, radio stations, podcasts, and websites.
  see also media

mass survey, 202 A way to measure public opinion by interviewing a large sample of the population.

Matthew Shepard and James Byrd Jr. Hate Crimes Prevention Act, 176
Mayhew, David, 371
McCain, John, 270, 382, 406
McCain-Feingold Act, *see* Bipartisan Campaign Reform Act (BCRA)
McCarthy, Kevin, 389, 402
McCaskill, Claire, 362
McConnell, Mitch, *321*, 474
McCulloch v. Maryland, 54, 57–58, 72, 74, *74*
McCutcheon v. Federal Election Commission, 310
McDonald v. Chicago, 109
McHenry, James, 45
media, 224–51
  by-product theory of information transmission and, 231–32
  deregulation of, 228
  election coverage and, 8, 13
    in 2016 election, 224, *225, 226*, 239, 248

media, (*Continued*)
 historical overview of, 226–28, *227*
 Internet-based news sources in, 228–31, *230*, *231*
 leaks, sources, and, 234–36
 in lobbying campaigns, 352
 "off the record" in, 233
 "on background" in, 233
 politicians and, 233–36, *234*, 249
 politics and, 236–42, *237*, *241*, *242*, 249, *250*
 regulation of, 227–28, *228*
 role of, in democracy, 244–47, *245*, 250
  lack of citizen interest and, 244–45, *245*
  market forces and, 244–45, *245*, 247
 sources, 228–31, *230*, *231*, 232
 violent crime coverage by, 243

media conglomerates, 228 Companies that control a large number of media sources across several types of media outlets.

media effects, 237, 237–40 The influence of media coverage on average citizens' opinions and actions.

Medicaid, 56, 85, 86, 90, 410
medical marijuana, 91, 92, *92*
Medicare, 26, 354, *354*, 410, *448*
Merkel, Angela, 130
Mexican Americans, *148*, 148–49
Mexican-American War, 148, 408, 414
Mexico, 144
Michael M. v. Superior Court, 171
Michigan
 busing in Detroit, 165
 Flint's public water supply, 154, 440, *441*, *442*, *467*, 469–70
military, U.S., 7
 gays in, 177, *177*, 185
 sexual assault and, 362, *363*, 364
 unilateral action and, 429
 women in, *150*
military funerals, protests of, *115*, 115–16, 138
millennials, political affiliation of, 19

Miller test, 123 Established in *Miller v. California*, this three-part test is used by the Supreme Court to determine whether speech meets the criteria for obscenity. If so, it can be restricted by the government.

Miller v. California, 123
"Millionaires" Amendment, 117
Minnesota, Near v., 109

Minority Leader, 384, *385* The elected head of the party holding the minority of seats in the House or Senate.

minority rights, 36
minor political parties, 277–79, *278*
Miranda, Ernesto, 131

Miranda rights, *131*, 131–32 The list of civil liberties described in the Fifth Amendment

that must be read to a suspect before anything the suspect says can be used in a trial.

Mischiefs of Faction, 229
Mississippi, 137, 147, *161*
Missouri, *116*, 156
Missouri Compromise, 74, 146

modified rules, 400 Conditions placed on a legislative debate by the House Rules Committee allowing certain amendments to a bill while barring others.

Moe, Terry, 429, 455
"Moms Demand Action for Gun Sense in America," 348

monarchy, 7, 21, 32 A form of government in which power is held by a single person, or monarch, who comes to power through inheritance rather than election.

Moniz, Ernest, 427
Monkey Cage, The, 229
monopolies, 72, *73*
Monroe, James, 408
Monroe Doctrine, 408
Montana, 86, 108, 408
Montgomery, Ala., civil rights movement in, 159–61, *160*, *161*

mootness, 495, 496 The irrelevance of a case by the time it is received by a federal court, causing the Court to decline to hear the case.

Morris, Gouverneur, 35
Morrison, United States v., 88
mortgage discrimination, 152
Motor Voter Act, 84
MoveOn.org, 339
Moynihan, Daniel Patrick, 104
multiculturalism, 182, 184–85, *185*
My Story (Parks), 159

NAACP (National Association for the Advancement of Colored People), 153, 163–64, 179
Nader, Ralph, 277–78, *278*
Nadler, Jerrold, 398
NAFTA (North American Free Trade Agreement), 411
NASA, 353, 440, 447, 460, 466
Nation, 240
National Aeronautics and Space Administration (NASA), 7
National Association for the Advancement of Colored People (NAACP), 153, 163–64, 179
National Association of Realtors, 335, 350–51
National Beer Wholesalers Association (NBWA), 336
National Cholesterol Education Month, 380

national committee, 258 An American political party's principal organization, comprising party representatives from each state.

"National Conversation on Race," 178
National Fair Housing Alliance, 152
National Federation of Independent Business v. Sebelius, 88
National Forest Service, 389
National Guard, 5, 177
National Independent Automobile Dealers Association (NIADA), 336
National Institutes of Health (NIH), 447
National Journal, 247
National Labor Relations Board v. Jones & Laughlin Steel, 74, 76
National Organization for Women (NOW), 118, 174
National Public Radio (NPR), 231
National Republican Congressional Committee (NRCC), 261
National Republican Senatorial Committee (NRSC), 261
National Rifle Association (NRA), 124, 190, 332, 354, 357
national security, 100–101, 138
National Security Agency (NSA), 52, 129–31, 137, 198, 235
National Security Council (NSC), 425
national supremacy, 69–70, 72, 84–85

national supremacy clause, 41 Part of Article VI, Section 2, of the Constitution stating that the Constitution and the laws and treaties of the United States are the "supreme Law of the Land," meaning national laws take precedence over state laws if the two conflict.

National Turkey Federation, 357, *357*
National Women's Soccer League (NWSL), 175
Nation of Islam, 17, 179
Native Americans, 145, 148
NATO (North Atlantic Treaty Organization), 68

natural rights, 33 Also known as "unalienable rights," the Declaration of Independence defines them as "Life, Liberty, and the pursuit of Happiness." The Founders believed that upholding these rights should be the government's central purpose.

NBWA (National Beer Wholesalers Association), 336
Near v. Minnesota, 109

necessary and proper clause, 47, 55, 69 Part of Article I, Section 8, of the Constitution that grants Congress the power to pass all laws related to its expressed powers; also known as the elastic clause.

Nevada Department of Human Resources v. Hibbs, 88

New Deal, 26, 83, 84, 256, 257, 409, *410*
    bureaucracy and, 452, *452*
    Supreme Court and, 488, 507
New Deal Coalition, 256
New Federalism, *80*, 81
New Hampshire, 46
New Haven, Conn., 181
New Jersey, *381*

New Jersey Plan, 38, 56 A plan that was in response to the Virginia Plan, in which smaller states at the Constitutional Convention proposed that each state should receive equal representation in the national legislature, regardless of size.

New London, Conn., 133
News Corp/21st Century Fox, 229
Newtown, Conn., school shootings, 201, 241, 414
New York (state), 44, 46, 72, *73*, 76
New York, Gitlow v., 108, *109*
New York, N.Y., 155-56, 256
New York Board of State Regents, 110
New York Sun, 227
New York Times, 120, 131, 231, 234
New York Tribune, 227
NIADA (National Independent Automobile Dealers Association), 336
NIH (National Institutes of Health), 447
1984 (Orwell), 130
Nineteenth Amendment, 56, *56*, 149, *158*, 159
Ninth Amendment, *106*, *109*, 135
Nixon, Richard, 81
    affirmative action and, 177, 180
    executive privilege used by, 422, 424
    justices appointed by, 489
    resignation of, 432
    Vietnam War and, 410
    Watergate and, *213*, 422, 424
Nixon, United States v., 422, 424
No Child Left Behind Act, *83*

nominating convention, 271, 272, 294, 294
A meeting held by each party every four years at which states' delegates select the party's presidential and vice-presidential nominees and approve the party platform.

nominations, 268-71, 272, 292-94
nonpartisan primaries, 269
nonviolent protest, *159*, 160-61, 160-63, *162*
North American Free Trade Agreement (NAFTA), 411
North Atlantic Treaty Organization (NATO), 68
North Carolina, 46, *159*
    redistricting in, 379-80, *380*
    sit-ins in, *159*, 160, *160*
North Carolina Supreme Court, 101
North Dakota, 137
Northern Securities Company, 409

notice-and-comment procedure, 443
A step in the rule-making process in which proposed rules are published in the *Federal*

Register and made available for debate by the general public.

NOW (National Organization for Women), 118, 174
NRA (National Rifle Association), 124, 190, 332, 354, 357
NRCC (National Republican Congressional Committee), 261
NRSC (National Republican Senatorial Committee), 261
NSA, *see* National Security Agency (NSA)
NSC (National Security Council), 425
nullification, 73
NWSL (National Women's Soccer League), 175

Obama, Barack, 130, 275, 389, 426, *426*, 428, *434*
    Affordable Care Act and, *395*
    Afghanistan war and, *51*
    appointments made by, 179, 413, 490
    approval ratings of, 194, *194*, 321, 432, *433*, 434-35, *435*
    bureaucracy and, 464
    civil rights and, *178*, 178-79
    Congress and, 50, *51*, 58, 421
    Dream Act and, 144, 412-13, *413*
    economic policy and, 85, 302
    in 2008 election, *298*, 377
    in 2012 election, *298*, 320-21, 324
    EOP staff and, 425, *426*
    Every Student Succeeds Act and, *11*
    executive orders of, 169, 320, 412-13, *413*, 414, *415*, 429
    executive privilege invoked by, *422*, 424
    on Flint's water supply, 154
    foreign policy of, 417, *421*
    gay rights and, 151, *151*
    Guantánamo Bay and, *49*, *430*, 431
    gun control and, 414
    on hate-crimes legislation, 176
    health care reform and, 26, 85, 201, *201*, 276, 321, 419
    immigration reform and, 184, 185
    Iraq and, 429
    judges appointed by, 490, *490*
    judges nominated by, 474, *488*, 490, 492
    lobbyists and, 338, *338*
    national supremacy and, 84-85
    omnibus spending bill and, *383*
    on racial discrimination, 152
    Supreme Court and, 510
    unilateral actions of, *429*
    vetoes and, 418-19, *419*
Obama, Michelle, 426
Obergefell, Jim, *69*
Obergefell v. Hodges, 10, *69*, 173
obscenity, 122-24
Occupational Safety and Health Administration (OSHA), 468
Occupy Wall Street, 163
O'Connor, Sandra Day, 133, 137, 173, *500*, 506, 507

Office of the United States Trade Representative, 425
Ogden, Gibbons v., 72, 74
Ohio, 115, 377
Ohio, Brandenburg v., 115
Ohio, Mapp v., 128
Oklahoma, 134, 148, *171*
Ollie's Barbeque, 165
O'Malley Dillon, Jennifer, 433

omnibus legislation, 398 Large bills that often cover several topics and may contain extraneous, or pork-barrel, projects.

omnibus spending bill, *383*

on background or off the record, 233 Comments a politician makes to the press on the condition that they can be reported only if they are not attributed to that politician.

open primary, 269, 272, 289 A primary election in which any registered voter can participate in the contest, regardless of party affiliation.

open rules, 400 Conditions placed on a legislative debate by the House Rules Committee allowing relevant amendments to a bill.

open seat, 300 An elected position for which there is no incumbent.

Operation Fast and Furious, *422*, 424
opinion writing in Supreme Court, 499-502, *500*
Opportunity rover, 440, 447

oral arguments, 498, 498-99 Spoken presentations made in person by the lawyers of each party to a judge or an appellate court outlining the legal reasons their side should prevail.

Oregon, 408
Oregon, DeJonge v., 109

original intent, 504 The theory that justices should surmise the intentions of the Founders when the language of the Constitution is unclear.

originalism, 54

original jurisdiction, 479 The authority of a court to handle a case first, as in the Supreme Court's authority to initially hear disputes between two states. However, original jurisdiction for the Supreme Court is not exclusive; it may assign such a case to a lower court.

from each of its donors and the amount it can spend on federal electioneering are strictly limited.

treat their own residents. This was meant to promote commerce and travel between states.

problem of control, 448, 448–50, 449 A difficulty faced by elected officials in ensuring that when bureaucrats implement policies they follow these officials' intentions but still have enough discretion to use their expertise.

procedures, influence on political process of, 8, 13
Progressive Era, 76–77, 451–52
Prohibition, 56
Project Censored, 241
property rights, 132–33

proportional allocation, 293 During the presidential primaries, the practice of determining the number of convention delegates allotted to each candidate based on the percentage of the popular vote cast for each candidate. All Democratic primaries and caucuses use this system, as do some states' Republican primaries and caucuses.

protectionism, 150 The idea under which some people have tried to rationalize discriminatory policies by claiming that some groups, like women or African Americans, should be denied certain rights for their own safety or well-being.

protests
at military funerals, *115*, 115–16, 138
nonviolent, *159*, 160–61, 160–63, *162*
during the Vietnam War, 116, 117, 163, *503*
Public Citizen, 347

public goods, 6 Services or actions (such as protecting the environment) that, once provided to one person, become available to everyone. Government is typically needed to provide public goods because they will be under-provided by the free market.

public health, 101, *101*

public opinion, 190–223 Citizens' views on politics and government actions.
abortion and, 11, 195
accuracy of, 208–10
on bureaucracy, 448–49, *449*
considerations and, *194*, 194–96, *195*, *196*
definition of, 192
on gays in the military, 185
on gun control, 190, *191*, 196, 201, 218–19
on health care, 208–10, 218
ideology and, 11, 193, *193*, 211–13
on immigration, 185, 218
influences on, 193–201, 221
latency of, 193, *193*
lobbying and mobilization of, 349
measuring of, 202–6, 208–11, *209*, 222
political influence of, *193*, 213–15, *214*, *215*, 218–19, 222

relevance of, *218*, 218–19
on same-sex marriage, 151, 185, 199, *199*
on spending cuts, *457*
Supreme Court and, 508–9
types of, 193, *193*

public safety, 67, 101, *101*, 110
Puerto Ricans and Puerto Rico, 149, 483
punishment, cruel and unusual, 134
Pure Food and Drug Act, 451
Puritans, 146

purposive benefits, 342 Satisfaction derived from the experience of working toward a desired policy goal, even if the goal is not achieved.

push polls, 206

R. J. Reynolds, 122
race
census data on, *18*
federal district judges and, *489*
juries and, 134
political conflict and, 17–18
political parties and, 17, *17*, 266, *266*, 324
poverty and, 154, *155*
redistricting and, 378, 379–80, *380*
voting and, 17, *17*, 152–54, *153*
racial discrimination, 147–49, 152–54, *155*, 158, 257
in employment, *158*, 166, *176*
immigration laws and, 142
in law enforcement, 157
racial profiling, 142, 179, 186
racial redistricting, 166–67, 378, 379–80, *380*
radio networks, 228
Raich, Gonzales v., 92
Randolph, Edmund, 35, 38

random sample, 204, 205, 206 A subsection of a population chosen to participate in a survey through a selection process in which every member of the population has an equal chance of being chosen. This kind of sampling improves the accuracy of public opinion data.

Rangel, Charles, 510

rational basis test, 167–68, *170*, 171 The use of evidence to suggest that differences in the behavior of two groups can rationalize unequal treatment of these groups.

Rayburn, Sam, 388
Reagan, Ronald, 81, 125, 149
assassination attempt on, 125
bureaucracy and, 453
foreign policy of, 410, *410*

realignment, 257 A change in the size or composition of the party coalitions or in the nature of the issues that divide the parties. Realignments typically occur within an

election cycle or two, but they can also occur gradually over the course of a decade or longer.

"reasonable" test, 167

recess appointment, 413 Selection by the president of a person to be an ambassador or the head of a department while the Senate is not in session, thereby bypassing Senate approval. Unless approved by a subsequent Senate vote, recess appointees serve only to the end of the congressional term.

Reconstruction, 75, 401
Redding, Savana, 127
reddit, 230

redistributive tax policies, 15, 25 Politics, generally favored by Democratic politicians, that use taxation to attempt to create social equality (for example, higher taxation of the rich to provide programs for the poor).

redistricting, 166–67, 377–80, 380 Re-drawing the geographic boundaries of legislative districts. This happens every 10 years to ensure that districts remain roughly equal in population.

"red states," 15–16, 25

red tape, 447–48 Excessive or unnecessarily complex regulations imposed by the bureaucracy.

Reed, Stanley, 500
Reed, Thomas, 399
Reed's Rules, 399
reelection, incumbents work toward, 371–72, 402, *402*

referendum, 352 A direct vote by citizens on a policy change proposed by a legislature or another government body. Referenda are common in state and local elections, but there is no mechanism for a national-level referendum.

Reform Party, 278, 291, *291*
Regents of the University of California, Hamilton v., 109
Regents of the University of California v. Bakke, 181

regulation, 442–46, 444, 446 A rule that allows the government to exercise control over individuals and corporations by restricting certain behaviors.
civil service, 459–60

regulatory capture, 449–50 A situation in which bureaucrats favor the interests of the groups or corporations they are supposed to regulate at the expense of the general public.

Rehnquist, William, 54, 500
Reid, Harry, *395*
religion
    government and, 103, 108, 110–13
    see also freedom of religion
Religious Freedom Restoration Act (RFRA), 113

remedial legislation, 87 National laws that address discriminatory state laws. Authority for such legislation comes from Section 5 of the Fourteenth Amendment.

Reno, Shaw v., 166–67
representative democracy, 20

republicanism, 32–33 As understood by James Madison and the framers, the belief that a form of government in which the interests of the people are represented through elected leaders is the best form of government. Our form of government is known as a republican democracy.

Republican National Committee (RNC), 254, 271
Republican Party, 199, 200, 254, *255*
    as brand name, 259, *260*
    campaign fund-raising and support provided by, 271, 274
    Civil War amendments passed by, 147
    congressional conference of, 261
    culture wars and election results of, 17
    economic policy and, 15
    formation of, 409
    founding and history of, 254–57, *255, 257*
    gender and, 17, *17*
    House controlled by, 275, 320
    identification with, 199, 200, 212
    ideology and, 19, 261–62, *262*
    immigration proposals and, 281
    party coalitions in, *266,* 266–67, *267*
    party identification in electorate of, 262, *264,* 264–65, 281
    party in government of, 261–62, *262*
    party organizations of, 258–60, *259, 260*
    presidential platforms of, 274–75
    race and, 17, *17,* 266, *266,* 324
    recruiting and nominating of candidates in, 268–71, 272, 280
    Senate controlled by, 320, *321,* 322, 384
    taxes and, 15
    see also elections
research and development, 446–47

reserved powers, 41 As defined in the Tenth Amendment, powers that are not given to the national government by the Constitution, or not prohibited to the states, are reserved by the states or the people.

resolutions, types of, 393
resources used by interest groups, 339–41, *340*
retrospective evaluations, 289
Revels, Hiram, *147*

reverse discrimination, 181, 182, *182*
revisionary power, 478
Revolutionary War, 50
    Articles of Confederation and, 30
    Constitution and, *30,* 31, 36
    newspaper coverage of, 226–27

revolving door, 338 The movement of individuals from government positions to jobs with interest groups or lobbying firms, and vice versa.

RFRA (Religious Freedom Restoration Act), 113
Rhode Island, 39, 44, 46
Richie, Nicole, 123
rights of criminal defendants, 126–34, *131,* 140–41
"rights revolution," 83–84
right to bear arms, 124–26, *125,* 140
right to legal counsel, 133
Rivkin, David, 64
RNC (Republican National Committee), 254, 271
Roberts, John G., Jr., 66, 476, 490, 499, *500, 506, 507, 507,* 510
Roberts, Pat, 260
Robinson, Jackie, 148
Robinson v. California, 109
Rock Hill, S.C., 161
Rodriguez, Alex, 129
Roe v. Wade, 135, *136,* 137, *159,* 507, 509
Rogers, Will, 260

roll call vote, 386 A recorded vote on legislation; members may vote yes, no, abstain, or present.

Romney, Mitt, 406
    2012 election and, 270, *298,* 320–21, 324
    as governor of Massachusetts, 91
Roof, Dylann, *156,* 158
Roosevelt, Franklin D., *70,* 256, 409, *410*
    court-packing plan of, 488
    New Deal and, *257,* 452, *452*
Roosevelt, Theodore, 26, 409
Rosen, Jeffrey, 118
Rubio, Marco, 269, 273, 291, 313
rules, influence on political process of, 8, 13
Rumsfeld, Hamdan v., 49

runoff election, 290 Under a majority voting system, a second election held only if no candidate wins a majority of the votes in the first general election. Only the top two vote-getters in the first election compete in the runoff.

Ryan, Paul, 252, 254–53, 261, *375, 388,* 389

Safford, Arizona, 127

salience, 356–57, *357* The level of familiarity with an interest group's goals among the general population.

Sallie Mae, 330, *333,* 333–34
same-sex marriage, *10,* 69, 71, 173, *177,* 179, *485*
    Defense of Marriage Act and, 71, 91, 173, 176
    marriage licenses for, 98, *99*
    public opinion on, 151, 185, 199, *199*

sample, 202, 203, 204, 205, 206 Within a population, the group of people surveyed in order to gauge the whole population's opinion. Researchers use samples because it would be impossible to interview the entire population.

sample size, 202, 204, 205

sampling error, 202, 204, 205 The predicted difference between the average opinion expressed by survey respondents and the average opinion in the population, sometimes called the *margin of error.* Increasing the number of respondents lowers the sampling error.

Sanders, Bernie, 291, *291,* 306, 320, 323
Sandford, Dred Scott v., 73, 74, *74*–75, 107, 146, 479
Sandoval, Alexander v., 182
Sandoval, Martha, 182
Sandy Hook Elementary School, 125–26, 241, 414
Saturday Night Live
    Trump on, 228, *228*
Scalia, Antonin, 128, 173, 474, 488, 490, 499, 505, 506, *507*
Schattschneider, E. E., 10
Schenck, Charles, 100
Schenck v. United States, 114
Schickler, Eric, 200
Schilb v. Kuebel, 109
school desegregation, 83, *160,* 163–65, 177
    Brown I and, 148
    Brown II and, 148
    busing and, *164*
school prayer, 110–11, *510*
Schultz, Debbie Wasserman, 260
Schumer, Charles, 290
Scott, Dred, 74
Scott, Walter, *156,* 158
SCOTUSblog (Supreme Court blog), 245
scrutiny, 114
searches and seizures, 105, 126–31, *127, 128, 130,* 135
search warrants, 127–28
Sears, David O., 200
Seattle, Wash., *164*
Sebelius, Kathleen, 401
Sebelius, National Federation of Independent Business v., 88
secession, 72–73, 146
Second Amendment, *106, 109,* 124–26, *125,* 140
Second Continental Congress, 29–30, *30*
second party system, *255,* 256
Sedition Act, 114

segregation, 75, 76, 159–60, 160
   de jure vs. de facto, 165
   separate but equal doctrine and, 147–48,
    159–60, 160, 163–64
Select Committee on Energy Independence
  and Global Warming, 389

select committees, 389 Committees in
the House or Senate created to address a
specific issue for one or two terms.

selective incentives, 342 Benefits that
can motivate participation in a group effort
because they are available only to those
who participate, such as member services
offered by interest groups.

selective incorporation, 108, 109 The
process through which the civil liberties
granted in the Bill of Rights were applied to
the states on a case-by-case basis through
the Fourteenth Amendment.

self-incrimination, 83, 131–32

semi-closed primary, 269, 289 A primary
where anyone who is a registered member
of the party or registered as an Independent
can vote.

Seminole Tribe v. Florida, 88
Senate, U.S.
   "advice and consent" of, 50, 50, 58, 401
   Agriculture Committee of, 389, 390
   appointments confirmed by, 413,
    488–90, 490, 492
   Appropriations Committee of, 390
   bills in, 398–400, 399
   Budget Committee of, 390
   constitutional requirements of candi-
    dates for, 292
   filibuster in, 490, 492, 492
   Finance Committee in, 390
   Foreign Relations Committee in, 390
   gun control and, 190
   House vs., 365
   incumbents in, 372–73, 373, 375
   Intelligence Committee of, 390
   Judiciary Committee of, 390, 490
   Majority Leader in, 242, 384, 385
   Minority Leader in, 384, 385
   president pro tempore of, 386
   reelection to, 372–73, 373
   Republican control of, 320, 321, 322, 384
   rules and procedures in, 13, 400
   sexual assault in the military bill and,
    362, 363, 364
   treaties approved by, 416

senatorial courtesy, 490 A norm in the
nomination of district court judges in which
the president consults with his or her party's
senators from the relevant state in choosing
the nominee.

Seneca Falls Convention (1848), 18, 158, 159
Senior Executive Service (SES), 462–63

seniority, 382 The informal congressional norm of choosing the member who has
served the longest on a particular committee to be the committee chair.

**"separate but equal" doctrine, 147–48,
163–64, 257** The idea that racial segregation was acceptable as long as the separate
facilities were of equal quality; supported by
Plessy v. Ferguson and struck down by *Brown
v. Board of Education*.

separation of church and state, 110, 110–11

separation of powers, 6, 47 The division
of government power across the judicial,
executive, and legislative branches.
   constitutional framework for, 47, 48–49,
    50–53
   Supreme Court in, 506

separatism, racial, 17–18
September 11, 2001, terrorist attacks
   domestic surveillance after, 127, 129,
    129–31, 198
   G. W. Bush and, 411
SES (Senior Executive Service), 462–63
Seventeenth Amendment, 56, 365
Seventh Amendment, 106, 109
sexual assaults in the military, 362, 363, 364
sexual discrimination, 158, 159, 168–69, 169,
   170, 172, 172, 176, 482
sexual harassment, 168
Shapiro, Robert, 201
Shaw v. Reno, 166–67
Shays, Daniel, 32

Shays's Rebellion, 31, 32 An uprising of
about 4,000 men in Massachusetts in 1786
and 1787 to protest oppressive laws and gain
payment of war debts. The unrest prompted
calls for a new Constitution.

Shelby, Richard, 290
Shelby County v. Holder, 88
Shepard, Matthew, 176
Sherman Antitrust Act, 409, 451
Shinseki, Eric, 401
Sierra Club, 339, 340

signing statement, 430 A document
issued by the president when signing a bill
into law explaining his or her interpretation
of the law, which often differs from the
interpretation of Congress, in an attempt to
influence how the law will be implemented.

Silver, Nate, 203
simple resolutions, 393
Simpson, O. J., 482
Simpsons, The, 192
Sinclair, Barbara, 392

single-member district, 279 An electoral
system in which every elected official
represents a geographically defined area,

such as a state or congressional district, and
each area elects one representative.

sit-ins, 159, 160, 160–61
Sixteenth Amendment, 56, 58
Sixth Amendment, 54, 106, 109, 133, 133–34
sixth party system, 255, 256–57
Slager, Michael, 156

slander, 121 Spoken false statements that
damage a person's reputation. They can be
regulated by the government but are often
difficult to distinguish from permissible
speech.

slavery, 73, 227
   abolition of, 56, 107
   civil rights and, 145–47, 146
   compromises on, 41–44, 42, 409
   Dred Scott and, 74, 74–75, 146, 479
   Emancipation Proclamation and, 409,
    429
   party systems aligned over issue of, 256
snake handling, 101, 101
Snake Salvation, 101
SNCC (Student Nonviolent Coordinating
  Committee), 160
Snow, Murray, 142
Snowden, Edward, 52, 130, 235–36
Socialist Party, 114
socialization, political, 197, 198
social media, cyberbullying and, 118
Social Security, 26
sodomy laws, 137, 137, 172, 173

soft money, 117, 310–11 Contributions
that can be used for voter mobilization or to
promote a policy proposal or point of view as
long as these efforts are not tied to supporting or opposing a particular candidate.

soft news, 247 Media coverage that aims
to entertain or shock, often through sensationalized reporting or by focusing on a
candidate or politician's personality.

solicitor general, 497 A presidential
appointee in the Justice Department who
conducts all litigation on behalf of the
federal government before the Supreme
Court and supervises litigation in the
federal appellate courts.

solidary benefits, 342 Satisfaction
derived from the experience of working
with like-minded people, even if the group's
efforts do not achieve the desired impact.

Sotomayor, Sonia, 129, 178, 413, 490, 490,
   499, 507
Souter, David, 487, 506
South
   civil rights in, 147
   Jim Crow laws in, 147–48
   secession of, 72–73, 146
   slavery and, 42–45, 73, 145–46, 146

symbolic speech, *116,* 116–17, *118* Nonverbal expression, such as the use of signs or symbols. It benefits from many of the same constitutional protections as verbal speech because of its expressive value.

Three-Fifths Compromise, 42–45 The states' decision during the Constitutional Convention to count each slave as three-fifths of a person in a state's population for the purposes of determining the number of House members and the distribution of taxes.

trade association, *333,* 336 An interest group composed of companies in the same business or industry (the same "trade") that lobbies for policies that benefit members of the group.

trustee, 368 A member of Congress who represents constituents' interests while also taking into account national, collective, and moral concerns that sometimes cause the member to vote against the preference of a majority of constituents.

turkey farms, 462 Agencies to which campaign workers and donors can be appointed in reward for their service because it is unlikely that their lack of qualifications will lead to bad policy.

unfunded mandates, 81 Federal laws that require the states to do certain things but do not provide state governments with funding to implement these policies.

unified government, 277 A situation in which one party holds a majority of seats in the House and Senate and the president is a member of that same party.

unilateral action (presidential), 429, 430–32, *431* Any policy decision made and acted upon by the president and presidential staff without the explicit approval or consent of Congress.

unitary executive theory, 429 The idea that the vesting clause of the Constitution gives the president the authority to issue orders and policy directives that cannot be undone by Congress.

unitary government, 68 A system in which the national, centralized government holds ultimate authority. It is the most common form of government in the world.

United Farm Workers Union, *148*, 148–49
United Nations (UN), 68
United States, Schenck v., 114
United States v. Bond, 88
United States v. Lopez, 88, 89
United States v. Morrison, 88
United States v. Nixon, 422, 424
United States v. Virginia, 171
United States v. Windsor, 88
Univ. of Texas, Fisher v., 171
University of Michigan, 118, *171*, 181, 183
University of Missouri, 118
University of Texas, 182, *182*, 183, *183*, 476
Unorthodox Lawmaking (Sinclair), 392
unreasonable searches and seizures, 126–31, *127*, *128*, *130*, 135
Unruh, Jessie, 336
urbanization, 77
U.S. Commission on Civil Rights, 145, 153
USA PATRIOT Act, 127, 398

Van Buren, Martin, 408
Van Hollen, Chris, *434*
Verizon, 130

vesting clause, 411–12, 429 Article II, Section 1, of the Constitution, which states: "The executive Power shall be vested in a President of the United States of America," making the president both the head of government and the head of state.

Veterans of Foreign Wars, 116

veto The president's rejection of a bill that has been passed by Congress. A veto can be overridden by a two-thirds vote in both the House and Senate.
    executive power of, 6, 40, 397, 417–19, *419*, *420*
    overriding of, by Congress, 397, 417, *419*, *420*
    pocket, 397, 417, *419*
    process, *418*

vice president, U.S., *426*, *426*
video games, 124
Vietnam War, 51, 120, *213*, 410
    protest against, 116, 117, 163, *503*
Violence Against Women Act, *88*, 89, 175
Virginia, *42*, 44, 46
Virginia, United States v., 171
Virginia Military Institute, 168

Virginia Plan, 38, 39, 56 A plan proposed by the larger states during the Constitutional Convention that based representation in the national legislature on population. The plan also included a variety of other proposals to strengthen the national government.

Vitale, Engle v., 110
voting
    of African Americans, 316, 324
    of Asian Americans, 17, 149, 153, 324
    citizen turnout in, 152–53, *153*, *315*, 315–16

cues in, *316*, 316–18, *317*
cultural values and, 16
early or absentee, 153–54
2008 election problems with, 153
gender patterns of, 17
of Latinos, 17, 153, *153*, 324
majority, 290
methods of, *291*, 291–92
paradox of, 315–16
plurality, 279, 290
polling places for, 289
race and, 17, *17*, 152–54, *153*, 324
requirements for, 290
in wave elections, *318*, 318–19

voting cues, 316, 316–18, 317 Pieces of information about a candidate that are readily available, easy to interpret, and lead a citizen to decide to vote for a particular candidate.

voting rights, 17, 21–22, *22*, 410
    of African Americans, 17, *17*, 56, 75, 84, 87, 147, 152–54, *153*, 173
    of women, 56, *56*, 149, *158*, 159
Voting Rights Act, 17, 84, 87, 88, 153–54, *161*, 165, 167, 173–74, 179, 378
Vox, 229

Wade, Roe v., 135, *136*, 137, *159*, 507, 509
Wainwright, Gideon v., 109, 133
Wallace, George, 278
Walmart, 169, 172, *172*, 482
Walters, LeeAnne, *441*
war-making power, 414, 416
War of 1812, 414
War on Terror, *49*, 100–101, *133*
    see also terrorism
War Powers Resolution, 414, 416, 429
Warren, Earl, 164, 487
Warren, Elizabeth, 164
Washington, 408
Washington, George, 35, 47, *51*, 72, 365, 408
    on constitutional amendments, 55
    national foreign policy and, 57
    as presidential ideal, *409*
Washington Post, 235–36
Washington v. Texas, 109
Watergate, *213*, 422, 424
WBC (Westboro Baptist Church), *115*, 115–16, 138
welfare, 6–7, 71, 86
    reform of, 81, 91, 411
West, Kanye, 121
Westboro Baptist Church (WBC), *115*, 115–16, 138
West Wing of the White House, 425
Whig Party, 256

whip system, 384 An organization of House leaders who work to disseminate information and promote party unity in voting on legislation.

white flight, 165
White House Office, 425

white primary, 147, 148
whites, voting history of, 17, *17*
WikiLeaks, *120*, 120–21
Wilcox, John A., *365*
Williams, George, 489
Wilson, Darren, *116*
Wilson, James, 35
Wilson, Woodrow, 409
Windsor, United States v., 88

winner-take-all, 273, 293 During the presidential primaries, the practice of assigning all of a given state's delegates to the candidate who receives the most popular votes. Some states' Republican primaries and caucuses use this system.

Wired magazine, 236
wiretapping, 126, 131
Wisconsin, 94, *94*
Wisconsin Territory, 74
WNBA (Women's National Basketball Association), 175
Wolf v. Colorado, 109
women and women's rights, 17, 18
    civil rights of, 149–50, *150*, 158–59, *159*, 163, 167–69, *169*, 170, 171, 172, *172*, 174–75, *175*
    as federal district judges, *383*
    in military, *150*
    protectionism and, 150
    sexual assault of, in the military, 362, *363*, 364
    Supreme Court and, 167–69, 172, *172*
    voting rights of, 56, *56*, 149, *158*, 159
Women's National Basketball Association (WNBA), 175
World Trade Organization (WTO), 163
World War I, 114, 148, 409, 414
World War II, 47, 83, 414
    African Americans in, 148
    internment of Japanese Americans during, 149, 508

writ of *certiorari*, 494 The most common way for a case to reach the Supreme Court, in which at least four of the nine justices agree to hear a case that has reached them via an appeal from the losing party in a lower court's ruling.

WTO (World Trade Organization), 163
Wyoming, 125, *158*, 408

Yaqui Indians, 142

yellow journalism, 227 A style of newspaper reporting popular in the late 1800s that featured sensationalized stories, bold headlines, and illustrations to increase readership.

Zaller, John, 198
Zimmerman, George, 156

Voter Registration Information

State	Registration Deadline before Election*	Early Voting Permitted?**	Identification Required to Vote?**	More Information
Alabama	14 days	No	Photo ID requested	alabamavotes.gov
Alaska	30 days	Yes	ID requested; photo not required	elections.alaska.gov
Arizona	29 days	Yes	ID required; photo not required	azsos.gov/election
Arkansas	30 days	Yes	ID requested; photo not required	sos.arkansas.gov
California	15 days	Yes	No	sos.ca.gov
Colorado	8 days by mail or online; no in-person deadline	Yes (all voting by mail)	ID requested; photo not required	sos.state.co.us
Connecticut	14 days by mail; 7 days in person; election-day registration permitted	No	ID requested; photo not required	ct.gov/sots
Delaware	24 days	No	ID requested; photo not required	elections.delaware.gov
District of Columbia	30 days by mail or online; no in-person deadline	Yes	No	dcboee.org
Florida	29 days	Yes	Photo ID requested	dos.myflorida.com/elections
Georgia	28 days	Yes	Photo ID required	sos.ga.gov
Hawaii	30 days	Yes	Photo ID requested	hawaii.gov/elections
Idaho	25 days	Yes	Photo ID requested	idahovotes.gov
Illinois	27 days	Yes	No	elections.il.gov
Indiana	29 days	Yes	Photo ID required	in.gov/sos/elections
Iowa	10 days	Yes	No	sos.iowa.gov
Kansas	21 days	Yes	Photo ID required	kssos.org
Kentucky	29 days	No	ID requested; photo not required	elect.ky.gov
Louisiana	30 days	Yes	Photo ID requested	sos.la.gov
Maine	21 days by mail; no in-person deadline	Yes	No	maine.gov/sos
Maryland	21 days	Yes	No	elections.state.md.us
Massachusetts	20 days	No	No	www.sec.state.ma.us
Michigan	30 days	No	Photo ID requested	michigan.gov/sos
Minnesota	21 days	Yes	No	mnvotes.org
Mississippi	30 days	No	Photo ID required	sos.ms.gov
Missouri	Fourth Wednesday prior to election	No	ID requested; photo not required	sos.mo.gov
Montana	30 days by mail; no in-person deadline	Yes	ID requested; photo not required	sos.mt.gov

State	Registration Deadline before Election*	Early Voting Permitted?**	Identification Required to Vote?**	More Information
Nebraska	Third Friday prior to election by mail; second Friday prior to election in person	Yes	No	www.sos.ne.gov
Nevada	31 days by mail; 21 days in person	Yes	No	nvsos.gov
New Hampshire	10 days; election-day registration permitted	No	ID requested; photo not required	sos.nh.gov
New Jersey	21 days	Yes	No	njelections.org
New Mexico	28 days	Yes	No	sos.state.nm.us
New York	25 days	No	No	www.elections.ny.gov
North Carolina	25 days	Yes	No	ncsbe.gov
North Dakota	No voter registration required	Yes	Photo ID required	vote.nd.gov
Ohio	30 days	Yes	ID required; photo not required	sos.state.oh.us
Oklahoma	24 days	Yes	ID requested; photo not required	ok.gov/elections
Oregon	21 days	Yes (all voting by mail)	No	sos.oregon.gov
Pennsylvania	30 days	No	No	votespa.com
Rhode Island	30 days; election-day registration permitted	No	Photo ID requested	www.elections.state.ri.us
South Carolina	30 days	No	ID requested; photo not required	scvotes.org
South Dakota	15 days	Yes	Photo ID requested	sdsos.gov
Tennessee	30 days	Yes	Photo ID required	tn.gov/sos/election
Texas	30 days	Yes	Photo ID requested	votetexas.gov
Utah	30 days by mail; 7 days in person	Yes	ID requested; photo not required	elections.utah.gov
Vermont	Wednesday before the election	Yes	No	www.sec.state.vt.us/elections
Virginia	22 days	No	Photo ID required	sbe.virginia.gov
Washington	30 days by mail and online; 8 days in person	Yes (all voting by mail)	ID requested; photo not required	sos.wa.gov/elections/
West Virginia	21 days	Yes	No	sos.wv.gov
Wisconsin	20 days by mail; election-day registration permitted	Yes	Photo ID required	www.sos.state.wi.us
Wyoming	14 days; election-day registration permitted	Yes	No	soswy.state.wy.us

* Information collected from Project Vote Smart, votesmart.org/elections/voter-registration (accessed 9/1/16).

** Information collected from National Conference of State Legislatures, www.ncsl.org (accessed 9/1/16). In states where an ID is "requested," voters who do not bring ID to the polls may be required to sign an affidavit of identity, vote on a provisional ballot, have a poll worker vouch for their identity, or take additional steps after Election Day to make sure their vote is counted.

Study smarter with
INQUIZITIVE

digital.wwnorton.com/amerpoltoday5core

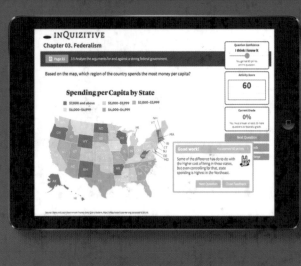

Cover design by Open, N.Y.

Cover photograph: Andrew Burton/Getty Images

 W. W. NORTON New York • London

wwnorton.com

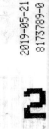